36480000006470

BLS Handbook of Methods

U.S. Department of Labor
Lynn Martin, Secretary

Bureau of Labor Statistics

September 1992

Bulletin 2414

RECEIVED

APR 12 1993

DEPARTMENT OF LABOR
LIBRARY
TRENTON, N.J. 08625

For sale by the U.S. Government Printing Office
Superintendent of Documents, Mail Stop: SSOP, Washington, DC 20402-9328
ISBN 0-16-038205-X

Preface

The *BLS Handbook of Methods* presents detailed explanations of how the Bureau of Labor Statistics obtains and prepares the economic data it publishes. BLS statistics are used for many purposes, and sometimes data well suited to one purpose may have limitations for another. This edition of the *Handbook*, like its predecessors, aims to provide users of BLS data with the information necessary to evaluate the suitability of the statistics for their needs.

Chapters for each major Bureau program give a brief account of the program's origin and development and then follow with comprehensive information on concepts and definitions, sources of data and methods of collection, statistical procedures, where the data are published, and their uses and limitations. Sources of additional technical information are given at the end of most chapters. Information on the most recent addition to the Bureau's programs is presented in chapter 20, "National Longitudinal Surveys."

The *Handbook* was written by members of the staffs of the various BLS program offices. It was prepared for publication by Jerry Matheny and Eugene Becker in the Division of Editorial Services, Office of Publications.

Information in this bulletin will be made available to sensory impaired individuals upon request. Voice phone: 202–606–STAT; TDD phone: 202–606–5897; TDD message referral phone: 1–800–326–2577.

Material in this publication is in the public domain and, with appropriate credit, may be reproduced without permission.

Contents

Page

Introduction 1

Chapter:

Employment and Unemployment Statistics

1. Labor force, employment, and unemployment from the Current Population Survey 3
2. Employment, hours, and earnings from the establishment survey 14
3. Occupational employment statistics 29
4. Measurement of unemployment in States and local areas 32
5. Employment and wages covered by unemployment insurance 37

Compensation and Working Conditions

6. Occupational pay and employee benefits 42
7. Negotiated wage and benefit changes 51
8. Employment Cost Index 56
9. Employee benefits survey 67

Productivity and Technology

10. Productivity measures: Business sector and major subsectors 78
11. Productivity measures: Industries and government 89
12. Technological change 99
13. Foreign labor statistics 103

Occupational Safety and Health

14. Occupational safety and health statistics 111

Economic Growth and Employment Projections

15. Economic growth and employment projections 128

Prices and Living Conditions

16. Producer prices 140
17. International price indexes 161
18. Consumer expenditures and income 170
19. Consumer Price Index 176

National Longitudinal Surveys

20. National Longitudinal Surveys 236

Appendixes:

A. Seasonal adjustment methodology at BLS 243

B. Industrial classification 246

C. Geographic classification 250

Chapter Index 251

Introduction

When U. S. Commissioner of Labor Carroll Wright issued his first annual report in March 1886, he established the policy of explaining his statistical methods to his readers and of seeking to avoid misinterpretation of the figures presented. During the more than 100 years which have followed that initial report, the definitions, methods, and limitations of the data published by the Bureau of Labor and its successor, the Bureau of Labor Statistics (BLS), have been explained many times. The reason for this is to make readers aware of the known limitations of the Bureau's data, to guide them in the appropriate use of the information, and to assure them that proper statistical standards and techniques have been observed.

This volume continues that tradition by providing current descriptions of the Bureau's statistical series. For example, since the last edition of this bulletin, significant changes have been made in the Bureau's compensation and labor force statistics programs. These are described in full. The Bureau's role, organization, and approach to its data collection activities also are discussed briefly.

BLS role

Among Federal agencies collecting and issuing statistics, the Bureau of Labor Statistics is a general-purpose statistical collection agency in the broad field of labor economics. BLS statistics, however, are often quite specialized, yet they meet general economic and social data requirements. In this regard, the Bureau's data serve the needs of business, labor, Congress, the general public, and the administrative and executive agencies for information on economic and social trends. As the needs of users are likely to differ, no statistic is ideal for all. This makes it important that the characteristics of the measures and their limitations be well understood.

Organization

The statistical programs of the Bureau have been developed, for the most part, independently of each other, taking on characteristics suited to the requirements of the subject under observation. As a result, the Bureau is organized according to subject matter areas, an arrangement which has proved efficient and has been continued over the years. Expertise in techniques, economic analysis, and other staff activities across subject-matter lines provides better use of the Bureau's resources.

As the Bureau's collection activities increased, regional offices were established to administer the field programs, to disseminate data to local users, and to furnish technical advice and assistance to State agencies and other cooperating organizations. An important aspect of the work of the regional staffs has been explaining the concepts and techniques which the Bureau uses in compiling the statistics.

The Bureau's work extends beyond the initial collection and processing of data. Its findings frequently influence, and sometimes are crucial to, the determining and shaping of public policy. Over the years, it has developed a staff of professionals—economists, statisticians, computer analysts, and administrative specialists, among others—each playing a significant role to ensure that the information issued by the Bureau is of the highest quality.

Consultation and advice

A statistical program too much detached from the users of its data may fail in its principal mission. To remain responsive to those who rely on BLS data, the Bureau continuously invites advice and ideas from users and experts in business, labor, professional and academic organizations, and from members of the public. Although several commissions and committees have reviewed specific Bureau programs over the years and made valuable, the Commissioner of Labor Statistics retains final responsibility for all decisions on statistical policy.

The Commissioner established two standing research advisory committees in 1947. These groups are the Business Research Advisory Council and the Labor Research Advisory Council. A third council, the State Research Advisory Committee on Occupational Safety and Health, was established in 1989. These councils advise on technical problems and provide perspectives on Bureau programs in relation to needs of their members. The councils accomplish their work in general sessions and also through committees on specialized subject-matter fields. The councils formally express their opinion through resolutions or recommendations on appropriate matters, but such resolutions are merely advisory. Members of the councils and the subcommittees serve in their individual capacities, not as representatives of their organizations.

The members of the Business Research Advisory Council are designated by the Commissioner under authorization of the Secretary of Labor, after nomination by the council's membership committee. The committee consists of representatives from broad-based business organizations such as the National Association of Manufacturers, the U.S. Chamber of Commerce, and the National Federation of Independent Business. The members of the Labor Research Advisory Council are designated by the Commissioner under authorization of the Secretary of Labor, from nominations by the Director of Research, AFL-CIO. All research directors of international unions represented in the AFL-CIO are invited to attend the general meetings of the council. Members of the State Research Advisory Committee on Occupational Safety and Health are nominated by their respective jurisdictions, with no more than one member from each State, the District of Columbia, the Commonwealth of Puerto Rico, the Virgin Islands, American Samoa, and Guam. A chairperson is selected from the membership by the Commissioner and appointed by the Secretary of Labor.

Voluntary reporting and confidentiality

Voluntary reporting and assuring the confidential nature of reported data are important characteristics of BLS programs. For more than a century, the Bureau has asked millions of firms and individuals to provide information closely related to their daily affairs and their personal lives. Although Bureau data collectors often return to the same firms or individuals for later information on the same subject or for new types of information, the Bureau's respondents have been remarkable in their generosity. This high degree of voluntary cooperation is due in part to the great care BLS employees take to protect the confidentiality of the information that respondents furnish by combining the data reported by the different sources and issuing the findings in summary tables, analyses, and reports. Respondents are thereby assured that their reports will be used for statistical purposes only. All efforts to obtain legal access to individual respondents' reports have been successfully resisted.[1]

Bureau Commissioners and their staffs have been convinced over the years that these policies contribute to the reliability of BLS statistics.

[1] For example, see *Husted v. Norwood*, 529 F. SUPP. 323 (S.S. Fla. 1981).

Chapter 1. Labor Force, Employment, and Unemployment from the Current Population Survey

Each month, the Bureau analyzes and publishes statistics on the labor force, employment, unemployment, and persons not in the labor force, classified by a variety of demographic, social, and economic characteristics. These statistics are derived from the Current Population Survey (CPS), which is conducted by the Bureau of the Census for the BLS. This monthly survey of the population is conducted using a scientifically selected sample of households, representative of the civilian noninstitutional population of the United States.

Background

Specific concepts of the labor force, employment, and unemployment were introduced in the later stages of the depression of the 1930's. Before the 1930's, aside from attempts in some of the decennial censuses, no direct measurements were made of the number of jobless persons. Mass unemployment in the early 1930's increased the need for statistics, and widely conflicting estimates based on a variety of indirect techniques began to appear. Dissatisfied with these methods, many research groups, as well as State and municipal governments, began experimenting with direct surveys or samples of the population. In these surveys, an attempt was made to classify the population as employed, unemployed, or out of the labor force by means of a series of questions addressed to each individual. In most of the surveys, the employed were defined as persons with occupations ("gainful workers"), and the unemployed were defined as those who were not working but were "willing and able to work." These concepts did not meet the standards of objectivity that many technicians felt were necessary to measure either the level of unemployment at a point in time or changes over periods of time. Counts of gainful workers did not have a current dimension, and the criterion "willing and able to work," when applied in specific situations, appeared to be too intangible and too dependent upon the interpretation and attitude of the persons being interviewed.

A set of precise concepts was developed in the late 1930's to meet these various criticisms. The classification of an individual depended principally upon his or her actual *activity* within a designated time period, that is, was the individual working, looking for work, or engaged in other activities? These concepts were adopted for the national sample survey of households, called the Monthly Report of Unemployment, initiated in 1940 by the Works Progress Administration.

The household survey was transferred to the Bureau of the Census in late 1942, and its name was changed to the Monthly Report on the Labor Force. The survey title was changed once more in 1948 to the present Current Population Survey in order to reflect its expanding role as a source for a wide variety of demographic, social, and economic characteristics of the population. In 1959, responsibility for analyzing and publishing the CPS labor force data was transferred to BLS, and the Bureau of the Census continues to collect and tabulate the statistics.

Description of Survey

The CPS provides statistics on the labor force status of the civilian noninstitutional population 16 years of age and over. Persons under 16 years of age are excluded from the official definition of the labor force because child labor laws, compulsory school attendance, and general social custom prevent most of these children from working in the United States. The institutional population, which is also excluded from coverage, consists of inmates of penal and mental institutions, sanitariums, and homes for the aged, infirm, and needy.

The CPS is collected each month from a probability sample of approximately 60,000 occupied households. Respondents are assured that all information obtained is completely confidential and is used only for the purpose of statistical analysis. Although the survey is conducted on a strictly voluntary basis, refusals to cooperate have averaged about 2.5 percent or less since its inception.

The time period covered in the monthly survey is a calendar week. A calendar week was selected as the survey reference period because the period used must be short enough so that the data obtained are "current" but not so short that the occurrence of holidays or other accidental events might cause erratic fluctuations in the information obtained. A calendar week fulfills these conditions as well as being a convenient and easily defined period of time. Since July 1955, the calendar week, Sunday through Saturday, which includes the 12th day of the month has been defined as the reference week. The actual survey is conducted during the following week, which is the week containing the 19th day of the month.

Concepts

The criteria used in classifying persons on the basis of their labor force activity are as follows.

Employment. Employed persons comprise (1) all those who, during the survey week, did any work at all as paid employees, or in their own business, profession, or on their own farm, or who worked 15 hours or more as unpaid workers in a family-operated enterprise; and (2) all those who did not work but had jobs or businesses from which they were temporarily absent due to illness, bad weather, vacation, labor-management dispute, or various personal reasons—whether or not they were paid by their employers for the time off and whether or not they were seeking other jobs. Each employed person is counted only once, even if they hold more than one job. In multiple job situations, a person is counted in the job at which she/he worked the greatest number of hours during the survey week. Included in the total are employed citizens of foreign countries, temporarily in the United States, who are not living on the premises of an embassy. Excluded are persons whose only activity consisted of work around their own home (such as housework, painting, repairing, etc.) or volunteer work for religious, charitable, and similar organizations.

Unemployment. Unemployed persons include those who did not work at all during the survey week, were actively looking for work, and were available for work during the reference period (except for temporary illness). Those who had made specific efforts to find work within the preceding 4-week period—such as by registering at a public or private employment agency, writing letters of application, canvassing for work, etc.—are considered to be looking for work. Persons who are awaiting recall to a job from which they had been laid off or volunteer that they expect to report to a new job within 30 days need not be looking for work to be classified as unemployed. (As indicated below in the section, "The new CPS questionnaire," there will be a change in the treatment of persons expecting to report to a new job within 30 days beginning in 1994.)

Duration of unemployment represents the length of time (through the current survey week) during which persons classified as unemployed had been continuously looking for work and thus is a measure of an in-progress spell of joblessness. For persons on layoff, duration of unemployment represents the number of full weeks since the termination of their most recent employment. Two useful measures of the duration of unemployment are the mean and the median. Mean duration is the arithmetic average computed from single weeks of unemployment. Median duration is the midpoint of a distribution of weeks of unemployment.

The reasons for unemployment are divided into four major groups. (1) Job losers are persons whose employment ended involuntarily and who immediately began looking for work, and include those on layoff. (2) Job leavers are persons who quit or otherwise terminated their employment voluntarily and immediately began looking for work. (3) Reentrants are persons who previously worked at a full-time job lasting 2 weeks or longer but who were out of the labor force prior to beginning to look for work. (4) New entrants are persons who never worked at a full-time job lasting 2 weeks or longer.

Civilian labor force. The civilian labor force comprises the total of all civilians classified as employed and unemployed.

Unemployment rate. The unemployment rate represents the number of unemployed as a percent of the civilian labor force. This measure is also computed for various groups within the labor force classified by sex, age, race, Hispanic ethnicity, industry, occupation, etc., or for combinations of these characteristics. The job-loser, job-leaver, reentrant, and new-entrant rates are each calculated as a percent of the total civilian labor force; the sum of the percentages for the four groups thus equals the unemployment rate for all civilian workers.

Not in labor force. All civilians 16 years of age and over who are not classified as employed or unemployed are defined as "not in the labor force." These persons are further classified as "engaged in own housework," "in school," "unable to work" because of long-term physical or mental illness, "retired," or "other." The "other" group includes the voluntarily idle who do not fit into any of the other categories. Persons who are not in the labor force are also identified if they are "discouraged workers." Discouraged workers are persons who say that they want a job but did not look for work because they believed that no jobs were available. (See below, "The new CPS questionnaire," concerning a change in this measure to be introduced in 1994.)

Sampling

The CPS sample is traditionally redesigned after each decennial census and a new sample is then selected. The 1980 sample design in use during the 1985-94 period includes about 72,000 housing units per month located in 727 selected geographic areas called primary sampling units. The sample was initially selected so that specific reliability criteria were met nationally, for each of the 50 States, for the District of Columbia, and for the sub-State areas of New York City and the Los Angeles-Long Beach metropolitan area. Since 1985, these reliability criteria have been maintained through periodic additions and deletions in the State samples. The criteria, given below, are based on the coefficient of variation (CV) of the unemployment rate, where the CV is defined as the standard error of the estimate divided by the estimate, expressed as a percentage. These CV controls assume a 6-percent unemployment rate in the denominator of this formula to establish a consistent specification of sampling error.

Nationally, a 1.8-percent CV is maintained on the monthly unemployment rate estimate. This means that a change of 0.2 percentage point in the unemployment rate is significant at a 90-percent confidence level.

In 11 states—California, Florida, Illinois, Massachusetts, Michigan, New Jersey, New York, North Carolina, Ohio, Pennsylvania, and Texas—the most populous States at the time of the 1980 decennial census, an 8-percent CV is maintained on the monthly unemployment rate estimate.

In the other 39 States and the District of Columbia, an 8-percent CV is maintained on the annual unemployment rate estimate.

In New York City and the Los Angeles-Long Beach metropolitan area, a 9-percent CV is maintained on the monthly unemployment rate.

In the first stage of sampling, the 727 primary sampling units were chosen. In the second stage, ultimate sampling unit clusters composed of about four housing units each were selected. Each month, about 72,000 housing units are assigned for data collection, of which about 60,000 are occupied and thus eligible for interview. The remainder are units found to be destroyed, vacant, converted to nonresidential use, containing persons whose usual place of residence is elsewhere, or ineligible for other reasons. Of the 60,000 housing units, 4 to 5 percent are not interviewed in a given month due to temporary absence (vacation, etc.), other failures to make contact after repeated attempts, inability of persons contacted to respond, unavailability for other reasons, and refusals to cooperate (about half of the noninterviews). Information is obtained each month for about 113,000 persons 16 years of age and older.

Selection of sample areas. The entire area of the United States, consisting of 3,137 counties and independent cities, is divided into 1,973 primary sampling units (PSU's). In most States, a PSU consists of a county or a number of contiguous counties. In New England and Hawaii, minor civil divisions are used instead of counties.

Metropolitan areas within a State are used as a basis for forming PSU's. Outside of metropolitan areas, counties normally are combined, except where the geographic area of the sample county is very large. Combining counties to form PSU's provides greater heterogeneity; a typical PSU includes urban and rural residents of both high and low economic levels and encompasses, to the extent feasible, diverse occupations and industries. Another important consideration is to have the PSU sufficiently compact so that, with a small sample spread throughout, it can be efficiently canvassed without undue travel cost.

The 1,973 PSU's are grouped into strata within each State. Then one PSU is selected from each stratum with the probability of selection proportional to the population of the PSU. There are 314 PSU's in strata by themselves that are self-representing, and generally these are the most populated PSU's in each State. The remaining strata are formed by combining PSU's that are similar in such characteristics as population growth; proportions of blacks and of Hispanics (in certain States); and population distribution by occupation, industry, age, and sex. The PSU's, randomly selected from these strata, are non-self-representing, because each one chosen represents the entire stratum. The probability of selecting a particular PSU in a non-self-representing stratum is proportional to its 1980 population. For example, within a stratum, the chance that a PSU with a population of 50,000 would be selected for the sample is twice that for a PSU having a population of 25,000.

Selection of sample households. Because the sample design is essentially State based, the sampling ratio differs by State and depends on the reliability requirements for estimates for each State. The State sampling ratios range roughly from 1 in every 200 households to 1 in every 2,500 households in each stratum of the State. The sampling ratio occasionally is modified slightly to hold the size of the sample relatively constant given the overall growth of the population. The sampling ratio used within a sample PSU depends on the probability of selection of the PSU and the sampling ratio for the State. In a sample PSU with a probability of selection of 1 in 10 with a State sampling ratio of 1 in 2,500, the within-PSU sampling ratio that results is 1 in 250, thereby achieving the desired ratio of 1 in 2,500 for the stratum.

Within each designated PSU, several steps are involved in selecting the housing units to be enumerated. First, the 1980 census enumeration districts (ED's), which are administrative units and contain on the average about 300 housing units, are ordered so that the sample would reflect the demographic and residential characteristics of the PSU. Within each ED, the housing units are sorted geographically and are grouped into clusters of approximately four housing units. Next, a systematic sample of these clusters of housing units is selected.

The indentification of the sample housing units within an ED is made wherever possible from the list of ED addresses compiled during the 1980 census. The address lists are used in about three-fourths of the ED's, primarily in urban areas. Area sampling is applied in the remaining ED's, mostly in rural areas. In ED's where address lists are used, automated methods are used to form clusters of geographically contiguous housing units. An effort is made to have all small, multi-unit addresses (two to four housing units) included in the same cluster. The methods use the within-PSU sampling ratio to identify appropriate clusters for the sample. Supplemental samples are also prepared to account for addresses in isolated geographic areas and to account for housing units not found on the address lists, including housing units newly contructed in the PSU since the census date. The addresses of these units are obtained mainly from records of building permits.

In those enumeration districts where area sampling methods are used, mainly rural areas, the ED's are subdivided into small land "chunks" with well-defined boundaries and having, in general, an expected "size" of about 8 to 12 housing units or other living quarters. For each subdivided ED, one chunk (or more) is designated for the sample. When a selected chunk contains about four households, for example, all units are included in the sample. When the size of the chunk is several times four units, an interviewer does not conduct interviews at all housing units in the chunk but uses a systematic sampling pattern to obtain approximately four households. The remaining housing units in the chunk are then available for further samples. Area ED's also make use of building permit lists to identify newly constructed housing units.

Rotation of sample. Part of the sample is changed each month. For each sample, eight representative subsamples or rotation groups are identified. A given rotation group is interviewed for a total of 8 months, divided into two equal periods. It is in the sample for 4 consecutive months, leaves the sample during the following 8 months, and then returns for another 4 consecutive months. In any 1 month, one-eighth of the rotation groups are in their first month of enumeration, another eighth is in their second month, and so on. Under this system, 75 percent of the sample segments are common from month to month and 50 percent from year to year. This procedure provides a substantial amount of month-to-month and year-to-year overlap in the sample, thus reducing discontinuities in the series of data without burdening any specific group of households with an unduly long period of inquiry.

Collection Methods

Each month, during the calendar week containing the 19th day, interviewers contact a "responsible" person in each of the sample households in the CPS. At the time of the first enumeration of a household, the interviewer visits the household and prepares a roster of the household members, including their personal characteristics (date of birth, sex, race, ethnic origin, marital status, educational attainment, veteran status, etc.) and their relationship to the person maintaining the household. This roster is brought up to date at each subsequent interview to take account of new or departed residents, changes in marital status, and similar items. The information on personal characteristics is thus available each month for identification purposes and for cross-classification with economic characteristics of the sample population.

Personal visits are required in the first and fifth months that the household is in the sample. In other months, the interview may be conducted by telephone if the respondent agrees to this procedure. Also, if no one is at home when the interviewer visits, the respondent may be contacted by telephone after the first month. Approximately 68 percent of the households in any given month are interviewed by telephone.

At each monthly visit, a questionnaire is completed for each household member 16 years of age and over. The interviewer asks a series of standard questions on economic activity during the preceding week. The primary purpose of these questions is to classify the sample population into the three basic economic groups: The employed, the unemployed, and those not in the labor force. (See the facsimile of the CPS standard questionnaire at the end of this chapter.)

Additional questions are asked each month to help clarify the information on labor force status. For the employed, information is obtained on hours worked during the survey week, together with a description of the current job. For those temporarily away from their jobs, the enumerator records their reason for not working during the survey week, whether or not they were paid for their time off, and whether they usually work full or part time. For the unemployed, information is obtained on (1) the method(s) used to find work during the 4 weeks prior to the interview, (2) the reasons the unemployed persons had started to look for work, (3) the length of time they had been looking for work, (4) whether they were seeking full- or part-time work, and (5) a description of their last full-time civilian job. For those outside the labor force, their principal status during the survey week—keeping house, going to school, etc.—is recorded. In addition, all households in the outgoing rotation groups are asked questions on the work history, reasons for nonparticipation, and job-seeking intentions of individuals not in the labor force. Data on union status and hourly and weekly earnings are obtained from a quarter of the sample households—those in the two outgoing rotation groups.

The information obtained for each person in the sample is subjected to an edit by the regional offices of the Bureau of the Census. The field edit serves to catch omissions, inconsistencies, illegible entries, and errors at the point where correction is possible.

After the field edit, the questionnaires are forwarded to the Jeffersonville, Indiana office of the Bureau of the Census by the end of the week after enumeration for data capture. The raw data are transferred to computer tape and transmitted to the Bureau of the Census computers in the Washington office where the data are checked for completeness and consistency.

Although the CPS interviewers are chiefly part-time workers, most have had several years of experience on the survey. They are given intensive training when first recruited and further training each month before the survey. Through editing of their completed questionnaires, repeated observation during enumeration, and a systematic reinterview of part of their assignments by the field supervisory staff, the work of the interviewers is monitored and errors or deficiencies are brought directly to their attention.

Estimation Methods

Under the estimation methods used in the CPS, all of the results for a given month become available simultaneously and are based on returns from the entire panel of respondents. The estimation procedure involves weighting the data from each sample person by the inverse of the probability of the person being in the sample. This gives a rough measure of the number of persons the sample person represents. Since 1985, almost all sample persons within the same State have had the same probability of selection (with the exception of New York and California, where the cities of New York and Los Angeles are sampled at a higher probability). These selection probabilities are then adjusted for noninterviews; ratio adjustments are made to known population controls; and composite estimation procedures are applied.

Noninterview adjustment. The weights for all interviewed households are adjusted to the extent needed to account for occupied sample households for which no information was obtained because of absence, impassable roads, refusals, or unavailability of the respondents for other reasons. This noninterview adjustment is made separately for clusters of similar sample areas that are usually, but not necessarily, contained within a State. Similarity of sample areas is based on Metropolitan Statistical Area (MSA) status and size. Within each cluster, there is a further breakdown by residence. Each MSA cluster is split by "central city" and "balance of the MSA." Each non-MSA cluster is split by "urban" and "rural" residence categories. The proportion of sample households not interviewed varies from 4 to 5 percent depending on weather, vacations, etc.

Ratio adjustment. The distribution of the population selected for the sample may differ somewhat, by chance, from that of the population as a whole, in such characteristics as age, race, sex, and residence. Because these characteristics are closely correlated with labor force participation and other principal measurements made from the sample, the survey estimates can be substantially improved when weighted appropriately by the known distribution of these population characteristics. This is accomplished through two stages of ratio estimation, as follows.

First-stage ratio adjustment. The non-self-representing PSU's are chosen to represent all PSU's in a stratum. The remaining PSU's are self-representing. The first-stage ratio adjustment reduces the portion of the variance resulting from requiring sample PSU's in a State to represent nonsampled PSU's in the same State and is not applied to self-representing PSU's. The adjustment is made at the State level for each of the 43 States that contain nonsample areas by race cells of black and nonblack. The procedure corrects for the differences that existed in each cell at the time of the 1980 census between the race distribution of the population in sample PSU's and the known race distribution of the State.

Second-stage ratio adjustment. In this stage, the sample proportions of persons in specific categories are adjusted to the distribution of independent current estimates of the civilian noninstitutional population in the same categories. The second-stage ratio adjustment, which further reduces variability of the estimates and corrects to some extent for CPS undercoverage relative to the decennial census, is carried out in three steps.

In the first step, the sample estimates are adjusted within each State and the District of Columbia to independent controls for the population 16 years and over. These controls are an arithmetic extrapolation of the trend in the growth of this segment of the population using the two most recent July 1 estimates, adjusted to a current estimate of the U.S. population of this group.

The second step involves an adjustment by Hispanic origin to a national estimate for 14 Hispanic age-sex and 5 non-Hispanic age-sex categories. The adjustment is prepared by carrying forward the 1980 census count for Hispanics by adding estimated Hispanic births and immigrants and subtracting estimated Hispanic deaths and emigrants to yield an estimate of the Hispanic population by age and sex.

In the third step, a national adjustment is made by the race categories of white, black, and other races to independent estimates by age and sex. The white and black categories contain 66 and 42 age-sex groups respectively; the other races category has 10 age-sex cells.

The entire second-stage adjustment procedure is iterated six times, each time beginning at the weights developed the previous time. This ensures that the sample estimates of the population for both State and national age-sex-race-origin categories will be virtually equal to the independent population control totals.

The "inflation-deflation" method is used in the preparation of the independent national controls used for the age-sex-race groups in the third step of the second-stage ratio estimation procedure. With the "inflation-deflation" method, the independent controls are prepared by inflating the 1980 census counts to include estimated undercounts by age, sex, and race, aging this population forward to each subsequent month, adding births and net migration and subtracting deaths. These postcensal population estimates are then deflated to reflect the pattern of net undercount in the most recent census by age, sex, and race. Because an estimate of undercount is first added and then subtracted, the size of each race-sex group is unaffected by the "inflation-deflation" method. Similarly, the final estimate is affected only by the age structure of the undercount, but not the level.

Composite estimate. The last step in the preparation of most CPS estimates makes use of a composite estimation procedure. The composite estimate consists of a weighted average of two factors: The two-stage ratio estimate based on the entire sample from the current month and the composite estimate for the previous month plus an estimate of the month-to-month change based on the six rotation groups common to both months. In addition, a bias adjustment term is added to the weighted average to account for relative bias associated with month-in-sample estimates. This month-in-sample bias is exhibited by unemployment estimates for persons in their first and fifth months in the CPS being generally higher than estimates obtained for the other months.

The composite estimate results in a reduction in the sampling error beyond that which is achieved after the two stages of ratio adjustment. For some items, the reduction is substantial. The resultant gains in reliability are greatest in estimates of month-to-month change, although gains are also usually obtained for estimates of level in a given month, change from year to year, and change over other intervals of time.

Seasonal adjustment. Seasonal events such as weather changes, major holidays, and school openings and closings cause fluctuations in employment and unemployment levels. Seasonality, which may account for as much as 95 percent of month-to-month unemployment change, obscures nonseasonal trends and cyclical movements. Since seasonal fluctuations follow fairly regular annual patterns, their influence can often be easily estimated and removed from the data series using seasonal adjustment techniques. The procedure used by BLS is the X-11 ARIMA seasonal adjustment method, which is described in appendix A of this *Handbook*.

Seasonal adjustment involves using past data to approximate seasonal patterns. The seasonally adjusted series therefore have the same errors as the original series plus the uncertainties of the seasonal adjustment process. Adjusted series are, however, quite useful in analyzing nonseasonal economic and social trends.

Presentation and Uses

The CPS provides a large amount of detail on the economic and social characteristics of the population. It is the source of monthly estimates of total employment, both farm and nonfarm; of self-employed persons, domestics, and unpaid helpers in family enterprises, as well as wage and salaried employees; and of total unemployment. It is a comprehensive source of information on personal characteristics such as age, sex, race, Hispanic origin, educational attainment, and the marital and family status of the total civilian population (not in institutions) 16 years of age and over and of the employed, the unemployed, and those not in the labor force.

The survey provides distributions of workers by the number of hours worked, as distinguished from aggregate or average hours for an industry, permitting separate analyses of part-time workers, workers on overtime, etc. It is a comprehensive current source of information on the occupation of workers—whether teachers, stenographers, engineers, laborers, etc.—and the industries in which they work. It also provides data on the usual weekly earnings of wage and salary workers, which are published on a quarterly basis because the monthly detail is collected from only a quarter of the sample (the two "outgoing" rotation groups).

Information is available from the survey not only for persons currently in the labor force but also for those who are outside of the labor force. The characteristics of such persons—whether married women with or without young children, disabled persons, students, retired workers, etc.—can be determined. Also, through special inquiries, it is possible to obtain information on their skills and past work experience.

Each month, the employment and unemployment data are published initially in *The Employment Situation* news release 2 weeks after they are collected. The release includes a narrative summary and analysis of the major employment and unemployment developments together with tables containing statistics for the principal data series. The news release is also available electronically on a cost-for-service basis.

Subsequently, more detailed statistics are published in *Employment and Earnings.* The detailed tables in this periodical provide information on the labor force, employment, and unemployment by a number of characteristics, such as age, sex, race, marital status, industry, and occupation. Estimates of the labor force status and detailed characteristics of selected population groups not published on a monthly basis, such as Vietnam-era veterans, Hispanics, etc., are published every quarter. Additionally, data are published quarterly on employment and unemployment by family relationship and on median weekly earnings classified by a variety of characteristics. Approximately 250 of the most important estimates from the CPS are presented monthly and quarterly on a seasonally adjusted basis.

In addition, the January issue of *Employment and Earnings* provides annual averages on employment and earnings by detailed occupational categories, union affiliation, and employee absences.

Labor force data are available in machine-readable form and on BLS data diskettes. About 32,000 of the monthly labor force data series plus quarterly and annual averages are maintained on a one-reel tape. In many cases, these data are available from the inception of the series through the current month.

The CPS is used also for a program of special inquiries to obtain detailed information from particular segments, or for particular characteristics of the population and labor force. About four such special surveys are made each year. The inquiries are repeated annually in the same month for some topics, including the earnings and total incomes of individuals and families (published by the Bureau of the Census); the extent of work experience of the population during the calendar year; the marital and family characteristics of workers; the employment of school-age youth, high school graduates and dropouts, and recent college graduates; and the educational attainment of workers. Surveys are also made periodically on subjects such as job mobility, job tenure, displaced workers, and disabled veterans.

Generally, the persons who provide information for the monthly CPS questions also answer the supplemental questions. Occasionally, the kind of information sought in the special survey requires the respondent to be the person about whom the questions are asked. The results of these special surveys are first published as news releases and subsequently in the *Monthly Labor Review.*[1]

In addition to the regularly tabulated statistics described above, special data can be generated through the use of the CPS individual record (micro) tapes. These tape files contain records of the responses to the survey questionnaire for all individuals in the survey. While the tapes can be used simply to create additional cross-sectional detail, an important feature of their use is the ability to match the records of specific individuals at different points in time during their participation in the survey. By matching these records, data files can be created which lend themselves to some limited longitudinal analysis and the investigation of short-run labor market dynamics. An example is the statistics on gross labor force flows, which indicate how many persons move among the labor force status categories each month. Although a number of technical difficulties lie in the path of more complete utilization of these data files for the purposes of longitudinal analysis, this area is continually being investigated and holds considerable promise.

Limitations

Geographic. Although the present CPS sample is a State-based design, the CPS continues to produce reliable national monthly estimates. The sample does not permit the production of reliable monthly estimates for all States. Subnational data from the CPS are published monthly for the census regions and divisions, 11 large States, and two metropolitan areas. These data are limited to major labor force status categories. Demographic, social, and economic de-tail are published annually for the census regions and divisions, all States and the District of Columbia, 50 large metropolitan areas, and selected central cities. The production of subnational labor force and unemployment estimates is discussed in more detail in chapter 4 of this bulletin.

Sources of errors in the survey estimates. The estimates from the survey are subject to sampling errors, that is, errors arising from the fact that the estimates each month are based on information from a sample rather than the whole population. In addition, as in any survey, the results are subject to errors made in the field and in the process of compilation.

Classification errors in labor force surveys may be particularly large in the case of persons with marginal attachments to the labor force. These errors may be caused by interviewers, respondents, or both, or may arise from faulty questionnaire design. In spite of a continuous quality control program, interviewers may not always ask the questions in the prescribed fashion. To the extent that varying the wording of the question causes differences in response, errors or lack of uniformity in the statistics may result. Similarly, the data are limited by the adequacy of the information possessed by the respondent and the willingness to report accurately.

The estimates from the survey also are subject to various other types of errors. Some of these are:

Nonresponse. About 4 to 5 percent of occupied units are not interviewed in a typical month because of temporary absence of the occupants, refusals to cooperate, or other reasons. Although an adjustment is made in weights for interviewed households to account for noninterviews, they still represent a possible source of bias. Similarly, for a relatively few households, some of the information is omitted because of lack of knowledge on the part of the respondent or because of interviewer error. In processing the completed questionnaires, entries usually are imputed for omitted items on the basis of the distributions of these items for persons of similar characteristics.

Independent population estimates. The independent population estimates used in the estimation procedure may be a source of error although, on balance, their use substantially improves the statistical reliability of many of the figures. Errors may arise in the independent population estimates because of underenumeration of certain population groups or errors in age reporting in the last census (which serves as the base for the estimates) or similar problems in the components of population change (mortality, immigration, etc.) since that date.

[1] Historical data through 1987 for many of the CPS regular monthly and annual data series as well as those derived from the supplemental questions were published in *Labor Force Statistics Derived From the Current Population Survey*, 1948-87, Bulletin 2307 (U.S. Department of Labor, Bureau of Labor Statistics, 1988).

Processing errors. Although there is a quality control program on coding and a close control on all other phases of processing and tabulation of the returns, some processing errors are almost inevitable in a large statistical operation of this type. However, the net error arising from processing is probably fairly negligible.

Measuring the accuracy of results. Modern sampling theory provides methods for estimating the range of errors due to sampling where, as in the CPS sample, the probability of selection of each member of the population is known. Methods are also available for determining the effect of response variability in the CPS. A measure of sampling variability indicates the range of differences that may be expected because only a sample of the population is surveyed. A measure of response variability indicates the range of difference that may be expected as a result of compensating types of errors arising from practices of different interviewers and the replies of respondents; these would tend to cancel out in an enumeration of a large enough population. In practice, these two sources of error—sampling and response variability—are estimated jointly from the results of the survey. The computations, however, do not incorporate the effect of response bias, that is, any systematic errors of response. Response biases occur in the same way in a complete census as in a sample, and, in fact, may be smaller in a well-conducted sample survey where it may be feasible to collect the information more skillfully.

Estimates of sampling and response variability combined are provided in *Employment and Earnings* and in other reports based on CPS data, thus permitting the user to take this factor into account in interpreting the data. In general, the smaller figures and small differences between figures are subject to relatively large variation and should be interpreted with caution.

Estimation of response bias is one of the most difficult aspects of survey and census work. In many instances, available techniques are not sufficiently precise to provide satisfactory estimates. Continuing experimentation is carried out with the aim of developing more precise measurements and improving the overall accuracy of the series.

Planned Changes for the CPS

In 1986, the Bureau of Labor Statistics and the Bureau of the Census undertook an intensive investigation of the CPS that resulted in the commitment to a plan providingfor major improvements, to be implemented beginning in 1994. These improvements include a new questionnaire, automated data collection methods, and a modernized computer processing system. Concurrent with this effort, the CPS sample will be redesigned based on the 1990 decennial census.

The new CPS questionnaire

The CPS labor force questionnaire has been virtually unchanged since 1967, at which time changes had been introduced based on recommendations of the Gordon Committee (President's Committee to Appraise Employment and Unemployment, 1962). Additional changes were proposed in the late 1970's based on the Levitan Commission (National Commission on Employment and Unemployment, 1979); these, in part, formed the basis for the redesign of the questionnaire.

Beginning in 1986, the Bureau of Labor Statistics and the Bureau of the Census conducted a 5-year program of research and testing, which will result in a major redesign of the questionnaire (see Butz and Plewes, 1989). Rothgeb, et al. (1991) discussed five main objectives of the redesign program: (1) To better operationalize existing definitions and reduce reliance on volunteered responses; (2) to reduce the potential for response error in the questionnaire-respondent-interviewer interaction and improve measurement of CPS concepts; (3) to implement minor definitional changes on labor force classifications; (4) to expand the CPS labor force data base and improve longitudinal measures; and (5) to use computer-assisted interviewing techniques to improve data quality and reduce respondent burden. The new questionnaire will be implemented in January 1994.

The new questionnaire contains many more questions tailored toward certain demographic and labor force groups than the pre-1994 version. Interview time will not be meaningfully affected, however, primarily because of the use of automated data collection (see below) as well as the implementation of dependent interviewing, i.e., making use of information collected in the prior month, such as industry and occupational status. The 1994 revisions will provide precision to the measurement of labor force status, resulting in virtually no reliance upon volunteered information; provide more data for analysis, such as multiple jobholding and usual hours of all employed persons; and implement minor definitional changes.

In terms of definitional changes, there were two. One was the introduction of a revised measure for labor market discouragement, based on the Levitan Commission recommendations. Beginning in 1994, discouraged workers will be identified as persons who, though not working or seeking work, have a current desire for a job, have looked for one within the past year, and are currently available for work. (The data will be published monthly.) The second involves "persons expecting to report to a new job within 30 days" and is a miniscule change. Those volunteering such an expectation will no longer automatically be classified as unemployed but will, instead, be routed through the series of questions on job search like all other potentially unemployed persons (excepting those on layoff who anticipate returning to their jobs).

Computer-assisted interviewing

Starting in January 1994, CPS survey data will be collected using computer-assisted interviewing (CAI), which employs interactive computing to replace paper-and-pencil methods. The interviewer reads survey questions displayed on a computer screen to the respondent and enters his or her answers on the computer keyboard. CAI systems also help the interviewer schedule interviews and callbacks, check interview completion status, and maintain records of calls made, outcomes, and interview length.

There are two basic forms of CAI: Computer-assisted telephone interviewing (CATI) and computer-assisted personal interviewing (CAPI). CATI will use interactive mainframe computer facilities and be conducted from two central sites, located in Hagerstown, Maryland, and Tucson, Arizona. CAPI will use laptop computers to assist a geographically dispersed interviewing staff in conducting interviews in respondents' homes or in conducting telephone interviews from their own homes.

CATI and CAPI have many advantages over paper-and-pencil methods. A main advantage is the ability for dependent interviewing. In this mode, the computer is programmed to display a respondent's answers from the previous month's interview. The interviewer can then remind the respondent of his or her previous answer and ask if specific changes have occurred. This technique greatly reduces spurious, month-to-month changes and is especially useful for classifying individuals according to industry and occupation codes, for measuring length of unemployment spells more accurately, and for reducing respondent burden for the retired and the disabled.

In addition to providing enhanced management and supervisory information for control of interviewing operations, other advantages of CATI and CAPI include the elimination of interviewer errors resulting from incorrectly followed skip patterns and the elimination of errors resulting from survey operations such as printing and shipping of questionnaires, keypunching operations, and other clerical data processing.

The implementation of CAI in 1994 requires that CAPI be used for the first and fifth month-in-sample households (which are currently collected by personal visit), for subsequent month-in-sample cases in single interviewer PSU's, for households with language problems, for prior-month noninterviews, and for no-telephone households. All other household interviews for months-in-sample 2 through 4 and 6 through 8 will be collected by the centralized CATI facilities.

Redesign of the CPS sample

Since the inception of the CPS in 1940, it has been the practice to update and revise the sample after each decennial census. As the 1990 census data become available, minor revisions in the sample design will be made. Consistent with procedures following past censuses, new sample areas for the CPS will be introduced which, for the most part, will remain in the CPS sample until it is redesigned after the 2000 census. The CPS design and reliability requirements, however, will change relatively little from the 1980's State-based design (see Sampling).

Technical References

Rothgeb, J. M.; Polivka, A. E.; Creighton, K. P.; Cohany, S. R. (1991) "Development of the Proposed Revised Current Population Survey Questionnaire," *ASA Proceedings of the Section on Survey Methods Research* (in press).

Butz, W. P. and Plewes, T. J. (1989) "A Current Population Survey for the 21st Century," *Proceedings of the Fifth Annual Research Conference*, U.S. Department of Commerce, Bureau of the Census: Washington, DC, pp. 3-13.

Bregger, John E. "The Current Population Survey: A Historical View and BLS' Role," *Monthly Labor Review*, June 1984.

Dagum, Estela Bee. *The X-11 ARIMA Seasonal Adjustment Method.* Ottawa, Statistics Canada, January 1983 (Statistics Canada Catalogue No. 12-564E).

National Commission on Employment and Unemployment Statistics. *Counting the Labor Force*, 1979.

A comprehensive review of the entire labor market data system; includes an appraisal of current concepts and methodology and recommendations for further research and improvements.

U.S. Department of Commerce, Office of Federal Statistical Policy and Standards. "An Error Profile: Employment as Measured by the Current Population Survey," *Statistical Policy Working Paper 3*, 1978.

A description of the potential sources of error in the CPS as they affect the national employment statistics.

President's Committee to Appraise Employment and Unemployment Statistics. *Measuring Employment and Unemployment*, 1962.

A review of all Federal statistical series on employment and unemployment and a comparison of the sources and uses of each series; includes a brief history of the development of labor force statistics, an evaluation of concepts and techniques, and recommendations for further research and improvements.

Bureau of Labor Statistics

Employment and Earnings, Explanatory Notes, monthly.

An up-to-date, concise description of the concepts and methods used in the labor force data from the Current Population Survey. Provides tables which present the sampling errors for various labor force series.

Technical References—Continued

Geographic Profile of Employment and Unemployment, 1990, Bulletin 2381, 1991.

A tabular presentation of 1990 annual average data on the labor force characteristics of the population residing in the Census regions, the 50 States and the District of Columbia, 50 large metropolitan areas, and 17 central cities.

Labor Force Statistics Derived From the Current Population Survey, 1948-87, Bulletin 2307, 1988.

A compilation of historical data through 1987 for many of the data series obtained from the Current Population Survey.

How the Government Measures Unemployment, Report 742, 1987.

A short, nontechnical discussion of the concepts and methods used in obtaining labor force statistics from the Current Population Survey.

A Guide to Seasonal Adjustment of Labor Force Data, Bulletin 2114, 1982.

A nontechnical description of the concepts and techniques used in seasonally adjusting labor force statistics from the Current Population Survey.

18. LINE NUMBER

19. What was . . . doing most of LAST WEEK – Working / Keeping house / Going to school / or something else?

- Working (Skip to 20A) . . . . WK ○
- With a job but not at work . . J ○
- Looking for work . . . . LK ○
- Keeping house . . . . H ○
- Going to school . . . . S ○
- Unable to work (Skip to 24) . . U ○
- Retired . . . . R ○
- Other (Specify) . . . . OT ○

20. Did . . . do any work at all LAST WEEK, not counting work around the house? (Note: If farm or business operator in hh., ask about unpaid work.)

Yes ○ No ○ (Go to 21)

20A. How many hours did . . . work LAST WEEK at all jobs?

20B. INTERVIEWER CHECK ITEM

- 49+ ○ (Skip to item 23)
- 1–34 ○ (Go to 20C)
- 35–48 ○ (Go to 20D)

20C. Does . . . USUALLY work 35 hours or more a week at this job?

Yes ○ What is the reason . . . worked less than 35 hours LAST WEEK?

No ○ What is the reason . . . USUALLY works less than 35 hours a week?

(Mark the appropriate reason)

- Slack work . . . . ○
- Material shortage . . . . ○
- Plant or machine repair . . . . ○
- New job started during week . . ○
- Job terminated during week . . . ○
- Could find only part-time work ○
- Holiday (Legal or religious) . . . . ○
- Labor dispute . . . . ○
- Bad weather . . . . ○
- Own illness . . . . ○
- On vacation . . . . ○
- Too busy with housework, school, personal bus., etc. . . ○
- Did not want full-time work . . . ○
- Full-time work week under 35 hours . . . . ○
- Other reason (Specify) . . . . ○

(Skip to 23 and enter job worked at last week)

20D. Did . . . lose any time or take any time off LAST WEEK for any reason such as illness, holiday or slack work?

Yes ○ How many hours did . . . take off?

(Correct 20A if lost time not already deducted; if 20A reduced below 35, correct 20B and fill 20C)

No ○

20E. Did . . . work any overtime or at more than one job LAST WEEK?

Yes ○ How many extra hours did . . . work?

(Correct 20A and 20B as necessary if extra hours not already included and skip to 23.)

No ○ (Skip to 23)

21. (If J in 19, skip to 21A.) Did . . . have a job or business from which he/she was temporarily absent or on layoff LAST WEEK?

Yes ○ No ○ (Go to 22)

21A. Why was . . . absent from work LAST WEEK?

- Own illness . . . . . . ○
- On vacation . . . . . ○
- Bad weather . . . . . ○
- Labor dispute . . . . ○
- New job to begin within 30 days ○ (Skip to 22B and 22C2)
- Temporary layoff (Under 30 days) ○
- Indefinite layoff (30 days or more or no def. recall date) . . . . ○ (Skip to 22C3)
- Other (Specify) . . ○

21B. Is . . . receiving wages or salary from his/her employer for any of the time off LAST WEEK?

Yes ○

No ○

21C. Does . . . usually work 35 hours or more a week at this job?

Yes ○

No ○

(Skip to 23 and enter job held last week)

OFFICE USE ONLY

INDUSTRY	OCCUPATION
Ref. ○	Ref. ○
Unc. ○	Unc. ○

22. (If LK in 19, Skip to 22A.) Has . . . been looking for work during the past 4 weeks?

Yes ○ No ○ (Go to 24)

22A. What has . . . been doing in the last 4 weeks to find work? (Mark all methods used; do not read list.)

- Checked with – pub. employ. agency ○
- pvt. employ. agency ○
- employer directly . . . ○
- friends or relatives . . ○
- Placed or answered ads . . . . ○
- Nothing (Skip to 24) . . . . ○
- Other (Specify in notes, e.g., JTPA, union or prof. register, etc.) . . . . ○

22B. At the time . . . started looking for work, was it because he/she lost or quit a job or was there some other reason?

- Lost job . . . . ○
- Quit job . . . . ○
- Left school . . . . ○
- Wanted temporary work . . ○
- Change in home or family responsibilities ○
- Left military service . . . . . . ○
- Other (Specify in notes) . . . . ○

22C. 1) How many weeks has . . . been looking for work?

2) How many weeks ago did . . . start looking for work?

3) How many weeks ago was . . . laid off?

22D. Has . . . been looking for full-time or part-time work?

Full ○ Part ○

22E. Could . . . have taken a job LAST WEEK if one had been offered?

Yes ○ No ○ Why not?

- Already has a job . . . . . ○
- Temporary illness . . . . ○
- Going to school . . . . . . ○
- Other (Specify in notes) ○

22F. When did . . . last work at a full-time job or business lasting 2 consecutive weeks or more?

- Within last 12 months (Specify) . . ○ (Month) ________
- One to five years ago . . . . ○
- More than 5 years ago . . . . ○
- Never worked full-time 2 wks. or more . . . . ○
- Never worked at all . . . . ○

(SKIP to 23. If layoff entered in 21A, enter job, either full or part time, from which laid off. Else enter last full time job lasting 2 weeks or more, or "never worked.")

24. INTERVIEWER CHECK ITEM (Rotation number)

First digit of SEGMENT number is:

- ○ 1, 2, 4, 5, 6 or 8 (Skip to 26)
- ○ 3 or 7 (Go to 24A)

24A. When did . . . last work for pay at a regular job or business, either full- or part-time?

- Within past 12 months ○
- 1 up to 2 years ago . . . ○
- 2 up to 3 years ago . . . ○ (Go to 24B)
- 3 up to 4 years ago . . . ○
- 4 up to 5 years ago . . . ○
- 5 or more years ago . . ○ (Skip to 24C)
- Never worked . . . . ○

24B. Why did . . . leave that job?

- Personal, family (Incl. pregnancy) or school . . . . ○
- Health . . . . ○
- Retirement or old age . . . . ○
- Seasonal job completed . . . . ○
- Slack work or business conditions ○
- Temporary nonseasonal job completed . . . ○
- Unsatisfactory work arrangements (Hours, pay, etc.) ○
- Other . . . . ○

24C. Does . . . want a regular job now, either full- or part-time?

- Yes . . . . ○ (Go to 24D)
- Maybe – it depends ○ (Specify in notes)
- No . . . . ○ (Skip to 24E)
- Don't know . . . . . . ○

24D. What are the reasons . . . is not looking for work? (Mark each reason mentioned)

- Believes no work available in line of work or area ○
- Couldn't find any work . . . . ○
- Lacks nec. schooling, training, skills or experience . . . . ○
- Employers think too young or too old . . . . . ○
- Other pers. handicap in finding job ○
- Can't arrange child care . . . . ○
- Family responsibilities . . . . ○
- In school or other training . . . . ○
- Ill health, physical disability . . . . . . ○
- Other (Specify in notes) . . . . ○
- Don't know . . . . ○

24E. Does . . . intend to look for work of any kind in the next 12 months?

- Yes . . . . ○
- It depends (Specify in notes) ○
- No . . . . ○
- Don't know . . . . ○

(If entry in 24B, describe job in 23, otherwise, skip to 26)

25. INTERVIEWER CHECK ITEM (Rotation number)

First digit of SEGMENT number is:

- ○ 1, 2, 4, 5, 6 or 8 (Skip to 26)
- ○ 3 or 7 (Go to 25A)

25A. How many hours per week does . . . USUALLY work at this job?

25B. Is . . . paid by the hour on this job?

Yes ○ (Go to 25C)

No ○ (Skip to 25D)

25C. How much does . . . earn per hour?

Dollars Cents

$ ¢

REF ○ (Ask 25D)

25D. How much does . . . USUALLY earn per week at this job BEFORE deductions? Include any overtime pay, commissions, or tips usually received.

$

REF ○

25E. On this job, is . . . a member of a labor union or of an employee association similar to a union?

Yes ○ (Skip to 26)

No ○ (Ask 25F)

25F. On this job, is . . . covered by a union or employee association contract?

Yes ○ (Go to 26)

No ○

23. DESCRIPTION OF JOB OR BUSINESS

23A. For whom did . . . work? (Name of company, business, organization or other employer.)

23B. What kind of business or industry is this? (For example: TV and radio mfg., retail shoe store, State Labor Dept., farm.)

23C. What kind of work was . . . doing? (For example: electrical engineer, stock clerk, typist, farmer.)

23D. What were . . .'s most important activities or duties at this job? (For example: types, keeps account books, files, sells cars, operates printing press, finishes concrete.)

23E. Was this person

- An employee of a PRIVATE Co, bus., or individual for wages, salary or comm. . . P ○ (Go to 23F)
- A FEDERAL government employee . . . . F ○
- A STATE government employee . . . . S ○
- A LOCAL government employee . . . . L ○
- Self-empl. in OWN bus., prof. practice, or farm
  - Is the business incorporated? Yes . . . . I ○
  - No . . . . SE ○ (Skip to 26)
- Working WITHOUT PAY in fam. bus. or farm . . . WP ○
- NEVER WORKED . . . . NEV ○

23F. INTERVIEWER CHECK ITEM

- Entry (or NA) in item 20A ○ (Go to 25 at top of page)
- Entry (or NA) in item 21B ○
- All other cases ○ (Skip to 26)

Page 8

Chapter 2. Employment, Hours, and Earnings from the Establishment Survey

BLS cooperates with State employment security agencies in the Current Employment Statistics (CES) survey to collect data each month on employment, hours, and earnings from a sample of nonfarm establishments (including government). In early 1992, this sample included over 350,000 reporting units. From these data, a large number of employment, hours, and earnings series in considerable industry and geographic detail are prepared and published each month. The employment data include series on all employees, women workers, and production or nonsupervisory workers. Hours and earnings data include average weekly hours, average weekly overtime hours, and average hourly and weekly earnings. For many series, seasonally adjusted data are also published.

Background

The first monthly studies of employment and payrolls by BLS began in 1915 and covered four manufacturing industries. Before 1915, the principal sources of employment data in the United States were the census surveys—the decennial Census of Population and the quinquennial Census of Manufactures. No regular employment data were compiled between the censuses.

In 1916, the survey was expanded to cover employment and payrolls in 13 manufacturing industries; by 1923, the number had increased to 52, and by 1932, 91 manufacturing and 15 nonmanufacturing industries were covered by a monthly employment survey.

With the deepening economic crisis in 1930, President Hoover appointed an Advisory Committee on Employment Statistics which recommended extension of the Bureau's program to include the development of hours and earnings series. In 1932, Congress granted an increase in the BLS appropriation for the survey. In 1933, average hourly earnings and average weekly hours were published for the first time for total manufacturing, for 90 manufacturing industries, and for 14 nonmanufacturing categories.

During the Great Depression, there was controversy concerning the actual number of unemployed people; no reliable measures of employment or unemployment existed. This confusion stimulated efforts to develop comprehensive estimates of total wage and salary employment in nonfarm industries, and BLS survey data produced such a figure for the first time in 1936.

Interest in employment statistics for States and areas also grew. Even before BLS entered the field in 1915, Massachusetts, New York, and New Jersey were preparing employment statistics. In 1915, New York and Wisconsin entered into cooperative agreements with BLS, whereby sample data collected from employers by a State agency would be used jointly with BLS to prepare State and national series. By 1928, five other States had entered into such compacts, and another five were added by 1936. By 1940, estimates of total nonfarm employment for all 48 States and the District of Columbia were available. In 1991, cooperative arrangements were in effect with all 50 States, the District of Columbia, Puerto Rico, and the Virgin Islands.

Since 1949, the Current Employment Statistics (CES) program has been a fully integrated Federal-State project which provides employment, hours, and earnings information by industry on a national, State, and area basis. BLS is expanding the published industry detail for the service-producing sector, bringing it into parity with the goods-producing sector, and it is implementing computer-assisted reporting through telephone interviews, touch-tone self-reporting, and voice recognition systems.

Concepts

Establishment

An establishment is an economic unit, such as a factory, mine, or store which produces goods or services. It is generally at a single location and engaged predominantly in one type of economic activity. Where a single location encompasses two or more distinct activities, these are treated as separate establishments, provided that separate payroll records are available and certain other criteria are met.

Employment

Employment is the total number of persons employed full or part time in nonfarm establishments during a specified payroll period. Temporary employees are included. In general, data refer to persons who worked during, or received pay for, any part of the pay period that includes the 12th of the month, which is standard for all Federal agencies collecting employment data from business establishments. National employment figures for Federal Government establishments, however, represent the number of persons who were paid for the last full pay period of the calendar month; intermittent Federal Government workers are counted if they performed any service during the month.

Workers on an establishment payroll who are on paid

sick leave (when pay is received directly from the employer); on paid holiday or vacation; or who work during only a part of the specified pay period, even though they are unemployed or on strike during the rest of the pay period, are all counted as employed. Persons on the payroll of more than one establishment during the pay period are counted in each establishment which reports them, whether the duplication is due to turnover or dual jobholding. Persons are considered employed if they receive pay for any part of the specified pay period, but they are not considered employed if they receive no pay at all for the pay period. Since proprietors, the self-employed, and unpaid family workers do not have the status of paid employees, they are not included. Also excluded from the employed are domestic workers in households; persons who are on layoff, on leave without pay, or on strike for the entire pay period; and persons who were hired but have not yet started work during the pay period. The employment statistics for government refer to civilian employees only.

All persons who meet these specifications are included in the designation "all employees," regardless of industry. Major categories of employees are differentiated primarily to ensure the expeditious collection of current statistics on hours and earnings; these groups of employees are designated production workers, construction workers, or nonsupervisory workers, depending upon the industry.

In manufacturing industries, data also are collected for *production workers.* This group covers employees, up through the level of working supervisors, who engage directly in the manufacture of the establishment's product. Among those excluded from this category are persons in executive and managerial positions and persons engaged in activities such as accounting, sales, advertising, routine office work, professional and technical functions, and force-account construction. (Force-account construction is construction work performed by an establishment, primarily engaged in some business other than construction, for its own account and for use by its own employees.) Production workers in mining are defined in a similar manner. A more detailed description of the classes of employees included in the production and nonproduction worker categories in manufacturing is shown on the facsimile of the BLS 790 C schedule at the end of this chapter.

In construction, the term "construction workers" covers workers, up through the level of working supervisors, who are engaged directly on the construction project either at the site or in shops or yards at jobs ordinarily performed by members of construction trades. Excluded from this category are executive and managerial personnel, professional and technical employees, and workers in routine office jobs.

In the remaining industries (transportation, communications, and public utilities; wholesale and retail trade; finance, insurance, and real estate; and services) data are collected for nonsupervisory workers. Nonsupervisory workers include most employees except those in top executive and managerial positions. (See facsimile of BLS 790 E, the reporting form for wholesale and retail trade.)

An employment benchmark is a reasonably complete count of employment used to adjust estimates derived from a sample. Adjustment is usually done annually. The basic source of benchmark data for the CES survey is data collected from employers by State employment security agencies as a byproduct of the unemployment insurance (UI) system. About 98 percent of all employees on nonfarm payrolls are covered by the UI system. The compilation and use of benchmark data are explained in detail in later sections of this chapter.

Hours and earnings

The hours and earnings series are based on reports of gross payrolls and the corresponding paid hours for production workers, construction workers, or nonsupervisory workers. (See facsimile of BLS 790 C.) In government and private educational institutions, payroll data are for "all employees."

Aggregate payrolls include pay before deductions for Social Security, unemployment insurance, group insurance, withholding tax, salary reduction plans, bonds, and union dues. The payroll figures also include pay for overtime, shift premiums, holidays, vacations, and sick leave paid directly by the employer to employees for the pay period reported. They exclude bonuses, commissions, and other lump-sum payments (unless earned and paid regularly each pay period or month), or other pay not earned in the pay period concerned (e.g., retroactive pay). Tips and the value of free rent, fuel, meals, or other payments in kind are not included.

Total hours during the pay period include all hours worked (including overtime hours), hours paid for standby or reporting time, and equivalent hours for which employees received pay directly from the employer for sick leave, holidays, vacations, and other leave. Overtime or other premium pay hours are not converted to straight-time equivalent hours. The concept of total hours differs from scheduled hours or hours worked. The average weekly hours derived from the total hours reflect the effects of such factors as unpaid absenteeism, labor turnover, part-time work, and strikes, as well as fluctuations in work schedules.

Overtime hours are hours worked for which premiums were paid because they were in excess of the number of hours of either the straight-time workday or workweek. Saturday and Sunday hours (or 6- and 7th-day hours) are included as overtime only if overtime premiums were paid. Holiday hours worked as overtime are not included unless they are paid for at more than the straight-time rate. Hours for which only shift differential, hazard, incentive, or similar types of premiums were paid are excluded from overtime hours. Overtime hours data are collected only from establishments in manufacturing industries.

Average hourly earnings series, derived by dividing gross payrolls by total hours, reflect the actual earnings of workers, including premium pay. They differ from wage rates, which are the amounts stipulated for a given unit of work or time. Average hourly earnings do not represent total labor costs per hour for the employer, because they exclude retroactive payments and irregular bonuses, employee benefits, and the employer's share of payroll taxes. Earnings for those employees not covered under the production worker and nonsupervisory categories are not reflected in the estimates.

Real earnings data (those expressed in 1982 dollars) result from the adjustment of average hourly and weekly earnings by means of the Bureau's Consumer Price Index for Urban Wage Earners and Clerical Workers (CPI-W); they indicate the changes in the purchasing power of money earnings as a result of price changes for consumer goods and services. These data cannot be used to measure changes in living standards as a whole, which are affected by other factors such as total family income, the extension and incidence of various social services and benefits, and the duration and extent of employment and unemployment. The long-term trends of these earnings data are also affected by changing mixes of full-time/part-time workers, high-paid/low-paid workers, etc.

Straight-time average hourly earnings are approximated by adjusting average hourly earnings by eliminating only premium pay for overtime at a rate of time and one-half. Thus, no adjustment is made for other premium payment provisions such as holiday work, late shift work, and premium overtime rates other than those at time and one-half. Straight-time average hourly earnings are calculated only for manufacturing industries because data on overtime hours are not collected in other industries.

Industrial classification

Industrial classification refers to the grouping of reporting establishments into industries on the basis of their major product or activity as determined by the establishments' percentages of total sales or receipts for the previous calendar year. This information is collected as an administrative byproduct of the UI reporting system. All data for an establishment making more than one product or engaging in more than one activity are classified under the industry of the most important product or activity, based on the percentages reported.

Industries are classified in accordance with the 1987 *Standard Industrial Classification Manual*, Office of Management and Budget. (See appendix B of this bulletin for a description of this classification system.)

Data Sources and Collection Methods

Sample data

Each month, the State agencies cooperating with BLS in the survey collect data on employment, payrolls, and paid hours from a sample of establishments. Data are collected by mail from most respondents; phone collection is used to obtain higher response rates from selected respondents through computer-assisted interviews, touch-tone self-response, and voice recognition technology.

The respondents extract the requested data from their payroll records, which must be maintained for a variety of tax and accounting purposes. All firms with 250 employees or more are asked to participate in the survey, as well as a sample of smaller firms. Together, they comprise the largest monthly employer survey in existence, with a sample of over 350,000 establishments. Despite the voluntary nature of the survey, numerous establishments have reported regularly for many years.

A "shuttle" schedule (BLS form 790 series) is used for mail respondents. It is submitted each month by the respondent, edited by the State agency, and returned to the respondent for use again the following month. The shuttle schedule has been used since 1930, but there have been substantial changes in its design and in the data collected. The report forms are basically alike for each industry, but there are several variants tailored to the characteristics of different industries.

The technical characteristics of the shuttle schedule are particularly important in maintaining continuity and consistency in reporting from month to month. The shuttle design automatically exhibits the trends of the reported data covered by the schedule during the year; therefore, the relationship of the current data to the data for the previous months is shown. The schedule also has operational advantages. For example, accuracy and economy are achieved by entering the identification codes and the address of the reporter only once a year.

All schedules are edited by the State agencies each month to make sure that the data are correctly reported and that they are consistent with the data reported by the establishment in earlier months and with the data reported by other establishments in the industry. The State agencies forward the data, either on the schedules themselves or in machine-readable form, to BLS-Washington. They also use the information provided on the forms to develop State and area estimates of employment, hours, and earnings. At BLS, the data are edited again by computer to detect processing and reporting errors which may have been missed in the initial State editing. Questionable reports discovered at any stage of the editing process are discussed with the respondent for clarification or correction. The edited data are used to prepare national estimates.

It should be noted that for employment, the sum of the State figures will differ from the official U.S. national totals because of the effects of differing industrial and geographic stratification and differences in the timing of benchmark adjustments.

Benchmark data

Since about 1940, the basic source of benchmark information for "all employees" has been the periodic tabulations compiled by State employment security agencies from reports of establishments covered under State UI laws.

The State employment security agencies receive quarterly reports from each employer subject to the UI laws showing total employment in each month of the quarter and the total quarterly wages for all employees. The State agencies submit tabulations of these reports to BLS-Washington each quarter. (See chapter 5.)

For the few industries exempt from mandatory UI coverage, other sources are used for benchmark information. For example, data on employees covered under Social Security laws, published by the Bureau of the Census in *County Business Patterns*, are used to augment the UI data for religious organizations, private schools, and interns and trainees in hospitals. Data for interstate railroads are obtained from the Interstate Commerce Commission.

The Federal Government employment series is a complete count provided monthly by the Office of Personnel Management and, therefore, a benchmark is not necessary. The UI data for State and local government employment are supplemented as necessary with Bureau of the Census data derived from the Census of Governments for local elected officials and certain other groups.[1]

Sample Design

BLS uses sampling in the CES survey to collect data in most industries, because full coverage would be prohibitively costly and time consuming. The sampling plan for the program must: (a) Provide for the preparation of reliable monthly estimates of employment, hours of work, and weekly and hourly earnings, which can be published promptly and regularly; (b) through a single, general system, yield considerable industry detail for metropolitan areas, States, and the Nation; (c) be appropriate for the existing framework of operating procedures, administrative practices, resource availability, and other institutional characteristics of the program; and (d) provide maximum accuracy at minimum cost.

The primary sampling design is stratified random sampling of establishments, which produces an efficient and equitable sample distribution by stratifying the universe of establishments into homogeneous groups. The strata are arranged according to industry and size characteristics. Under optimum allocation for this design, a larger sample is usually required for a stratum of a certain size if that stratum has a greater number of units in the universe or if it has a high degree of variability. The optimum number of establishments included in each size of stratum in the national CES sample is determined by the number of establishments in a stratum's universe and the standard deviation of the establishments in that universe.

Under the assumption that the standard deviation of establishments within a stratum of a particular size is proportional to the average size of the establishments within that stratum, optimum allocation for this sample design becomes proportional to employment. This requires that the universe of establishments for each industry be stratified into employment-size classes. A total sample size sufficient to produce adequate employment estimates is then determined and distributed among the size classes in each industry based on the average employment per establishment and the relative importance of each size class to its industry. In practice, this amounts to distributing the total number of establishments needed in the sample among the cells according to the ratio of the employment in each cell to the total employment in the industry.

The likelihood that a certain establishment will be selected depends upon its employment level. Large establishments are certain of selection; smaller ones have less chance. Within each cell, sample members are selected at random. Sampling ratios are determined in order to aid this selection process. In nearly all industries, establishments with 250 or more employees are included in the sample with certainty; in many industries, the cutoff is lower. In a manufacturing industry in which a high proportion of total employment is concentrated in relatively few large establishments, a high percentage of total employment is included in the sample. Consequently, the sample design for such industries provides for a complete census of the large establishments with only a few chosen from among the smaller establishments. On the other hand, in an industry where a large proportion of total employment is in small establishments, the sample design calls for the inclusion of all large establishments, and also for a substantial number of the smaller establishments. Many industries in the trade and services divisions fall into this category.

This sample design, although aimed primarily at meeting the requirements for national estimates, provides a technical framework within which State and area needs can be met. It incorporates the trends in all size classes, reduces geographic bias, and reduces large-firm bias by giving smaller firms proper representation in the sample. Because the estimates for States and areas generally are not prepared at the same degree of industry detail as the national estimates, it may be necessary to modify the national sampling ratios in order to obtain a sufficient sample. The additional reports needed for State and area samples are added to the sample required by the national design.

Stratification

Since 1959, when all-employee benchmark data stratified by employment size became available, estimates have been prepared using a cell structure which uses size and, in some cases, regional stratification. In preparing the estimates, the nine size classes used for sampling are usually

[1] For a more detailed description of the benchmarking process, see Patricia M. Getz, "BLS Establishment Estimates Revised to March 1991 Benchmarks," *Employment and Earnings, June 1992.*

combined into no more than five size classes when stratification by size is needed.

Stratification by size class and geographic region was originally introduced to improve estimating efficiencies for the hours and earnings data series. There was an observed heterogeneity in earnings levels, particularly among establishments of different sizes and in geographic areas for particular industries. Because there is no universe data available for hours and earnings, sample averages data were used to specify strata using the following procedure.

National estimates of average weekly hours and average hourly earnings were prepared using eight size strata and four regional strata (Northeast, Midwest, South, and West); this represented the maximum stratification possible. These estimates served as a standard against which the published averages were compared. If this comparison indicated a need for regional and/or size stratification, these strata were created.

Later research, conducted in the early 1980's, indicated gains in employment estimation efficiencies could also be realized by detailed size stratification in the trade and services industries. These industries have relatively larger percentages of employment concentrated among small employers, which tend to grow at rates different from large employers. Stratification into four or five size classes in most industries within these divisions was implemented in the mid-1980's to capture the efficiencies. Employment is the primary characteristic of interest in the CES program, thus, size stratification patterns developed to improve employment estimates in trade and services took precedence over stratification derived from hours and earnings patterns.

Estimating Procedures

Employment

Employment estimates are made at what is termed the basic estimating cell level and aggregated upward to broader levels of industry detail by simple addition. Basic cells are defined by industry (usually at the 3- or 4-digit SIC level) and are stratified within industry by geographic region and/or size class in the majority of cases. Within the wholesale trade, retail trade, and services divisions, most industries are stratified into three to five size classes (beginning in 1984) because research demonstrated that estimates produced under this scheme require less benchmark revision. (See earlier section on benchmarks.) For other divisions, size and region strata are used when they improve the hours and earnings estimates.

To obtain all-employee estimates for a basic estimating cell, the following three steps are necessary:

1. A total employment figure (benchmark) for the basic estimating cell as of a specified month (usually March) is obtained.

2. For each cell, the ratio of all employees in 1 month to all employees in the preceding month (i.e., the link relative) is computed for sample establishments which reported for both months.

3. Beginning with the benchmark month, the all-employee estimate for each month is obtained by multiplying the all-employee estimate for the previous month by the link relative for the current month.

The following example illustrates how the estimating procedure is applied in preparing a series. Assume that the estimate of all employees for a given cell was 50,000 in July. The sample, composed of 60 establishments that reported both months, had 25,000 employees in July and 26,000 in August, a 4-percent increase. To derive the August estimate, the change for identical establishments reported in the July-August sample is applied to the July estimate:

$$50{,}000 \times \frac{26{,}000}{25{,}000} = 52{,}000$$

This procedure, known as the link relative technique, is efficient in that it takes advantage of a reliable, complete count of employment and of the high correlation between levels of employment in successive months in identical establishments.

Most national employment estimates are multiplied by bias adjustment factors to produce the monthly published estimates. Bias adjustment factors are used primarily to compensate for the inability to capture the entry of new firms on a timely basis. New firms contribute a substantial amount to employment growth each year, but there is a lag between the creation of a firm and its inclusion on the sample frame, i.e., the UI universe file. It is, therefore, necessary to use modeling techniques to capture this segment of the population. Without bias adjustment, the sample survey alone would seriously understate employment totals. The bias adjustment factors are derived based on a 3-year average of differences between benchmarks and sample estimates, and the rate of employment change in the most recent quarter. The 3-year average provides a baseline bias factor which takes into account a moving average of historically observed differences between purely sample-based estimates and complete population counts of benchmarks. The rate-of-change component enhances the sensitivity of the factors to recent trends in employment change. When employment grows rapidly, a larger bias adjustment is necessary. When employment growth slows or declines overall, smaller adjustments are required.

To obtain estimates of production, construction, or nonsupervisory worker employment, the ratio of production workers to all employees in the sample is assumed to equal the same ratio in the universe. The current month's production worker ratio is thus estimated and then multiplied by the all-employee estimate. The difference link and taper formula, described below in the section on hours and earnings, is used to estimate the current month's production worker ratio. This formula adds the change in the matched sample's production worker ratio (the link) to the prior month's estimate, which has been slightly modified for changes in the sample composition (the taper). A similar method is adopted to estimate the number of women workers.

The estimates for each type of series (all employees, production workers, and women workers) for individual basic estimating cells are summed to obtain corresponding totals for broader industry groupings and divisions.

All estimates back to the most recent benchmark month are subject to revision each year when new benchmarks become available. Because of the complexity of developing benchmarks, they are not available until at least 15 months after the benchmark month (usually March). For example, the revised estimates based on the March 1991 benchmarks were released in June 1992. The inter-benchmark revision period extended from April 1990 through February 1991. Estimates based on the new benchmark level were also released at that time for the post-benchmark period—April 1991 through May 1992. Subsequent estimates also are based on the 1991 benchmark levels until release of the 1992 benchmark.

Table 1. Percent differences between nonfarm employment estimates and benchmarks by industry, March 1989-91

Industry	1989	1990	1991
Total	(1)	-0.2	-0.6
Mining	-3.7	-3.3	-.6
Construction	-1.5	-.8	-.2
Manufacturing	-1.0	.3	.1
Transportation and public utilities	-1.7	-.3	-1.0
Wholesale trade	.8	-2.6	-.2
Retail trade	.5	-.3	-.3
Finance, insurance, and real estate	-1.1	-1.4	-.4
Services	.8	.3	-1.6
Government	.3	.2	-.3

[1] Less than 0.05 percent.

To determine the appropriate revisions, the new benchmarks for March are compared to the estimates previously made for that month. The differences represent: 1) Estimating errors that accumulated since the previous benchmark revision and 2) corrections to establishments' industry classification. These differences are assumed to have accumulated at a regular rate. The all-employee estimates are wedged, or tapered, in order to smooth out the differences between the new and old benchmarks. Estimates for the 15 months subsequent to the benchmark month are revised by applying the previously computed sample link relative to the new benchmark level. Estimates for women workers and production workers are recomputed using the revised all-employee estimates.

Although most national all-employee series are adjusted by this wedging technique, the benchmark source figures replace the CES monthly estimates, in a few cases, if this results in more accurate levels and trends. (In States, the replacement technique predominates.) A comparison of the national revisions made in recent years is presented in table 1.

Hours and earnings

Independent benchmarks are not available for the hours and earnings series; consequently, the levels derive directly from the CES sample averages.

Average weekly hours and average hourly earnings. To obtain average weekly hours for a basic estimating cell, the sum of the worker hours that the establishments classified in the cell reported is divided by the total number of production workers reported for the same establishments. In computing average hourly earnings, the reported payroll is divided by the reported worker hours.

First, the unmodified sample averages of average hourly earnings and average weekly hours are modified at the basic estimating cell level by a wedging technique designed to compensate for month-to-month changes in the sample of reporting establishments.

For example, unmodified sample averages for the current month, $\bar{x}_c$ is obtained from aggregates from a matched sample of establishments reporting for both the current month and the previous month. Similarly, unmodified sample averages for the previous month, $\bar{x}_p$, is calculated from the same matched sample. $\bar{x}_c$-$\bar{x}_p$ is a measure of the change between the 2 months.

Note is then taken of the estimate of average hourly earnings for the previous month, $\bar{X}_p$. Because the panel of establishments reporting in the sample is not fixed from month to month, $\bar{X}_p$ and $\bar{x}_p$ may differ. An estimate for the current month, $\bar{X}_c$, is obtained by using both pieces of information:

$$\bar{X}_c = (0.9\bar{X}_p + 0.1\bar{x}_p) + (\bar{x}_c - \bar{x}_p)$$

The procedure reflected in this formula has the following advantages: (1) It uses matched sample data; (2) it tapers the estimate toward the sample average for the previous month of the current matched sample ($\bar{x}_p$) before applying the current month's change; and (3) it promotes continuity by heavily favoring the estimate for the previous month ($\bar{X}_p$) when applying the numerical factors.

The user may modify the formula if the difference between $\bar{X}_p$ and $\bar{x}_p$ is great and if there is reason to believe it will be sustained (e.g., it results from a new sample member with significantly different hours or earnings). This is done by changing the numerical factors from 0.9 and 0.1 to 0.8 and 0.2, or 0.7 and 0.3, etc., or by using a special wedging procedure when the difference exceeds 3 percent in the same direction for 3 consecutive months.

Average weekly hours and average hourly earnings for industries and groups above the basic estimating cell level are weighted averages of the figures for component cells. The average weekly hours for each basic estimating cell are multiplied by the corresponding estimate of the number of production workers to derive aggregate worker hours. Payroll aggregates are the product of the aggregate worker hours and average hourly earnings. The payroll and worker hour aggregates for industry groups and divisions are the sum of the aggregates for the component industries.

Average weekly hours for industry groups are obtained by dividing the worker hour aggregates by the corresponding production worker estimates. Average hourly earnings for industry groups are computed by dividing the payroll aggregates by the worker hour aggregates. This method is equivalent to weighting average weekly hours by the estimated number of production workers in the universe and weighting average hourly earnings by the estimated worker hours for the universe.

For all levels, from basic estimating cells to major industry divisions, average weekly earnings are computed by multiplying average hourly earnings by average weekly hours.

Overtime hours. Average weekly overtime hours are estimated in basically the same way as average weekly hours. Overtime worker hour sample averages are used in the computations rather than the sample averages for total worker hours. The sample totals for production workers used in the computations are those for the reports containing overtime worker hours (including those reporting zero hours) as well as production workers, total payroll, and total worker hours. The wedging technique and the summary level estimating technique are also comparable to those used to estimate average weekly hours.

Average hourly and weekly earnings in 1982 dollars. Average hourly and weekly earnings are computed and published in terms of 1982 dollars to give an approximate measure of changes in "real" average earnings (earnings in constant dollars). These series are computed by dividing the average hourly and weekly earnings (in current dollars) by the BLS Consumer Price Index for Urban Wage Earners and Clerical Workers (CPI-W) for the same months.

Average hourly earnings, excluding overtime, for manufacturing industries. These are computed by dividing the total production worker payroll for an industry group by the sum of the total production worker hours and one-half of the total overtime worker hours, which is equivalent to the payroll divided by straight-time hours. This method excludes overtime earnings at an assumed rate of 1 1/2 times the straight-time rates; no further adjustment is made for other premium payment provisions.

Indexes of aggregate weekly hours and payrolls. These indexes are prepared by dividing the current month's aggregates by the annual average aggregate for 1982. The hours aggregates are the product of average weekly hours and production or nonsupervisory worker employment; the payroll aggregates are the product of the hours aggregates and average hourly earnings.

Indexes of diffusion of employment changes. These indexes measure the dispersion among industries of the change in employment over the specified time span. The overall indexes are calculated from 356 seasonally adjusted employment series (3-digit industries) covering all nonfarm payroll employment in the private sector. The manufacturing indexes are based on 139 3-digit industries. Each component series is assigned a value of 0, 50, or 100 percent, depending on whether its employment showed a decrease, no change, or an increase over a given time period. The average (mean) value is then calculated, and this percent is the diffusion index number. The reference point for interpreting the diffusion indexes is 50 percent, the value which indicates that the same number of component industries have increased as have decreased. The direction and distance of the index number from the 50 percent reference point indicate whether growing (above 50) or declining (below 50) industries predominate and by what magnitude. The margin between the percentage of industries that increased and the percentage that decreased employment equals twice the difference between the index number and 50 percent.

Seasonally adjusted series

Many economic statistics reflect a regularly recurring seasonal movement which can be measured from past experience. By eliminating that part of the change attributable to the normal seasonal variation, it is possible to observe the cyclical and other nonseasonal movements in these series. Seasonally adjusted series are published regularly for selected employment, hours, and earnings series.[2]

The seasonally adjusted series are computed by multiplying the unadjusted series by the appropriate seasonal adjustment factors. Seasonally adjusted employment series for broader industry groups are obtained by summing the seasonally adjusted data for the component industries. Seasonally adjusted hours and earnings averages for broader level industry groups are weighted averages of the seasonally adjusted component series.

Presentation

The CES program has continued to improve and expand since its inception; it currently uses payroll reports from over 350,000 establishments to provide monthly estimates of employment, hours, and earnings in considerable industry detail. National estimates are published at the 4-digit SIC level for most manufacturing industries and at the 3-digit SIC level for most nonmanufacturing industries. As part of an ongoing effort to increase data availability for the services sector, BLS published estimates for

[2] See appendix A of this bulletin for a description of the seasonal adjustment methodology.

10 additional industries in the service-producing sector in June 1991, coincident with the introduction of the March 1990 benchmarks; publication of 19 new industries was introduced in June 1992 with the March 1991 benchmarks. The Bureau plans additional expansion through 1995.

At the national level, the CES program currently produces more than 3,700 separately published series each month. Tables 2, 3, and 4 summarize the published national detail by major industry division. Table 2 describes the primary series produced by the program, that is, those computed directly from the sample and benchmark data. Table 3 indicates the special series obtained from the primary series by applying special adjustments, and table 4 lists the seasonally adjusted series.

In addition to the series published on a current monthly basis, employment in March of each year (based on benchmark data) is usually published in the June issue of *Employment and Earnings* for nearly 600 industries for which monthly estimates do not meet established publication standards.

The national series on employment, hours, and earnings appear in several BLS publications. The summary data are first published each month in *The Employment Situation* news release which contains preliminary national estimates of nonfarm employment, average weekly hours, and average hourly and weekly earnings in the preceding month, for major industries. The preliminary estimates are based on tabulations of data for less than the full sample to permit early release of these widely used economic indicators. This release is normally issued on Friday, 3 weeks after the week of reference for the data. The news release also includes a brief analysis of current trends in employment, hours, and earnings.

Most of the national estimates at the level of detail described in tables 2, 3, and 4 are published monthly in *Employment and Earnings*. The summary data are in the issue available about 5 weeks after the week of reference; preliminary estimates for the full industry detail, based on about 80 percent of the sample, are in the following month's issue. Final (pre-benchmarked) figures are issued 1 month later. Special articles describe technical developments in the program. The *Monthly Labor Review* also presents many of the national series.

Historical national statistics (monthly data and annual averages) derived from the CES program appear in *Employment, Hours, and Earnings, United States, 1909-90* (Bulletin 2370). Following each benchmark revision, a supplement which contains all revised data is published. The latest supplement, issued in August 1992, reflects all revisions resulting from the introduction of the March 1991 benchmarks.

Employment, hours, and earnings data are available in machine-readable form and on data diskettes on a cost-for-service basis. National data are also disseminated in the publications of other Federal agencies, e.g., the Department of Commerce, the Board of Governors of the Federal Reserve System, and the Council of Economic Advisers. They are also regularly republished in summary form or for specific industries in many trade association journals, the labor press, and in general reference works.

In addition to the national estimates, BLS publishes in *Employment and Earnings* monthly employment estimates for all 50 States, the District of Columbia, Puerto Rico, the Virgin Islands, and nearly 280 metropolitan areas.[3] (These estimates were adjusted to March 1991 benchmarks with the publication of January 1992 data.) The employment series cover total nonfarm employment, major industry divisions (e.g., mining, construction, and manufacturing) for each State and area. Hours and earnings data generally are limited to manufacturing production workers only. Detailed industry data are available monthly in releases published by the cooperating State agencies. The reference month for State and area data is about 1 month later than that for the national data.

Historical monthly and annual State and area data by detailed industry were last published in a 5-volume compendium, *Employment, Hours, and Earnings, States and Areas, 1972-87* (Bulletin 2320). Plans are underway to produce a supplement incorporating data through 1991.

Employment, hours, and earnings data by detailed industry for States and areas are available in machine-readable form and on data diskettes on a cost-for-service basis.

Comparison with the Current Population Survey

Total employment in nonfarm establishments from the CES or payroll survey is not directly comparable with the Bureau's estimates of the number of persons employed in nonagricultural industries obtained from the monthly household survey. (See chapter 1 for a description of the Current Population Survey, or household survey.) The two surveys have differences in concept and scope and employ different collection and estimating techniques.

The payroll survey excludes unpaid family workers, domestic workers in private homes, proprietors, and other self-employed persons, all of whom are covered by the household survey. Moreover, the payroll survey counts a person who is employed by two or more establishments at each place of employment, but the household survey counts a person only once, and classifies him or her according to the major activity. Certain persons on unpaid leave for the entire reference period are counted as employed under the household survey but are not included in the employment count derived from the payroll survey. Over time, however, they show similar trends in employment.

The household survey emphasizes the employment sta-

[3] Data for Puerto Rico and the Virgin Islands are not used in compiling national estimates.

Table 2. Number of "primary" national series on employment, hours, and earnings published from the Current Employment Statistics program by industry, June 1992

Industry	All employees	Production or nonsupervisory workers[1]	Women workers	Average weekly hours	Average weekly overtime hours	Average hourly earnings	Average weekly earnings
Total	629	497	558	496	324	496	494
Total nonfarm	1	—	1	—	—	—	—
Total private	1	1	1	1	—	1	1
Goods-producing	1	1	1	—	—	—	—
Mining	13	11	9	11	—	11	11
Construction	15	15	15	15	—	15	15
Manufacturing	325	324	276	324	324	324	322
Service-producing	1	—	1	—	—	—	—
Private service-producing	1	1	1	—	—	—	—
Transportation and public utilities	35	22	30	23	—	23	23
Wholesale trade	47	22	47	22	—	22	22
Retail trade	48	36	48	36	—	36	36
Finance, insurance, and real estate	30	11	30	11	—	11	11
Services	89	53	87	53	—	53	53
Government	22	—	11	—	—	—	—

[1] Production workers in manufacturing and mining, construction workers in construction, and nonsupervisory workers in all other industries.

Table 3. Number of "special" national series on employment, hours, and earnings published from the Current Employment Statistics program by industry, June 1992

Industry	Indexes of aggregate weekly hours	Indexes of aggregate weekly payrolls	Average hourly earnings, excluding overtime	Average hourly earnings (1982=100)	Average weekly earnings (1982=100)
Total	35	35	23	9	9
Total private	1	1	—	1	1
Goods-producing	1	1	—	—	—
Mining	1	1	—	1	1
Construction	1	1	—	1	1
Manufacturing	25	25	23	1	1
Service-producing	1	1	—	—	—
Transportation and public utilities	1	1	—	1	1
Wholesale trade	1	1	—	1	1
Retail trade	1	1	—	1	1
Finance, insurance, and real estate	1	1	—	1	1
Services	1	1	—	1	1

Table 4. Number of "seasonally adjusted" national series on employment, hours, and earnings published from the Current Employment Statistics program by industry, June 1992

Industry	All employees	Production or nonsupervisory workers[1]	Women workers	Average weekly hours	Indexes of aggregate weekly hours	Average overtime hours	Average hourly earnings		Average weekly earnings	
							Current dollars	1982 dollars	Current dollars	1982 dollars
Total	56	35	39	29	35	3	10	1	1	1
Total nonfarm	1	—	1	—	—	—	—	—	—	—
Total private	1	1	1	1	1	—	1	1	1	1
Goods-producing	1	1	1	—	1	—	—	—	—	—
Mining	2	1	1	1	1	—	1	—	—	—
Construction	2	1	1	—	1	—	1	—	—	—
Manufacturing	25	25	23	23	25	3	2	—	—	—
Service-producing	2	1	2	—	1	—	—	—	—	—
Transportation and public utilities	3	1	1	1	1	—	1	—	—	—
Wholesale trade	3	1	1	1	1	—	1	—	—	—
Retail trade	5	1	1	1	1	—	1	—	—	—
Finance, insurance, and real estate	4	1	1	—	1	—	1	—	—	—
Services	3	1	1	1	1	—	1	—	—	—
Government	4	—	4	—	—	—	—	—	—	—

[1] Production workers in manufacturing and mining, construction workers in construction, and nonsupervisory workers in all other industries.

tus of individuals and also provides much information on the demographic characteristics (sex, age, race) of the labor force. The survey is not well suited to furnishing detailed information on the industrial and geographic distribution of employment. The establishment survey provides limited information on personal characteristics of workers, however, it is an excellent source for detailed industrial and geographic data; in addition, it provides hours and earnings information which relates directly to the employment figures. The payroll and household surveys thus complement each other.

Uses

Data from the Current Employment Statistics program, along with the Current Population Survey data, are usually the first major economic indicators to be released each month. As such, they are used in the formulation of fiscal and economic policy. CES employment estimates are the primary component of the Index of Coincident Economic Indicators and have proved to be an extremely reliable measure of current economic activity. The manufacturing average weekly hours series is used in the Index of Leading Economic Indicators, which predicts swings in the business cycle.

Aggregate earnings data are the major component of Personal Income in the National Income and Product Accounts. Productivity measures (chapters 11 and 12) and the Industrial Production Index use aggregate hours. Indicating changes in the growth of individual industries, employment series are a basic input for employment projections by BLS (chapter 16) and State employment security agencies.

The series are also used in the private sector by business firms, labor unions, universities, trade associations, and private research organizations to study economic conditions and to develop plans for the future. Business firms, for example, use the employment, hours, and earnings data for guidance in plant location, sales, and purchases. In addition, firms negotiating long-term purchase contracts often use escalation clauses based on the average hourly earnings series as an aid to adjust payments for changes in wages. Escalation clauses permit an adjustment of the contract price of the products or services being purchased depending on the movement of average hourly earnings in a selected industry.

Both labor and business have shown wide need for industry series on hourly earnings and weekly hours to provide a basis for labor-management negotiations. They not only furnish current and historical information on a given industry but also provide comparative data on related industries.

Reliability of Estimates

Although the relatively large size of the CES sample assures a high degree of accuracy, the estimates derived from it may differ from the figures that would be obtained if it were possible to take a complete census using the same schedules and procedures. Although the estimates are adjusted annually to new benchmarks, estimates subsequent to the benchmark month have several potential sources of error. The amount added each month for new establishments, for example, may be too high or too low. Changes in the industrial classification of establishments that result from changes in their product or activity between benchmark months are not reflected. In addition, small sampling and response errors may accumulate over several months as a result of the link relative technique of estimation used between benchmarks.

One measure of the reliability of the employment estimates for individual industries is the root-mean-square error (RMSE). This measure is the standard deviation adjusted for the bias in the estimates:

$$\text{RMSE} = \sqrt{(\text{standard deviation})^2 + (\text{bias})^2}$$

If the bias is small, the chances are about 2 out of 3 that an estimate based on the sample would differ from its benchmark by less than the root-mean-square error. The chances are about 19 out of 20 that the difference would be less than twice the root-mean-square error.

Hours and earnings estimates are not subject to benchmark revisions, although the broader industry groupings may be affected slightly by changes in the production-worker weights. The hours and earnings estimates, however, are subject to sampling errors which may be expressed as relative errors. (A relative error is a standard error expressed as a percent of the estimate.) Measures of root-mean-square errors for employment estimates and relative errors for hours and earnings estimates are provided in the Explanatory Notes of *Employment and Earnings.*

Technical References

Bureau of Labor Statistics

Current Employment Statistics State Operating Manual, October 1989.

Employment and Earnings, Explanatory Notes, monthly.

An up-to-date, concise description of the concepts and methods used in establishment-based employment, hours, and earnings data from the Current Employment Statistics program. Provides tables which present measures of the reliability of the data and the magnitude of revisions due to benchmark adjustments.

Employment, Hours, and Earnings, United States, 1909-90, volumes I and II, Bulletin 2370, March 1991, annual supplement, August 1992.

A compilation of historical and current data from all national series published from the Current Employment Statistics program.

Getz, Patricia. "BLS Establishment Estimates Revised to March 1989 Benchmarks and 1987 SIC Codes," *Employment and Earnings*, September 1990, and "BLS Establishment Estimates Revised to March 1991 Benchmarks", *Employment and Earnings*, June 1992.

Green, Gloria P. "Comparing Employment Estimates From Household and Payroll Surveys," *Monthly Labor Review*, December 1969.

Manual on Series Available and Estimating Methods, BLS Current Employment Statistics Program, March 1991.

A summary of the SIC codes, industry titles, sample coverage, stratification pattern, etc., of the national employment, hours, and earnings series produced and published from the Current Employment Statistics program.

Stinson, John F., Jr. "Comparison of Nonagricultural Employment Estimates From Two Surveys," *Employment and Earnings*, March 1984.

Thomas, Anderia D. "Establishment Estimates Revised to March 1990 Benchmarks," *Employment and Earnings*, June 1991.

Other

Dagum, Estela Bee. *The X-11 ARIMA Seasonal Adjustment Method.* Ottawa, Statistics Canada, January 1983. Statistics Canada Catalogue No. 12-564E.

National Commission on Employment and Unemployment Statistics. *Counting the Labor Force*, 1979.

A comprehensive review and critique of the methods and concepts used by various Federal Government programs providing statistics on employment, unemployment, and the labor force in the United States.

Bureau of Labor Statistics Report on Employment, Payroll, and Hours—**Manufacturing**

U.S. Department of Labor

This report is authorized by law 29 U.S.C. 2. Your voluntary cooperation is needed to make the results of this survey comprehensive, accurate, and timely. The information collected on this form by the Bureau of Labor Statistics and the States cooperating in its statistical programs will be held in confidence and will be used for statistical purposes only.

Form Approved
O.M.B. No. 1220-0011

State	Report Number	Industry	We estimate that it will take an average of 7 minutes to complete this form each month including time for reviewing instructions, searching existing data sources, gathering and maintaining the data needed, and completing and reviewing this information. If you have any comments regarding these estimates or any other aspect of this survey, send them to the Bureau of Labor Statistics, Division of Management Systems (1220-0011), 441 G Street NW, Washington, D.C. 20212 and to the Office of Management and Budget, Paperwork Reduction Project (1220-0011), Washington, D.C. 20503.

Please return promptly each month in the enclosed postage paid envelope.
Change name and mailing address if incorrect and include Zip code.

Return to:

SAMPLE COPY

A. Please provide the following information in case questions arise concerning this report.

Your Name **Title** **Phone Number** ( )

B. Please provide the number and location of establishments covered by this report.

Number of establishments **City** **County** **State**

C. Please check one: Production workers are paid ☐ each week ☐ every 2 weeks ☐ twice a month ☐ once a month ☐ other, specify:

D. Please complete columns 1-6 for the single pay period checked above which includes the 12th of the month. Detailed directions are on the reverse side.

Reference Period Please report data **only** for the pay period which includes the 12th of the month	(1) **All Employees:** Report the number of paid employees who worked during or received pay for any part of the pay period which includes the 12th of the month	(2) **Women Employees:** Report the number of employees from column 1 that are women	(3) **Production Workers:** Report the number of employees from column 1 that are production workers	(4) **Production Worker Payroll:** Report the total production worker payroll, including overtime and excluding lump sum payments for the pay period which includes the 12th of the month (omit cents)	(5) **Production Worker Hours:** Report the total production worker hours paid, including overtime, for the pay period which includes the 12th of the month (omit fractions)	(6) **Production Worker Overtime Hours:** Report the total production worker overtime hours paid included in column 5 (omit fractions)	**OFFICE USE ONLY** Expl code	L/P code
DEC				$				
JAN								
FEB								
MAR								
APR								
MAY								
JUN								
JUL								
AUG								
SEP								
OCT								
NOV								
DEC								

E. Please report comments on significant changes in your employment, payroll, or hours on the reverse. ▷

BLS-790 C Rev Jun 89

Detailed Directions for Entering Data

For what time period should I complete this form?

Complete this form only for the **single** pay period checked in Part C (weekly, monthly, etc.) that includes the 12th day of the month. Payroll and hours (Part D, columns 4-6) should be reported for the entire pay period checked in Part C, regardless of its length.

If your pay period is Monday through Friday, and the 12th falls on a Saturday, please report for the week of the 6th through the 12th. When the 12th falls on a Sunday, report for the week of the 12th through the 18th.

Column 1 All Employees:
Enter the total number of persons who worked full- or part-time or received pay for any part of the pay period including the 12th of the month.

"All Employees" **includes:**

- * salaried officials of corporations
- * executives and their staff
- * persons on paid vacation
- persons on paid sick leave
- persons on other paid leave
- part-time employees
- trainees

COMMON REPORTING ADJUSTMENTS:
Please pay special attention to items marked with an asterisk (*).

"All Employees" **excludes:**

- proprietors
- pensioners
- unpaid family workers
- partners of unincorporated firms
- persons on strike the entire pay period
- * persons on leave without pay the entire pay period
- armed forces personnel on active duty the entire pay period
- outside contractors and their employees

Column 2 Women Employees:
Enter the number of employees from column 1 that are women.

Column 3 Production Workers:
Enter the number of employees from column 1 that are production workers. "Production workers" **includes** all nonsupervisory workers engaged in such occupations as:

fabricating	shipping	processing
storage	trucking	assembling
receiving	packing	janitorial
warehousing	handling	repair

maintenance
product development
recordkeeping (clerical) related to production

"Production workers" also **includes** working supervisors and group leaders who may be "in charge" of a group of employees, but whose supervisory functions are only incidental to their regular work.

"Production workers" **excludes:**

executives	personnel	cafeterias
finance	medical	accounting
technical	professional	legal
advertising	credit	sales
collection	sales-delivery	purchasing

recordkeeping (clerical) not related to production
force account construction
installation of products
servicing of products

Column 4 Production Worker Payroll:
Enter the total amount of pay earned during the entire pay period checked in Part C (weekly, etc.) for all production workers in column 3.

Report pay ***before*** employee deductions for:

- FICA (social security)
- unemployment insurance
- health insurance
- pensions
- pay deferral plans (401K plans)
- Federal, State, and local income taxes
- bonds
- union dues

Include pay for:

- * bonuses paid each pay period
- overtime
- holidays
- vacations
- sick leave
- other paid leave
- incentive pay
- commissions paid monthly

Exclude:

- * bonuses not paid each pay period
- * lump sum payments
- * retroactive pay
- pay advances
- payments-in-kind
- annual pay for unused leave

Column 5 Production Worker Hours:
Enter the total number of hours paid for during the entire pay period checked in Part C (weekly, etc.) for all production workers in column 3. Do not convert overtime or other premium hours to straight-time equivalent hours. "Hours paid for" is the sum of:

1. Hours worked, including overtime hours.
2. Hours paid for stand-by or reporting time.
3. Hours not worked, but for which pay was received directly from the firm. Included are holidays, vacations, sick leave, or other paid leave.

Column 6 Production Worker Overtime Hours:
Enter the total number of hours from column 5 for which overtime premiums were paid because the hours were in excess of the regularly scheduled hours. Include Saturday, Sunday, 6th day, 7th day, and holiday hours only if overtime premiums were paid. Exclude hours for which only shift differential, hazard, incentive, or other similar types of premiums were paid.

If there were no overtime hours, enter "O" in column 6.

E. Your Comments. Check the box which best indicates the reason for significant changes in employment (Emp), payroll (PR), or hours (Hrs). Circle the item(s) (Emp, PR, or Hrs) to which the comment applies.

				seasonal increase	seasonal decrease	more business (new orders)	less business (lack of orders)	majority on paid vacation	majority on unpaid vacation	more overtime	less overtime	longer scheduled workweek	shorter scheduled workweek	higher earnings for piece work or incentive pay	lower earnings for piece work or incentive pay	general wage change—COLA	temporary shutdown	permanent shutdown	strike	If none of the checkboxes apply, write your own comments here.
JAN	Emp	PR	Hrs																	
FEB	Emp	PR	Hrs																	
MAR	Emp	PR	Hrs																	
APR	Emp	PR	Hrs																	
MAY	Emp	PR	Hrs																	
JUN	Emp	PR	Hrs																	
JUL	Emp	PR	Hrs																	
AUG	Emp	PR	Hrs																	
SEP	Emp	PR	Hrs																	
OCT	Emp	PR	Hrs																	
NOV	Emp	PR	Hrs																	
DEC	Emp	PR	Hrs																	

BLS-790 C Rev Jun 89

Bureau of Labor Statistics Report on
Employment, Payroll, and Hours—**Trade**

U.S. Department of Labor

This report is authorized by law 29 U.S.C. 2. Your voluntary cooperation is needed to make the results of this survey comprehensive, accurate, and timely. The information collected on this form by the Bureau of Labor Statistics and the States cooperating in its statistical programs will be held in confidence and will be used for statistical purposes only.

Form Approved
O.M.B. No. 1220-0011

State	Report Number	Industry	We estimate that it will take an average of 7 minutes to complete this form each month including time for reviewing instructions, searching existing data sources, gathering and maintaining the data needed, and completing and reviewing this information. If you have any comments regarding these estimates or any other aspect of this survey, send them to the Bureau of Labor Statistics, Division of Management Systems (1220-0011), 441 G Street NW, Washington, D.C. 20212 and to the Office of Management and Budget, Paperwork Reduction Project (1220-0011), Washington, D.C. 20503.

Please return promptly each month in the enclosed postage paid envelope.
Change name and mailing address if incorrect and include Zip code.

Return to:

SAMPLE COPY

A. Please provide the following information in case questions arise concerning this report.
Your Name **Title** **Phone Number**
( )

B. Please provide the number and location of establishments covered by this report.
Number of establishments **City** **County** **State**

C. Please check one.
Nonsupervisory employees are paid:
☐ each week ☐ every 2 weeks ☐ twice a month ☐ once a month
☐ other, specify:

D. Please check one.
Nonsupervisory employees are paid commissions:
☐ each week ☐ every 2 weeks ☐ twice a month ☐ once a month
☐ no commissions are paid ☐ other, specify:

E. Please complete columns 1-4 and 6 for the single pay period checked in C above which includes the 12th of the month. Complete column 5 for the commission period checked in D above which includes the 12th of the month. Detailed directions are on the reverse side.

Reference Period Please report data **only** for the pay period which includes the 12th of the month	(1) **All Employees:** Report the number of paid employees who worked during or received pay for any part of the pay period which includes the 12th of the month	(2) **Women Employees:** Report the number of employees from column 1 that are women	(3) **Nonsupervisory Employees:** Report the number of employees from column 1 that are nonsupervisory employees	(4) **Nonsupervisory Employee Payroll:** Report the total nonsupervisory employee payroll, excluding commissions and lump sum payments for the pay period including the 12th of the month (omit cents)	(5) **Commissions of Nonsupervisory Employees:** Report the total commissions paid for the period including the 12th of the month (omit cents)	**DO NOT USE** **OFFICE USE ONLY** PR	(6) **Nonsupervisory Employee Hours:** Report the total nonsupervisory employee hours paid including overtime, for the pay period including the 12th of the month (omit fractions)	**DO NOT USE** **OFFICE USE ONLY** Expl code	L/P code
DEC				$	$				
JAN									
FEB									
MAR									
APR									
MAY									
JUN									
JUL									
AUG									
SEP									
OCT									
NOV									
DEC									

F. Please report comments on significant changes in your employment, payroll, hours, or commissions on the reverse. ➔

BLS-790 E Rev Jun 89

Detailed Directions for Entering Data

For what time period should I complete this form?

Complete Part E, columns 1-4 and 6, only for the **single** pay period checked in Part C (weekly, monthly, etc.) that includes the 12th day of the month. Payroll and hours (Part E, columns 4 and 6) should be reported for the entire pay period checked in Part C, regardless of its length.

Commissions (Part E, column 5) should be reported for the entire commission period checked in Part D, regardless of its length. If your commission period ends more than 2 weeks after the end of the pay period checked in Part C, do not delay this report. Instead, report commissions on a one month lag, the next time you receive this form.

If your pay period checked in Part C is Monday through Friday, and the 12th falls on a Saturday, please report for the week of the 6th through the 12th. When the 12th falls on a Sunday, report for the week of the 12th through the 18th.

Column 1 All Employees:
Enter the total number of persons who worked full- or part-time or received pay for any part of the pay period including the 12th of the month.

"All Employees" **includes:**

- * salaried officials of corporations
- * executives and their staff
- * persons on paid vacation
- persons on paid sick leave
- persons on other paid leave
- part-time employees
- trainees

COMMON REPORTING ADJUSTMENTS:
Please pay special attention
to items marked with an asterisk (*).

"All Employees" **excludes:**

- proprietors
- pensioners
- unpaid family workers
- partners of unincorporated firms
- persons on strike the entire pay period
- * persons on leave without pay the entire pay period
- armed forces personnel on active duty the entire pay period
- outside contractors and their employees

Column 2 Women Employees:
Enter the number of employees from column 1 that are women.

Column 3 Nonsupervisory Employees:
Enter the number of employees from column 1 that are nonsupervisory employees. Nonsupervisory employees **excludes** all employees in column 1 who are:

- officers of corporations
- executives
- department heads
- managers

"Nonsupervisory employees" **includes** working supervisors and group leaders who may be "in charge" of a group of employees, but whose supervisory functions are only incidental to their regular work.

In other words, "nonsupervisory employees" **includes** every employee except those whose major responsibility is to supervise, plan, or direct the work of others.

Column 4 Nonsupervisory Employee Payroll:
Enter the total amount of pay earned during the entire pay period checked in Part C (weekly, etc.) for all nonsupervisory employees in column 3. Do not include commissions. Commissions are reported in column 5.

Report pay ***before*** employee deductions for:

- FICA (social security)
- unemployment insurance
- health insurance
- pensions
- pay deferral plans (401K plans)
- Federal, State, and local income taxes
- bonds
- union dues

Include pay for:

- * bonuses paid each pay period
- overtime
- holidays
- vacations
- sick leave
- other paid leave

Exclude:

- annual pay for unused leave
- tips
- commissions
- * lump sum payments
- * retroactive pay
- pay advances
- payments-in-kind (meals, etc.)
- * bonuses not paid each pay period
- travel expenses

Column 5 Commissions of Nonsupervisory Employees:
Enter commissions (not base pay, drawing accounts, or basic guarantees) earned to all nonsupervisory employees in column 3 during the entire commission period checked in Part D (weekly, etc.). If no commissions are paid, check the appropriate box in Part D and leave column 5 blank.

Column 6 Nonsupervisory Employee Hours:
Enter the total number of hours paid for during the entire pay period checked in Part C (weekly, etc.) for all nonsupervisory employees in column 3. Do not convert overtime or other premium hours to straight-time equivalent hours. "Hours paid for" is the sum of:

1. Hours worked, including overtime hours.
2. Hours paid for stand-by or reporting time.
3. Hours not worked, but for which pay was received directly from the firm. Included are holidays, vacations, sick leave, or other paid leave.

F. Your Comments. Check the box which best indicates the reason for significant changes in employment (Emp), payroll (PR), or hours (Hrs). Circle the item(s) (Emp, PR, or Hrs) to which the comment applies.

				seasonal increase	seasonal decrease	more business (not seasonal)	less business (not seasonal)	more overtime	less overtime	longer scheduled workweek	shorter scheduled workweek	more commissions earned	less commissions earned	general wage change—COLA	temporary shutdown	permanent shutdown	strike	If none of the checkboxes apply, write your own comments here.
JAN	Emp	PR	Hrs															
FEB	Emp	PR	Hrs															
MAR	Emp	PR	Hrs															
APR	Emp	PR	Hrs															
MAY	Emp	PR	Hrs															
JUN	Emp	PR	Hrs															
JUL	Emp	PR	Hrs															
AUG	Emp	PR	Hrs															
SEP	Emp	PR	Hrs															
OCT	Emp	PR	Hrs															
NOV	Emp	PR	Hrs															
DEC	Emp	PR	Hrs															

BLS-790 E Rev Jun 89

Chapter 3. Occupational Employment Statistics

The Occupational Employment Statistics (OES) survey is a periodic mail survey of nonfarm establishments that collects occupational employment data on workers by industry. The OES program surveys approximately 725,000 establishments in 400 detailed industries. The overall response rate is 79 percent. BLS provides the procedures and technical assistance for the survey; State employment security agencies collect the data. These data are used to estimate total employment by occupation for the Nation, each State, and selected areas.

Background

In 1971, questionnaires were sent to 50,000 manufacturing establishments throughout the United States, marking the beginning of the OES survey. This survey was conducted in cooperation with the Employment and Training Administration and 15 State employment security agencies. It was designed to obtain national, State, and area occupational estimates for the cooperating States. Following the completion of the manufacturing survey, similar surveys were developed for nonmanufacturing industries and State and local governments.

The OES survey follows a 3-year cycle. Three surveys are conducted alternately for manufacturing, nonmanufacturing, and the balance of nonmanufacturing industries. The manufacturing survey covers manufacturing industries and hospitals. The nonmanufacturing survey covers mining; construction; finance, insurance, and real estate; and services. The third survey covers the balance of the nonmanufacturing industries: Wholesale and retail trade, transportation, communications, public utilities, State and local government, and educational services. Hospitals were added to the manufacturing survey in 1980 and educational services were added to the third survey in 1985. Agricultural services were surveyed for the first time at the national level with the 1992 manufacturing survey. The 50 States, the District of Columbia, Puerto Rico, Guam, and American Samoa cooperate in this effort.

Concepts

An *establishment* is an economic unit which processes goods or provides services, such as a factory, mine, or store. It is generally at a single physical location and is engaged primarily in one type of economic activity. Single physical locations that encompass two or more distinct economic activities are treated as two or more establishments, provided that separate payroll records are available and certain other criteria are met.

Unit total employment is the number of workers who can be classified as full time or part time, workers on paid vacations or other types of leave, workers on unpaid or short-term absences (i.e., illness, bad weather, temporary layoff, jury duty), salaried officers, executives, staff members of incorporated firms, employees temporarily assigned to other units, and employees for whom this unit is their permanent (home) duty station regardless of whether this unit prepares their paycheck. Unit total employment excludes proprietors (owners and partners) of unincorporated firms, unpaid family workers, workers on extended leave (i.e., pensioners and members of the Armed Forces), and workers on long-term layoff.

Employees are reported in the occupation in which they are working, even if they have been trained for a different occupation. For example, an employee trained as an engineer but working as a drafter is reported as a drafter.

Working supervisors, those spending 20 percent or more of their time at work similar to that performed by workers under their supervision, are reported in the occupations which are most closely related to their work.

Part-time workers, learners, and apprentices are reported in the occupation in which they ordinarily work.

Industrial classification

The industrial classification system currently used for compiling and publishing OES survey data is defined in the 1987 *Standard Industrial Classification Manual.* (See appendix B for a detailed description of this system.)

Under the Standard Industrial Classification (SIC) system, reporting establishments are classified on the basis of major product or activity.

Occupational classification

The OES classification system emphasizes occupations of special interest to many data users, such as technology-related occupations and those which require substantial training. In addition, the system is concise and compatible with the 1980 Standard Occupational Classification (SOC) system. The titles and descriptions of occupations are principally derived from the *Dictionary of Occupation*

Titles (DOT). The classification of occupations, with some exceptions, follows the SOC principles which group occupations by function, industry, and skill.

A "crosswalk," which relates OES occupations to the SOC, the 1990 census classification system, and the DOT, has been developed so that users can use OES data in conjunction with these other sources. With crosswalks, each classification system can be used as a common denominator.

Data Sources and Collection Methods

Employers are the ultimate source of occupational data. Within establishments, the main source of occupational data reported by respondents is personnel records. In addition, there are cases, especially for the small reporting units, where personal knowledge of persons completing the reports is also used.

Employment benchmarks for this survey are derived from employment data tabulated from the reports of the Unemployment Insurance program. In some nonmanufacturing industries, supplemental sources are used to obtain lists of establishments that are not covered by unemployment insurance laws. For example, the unemployment insurance file is supplemented by the Federal Railroad Administration's list of railroad establishments when railroad transportation is sampled.

Employment information is currently being collected for approximately 750 occupations in 7 major divisions. A list of occupations has been designed for each industry or for each group of industries having a similar occupational structure.

Two types of survey questionnaires, long and short, are used. Both forms include specific occupational titles and definitions, establishment identification information, and several questions concerning the exact economic activity of the business. In addition, the questionnaire provides descriptions of 3-digit SIC industries to reduce industry misclassifications.

The long form specifies an extensive list of occupations selected for each industry grouped under broad headings such as Clerical Occupations, Professional and Technical Occupations, and Service Occupations. The long form includes supplemental sheets for respondents to report significant occupations that could not be reported in a detailed occupation, and thus reported in an "all other" residual category. Experience with previous surveys has shown that the supplemental sheets can be a valuable tool in improving the occupational lists and definitions for future surveys, as well as clarifying and correcting reported data.

The short form includes abbreviated occupational lists with accompanying definitions. Broad groups are not specified. Respondents are asked to identify and briefly describe jobs that cannot be matched to the occupations listed on the forms. When the questionnaires are returned, these additional occupations are coded according to the corresponding long-form occupational content. The short form was developed to reduce the reporting burden in smaller establishments by including more industry specific occupations and fewer general occupations.

Data are collected from respondents primarily by mail. Occasionally, visits are made to large employers and to other respondents who indicate particular difficulty in completing the questionnaires. Ordinarily, two mailings follow the initial mailing. After the third mailing, a subsample of the remaining nonrespondents is drawn and contacted by telephone.

Occupational employment data are requested for the pay period including the 12th day of April, May, or June, depending upon the industry surveyed.

Sampling

The OES sample is designed to yield reliable industry occupational estimates for all States and selected areas within those States. The sample is selected primarily from the lists of establishments reporting to the State unemployment insurance program.

The sample design initially stratifies the universe of establishments by 3-digit industry code and size class. All establishments employing 250 employees or more are automatically included in the sample. For establishments with fewer than 250 but more than 4 employees, each size class is sampled with probability proportionate to the amount of employment contained in the size class. Establishments with one to four employees are not sampled. Instead, they are represented by assigning larger weights to establishments with five to nine employees. Within each industry size cell, the sample members are systematically selected using a single random start.

Estimating Procedures

After data are edited and reconciled for apparent inconsistencies and completeness, the estimation process begins with the calculation of weight adjustments for nonrespondents within each sampling cell. The OES survey uses a separate ratio estimator, where separate occupational employment estimates are calculated by size class (or group of size classes) for each 3-digit industry within States and in the Nation. For each size class within an industry and State (Nation), the occupational distribution is estimated by calculating a ratio for each occupation. This ratio is the sum of the total weighted employment of an occupation to the sum of the total weighted employment of all reporting establishments. These ratios are then multiplied by a known total employment figure (benchmark value) for that size class. Final occupational estimates for each industry (all size classes) are then derived by summing the detailed industry size class estimates to the industry level. Estimates for higher levels of industry are derived by summing estimates from lower industry levels. Estimates of standard errors are calculated using a jackknife random group variance estimator.

Presentation

A report on the results of each OES survey is published by the cooperating States. BLS published national occupational employment estimates for the survey years 1971 and 1977 to the present. Each report consists of an analytical interpretation of the findings supported by statistical tables showing estimates of occupational employment and measurements of the sampling error associated with the estimates.

Uses and Limitations

Occupational employment data obtained by the OES survey are used to develop information regarding current and projected employment needs and job opportunities. Such information is used in the development of State vocational education plans. These data also enable the analysis of the occupational composition of different industries, of different establishments in the same industry, and changes in industry employment and staffing patterns over time. OES employment estimates also are used as job replacement aids by helping to identify industries that employ the skills gained by enrollees in vocational training programs. OES survey data also serve as the primary ingredients in the development of occupational information systems designed for use by those who are exploring career opportunities or those assisting others in career decision making. In addition, OES survey data are used to compare the occupational staffing patterns of foreign owned firms to those of U.S. firms, as part of the Foreign Direct Investment program.

All surveys are subject to response and processing errors. Errors are reduced through reviewing, editing, and screening procedures and, if necessary, through contact with respondents whose data are internally inconsistent or appear to involve misinterpretation of definitions or other instructions. In addition, estimates derived from sample surveys are subject to sampling error. Sampling errors for occupational employment estimates are calculated and published with the estimates.

Technical References

U.S. Department of Labor, Bureau of Labor Statistics. *Occupational Employment in Selected Nonmanufacturing Industries,* Bulletin 2397, May 1992.

Presents occupational employment data collected in 1990 for the mining; construction; finance, insurance, and real estate; and services industries.

U.S. Department of Labor, Employment and Training Administration. *Dictionary of Occupational Titles,* Revised fourth edition, vols. 1 and 2, 1991.

Comprehensive descriptions of more than 13,000 jobs coded by work requirements and duties performed.

U.S. Department of Labor, Bureau of Labor Statistics. *Occupational Employment in Manufacturing Industries,* Bulletin 2376, March 1991.

Presents occupational employment data collected in 1989 for manufacturing industries.

U.S. Department of Labor, Bureau of Labor Statistics. *Occupational Employment in Selected Nonmanufacturing Industries,* Bulletin 2348, March 1990.

Presents occupational employment data collected in 1988 for the transportation, communications, utilities, trade, educational services, and State and local government industries.

U.S. Department of Commerce, Bureau of the Census. *1980 Census of Population Classified Index of Industries and Occupations,* November 1982.

Thompson, John. "BLS Job Cross-classification System Relates Information From Six Sources," *Monthly Labor Review,* November 1981.

Describes the relationships of several major classification systems to the Occupational Employment Statistics classification system.

U.S. Department of Education, Office of Educational Research and Improvement, National Center for Education Statistics. *A Classification of International Programs,* 1981.

U.S. Department of Commerce, Office of Federal Statistical Policy and Standards. *Standard Occupational Classification Manual,* 1980.

Chapter 4. Measurement of Unemployment in States and Local Areas

Unemployment estimates for States and local areas are key indicators of local economic conditions. These estimates, which are produced by State employment security agencies, are used by State and local governments for planning and budgetary purposes and as determinants of the need for local employment and training services and programs. Local area unemployment estimates are also used to determine the eligibility of an area for benefits in various Federal assistance programs.

Under the Federal-State cooperative program, the Department of Labor develops the concepts, definitions, and technical procedures which are used by State agencies for the preparation of labor force and unemployment estimates. Currently, monthly estimates of employment and unemployment are prepared in State agencies for some 5,400 geographic areas, which include all States, labor market areas (LMA's), and counties and cities having a population of 25,000 or more.

Background

Unemployment estimates have been developed for LMA's for over 40 years. The program began during World War II under the War Manpower Commission to identify areas where labor market imbalance was created as a result of an inadequate labor supply, material shortages, and transportation difficulties. After the war, emphasis was placed on identifying areas of labor surplus, and the program of classifying areas in accordance with severity of unemployment was established.

In 1950, the Department of Labor's Bureau of Employment Security (now Employment and Training Administration) published a handbook, *Techniques for Estimating Unemployment,* so that comparable estimates of the unemployment rate could be produced among the States. This led, during the late 1950's, to the formulation of the "Handbook method," a series of computational steps designed to produce local employment and unemployment estimates. This method relied heavily on data derived from the unemployment insurance (UI) system. (See section on "Estimates for sub-State areas—the Handbook method.")

In 1972, the Bureau of Labor Statistics began to develop the concepts and methods to be used by States to estimate labor force, employment, and unemployment. In 1973, a new system for developing labor force estimates was introduced which combined the Handbook method with the concepts, definitions, and estimation controls from the Current Population Survey (CPS), the Bureau of Census survey sponsored by BLS used to measure the labor force status of individuals. The CPS estimates are based on a household survey sample selected in a way to provide unbiased estimates. (See chapter 1.)

Since 1976, State samples of the CPS have been increased in size several times to improve the quality of State labor force estimates. Also in 1976, the CPS was extended to all States as an estimation control. As a criterion for using the monthly CPS data directly for official publication of labor force estimates, BLS established a maximum expected coefficient of variation (CV) of 10 percent for unemployment assuming an unemployment rate of 6 percent. (The coefficient of variation of an estimate can be defined as the standard error of the estimate divided by the estimate.) Based on this criterion, monthly CPS data were used, beginning in 1978, for official statewide labor force estimates for the 10 largest States—California, Florida, Illinois, Massachusetts, Michigan, New Jersey, New York, Ohio, Pennsylvania, and Texas—and for 2 sub-State areas—the Los Angeles-Long Beach Metropolitan Statistical Area and New York City.

In 1985, a State-based design for the CPS was fully implemented to incorporate the 1980 census information and to provide for improved reliability requirements for each of the 50 States and the District of Columbia. North Carolina was added as another "direct-use" State, and the CV requirement for monthly unemployment was reduced to 8 percent for these 11 large States. For each of the 39 (non-direct-use) States and the District of Columbia, the reliability requirement was established at an 8 percent CV for annual average unemployment, assuming a 6-percent unemployment rate.

Until 1989, official monthly estimates for the non-direct-use States and sub-State areas were based on the Handbook method. Since 1989, estimates for these 39 States and the District of Columbia have been based on time series models developed by BLS and tested by State employment security agencies, using standardized procedures. Estimates for all other sub-State areas are based on the Handbook method, adjusted to annual State control totals. (See the sampling section of chapter 1.)

Over the years, other major improvements have been made to the UI database, an integral input to State and area estimation. The UI database project, conducted in 1976-78, standardized all UI claims data used in State and area labor force estimates, so that these data would be more consistent with the conceptual underpinnings of unemployment used in the CPS. The result of this project was the regular development, from computer files, of data on UI claimants, in the week including the 12th day of the month (the CPS reference week). These data are based on the claimants' State/county/city of residence and exclude those who had earnings from employment in the certification week.

Estimation Methodology

Estimates for States

The CPS is the direct source of monthly labor force data for 11 large States. For the 39 smaller States and the District of Columbia, monthly labor force estimates are developed using models which treat the observed monthly CPS estimate as the sum of a "signal" or (true labor force value) plus "noise" (error due to sampling only a portion of the population). The goal is to reduce the sampling variability in the CPS data by estimating the true labor force value, the CPS with its noise removed. This is done by modeling the true values by a time series regression with variable coefficients and the sampling error as a correlated noise component. Given these models, the Kalman filter algorithm is used to disaggregate the observed CPS into a "signal" and "noise" component.

Under this algorithm, the current model estimates are updated as new data become available each month. Under the model's assumptions, the Kalman filter provides optimal estimates of the current value of the "signal" using all available information. Estimates prior to the current period are not updated as new data become available. At the end of each year, however, the estimates are revised by processing the entire data series through a process called "smoothing," which uses the data both before and following a given month.

Using more than 10 years of data from three major sources (CPS, the Current Employment Statistics (CES) survey, and UI data), two models were developed for each State—one to estimate the employment level and one to estimate the unemployment rate. Each State has separately determined models that have been specially tailored to its historical and current data.

Employment level models. The signal component of the employment level model consists of a time varying stochastic intercept, a base variable common to all models; other explanatory variables; and seasonal variables. The coefficients of the explanatory variables are time varying to reflect changing relationships between the explanatory variables.

The time varying intercept is a trend variable that accounts for long-run variation in employment not accounted for by the other variables in the model. The base variable for the employment level models is the statewide monthly estimate of workers on payrolls in nonfarm industries from the CES program. As a predictor variable, this estimate provides for the largest portion of the total employed estimate.

Other explanatory variables are included in the employment level models to account for workers that are either not covered or only partially covered by UI, including self-employed workers, unpaid family workers, private household workers, agricultural workers, and agricultural service workers. Additional seasonal variables are used in the models when it is recognized that, for given months, some variables are not sensitive enough to capture the seasonality of the series being estimated.

Unemployment rate models. These models are specified to estimate the unemployment rate rather than the level of unemployment. This was done because the unemployment rate can be more accurately modeled than the unemployment level. Like the employment model, the rate model includes time varying intercept and coefficients. The base variable for the unemployment rate models is the statewide UI claims rate. This rate is a relative measure of the number of workers who are currently collecting UI benefits and is defined in percentage terms as a ratio of State continued claims without earnings to total State nonfarm wage and salary payroll employment. Other explanatory variables include an employment-to-population (E/P) ratio and an entrant rate. The E/P ratio is used as a measure of labor market tightness. The entrant rate is included to account for unemployment of new entrants and reentrants into the labor force and is used to measure seasonal movements of the unemployment rate in a State.

Benchmarking. This process is a general statistical procedure used to adjust estimates to a control total. Each year, monthly State employment and unemployment estimates prepared by State employment security agencies using regression models are adjusted, or benchmarked, to the annual average CPS State estimates of employment and unemployment. The benchmarking process involves adjusting the time series of monthly estimates so that their annual average equals that of the CPS.

The goal of benchmarking is twofold: (1) To insure that the annual average of the final benchmarked series equals the CPS annual average, and (2) to preserve the pattern of the model series as much as possible. In practice, these two goals are conflicting, and some changes to the pattern of the time series are made to meet the first goal. The Denton benchmarking method—a statistical procedure that minimizes the changes to the time series pattern and resolves discontinuities, or breaks, between December and January estimates—has been used since the introduction of model-based estimates in 1989.

Estimates for sub-State areas—the Handbook method

Until 1973, the Handbook method was the only means used to develop State and local area labor force and unemployment estimates. With the exception of the Los Angeles metropolitan area and New York City, it continues to be the method used for sub-State estimation. It is an effort to estimate unemployment for an area, comparable to what would be produced by a random sample of households in the area, using available information without the expense of a large labor force survey like the CPS. The Handbook presents a series of estimating "building blocks," where categories of unemployed workers are classified by their previous status. Three broad categories of unemployed persons are: (1) Those who were last employed in industries covered by State UI laws, (2) those who were last employed in noncovered industries, and (3) those who either entered the labor force for the first time or reentered after a period of separation.

Unemployment. In the current month, the estimate of unemployment is an aggregate of the estimates for each of the three building-block categories. The "covered" category consists of four unemployed worker groups: 1) Those who are currently collecting UI benefits, 2) those who have exhausted their benefits, 3) those who have been disqualified from receiving benefits because of the reason for their separation, and 4) those who have delayed filing for benefits.

Within the covered category, only the insured unemployed are obtained directly from an actual count of current UI claimants for the reference week. All other components in this and the other two covered categories are based on special estimating equations. The estimates of persons who have exhausted their benefits and those in a disqualified status are based upon the number actually counted in the current period, plus an estimate of those expected still to be unemployed from previous periods.

For the "noncovered" category, an estimate of unemployment is developed for each industry or class-of-worker subgroup, based primarily on the "State-covered unemployment rate" (the ratio of covered unemployment to covered employment) and the estimate of current employment for the subgroup.

The third category, "new entrants and reentrants into the labor force," cannot be estimated directly from UI statistics because unemployment for these persons is not immediately preceded by the period of employment required to receive UI benefits. Instead, total entrants into the labor force are estimated on the basis of the national historical relationship of entrants to the experienced unemployed and the experienced labor force. The Handbook estimate of entrants into the labor force is a function of: (1) The particular month of the year, (2) the level of the experienced unemployed, (3) the level of the experienced labor force, and (4) the youth proportion of the working-age population. The estimate of total entrants for a given month is derived from the following equation:

$$ENT = A(X+E) + BX$$

where:

ENT = total entrant unemployment
E = total employment
X = total experienced unemployment
A, B = synthetic factors incorporating both seasonal variations, and the assumed relationship between the proportion of youth in the working-age population and the historical relationship of entrants to either the experienced unemployed (B factor) or the experienced labor force (A factor).

Employment. The total employment estimate is based on data from several sources. The primary source is surveys of establishments either directly from the Federal-State CES survey or conducted by the States themselves. These are designed to produce estimates of the total number of employees on payrolls in nonfarm industries for the particular area.

These "place-of-work" employment estimates must be adjusted to refer to place-of-residence estimates, as in the CPS. Estimated adjustment factors for several categories of employment have been developed on the basis of employment relationships which existed at the time of the most recent decennial census. These factors are applied to the place-of-work employment estimates for the current period to obtain adjusted employment estimates, to which are added synthetically developed estimates for employment not represented in the establishment series—agricultural workers, nonfarm self-employed and unpaid family workers, and private household workers.

Sub-State adjustment for consistency and additivity. Each month, Handbook estimates are prepared for labor market areas that exhaust the entire State area. To obtain an estimate for a given area, a "Handbook share" is computed for that area which is defined as the ratio of that area's Handbook estimate to the sum of the Handbook estimates for all LMA's in the State. This ratio is then multiplied by the current, statewide estimate for each State—either the model-based estimate used for 39 States, or the CPS estimate used for the 11 direct-use States—to produce the final adjusted LMA estimates:

$$U_a(t) = U_s(t) * \left[\frac{UHB_a(t)}{\Sigma UHB_a(t)} \right]$$

where:

U = total unemployment
UHB = Handbook unemployment
a = area
s = State
t = time

Benchmark correction. At the end of each year, sub-State estimates are revised to incorporate any changes in the inputs, such as revisions in the place-of-work-based employment estimates, corrections in claims data, and updated historical relationships. These corrected estimates are then readjusted to sum to the revised (benchmarked) State estimates of employment and unemployment.

Producing estimates for parts of LMA's

Current labor force estimates at the sub-LMA level are required by several Federal programs. However, for areas this small, the data required to compute independent Handbook estimates are generally not available. Based on data availability, two alternative methods are used to disaggregate the LMA estimates to the subarea level.

The population-claims method is the preferred technique. If residence-based UI claims data are available for the subareas within the labor market area, the ratio of the subarea to the total number of claims within the LMA is used to disaggregate the Handbook estimate of experienced unemployed to the subarea level. The Handbook estimates of unemployed entrants are allocated based on the latest available census distribution of adult and teenage population groups. Employment is disaggregated using current population distributions prepared by the Bureau of the Census and weighted by each area's decennial census relative share of employment to population.

If the necessary UI claims data are not available, the census-share method is used. This method uses each subarea's decennial census share of total LMA employment and unemployment, respectively, in order to disaggregate Handbook employment and unemployment.

Uses and Limitations

Estimates of unemployment and the unemployment rate are used by Federal agencies to determine the eligibility of an area for benefits in various Federal programs. These include the Job Training Partnership Act (JTPA), the Emergency Unemployment Compensation Act (EUCA), the Emergency Food and Shelter Program (EFSP), the Public Works Program (PWP), the Temporary Emergency Food Assistance Program (TEFAP), and Labor Surplus Area designation. Under JTPA, EFSP, PWP, and TEFAP, unemployment data are used to determine the distribution of funds to be allocated to each eligible area. In the case of the Labor Surplus Area designations, the data are used in the determination of area eligibility for benefits. Under EUCA, the State total unemployment rate is one of two triggers for paying extended unemployment benefits.

Labor force estimates for States and areas are based on sample survey and administrative data and thus are subject to sampling, nonsampling, and other types of error.

The annual CPS estimates used to benchmark monthly, statewide labor force estimates for the 39 States and the monthly CPS estimates used directly for 11 States and 2 areas are based on probability samples of households and are subject to both sampling and nonsampling errors. (See Limitations under chapter 1 for a discussion of errors in the CPS.)

Approximate error measures for annual average estimates of major labor force characteristics for State and sub-State areas are published in *Geographic Profile of Employment and Unemployment.* These error estimates are developed from generalized variance functions which use CPS data for the areas and independently developed parameters. As with all sampling error tables produced for CPS State and area data, a number of approximations are required; as a result, the sampling errors from generalized variance functions should be interpreted with caution.

Estimates not directly derived from sample surveys are subject to errors resulting from the estimation processes used as well as the limitations of the data sources used. The error structure associated with these estimates is complex, and information on the magnitude of the overall errors is not available.

Technical References

Bell, W.R. and Hillmer, S.C. "The Time Series Approach to Estimation for Repeated Surveys," *Survey Methodology,* 1990, pp. 195-215.

Tiller, Richard B. "An Application of Time Series Methods to Labor Force Estimation Using CPS Data," *Proceedings of the Survey Research Methods Section,* American Statistical Association, 1990.

Tiller, Richard B. "A Kalman Filter Approach to Labor Force Estimation Using Survey Data," *Proceedings of the Survey Research Methods Section,* American Statistical Association, 1989, pp. 16-25.

U.S. Department of Labor, Bureau of Labor Statistics. *Questions and Answers on the New Method for Developing State Employment and Unemployment Estimates,* January 1989.

U.S. Department of Labor, Bureau of Labor Statistics. *Manual for Developing Local Area Unemployment Statistics,* July 1979.

Scott, A.J.; Smith, T.M.F.; and Jones, R.G. "Analysis of Repeated Surveys Using Time Series Methods," *Journal of the American Statistical Association,* 1974, pp. 674-678.

Denton, F.T. "Adjustment of Monthly or Quarterly Series to Annual Totals: An Approach Based on Quadratic Minimization," *Journal of the American Statistical Association,* 1971, Volume 66, pp. 99-102.

U.S. Department of Labor, Bureau of Employment Security. *Handbook on Estimating Unemployment,* Employment Security Research Methods, Handbook Series (BLS Reprint No. R-185), 1960.

Chapter 5. Employment and Wages Covered by Unemployment Insurance

The Covered Employment and Wages program, commonly called the ES-202 program, is a cooperative endeavor of BLS and the employment security agencies of the 50 States, the District of Columbia, Puerto Rico, and the Virgin Islands. Using quarterly data submitted on magnetic tapes or cartridges by the agencies, BLS summarizes employment and wage data for workers covered by State unemployment insurance (UI) laws and for civilian workers covered by the program of Unemployment Compensation for Federal Employees (UCFE).

The ES-202 program is a comprehensive and accurate source of employment and wage data, by industry, at the national, State, and county levels. It provides a virtual census of nonagricultural employees and their wages. In addition, about 44 percent of all workers in agricultural industries are covered.

Background

The ES-202 program can trace its origins back to the Social Security Act of 1935, which authorized collection of information to determine if State unemployment compensation programs were in compliance with the act. From the inception of the national UI system in 1938, when the Federal Unemployment Tax Act (FUTA) became effective, until 1972, collection of the data, publication, and technical expertise were the responsibilities of the U.S. Department of Labor's Manpower Administration or its predecessor agencies. Semiannual reports summarizing the data were issued until 1950, when the periodical *Employment and Wages* began quarterly publication. In 1972, BLS assumed responsibility and continued quarterly publication until 1975. *Employment and Wages* then became an annual publication.

Concepts and Methodology

Scope of coverage

In 1938, UI coverage and, consequently, ES-202 reporting requirements, extended only to private firms employing eight or more persons at least 20 weeks a year; certain employee groups were exempt. Insurance coverage was successively broadened, to include Federal civilian employees[1] (1955); firms employing four to seven employees (1956) and ex-military personnel[2] (1958); and firms employing one to three employees and State colleges, universities, and hospitals (1972). In 1978, coverage was extended to nearly all other State and local public employees, to agricultural firms employing a minimum of 10 workers in at least 20 weeks a year or having a $20,000 quarterly payroll; and to employers paying a quarterly minimum of $1,000 to domestic workers.

UI coverage is broad and basically comparable from State to State. In 1991, UI and UCFE covered 107 million jobs, or 98 percent of total wage and salary civilian employment. Covered workers received $2.6 trillion in pay or 94.3 percent of the wage and salary component of national income.

Over the years, many States have legislated unemployment insurance protection for additional categories of workers above the base established through Federal legislation. Details on coverage laws are provided in *Comparisons of State Unemployment Insurance Laws,* available upon request from the Employment and Training Administration of the Department of Labor.

When UI-covered private industry employment data are compared directly with other employment series, the industry exclusions also should be taken into account. Excluded from private-sector coverage in 1991 were approximately 0.3 million wage and salary agricultural employees, 1.5 million self-employed farmers, 8.9 million self-employed nonagricultural workers, 0.7 million domestic workers, and 0.3 million unpaid family workers. Also excluded were 1.6 million members of the Armed Forces stationed in the United States, 0.3 million workers covered by the railroad unemployment insurance system, and about 0.6 million State and local government workers. In addition, certain types of nonprofit employers, e.g., religious organizations, are given a choice of coverage or noncoverage in a number of States.

Reporting units and establishments

A reporting unit is the economic unit for which the employer submits a quarterly UI Contribution Report or provides employment and wage data for separate locations on a separate form that supplements the regular contribution report.

An establishment is an economic unit, such as a farm, mine, factory, or store, which produces goods or provides

[1] Under the Unemployment Compensation for Federal Employees (UCFE) program.

[2] Under the Unemployment Compensation for Ex-Servicemen (UCX) program.

services. It usually is at a single physical location and engaged in one, or predominantly one, type of economic activity, for which a single industrial classification may be applied. Occasionally, a single physical location encompasses two or more distinct and significant activities. Each activity should be reported as a separate establishment if separate records are kept and the various activities are classified under different 4-digit Standard Industrial Classification (SIC) codes.

Most employers have only one establishment; thus, the establishment is the predominant reporting unit or statistical entity for reporting employment and wage data. Most employers who operate more than one establishment in a State file a Multiple Worksite Report (MWR) each quarter, in addition to their quarterly UI Contribution Report. The MWR form is used to collect separate employment and wage data for each establishment of these employers. Some very small multi-establishment employers do not file a Multiple Worksite Report. When the total employment in an employer's secondary establishments (all establishments other than the largest) is less than 10, the employer will generally file a consolidated report for all establishments. Some employers either cannot or will not report at the establishment level and thus group establishments into one consolidated unit, or possibly several units, though not at the establishment level.

In government, the reporting unit is the installation (a single location at which a department, agency, or other government instrumentality has civilian employees). Federal agencies follow slightly different criteria from private employers in breaking down their reports by installation. They are permitted to combine as a single statewide unit (1) all installations with 10 workers or fewer and (2) all installations which have a combined total in the State of fewer than 50 workers. In addition, when there are fewer than 25 workers in all secondary installations in a State, they may be combined and reported with the major installations. Lastly, if a Federal agency has fewer than five employees in a State, the agency headquarters office (regional office, district office) serving each State may consolidate the wage and employment data for that State with the data reported to the State in which the headquarters is located.

As a result of these reporting rules, the number of reporting units is always larger than the number of employers (or government agencies) but smaller than the number of establishments (or installations).

Employment

Employment data represent the number of workers on the payroll during the pay period including the 12th day of the month. The pay period varies in length from employer to employer; for most employers, it is a 7-day period but not necessarily a calendar week. An employer who pays on more than one basis (such as weekly for production employees and semimonthly for office employees) reports the sum of the number of workers on each type of payroll for the period.

The employment count includes all corporation officials, executives, supervisory personnel, clerical workers, wage earners, pieceworkers, and part-time workers. Workers are reported in the State and county of the physical location of their job. Persons on paid sick leave, paid holiday, paid vacation, and so forth are included, but those on leave without pay for the entire payroll period are excluded.

Persons on the payroll of more than one firm are counted in each firm. Workers are counted even though their wages may be nontaxable for UI purposes during that period (having reached the taxable limit for the year).

The employment count excludes employees who earned no wages during the entire applicable period because of work stoppages, temporary layoffs, illness, or unpaid vacations, and employees who earned wages during the month but not during the applicable pay period.

Total wages

Total wages, for purposes of the quarterly UI reports submitted by employers in private industry in most States, include gross wages and salaries, bonuses, tips and other gratuities, and the value of meals and lodging, where supplied. In a majority of the States, employer contributions to certain deferred compensation plans, such as 401(k) plans, are included in total wages. Total wages, however, do not include employer contributions to Old-age, Survivors', and Disability Insurance (OASDI); health insurance; unemployment insurance; workers' compensation; and private pension and welfare funds.[3]

In most States, firms report the total wages paid during the calendar quarter, regardless of the timing of the services performed. Under laws of a few States, however, the employers report total wages earned during the quarter (payable) rather than actual amounts paid.

For Federal workers, wages represent the gross amount of all payrolls for all pay periods ending within the quarter. This gross amount includes cash allowances and the cash equivalent of any type of remuneration. It includes all lump-sum payments for terminal leave, withholding taxes, and retirement deductions. Federal employee remuneration generally covers the same types of services as those for workers in private industry.

Taxable wages and contributions

Taxable wages are that part of wages subject to the State unemployment insurance contribution tax. Contributions (i.e., monies that are deposited in trust funds in order to pay unemployment claims) are calculated on taxable wages and are reported quarterly.

Under Federal Law, certain units of State and local goverrnments and certain nonprofit establishments may elect

[3] Employee contributions for the same purposes, as well as money withheld from the employee's gross pay for income taxes, union dues, etc., are included in the UI reports.

to reimburse the State for any unemployment insurance claims that have been filed against them. These reimbursable accounts are not subject to the quarterly assessment for unemployment insurance funds; therefore, their taxable wages and contributions are not reported.

In mid-1990, approximately 30 percent of the States required that employers pay UI taxes on the first $7,000 of employee wages—the minimum established by Federal laws. The remaining States established higher limits on taxable earnings. The portion of wages subject to taxation has varied substantially over time. In mid-1990, about two-fifths of the States allowed employers to obtain lower tax rates by making voluntary contributions to the unemployment tax fund. The few States which tax employees in addition to employers are requested to include employees' contributions in their ES-202 report.

Industrial classification

Employment and wage data under the ES-202 program have been classified by industry since 1938. Industrial codes are assigned by State agencies to each reporting unit based on responses to questionnaires in which employers indicate their principal product or activity. If a private or government employer conducts different activities at various establishments or installations, separate industrial codes are assigned to each establishment, to the extent possible.

Since 1938, the industrial classification of business establishments and government installations has undergone a number of modifications. (See table 1.) Until 1945, classification was based on the *Social Security Board Classification Manual.* At that time, the basis was changed to the *Standard Industrial Classification Manual,* which has since been revised several times. Establishments were originally classified into 20 manufacturing and 60 nonmanufacturing groups, on a 2-digit basis. The number of such groups has remained fairly constant. Three-digit groupings were added in 1942, and 4-digit groupings were added for manufacturing in 1956 and for nonmanufacturing in 1968. In the Covered Employment and Wages program, statewide 4-digit classification of nonmanufacturing became mandatory in 1978.

Since 1988, the *1987 Standard Industrial Classification Manual* has been used to classify the industry of each establishment. The manual provides for 1,005 4-digit industries, 416 3-digit industries, 83 major industry groups, and 11 industry divisions. Of the 1,005 4-digit industries, 7 are not used in the Covered Employment and Wages program because of problems in obtaining systematic and accurate information to code sufficiently at the 4-digit level.

In order to insure the highest possible quality of data from the ES-202 program, BLS and the States verify and update, if necessary, the SIC, location, and ownership classifications of all units on a 3-year cycle. Government units in the public administration industry division, however, are verified on a 5-year cycle.

Collection methods

State agencies collect ES-202 data on the quarterly UI Contribution Report or MWR as a byproduct of the administration of the UI program. Once new employers have met the criteria for UI liability and registered with the State agency, they begin the ongoing process of submitting a quarterly UI report. Employers who have ceased operations no longer report and are dropped from ES-202 data.

Table 1. Industrial classification of employment and wage data, 1938-92

Period	Number of industry groups by:			Basis of industrial classification							
				Social Security Board (SSB)		Standard Industrial Classification (SIC)					
	2-digit code	3-digit code	4-digit code	1939 edition	1942 edition	1945 edition	1957 edition	1967 edition	1972 edition	1977 supplement	1987 edition
Manufacturing											
1938-41	20			X							
1942-46	21	146			X						
1947-55	21	150				X					
1956-57	21	150	[1]469			X					
1958-67	21	148	[1]433				X				
1968-74	21	148	[1]417					X			
1975-78	20	143	451						X		
1979-87	20	143	452							X	
1988[2]	20	143	452						X	X	
1988 to present	20	140	459								X
Nonmanufacturing											
1938-41	60			X							
1942-57	56	256			X						
1958-67	58	236					X				
1968-74	62	235	[3]494					X			
1975-77	64	277	[3]553						X		
1978	64	277	553						X	X	
1979-87	64	277	553							X	
1988[2]	64	277	553						X	X	
1988 to present	63	276	546								X

[1] First quarter (January-March) only.
[2] First quarter 1988 data were coded under both the 1972/77 and 1987 SIC Manual.
[3] Not coded on a mandatory basis.

State agencies send their magnetic tapes or cartridges of ES-202 data for over 6.0 million active establishments to BLS each quarter. Each establishment is classified by its industrial activity and then independently by 1 of 5 ownership categories. Private industry has 5.3 million reporting units; Federal Government, 42,000; State government, 52,000; local government, 98,000; and foreign or international government, about 25.

The State agencies code and summarize the raw data from the UI Contribution and Multiple Worksite Reports; check for missing information and errors; prepare imputations of data for delinquent reports; and finally, machine process the data onto magnetic tapes. Five months following the end of each quarter, the agencies send tapes containing these data to Washington.

In order to assure accurate data, BLS conducts several additional edits of the data each quarter and then requests State agencies to review questionable entries and provide updates or explanations where necessary. BLS has also developed an exportable macro-edit system for State agency use so that there may be consistent and efficient review of the ES-202 report. The macro-edit permits State agencies to use their resources effectively in the processing, review, and correction of data.

Comparison of the ES-202 Program with Other Series

A number of other statistical data series are comparable in some respects to those provided in the ES-202 program. These series all have certain applications, strengths, and shortcomings. Because of its broad universe coverage, continuity, and currency, the ES-202 program is one of the most useful.

Current Employment Statistics

The Current Employment Statistics (CES) program uses a sample of over 350,000 establishments to provide current estimates of monthly nonfarm employment, average weekly hours, and average hourly and weekly earnings. Employment estimates derived from the CES are benchmarked primarily to ES-202 records, which cover about 98 percent of all nonfarm employees and 99 percent of those in the private nonfarm sector. For the remaining industries, the CES program uses other sources to estimate employment not covered by State UI laws.

In addition to being both sample-based rather than a universe count and more current, the CES program differs from the ES-202 program in that CES provides paid hours and weighted weekly earnings estimates for production workers in manufacturing and nonsupervisory workers in nonmanufacturing. The ES-202 program provides total quarterly payroll data for all employees, unrelated to hours paid. Also, CES data are available monthly, whereas ES-202 data are available quarterly.

Current Population Survey

The Current Population Survey (CPS) is a sample survey of about 60,000 households selected to represent the entire civilian noninstitutional population and designed to measure overall employment, unemployment, and those not in the labor force. In terms of employment, the sample thus includes categories of workers which are entirely or partly excluded from the ES-202 program: Certain farm and domestic workers, the self-employed, persons working 15 hours or more in the survey week as unpaid workers in a family-operated enterprise, employees of certain nonprofit organizations, and railroad workers. The CPS also counts employees uncompensated because of temporary absence but excludes workers under 16 years old.

Because the CPS is a sample and surveys households rather than establishments, it cannot present employment and wage data in the industrial and geographical detail available under the ES-202 program, but it does provide demographic characteristics. As a household survey, its focus is on individuals, whereas establishment-based surveys such as the ES-202 program focus on jobs. When providing geographic information, the CPS program tabulates data by the location of the residence. On the other hand, the ES-202 program provides its State and county data by the location of the job. Both CPS and CES data are released within 1 month of the reference period; ES-202 data become available several months after the reference quarter.

County Business Patterns

Covered employment and wages data from the ES-202 program differ from employment data published in *County Business Patterns* (CBP) of the Census Bureau in the following major areas: (1) CBP data exclude administrative and auxiliary units from "operating" unit data at the 4-digit level and include these data at the industry division level only. ES-202 covered employment, on the other hand, includes data for these units at the 4-digit SIC level. (2) CBP excludes agricultural production workers and household workers, some of whom are included in ES-202 covered employment data. CBP also excludes government units, all of which are included in the ES-202 program. (3) Every 5 years, data are collected for all multi-units within the scope of business and economic censuses and included in the CBP for that year. Annual updates for the larger multi-units are obtained from the sample selected for the Report of Organization Survey, and data for nonsample multi-units are estimated. Annual updates for single units come from the Internal Revenue Service and the Social Security Administration. ES-202 covered employment and wages data, on the other hand, includes data collected from all active units each quarter.

Office of Personnel Management data

The Office of Personnel Management (OPM) maintains and publishes a statistical series on Federal employment and payrolls with information by agency, type of position and appointment, and characteristics of employees. Both the OPM and ES-202 series exclude the Central Intelligence Agency and the National Security Agency, the Armed Forces, temporary emergency workers employed to cope with catastrophes, and officers and crews of certain American vessels. OPM data, but not ES-202 data, include employees working in foreign countries, workers paid on a fee or commission basis, and paid patients, inmates, and certain employees of Federal institutions. Conversely, ES-202 data, but not OPM data, include Department of Defense employees paid from nonappropriated funds as well as employees with Federal appointments to the Agricultural Extension Service, County Agricultural Stabilization and Conservation Committees, and State and Area Marketing Committees.

In comparison with the OPM data, ES-202 program data provide more industry, local employment, and wage detail and more frequently updated detail on employment by State. The OPM data series, of course, have certain statistics that have no parallel in the ES-202 program.

Presentation

Employment and Wages, an annual BLS publication, presents State and national totals for covered employment and wages by broad industry division, major industry group, and detailed 4-digit industry. Data for government workers are shown by State and selected industries. The publication includes distributions of employment and wages by size of reporting unit for each major industry division for the United States as a whole. These data are distributed into 10 employment-size categories.

To preserve the anonymity of establishments, BLS withholds publication of data for any geographic industry level in which there are fewer than three firms or in which the employment of a single firm accounts for over 80 percent of the industry. At the request of a State, data are also withheld where there is reason to believe that the "fewer than three" rule would not prevent disclosure of information pertaining to an individual firm or would otherwise violate the State's disclosure provisions. Information concerning Federal employees, however, is fully disclosable.

In addition to published information, county and metropolitan data and historical information are available from the BLS Washington office either on hard copy or on machine-readable media such as magnetic tapes and diskettes on a cost reimbursable basis. The charge for this service varies according to the complexity and volume of the request. Write to the Division of Occupational and Administrative Statistics, Office of Employment and Unemployment Statistics, U.S. Department of Labor, Bureau of Labor Statistics, Washington, DC 20212.

The individual States, which have a wide variety of uses for the data, usually publish their own reports containing ES-202 data.

Uses

The ES-202 data series is the most complete universe of monthly employment and quarterly wage information by industry, county, and State. The series have broad economic significance in evaluating labor trends and major industry developments in time series analyses and industry comparisons, and in special studies such as analyses of wages by size of establishment.

The program provides data necessary to both the Employment and Training Administration and the various State employment security agencies in administering the employment security program. The data accurately reflect the extent of coverage of the State unemployment laws and are used to measure UI revenues; National, State, and local area employment; and total and taxable wage trends. The information is used as an input for actuarial studies, determination of experience ratings, maximum benefit levels, and areas needing Federal assistance. It also assists in determining the solvency of unemployment insurance funds.

The ES-202 data are used by a variety of other BLS programs. They serve, for example, as the basic source of benchmark information for employment by industry and by size of establishment in the Current Employment Statistics program. The Unemployment Insurance Name and Address File, developed in conjunction with the ES-202 report, also serves as a national sampling frame for establishment surveys by the Producer Price Index, Occupational Safety and Health Statistics, and Employment Cost Index and other compensation programs.

The Bureau of Economic Analysis of the Department of Commerce uses ES-202 wage data as a base for estimating a large part of the wage and salary component of national income and gross domestic product. A subdivision of these accounts, personal income, is instrumental in determining Federal allocation of program grants to State and local governments. The Social Security Administration and State governments also use ES-202 data in updating economic assumptions and forecasting trends in their taxable wage base.

Finally, business and public and private research organizations find the ES-202 program one of the best sources of detailed employment and wage statistics.

Technical References

U.S. Department of Labor, Bureau of Labor Statistics. *Employment and Wages, Annual Averages, 1990,* Bulletin 2393, November 1991.

U.S. Department of Labor, Bureau of Labor Statistics. *Employment Data Under the New Standard Industrial Classification, First Quarter 1988,* Report 772, October 1989.

Bureau of Labor Statistics. "ES-202, Operating Manual," *Employment Security Manual,* Part III, Sections 0400-0599, revised on a regular basis.

U.S. Department of Labor, Employment and Training Administration. "Comparison of State Unemployment Insurance Laws," revised on a regular basis.

Chapter 6. Occupational Pay and Employee Benefits

Background

For many decades, the Bureau of Labor Statistics has conducted studies of wages by occupation and industry. The best known of the early Bureau studies stemmed from a Senate resolution of March 3, 1891, which instructed its Committee on Finance to investigate the effects of tariff legislation on wages and prices. At the request of the committee, the Bureau developed detailed data for 1889-91 and a more limited wage rate history extending back to 1860, and in some cases to 1840.

Systematic collection of wage data by occupation and industry continued after the turn of the century, with changes in coverage dictated mainly by government data needs. Thus, a large survey program undertaken for the War Industries Board in 1919 produced occupational pay rates by industry and State, and (for some industries) by city. Between 1934 and 1940, the selection of industries studied was determined largely by administrative needs under the National Industrial Recovery Act, the Public Contracts Act, and the Fair Labor Standards Act, with emphasis on nationwide data for relatively low-wage industries.

Survey activity shifted in the early 1940's defense period to heavy industries essential to war production. Implementation of wage stabilization policy during the war required a large-scale program of occupational wage studies by industry and locality. The emphasis on data by locality continued after 1945 within the framework of industry studies generally designed to yield national and regional estimates. In addition, the Bureau developed two new types of occupational wage surveys.

Area wage surveys, initiated in the late 1940's, were designed to meet the growing demand for pay data related to office clerical and manual jobs that are common to a wide variety of manufacturing and nonmanufacturing industries within a metropolitan area. This survey program was firmly established and temporarily expanded for use in the wage stabilization effort during the Korean emergency. In 1960, the program was converted from a study of metropolitan areas of special interest to a statistically selected group of areas from which data could be projected to represent all metropolitan areas of the United States, excluding Alaska and Hawaii.

Also in 1960, the Bureau began conducting an annual nationwide survey of professional, administrative, technical, and clerical jobs in a broad spectrum of private industries. The survey was begun in preparation for the Federal Salary Reform Act of 1962 and was used in administering both that act and the subsequent Federal Pay Comparability Act of 1970. These statutes called for comparability on a nationwide basis of salaries of Federal Government employees and those in the private sector. They governed adjustments in pay of most Federal white-collar employees until the passage of the Federal Employees Pay Comparability Act of 1990.

The 1990 legislation provides for local variations in Federal white-collar pay scales in accordance with area differences in pay levels. Such area differences are to be determined using the results of Bureau surveys and, consequently, the BLS occupational wage survey program is being restructured to give greater emphasis to locality studies. Because the restructuring is currently in progress, and results are not yet visible in published survey findings, the following discussion considers both the pre-1990 program and planned modifications of that program.

Description of Surveys

Even when differing in industrial, geographic, and occupational coverage, the surveys have been components of an integrated program of occupational wage studies based upon a common set of administrative forms, a single manual of procedures, and common concepts and definitions. Survey data, collected largely by personal visits, are provided by employers on a voluntary basis. In return, the Bureau pledges confidentiality for the information and publishes it in a manner that will avoid possible disclosure of an establishment's pay rates. In all surveys, establishments are classified by industry as defined in the *Standard Industrial Classification Manual* (SIC) prepared by the U.S. Office of Management and Budget.[1] Survey reports identify the minimum size of the establishments (measured by total employment) studied. Metropolitan Statistical Area definitions are used in all programs,[2] but for selected surveys, the geographic scope may not coincide with MSA definitions.

Area Wage Surveys, conducted in a sample of metropolitan areas, have provided wage data annually or every

[1] See appendix B.
[2] See appendix C.

second year for selected office clerical, professional, technical, maintenance, toolroom, powerplant, material movement, and custodial occupations common to a wide variety of industries in the areas surveyed. The occupations studied have provided representation of the range of duties and responsibilities associated with white-collar jobs, skilled maintenance trades, and custodial and material movement jobs. In many instances, occupations have been divided into two or more work levels, based on differences in incumbents' experience and responsibilities. Weekly salaries reported for individuals in white-collar jobs relate to regular straight-time salaries paid for standard workweeks. Earnings information for plant workers excludes late-shift differentials and premium pay for overtime.

Over the years, industry divisions included in these surveys were: (1) Manufacturing; (2) transportation, communications, and other public utilities; (3) wholesale trade; (4) retail trade; (5) finance, insurance, and real estate; and (6) selected service industries. Establishments employing fewer than 50 workers were excluded. However, in the 19 largest areas, establishments in manufacturing; transportation, communications, and other public utilities; and retail trade had to employ a minimum of 100 workers to be included in the survey.

In addition to the all-industry pay averages and distributions of workers by earnings classes, separate data were provided for manufacturing and nonmanufacturing in each area, and for transportation, communications, and other public utilities in all but nine areas. In 31 of the larger areas, wage data were presented separately for establishments with 500 workers or more. In 1987, the program increased its sample of areas from 70 to 90, with 61 being studied each year. The 32 largest areas, in terms of nonagricultural employment, were surveyed annually, and two groups of 29 areas each were surveyed in alternate years. All of the areas were Metropolitan Statistical Areas or Primary Metropolitan Statistical Areas as defined by the Office of Management and Budget through October 1984.

Data on weekly work schedules; paid holiday and vacation practices; and health, insurance, and retirement plans were recorded separately for nonsupervisory office workers and for production and related workers. Information relating to shift operations and shift pay differentials was published for production workers in manufacturing, while data on minimum entrance rates were collected for inexperienced office workers in all industries. While the wage data were collected annually or every 2 years, establishment practices and benefit items were studied every 3 or 4 years.

Beginning with surveys fielded in September 1991, the area wage survey program is being expanded to provide the locality data to be used by the President's Pay Agent[3] in administering the Federal Employees Pay Comparability Act of 1990. This expansion, of course, will also yield additional information to other users of occupational wage survey data.

Plans for the immediate future call for annual surveys in 60-65 metropolitan areas, roughly half of which are of special interest to the Pay Agent. In all areas, although wage data will be collected each year, information on employee benefits will be obtained at less frequent intervals.

The number of establishments in an area within the scope of the survey will grow, in part through coverage of all establishments with 50 workers or more. In addition, in areas surveyed for the Pay Agent, coverage will extend to all private nonagricultural industries except households, plus State and local governments. In other areas, while State and local governments will be surveyed, mining, construction, and parts of services will remain outside the scope of the program. Also being modified are the lists of surveyed occupations, particularly in areas studied for the Pay Agent. The most significant change is an expansion in the number of professional and administrative occupations in areas studied for the Pay Agent (see table 1).

Increases in the number of establishments visited will permit publication of greater industry detail. This will be particularly true in areas studied for the Pay Agent, where separate detail may be publishable for all industries studied, State and local governments, private industries, goods-producing industries, service-producing industries, manufacturing, and transportation and utilities. In other areas, planned publication of data will be for all industries studied, State and local governments, private industries, manufacturing, service-producing industries, and transportation and utilities. However, current occupational averages for men and women separately will be dropped. Information on employee benefits will parallel that previously published, although temporarily limited to paid holidays, vacations, and the incidence of health insurance and retirement plans. Information on benefits will be shown separately for white-and blue-collar workers, rather than for nonsupervisory office and production workers, as in earlier years.

Area type wage surveys have also been conducted since 1967 at the request of the Employment Standards Administration of the U.S. Department of Labor for use in administering the Service Contract Act of 1965. Survey scope and method were the same as for the Bureau's regular area surveys, but a more limited number of occupations and benefits were studied. Beginning in September 1991, however, the revised job list being introduced in the area wage survey program is also being introduced in Service Contract Area surveys. However, changes in the size of establishments and industries studied in area wage surveys are not being made in the Service Contract Act surveys. In some cases, surveys relate to geographic areas other than Metropolitan Statistical Areas. Wage data are published annually or every

[3] The Secretary of Labor and the Directors of the Office of Personnel Management and the Office of Management and Budget. The Agent has responsibility for making salary comparisons between Federal white-collar workers and their non-Federal counterparts and recommending pay increases for Federal white-collar workers based on these comparisons.

annually or every second year and benefits data every 3 or 4 years for all industries combined.

Both programs of area wage surveys are conducted throughout the calendar year, with each survey relating to a specific month.

The White-Collar Pay Survey (WCP)—until 1989 called the National Survey of Professional, Administrative, Technical, and Clerical Pay (PATC)—has provided broadly based information on white-collar salary levels and distributions in private employment, as of March each year. Approximately 150 occupational work levels were studied in 1990, selected from the following fields: Accounting, legal services, personnel management, engineering and chemistry, nursing, purchasing, photography, drafting, computer science, and clerical. Definitions for these occupations provided for classification of employees into appropriate work levels. Although reflecting duties and responsibilities in private industry, the definitions were designed to be translatable to specific pay grades of Federal white-collar employees. This stemmed from the design of the survey as a vehicle for obtaining information suitable for use in comparing pay of salaried employees in the Federal civil service with pay of their counterparts in private industry.

Monthly and annual average salaries were reported by occupational work level. Data related to the straight-time salary corresponding to the employee's normal work schedule, excluding overtime hours. Salary averages were presented for all establishments covered by the survey, establishments employing 2,500 workers or more, and for metropolitan areas as a group. Although limited industry detail was reported, regional and area breakouts were not possible.

Industry divisions included in the WCP survey were: (1) Mining; (2) construction; (3) manufacturing; (4) transportation, communications, electric, gas, and sanitary services; (5) wholesale trade; (6) retail trade; (7) finance, insurance, and real estate; and (8) services.

Limited to the Nation's metropolitan areas during 1960-64, the annual survey was expanded in 1965 to include nonmetropolitan counties. In 1990, the survey included establishments with 50 or more employees. This minimum had been adjusted at various times in earlier years in response to the specifications of the President's Pay Agent.

The Pay Agent's growing interest in locality pay and the consequent expansion of the area wage survey program has affected the national white-collar pay report. Beginning with the report for 1992, data will come, not from a separate survey, but from the data base developed from the area wage surveys.[4] Information to be reported will parallel that presented in earlier years. However, some major changes—such as the expansion of the industrial scope to include State and local governments, the addition of blue-collar occupations, and the restructuring of the list of white-collar jobs—will be reflected in the 1992 report.

Industry Wage Surveys, conducted in selected manufacturing and nonmanufacturing industries, have provided data for occupations representing a range of activities performed by workers in the industry during a specified payroll month. In selecting the occupations, primarily nonsupervisory, consideration has been given to their prevalence in the industry, definiteness and clarity of duties, use as reference points in collective bargaining, and importance in representing the industry's wage structure.

In addition to reporting straight-time first-shift wage rates of individuals in the selected occupations (or hours and earnings for incentive workers), surveys in most industries have also provided pay distributions for broad employee groups, such as all production and related workers or all nonsupervisory workers.

Weekly work schedules; shift operations and shift pay differentials; paid holiday and vacation practices; and incidence of health, insurance, and retirement plans have been included in the information collected, along with other items of interest in a particular industry, for example, incidence of cost-of-living adjustment (COLA) provisions or extent of company-provided work clothing. The studies have also provided estimates of workers covered by labor-management agreements, proportions employed under incentive pay plans, and the extent to which establishments have a single pay rate or a range of rates for individual job categories.

Roughly 25 manufacturing and 15 nonmanufacturing industries, defined at the 3- or 4-digit SIC level of industry detail, have been studied. A majority were on a 5-year cycle, but a number of comparatively low-wage industries were on a 3-year cycle. The program covered a broad cross-section of the Nation's economy, including automobile and steel manufacturing as well as banking, computer data services, and hospitals.

Nearly all of the manufacturing, utility, and mining industries were studied on a nationwide basis, and estimates were provided also for broad regions and major local areas of employment concentration wherever possible.

Surveys in trade, finance, and service industries usually were limited to about two dozen metropolitan areas. Nationwide surveys generally developed separate employment and wage estimates by size of establishment, type of area (metropolitan or nonmetropolitan), labor-management agreement coverage status, and type of product or plant group. Because of budget curtailments, the industry wage survey program is currently being suspended.

Concepts

The Bureau's occupational pay surveys summarize a highly specific wage measure—the rate of pay for indi-

[4] A survey of the nonmetropolitan portions of the country outside the scope of the area wage survey program will permit the development of nationwide estimates.

vidual workers, excluding premium pay for overtime and for work on weekends, holidays, and late shifts. Also excluded are performance bonuses and lump-sum payments of the type negotiated in the auto and aerospace industries, as well as profit-sharing payments, attendance bonuses, Christmas or yearend bonuses, and other nonproduction bonuses. Pay increases—but not bonuses—under cost-of-living allowance clauses and incentive payments, however, are included. For workers paid under piecework or other types of production incentive pay plans, an hourly earnings figure serves as a proxy for the wage rate; it is computed by dividing straight-time earnings over a time period by corresponding hours worked.

Unless stated otherwise, rates do not include tips or allowances for the value of meals, room, uniforms, etc. The earnings figures, thus, represent cash wages (prior to deductions for Social Security and income taxes, savings bonds, premium payments for group insurance, meals, room, or uniforms) after the exclusion of premium pay for overtime, weekend, holiday, or late-shift work.

Hours shown for salaried occupations relate to standard weekly hours for which the employee receives regular straight-time salary.

Survey occupations are defined in advance in a uniform set of job descriptions. Because of the emphasis on comparability of occupational content across establishments, the Bureau's job descriptions may differ significantly from those in use in individual establishments or those used for other purposes. The primary objective of the description is to identify the essential elements of skill, difficulty, and responsibility that establish the basic concept of the job.[5] In general, the Bureau's survey job descriptions are more specific than those published in the *Standard Occupational Classification Manual,* prepared by the U.S. Department of Commerce.

Although work arrangements in any one establishment may not correspond precisely to those described, workers meeting the basic requirements established for the job are included.[6]

In applying the survey job descriptions, the Bureau's field representatives exclude working supervisors and those paid less than the established job rate, such as apprentices, learners, beginners, trainees, handicapped workers whose rates are reduced because of their handicap, part-time or temporary workers, and probationary workers unless provision for their inclusion is specifically stated. Tabulations of the incidence of paid holidays, paid vacations, and health, insurance, and retirement plans are based on the assumption that plans are applicable to all covered workers if a majority of such workers are eligible or can expect eventually to qualify for the practices listed. Data for health, insurance, and retirement plans are limited to plans for which at least a part of the cost is borne by the employer. Informal provisions are excluded. (For a description of the Bureau's comprehensive study of employee benefits in medium and large firms, see chapter 9 of this bulletin.) Expansion of survey coverage to governmental units has led to a clarification of the definition of workers covered by collective bargaining agreements. It is now specified explicitly that collective bargaining must cover wage rates.

Survey Methods

Planning. The needs of major users are a prime consideration in designing the Bureau's occupational wage surveys. Consultations are held with appropriate management, labor, and government representatives to obtain views and recommendations related to scope, timing, selection, and definitions of survey items, and types of tabulations.

Reflecting its use in evaluating of Federal white-collar pay, the design of the White-Collar Pay Survey was developed in conjunction with the Office of Management and Budget and the Office of Personnel Management. Changes in the survey scope, item coverage, and job definitions were initiated by these agencies. Similarly, the recent modifications of the area wage survey program were developed after extensive discussions with representatives of the Pay Agent.

The industrial scope of each survey is identified in terms of the classification system provided in the *Standard Industrial Classification Manual.* The scope may range from part of a 4-digit code for an industry study to the entire nonfarm economy, excluding households and the Federal Government.

The minimum establishment size included in a survey is greatly influenced by budget considerations. It is set at a point where the possible contribution of the excluded establishments to the pay averages is regarded as negligible for most of the occupations surveyed. Another practical reason for the adoption of size limitations is the difficulty encountered in classifying workers in small establishments where they do not perform the specialized duties indicated in the survey job definitions.

[5] An example of a job description is Maintenance Machinist: Produces replacement parts and new parts in making repairs of metal parts of mechanical equipment. Work involves most of the following: Interpreting written instructions and specifications; planning and laying out of work; using a variety of machinist's handtools and precision measuring instruments; setting up and operating standard machine tools; shaping of metal parts to close tolerances; making standard shop computations relating to dimensions of work, tooling, feeds, and speeds of machining; knowledge of the working properties of the common metals; selecting standard materials, parts, and equipment required for this work; and fitting and assembling parts into mechanical equipment. In general, the machinist's work normally requires a rounded training in machine-shop practice usually acquired through a formal apprenticeship or equivalent training and experience.

[6] In general, workers are included in a classification if the described duties are performed a major part of the time and the remainder is spent on related duties requiring similar or lesser skill and responsibility. However, in some jobs, particularly office and skilled production-worker categories, workers may regularly perform a combination of duties involving more than one occupation. Unless indicated otherwise in the description, in these situations consideration for classification purposes is given to those elements of the job which are most important in determining its level for pay purposes.

The types of occupations studied and the criteria used in their selection are identified in the descriptions of the various types of surveys. The job list for each survey is selected to represent a reasonably complete range of rates in the wage structure for the employment categories in the study.

User interest, particularly views of the Pay Agent regarding content of area wage surveys, and the extent to which occupations can be defined and surveyed are key elements in the selection of specific jobs. The established hierarchy of job rates to be found within establishments and industries permits the use of pay data for such key or benchmark jobs for interpolating rates of other jobs. Technological developments or user interests may dictate changes over time in the job lists and definitions. New definitions for jobs usually are pretested in a variety of establishments prior to their use in a full-scale survey.

Questionnaires. Two basic reporting forms are used in all surveys. The first (BLS 2751A) includes items relating to products or services, employment, shift operations and differentials, work schedules, wage payment plans, paid holidays and vacations, insurance and retirement plans, union contract coverage, and other items applicable to the establishments. The second (BLS 2753G) is used in recording such information as occupation, method of wage payment, hours, and pay rate or earnings for each worker studied. Supplementary forms are used to meet particular needs.

Data collection. Bureau field representatives typically visit the sample establishments in a survey and collect data for a specified payroll period. They carefully compare job functions and factors in the establishment with those included in the Bureau job definitions. This job-matching process may involve review of records (such as pay structure plans, organizational charts, and company position descriptions), interviews with appropriate officials, and, on occasion, observation of jobs within establishments. A satisfactory completion of job matching permits acceptance of company-prepared reports where this procedure is preferred by the respondent. Generally, however, the field representative secures wage or salary rates (or hours and earnings data, when needed) from payroll or other records, and data on the selected employer practices and employee benefits from company officials, company booklets, or labor-management agreements.

Area wage surveys in each locality are now conducted by personal visits every other year, with partial collection by mail or telephone in the intervening years. Establishments participating in the mail collection receive a transcript of the job-matching and wage data obtained previously, together with the job definitions. The returns are scrutinized, and questionable entries are checked with the respondent. Visits are made to establishments not suitable for other types of collection, those not responding to the mail or telephone request, and those reporting unusual changes from previous survey data.

Selected respondents to the surveys are contacted by regional and national office staff to systematically verify that data collection procedures and concepts were correctly applied by the Bureau's field staff. Results of these contacts are used in staff development and to improve data collection materials and procedures and survey definitions.

Sampling

All surveys are conducted on a sample basis using a suitable sampling "frame," that is, a list of establishments which fall within the designated scope of the survey. The frame is as close to the universe as possible but is often incomplete. BLS uses frames primarily compiled from lists provided by administrative or regulatory government agencies (primarily State unemployment insurance agencies). These may be supplemented by data from directories, trade associations, labor unions, and other sources as needed. For survey purposes, an "establishment" generally refers to a single physical location in manufacturing industries and to all outlets of a company within an area or county in nonmanufacturing industry divisions.

The survey design employs a high degree of stratification. Each geographic-industry unit for which a separate analysis is to be presented is sampled independently. Within these broad groupings, a finer stratification by product (or other pertinent attribute) and size of establishment is made. Stratification has been carried still further in certain industry wage surveys: Coal mines, for instance, have been classified into underground and surface mines. Such stratification is important if the occupational structure differs widely among the various industry segments.

The sample for each industry-area group is a probability sample, that is, each establishment has a predetermined chance of selection. However, in order to secure maximum accuracy at a fixed level of cost (or a fixed level of accuracy at minimum cost), the sampling fraction used in the various strata, or sampling cells, ranges downward from all large establishments through progressively declining proportions of the establishments in each smaller size group. This procedure follows the principles of optimum allocation using the average employment in the stratum as the design variable. Thus, each sampled stratum will be represented in the sample by a number of establishments roughly proportionate to its share of total employment. The method of estimation used yields unbiased estimates by the assignment of proper weights to the sampled establishments.

The size of the sample in a particular survey depends on the size of the universe, the diversity of occupations and their distribution, the relative dispersion of earnings among establishments, the distribution of the establishments by size, and the degree of accuracy required.

Area wage surveys are limited to selected metropolitan areas, which form a sample of all such areas and, when properly combined (weighted), yield employment and wage estimates at the national and regional levels. The sample of areas is based on the selection of one area from a stratum of similar areas. The criteria for stratification are region, type of industrial activity as measured by percent of employment in manufacturing, and major industries. Each area within a stratum is selected with its probability of selection proportionate to its nonagricultural employment. The larger metropolitan areas are self representing, i.e., each one forms a stratum by itself and is certain of inclusion in the area sample.

Estimating Procedures

Estimated average earnings (hourly, weekly, monthly, or annual) for an industry or an occupation are computed as the arithmetic mean of individual employee earnings.

All estimates are derived from the sample data. The averages for occupations, as well as for industries, are weighted averages of individual earnings and are not computed on an establishment basis. Employee benefit provisions which apply to a majority of the blue- or white-collar workers in an establishment are considered to apply to all such workers in that establishment and are considered nonexistent when they apply to less than a majority.

To obtain unbiased estimates, each establishment is assigned a weight that is the inverse of the sampling ratio for the stratum from which it was selected; e.g., if a third of the establishments in one stratum are selected, each of the sampled establishments is given a weight of 3.

To illustrate the use of weights, suppose the universe was seven establishments, from which a sample of three was selected. Assume that establishment A was one of two establishments in its stratum. It was chosen for the sample and is given a weight of 2. Establishment B, on the other hand, was taken with certainty (or a probability of 1) and is thus given a weight of 1. Establishment C was taken from the remaining group where one of the four establishments was used in the sample, and hence is given a weight of 4. The following calculations are made in estimating average earnings for a given occupation.

		Workers in occupation in sample establishments		*Estimates of total in stratum*	
Establishment	*Weight*	*Actual employment in occupation*	*Average hourly earnings*	*Workers*	*Earnings*
A	2	40	$10.40	2x40	2x40x $10.40
B	1	50	11.20	1x50	1x50x 11.20
C	4	10	10.60	4x10	4x10x 10.60
Estimated universe				170	$1,816.00

A similar method applies to any characteristic estimated from the sample. For instance, to estimate the proportion of employees in establishments granting paid vacations of 2 weeks after 2 years of service, the establishments are classified according to the length of vacation granted after 2 years' service, establishment weights are applied to employment, as in the previous example, and the proportion of the estimated employment in the 2-week category is computed. Using the three establishments in the previous example, this can be illustrated as follows.

Establishment	*Weight*	*Actual total establishment employment*	*Weighed employment*	*Vacation provisions after 2 years*
A	2	100	200	1 week
B	1	500	500	2 weeks
C	4	75	300	1 week
Estimated universe			1,000	

Thus, the estimated percentage of workers in establishments granting 2 weeks' vacation after 2 years of service is $\frac{500}{1,000}$ or 50 percent.

In the area wage survey program, where a sample of selected metropolitan areas is used to represent the totality of such areas, a second stage of weighting is used to expand the individual area estimates to regional and national levels. Since each area represents a stratum of similar areas, the total from each area is weighted to the estimated stratum totals by multiplying by the inverse of the chance of selection. Summing all such estimated stratum totals yields the earnings and employment totals for the regional and the national estimates.

BLS occupational wage surveys have response rates generally exceeding 80 percent of establishments contacted. However, when a sample establishment does not provide data, the weights of responding sample establishments from the same stratum are increased to adjust for the missing data. Establishments that are out of business or outside the scope of a survey (and their sampling weights) are dropped from survey estimates.

Analysis and Presentation

Survey results are published in BLS bulletins, reports, news releases, and the Bureau's *Monthly Labor Review*. Reports and bulletins are issued throughout the year as the surveys are completed. Copies of BLS reports and releases are available upon request. Bulletins may be purchased by contacting New Orders, Superintendent of Documents, P.O. Box 371954, Pittsburgh, PA 15250-7954; GPO bookstores; or the BLS Chicago Regional Office, Publications Sales Center, P.O. Box 2145, Chicago, IL 60690. A brief discussion of some features related to these publications follows.

Where an industry survey has been designed to yield estimates for selected States or areas, individual summary reports have been published separately as this local information has become available. Industry surveys limited to selected areas have not provided the pay tabulations by type of area, size of establishment, product, or labor-management agreement coverage that generally have been included in reports on nationwide surveys. Regardless of geographic scope, industry reports have recorded the incidence of incentive pay plans and, to the extent possible, have shown pay data separately for time and incentive workers.

Area wage survey reports and bulletins have included tabulations of percentage pay increases, adjusted for changes in employment, for industrial nurses and four broad occupational groups: Office clerical, electronic data processing, skilled maintenance, and unskilled plant workers. These increases have been computed for all industries combined, and for manufacturing and nonmanufacturing separately, for each metropolitan area studied. The computations have included data only from establishments included in both years of the survey being compared. Because of the current restructuring of the area wage survey program, calculation of these percentage increases will be suspended for the next few years.

Pay relatives for broad occupational categories, expressing area average pay as a percentage of the national average, are published each year in two reports: *Wage Differences Among Metropolitan Areas* and *Wage Differences Among Selected Areas.* (The first of these reports covers the areas in the area wage survey program; the latter covers areas surveyed for the Employment Standards Administration.) These reports permit ready comparisons of average pay levels among areas.

The annual bulletins reporting findings of the white-collar pay survey have presented occupational salary averages and distributions on an all-industry basis, nationwide and separately for all metropolitan areas combined, and for establishments employing 2,500 workers or more. Average pay levels by industry division have been shown as percentages of the all-industry averages. Salary trend estimates for the occupations studied have been included as a byproduct of the survey. Prior to 1987, survey coverage extended fully to all private-sector industry divisions except services, in which coverage was limited.[7] The 1987 survey, in contrast, was restricted to services but covered the entire industry division. Coverage in 1988 extended to private nonservice industries, in 1989 to private service-producing industries, and in 1990 to private goods-producing industries.

The *Monthly Labor Review* publishes two types of articles on the occupational wage surveys. Research summaries alert interested parties to a survey that has been completed by providing highlights of the findings. Special topical articles provide in-depth analyses of wages and related benefits. (See references at the end of this chapter for specific *Monthly Labor Review* articles.)

In addition to the survey publications, BLS has made computer tapes available for sale on the area wage and white-collar pay surveys. Requests for computer tapes on industry wage surveys have been considered on an individual survey basis. Filling such requests has primarily depended upon the Bureau's ability to protect the identity of respondents and their data.

Uses and Limitations

Occupational wage and benefit data developed in BLS surveys have a variety of uses. Federal, State, and local agencies use them in compensation administration and in the formulation of public policy on compensation as in minimum wage legislation. They are of value to Federal and State mediation and conciliation services and to State unemployment compensation agencies in judging the suitability of job offers.

Bureau data also are used in private compensation determinations by employers or through the collective bargaining process. To the extent that wages and benefits are a factor, survey data are considered by employers in selecting locations for new facilities and in cost estimating related to contract work.

In addition, the data are important for economic analysis. Knowledge of levels, structures, and trends of pay rates by occupation, industry, locality, and region is required in the analysis of current economic developments and in studies relating to wage dispersion and differentials.

Occupational wage survey programs, however, are not designed to supply mechanical answers to questions of pay policy. As suggested earlier, limitations are imposed in the selection and definition of industries examined, of geographic units for which estimates are developed, of occupations and associated items studied, and in the determination of periodicity and timing of particular surveys. Depending upon user needs, it may be necessary to interpolate for occupations or areas missing from a survey on the basis of knowledge of pay relationships.

Because of variation among establishments in the proportion of workers in the jobs studied and in the general level of pay, the survey averages do not necessarily reflect either the absolute or relative relationship found within the majority of individual establishments. Because of this, area wage survey bulletins provide some insights into pay relationships within establishments through special analytical tables.

The incidence of incentive pay systems may vary greatly among the occupations and establishments studied. Because average hourly earnings of incentive workers generally exceed those of time-rated workers in the same job, data have been shown separately wherever possible for the two groups in industry surveys. Incentive plans apply to only a very small proportion of the workers in the indirect plant jobs studied in the area wage and white-collar pay survey programs.

Although survey-to-survey changes in pay averages for a job or job group primarily reflect general wage and salary changes or merit increases received by individuals, these

[7] The 1986 coverage of services was limited to engineering, architectural, and surveying services; commercially operated research, development, and testing laboratories; credit reporting and collection agencies; computer and data processing services; management, consulting, and public relations services; noncommercial educational, scientific, and research organizations; and accounting, auditing, and bookkeeping services.

averages also may be affected by other factors. Common among these are labor turnover, labor force expansions and reductions, and changes in the proportion of workers employed in high- and low-paying establishments. A labor force expansion might increase the proportion of workers in lower paid, entry type jobs and thereby tend to lower the average; or the closing of a relatively high-paying establishment could cause average earnings in the area to drop.

Much of this problem has been overcome for area wage survey measures of pay change by holding establishment employment constant while computing percent increases in earnings. That is, the previous and current survey earnings of each establishment are weighted by that establishment's employment at the time of the previous survey. Under this system, measurement of change is limited to establishments included in two consecutive surveys. (As noted above, calculation of these percentage increases is being temporarily suspended.)

The effect of employment shifts among occupations between survey dates also has been eliminated in measuring average earnings increases for workers covered by the white-collar pay survey and by the machinery industry wage survey. Employment shifts among establishments or turnover of establishments included in survey samples, however, are not controlled in these computations, as they are in calculating area wage survey trends.

In general, the occupational wage survey programs are designed to measure pay levels and pay structures at specified points of time, rather than wage trends. For this reason, users are directed to other BLS series that are more appropriate indicators of wage change, such as the Employment Cost Index (see chapter 8 of this bulletin).

Reliability of surveys. Results of the surveys are subject to both sampling and nonsampling error. Sampling errors occur because observations come from a scientifically selected probability sample, rather than a census of the entire population. Sample-based estimates may differ from the results obtained from a census of the population. The sample used was one of many possible samples, each of which could have produced different estimates. The variation in the sample estimates across all possible samples that could have been drawn is measured by the standard error. The standard error is used to calculate a "confidence interval" around a sample estimate.

The 90-percent confidence interval is the interval centered at the sample estimate and includes all values within 1.6 times the estimate's standard error. If several different samples were selected to estimate the population value, the 90-percent confidence interval would include the true population value approximately 90 percent of the time.

Sampling errors are not uniform for the occupations studied because the dispersion of earnings among establishments and the frequency of occurrence of the occupations differ. The sample is designed so that the chances are 9 out of 10 that the published estimates on average earnings generally do not differ by more than 5 percent from the average that would be obtained by studying all establishments in the survey universe.

The sampling error of the percentage of workers receiving any given employee benefit differs with the size of the percentage. However, the error is such that rankings of predominant practices almost always will appear in their true position. Small percentages may be subject to considerable error but will always remain in the same scale of magnitude. For instance, the proportion of employees in establishments providing more than 5 weeks' paid vacation to long-service employees may be given as 2 percent, when the percentage for all establishments might be only 1 percent. Such a sampling error, while considerable, does not affect the essential inference that the practice is a rare one.

Estimates of the number of workers in a given occupation may have considerable sampling error, due to the wide variation among establishments in the proportion of workers found in individual occupations. (It is not unusual to find sampling errors of as much as 20 percent.) Hence, the estimated number of workers can be interpreted only as a rough indicator of the relative importance of various occupations. The greatest degree of accuracy in these employment counts is for occupations found principally in large establishments.

Since completely current and accurate information regarding establishment products and the creation of new establishments is not available, the universe from which the sample is drawn may be incomplete. Sample firms incorrectly classified are accounted for in the actual field work, and the universe estimates are revised accordingly. Those firms which should have been included but were classified erroneously in other industries cannot be accounted for.

Since some measure of judgment enters into the classification of occupations and other characteristics, there is some reporting variability in the results. A repetition of the survey in an establishment with different interviewers and respondents would undoubtedly produce slightly different results. Hence, analyses based on a small number of respondents must be used with care, even when all eligible establishments are included. However, when spread over a large number of establishments the differences, being random, would tend to balance out. No evidence of any consistent error has been uncovered.

Nonsampling errors can come from a number of other sources, including inability to obtain information from some establishments, definitional difficulties, inability of respondents to provide correct information, and errors in recording and coding the data obtained or estimating for missing data. Although not specifically measured, the surveys' nonsampling errors are likely to be minimal due to relatively high response rates, well-trained field representatives, careful review of the data, and other survey controls and procedures.

Technical References

Anderson, Kay E., Doyle, Philip M., and Schwenk, Albert E. "Measuring Union-Nonunion Earnings Differences," *Monthly Labor Review,* June 1990, pp. 26-38.

Barsky, Carl B., and Personick, Martin E. "Measuring Wage Dispersion: Pay Ranges Reflect Industry Traits," *Monthly Labor Review,* April 1981, pp. 35-41.

Buckley, John E. "Wage Differences Among Workers in the Same Job and Establishment," *Monthly Labor Review,* March 1985, pp. 11-16.

Buckley, John E. "Variations in Holidays, Vacations, and Area Pay Levels," *Monthly Labor Review,* February 1989, pp. 24-30.

Carlson, Norma W. "Time Rates Tighten Their Grip on Manufacturing Industries," *Monthly Labor Review,* May 1982, pp. 15-22.

Douty, N.M. "A Century of Wage Statistics: The BLS Contribution," *Monthly Labor Review,* November 1984, pp. 16-28.

Doyle, Philip M. "Area Wage Surveys Shed Light on Declines in Unionization," *Monthly Labor Review,* September 1985, pp. 13-20.

King, Sandra L., and Williams, Harry B. "Shift Work Pay Differentials and Practices in Manufacturing," *Monthly Labor Review,* December 1985, pp. 26-33.

Personick, Martin E. "White-collar Pay Determination Under Range-of-rate Systems," *Monthly Labor Review,* December 1984, pp. 25-30.

Personick, Martin E., and Barsky, Carl B. "White-collar Pay Levels Linked to Corporate Work Force Size," *Monthly Labor Review,* May 1982, pp. 23-28.

Van Giezen, Robert W. "A New Look at Occupational Wages Within Individual Establishments," *Monthly Labor Review,* November 1982, pp. 22-28.

Williams, Harry B. "What Temporary Workers Earn: Findings From New BLS Survey," *Monthly Labor Review,* March 1989, pp. 3-6.

U.S. Department of Labor, Bureau of Labor Statistics. *BLS Measures of Compensation,* Bulletin 2239, 1986.

Chapter 7. Negotiated Wage and Benefit Changes

The Bureau of Labor Statistics prepares information on current changes in wages and benefits agreed to in collective bargaining. The information includes monthly listings of companies, employer associations, or governmental units in which such changes have occurred, the unions involved, and the nature of the change. BLS also prepares quarterly and annual statistical summaries of negotiated wage changes in all major collective bargaining situations in private industry, and semiannual summaries for State and local government bargaining units.

Background

BLS began publishing a monthly listing of collective bargaining settlements in 1948, when prices and wage rates were rising rapidly and interest grew in determining the extent to which settlement patterns spread from industry to industry. The statistical series summarizing wage changes was initiated in 1949; regular quarterly publication was begun in 1954. In 1964, with the increasing importance of supplementary benefits such as various forms of premium pay, paid leave, and employer payments for health and life insurance and retirement benefits, the Bureau began to publish estimates of the size of negotiated changes in rates of compensation—the wage and benefit package—in selected private industries. The series was expanded to cover all private industry in 1968. Similar data have been published for State and local government bargaining units since 1979. Beginning with data for 1988, a new series was introduced accounting for the effects of the timing of wage and benefit changes on employer costs over the contract term and incorporating additional elements of compensation.

Description of Statistical Series

Coverage

Private industry agreements. The series summarizes wage-rate changes in major collective bargaining settlements (settlements covering 1,000 workers or more) for production and related workers in manufacturing and nonsupervisory workers in nonmanufacturing. Changes in total compensation are measured for agreements covering 5,000 workers or more in all industries and 1,000 workers or more in construction.

A contract covering a multiunit firm is included if it covers 1,000 workers even though each unit employs fewer workers. A contract covering a trade association, or two or more firms that bargain as a group, is included if it covers 1,000 workers even if the individual firms are not associated formally and each has fewer than the minimum number of workers within the scope of the series. Similarly, a contract covering two or more unions, which together represent at least 1,000 workers, is included even if each union represents fewer than 1,000 workers. In its present configuration, the series dates back to 1968 and, as of 1991, covered about 1,200 agreements and 5.6 million workers, for virtually complete coverage of major agreements.

State and local government agreements. This series summarizes wage and benefit changes for workers in State and local governments where: (1) A labor organization is recognized as the bargaining agent for a group of workers; (2) settlements are embodied in signed, mutually binding contracts; and (3) wages are determined by collective bargaining. When introduced in 1979, this series presented wage and benefit measures for units of 5,000 workers or more. Beginning with 1984 data, the coverage for wage data was expanded to units of 1,000 workers or more. As of 1991, this series covered 680 bargaining units and 2.7 million workers, about one-half of all State and local government employees covered by collective bargaining agreements.

Data presented

Wage-rate changes. Two types of information are presented on wage-rate changes. Settlement data measure wage-rate changes specified in bargaining settlements reached during the reference period (e.g., a particular quarter or year). They reflect decisions to increase, decrease, or not alter wage rates. These data exclude wage-rate changes that may occur under cost-of-living adjustment (COLA) clauses which link the size of future wage-rate changes to changes in the Consumer Price Index. Lump-sum payments are also excluded. Lump sums are one-time payments to workers that, unlike wages and benefits, are limited to a specific contract and typically are not continued in future contracts unless renegotiated. Both first-year changes, those scheduled during the first 12 months of the contract, and total changes scheduled over the contract term, expressed as an annual rate, are presented.

The second type of information presents net wage-rate changes under all major agreements. These include increases, decreases, and no alteration in wage rates during the reference period under all contracts, regardless of the contract settlement date. Included are increases and decreases stemming from settlements reached in the calendar year, agreements reached in a prior year, and COLA clauses.

Compensation changes. Although at one time the economic terms of collective bargaining settlements involved wage rates almost exclusively, today, a wide variety of benefits are also involved. "Compensation" refers to the total of wages and benefits. As with wage data, the Bureau publishes compensation data for settlements reached during the reference period, but limited to settlements covering 5,000 workers or more in all industries and 1,000 workers or more in construction.

Two measures of negotiated change in compensation are presented. The first, *compensation rate* change, has been published since 1964. The second, *compensation cost* change, was initiated with publication of settlement data for 1988.

Compensation rate change data provide a prospective estimate of how much compensation rates will be changed (increased, decreased, or left unaltered) as a result of collective bargaining settlements reached during specified reference periods. In the compensation rate series, compensation includes: Straight-time pay for time worked, including incentive earnings, production bonuses, and cost-of-living adjustments actually paid; premium pay for overtime, weekend, holiday, and late-shift work; pay for leave, including vacations, holidays, sick leave, and personal leave; negotiated payments for life insurance, health insurance, and sickness and accident insurance; pension and other retirement plans; severance pay; vacation and holiday funds; supplemental unemployment benefit plans; and legally required payments for Social Security; railroad retirement; Federal, State, and railroad unemployment insurance; workers' compensation; State temporary disability insurance, and other legally required insurance. Also included are changes in contract provisions specifying paid time for clothes change, washup, and lunch periods.

Lump-sum payments and cost-of-living adjustments tied to future changes in prices are excluded (as are items which, although related to compensation, are not normally considered part of compensation, such as per diem payments, moving expense reimbursements, payments for safety clothing, and provision of facilities or services such as parking lots and health units). Indirect effects of settlements are ignored; factors such as possible extension of settlement terms to nonunion workers in the same firm or to members of other bargaining units are not considered. Similarly, though the cost of providing lengthened vacations is measured (by the wages and salaries paid for the additional time off), the cost of hiring vacation replacements, if necessary, is not measured.

The compensation cost series takes into account the timing of specified changes in compensation rates. It includes items of compensation included in the rate series plus the cost of specified (guaranteed) lump-sum payments, the cost of contractually required training programs that are clearly not a cost of doing business, and the additional costs of changes in legally required insurance known at the time of settlement to be mandated during the contract term.

Data Sources

Calculations of the size of negotiated wage and benefit changes are based on actual characteristics of the workforce affected by the settlements. These include the distribution of workers by occupation, earnings, and length of service. When estimates of compensation changes are made, data are also obtained on employer costs for various benefits. The data on workforce characteristics and benefit costs are usually obtained directly from the companies as part of a variety of BLS surveys. (Data for these surveys are collected under a pledge that they will be kept confidential and not released outside the Bureau.) Other data sources for these calculations include the file of union contracts maintained by BLS, the file of pension and insurance benefit agreements and financial information maintained by the Department of Labor's Office of Labor-Management Standards, and secondary sources. Secondary sources, including general circulation newspapers and periodicals and union, management, and trade publications, are used in producing listings of agreements.

Estimating rates and costs

Since a value is placed on settlements at the time they are reached, the rates and costs attributed to them are estimates of outlays to be made in the future; they cannot be taken from employers' accounting records. The estimates are made on the assumption that conditions existing at the time the contract is negotiated will not change. For example, analysts assume that methods of financing pensions will not change, and that expenditures for insurance will not change except as a result of altered benefit provisions or modified participation because of changes in company contributions. They also assume that the composition of the labor force will not change.

Wage-rate changes that may result from COLA clauses are excluded because it is impossible to predict changes in the Consumer Price Index. ("Guaranteed" COLA increases, however, are treated as deferred changes.)

Estimates of compensation changes attempt to measure rates and costs associated with actual characteristics of the work force affected by the settlements, not those for some hypothetical employee group. Estimates based on the actual age, length of service, sex, and skill characteristics of the workers involved recognize that the choice in incorporating alternative benefit changes into contracts is affected by their costs, which, in turn, are affected by the character of the workforce. For example, an extra week of vacation after 15 years of service will cost very little when only 10 percent of the workers have that much service, but will add about 1 percent to the annual cost of straight-time pay for working time when half of the workers have been employed for 15 years or more. Changes in wage rates affect costs for certain benefits that are linked to wage rates such as paid leave, Social Security, and pensions based on earnings. This effect, variously referred to as "creep," "bulge," or "rollup," is reflected in estimates of changes in compensation.

Many items in a collective bargaining agreement are priced without difficulty. This is particularly true when settlement terms are expressed as cents-per-hour adjustments; e.g., a 20-cent-an-hour general wage increase or a 5-cent increase in employer contributions to a health and welfare fund. These stipulated cents-per-hour figures are used as the costs of the settlement provisions. Percentage wage adjustments are converted to cents-per-hour figures on the basis of current average straight-time hourly earnings in the bargaining unit.

Other settlement terms are more difficult to price. For example, the cost of an unfunded severance pay plan depends not only on plan provisions but on the frequency of layoffs, which is difficult to estimate. Pension improvement costs are particularly difficult to estimate because employers often have considerable discretion in funding their obligations. BLS assumes that a pension benefit change will change existing expenditures for current service proportionately. Since employer contributions for pensions frequently vary widely from year to year, outlays in several past years are examined to develop a measure of current payments.

For most benefit provisions, BLS estimates are of actual cash outlays to be made by employers. In the case of paid leave provisions, however, modifications may entail changes in hours worked for workers, without changing cash payments by the employer. In these cases, the changes in payment per hour worked are taken as the cost effect of the settlement provision. When the changes in hours worked, such as additional time off, have an eligibility requirement, the number of workers with the specified eligibility must be determined. A change in the basic workweek may be accompanied by changes in overtime work; unless this overtime is specified in the agreement, it is ignored in the cost estimate. The impact of any changes in work hours on the per-hour-worked cost of benefits is also captured.

Expressing rates and costs

The series on major collective bargaining settlements estimates how much wage and compensation rates and compensation costs will change from existing levels as a result of new collective bargaining agreements reached during specified reference periods.

Wage and compensation rate changes under settlements. The rate change for a settlement is the percent difference between the average rate just prior to the start of a new agreement and the average rate that would exist at the end of the first 365 days of the new agreement (first-year measure) or at its expiration date (over-the-life measure, expressed as an annual average change). The average rate change for all settlements is calculated by first multiplying the rate change for each settlement by the number of workers under the settlement. Next, the resulting products are summed, and the sum is divided by the total number of workers under all settlements. The result is the average change for all settlements.

Compensation cost changes. The compensation cost change for a settlement is the percent difference between the average cost of compensation per work hour just prior to the start of a new agreement (including the hourly cost of lump-sum payments made during the term of the expiring agreement) and the average cost of compensation per work hour under the settlement.

The average cost of compensation under the settlement is calculated in two steps. First, each hourly compensation rate (excluding lump-sum payments) is multiplied by the number of hours it is to be paid during the agreement, the products are summed, and the total is divided by the number of work hours over the agreement term. The result is the cost per work hour of compensation excluding specified lump-sum payments. Second, the cost per work hour of specified lump-sum payments is computed by dividing the total amount of the lump sum by the total number of work hours over the agreement term. The sum of the results of steps one and two is the estimated average cost of compensation per work hour over the term of the new agreement. The percent difference between this amount and the average cost at the end of the expiring agreement is the average cost change under the settlement.

The average cost change under all settlements is calculated by multiplying the percent change in cost under each settlement by the number of workers under the settlement. The results are summed, and the sum is divided by the total number of workers under all settlements.

The following example illustrates one of the major differences between the compensation rate series and the compensation cost series. Two agreements, A and B, expire. At expiration, compensation under each agreement is $10 an hour. The agreements are replaced by new settlements that run for 1 year. The settlement replacing agreement A immediately increases compensation from $10 an hour to $10.50 an hour. The settlement replacing agreement B leaves compensation unchanged for the first 6 months and then increases compensation from $10 an hour to $10.50 an hour.

The rate series measures the size of each settlement by calculating the difference between compensation at the expiration of the old agreement and compensation at the expiration of the new agreement and computing the percent change. Thus, it measures each settlement as providing a 5-percent ($.50/$10) compensation rate increase over the 1-year term.

The cost series measures the size of each settlement by comparing employer costs for compensation under the settlement with what they were under the expiring agreement prior to renegotiation as follows: When each agreement expired, an employee who worked 2,000 hours over the year would cost the employer $20,000 (2,000 hours at $10). Under the settlement replacing agreement A (with the immediate increase), the employer would pay for 2,000 hours at $10.50 an hour, or $21,000 for the year, a 5-percent increase over the $20,000. Under the settlement replacing agreement B (with the delayed increase), the employer would pay for 1,000 hours at $10 an hour and for 1,000 hours at $10.50 an hour, or $20,500 for the year, a 2.5-percent increase over the $20,000. Thus, the cost series reflects the influence of timing of changes during the agreement term which is not reflected by the rate series.

Wage-rate changes under all contracts. The series on all major collective bargaining contracts estimates average wage-rate changes during the reference period under settlements reached during the calendar year as well as under major agreements reached earlier and remaining in force during the period. The average change under all contracts in force during a period is computed by multiplying the percent change (including zero) under each contract by the number of workers covered, adding the products, and dividing the sum by the total number of workers under all contracts, including those with no wage-rate change.

The average rate change reflects net rate increases, decreases, and zero changes during the reference period. Rate increases and decreases stem from settlements in the calendar year that call for increases or decreases during the period, from agreements reached earlier with increases or decreases deferred to the period, and from COLA clauses. (Although wage increases and decreases from COLA clauses are not incorporated into base wage rates under all agreements, they are included in the wage rate change measure for all contracts.)

Contracts are considered to run from their effective dates to their termination dates. However, where there are wage reopening clauses, the reopening date is taken as the termination date, and any agreement under the reopening clause is treated as a new settlement. Sometimes, the parties to a contract agree to an unscheduled contract reopening. Beginning with full-year data for 1981 (published in January 1982), compensation changes negotiated under unscheduled reopenings are included in the data for new settlements. Their exclusion from earlier data on settlements made no noticeable difference because, prior to 1981, they were rare; and, when they occurred, they usually changed compensation for the balance of the contract that was already in place, typically no more than 1 year. In 1981, unscheduled reopenings became more frequent and usually resulted in new contracts that ran 2 to 3 years.

Presentation

The listing of current changes in wages and benefits is published monthly in the periodical *Compensation and Working Conditions (CWC)*. Summaries are grouped by industry. The listings include the name of the employer and the union, the number of workers involved, the amount and effective date of the change, details of complex changes, and the reason for the change (i.e., whether it is a new settlement, a deferred increase, or a COLA).

Statistical summaries of preliminary data on settlements and wage changes under all major agreements in private industry are issued first in news releases in the month following each quarter and then in *CWC*. Final quarterly and annual data are presented in a summary article published in the *Monthly Labor Review*, and detailed data are published in *CWC* each year.

Statistical summaries of State and local government bargaining settlements and wage changes under all major agreements are issued in news releases semiannually in February and August and also appear in *CWC*.

Uses and Limitations

The series on wage and compensation adjustments resulting from collective bargaining is one of the Federal Government's principal economic indicators. As such, it is used by a variety of Federal agencies including the Council of Economic Advisers, the Federal Reserve System, and the Congressional Budget Office, for a broad range of purposes including determining trends in compensation and forecasting changes in wage and salary income and gross national product. The statistics, as well as the monthly listings, are used by the Federal Mediation and Conciliation Service; State and local government agencies; employer and employee organizations; economic consultants; and researchers and practitioners in industrial relations, collective bargaining, and economic forecasting.

The user of the compensation data should remember that the series does not measure all changes in average hourly expenditures for employee compensation. The data are estimates of negotiated change, not total changes in employer cost. In calculating compensation change estimates, a value is put on the benefit portion of the settlements at the time they are reached on the assumption that conditions existing at the time of settlement will not change.

However, changes in the existing conditions do occur, for example, in the volume of overtime and shift work, in the composition of the workforce, the level and stability of employment, and in factors affecting incentive earnings. These changes influence outlays for employee compensation. In some instances, these changes are introduced by management specifically to offset costs of new labor agreements. In other cases, changes are the result of modified production schedules or of technological developments independent of collective bargaining, and may influence the cost of the union-management settlement.

Public- and private-sector negotiated compensation data are not strictly comparable because of differences in bargaining practices and settlement characteristics. Two differences are the incidence of lump-sum payments and cost-of-living (COLA) clauses. Lump-sum payments are rare in government but common in private industry. COLA clauses are included in about 10 percent of the State and local government agreements and in about 32 percent of private industry agreements. Furthermore, State and local government bargaining frequently excludes pension benefits, which are often prescribed by law. In private industry, pensions are typically a bargaining issue.

Techinical Reference

Bauman, Alvin. "A New Measure of Compensation Cost Adjustments." *Monthly Labort Review,* August 1990, pp. 11–18.

Chapter 8. Employment Cost Index

The Employment Cost Index (ECI) measures the rate of change in employee compensation, which includes wages, salaries, and employers' cost for employee benefits. The ECI was developed in response to a frequently expressed need for such a statistical series. Existing measures, while adequate for specific purposes, were found to be fragmented, limited in industrial and occupational coverage, insufficiently timely or detailed, or subject to influences unrelated to the basic trend in employee compensation.

Several elements distinguish the ECI from other surveys of employee compensation. It is comprehensive in that it (1) includes costs incurred by employers for employee benefits in addition to wages and salaries; and (2) covers all establishments and occupations in both the private nonfarm and public sectors.[1] It measures the change in cost of employing a fixed set of labor inputs, so it is not affected over time by changes in the occupational composition of the labor force. The survey is timely in that statistics are published quarterly, approximately 1 month after their reference date. The ECI also enables users to compare rates of change in detailed occupational, industrial, geographic, union coverage, and ownership (public-private) submeasures.

Background

The ECI survey has been implemented in stages. Initially, beginning in 1976, published statistics covered quarterly changes in wages and salaries for the private nonfarm economy, excluding establishments in Alaska and Hawaii, and private household workers. In November 1978, the survey was expanded to include establishments in Alaska and Hawaii, and an additional 13 statistical series (union/nonunion, manufacturing/nonmanufacturing, for example) were published.

The second major stage was completed in 1980 with the publication of quarterly changes in total employee compensation.

The third stage involved expansion of the survey to State and local government units. With the inclusion of these government units in November 1981, the overall series now represents the civilian nonfarm economy, excluding households and the Federal Government.

[1] Coverage of the private sector is limited to the private nonfarm economy, excluding private household workers. Public sector coverage includes employees of State and local governments, but excludes workers in the Federal Government.

The most recent major development of the ECI was the publication in 1987 of compensation cost levels. Data collected for the ECI can be used to calculate cost levels with no additional burden on survey respondents. The cost levels use current employment weights derived from BLS's Current Employment Statistics survey and the ECI sample. The cost levels, with a March reference date, are published annually during midsummer.

Another recent development involved the publication in 1991 of seasonally adjusted statistics for the major industry and occupational series. Seasonal adjustment of selected ECI series is discussed in the section dealing with index computation.

Future development of the ECI will include increases in the number of published series, especially in the service-producing sector of the economy, and expansion to include the Federal Government.

Description of the ECI

Major features

The ECI is a measure of change in the price of labor defined as compensation per employee hour worked. The self-employed, owner-managers, and unpaid family workers are excluded from coverage.

The ECI is designed as a Laspeyres, fixed-weight index at the occupational level, thus eliminating the effects of employment shifts among occupations. The index weights are derived from occupational employment for ECI industries reported in the 1980 Census of Population. The weights remain fixed from period to period pending a major index revision, next scheduled to occur when the results of the 1990 census are incorporated.

The index is computed from data on compensation by occupation collected from a sample of establishments and occupations weighted to represent the universe of establishments and occupations in the economy. The wage and salary component of the index is represented by average straight-time hourly earnings in an occupation. Straight-time earnings are defined as total earnings before deductions, excluding premium payments for overtime, weekend, and late-shift work. Earnings include production bonuses, commissions, and cost-of-living allowances but exclude nonproduction bonuses (which are considered a benefit in the ECI), payments in kind, room and board, and tips.

All earnings are computed on an hourly basis, whether or not this is the actual basis of payment. Earnings of salaried employees and those paid under incentive systems are converted to an hourly basis. Benefit cost data are also converted to an hourly basis. Thus, occupational hourly earnings plus the employer's cost per hour worked for employee benefits constitute the price of labor in the ECI.

Since pay rates generally relate to the job rather than to the incumbent workers, the basic unit of data collection is a job, as defined by the firm, in an establishment. Shifts in employment among jobs and establishments are controlled by measuring wage change for the same jobs in the same establishments and applying fixed employment weights to the results. The unit of observation is standardized to a certain extent below the job level by measuring only selected types of labor within the job; e.g., full or part time and incentive or time rated.

The benefit data portion of the ECI encompasses 22 distinct benefit categories, which can be grouped as follows:

Paid leave benefits

1. Vacations
2. Holidays
3. Sick leave
4. Other paid leave

Supplemental pay

5. Premium pay for overtime and work on holidays and weekends
6. Shift differentials
7. Nonproduction bonuses

Insurance

8. Life insurance
9. Health benefits
10. Sickness and accident insurance

Pension and savings plans

11. Pension and retirement benefits
12. Savings and thrift plans

Legally required benefits

13. Social Security
14. Railroad retirement
15. Railroad supplemental retirement
16. Railroad unemployment insurance
17. Federal Unemployment Tax Act
18. State unemployment insurance
19. Workers' compensation
20. Other legally required benefits

Other benefits

21. Severance pay
22. Supplemental unemployment benefit funds

The benefit data supplied by respondents normally consist of data elements which are used to compute the cents-per-hour-worked cost of each benefit provided employees in an occupation. For example, the data element for vacations might be expressed as follows: For an occupation in an establishment, the average worker received 2.8 weeks of paid vacation. In order to convert the data element to a cents-per-hour-worked cost, additional information covering workers in the occupation is needed, Therefore, data are also collected on scheduled daily and weekly hours and annual weeks. The following example illustrates the calculation of the cents-per-hour-worked cost for a benefit:

Calculating the cost per hour worked of a benefit

Data element—2.8 average weeks of vacation

Scheduled weekly hours—40

Straight-time average hourly rate—$6.95

Annual hours worked (computed by data processing system)—1,950

$$\frac{\text{2.8 weeks/year x 40 hours/week x \$6.95/hour}}{\text{1,950 hours/year}} = \text{\$0.399/hour}$$

This equation can be broken into the following steps:

2.8 weeks/year x 40 hours/week = 112 (average annual hours of vacation)

112 hours/year x $6.95/hour = $778.40 (average annual cost of vacation)

($778.40/year) / (1,950 hours/year) = $0.399 (average cost per hour worked for vacation)

Note that average annual hours of vacation are also used by the data processing system to compute annual hours worked.

The nature of the data collected varies somewhat depending upon the particular benefit. For paid leave benefits, the data element is usually expressed in terms of average number of days, weeks, or hours per year. For the insurance benefits, the data element may consist of a rate per thousand dollars of life insurance coverage or of a rate per month for family medical insurance coverage. In the case of the legally required benefits, a tax rate and taxable earnings ceiling are usually collected. Whatever the form of the data element, the benefit cost is always converted to cents per hour worked.

Occupational classification

The ECI occupational classification system was originally based on the classification system used for the 1970 Census of Population. In June 1986, the occupations being surveyed were recoded to the classification system used in the 1980 census, which is based on the Standard Occupational Classification (SOC) system.[2] The census system classifies all occupations reported into 503 3-digit occupational categories (such as accountant, stockhandler, etc.) which are then combined into 13 major occupational groups.

For ECI purposes, four of the census groups are combined into two groups (professional and technical workers are combined, as are two categories of service workers). Also, the census groups covering private household occupations and some farming, forestry, and fishing occupations include workers outside the scope of the survey and are, therefore, excluded. As a result of these modifications, the ECI includes the following nine major occupational groups.

1. Professional specialty and technical occupations
2. Executive, administrative, and managerial occupations
3. Sales occupations
4. Administrative support, including clerical occupations
5. Precision production, craft, and repair occupations
6. Machine operator, assembler, and inspector occupations
7. Transportation and material moving occupations
8. Handler, equipment cleaner, helper, and laborer occupations (including forestry and fishing occupations within the scope of the ECI)
9. Service occupations

The census occupational classification system only lists occupations to be included under each of the 503 occupational categories. For data collection purposes, definitions of the census occupations have been developed.[3]

Industrial classification

The ECI currently covers all nonfarm establishments classified in the 1987 edition of the *Standard Industrial Classification Manual* (SIC), with the exception of private households and the Federal Government. No minimum establishment size cutoff is used. The ECI publishes statistics for all major industry divisions with the , durable and nondurable goods and within services, health services exception of mining. Selected industry divisions are presented in more detail; for example, within manufacturingand hospitals. Statistics are also published for goods-producing and service-producing industries.

Geographic classification

The geographic coverage of the ECI includes all States and the District of Columbia. Rates of change in wages and salaries are published using the four-region classification system shown in appendix C. Statistics are also published for metropolitan areas (establishments located in a Metropolitan Statistical Area) and for other areas.

Union classification

Occupations surveyed within an establishment are classified as union if: (1) The majority of workers in the occupation are represented by a labor organization which is recognized as their bargaining agent; (2) wages are determined by collective bargaining; and (3) settlements are embodied in signed, mutually binding collective bargaining contracts.

Data Sources and Collection Methods

The wage, salary, and benefit cost data from which the ECI is computed are obtained from a sample of more than nearly 23,000 occupations within 4,400 establishments in the private sector and 8,800 occupations within about 1,300 establishments in State and local government.

Data collection is initiated by BLS field economists who visit the establishments. The purposes of the initial visit are to introduce the ECI program and obtain cooperation, determine organizational unit or units for establishment coverage, select occupations, develop establishment reporting procedures, and complete the first schedule. The field economist obtains the required wage, salary, and benefit cost data and records it on a form. Respondents do not complete a questionnaire during the initial stage of data collection. The initial personal visit lasts about 4 hours. Quarterly reports thereafter are normally collected by mail or telephone by field economists located in BLS's regional offices. An average of about 30 minutes of respondent time is required to report quarterly updates of the wage and benefit data.

Prior to 1987, a major task in the initial contact by a BLS field representative was to classify all company jobs into major occupational groups. The job-matching procedure sought to obtain at least one match for each of the nine major occupational groups surveyed by the ECI. Wage, salary, and benefit cost data were then collected for the selected jobs. In certain cases, data were requested for two or more company jobs within a single major

[2] *Classified Index of Industries and Occupations, 1980 Census of Population* (Bureau of the Census, 1980).

[3] *Employment Cost Index Occupation Classification System Manual—1980* (Bureau of Labor Statistics, March 1988).

occupational group if it accounted for a significant proportion of employment in an industry. Beginning with companies visited in 1987, the ECI uses a Reduced Job Match procedure which involves a request of data for four to eight company jobs, with the jobs selected strictly on a probability-proportionate-to-size basis. There is no longer an attempt to obtain at least one observation for each of the nine major occupational groups. The number of job matches sought varies with establishment employment size.

The job-matching process results in the selection of company jobs which are at the most detailed level recognized by that company. Examples would be clerk III and senior attorney litigation. During the job-matching process, characteristics of the company jobs are also determined—whether the groups selected consist of full- or part-time workers, time or incentive workers, and whether they are covered by collective bargaining agreements.

The wage data are collected on a "shuttle" form which is sent to the respondent each quarter for the addition of new data (see ECI Wage Data Form at the end of this chapter). The survey months are March, June, September, and December; the data relate to the pay period which includes the 12th day of the month.

Benefit data are initially reported in detail, including such information as vacation provisions by length-of-service categories; the length-of-service distribution of occupational employment (used to compute the cost of vacations); and employer contributions for pensions, insurance, and other benefits. Then, each quarter, the information on benefit provisions is summarized and sent to the respondents to review and to report any changes which have occurred since the prior quarter. For example, in the prior quarter, the respondent might have reported that 9 of the 10 employees in a surveyed occupation subscribed to a health insurance plan which cost $115 per month. During the quarterly update, the respondent indicates that the cost of the plan has increased to $129 per month. In both the prior and current quarter, the employer assumed 50 percent of the plan's cost.

For ECI purposes, the average cost for workers in the prior quarter equalled $51.75 per month. (The employer's share of the cost for each worker participating in the plan is $57.50. Ninety percent of the workers participate, $57.50 x 0.90 = $51.75.) The current quarter's cost of the plan would equal $58.05 ($64.50 x 0.90 = $58.05). Note that the 90-percent participation rate was held constant. This would be changed only if the employee contribution rate (50 percent of plan cost) increased or decreased. Holding the participation rate constant eliminates the effects of forces such as shifts in workforce composition on the measurement of the cost change.

Similarly, when an employer changes an overtime pay provision, new overtime hours worked are not normally collected. Instead, the base period overtime hours worked pertaining to the altered provision are repriced using the new overtime rate. This practice restricts changes in overtime cost to changes caused only by the adoption of a new overtime rate and eliminates the effect of changes in the number of hours of overtime worked.

Survey Design

The ECI sample design has evolved over the 15-year history of the program. Separate designs have been used for the public and private sectors of the economy, although, since 1987, the designs of all replacement samples are similar.

Private sector—respondent universe and sample design

The original sample design used for the selection of the ECI sample in 1975 consisted of a two-phase controlled selection.[4] In the first phase, approximately 23 occupations were identified for each 2-digit SIC. Using the 1970 Census of Population, the largest five occupations in each 2-digit SIC were selected with certainty. Then one to four, but generally two, occupations were selected from each major occupational group within the 2-digit SIC using a probability-proportionate-to-size method. A sample of approximately 10,000 establishments[5] was selected from a larger BLS survey of approximately 200,000 establishments drawn primarily from the unemployment insurance universe. The first phase of the ECI survey determined the occupational employment within each of the 10,000 sampled establishments for each of the 23 selected occupations for the 2-digit SIC. Imputation was used for partial and complete nonrespondents. Using measures of size designed to enhance the probability of selection of establishments with a large proportion of the employment in any of the 23 occupations, a subsample of approximately 2,000 establishments was selected, the selection being done separately within each 2-digit SIC. Data were collected for the selected occupations within the selected establishments.

Beginning in 1981, the ECI began replacing the entire private sector sample using a new sample design. Within each 2-digit SIC, all detailed census occupations were assigned to 1 of 9 to 15 occupational groups, each

[4] Goodman, R. and Kish, L. "Controlled Selection, a Technique in Probability Sampling," *Journal of the American Statistical Association*, Vol. 45, 1950, pp. 350-72.

[5] The term establishment generally indicates a single physical location. In the public sector, many of the establishments have units at more than one location. For example, school districts meet the SIC manual's criteria for an establishment, but the majority of school districts are comprised of units in several different locations.

consisting either of all of the occupations within a major occupational group, 1 or more closely related occupations within a major occupational group, or the residual occupations within one. The 2-digit SIC's were divided into 12 groups that replaced the existing samples over a 4-year period. The new design was completely implemented in 1986. Allocation of the sample was made proportionate to the employment of each 2-digit SIC with an initial total sample size of about 2,000 establishments.[6] Within each establishment, one occupation was selected from each occupational group with probability of selection proportionate to the employment of the occupation within the group. This was the sample in use at the time of publication in 1987.

Beginning in 1987, the within-establishment occupation selection methodology was changed to eliminate the initial classification of all establishment jobs into groups. This change reduced the collection burden on both respondents and BLS and improved weight computation. With the new Reduced Job Match procedure, a sample of four to eight jobs, the number depending on the size of the establishment, is selected. The jobs are selected from either a list of establishment employees or a list of establishment employment by job title, using probability proportionate to employment in the selection of the jobs. Data are collected for a homogeneous group of employees, matching characteristics of either a selected individual or a selected job. The first data collected using this new methodology were introduced into the ECI in 1988. The entire private sector sample will be replaced using this methodology by 1993.

Public sector—respondent universe and sample design

Because of the nature of the available sampling frames, the initial public sector sample was divided into four parts: Schools, hospitals, State and large local governments, and small local governments. Each had a somewhat different sample design. The unemployment insurance file's coverage of the public sector has since been improved so that the new sample of government units was selected in a manner similar to that for the private sector.

Data collection from the new public sector sample occurred over a three year period—1988 to 1991.

Sample replacement

Beginning in 1981, the existing sample of private sector establishments was gradually replaced by a new sample. A few large establishments were included in both the old and new samples. Sample replacement is necessary to ensure that sample sizes remain adequate for publication and that new establishments are represented in the sample, and to limit the burden on individual establishments. The entire sample will be replaced every 4 to 5 years. Replacement is done in stages, with part of the sample being replaced each quarter.

Adjustments for sample nonresponse

When base-period data collection is completed, nonresponse adjustment factors are calculated for permanent refusals and applied to the sample weights of responding establishment/occupations in the same major industry division, major occupational group, and size class. The application of the nonresponse adjustment factors compensates for the loss of data due to base-period refusals only. Because the adjustment factors are calculated and applied only once, their effects on the estimates are constant for the duration of the sample.

For wage change estimation after the base period, values are imputed when there is a temporary nonresponse. The basic assumption is that nonrespondents have, on the average, the same wage movement that respondents have. Therefore, for a temporary nonresponse, the prior-quarter data for an establishment/occupation are moved by the average occupational wage change estimated from similar establishment/occupations. Establishment/occupations are considered similar if the establishments are in the same 2-digit SIC and the occupations are in the same major occupational group. If there are not sufficient data at this level, a broader level of aggregation is used. Prior-quarter data are not adjusted when nonresponse is the result of seasonal closing of an establishment.

Imputations are also made to fill in any gaps in a respondent's benefit data. Imputation for benefits is done separately for each benefit both in the base period and on a quarterly basis. A benefit cost is imputed based on the average cost for the same benefit in similar establishment/occupations.

Index Computation

The basic computational framework is the standard formula for an index number with fixed weights, as modified by the special statistical conditions that apply to the ECI. This discussion focuses on the ECI measure of wage changes, but indexes of compensation changes are calculated in essentially the same fashion.

An index for the ECI is simply a weighted average of the cumulative average wage changes within each establishment cell, with base-period wage bills as the fixed weights.

The simplified formula is:

$$I_t = \frac{\Sigma W_{o,i} M_{t,i}}{\Sigma W_{o,i}} \times 100$$

where:

$M_{t,i} = M_{t-1,i} * R_{t,i}$ and

I^t is the symbol for the index.

[6] The total private sector sample size had grown to about 4,400 establishments by 1991. Allocation to 2-digit SIC's is now based partly on generalized variance estimates so as to minimize the variance of national estimates of annual relatives of total compensation.

The other variables are defined as follows:

$W_{o,i}$ is the estimated base-period wage bill for the ith cell. A cell generally is an occupation in a 2-digit SIC industry, while the wage bill is the average wage of workers in the cell times the number of workers represented by the cell.

$M_{t,i}$ is the cumulative average wage change in the ith cell from time 0 (base period) to time t (current quarter).

$R_{t,i}$ is the ratio of the current-quarter weighted average wage in the cell to the prior-quarter weighted average wage in the cell, both calculated in the current quarter using matched establishment/occupation wage quotations. The weights applied are the sample weights described in the next section.

All wage indexes are computed from the following data:

Average straight-time hourly earnings for 3-digit census code occupations, or groups of those occupations, in those sample establishments for which data are available for both the current and prior survey periods. The occupational wage data are identified by major occupational group, industry, geographic location, metropolitan area, and union status.

Employment in 1980, in the 3-digit census code occupation or group of occupations in an industry, obtained from the decennial census.

Sample weights derived from an occupational employment survey or the initial employment reported on the survey schedule. These weights reflect both employment in each establishment/occupation surveyed and the probability of selection of that establishment/occupation.

The index computation involves essentially five steps:

1. Establishment/occupation sample weights are applied to the occupational earnings to obtain weighted average earnings for each estimation cell for the current and prior survey periods. The estimation cell is defined on the basis of owner/industry/occupation. For the private sector, 67 SIC industries have been identified, most at the 2-digit level. For the public sector, separate cells are identified for State and local governments. Industries as broad as "public administration" and as narrow as "colleges and universities" are treated as separate estimation cell industries. For example, one estimation cell is identified as State government/public administration/clerical workers.

2. Each quarter, the ratio of the current-quarter weighted average wage to the prior-quarter weighted average wage is, in effect, multiplied by the prior-quarter cumulative average wage change for the cell. The product is a measure of the cumulative percentage wage change in the cell since the base period.

3. This measure of cumulative percentage wage change is multiplied by the base-period wage bill to generate an estimate of the current-quarter wage bill for the cell.

4. Both the current-quarter and the base-period wage bills are then summed over all cells within the scope of the index.

5. The summed current-quarter wage bill is divided by the summed base-period wage bill. The result, when multiplied by 100, is the current-quarter index. That index is divided by the prior-quarter index to provide a measure of quarter-to-quarter change, the link relative.

The table below illustrates the procedures for a particular industry. The computations for the occupation- and industry groups follow the same procedures as those

Occupation	Prior-quarter cumulation change (a)	Current-quarter weighted average earnings (b)	Prior-quarter weighted average earnings (c)	Relative (b/c) (d)	Current-quarter cumulative change (a x d) (e)	Current-quarter wage cbill (f x d) (f)	Base period wage bill (g)	Prior-quarter wage bill (f x a) (h)
Electricians	1.23567	$5.50	$5.25	1.04762	1.29451	$12,613.40	$16,328.17	$15,586.00
Carpenters	1.15435	7.20	7.15	1.00699	1.16242	8,316.37	9,667.11	9,600.00
Total						20,929.77	25,995.28	25,186.00

for all overall indexes except for the summation. The wage bills for the occupational groups are summed across industries and regions for each group; the wage bills for the industry division are summed across occupational groups and regions for each industry division.

Computational procedures for the regional, union/nonunion and metropolitan/nonmetropolitan measures of change differ from those of the national indexes because the current sample is not large enough to hold constant the wage bills at that level of detail. For these nonnational series, each quarter, the prevailing distribution in the sample between, for example, union and nonunion within each industry/occupation cell, is used to apportion the prior-quarter wage bill in that cell between the union and nonunion series. The portion of the wage bill assigned to the union sector is then moved by the percentage change in union wages in the cell, and similarly for the nonunion sector. Thus, the relative employment of the union sector in each cell is not held constant over time. Since the relative weights of the region, the union, and the metropolitan area subcells are allowed to vary over time, it is not possible to calculate Laspeyres indexes for the nonnational series.

Seasonal adjustment

Over the course of a year, the rate of wage and benefit cost change is affected by events that follow a more or less regular pattern each year. For example, wage and benefit adjustments in State and local governments, especially schools, are concentrated in the June-September period. Increases in the Social Security tax rate and earnings ceiling, when they occur, always take effect in the December-March period. Wage and benefit adjustments in construction occur in the summer when there is the most activity in the industry.

Adjusting for these seasonal patterns makes it easier to observe the cyclical and other nonseasonal movements in the series. In evaluating changes in a seasonally adjusted series, it is important to note that seasonal adjustment is merely an approximation based on past experience. Seasonally adjusted estimates have a broader margin of possible error than the original data on which they are based, since they are subject not only to sampling and other errors but are also affected by the uncertainties of the seasonal adjustment process itself.

Beginning with the December 1990 ECI statistics, major industry and occupational series are seasonally adjusted using a procedure called X-11 ARIMA (Auto-Regressive Integrated Moving Average). This procedure was developed at Statistics Canada as an extension of the standard X-11 method. (See appendix A for a description of the Bureau's seasonal adjustment methodology.)

At the beginning of each calendar year, seasonal adjustment factors are calculated for use during the coming year. The seasonal factors for the coming year are published in the March issue of the Bureau publication *Compensation and Working Conditions* (CWC). Revisions of historical seasonally adjusted data for the most recent 5 years also appear in the March CWC.

ECI series are seasonally adjusted using either direct or composite estimates. Most industry and occupational series such as construction, for example, are adjusted directly. The civilian, State and local governments, A private, and manufacturing series are adjusted using composite estimates. The seasonally adjusted civilian compensation series, for example, is computed by aggregating the following independently adjusted series: Private goods-producing wages, private goods-producing benefits, private service-producing wages, private service-producing benefits, State and local governments wages, and State and local government benefits. (Goods-producing wages has no identifiable seasonality, so the seasonally adjusted and unadjusted series are identical.)

Reliability of the estimates

There are two types of errors possible in the estimates from the ECI as well as any other sample survey—sampling and nonsampling errors.

Nonsampling errors have a number of potential sources. The primary sources are (1) survey nonresponse and (2) data collection and processing errors.

Nonsampling errors are not measured. The ECI program has implemented procedures for reducing nonsampling errors, however, primarily through quality assurance programs. The quality assurance programs include the use of data collection reinterviews, observed interviews, computer edits of the data, and systematic professional review of the reports on which the data are recorded. These programs serve as a training device to provide feedback to the field economists on errors. They also provide information on the sources of error which can be remedied by improved collection instructions or computer processing edits. Extensive training of field economists is also conducted to maintain high standards in data collection.

Sampling errors are differences that occur between the results computed from a sample of observations and those computed from all observations in the population. The estimates derived from different samples selected using the same sample design may differ from each other.

A measure of the variation among these differing estimates is the standard error. It can be used to measure the precision with which an estimate from a particular sample approximates the average result of all possible samples. The standard error can be used to define a range (confidence interval) around the estimate. The 95-percent confidence level means that if all possible samples were selected and an estimate of the value and its sampling error were computed for each, then, for approximately 95 percent of the samples, the intervals from 2 standard errors below the estimates to 2 standard errors above the estimates would include the "true" average value. For example, the 95-percent confidence interval for a cost estimate of $10 with a standard error of 10 cents would be $10.00 plus or minus 20 cents (2 x 10 cents) or $9.80 to $10.20.

The method used to compute the standard errors for both the 12-month percent change in the ECI and the cost levels is called "balanced repeated replication." Each industry sample is divided into a number of variance strata, and the sample in each variance stratum is divided into half-samples. The cost level or percent-change estimates are replicated 64 times using the data from one half-sample from each stratum instead of the data from both half-samples.

The formula used for calculating the variances, and in turn the standard errors, for the percent changes is:

$$VAR\,(R_{s,t,o}) = \sum_{i=1}^{64} [(R_{s,t,o}-R_{s,t,i})^2]/64$$

where:

$R_{s,t,o}$ is the annual relative for some cell from time s to time t calculated using the full sample.

$R_{s,t,i}$ is the annual relative for the same cell from time s to time t calculated using the ith balanced half-sample.

The standard error is the square root of the variance.

The formula for calculating the variances, and in turn the standard errors, for the cost levels is:

$$VAR\,x(0) = \sum_{i=1}^{64} [(x_i x_o)^2]/64$$

where:

x_o is the full sample level estimate for some cell and is the ith half-sample estimate for the same cell.

Standard errors for both the indexes and cost levels are presented in the ECI's annual bulletin.

Presentation

ECI statistics are published quarterly in the month after the survey period. For example, statistics computed from the survey data for June are published in July. Initially, the statistics are presented in a news release which includes descriptions of quarter-to-quarter and year-to-year trends, tables, and an explanatory note about the survey. The data are published later in *Compensation and Working Conditions* and the *Monthly Labor Review*, monthly BLS periodicals. The data are also available on IBM-compatible microcomputer diskettes.

Uses and Limitations

The Employment Cost Index has been designated as a principal Federal economic indicator by the Office of Management and Budget. It is the only measure of labor costs that treats wages and salaries and total compensation consistently, and provides consistent subseries by occupation and industry. Special wage and salary indexes are also provided for union status, geographic region, and metropolitan area status. The ECI is used by the Federal Reserve Board in monitoring the effects of monetary and fiscal policies and in formulating those policies. It enables analysts and policymakers to assess the impact of labor cost changes on the economy, both in the aggregate and by sectors. The ECI is particularly important in studies of the relationships between prices, productivity, labor costs, and employment. It is also used as an escalator of labor costs. For example, the Federal Health Care Financing Administration uses the ECI as part of an input price index in determining allowable increases in hospital charges under Medicare's Inpatient Hospital Prospective Payment System.

The Ethics Reform Act of 1989 specifies that, beginning in January 1991, the ECI will be used to adjust the pay of members of Congress, Federal judges, and senior government executives. Their pay will be raised by 0.5 percentage points less than the ECI 12-month percent change in wages and salaries for private industry workers. The law limits any increase to 5 percent. The Federal Employees Pay Comparability Act of 1990 provides that the ECI will be used to adjust the pay of white-collar Federal employees. In 1992 and 1993 the increase will be the full ECI 12-month change in wages and salaries for private industry workers. In 1994 and beyond, as locality pay differentials are instituted, the pay increase will reflect the 12-month change in ECI wages and salaries minus 0.5 percentage points.

While the ECI statistics have many uses, the limitations of the index must be kept in mind. The index is not a measure of change in the total cost of employing labor. Not all labor costs (e.g., training expenses, retroactive pay, etc.) fall under the ECI definition of compensation. Currently, the ECI does not cover all employers and employees, although it does cover nearly all workers in the civilian (non-Federal) nonfarm economy. Finally, the index is not an exact measure of wage or compensation change. It is subject to sampling errors which may cause it to deviate from the results which would be obtained if the actual records of all establishments could be used in the index calculation.

Technical References

U. S. Department of Labor, Bureau of Labor Statistics. *Employment Cost Indexes and Levels, 1975-91,* Bulletin 2389.

Schwenk, Albert E. "Employment Cost Index Rebased to June 1989," *Monthly Labor Review,* April 1990.

O'Connor, Karen and Wong, William. "Measuring the Precision of the Employment Cost Index," *Monthly Labor Review,* March 1989.

Nathan, Felicia. "Analyzing Employers' Costs for Wages, Salaries, and Benefits, " *Monthly Labor Review,* October 1987.

Schwenk, Albert E. "Introducing New Weights for the Employment Cost Index," *Monthly Labor Review,* June 1985.

U.S. Department of Labor, Bureau of Labor Statistics. *Employment Cost Index Occupation Classification System Manual—1980,* 1985.

Wood, G. Donald. "Estimation Procedures for the Employment Cost Index," *Monthly Labor Review,* May 1982.

U.S. Department of Commerce, Bureau of the Census. *Classified Index of Industries and Occupations,* 1980 Census of Population, 1980.

Sheifer, Victor J. "How Benefits Will Be Incorporated into the Employment Cost Index," *Monthly Labor Review,* January 1978.

Sheifer, Victor J. "Employment Cost Index: A Measure of Change in the 'Price of Labor'," *Monthly Labor Review* July 1975.

Bureau of Labor Statistics
ECI Wage Data Form

U.S. Department of Labor

The information collected on this form by the Bureau of Labor Statistics will be held in confidence and will be used for statistical purposes only.

This report is authorized by law, 29 U.S.C. 2. Your voluntary cooperation is needed to make the results of this survey comprehensive, accurate, and timely.

Form Approved
O.M.B. No. 1220-0038

We estimate that it will take an average of 35 minutes to complete this form, including time for reviewing instructions, searching existing data sources, gathering and maintaining the data needed, and completing and reviewing this information. If you have any comments regarding this estimate or any other aspect of this survey, send them to the Bureau of Labor Statistics, Division of Management Systems (1220-0038), 441 G Street N.W., Washington, D.C. 20212 and to the Office of Management and Budget, Paperwork Reduction Project (1220-0038), Washington, D.C. 20503.

Establishment Name ______________________ **Schedule Number** [ ][ ][ ][ ][ ] [ ] [ ] Page _____ of _____

Line No.	BLS Occ./ Quote Code	Identification of Survey Occupations, Establishment Jobs, or Individuals for whom Wage Information is being reported on each line (1)	Reference Date , 19____ Hourly Rate (2)	OR Hours and Earnings (3)		Number of Workers Per Line (4)	FOR BLS USE ONLY	, 19____ Hourly Rate (2)	OR Hours and Earnings (3)		Number of Workers Per Line (4)	FOR BLS USE ONLY
1												
2												
3												
4												
5												
6												
7												
8												
9												
10												
11												
12												
13												
14												
15												
16												
17												
18												

*** Please use the back of this form to explain significant earnings changes (i.e., decreases or large increases in the average rate of pay for an occupation) from one reporting period to the next.**

BLS 3038B (Rev. June 1989)

VACATION

Benefit 02 _____

Plan Name | Eligibility Requirement | Most Recent Change

Schedule #: |_|_|_|_|_|_|

Contact: ____________________

1. Description

2. Occupational Distribution

Quote Code																	
Length of Service	Wks _____ % _____	Wkrs.	Wt. Weeks	Wkrs.	Wt. Weeks	Wkrs.	Wt. Weeks	Wkrs.	Wt. Weeks	Wkrs.	Wt. Weeks	Wkrs.	Wt. Weeks	Wkrs.	Wt. Weeks	Wkrs.	Wt. Weeks
Totals																	
Paid Weeks																	

3. Data Entries

Quote Code	Status Code	Value Entry	Conversion Code	Paid Weeks	Unpaid Weeks	Alt. W.S.
		•		•	•	
		•		•	•	
		•		•	•	
		•		•	•	
		•		•	•	
		•		•	•	
		•		•	•	
		•		•	•	

NOTE: This benefit does ***not*** allow multiple plans.

Page 02 _____

Chapter 9. The Employee Benefits Survey

Background

The Bureau of Labor Statistics has analyzed and presented data on the availability and characteristics of employee benefits since the beginning of the 20th century. Early studies were often one-time looks at a particular benefit, such as retirement income plans, or at the benefit activity of a particular establishment or labor union. The lack of a consistent series of data prior to World War II is not surprising, as employee benefits were uncommon and made up only a small portion of total compensation.[1]

During the 1940's, a number of factors led to the expansion of employee benefit plans. These included: Wage controls during World War II and the early postwar period that permitted supplementary benefit improvements while denying wage increases; National Labor Relations Board decisions bringing pensions and other benefits within the scope of compulsory collective bargaining; a 1949 report of the Steel Industry Fact Finding Board stating that industry had an obligation to provide workers with social insurance and pensions; and clarifications of the Internal Revenue Code requiring employers providing pensions to treat all workers equally. The Bureau recognized these trends and began to track employee benefits on a more regular basis.[2]

The first recurring study of employee benefits began in the mid-1940's as part of the Bureau's occupational wage studies. These surveys yielded data on the incidence and provisions of paid vacation and sick leave plans and the incidence of insurance and pension plans for plant and office workers. This series, described in chapter 6 of this *Handbook*, continues today.

Analysis of employee benefits expanded to emphasize provisions of individual plans. Based on small samples, these analyses were designed to provide information about the particular benefit plans, such as health insurance and pensions. Published data included details of benefits established through collective bargaining as well as more general surveys of benefits provided by individual establishments.[3]

In 1959, the Bureau initiated a series of surveys of employer expenditures for employee compensation. This program, which continued until 1977, measured outlays for individual elements of compensation, including pay for leave and contributions to private and public welfare and retirement plans.[4]

In 1976, the Bureau inaugurated the Employment Cost Index, which tracks quarterly changes in employer costs for employee compensation, including benefits. Cost level data, similar to the earlier expenditure series, became available from the Employment Cost Index in 1987. (More details on the Employment Cost Index may be found in chapter 8 of this *Handbook*.)

The most recent development in the Bureau's analysis of employee benefit plans occurred in the late 1970's, at the request of the U.S. Civil Service Commission (now the Office of Personnel Management). At that time, the Bureau was conducting annual white-collar salary surveys for use in comparing private-sector and Federal pay (and setting Federal white-collar pay levels).[5]

The rapid growth of employee benefits raised questions about the validity of a comparability process limited to wages and salaries alone. In the 1970's, the General Accounting Office and two Presidential review groups recommended that the Federal pay comparability system be expanded to include both pay and benefits.

In response to these recommendations, the Office of Personnel Management (OPM) initiated its Total Compensation Comparability (TCC) project, designed to compare Federal and private pay and benefits. Because of the Bureau's long experience in studying employee benefits, OPM asked the Bureau to participate in the gathering of data on plan provisions and characteristics. The Employee Benefits Survey (EBS) was then developed. In 1979, a test survey was conducted in conjunction with the Bureau's collection of white-collar salary data. Annual full-scale surveys began in 1980.

[1] William J. Wiatrowski, "Family-Related Benefits in the Workplace," *Monthly Labor Review, March 1990, pp. 28-33.*

[2] Alvin Bauman, "Measuring Employee Compensation in U.S. Industry," *Monthly Labor Review,* October 1970, pp. 17-24.

[3] See, for example, *Health-Benefit Programs Established Through Collective Bargaining,* Bulletin 841 (Bureau of Labor Statistics, 1945). In addition, the *Digest of Selected Health and Insurance Plans* and *Digest of Selected Pension Plans* were published every 3 or 4 years until 1978, when the program was discontinued.

[4] *Employee Compensation in the Private Nonfarm Economy,* 1977, Summary 80-5 (Bureau of Labor Statistics, 1980).

[5] The Federal Salary Reform Act of 1962 and its successor, the Federal Pay Comparability Act of 1970, provided for annual adjustments in salaries of Federal white-collar employees to achieve comparability with pay rates in private enterprise for the same levels of work. The Bureau's National Survey of Professional, Administrative, Technical, and Clerical Pay (later the White-collar Pay Survey) provided the data on private industry salaries used in administering this legislation. Due to changes in the law, the Bureau's Occupational Compensation Surveys Program and Employment Cost Index now provide data for private-Federal pay comparisons.

The TCC project was discontinued in the early 1980's. However, the Bureau continued the Employee Benefits Survey as part of its comprehensive series of compensation data. Since then, the survey has undergone significant expansions and improvements toward the goal of providing accurate and timely data on the rapidly changing details of employee benefits throughout the U.S. economy.

Description of the Survey

The Employee Benefits Survey is currently conducted in three stages during a 2-year cycle. During each cycle, comprehensive data on the incidence and characteristics of employee benefits for full- and part-time employees in private establishments and State and local governments are collected and presented. Data for small private establishments (fewer than 100 workers) and governments are collected in even-numbered years; data for medium and large private establishments (100 workers or more[6]) are collected in odd-numbered years.[7]

Data are collected individually for narrowly defined occupations that are sampled within establishments. Each of these narrowly defined occupations is classified into one of three broad occupational groups. In the private-industry surveys, the broad occupational groups are as follows.

Professional, technical, and related. Includes professional, technical, executive, administrative, managerial, and related occupations.

Clerical and sales. Includes clerical, administrative support, and sales occupations.

Production and service. Includes precision production, craft, and repair occupations; machine operators and inspectors; transportation and moving occupations; handlers, equipment cleaners, helpers, and laborers; and service occupations.[8]

In governments, the broad occupational groups are as follows.

Regular employees. Includes professional, technical, executive, administrative, and managerial occupations; clerical, administrative support, and sales occupations; precision production, craft, and repair occupations; machine operators and inspectors; transportation and moving occupations; handlers, equipment cleaners, helpers, and laborers; and service occupations. Teachers, police officers, and firefighters are excluded.

Teachers. Includes all personnel in primary and secondary schools, junior colleges, colleges, and universities whose primary duty is teaching or closely related activities, such as research or counseling. This category includes professors, lecturers, teachers, instructors, athletic coaches, department heads, librarians, and research scientists (if considered faculty). Employees whose primary function is administrative, such as deans, principals, and assistant principals, are classified as regular employees, as are full-time teaching assistants, teachers' aides, and workers in day-care centers performing child-care functions.

Police and firefighters. Includes firefighters, personnel whose main duty is law enforcement, such as State and local uniformed police, detectives and sheriffs, and personnel engaged in the administration of law enforcement, such as desk sergeants, lieutenants, and captains. Corrections officers (guards and jailers), officers of the court (bailiffs), sheriffs performing corrections officer or officer of the court duties, campus police, and fire inspectors are considered to be regular employees.

Employees excluded from the survey are the self-employed, proprietors, major stockholders, members of a corporate board who are not otherwise officers of the corporation, volunteers, unpaid workers, family members paid token wages, persons permanently disabled, partners in unincorporated firms, and U.S. citizens working overseas.[9]

Sampled establishments are requested to provide data for a sample of their occupations on work schedules and details of plans in each of the following benefit areas: Paid lunch periods, paid rest periods, paid holidays, paid vacations, paid personal leave, paid funeral leave, paid military leave, paid jury-duty leave, paid and unpaid parental leave, paid sick leave, sickness and accident insurance, long-term disability insurance, medical, dental, and vision care, life insurance, retirement and capital accumulation plans, flexible benefit plans, and reimbursement accounts.

Data are also collected on the incidence of the following additional benefits: Severance pay, supplemental unemployment benefits, parking, subsidized commuting, travel accident insurance, nonproduction cash bonuses, financial counseling, prepaid legal services, gifts, child care, adoption assistance, eldercare, in-house infirmaries, long-

[6] The establishments included in the private sector surveys are determined in advance of the actual collection. Establishments are classified by size as of the reference date of the sampling frame. All establishments that were sampled with fewer than 100 employees are included in the small establishment survey and all establishments sampled with 100 or more workers are included in the medium and large establishment survey, even if their employment had gone beyond the threshold at the time of data collection.

[7] The industrial coverage, establishment size coverage, and geographic coverage for the survey differed prior to 1990. The surveys conducted from 1979 to 1986 excluded most of the service industries and included private establishments that employed at least 50, 100, or 250 workers, depending on the industry. The survey conducted in 1987 consisted of State and local governments with 50 or more employees. The surveys conducted in 1988 and 1989 included all private sector establishments that employed 100 or more employees. All surveys conducted from 1979 to 1989 excluded establishments in Alaska and Hawaii.

[8] In private-sector surveys prior to 1990, employees were classified as either professional and administrative, technical and clerical, or production and service workers.

[9] Prior to 1990, employees excluded from the survey also included executive management employees (defined as those whose decisions have direct and substantial effects on an organization's policymaking); part-time, temporary, and seasonal employees; and operating employees in continuous travel status, such as airline flight crews and long-distance truckdrivers.

term care insurance, wellness programs, recreation facilities, subsidized meals, employee discounts, relocation allowances, job-related and non-job-related educational assistance, employee assistance programs, and sabbatical leave.

Survey Design

The list of establishments from which the sample is selected (called the sampling frame) is the State Unemployment Insurance (UI) reports for the 50 States and the District of Columbia.[10] The reference date of the UI reports that are sampled varies by industry. This is due to the nature of the sample selection and replacement, which is described below.

A single sample is selected for the Employee Benefits Survey and the Bureau's Employment Cost Index. The sample design for the surveys is a 2-stage probability sample of detailed occupations. The first stage of sample selection is a probability sample of establishments, while the second stage of sample selection is a probability sample of occupations within the sampled establishments.

The sample is updated periodically over a 4-year cycle. Each year, new sample establishments are introduced into the survey in selected industries and replace the sample units that were previously selected in those same industries. Using this procedure, the entire sample is replaced approximately every 4 years.

The sample of establishments is selected by first stratifying the sampling frame by industry group and size of establishment (as measured by employment). The industry groups usually consist of 3-digit Standard Industrial Classification groups, as defined by the Office of Management and Budget, which are covered by the survey.

The number of sample establishments allocated to each stratum is approximately proportional to the total employment of all sampling frame establishments in the stratum. Thus, a stratum that contained 1 percent of the total employment within the scope of the survey receives approximately 1 percent of the total sample establishments. Some industries are sampled at a higher rate than other industries because of publication requirements or highly variable data.

Each sampled establishment is selected within a stratum with a probability proportional to its employment. For example, consider two establishments, A and B, with respective employment of 5,000 and 1,000. Establishment A is five times more likely to be selected than establishment B.

At the beginning of each field visit by a Bureau field economist to collect data from a sampled establishment, a second-stage probability sample of occupations is selected from the establishment. Data are collected for these sampled occupations. The number of occupations selected from an establishment varies from four in the smallest establishments to eight in the largest establishments. The probability of an occupation being selected is proportionate to its employment within the establishment.[11]

Data Collection

Data for the survey are collected by visits of Bureau field economists to the sampled establishments. Field economists use a structured collection form (see exhibit) to record respondent data on the existence of benefits, the number of workers in selected occupations who participate in specific benefit plans, and the detailed characteristics of leave benefits. To reduce the reporting burden, respondents are asked to provide documents describing their flexible benefits plans, reimbursement accounts, retirement and capital accumulation plans, medical, dental, and vision care plans, and insurance plans. These are analyzed by BLS staff in Washington to obtain the required data on plan provisions.

Field data collection takes place simultaneously for the Bureau's Employee Benefits Survey and Employment Cost Index. Because the surveys require many of the same data items, the interview is generally structured to ask all questions required in both surveys for a given benefit at one time, and then move on. Because data are being collected for two surveys and follow-up visits to collect benefit plan documents are often required, the data collection process can vary significantly from one establishment to another. Total data collection time can range from several hours to several days per sampled establishment.

Field economists are professional economists hired specifically to collect Employee Benefits Survey and Employ-

[10] For this survey, an establishment is an economic unit that produces goods or services, a central administrative office, or an auxiliary unit providing support services to a company. In manufacturing industries, the establishment is usually a single physical location. In nonmanufacturing industries, all locations of an individual company within a Metropolitan Statistical Area (MSA), a Primary Metropolitan Statistical Area (PMSA), or a nonmetropolitan county are usually considered a single establishment.

[11] Prior to 1990, the Employee Benefits Survey sample was a subsample of the Bureau's White-collar Pay Survey. The list of establishments from which the sample was selected was the most recently available State unemployment insurance reports for the 48 contiguous States and the District of Columbia.

The sample of establishments was selected by first stratifying the sampling frame by broad industry group and establishment size group based on the total employment in the establishment. Within each stratum, a random sample was selected using a probability technique to maximize the probability of retaining establishments that were selected in the previous survey. This method of selection reduced collection costs by decreasing the number of new establishments in the sample.

In 1987, the State and local government survey used an independent sample of 24 States and 850 local governments. The 48 States within the scope of the survey were stratified into the four Census Economic Regions, and a sample was then selected with the probability of inclusion being proportional to employment. Local governments were selected in a three-stage procedure. First, a sample of Metropolitan Statistical Areas and nonmetropolitan counties was selected. Next, within each area or county selected, governmental units were stratified into four broad industrial groups—general government, schools, health services, and special districts. Finally, within each of these industrial groups, a sample of governments was selected, with probability proportional to employment.

ment Cost Index data. Their training includes a 2-week introductory course, a 3-day update course several months after the introductory course, an annual training conference, and on-the-job training. In addition, a formal quality assurance program, consisting of interview observations and recontacts, is performed on every field economist by senior personnel.

Collection of the provisions of insurance, medical, dental, and vision care, retirement and capital accumulation, flexible benefits, and reimbursement account plans is conducted by the survey's national office staff of professional economists. Data from plan documents provided by field economists are recorded in coding manuals designed to capture a wide variety of provision information. (See exhibit.) Coding manuals are revised annually to capture the most recent benefit plan innovations.

Economists are trained in benefit plan analysis by senior staff and supervisors. All data are reviewed by a benefit area expert prior to entry on a data base. Individual plan analysis can take from 10-15 minutes for disability benefit plans to several hours for defined benefit pension and medical care plans.

Survey response

The following tabulation indicates the number of establishments surveyed in three recent Employee Benefits Surveys, as well as the percentage of those establishments providing data for the survey. The response to the survey was sufficient to provide reliable estimates of employee benefits data.

	Medium and large private establishments, 1989	*Small private establishments, 1990*	*State and local governments, 1990*
Total sample	1,970	3,567	1,464
Percent of total:			
Providing data	84	57	91
Refusing to respond	15	22	6
Out-of-business and out-of-scope	1	21	3

Data Processing

Information obtained from respondents and plan documents is entered on computer files. At present, data entry is by batch processing, with completed data keypunched and added to the survey's data bases periodically. Three data bases are created—one for establishment control data, another for leave plan provisions, and a third for retirement and insurance plan provisions. The control data base contains information on the establishments surveyed, including number of employees, number of plan participants, industry, geographic location, and sampling weight.

The plan data bases contain the provisions of each plan for which information was obtained. Plan identification codes are such that a plan, once analyzed, need not be analyzed again regardless of how many establishments report it (for example, a companywide health insurance program or a multiemployer pension plan).

Once data items are entered on one of the survey's data bases, extensive computer checks are made to ensure data consistency and reasonableness. When these edits fail, data corrections are made by survey economists. In addition, when data are tabulated, an extensive professional review is made to guarantee data accuracy.

Estimation

The estimation procedure followed in the Employee Benefits Survey reflects the two-stage sampling design, that is, the separate sampling of establishments and occupations within establishments. Two weight adjustment factors are applied to the establishment data. The first factor is introduced to account for the establishment nonresponse[12] and a second post-stratification factor is introduced to adjust the estimated employment totals to actual counts of the employment by industry for the survey reference date. These actual employment figures are obtained from the State Unemployment Insurance reports that correspond most closely to the reference date of the survey.

The form of the estimator used to derive population total Y is:

$$Y = \sum_{i=1}^{n'} \frac{f2_i \; f1_i}{P_i} \sum_{j=1}^{o_i} \frac{Y_{ij}}{P_{ij}}$$

where:

n' = number of responding sample establishments

o_i = occupation sample size selected from the ith establishment

Y_{ij} = value for the characteristics of the jth selected occupation in the ith selected establishment

P_i = the probability of including the ith establishment in the sample

P_{ij} = the probability of including the jth occupation in the sample of occupations from the ith establishment

$f1_i$ = weight adjustment factor for nonresponse for the ith establishment

$f2_i$ = weight adjustment factor for post-stratification totals for the ith establishment

[12] This technique assumes that the mean value of the nonrespondents is equal to the mean value of the respondents at some detailed "cell" level. These cells are defined in a manner that groups establishments together that are homogeneous with respect to the characteristics of interest. In most cases, these cells are the same as those used for sample selection.

Procedures are necessary to adjust for missing data from partial schedules. First, imputations for the number of plan participants are made where this number was not reported. Each of these participant values is imputed by randomly selecting a similar plan from another establishment in a similar industry and establishment size class. The participant rate from this randomly selected plan is then used to approximate the number of participants for the plan that is missing a participation value. Second, imputations for plan provisions are made where they are not available in a partially responding establishment. These plan provisions are imputed by randomly selecting a similar plan from another establishment in a similar industry and establishment size class. The plan provisions from this randomly selected plan are then used to represent the plan that is missing plan provision data.

One other form of missing data occurs when an establishment cooperates in the survey but refuses all information concerning one or more of the selected occupations. No adjustment is made for these missing data at present. However, methods to impute for these data are being explored for future surveys.

Sampling and estimating procedures are designed to yield national data for all studied industries combined. Estimates for individual industries or geographic regions generally do not meet reliability standards. Data are, however, reported separately for three occupational groups.

Reliability of Estimates

Employee Benefits Survey estimates are derived from a sample, rather than from all employees in all establishments within the scope of the survey. Consequently, the estimates are subject to sampling errors, as well as nonsampling errors.

Sampling errors are the differences that can arise between results derived from a sample and those computed from observations of all units in the population being studied. When probability techniques are used to select a sample, as in the Employee Benefits Survey, statistical measures called "standard errors" can be calculated to measure the size of sampling errors.

This evaluation of survey results involves the formation of confidence intervals that can be interpreted in the following manner: Assume that repeated random samples of the same size were drawn from a given population and an estimate of some value, such as a mean or percentage, was made from each sample. Intervals described by one standard error below each sample's estimate and one standard error above would include the population value for 68 percent of the samples. Confidence of inclusion rises to 90 percent if the intervals surrounding the sample estimates are widened to plus and minus 1.6 standard errors, and to 95 percent if the intervals are increased to plus and minus 2 standard errors.

Chart A-1 Generalized standard errors, medium and large firms, 1989

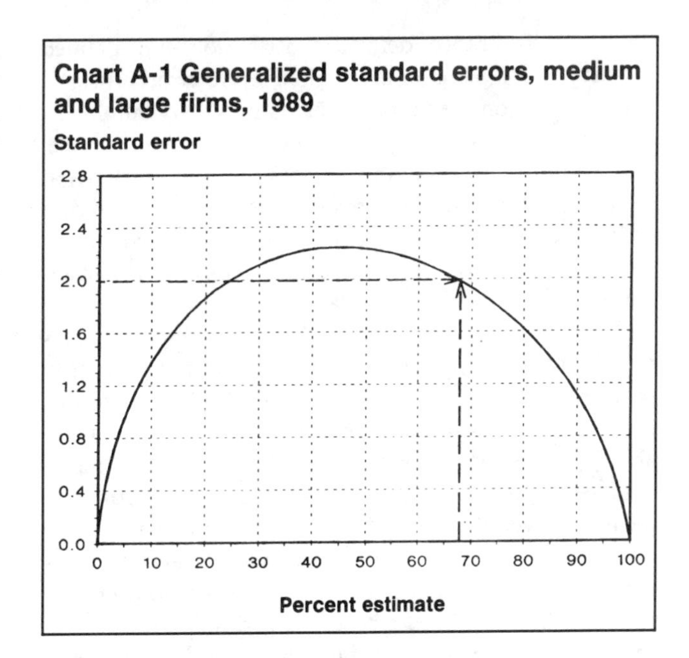

The accompanying chart provides standard errors for the estimates from the 1989 survey of medium and large private establishments. For example, the 1989 data indicate that 68 percent of full-time employees in medium and large establishments participated in a sick leave plan. The chart shows a standard error of approximately 2.0 percent for this estimate. Thus, at the 95 percent level, the confidence interval for this estimate is 64 percent to 72 percent (68 plus and minus 2 times 2.0 percent). Data used to develop the chart were derived using regression techniques based on standard errors from a representative portion of the estimates.

Nonsampling errors also affect survey results. They can be attributed to many sources: Inability to obtain information about all establishments in the sample; definitional difficulties; differences in the interpretation of questions; inability or unwillingness of respondents to provide correct information; mistakes in recording or coding the data; and other errors of collection, response, processing, coverage, and estimation for missing data.

Through the use of computer edits of the data and professional review of both individual and summarized data, efforts are made to reduce the nonsampling errors in recording, coding, and processing the data. However, to the extent that the characteristics of nonrespondents are not the same as those of respondents, nonsampling errors are introduced in the development of estimates. Because the impact of these limitations on the Employee Benefits Survey estimates is unknown, reliability measurements are incomplete.

Presentation

Survey results are published in a news release and a BLS bulletin. Estimates in these publications show the percent of employees that are covered by leave plans; participate in insurance, defined contribution, and defined benefit pension plans; or are eligible for other benefits. All workers are considered participants in wholly employer-financed plans that require a minimum length of service, even if some workers have not met those requirements at the time of the survey. Where plans—such as medical care or life insurance—require an employee to pay part of the cost (contributory plans), workers are considered participants only if they elect the plan.

The survey provides data on the incidence and characteristics of employee benefits that are paid for, at least in part, by the employer. There are a few exceptions to this general rule. The survey provides estimates on the availability of postretirement life insurance, dependent life insurance, supplemental life insurance, and long-term care insurance even if such coverage must be fully paid for by an employee or retiree. This is because the guarantee of insurability and availability of coverage at group premium rates can be considered a benefit. In addition, reimbursement accounts, salary reduction plans, and parental leave plans are tabulated even if there is no employer cost involved, beyond administrative expenses.

Most of the Employee Benefits Survey data presented by BLS show the percent of workers covered by individual benefit plans or plan provisions. Percentages are calculated in three ways. One technique shows the number of covered or eligible workers as a percent of all workers within the scope of the survey.

A second approach shows the number of workers covered by specific features in a benefit area as a percent of all employees who participate in that general benefit area. It answers questions concerning the typical coverage provided to persons with a given medical, dental, and vision care, insurance, retirement, or capital accumulation plan; for example, what percent of all employees with medical care receive mental health care coverage?

The third approach provides a close look at an important plan feature, for example, what percent of all employees with accidental death and dismemberment benefits have coverage equal to their life insurance benefits? A few tables use a combined approach, indicating in the first row of data the percent of persons who have a particular coverage, while the remainder of the table is based on employees with that coverage.

This multilevel approach has the advantage of clearly pointing out typical benefit plan characteristics after the incidence of the benefit has been established. Any of the second or third types of tables, if desired, can be converted to the first type by multiplying each data cell by appropriate factors. Thus, to calculate the percent of all employees in plans specifying a maximum payment for orthodontia, multiply the percent of those with orthodontia coverage subject to a maximum payment (for example, 90 percent) by the percent of dental care participants with orthodontia coverage (66 percent), and multiply that product by the percent of all employees who have dental care coverage (30 percent). In this example, 18 percent (.90 X .66 X .30) of employees are in plans that impose a maximum on orthodontia payments.

A few tables display average benefit values rather than percentages of workers. These tables present the averages for all covered employees; calculations exclude workers without the benefit.

The tables published by BLS present the major findings of the Employee Benefits Survey. Results of additional research appear in the *Monthly Labor Review*. Included among the articles published are detailed looks at important benefits, such as substance abuse treatment and parental leave. Articles are also used to introduce new data series. For example, data on defined benefit pension plan replacement rates (indicating the percent of preretirement income that pension benefits will provide) were first presented in the *Monthly Labor Review* before being incorporated in regular survey publications.

BLS publications, while detailed, can not include all Employee Benefits Survey information collected. Therefore, additional unpublished information is available for purchase on magnetic tape. Tapes containing the information supplied by individual respondents are currently available for the 1981-90 surveys.[13] Because of the Bureau's pledge of confidentiality to survey respondents, the tapes have been carefully screened to remove or alter any data that would reveal the identity of individual establishments.

The magnetic tapes, which consist of a control file and plan data files for each benefit area, may be used to derive national estimates, similar to those published by BLS, for those provisions not tabulated by BLS. The tapes may not yield reliable estimates for individual industries, geographic regions, or establishment size classes. Full documentation accompanies the tapes, including examples of estimating formulas.

Uses and Limitations

The extensive body of information on employee benefits generated in this survey provides a unique data resource. It is a major source of information for labor and management representatives involved in contract negotiations. Employers frequently seek information permitting comparison of their benefit plans with prevailing practices. Labor unions also use benefit data to assess potential areas for increasing nonwage compensation.

Employee Benefits Survey findings have been the primary data source for several recent research studies. For example:

[13] The tapes may be purchased from the Office of Compensation and Working Conditions, Bureau of Labor Statistics, Washington, DC 20212. Lists of data items on the computer files are available upon request.

The General Accounting Office (GAO) conducted a study of prevailing practices in private pension plans. This particular study was used by Congress when it created the new Federal Employees Retirement System for employees hired after 1983. The GAO also made a comparison of Federal and non-Federal life insurance coverage to determine the adequacy of Federal life insurance plans.

The Congressional Research Service (CRS) conducted an analysis, using EBS pension data, with an emphasis on pension plans integrated with Social Security benefits. CRS also recently completed a study of prevailing practices among health care plans offered by private firms and State and local governments, to brief Federal policymakers about prevailing non-Federal health provisions.

The Office of National Drug Control Policy used EBS data on substance abuse coverage provided through employer-provided health care plans in establishing the Nation's drug abuse treatment policies.

The Small Business Administration used the survey's data in its May 1985 report to the President, "The State of Small Business," to compare employee benefits in small businesses with those in larger firms.

The National Institute on Alcohol Abuse and Alcoholism used special questions EBS included in its survey to measure coverage for alcohol and drug abuse treatment across the Nation.

The National Association of Governors used information on public and private pensions in its analysis of State pension systems.

The District of Columbia City Council used EBS data on flexible benefits, health insurance, and pensions to compare benefits it provides with those provided by other localities.

The State of Washington used EBS data on the availability and details of health care benefits in its analysis of the need for government-mandated health care benefits.

The government of Japan recently approached EBS with sophisticated questions about retirement ages in the United States. Japan is considering changing its official retirement age and is attempting to estimate what effects such a change would have on its society.

The government of Austria has come to EBS in search of data pertaining to average United States workweek length, leave, and paid holidays. Austria is considering a policy change to a shorter workweek and is attempting to predict the outcome for its society.

Many labor organizations and unions use EBS data in their negotiations for benefit packages. The U.S. railroad industry recently used EBS data on health benefits in contract negotiations. EBS has also received numerous requests from the AFL-CIO and individual unions for the most current information available on employee benefits.

A researcher of the Kia Economic Research Institute, of Seoul, Korea, used EBS data to help design the employee benefits system for a large Korean motor company.

The Conference Board, a New York research organization, used EBS information as the foundation for a special publication about employer-provided family-related benefits, "A Life Cycle Approach To Family Benefits and Policies."

Brandeis University recently published "The Incidence of Integration Provisions in Private Pension Plans", based on EBS pension statistics.

A researcher from the University of Illinois published "Cost Sharing and the Changing Pattern of Employer-sponsored Health Benefits," based on EBS data, in the Milbank Quarterly (1987). The University of Illinois also contributed to the Final Report of the State of Illinois Reimbursement Task Force, "Third Party Coverage for Alcohol and Substance Abuse Treatment in Illinois" (1987).

While the Employee Benefits Survey is widely used, the data do have limitations. Because data collection is restricted to provisions of formal plans, the extent of such benefits as rest periods and personal leave may be understated. Furthermore, the data show the availability of benefit plans but not the actual use of these benefits; for example, results of the survey may indicate an average of 15 paid sick leave days available per year, but will not indicate the number actually taken.

At present, reliable estimates can be produced only at the national level, with no geographic or industry detail. Data for selected industries are available from industry wage surveys and, for selected geographic regions, from area wage surveys. These occupational wage surveys provide data on paid holiday and vacation practices and the incidence of welfare and pension plans, but not detailed provisions of benefits (see chapter 6).

The EBS is designed to yield estimates of the percent of employees with specific benefit provisions in the survey year, not the change in plan provisions over time. Some plan provisions are found mainly in one or two industries. When employment changes do not occur evenly across industries, shifts in survey findings regarding relative incidence of types of benefit plans may stem, not from changes in plans, but from disproportionate changes in the number of employees covered by different types of plans.

Quality Control and Future Research

The Employee Benefits Survey includes an ongoing quality control program designed to scrutinize survey processes, keep abreast of innovations in employee benefits, and provide information that is useful to data users. Survey processes are periodically reviewed by survey economists, who are asked to submit written reports of their recent survey experiences and suggestions for improvements. These reports have always been invaluable and have led to numerous improvements in data collection forms, instructions, and procedures. Recent improvements stemming from this process include multi-year collection forms and written summaries of unusual situations likely to be encountered during Statewide data collection.

The multitude of changes in the employee benefits field in recent years have made it necessary for the Employee Benefits Survey to undergo frequent change. To keep the survey up-to-date, survey economists undertake extensive research in the legal, financial, and accounting aspects of employee benefits. Among the products generated from this research is a periodic look at Federal and State legislation affecting employee benefits. This information is then used to assist in the collection and analysis of employee benefits data.

Finally, the Employee Benefits Survey seeks information from data users concerning whether the survey is meeting their needs. Included in these activities are routine discussions and meetings with frequent survey users and questionnaires designed to solicit opinions about the survey from a broader range of data users. These activities have resulted in improvements in published survey data.

Research is currently under way in a number of areas in an effort toward publishing more survey results, improving survey processes, and increasing survey response. Among the items being studied are benefit incidence and provisions by industry, new measures of employer-provided health care benefits, and a revised format for the survey bulletin. Direct entry of survey data via interactive computer systems is among the improved processes being developed. Such a system will save time and money while improving data reliability. Finally, efforts are underway to improve the rate of response to the survey, and to improve the amount of usable data obtained from each respondent.

Technical References

Bulletins:

Employee Benefits in State and Local Governments, 1990, Bulletin 2398, February 1992.

Employee Benefits in Small Private Establishments, 1990, Bulletin 2388, September 1991.

Employee Benefits in Medium and Large Establishments, 1989, Bulletin 2363, June 1990.

Employee Benefits Survey: An MLR Reader, Bulletin 2362, June 1990.

Articles in the *Monthly Labor Review:*

General

Burke, Thomas P. and Morton, John D. "How Firm Size and Industry Affect Employee Benefits," December 1990, pp. 35-43.

Wiatrowski, William J. "Comparing Employee Benefits in the Public and Private Sectors," December 1988, pp. 3-8.

Frumkin, Robert N. and Wiatrowski, William J. "Bureau of Labor Statistics Takes A New Look at Employee Benefits," August 1982, pp. 41-45.

Retirement

Wiatrowski, William J. "New Survey Data on Pension Benefits," August 1991, pp. 8-22.

Coates, Edward M., III "Profit Sharing Today: Plans and Provisions," April 1991, pp. 19-25.

Bucci, Michael. "Contributions to Saving and Thrift Plans," November 1990, pp. 28-36.

Wiatrowski, William J. "Supplementing Retirement until Social Security Begins," February 1990, pp. 25-29.

Lovejoy, Lora Mills. "The Comparative Value Of Pensions In the Public and Private Sectors," December 1988, pp. 18-26.

Graham, Avy D. "How Has Vesting Changed Since Passage of Employee Retirement Income Security Act?" August 1988, pp. 20-25.

Bell, Donald R. and Marclay, William. "Trends in Retirement Eligibility and Pension Benefits, 1974-83," April 1987, pp. 18-25.

Schmitt, Donald G. "Today's Pension Plans: How Much Do They Pay?" December 1985, pp. 19-25.

Schmitt, Donald G. "Postretirement Increases Under Private Pension Plans," September 1984, pp. 3-8.

Bell, Donald R. and Hill, Diane. "How Social Security Payments Affect Private Pensions," May 1984, pp. 15-20.

Bell, Donald R. and Graham, Avy. "Surviving Spouse's Benefits in Private Pension Plans," April 1984, pp. 23-31.

Bell, Donald R. and Wiatrowski, William J. "Disability Benefits for Employees in Private Pension Plans," August 1982, pp. 36-40.

Technical References—Continued

Health care benefits

Kronson, Marc E. "Substance Abuse Coverage in Employer Medical Plans," April 1991, pp 3-10.

Baker, Cathy and Kramer, Natalie. "Employer-Sponsored Prescription Drug Benefits," February 1991, pp. 31-35.

Burke, Thomas P. and Jain, Rita S. "Trends in Employer-Provided Health Care Benefits," February 1991, pp. 24-30.

Blostin, Allan P., Burke, Thomas P. and Lovejoy, Lora M. "Disability and Insurance Plans in the Public and Private Sectors," December 1988, pp. 9-17.

Jain, Rita S. "Employer-sponsored Dental Insurance Eases the Pain," October 1988, pp. 18-23.

Jain, Rita S. "Employer-sponsored Vision Care Brought Into Focus," September 1988, pp. 19-23.

Blostin, Allan P. "Mental Health Benefits Financed by Employers," July 1987, pp. 23-27.

Frumkin, Robert N. "Health Insurance Trends in Cost Control and Coverage," September 1986, pp. 3-8.

Hedger, Douglas and Schmitt, Donald G. "Trends in Major Medical Coverage During a Period of Rising Costs," July 1983, pp 11-16.

Blostin, Allan P. and Marclay, William. "HMOs and Other Health Plans: Coverage and Employee Premiums," June 1983, pp. 28-33.

Life insurance

Bucci, Michael. "The Growth of Employer-sponsored Life Insurance," October 1991, pp. 25-32.

Ott, David E. "Employer-provided Survivor Benefits," June 1991, pp. 13-18.

Hyland, Stephanie L. "Age-related Reductions in Life Insurance Benefits," February 1991, pp. 36-38.

Simons, Margaret and Thompson, Cynthia. "Life Insurance Benefits for Retired Workers," September 1990, pp. 17-21.

Bellet, Adam Z. "Employer-sponsored Life Insurance: A New Look," October 1989, pp. 25-28.

Thompson, Cynthia. "Compensation for Death and Dismemberment," September 1989, pp. 13-17.

Miller, Michael A. "Age-related Reductions in Workers' Life Insurance," September 1985, pp. 29-34.

Disability benefits

Houff, James N. and Wiatrowski, William J. "Analyzing Short-term Disability Benefits," June 1989, pp. 3-9.

Hill, Diane B. "Employer-sponsored Long-term Disability Insurance," July 1987, pp. 16-22.

Wiatrowski, William J. "Employee Income Protection Against Short-term Disabilities," February 1985, pp. 32-38.

Emerging benefits

Hyland, Stephanie L. "Helping Employees with Family Care," September 1990, pp. 22-26.

Wiatrowski, William J. "Family-Related Benefits in the Workplace," March 1990, pp. 28-33.

Meisenheimer, Joseph R., II and Wiatrowski, William J. "Flexible Benefits Plans: Employees Who Have a Choice," December 1989, pp. 17-23.

Meisenheimer, Joseph R., II. "Employer Provisions for Parental Leave," October 1989, pp. 20-24.

PAID HOLIDAYS

PLAN 1

Date of most recent change ____

1. Benefit/Plan Identification Information:

Record	BA	BLS Plan No.	Response Code
010	08	01	
(1–3)	(16–17)	(18–19)	(20)

2. Name of Plan:

____

(21–44)

3. Indicate relationship of holidays to work schedule.

Year 1	Year 2
(45)	(45)

Code	Provision
Blank	– Holidays based on regular work schedule
1	– Holidays based on alternate work schedule
9	– Other (Describe in Remarks.)

4. How many paid holidays (whole and decimal) are given as part of a "continuing holiday plan"? (Enter 9 whole days and 3 half days as 10.5; enter 10 days as 10.0.)

Year 1

Whole Days	Decimal Days	nc =7 nav =8
(46–47)	(48–49)	(50)

Year 2

Whole Days	Decimal Days	nc =7 nav =8
(46–47)	(48–49)	(50)

5. What is the establishment's policy when a holiday falls on a scheduled day off, such as a Saturday or Sunday? (Enter one of the following codes in box [51] below.)

Code	Policy
1	– The holiday is not observed.
2	– Another day off is granted or holidays are scheduled not to fall on a scheduled day off.
3	– An additional day's pay is granted.
4	– Either another day off or an additional day's pay is granted, depending on when the holiday falls.
5	– Either another day off is granted or the holiday is lost, depending on when the holiday falls.
8	– Data not available
9	– Other provision (Specify in Remarks.)

Year 1 Policy	Year 2 Policy
(51)	(51)

Remarks:

____

____

____

____

____

6. Participation:

If all employees participate, enter ALL in participants for Hit #1. No additional entries are needed.

Hit #	Year 1 Participants	Year 1 Gr. Size	Year 2 Participants	Year 2 Gr. Size
1	(52–58)	(59)	(52–58)	(59)
2	(60–66)	(67)	(60–66)	(67)
3	(68–74)	(75)	(68–74)	(75)
4	(76–82)	(83)	(76–82)	(83)
5	(84–90)	(91)	(84–90)	(91)
6	(92–98)	(99)	(92–98)	(99)
7	(100–106)	(107)	(100–106)	(107)
8	(108–114)	(115)	(108–114)	(115)
		D.C. Use (116)		D.C. Use (116)

Remarks:

____

____

____

____

____

____

____

____

____

____

____

____

____

____

310
1-3

What are the minimum age, service, and age plus service requirements needed for early retirement at the employee's election? If more than one set of requirements exist, describe first those requirements applying to the earliest possible age. If no minimum requirement exists for age, service, or age plus service, code "0". Check appropriate spaces.

		AGE	SERVICE	AGE PLUS SERVICE
___ 20	Earliest age	___ 21-22	___ 23-24	___ 25-27
___ 28	Alternative #1	___ 29-30	___ 31-32	___ 33-35
___ 36	Alternative #2	___ 37-38	___ 39-40	___ 41-43
___ 44	Other			
___ 45	Remarks			
___ 46	Not determinable			
___ 47	Not applicable			
___ 48	Action code			

Chapter 10. Productivity Measures: Business Sector and Major Subsectors

Background

Indexes of labor productivity, multifactor productivity, and related measures for broad economic sectors and manufacturing industries are published by the Bureau of Labor Statistics. Quarterly and annual measures of output per hour, together with comparable measures of compensation per hour and unit labor costs, are maintained for business and nonfarm business, from 1947 to the present. Similar measures are also available for manufacturing (total, durable, and nondurable) and for nonfinancial corporations.

The multifactor productivity indexes for major sectors measure output per combined unit of labor and capital input in private business, private nonfarm business, and manufacturing. Multifactor productivity indexes for 20 manufacturing industries measure output per combined unit of capital (K), labor (L), energy (E), materials (M), and purchased business services (S) inputs—KLEMS inputs.

Table 1 summarizes the availability of productivity measures for major sectors of the U.S. economy.

Table 1. Availability of productivity measures for major sectors and subsectors of the economy

Productivity measure	Input	Index Available
Labor productivity:[1]		
Business[1]	Labor	Quarterly
Nonfarm business	Labor	Quarterly
Nonfinancial corporations	Labor	Quarterly
Manufacturing, total	Labor	Quarterly
Durable	Labor	Quarterly
Nondurable	Labor	Quarterly
Multifactor productivity:		
Private business	Labor, capital	Annually
Private nonfarm business	Labor, capital	Annually
Manufacturing, total	Labor, capital	Annually
KLEMS[2] multifactor productivity:		
Manufacturing and 20 2-digit SIC manufacturing industries	Labor, capital, energy, materials, services	Annually

[1] Includes government enterprises; multifactor productivity measures exclude such enterprises.

[2] Capital (K), labor (L), energy (E), materials (M), and purchased business services (S) inputs.

Description of Measures

The Bureau publishes three sets of productivity measures for major sectors and subsectors of the U.S. economy, each using a distinct methodology. These measures include labor productivity measures for major sectors and durable and nondurable manufacturing subsectors, multifactor productivity measures for major sectors, and multifactor productivity measures for total manufacturing and 20 Standard Industrial Classification manufacturing industries. Each set of measures involves a comparison of output and input measures.

The traditional measure of labor productivity—output per hour—was first published in 1959, and represents the culmination of a long series of developments in productivity measurement in the Bureau.[1] Output, measured as real gross product originating (GPO) in a sector, is compared to labor input, measured as hours at work in the corresponding sector.[2] These measures are prepared for the business sector, the nonfarm business sector, nonfinancial corporations, and manufacturing, along with subsectors of durable and nondurable goods manufacturing. These measures are available quarterly and are updated and revised eight times a year.

The second set of measures covers multifactor productivity for major U.S. sectors.[3] In these measures, output is again measured as GPO, but the input measure is an aggregate of hours at work and capital service flows. These measures have been developed in recognition of the role capital growth plays in output growth. They are updated annually.

The third set of measures involves comparisons of broader measures of both output and input. Output is defined as the real value of production less the change in real inventories. Input includes labor and capital, and also energy, nonenergy materials, and purchased business ser-

[1] *Trends in Output per Man-Hour in the Private Economy, 1909-58,* Bulletin 1249 (Bureau of Labor Statistics, 1959).

[2] GPO represents deliveries of final goods and services by the sector. GPO is gross in the sense that neither capital consumption allowances nor purchases of capital goods are deducted, but it is net in the sense that inter-industry transactions in consumable materials and services are excluded from output. These transactions are excluded to avoid double counting. For example, the output of the steel industry is excluded to the extent that it is incorporated in final products such as automobiles. This focus on final outputs is appropriate for major economic sectors.

[3] *Trends in Multifactor Productivity, 1948-81,* Bulletin 2178 (Bureau of Labor Statistics, 1983).

vices. These measures are available for a comprehensive set of 20 manufacturing industries (corresponding to the 2-digit Standard Industrial Classification (SIC) level) as well as for total manufacturing. When the focus narrows to the productivity of a particular industry, the outputs are important regardless of whether they are delivered to other industries or to final users and the inputs from other industries are relevant. This set of measures consists of annual data and is updated approximately every 2 years.

Data Sources and Estimating Procedures

Output Per Hour Measures

Output

Real gross domestic product originating in the business sectors and subsectors is the basis of the output components of the major sector labor productivity and multifactor productivity measures. These output components are based on and are consistent with the National Income and Product Accounts (NIPA), including the gross national product (GNP) measure, prepared by the Bureau of Economic Analysis (BEA) of the U.S. Department of Commerce.

Computation of business sector GPO begins with GNP. Output measures are computed in constant dollars while labor's cost share and the implicit price deflator for business sector output are computed in current dollars. Gross domestic product (GDP) is simply GNP less "rest-of-world" output, that is, less net factor payments to domestic owners of factors of production located outside the United States. Next, the statistical discrepancy is subtracted, the result being a measure of income received by labor and property owners for services rendered in the current production of goods and services. (In current dollars, property income in the NIPA is dispersed as corporate profits, proprietors' and partners' income, net interest, capital consumption allowances, indirect business taxes, and several other items.)

Business sector output is computed by further subtracting general government, output of nonprofit institutions, output of paid employees of private households, and the rental value of owner-occupied real estate. The business sector thereby excludes many activities where it is difficult to draw inferences on productivity from NIPA output measures. Such inferences would be questionable mainly because the output measures are based largely on incomes of input factors.[4] The farm sector, which is subject to unique external forces, is subtracted to yield the nonfarm business sector, the principal focus of many productivity studies.

Output data for the manufacturing sector based on gross product are computed by the BEA on an annual basis only. In order to achieve quarterly estimates of manufacturing output consistent with the BEA's gross product concept, BLS uses the quarterly changes in the Federal Reserve Board monthly index of industrial production to move the gross product data. The results are benchmarked annually to the published BEA output levels. Thus, the output data used for all major sectors are consistent with the output concepts embodied in the National Income and Product Accounts.

Labor input

The primary source of hours and employment data is the BLS Current Employment Statistics (CES) program, which provides monthly survey data on total employment and average weekly hours of production and nonsupervisory workers in nonagricultural establishments. Jobs rather than persons are counted, so that multiple jobholders are counted more than once.

The CES data are based on payroll records from a sample of establishments in which the probability of sample selection is related to the establishment size. Data on employment, hours, and earnings are collected monthly; the reference period for these data is the payroll period including the 12th of the month. (The CES methods are described in chapter 2.) Establishment data are published monthly in *Employment and Earnings.*

Because CES data include only nonfarm wage and salary workers, data from the Current Population Survey (CPS) are used for farm employment. In the nonfarm sector, the CPS is also used for proprietors, unpaid family workers, and paid employees of private households. Government enterprise hours are developed from the National Income and Product Accounts estimates of employment and CPS data on average weekly hours.

Separate estimates for employment and hours paid are developed for each major sector, converted to an hours-at-work definition, and are aggregated to business and nonfarm business levels. Hours of labor input are treated as homogeneous units; no distinction is made among workers with different skill levels or wages.

For nonmanufacturing sectors, employment and average weekly hours are computed from the CES, CPS, and NIPA sources. Although CES data on average weekly hours refer only to nonsupervisory workers, it is assumed for hours computation that the length of the workweek in each nonmanufacturing industry is the same for all wage and salary workers.

In manufacturing, separate measures for production and nonproduction workers' hours are derived and aggregated to the manufacturing total. Employment and aver-

[4] A detailed description of the methods and procedures for estimating GNP and GDP in current and constant dollars is given in Carol S. Carson, "GNP: An Overview of Sources Data and Estimating Methods," *Survey of Current Business,* July 1987, pp. 103-26. Also see Methodology Paper No. 1 "Introduction to National Income Accounting" (Bureau of Economic Analysis, 1985). Further information on estimates for major industry sectors is presented in the October 1962 issue of the *Survey of Current Business.* Derivation of business sector output is discussed also in Jerome A. Mark, "Measuring Single-Factor and Multifactor Productivity," *Monthly Labor Review,* December 1986, pp. 3-11.

age weekly hours for production workers and employment for nonproduction workers are taken directly from CES data. Average weekly hours for nonproduction workers are developed from BLS studies of wages and supplements in manufacturing which provide data on the regularly scheduled workweek of white-collar employees.

In the CES, weekly hours are measured as hours paid rather than hours at work. The Hours at Work Survey is used to convert the hours paid of nonagricultural production and nonsupervisory employees to an hours-at-work basis.[5] Hours at work excludes all forms of paid leave, but includes paid time to travel between job sites, coffee breaks, and machine downtime. This survey of about 5,500 establishments has collected quarterly and annual ratios of hours at work to hours paid since 1981.[6] (See BLS form 2000P at end of this chapter for a sample data collection form for manufacturing industries. Form 2000N is a virtually identical form for nonmanufacturing industries and is not reproduced.) Ratios are developed for each 2-digit SIC industry within manufacturing and for each 1-digit SIC industry outside of manufacturing.

Unpublished data and one-time surveys have been used to extend the annual ratios back to 1948 as well as develop ratios for nonproduction and supervisory workers.[7] The quarterly ratios are not currently used in the quarterly measures of labor input. Instead, a quadratic minimization formula devised by Frank Denton is used to generate quarterly ratios.[8]

The resultant quarterly measures are used to convert the paid hours of nonfarm employees to an hours-at-work basis. The estimates of hours of farm workers, proprietors, unpaid family workers, employees of government enterprises, and paid employees of private households are on an hours-at-work basis, and so no adjustment is required for these workers.

Compensation and labor costs

Indexes of compensation per hour measure the hourly cost to employers of wages and salaries, as well as supplemental payments, which include employers' contributions to Social Security, unemployment insurance taxes, and payments for private health insurance and pension plans. Measures of real compensation per hour reflect the adjustment of hourly compensation for changes in the Consumer Price Index for All Urban Consumers (CPI-U).

Unit labor costs measure the cost of labor input required to produce one unit of output and are derived by dividing compensation in current dollars by output in constant dollars. Unit nonlabor payments measure the cost of nonlabor items such as depreciation, rent, interest, and indirect business taxes, in addition to corporate profits and profit-type income of proprietorships and partnerships.

Multifactor Productivity Measures for Major Sectors

The multifactor productivity (MFP) indexes for major sectors measure output per combined unit of labor and capital input in private business, private nonfarm business, and manufacturing. The output measures for private business and private nonfarm business are GPO measures, but differ from output in business and nonfarm business, respectively, in that output of government enterprises is omitted. MFP measures have not been developed for the broader sectors because, due to subsidies, estimates of the appropriate weights for labor and capital in government enterprises cannot be made. Labor input for the MFP measures in these sectors is also adjusted to exclude government enterprises.

Capital inputs for the MFP measures are computed in accordance with a service flow concept for physical capital assets—equipment, structures, inventories, and land. Capital inputs for major sectors are determined in three main steps: 1) A very detailed array of capital stocks is developed for various asset types in various industries; 2) asset-type capital stocks are aggregated for each industry to measure capital input for the industry; and 3) industry capital inputs are aggregated to measure sectoral level capital input.

The asset detail consists of 28 types of equipment, 22 types of nonresidential structures, 9 types of residential structures (owner occupied housing is excluded), 3 types of inventories (by stage of processing), and land. BLS measures of capital stocks for equipment and structures are prepared using NIPA data on real gross investment. Real stocks are constructed as vintage aggregates of historical investments (in real terms) in accordance with an "efficiency" or service flow concept (as distinct from a price or value concept). The efficiency of each asset is assumed to deteriorate only gradually during the early years of an asset's service life and then more quickly later in its life. These "age/efficiency" schedules are hyperbolic in form and based in part on empirical evidence on capital deterioration. Inventory stocks are developed using data from the NIPA. Farm land input is based on data from the Economic Research Service of the U.S. Department of Agriculture. A benchmark for nonfarm land is estimated by applying a land-structure ratio based on unpublished estimates by the U.S. Bureau of the Census to BLS estimates

[5] Kent Kunze, "A New BLS Survey Measures the Ratio of Hours Worked to Hours Paid," *Monthly Labor Review*, June 1984, pp. 3-7.

[6] The sample design and universe of establishments for the Hours at Work survey are essentially the same as those used in the Current Establishment Statistics program. The response rate has ranged from 70 to more than 80 percent including responses obtained through computer assisted telephone interviews.

[7] A description of the hours at work ratios for the period 1948 through 1988 can be found in Jablonski, Kunze, and Otto, "Hours at Work: A New Base for Productivity Statistics," *Monthly Labor Review*, February 1990, pp. 17-24.

[8] See Frank T. Denton, "Adjustment of Monthly and Quarterly Series to Annual Totals: An Approach Based on Quadratic Minimization," *Journal of the American Statistical Association*, March 1971, pp. 99-102. This method is also used to produce quarterly ratios prior to 1981.

of the value of stuctures. This benchmark is extrapolated using gross stocks of structures calculated from U.S. Bureau of Economic Analysis investment data. The resulting nonfarm land data series is allocated to industries based on Internal Revenue Service data on book values of land.[9]

For each industry (the BLS procedures are applied to 57 industries in the private business sector corresponding, approximately, to the 2-digit SIC level), these measures of capital stocks are aggregated using a Tornqvist chain index procedure (described below). Weights for each asset type are based on the share of property income estimated to be accruing to that asset type in each year. Payments are allocated to asset types by employing estimates of the implicit rental price of each asset type.[10] The implicit rental price concept (which is an income side counterpart to the user cost of capital) is based on the neoclassical theory of the firm and provides a framework for deriving weights for asset-type capital stocks. Because some asset types tend to deteriorate much more quickly than others and because of tax rules specific to asset types, the real economic cost of employing a dollar's worth of stock varies substantially by asset type.

Each sector's capital input is measured as a Tornqvist chain index of the capital inputs for each industry within the sector. Weights are determined annually by the industry's share of total nonlabor payments in the sector.

Once the sector's capital input is measured, total input is computed by combining capital and labor using, again, the Tornqvist procedure. For each input, the weight is the input's share of total costs and is derived from NIPA data on the components of nominal GPO by industry. At both the sector and the industry level, labor costs are measured as compensation to employees (wages, salaries, and supplements) plus a portion of noncorporate income.[11] Most other components of nominal GPO are assigned to capital.[12] The exception is those indirect taxes which are not assigned either to capital or labor (notably sales and excise taxes). Thus total cost is less than GPO by an amount equal to these taxes. Labor and capital shares *in total cost* are computed and then used in the aforementioned aggregation of capital and labor. Finally, major sector MFP indexes are calculated as the ratio of output (the sector's real GPO) to input.

[9] These methods are described in detail in *Trends in Multifactor Productivity, 1948-81*, appendix C.

[10] The rental price formula and related methodology and data sources are described in *Trends in Multifactor Productivity*, 1948-81, appendix C. The rental price formulas described in this publication have been modified to eliminate large fluctuations due to inflation in new goods prices. Research on this issue is reported by Michael J. Harper, Ernst R. Berndt and David O. Wood, "Rates of Return and Capital Aggregation Using Alternative Rental Prices," in Dale W. Jorgenson and Ralph Landau, *Technology and Capital Formation*, 1989, MIT Press, pp. 331-37.

[11] Noncorporate income is allocated to labor and capital costs in each year using the following assumption: The ratio of self-employed persons' compensation per hour to employees' compensation per hour equals the ratio of the noncorporate rate of return to capital to the corporate rate of return. This treats any apparent excess or deficiency in noncorporate income neutrally with respect to labor and capital.

[12] Capital costs are the sum of 1) the balance of noncorporate income, 2) corporate profits, 3) net interest, 4) rental income, 5) adjusted capital consumption allowances, 6) inventory valuation adjustments, and 7) portions of indirect taxes assumed to be associated with capital (notably motor vehicle and property taxes), 8) the sum of business transfers, government subsidies.

Multifactor Productivity Measures for Manufacturing Industries

Multifactor productivity indexes for 20 manufacturing industries also measure output per unit of input. In this case, input is a weighted aggregate of capital, labor, energy, nonenergy materials, and purchased business services inputs.[13]

For these manufacturing MFP measures, output is the deflated value of production of an industry; hence it differs from the GPO output measures used for the major sector output per hour and MFP indexes. The value of production is shipments, adjusted for inventory change, to purchasers outside the industry. Capital is measured as it is for the major sector MFP indexes; rental prices of capital are computed for each industry. Labor is also measured as it is for major sector MFP.

The inclusion in the industry MFP measures of all intermediate inputs—energy, nonenergy materials, and purchased business services—is consistent with the use of total value of production as the output measure. Energy input is constructed using data on price and quantity of fuels purchased for use as heat or power. Nonenergy materials input includes all commodity inputs exclusive of fuels but inclusive of fuel-type inputs used as raw materials in manufacturing. The measures of purchased business services are constructed using price and value data on services purchased by manufacturing industries from service industries. Data sources used in constructing these three inputs include input-output tables, surveys of establishments in manufacturing and other industries, and price indexes.

Total input is computed from components as a Tornqvist chain index number series. The weight for each input is its share in total input cost. The industry MFP measures are available for 1949 to the present.

Analysis and Presentation

Indexes of labor productivity show changes in the ratio of output to hours of labor input. Similarly, indexes of multifactor productivity show changes in the ratio of output to combined inputs. However, these indexes should not be interpreted as presenting the contribution of the particular input, or combination of inputs, to production. Rather, changes over time in the output, labor input, or

[13] An explanation of the methods and some results are presented in William Gullickson and Michael J. Harper, "Multifactor Productivity in U.S. Manufacturing, 1949-83," *Monthly Labor Review*, October 1987, pp. 18-28.

combined input measures underlying these productivity indexes may reflect the influence of other factors including variations in the characteristics and efforts of the workforce, changes in the managerial skill, changes in the organization of production, and new technology.

Compensation and labor costs

BEA develops employee compensation data as part of the national income accounts. These quarterly data include direct payments to labor—wages and salaries (including executive compensation), commissions, tips, bonuses, and payments in kind representing income to the recipients—and supplements to these direct payments. Supplements consist of vacation and holiday pay, all other types of paid leave, employer contributions to funds for social insurance, private pension and health and welfare plans, compensation for injuries, etc.

The compensation measures taken from establishment payrolls refer exclusively to wage and salary workers. Labor cost would be seriously understated by this measure of employee compensation alone in sectors such as farm and retail trade, where hours at work by proprietors represent a substantial portion of total labor input. BLS, therefore, imputes a compensation cost for labor services of proprietors and includes the hours of unpaid family workers in the hours of all employees engaged in a sector. Labor compensation per hour for proprietors is assumed to be the same as that of the average employee in that sector.

Unit labor and nonlabor costs

The Bureau also prepares data on labor and nonlabor costs per unit of output for the business sector and its major components. Unit labor costs relate hourly compensation of all persons to output per hour and are defined as compensation per unit of constant-dollar output. Nonlabor *payments* are the excess of gross product originating in an economic sector over corresponding labor compensation, and include nonlabor *costs* as well as corporate profits and the profit-type income of proprietors. Nonlabor costs include interest, depreciation, rent, and indirect business taxes.

In aggregate sectors, productivity changes through time reflect movements within the various component industries as well as shifts in the relative importance of each of the industries. For example, changes in labor productivity and multifactor productivity are influenced by the relative shift of inputs (labor and capital) from low- to high-productivity industries and by productivity changes in the component subsectors.[14]

Short-term movements in productivity and unit labor costs often result from cyclical variation in output, as noted below, and may also reflect unusual events such as drought. These short-term movements are sometimes substantially greater or smaller than long-term averages of productivity and cost movements. For example, productivity growth for 1 or 2 years can be substantially greater than the average for the business cycle that includes these years.

[14] The farm-nonfarm shift is examined in some detail by J. R. Norsworthy and L. J. Fulco in "Productivity and Costs in the Private Economy," *Monthly Labor Review*, June 1974, pp. 3-9.

Availability of results

Indexes of output per hour, compensation per hour, and related cost data are published twice each quarter in the BLS news release, "Productivity and Costs." In addition, quarterly and annual analyses are published from time to time in the *Monthly Labor Review.* Historical indexes of these and related data are available on request, as are detailed descriptions of data sources and computational procedures.

Multifactor productivity measures are announced each year in the "Multifactor Productivity Measures" news release. Included are annual indexes of multifactor productivity, capital inputs, and related measures for private business, private nonfarm business, and manufacturing.

Indexes of productivity and related cost data are available monthly in *Employment and Earnings* and the *Monthly Labor Review*, on LABSTAT (the Bureau's labor statistics data base) data tapes, and BLS data diskettes.

Information on trends in KLEMS productivity in manufacturing and the ratio of hours at work to hours paid is available on request from the Bureau.

Calculation Procedures

Labor productivity

Labor productivity, or output per hour, is computed as:

$$\text{Labor productivity} = \frac{\text{Constant-dollar output}}{\text{Hours of labor input}}$$

or

$$P = O/H$$

In instances where several sectors are involved, labor productivity can be computed equivalently as:

$$P = (\Sigma_i O_i) / \Sigma_i H_i$$

or as

$$P = \Sigma_i W_i (O_i/H_i)$$

where:

O_i is constant-dollar output in sector i,

H_i is hours of labor input in sector i,

$W_i = H_i/\Sigma_i H_i$ is the hours-based weighting factor for sector i,

P is average labor productivity for the aggregate sector.

The computation of labor compensation per hour parallels the computation of output per hour. Unit labor costs (ULC) are computed as labor compensation (C) per unit of (constant-dollar) output, but are often represented as:

$$ULC = (C/H) / (O/H)$$

This form highlights the relationships between unit labor costs, hourly compensation, and labor productivity.

Real compensation per hour (RC) is computed as hourly compensation deflated by the seasonally adjusted Consumer Price Index for All Urban Consumers (CPI-U):

$$RC = (C/H) / CPI\text{-}U$$

Unit nonlabor payments (UNLP) include all nonlabor components of gross product originating in a given sector—depreciation, rent, interest, and indirect business taxes as well as profits and profit-type income—whereas unit nonlabor cost (UNLC) excludes profit. These measures are computed as:

$$UNLP = (CU - C)/O$$

and

$$UNLC = (CU - C - PR)/O$$

where:

CU is current-dollar output,
C is current-dollar compensation,
O is constant-dollar output,
PR is current-dollar profits.

Labor's share in current dollar output in a given sector is simply the ratio of labor compensation paid in that sector to current dollar output:

$$LS = C/CU$$

and, analogously, the nonlabor or capital share is defined as:

$$NLS = (CU - C)/CU = 1 - LS$$

Most of the measures noted above are presented quarterly in index form. Indexes are computed from basic data or analytic ratios by dividing the series by its own base year annual value (presently 1982) and multiplying by 100. In addition, quarterly percent changes at a compound annual rate and percent changes from the same quarter in the previous year are computed:[15]

$$Q_t = 100\,(V_t/V_{t-1})^4 - 100$$
$$Y_t = 100\,(V_t/V_{t-4}) - 100$$

where:

t is a time subscript denoting the quarter,
V is a series described above,
Q_t is the quarterly percentage change in series V from quarter t-1 to quarter t, measured at a compound annual rate,
Y_t is the percentage change in series V from quarter t-4 (the same quarter 1 year before) to quarter t.

Indexes and percent changes are published to one decimal point. In order not to lose precision, all computations are made from the underlying measures themselves rather than from the published indexes.

Multifactor productivity

The procedure used by BLS to aggregate inputs for its multifactor productivity measures is the Tornqvist chain index. Some of the basic properties of this index are: It is calculated as a weighted average of growth rates of the components; the weights are allowed to vary for each time period; and the weights are defined as the mean of the relative compensation shares of the components in two adjacent time periods. Hence, the growth rate of the index ($\dot{I}/I$) is the proportional change over time (the dot notation refers to continuous change with respect to time), such that:

$$\dot{I}/I = \Sigma_i w_{it}(\dot{x}_{it}/x_{it})$$

where $\dot{x}_{it}/x_{it}$ is the growth rate of the ith input calculated as:

$$\dot{x}_{it}/x_{it} = \ln x_{it} - \ln x_{it-1}$$

The weights (w_{it}) are defined as the means of the relative compensation shares of all the inputs:

$$w_{it} = (s_{it} + s_{it-1})/2$$

$$s_{it} = \frac{p_{it}x_{it}}{\Sigma_i p_{it}x_{it}}$$

where:

p_{it} = price or wage of input x_i in period t.

Multifactor productivity growth is defined as the growth rate in output ($\dot{O}/O$) less the growth rate in aggregated inputs:

$$MFP = \dot{O}/O - \dot{I}/I$$

For MFP measures of output per combined unit of labor

[15] The estimation of quarterly (or subannual) changes at compound annual rates as the diffences between movements in the underlying series involves approximations. For changes in the neighborhood of 1 or 2 percent, these approximations are good; however, the inexactness of these approximations is amplified by relatively large changes in the economic measures such as those experienced during periods of inflation, sharp recession, and rapid recovery.

Since most of the productivity and costs measures are reported as percentages to one decimal place, e.g., 2.6 percent, questions sometimes arise because the greater precision carried in the automated computation results in differences in related measures in the final decimal place.

and capital inputs, this formula is implemented as:

$$\dot{I}/I = w_k\dot{K}/K + w_l\,\dot{L}/L$$

where:

w_k = capital's share of total costs,
w_l = labor's share of total costs,
$\dot{K}/K$ = growth in capital services,
$\dot{L}/L$ = growth in hours.

Uses and Limitations

Measures of output per hour (labor productivity), output per unit of capital (capital productivity), and output per combined unit of multifactor input (multifactor productivity) and related measures of costs are designed for use in economic analysis and public and private policy planning. The data are used in forecasting and analysis of prices, wages, and technological change.

The labor productivity, multifactor productivity, and related cost measures are useful in investigating the relationships between productivity, wages, prices, profits, and costs of production. As noted above, gross domestic product represents the sum of all production costs: Labor compensation, profits, depreciation, interest, rent, indirect business taxes, and other minor items. Unit labor costs, or compensation per unit of output, represent a major portion of total unit costs and reflect the combined effect of changes in output per hour and compensation per hour; thus, an increase in compensation per hour tends to increase unit labor costs while an increase in output per hour tends to reduce it, other things being equal. Therefore, through its impact on unit labor costs, output per hour is an important element in the wage-price relationship because it is an indicator of the extent to which compensation gains can occur without putting pressure on prices or reducing payments to other input factors.

Certain characteristics of the productivity and related cost data should be recognized in order to apply them appropriately to specific situations. First, the data for aggregate sectors reflect changes within various constituent industries as well as shifts in the relative importance of these industries: A portion of labor productivity growth from 1947 to the mid-1960's is attributable to the shift of workers from farm to nonfarm occupations. Second, the relationships among variables are often difficult to identify over short time periods. Third, data and other resources available for their preparation somewhat limit the productivity, output, compensation, and employment measures which can be constructed. In several sectors where output is difficult to define in a satisfactory way, productivity measures are correspondingly weak. Examples are the construction industry and the financial services sector, where output is an imputed value of labor and other inputs. The productivity and costs measures for these sectors should be interpreted with caution.

Technical References

Bureau of Labor Statistics

Productivity: A Selected Annotated Bibliography 1983-1987, Bulletin 2360, 1990.
Recent references concerning productivity and productivity measurement. Each reference includes a brief annotation.

The Impact of Research and Development of Productivity Growth, Bulletin 2331, 1989.
Presents annual measures of the stock of research and development and its contribution to productivity growth in the nonfarm business sector. The data cover 1948 to 1987.

Productivity: A Selected Annotated Bibliography 1979-1982, Bulletin 2212, 1984.
Over 1,400 references concerning productivity and productivity measurement. Each reference includes a brief annotation.

Trends in Multifactor Productivity, 1948-81, Bulletin 2178, 1983.
Presents BLS annual indexes of multifactor productivity for private business, private nonfarm business, and manufacturing for the period 1948 through 1981. Also presents BLS annual measures of output per unit of capital services input for the three sectors.

Fulco, L. J.; Harper, Michael; and Powers, Susan G. "Cyclicality in Labor Productivity Measures," *Monthly Labor Review*, forthcoming.
Analysis of the relationship between labor productivity and related variables over the business cycle to examine short run increasing returns to labor. No relationship between a fixed component of labor input and procyclical movements in labor productivity was found.

Gullickson, William. "Multifactor Productivity in U.S. Manufacturing Industries, 1948-88," *Monthly Labor Review*, forthcoming.
Updates multifactor productivity measures for each 2-digit SIC using gross output and inputs of capital, labor, energy, materials, and purchased business services.

Jablonski, Mary; Kunze, Kent; and Otto, Phyllis Flohr. "Hours at Work: A New Base for BLS Productivity Statistics," *Monthly Labor Review*, February 1990.
A description of the methodology used to develop measures of the ratio of hours at work to hours paid for the period 1948 to the present by linking the Hours at Work survey to early periodic surveys and unpublished data sources.

Harper, Michael J.; Berndt, Ernst R.; and Wood, David O. "Rates of Return and Capital Aggregation Using Alternative Rental Prices," in D.W. Jorgenson and R. London,

Technology and Capital Formation, MIT Press, 1989.
Examines the theoretical rationale for and empirical implementation of rental price formulas for use in weighting capital assets for multifactor productivity measurement.

Hulten, Charles R.; Robertson, James W.; and Wykoff, Frank C. "Energy, Obsolescence, and the Productivity Slowdown," in D.W. Jorgenson and R. London, *Technology and Capital Formation*, MIT Press, 1989.
An empirical examination of the hypothesis that high energy prices contributed to the post-1973 productivity slowdown by inducing capital obsolescence.

Dean, Edwin; Kunze, Kent; and Rosenblum, Larry. "Productivity Change and the Measurement of Heterogeneous Labor Inputs," prepared for Conference on New Measurement Procedures for U.S. Agricultural Productivity, March 1989.
Changes in the education and experience distribution of the workforce (based on a new model) show a modest contribution to productivity growth (0.2 percent annually) and very little explanation of the productivity slowdown.

Harper, Michael J. and Gullickson, William. "Cost Function Models and Accounting for Growth in U.S. Manufacturing, 1949-86," prepared for the National Bureau of Economic Research Summer Institute, 1989.
The effects of factor substitution induced by relative price changes on labor productivity are assessed using an econometric cost function model.

Powers, Susan G. "The Role of Capital Discards in Multifactor Productivity Measurement," *Monthly Labor Review*, June 1988.
Current measures of capital stocks do not reflect a firm's choice of when to discard capital. Capital stocks based on variations in capital discards over the business cycle are constructed. It is shown that multifactor productivity measures using these stocks do not significantly differ from the current productivity measures.

Dean, Edwin R. and Kunze, Kent. "United States Multifactor Productivity Growth, 1948-86," *Monthly Labor Review*, May 1988.
Presents growth rates of multifactor productivity for the periods 1948-73, 1973-79, and 1979-86 for private business, nonfarm business, and manufacturing. Analyzes trends in multifactor measures and describes data revisions and methodological improvements that have been incorporated into these measures.

Gullickson, William and Harper, Michael J. "Multifactor Productivity in 20 U.S. Manufacturing Industries, 1949-83," *Monthly Labor Review*, October 1987.
Presents multifactor productivity measures for 20 manufacturing industries and for total manufacturing, based on annual measures of output and inputs of capital, labor, energy, materials, and purchased business services. Analyzes multifactor growth rates in manufacturing industries.

Fulco, L. J. "U.S. Productivity Growth Since 1982: The Post-Recession Experience," *Monthly Labor Review*, December 1986.
A review of current developments in major sectors of the economy focusing on the first 14 quarters of the recovery phase of the business cycle. Contrasts experience during the recovery which began in the fourth quarter of 1982 with all previous post-World War II cycles.

Mark, Jerome A. "Problems Encountered in Measuring Single-Factor and Multifactor Productivity," *Monthly Labor Review*, December 1986.
Development of new data sources, better use of existing sources, and broader coverage are some of the ways in which BLS has improved its productivity measures; progress has been made, but inadequacies remain.

Sveikauskas, Leo. "The Contribution of R&D to Productivity Growth," *Monthly Labor Review*, March 1986.
Results of a BLS study suggest that the direct contribution of research and development to post-War productivity growth was between 0.1 and 0.2 percent annually in the nonfarm business sector; R&D had no substantial effect on the post-1973 productivity slowdown.

Fulco, L. J. "The Decline in Productivity During the First Half of 1985," *Monthly Labor Review*, December 1985.
A summary of movements in published major sectors: Business, nonfarm business, manufacturing, and nonfinancial corporations—during the first two quarters of 1985.

Fulco, L. J. "Productivity and Costs During 1984," *Monthly Labor Review*, June 1985. Annual review article for 1984.
Examines productivity movements during the year and charts changes in productivity, hourly compensation, and unit labor costs from 1973 forward.

Kunze, Kent. "A New BLS Survey Measures the Ratio of Hours Worked to Hours Paid," *Monthly Labor Review*, June 1984.
Hours at work accounted for about 93 percent of hours paid for production and nonsupervisory workers in 1982, according to an annual survey which includes only the time required to be on the job site, thereby excluding paid holidays, sick leave, and vacations.

Harper, Michael J. "The Measurement of Productive Capital Stock, Capital Wealth and Capital Services," BLS Working Paper No. 128, 1982.
Analysis of the computation of capital depreciation for productivity measurement.

Mark, Jerome A. and Waldorf, William H. "Multifactor Productivity: A New BLS Measure," *Monthly Labor Review*, December 1983.
Annual indexes for private business show that advances in multifactor productivity account for most of the growth of output per hour of all persons during 1948-81.

Other publications

Baily, Martin Neil and Gordon, Robert J. "Measurement Issues, the Productivity Slowdown, and the Explosion of Computer Power," *Brookings Papers on Economic Activity*. Washington, DC, The Brookings Institution, 1989.

Jorgenson, Dale; Gollop, Frank; and Fraumeni, Barbara. *Productivity and U.S. Economic Growth*, Cambridge, MA, The Harvard University Press, 1987.

Technical References—Continued

Denison, Edward F. *Trends in American Economic Growth, 1929-1982.* The Brookings Institution, Washington, DC, 1985.

Caves, Douglas W.; Christensen, Laurits R.; and Diewert, W. Erwin. "The Economic Theory of Index Numbers and the Measurement of Input, Output, and Productivity," *Econometrica,* Vol. 50, No. 6, 1983, pp. 1393-1414.

Kendrick, John W. and Vaccara, Beatrice N., editors. *New Developments in Productivity Measurement and Analysis.* Chicago, The University of Chicago Press, 1980.

Usher, Dan, ed. *The Measurement of Capital.* Chicago, The University of Chicago Press, 1980.

National Research Council's Panel to Review Productivity Statistics. *Measurement and Interpretation of Productivity.* Washington, DC, The National Academy of Sciences, 1979.

Christensen, Laurits and Jorgenson, Dale. "The Measurement of U.S. Real Capital Input, 1929-67," *Review of Income and Wealth,* December 1969.

Bureau of Labor Statistics
Hours at Work Report
Production Workers-BLS 2000P

U.S. Department of Labor

SEE ESTIMATED TIME FOR COMPLETION ON REVERSE SIDE

The information collected on this form by the Bureau of Labor Statistics will be held in confidence and will be used for statistical purposes only.

This report is authorized by law, 29 U.S.C. Your voluntary cooperation is needed to make the results of this survey comprehensive, accurate, and timely.

Form Approved
O.M.B. No. 1220-0076
Approval Expires 07/31/93

RETURN TO:
BUREAU OF LABOR STATISTICS
Room 2068, MAIL CODE 13
441 G STREET, NW
WASHINGTON, DC 20212

BLS Use Only
RC (9-10)

FOR ASSISTANCE CALL :

TELEPHONE ***COLLECT***:

REPORT FOR UNIT AT:

PLEASE READ BEFORE COMPLETING FORM

FAX NUMBER: (202) 523-2899

1. **ALL EMPLOYEES**-- Enter the total number of employees at this establishment during the payroll period that includes March 12, 1991.
2. **PRODUCTION WORKERS**-- Enter the number of employees who are not administrative or managerial.
3. **HOURS PAID**-- Enter the total number of hours for which **PRODUCTION WORKERS** were paid during each quarter. This includes all hours actually worked, ***PLUS*** paid holidays, vacation, sick days, jury duty, military leave, and other paid personal or administrative leave.
4. **HOURS AT WORK**-- Subtract from the **"HOURS PAID"** entry for each quarter the hours of paid leave time (holidays, vacation, sick days, jury duty, military leave, and other paid personal or administrative leave) and enter the difference in this column.

PLEASE SEE THE DETAILED DEFINITIONS/INSTRUCTIONS ON THE OTHER SIDE.

Number of Employees During Payroll Period Which Includes March 12, 1991	1. **ALL EMPLOYEES**	2. **PRODUCTION WORKERS**	BLS Use Only
	11-15	16-20	21-22

Hours Information for Production Workers Only QUARTERLY PERIOD	3. **HOURS PAID**	4. **HOURS AT WORK**	
First Quarter 1991 January - March	23-30	31-38	39-40
Second Quarter 1991 April - June	41-48	49-56	57-58
Third Quarter 1991 July - September	59-66	67-74	75-76
Fourth Quarter 1991 October - December	77-84	85-92	93-94
Annual Total 1991 January - December	95-103	104-112	113-114

5a. What records did you use to compile the above information? — 115

1 ☐ **Payroll** 2 ☐ **Personnel** 3 ☐ **Other** ____________

b. Are these records computerized? 1 ☐ **Yes** 2 ☐ **No** — 116

6. What types of paid leave do you offer? — 117-121

1 ☐ **Vacation** 2 ☐ **Sick** 3 ☐ **Holiday** 4 ☐ **Personal/Administrative** 5 ☐ **Other** 6 ☐ **None**

7. Enter below any unusual factors responsible for significant differences from normal hours worked during any quarter. Please indicate in which quarter these factors occurred. Examples are: more business, layoffs, strikes, fire, weather, seasonal, etc.

____

____

If questions arise concerning this report, whom should we contact? *(Please print)*			
NAME 122-146	TITLE	DATE	TELEPHONE 147-156 ( )

BLS 2000P (REV. SEPT. 1991)

1 - BLS COPY

INSTRUCTIONS FOR COMPLETING REPORT (BLS 2000P)

ESTIMATED TIME FOR COMPLETION

We estimate that it will take an average of 15 minutes to complete this information collection including time for reviewing instructions, searching existing data sources, gathering and maintaining the data needed, and completing and reviewing this information. If you have any comments regarding these estimates or any other aspect of this survey, send them to: Bureau of Labor Statistics, Division of Management Systems (1220-0076), 441 G Street NW, Washington, DC 20212, and to the Office of Management and Budget, Paperwork Reduction Project (1220-0076), Washington, DC 20503.

DATA REQUEST IS FOR CALENDAR YEAR 1991

ALL EMPLOYEES: Enter the total number of persons on the payroll(s) who worked full or part time or received pay for any part of the pay period which includes March 12, 1991. Check the appropriate box if: **1)** the establishment(s) closed down (either temporarily or permanently) during 1991. Provide the data for the time the establishment(s) was in operation. **2)** the establishment(s) merged or changed ownership. If you cannot provide the data for the entire year, enter the name and telephone number of whoever can provide the data for the payroll period which includes March 12, 1991, in the space below.

❑ TEMPORARILY CLOSED ❑ MERGED

❑ OUT OF BUSINESS ❑ CHANGED OWNERSHIP

CONTACT NAME: ______________________ TELEPHONE (   ) _____-__________

PRODUCTION WORKERS: Enter the total number of PRODUCTION WORKERS both full and part time on your payroll(s), whether wage or salaried, who worked during or received pay for any part of the pay period which includes March 12.

The term "production worker" refers to all occupational groups whose work is not primarily administrative or managerial, regardless of skill level, within the following industries: Mining and quarrying; crude petroleum, natural gas, and gasoline production; and the construction and manufacturing industries. These occupational groups include: Working supervisors and all nonsupervisory workers **(including group leaders and trainees)** engaged in excavation, hauling, trucking,hoisting, ventilation, drainage, pumping, drilling, blasting,loading, crushing, processing, inspection, storage, handling, warehousing, shipping, maintenance and repair, janitorial, record keeping, fabricating and assembly, as well as craft workers, mechanics, apprentices, helpers, laborers, plumbers, painters, plasterers, carpenters, masons, welders, or any of the special trades. Also include all other nonsupervisory employees whose services are closely associated with those of employees above.

The term "production worker" **excludes** employees engaged in the following activities: Executive, purchasing, finance, accounting, legal, personnel, cafeteria, medical, professional and technical activities, sales, advertising, credit collection, and in the installation and servicing of own products, routine office functions, and factory supervision **(above working supervisor's level). (Employees in the above activities, however, should be included in the ALL EMPLOYEES figure).**

QUARTERLY PERIOD: Normally, data will refer to the calendar quarter, i.e., from January 1 through March 31; April 1 through June 30; July 1 through September 30; and October 1 through December 31. If your records relate to a period other than the calendar quarter, please indicate beginning and closing dates.

HOURS PAID: **Include** all hours for which pay is received directly from the employer. **Include** paid vacation time, paid sick leave, paid holidays, and other paid personal or administrative leave (such as jury duty or military leave). If payments are made in lieu of time off, report the hours equivalent to the payments made. For example, 3 hours of leave time at two-thirds the regular rate should be reported as 2 hours paid. **Exclude** hours associated with unpaid leave, normal travel time from home to work, unpaid washup time, and unpaid meal time.

HOURS AT WORK: **Include** all time an employee is required to be on the employer's premises, on duty, or at a prescribed work place. **Include**, besides normal working hours, rest periods, stand-by time, downtime, travel time from job site during the working day, and travel time away from home if it cuts across the working day. ***Do not convert overtime or premium paid hours to straight-time-equivalent hours.***

NOTE: For survey purposes, **HOURS AT WORK** equals **HOURS PAID** less paid leave time (vacation, sick leave, holidays, and other paid personal or administrative leave).

ANNUAL TOTAL: The sum of **HOURS PAID** for each quarter should equal the **ANNUAL TOTAL, HOURS PAID** figure. Likewise, the sum of **HOURS AT WORK** for each quarter should equal the **ANNUAL TOTAL, HOURS AT WORK** figure.

Chapter 11. Productivity Measures: Industries and Government

Background

Studies of output per employee hour in individual industries have long been a part of the BLS program. A study of 60 manufacturing industries in 1898, prompted by congressional concern that human labor was being displaced by machinery, was presented in the report *Hand and Machine Labor;* this provided striking evidence of the savings in labor resulting from mechanization in the last half of the 19th century. The impact of productivity advance upon employment remained an important focus of BLS throughout the 1920's and 1930's. Also during this period, the Bureau began the preparation and publication of industry indexes of output per employee hour, which were based on available production data from the periodic *Census of Manufactures* and employment statistics collected by BLS.

In 1940, Congress authorized the Bureau of Labor Statistics to undertake continuing studies of productivity and technological changes. The Bureau extended earlier indexes of output per employee hour developed by the National Research Project of the Works Progress Administration, and published measures for selected industries. This work, however, was reduced in volume during World War II, owing to the lack of meaningful production and employee hour data for many manufacturing industries.

The advent of World War II also caused a change in the emphasis of the program from problems of unemployment to concern with the most efficient utilization of scarce labor resources. BLS undertook a number of studies of labor requirements for defense industries, such as synthetic rubber and shipbuilding. After the war, the industry studies program resumed on a regular basis, and was supplemented by a number of industry studies based on the direct collection of data from employers. Budget restrictions after 1952 prevented the continuation of direct collection of data. Consequently, the preparation of industry measures is largely limited to those industries where data are readily available.

In recent years, public interest in productivity has grown, and increases in output per employee hour have been recognized as important indicators of economic progress and a means to higher income levels, rather than merely a threat to job opportunities.

The industry studies cover a variety of manufacturing and nonmanufacturing industries at the 2-, 3-, and 4-digit Standard Industrial Classification levels. Measures for these industries are published on an annual basis and are provided for periods beginning as early as 1947 and continuing through the most recent year for which data are available.

Coverage includes industries in the manufacturing, mining, trade, transportation, communication, public utilities, finance, and business and personal services sectors. Productivity measures for selected government functions, and the Federal Government as a whole, are published annually. In addition, productivity measures are published for selected service areas of State and local governments.

The Bureau has been expanding its industry productivity measurement program by developing measures which include other inputs besides labor. The industry multifactor productivity indexes measure changes in an industry's output in relation to changes in labor, capital, and intermediate purchases. In addition to providing indicators of productivity change useful for analysis in their own right, such measures also are helpful in analyzing the causes of change in output per hour.

Labor Productivity Measures

Concepts

Indexes of output per employee hour measure changes in the relationship between an industry's output and the employee hours expended in producing that output. BLS computes an index of output per employee hour by dividing an output index by an index of aggregate employee hours. For most manufacturing industries, measures are prepared separately relating output to all employee hours and all employees. Since industries in trade and services often have a substantial number of self-employed and unpaid family workers in addition to employees, measures for these industries relate output to all-person hours and all persons.

The output per employee hour measures relate output to one input—labor time; they do not measure the specific contribution of labor, capital, or any other factor of production. Rather, they reflect the joint effect of a number of interrelated influences such as changes in technology, capital investment per worker, utilization of capacity, intermediate inputs per worker, layout and flow of material, skill and effort of the work force, managerial skill, and labor-management relations.

For an industry producing a single uniform output, this index of productivity may be expressed as follows:

$$P_i = \frac{q_i}{q_o} \div \frac{L_i}{L_o} = \frac{q_i(q_o l_o)}{q_o(q_i l_i)} = \frac{l_o}{l_i}$$

where:

P_i = the index of productivity or output per employee hour in the current year

q_i and q_o = the output quantities in the current and base years, respectively

L_i = the aggregate employee hours in the current year

L_o = the aggregate employee hours in the base year

l_i = unit labor requirement in the current year

l_o = unit labor requirement in the base year

Thus, for an industry producing a single uniform output, the index of productivity turns out to be simply the ratio of the unit labor requirement in the base year to the unit labor requirement in the current year. If l_o is greater (less) than l_i, the ratio (or productivity) is said to have increased (decreased) over the time period studied.

For an industry producing a number of different products or services (the more typical case), the output per employee hour index is the ratio for two periods of the total hours required to produce a given composite of products or services. Indexes of such industries vary with the composite and can take many forms. Two of these forms are:

a. Using a current-period composite

$$P_i = \frac{\Sigma q_i l_o}{\Sigma q_i l_i}$$

b. Using a base-period composite

$$P_i = \frac{\Sigma q_o l_o}{\Sigma q_o l_i}$$

An index constructed according to (a) compares the employee hours that would have been required in the base year to produce the current composite with the hours actually expended in their production. An index constructed according to (b) compares the employee hours that were expended in the base year to produce the base-year composite with the hours that would have been required in the current year to produce the same composite. Thus, these composite indexes eliminate the effects of shifts, over time, in the relative importance of products or services on output per hour.

In either form, an index of output per employee hour expressed as the quotient of an index of weighted output and an index of employee hours becomes:

$$\frac{\text{Output index (Laspeyres)}}{\text{Employee hours index}} = \text{Output per employee hour index (Paasche)}$$

$$P_i = \frac{\Sigma\, l_o\, q_i}{\Sigma\, l_o\, q_o} \div \frac{\Sigma\, l_i\, q_i}{\Sigma\, l_o\, q_o} = \frac{\Sigma\, l_o\, q_i}{\Sigma\, l_i\, q_i}$$

$$\frac{\text{Output index (Paasche)}}{\text{Employee hours index}} = \text{Output per employee hour index (Laspeyres)}$$

$$P_i = \frac{\Sigma\, l_i\, q_i}{\Sigma\, l_i\, q_o} \div \frac{\Sigma\, l_i\, q_i}{\Sigma\, l_o\, q_o} = \frac{\Sigma\, l_o\, q_o}{\Sigma\, l_i\, q_o}$$

The employee hours index measures the change in aggregate employee hours between the base and current periods. The employee hours data are the total hours expended by employees in establishments classified in the industry to produce the base-period and current-period composites.

As can be seen in the formulas, the appropriate output index is one which compares the quantities of the various products or services in the current and the base periods, each weighted by the employee hours expended per unit produced in a given period. A current-period weighted output per hour index uses a base-period weighted output index divided by the employee hours index. Conversely, a base-period weighted output per employee hour index is consistent with an output index which utilizes current-period weights.

Methods and Sources

Industries

Output

BLS industry output indexes are based on physical or deflated value of production of an industry combined with fixed-period weights. Whenever possible, physical quantities are used as the unit of measurement. For those industries lacking quantity data, constant-dollar value of shipments, sales, or revenue data are used to develop the output series. Quantity data on physical output are usually most comprehensive for years covered by an economic census. To make maximum use of the comprehensive census data, output indexes are derived from data for two consecutive censuses; these indexes are referred to as benchmark indexes. For intercensal years, annual indexes are based on either physical output data (generally in less detail than for census years) or, if such data are not available, value of output adjusted for price change (the value of output in constant dollars). The annual series subsequently are adjusted to the benchmark levels for the census years.

Weights. In order to derive a labor productivity index for an industry that is a mean of the productivity movements of the component outputs, the various products are combined with unit employee hour weights. Such weights are derived from special surveys or from data for specialized establishments published in the *Census of Manufactures.* In some industries, however, unit employee hour information is not available for individual products. In these cases, BLS uses substitute weights when it is believed that they are proportional to unit employee hour weights; these are usually unit value weights. Unit value weights are computed from census or survey data on the quantity and value of shipments of the primary products of the industry. The introduction of these substitute weights results in an industry output per employee hour index which reflects shifts in value per employee hour of the various products in the industry. Thus, a change can occur in the index without any change in the output per employee hour for any product of the industry.

The extent to which error or bias may be introduced by the use of unit value weights is not known. The index is equivalent to one weighted with unit employee hours if the unit employee hours and unit values among the products are proportional. There is evidence that unit values are fairly reliable approximations for individual products in instances where wages constitute a large proportion of total value of output. An error generated in the output index by an error in the substitute weights usually is considerably smaller than any error in the weights themselves.

In some industries, unit value weights for specific products and unit employee hour weights for product groups are used at different stages in constructing the industry output indexes. When this procedure is used, the individual products are first aggregated into product group indexes with unit value weights. These indexes are then combined into an industry output index with product group employee hours. The product group employee hours relate to a base period, as do the value weights.

To obtain product group employee hour weights, total employee hours for plants specializing in each product class, derived from published census data on production worker hours and nonproduction worker employment, are supplemented by unpublished BLS estimates of nonproduction worker hours. (See section on employee hours later in this chapter for the procedures used to estimate nonproduction worker employee hours.)

Most published industry indexes have used: 1947 weights for the 1947-58 period, 1958 weights for 1959-63, 1963 weights for 1964-67, 1967 weights for 1968-72, 1972 weights for 1973-77, 1977 weights for 1978-82, 1982 weights for 1983-87, and 1987 weights for years after 1987. The Bureau updates the weights as data become available from the periodic censuses.

Benchmark indexes. For many manufacturing, mining, trade, and service industries, indexes reflecting changes in output between census years are constructed. These are called benchmark indexes and are generally available for the nonregulated industries for which census data are collected.

For manufacturing industries, the procedure for developing benchmark output indexes involves several levels of aggregation. First, value-of-shipments indexes for 5-digit SIC product class groups are derived by the deflated-value method. Next, these product class indexes are combined with employee hour weights to derive an industry shipments index. Additionally, to develop an industry production index, adjustments are made to reflect both inventory and coverage changes.

Benchmark indexes are developed every 5 years based on data from the quinquennial *Census of Manufacturers.* The most recent benchmark, 1982-87, is developed using the following procedure.

At the 5-digit level, current value indexes are derived by dividing the current-year value of shipments by the base-year value of shipments. The value of shipments include both primary and secondary products and are obtained from Census table 5A, Industry Statistics by Industry and Primary Product Class Specialization.

Where available, 5-digit BLS producer price indexes (PPI's) are used to deflate current value indexes, resulting in product class quantity indexes. In the absence of PPI's other BLS price indexes or Census 7-digit unit value relatives are used as deflators.

The resulting product-class quantity indexes are combined with employee hour weights to develop an industry quantity-of-shipments index. Total employee hours for plants specializing in each 5-digit product class are derived from data on production worker hours, number of nonproduction workers (as reported in the *Census of Manufacturers)* and from BLS estimates of average annual hours of nonproduction workers. Employee hour weights for 1982 are used for the 1982-87 benchmark.

The industry quantity-of-shipments index is adjusted for inventory change and "coverage." The change in finished goods and work in process is added to the value of shipments to derive an estimated value of production. The value of production is divided by the value of shipments to obtain an inventory adjustment ratio. The industry quantity-of-shipments index is multiplied by the inventory adjustment ratio, resulting in a production index. To represent the total output of the industry, this production index is further adjusted for "coverage" inasmuch as not all industry shipments are captured in the product class statistics. The coverage adjustment used is the ratio of the total industry shipments to the measured portion of the 5-digit product class shipments.

Benchmark indexes for the mining industries are computed from data as reported in the *Census of Mineral Industries.* For trade and service industries, benchmark indexes are computed from sales data reported in the *Census of Business.*

Annual indexes. Annual output indexes are constructed by the following procedures. The annual indexes are adjusted, if necessary, to the levels of the benchmark indexes previously described. The adjustment factors for 2 census years are used to determine the adjustment factors for the intervening years by linear interpolation.

1. *Physical output.* Most physical output indexes are based on quantities of products combined with fixed-period unit employee hour or unit value weights. The basic quantity data are generally primary products of an industry classified into product groups; the finest level of detail available is used. The quantity data relate to primary products "wherever made" and, in some cases, to shipments of the products.

The Bureau's annual measures of production are constructed from data on physical quantities of products which comprise a high percent of the total value of an industry's output. Coverage varies between 80 and 100 percent.

2. *Deflated value.* When physical quantity data are not used, indexes are derived from data on the value of industry output adjusted for price change. Since the adjustment for price change is most often downward, the indexes usually are called "deflated value" indexes. Such indexes are conceptually equivalent to indexes which use data on physical quantities of products combined with unit value weights. These indexes are derived by dividing the value of an industry's output by an industry price index. An index of these deflated values shows the change in the real value of output between the past and current periods.[1]

For manufacturing industries, the value of shipments for each primary product (wherever made) is deflated by an appropriate price index. BLS industry sector price indexes (ISPI's) and producer price indexes (PPI's) are used if available. If these product-class price indexes are not available, deflators are developed by weighting together individual PPI's with base-year value of shipments' weights.

Indexes of the constant dollar values at the product class level are combined into a wherever-made product index by weighting the indexes with the base-year employee hour weights.

For each year, special coverage ratios for the industry (total value of industry shipments of all products, to total value of primary products wherever made) are used to adjust the wherever-made indexes to the industry basis. The resultant industry indexes are further adjusted by the ratio of total value of industry production to total value of industry shipments to reflect changes in inventories. These adjustments yield the estimated industry indexes of production.

For industries in trade and services, data on the value of sales for each year are divided by a specially constructed industry price index to derive a measure of the change in the industries' real output. These industry price indexes are, for the most part, producer and consumer price indexes developed by BLS.

Sources. Industry output indexes are prepared from basic data published by various public and private agencies, using the greatest level of detail available.

Data from the Bureau of the Census, U.S. Department of Commerce, are used extensively in developing output statistics for manufacturing, trade, and service industries. The Bureau of Mines, U.S. Department of the Interior, compiles most of the information for the mining and cement industries. Other important Government sources include the U.S. Department of Energy, the U.S. Department of Agriculture, the U.S. Department of Transportation, the U.S. Department of the Treasury, the Interstate Commerce Commission, the Federal Railroad Administration, the Federal Reserve Board, the Federal Deposit Insurance Corporation, and the U.S. Department of Housing and Urban Development. Important sources of trade association data include the Textile Economics Bureau, Inc., National Association of Hosiery Manufacturers, Inc., National Canners Association, Rubber Manufacturers Association, the American Iron and Steel Institute, Association of American Railroads, Ward's Communications, Rice Miller's Association, National Automobile Dealers Association, Pharmaceutical Manufacturers Association, American Bus Association, International Sleep Products Association, American Truck Association, American Paper Institute, Anti Friction Bearing Manufacturers' Association, Fiber Box Association, Institutional Furniture Manufacturers' Association, VISA-CARD Network and Interbank Card Network Association, National Automatic Clearing House Association, Agricultural Chemicals Association, Association of Oil Pipelines, and the American Gas Association.

Employee hours

An index of employee hours is computed by dividing the aggregate employee hours for each year by the base-period aggregate. Because of data limitations, employee hours are treated as homogeneous and additive with no distinction made between hours of different groups of employees. For industries in which the self-employed are important, indexes are constructed for the hours of all persons, which includes paid employees, partners, proprietors, and unpaid family workers.

[1] For example:
Value index/Price index (Paasche) = Output index (Laspeyres)

$$\frac{\Sigma p_i q_i}{\Sigma p_o q_o} \div \frac{\Sigma p_i q_i}{\Sigma p_o q_i} = \frac{\Sigma p_o q_i}{\Sigma p_o q_o}$$

where p_i and p_o represent prices of products in the industry in the current and base periods, respectively. This index requires quantities of all items produced in each year. These data are not available for the particular industries where this measure is used, and quantity data are usually available for the base year only. Accordingly, the deflated value indexes employed usually take the following form:
Value index/Price index (Laspeyres) = Output index (Paasche)

$$\frac{\Sigma p_i q_i}{\Sigma p_o q_o} \div \frac{\Sigma p_i q_o}{\Sigma p_o q_o} = \frac{\Sigma p_i q_i}{\Sigma p_i q_o}$$

Sources. Industry employment and employee hour indexes are developed from basic data compiled by the Bureau of Labor Statistics, the Bureau of the Census, and other sources. For most private nonagricultural industries, BLS publishes employment and average weekly hours data for production or nonsupervisory workers and employment data for all employees. The Bureau of the Census publishes employment and aggregate hours data for production workers and employment data for all employees.

BLS and the Bureau of the Census differ in their definition of employee hours and in their sampling and reporting methods. In general, BLS data are the preferred source for measuring industry employment and hours. Census employment is the average of production workers plus the number of other employees in mid-March. The number of production workers is the average for the payroll periods for the 12th of March, May, August, and November. In contrast, the BLS (790) employment statistics program is a cooperative Federal and State project. Employment and hours are collected monthly and are benchmarked each year to comprehensive data from the State unemployment insurance programs.

Only employment data are available for nonproduction workers. The average annual hours of these workers must be estimated. The estimates of aggregate nonproduction worker employee hours for the manufacturing industries are derived from published employment data, and estimates of average annual hours worked or paid per nonproduction worker.

For years prior to 1968, the estimates of average annual hours worked were calculated by multiplying the number of workweeks in the year times the scheduled weekly hours. This produced an estimate of annual hours paid. Estimated hours for vacations, holidays, disability, and personal time off were subtracted from average annual hours paid to obtain an estimate for average annual hours worked.

Estimated hours for vacations, holidays, and disabilities were based on data from various BLS surveys and studies of the U.S. Department of Health and Human Services. Personal time off was estimated as a constant from references in relevant publications.

From 1968 to 1977, the estimates of average annual hours paid and hours worked were based on data collected in the BLS biennial surveys of employee compensation in the private nonfarm economy. Since these surveys are no longer conducted, the 1977 levels are being carried forward until other data become available.

For the mining industries, estimates for the hours of nonproduction workers are based on data collected by the Mine Safety and Health Administration. For the trade and service industries, estimates are made for the hours of partners, proprietors, and unpaid family workers using unpublished data collected in the Current Population Survey, and for supervisory workers using data from the *Census of Population.*

All-employee hours estimates for manufacturing industries are derived by summing the aggregate hours for production workers and the estimated aggregate hours for nonproduction workers. For trade and service industries, all-person hours estimates are derived by summing the aggregate hours for paid employees and the estimated aggregate hours for partners, proprietors, and unpaid family workers.

Comparability of output and employee hours data

For manufacturing industries, employee hours data are based on total employee hours of establishments classified in an industry. Annual physical output data, however, usually include the products which are primary to an industry that are reported on a "wherever made" basis. Thus, there can be some discrepancy in the coverage of output and employee hours measures. This is not a serious problem unless there is considerable variation from year to year in the proportion of primary products to total products of an industry, or if there is a change in the proportion of primary products which are made in other industries. The comparability of the employee hours and output data is indicated by the specialization and coverage ratios which the Bureau of the Census publishes.[2] All industries in the BLS industry measurement program have high and stable specialization and coverage ratios.

In selecting industries for the measurement program, attention is also given to changes in the degree of vertical integration. Employee hours relate to all operations performed by establishments of an industry, while output usually is measured in terms of the final product. If establishments undertake additional operations (such as the manufacture of components which had previously been purchased from suppliers) employee hours will increase but there will be no corresponding increase in final output. Thus, output per employee hour indexes would be biased. In developing industry indexes, BLS examines data such as the ratio of cost of materials to value of shipments for

[2] The "specialization ratio" is the value of shipments of primary products of plants in the industry expressed as a percent of total shipments of all products (primary plus secondary) made by these same establishments. The "coverage ratio" is the value of shipments of the primary products made by plants classified in the industry as a percent of the total shipments of the industry's primary products made by all producers, both in and out of the specified industry.

any indication of a change in the degree of vertical integration.

Government

Federal

Indexes of output per employee year, output, and employee years for selected functional areas of Government[3] and for over 300 participating organizations are constructed in a manner similar to that described for industries. At the present time, these measures cover about 64 percent (2.0 million employee years) of the Executive Branch civilian work force.

Ideally, a productivity index should relate final outputs to their associated direct and indirect input(s), and, in fact, the output data are final from the perspective of the functional areas within which these data are classified. However, since the outputs of one organization may be consumed wholly or partially by another Federal organization in the production of its final outputs, all output indicators in the measured portion of the Federal Government may not be final from the perspective of a higher level of organization (for example, the entire Federal Government). Therefore, the overall statistics do not represent "Federal productivity" but rather, the weighted average of the productivity changes of the measured Federal organizations.

Through an annual collection process, most data are submitted directly by agencies to BLS, but in some cases data are obtained from secondary sources such as agency budgets and annual reports. In the Federal measure, about 2,500 products and services are aggregated into output indexes by combining the quantities of each type of output by their respective base-year labor requirements. These weights are constructed from the detailed output and input data provided by each organization. Although the weights relate to fixed periods, they are updated every 5 years. The output segments are linked and referenced to a fiscal year 1982 base.

The organizational indexes are grouped into 28 government functions, based on similarity of activity. Some of these functions, such as printing and duplication, are more homogeneous than others, such as general support services, which include many diverse activities. Nonetheless, these categories provide insight into the trends for the major functional areas underlying the overall measure. Although productivity, output, and input indexes are constructed for each participating organization, these are not published but are returned to each organization for its own use (for example, to stimulate further examination of the causes of productivity change within each organization). This is one method used by BLS to validate the basic data (that is, by examining the reasonableness of the derived trends).

Employee year indexes are developed from agency data submissions and secondary sources. As in all labor input measures used by the Bureau to develop productivity indexes, employee years are considered homogeneous and additive. Each employee year reflects the regularly scheduled time, overtime, and leave time of all full-time, part-time, or intermittent employees. An employee year is equivalent to one individual paid for 2,087 hours.

State and local

Government measurements are being extended to include indexes of output per employee year, output, and employee years for selected State and local services. A cross-section of services is being examined and indexes computed using concepts and methods similar to those for industries and the Federal Government. This research, which uses published and readily available secondary data, is keyed to the Standard Industrial Classification system.

Output indexes reflect final services to the public. The consequences or effectiveness of government service are not measured. The focus is on government production. Prison system outputs, for example, are the number of prisoners housed and to whom treatment is administered, not the effectiveness of rehabilitation or community safety. Output data are taken from Federal agencies such as the Departments of Labor, Justice, and Transportation and industry groups such as the American Public Power Association, American Public Transit Association, and Distilled Spirits Council of the U.S.

Employee year index computations use the same general concepts as those found in the Federal measurements. The primary source of employment data is the Bureau of the Census' Annual Public Employment Survey. This is supplemented by data from Federal agencies and industry associations when available.

Multifactor Productivity Measures

Concepts

The industry multifactor productivity indexes calculate productivity growth by measuring changes in the relationship between the quantity of an industry's output and the quantity of inputs consumed in producing that output, where measured inputs include capital and intermediate purchases (including raw materials, purchased services, and purchased energy) as well as labor input.

The index used to calculate multifactor productivity is the Tornqvist index and is of the form:

[3] The 28 functions are: Audit of operations; buildings and grounds; communications; education and training; electric power production and distribution; equipment maintenance; finance and accounting; general support services; information services; legal and judicial activities; library services; loans and grants; medical services; military base services; natural resources and environmental management; personnel investigations; personnel management; postal services; printing and duplication; procurement; records management; regulation—compliance and enforcement; regulation—rulemaking and licensing; social services and benefits; specialized manufacturing; supply and inventory control; traffic management; and transportation.

$$\ln\left(\frac{A_t}{A_{t-1}}\right) = \ln\left(\frac{Q_t}{Q_{t-1}}\right) - \left[W_K\left(\ln\frac{K_t}{K_{t-1}}\right) + W_L\left(\ln\frac{L_t}{L_{t-1}}\right) + W_{IP}\left(\ln\frac{IP_t}{IP_{t-1}}\right)\right]$$

where:

$\ln$ = the natural logarithm of the variable

A = multifactor productivity

Q = output

K = capital input

L = labor input

IP = intermediate purchases input

W_K, W_L, W_{IP} = compensation share weights

The weights are the means of the compensation shares (S) in two adjoining time periods.

$$W_i = \frac{(S_i^t + S_i^{t-1})}{2}$$

where:

$$S_i^t = \frac{P_i^t X_i^t}{\Sigma(P_i^t X_i^t)}$$

P_i^t = price of input X_i in period t

The Tornqvist formula yields growth rates which are differences in logarithms. The antilogs of these rates are chained together to form the index.

Methods and Sources

Output

The multifactor productivity output measures are calculated using, whenever possible, the same units of products or services of the industry as are used in measuring output for the industry labor productivity measures. Whenever possible, physical quantities are used as the unit of measurement; when physical quantities are unavailable, constant-dollar value of shipments, sales, or revenue data are used. The multifactor productivity output measures differ from the labor productivity output measures primarily in the method used for weighting together the various categories of output, as explained below.

Weights. The multifactor productivity output measure uses price weights for combining the various categories of output of an industry. The price of each output category is multiplied by its corresponding quantity and then expressed as a share of the total value of output. These value shares are averaged at time t and t-1.

Sources. Data sources are the same as those used in calculating indexes for the labor productivity measures.

Employee hours

Employee hour indexes are calculated in the same way as those used in measuring industry labor productivity. As with the labor productivity measure, employee hours are treated as homogeneous and additive with no distinction made between hours of different groups of employees. The index is computed by simply dividing the aggregate employee hours for each year by the base-period total.

Sources. Data sources are the same as those used in calculating employee hour indexes for the labor productivity measures.

Capital

The measure of capital input is based on the flow of services derived from the stock of physical assets. Physical capital is composed of equipment, structures, land, and inventories. Financial capital is excluded. Capital services are estimated by calculating capital stocks; changes in the stocks are assumed proportional to changes in capital services for each asset. Stocks of different asset types are Tornqvist-aggregated, using estimated rental prices to construct the weights for assets of different types.

Capital stocks are calculated using the perpetual inventory method, which takes into account the continual additions to and subtractions from the stock of capital as new investment and retirement of old capital take place. The perpetual inventory method measures stocks at the end of a year equal to a weighted sum of all past investments, where the weights are the asset's efficiency relative to a new asset. A hyperbolic age-efficiency function is used to calculate the relative efficiency of an asset at different ages. The hyperbolic age-efficiency function can be expressed:

$$S_t = (L - t) / (L - (B)t)$$

where:

S_t = the relative efficiency of a t-year-old asset

L = the service life

t = the age of the asset

B = the parameter of efficiency decline

The parameter of efficiency decline is assumed to be 0.5 for equipment and 0.75 for structures. These parameters yield a function in which assets lose efficiency more slowly at first, then rapidly later in life.

Stocks of equipment, structures, inventories, and land are estimated separately. Individual price deflators for each asset category are constructed and used to convert the current-dollar investment to constant dollars. Industry-specific service lives are computed for each type of equipment asset for use in the perpetual inventory method.

Current-dollar values of inventory stocks are calculated for three separate categories of manufacturers' inventories: Finished goods, work in process, and materials and supplies. Inventory stocks for each year are calculated as the average of the end-of-year stocks in years t and t-1 to represent the average utilized during the year as a whole. This is also done with equipment, structures, and land. Current-dollar inventory values for the three categories of inventories are deflated with appropriate price indexes.

Land stocks are estimated as a function of the movement in constant-dollar gross structures stocks for the given industry.

Weights. The various equipment, structure, inventory, and land stock series in constant dollars are aggregated into one capital input measure using estimated rental prices to construct the weights. Rental prices are calculated for each asset as:

$$RP = [(P \times R) + (P \times D) - (P^{t} - P^{t-1})] \times (1\text{-}uz\text{-}k)/(1\text{-}u)$$

where:

RP = the rental price

P = the deflator for the given asset type

R = the internal rate of return

D = the rate of depreciation for a given asset type

$P^{t}\text{-}P^{t-1}$ = the capital gain term for the asset

(l-uz-k)/(l-u) reflects the effects of taxation where:

u = the corporate tax rate

z = the present value of $1 of depreciation deductions

k = the effective investment tax credit rate

This method of calculating rental prices is similar to that used in calculating multifactor productivity for major sectors of the economy except that no attempt is made incorporate the effects of indirect business taxes, for which data are lacking at the industry level.

The rental prices are expressed in rates per constant dollar of productive capital stocks. Each rental price is multiplied by its constant-dollar capital stock to obtain current-dollar capital costs which are then converted to value shares for Tornqvist aggregation.

Sources. Industry capital indexes are developed from basic data published and maintained by the Bureau of the Census and the Bureau of Economic Analysis, U.S. Department of Commerce; and the Office of Employment Projections, Bureau of Labor Statistics. Price indexes are derived from producer price indexes developed by BLS.

Intermediate purchases

The index of intermediate purchases input is a Tornqvist aggregate of separate indexes of change in real materials, services, fuels, and electricity consumed by an industry. With the exception of electricity, for which both price and quantity data are available, the above indexes are calculated by dividing annual current-dollar values by appropriate price indexes to obtain constant-dollar annual estimates. Separate price deflators for materials and fuels for each industry are constructed using detailed price and value data for individual subcomponents of each group. The aggregate deflators are divided into the current-dollar values to derive constant-dollar estimates. The constant-dollar series for each component are indexed by dividing each year's estimate by the base-period aggregate.

Weights. The indexes of change in real materials, services, fuels, and electricity are weighted together with value share weights to derive an aggregate intermediate purchases index. These weights are derived by dividing the current-dollar values of each by the total combined value of intermediate purchases, and averaging these weights at times t and t-1.

Sources. Industry intermediate purchases indexes are developed from basic data published by the Bureau of the Census and the Bureau of Economic Analysis.

Weights for major input components

The indexes representing quantity change for each of the three major inputs are weighted together to compute the index of combined inputs. The relative weights for each year are derived from total costs for each input. All employee labor costs from Census data are used for the labor weight. The sum of current-dollar values for materials, services, fuels, and electricity constitute the weight for intermediate purchases. The weight for capital is derived by subtracting labor costs and an estimate of purchased services from Census value-added data. These compensation shares are averaged at time t and t-1.

Presentation

BLS industry and government indexes are published annually in the bulletin, *Productivity Measures for Selected Industries and Government Services.* A limited amount of the most current data is provided in an annual news release. As new industry indexes are developed, they are presented as articles in the *Monthly Labor Review.* The articles contain an analysis of productivity, output, and employment trends in the industry. Technical notes describing the methodology used to develop the indexes are available on request. Unpublished indexes for all 4-, 3-, and 2-digit SIC manufacturing industries are available for analytical purposes upon request.

Indexes of output per employee hour also are published in the *Statistical Abstract of the United States* and in the *Handbook of Labor Statistics,* and are available in the Bureau's LABSTAT database, and on BLS data diskettes. Some indexes for earlier years are published in *Historical Statistics of the United States.*

BLS Federal Government indexes are also available in the *Handbook of Labor Statistics,* on LABSTAT data tapes, and on BLS data diskettes. More detailed Federal data and State and local government data are available from BLS.

Uses and Limitations

Measures of output per employee hour are particularly useful for studying changes in labor use, projecting future employment requirements, analyzing trends in labor costs, comparing productivity progress among countries, examining the effects of technological improvements on employment and unemployment, and analyzing related economic and industrial activities. Such analysis usually requires that indexes of output per employee hour be used in conjunction with other data. Specifically, related data on production and employment are useful in studying technological effects; to study trends in labor costs, data on earnings and other labor expenditures are necessary.

These productivity measures of output per employee hour are subject to certain qualifications. First, existing techniques may not fully take into account changes in the quality of goods and services produced. Second, although efforts have been made to maintain consistency of coverage between the output and labor input estimates, some statistical differences may remain. Third, changes in the degree of plant integration and specialization often are not reflected adequately in the production statistics. This may result in overstatement of productivity gains in some years and understatement in others. Fourth, estimates of nonproduction worker hours are subject to a wider margin of error than are the estimates of production worker hours because of the technique for estimating average employee hours of nonproduction workers. Errors in estimating hours of nonproduction workers, however, have a relatively insignificant effect on the estimates of hours for all employees. Fifth, industries in which all person hours are used as the denominator are subject to a wider margin of error because of the limited data available for unpaid family workers, the self-employed, and paid managers. Finally, year-to-year changes in output per employee hour are irregular, and, therefore, are not necessarily indicative of basic changes in long-term trends. Conversely, long-term trends are not necessarily applicable to any one year or to any period in the future. Because of these and other statistical limitations, these indexes cannot be considered precise measures; instead they should be interpreted as general indicators of movements of output per employee hour.

The output per hour measures relate output to only one input—labor time—as noted earlier. They reflect the joint effect of a number of influences including changes in technology, capital per worker, utilization of capacity, intermediate inputs per worker, layout and flow of material, skill and effort of the workforce, managerial skill, and labor-management relations. Indexes of multifactor productivity are subject to many of the same limitations previously mentioned with the exception of the effects of changes in the ratio of other factor inputs to labor. The construction of multifactor productivity measures permits an analysis of the effects of the changes in capital per hour and intermediate purchases per hour on output per hour. Labor productivity is related to multifactor productivity in the manner given by the following formula:

$$\ln\left(\frac{Q_t}{Q_{t-1}}\right) - \ln\left(\frac{L_t}{L_{t-1}}\right) = \ln\left(\frac{A_t}{A_{t-1}}\right) + W_K\left[\ln\left(\frac{K_t}{K_{t-1}}\right) - \ln\left(\frac{L_t}{L_{t-1}}\right)\right] + W_{IP}\left[\ln\left(\frac{IP_t}{IP_{t-1}}\right) - \ln\left(\frac{L_t}{L_{t-1}}\right)\right]$$

Labor productivity, on the left side of the equation above, is the difference between the rate of change in output and the rate of change in labor input. On the right side of the equation are the rates of change in multifactor productivity, and the rates of change in the weighted capital-labor ratio and the weighted intermediate-purchases-labor ratio. Thus, changes in labor productivity can be analyzed in terms of changes in multifactor productivity versus changes in the inputs of capital relative to labor and intermediate purchases relative to labor.

Technical References

Bureau of Labor Statistics

Fisk, Donald M. *Measuring Productivity in State and Local Government,* BLS Bulletin 2166, December 1983.

Reports on a study of ways that national labor productivity trends might be calculated for State and local government. Reviews past research and studies, examines available national data, and outlines a strategy for further work.

Kutscher, Ronald E. and Mark, Jerome A. "The Service Producing Sector: Some Common Perceptions Reviewed," *Monthly Labor Review,* April 1983.

Compares the growth in output per hour in the service-producing industries to the goods-producing industries. Also examines the level of capital intensity in each sector and the underlying employment shifts between the two sectors.

Mark, Jerome A. "Industry Indexes of Output Per Man-Hour," *Monthly Labor Review,* November 1962.

Describes the methods used in constructing BLS indexes of output per employee hour. Covers methods and sources, construction of production and employee hour indexes, and limitations.

Sherwood, Mark. "Multifactor Productivity in the Steel and Motor Vehicle Industries," *Monthly Labor Review,* August, 1987.

Describes new multifactor productivity measures for two industries. Explains the relationship of multifactor productivity to labor productivity and discusses underlying trends in output and inputs of labor, capital, and intermediate purchases.

Siegel, Irving H. "Concepts and Measurement of Production and Productivity," Working Paper of the National Conference on Productivity, Bureau of Labor Statistics, U.S. Department of Labor, 1952.

Provides a foundation for the methods and concepts describing the construction of labor productivity indexes and measures.

Other publications

Dean, Edwin R. and Kunze, Kent. "Productivity Measurement in Service Industries," Conference on Output Measurement in the Service Sector, May 1990.

Describes the method for the construction of industry productivity measure in the service sector. Compares BLS industry output measures with industry output measures developed by the Bureau of Economic Analysis for service sector industries.

Forte, Darlene. "Measuring Federal Government Productivity," *Handbook for Productivity Measurement and Improvement,* forthcoming.

Discusses the Federal Productivity Measurement System including the history of the program, the measurement process and problems, and output developement and weighting. Includes a description of the 28 government functions that are published on an annual basis.

Kendrick, John W. and Vaccara, Beatrice N., eds. *New Developments in Productivity Measurement and Analysis,* Studies in Income and Wealth, Vol. 44. Chicago, The University of Chicago Press, 1980.

Collection of papers on such subjects as labor and multifactor productivity by industry; productivity in selected service sectors; and international comparisons of productivity. Includes a study of high and low productivity establishments; current efforts to measure productivity in the public sector; effects of research and development on industry productivity growth; and energy and pollution effects on productivity and international comparisons of economic growth.

National Academy of Sciences. *Measurement and Interpretation of Productivity,* Washington DC, 1979.

Collection of papers on such topics as the concepts and measurement of productivity; the limitations of productivity statistics; the measurement of outputs and inputs; the sources of economic growth; measures of company productivity; and international comparisons of productivity.

Siegel, Irving H. "On the Design of Constant Output and Input Indexes for Productivity Measurement," Conference on Research in Income and Wealth, *A Report of the National Bureau of Economic Research,* Princeton University Press, 1961, pp. 23-41.

Discusses the choice of index-number formulas that can be used in measuring input, output, and productivity. Covers both labor productivity and multifactor productivity index-number formulas.

Chapter 12. Technological Change

Background

Studies of technological changes and their labor implications have been undertaken by BLS over the years for a variety of purposes. During the 1930's, public interest focused on the unemployed, and reports were prepared on displacement of workers resulting from technological change in various industries. During World War II, emerging technologies were studied for purposes of improving work force utilization.

Beginning in the mid-1950's, nationwide attention was focused on the implications of new developments classified under the general term "automation." BLS made a series of studies on a plant basis in the insurance, petroleum refining, bakery, airline, and electronics industries, to explore the labor implications of various changes. Later, broader studies were undertaken, including a survey of the labor impact of changeover to electronic computers in 20 large companies and intensive studies of technological change in the coal and paper industries.

These studies formed the basis, beginning in the early 1960's, for a more systematic investigation of likely future changes. The first report, entitled *Technological Trends in 36 Major American Industries,* was issued by the President's Advisory Committee on Labor Management Policy in 1964. A revised edition covering 40 industries was published in 1966. More recent industry studies have been published as they were completed.

Description of Studies

To provide a broad overview of significant trends in the economy, the Bureau prepares a summary report, applying to key industries, on new types of machinery, processes, and products which are believed likely to have an important effect over the next 5 to 10 years. The industries covered comprise a cross-section of the economy and include those where the pace may be slow as well as those where rapid change is expected.

The emphasis of these studies is on technological developments within each industry in an early stage of the innovation's commercial use, i.e., the period after introduction on the market but before widespread adoption. Inventions and discoveries still in the formative stage are considered unlikely to have as much impact over the next decade as those already tested, and are generally not discussed.

The reports briefly describe recent technological developments, indicating insofar as practicable some economic advantages of various types of new equipment, processes, or products; their importance in terms of the employee hours engaged in the operations affected; estimated extent of use currently and in 5 to 10 years; and some factors affecting adoption such as the volume of investment and expenditures for research and development. The advantages described include not only labor savings per unit, but also quality improvements, fuel and material economies, greater accuracy, new markets, etc. A limited number of industry reports also include BLS data on diffusion of major new technologies, and case studies of their impact on productivity and employment in selected plants.

In assessing the employment implications of technological changes, account is taken of the possible rate of growth in output per employee hour and in the industry's total output. Appraisal also is made of the changes in occupational structure and of some issues and examples of adjustment of workers to technological change.

Some technological innovations have applicability in many industries. Among these are such developments as computers, numerical control of machine tools, material handling equipment, and control instruments. Because of their far-reaching impact, special studies have been made of the nature, status, prospects for adoption, and implications for unit labor requirements, occupational change, training needs, and problems of industrial relations. In analyzing their effects in different industries, differences as well as similarities are revealed.

Data Sources and Collection Methods

A variety of data sources and collection methods are used in making studies of technological change and its impact.

Personal interviews

In making studies, analysts personally conduct intensive interviews with plant managers, personnel directors, and other officials who have direct knowledge of changes at their plant. Union officials at the plant and, in some cases, individual workers are interviewed. The analyst uses a checklist of questions in conducting informal interviews in order to elicit the maximum amount of data. Plants and offices included in these studies are selected on the basis of having recently made a major change in their equipment, products, or methods of production.

Personal interviews also are used to help determine industry trends. Informal interviews are conducted with engineers, scientists, economists, and other experts in companies which produce and use new technology, and with unions, trade associations, government agencies, universities, etc., who have specialized knowledge of a particular technological development or industry trend. One objective in these cases is to obtain expert judgement about the nature, pace of introduction, and possible impact of developments with which few plants have had any experience. The emphasis in these interviews is on the technological change rather than on experiences in adjusting.

Trade and technical publications

Important sources of information concerning technological trends are trade journals, technical magazines and books, conference proceedings, government hearings, and company reports. Annual reports of leading corporations and company house organs often contain useful information on current technological developments in some industries. These publications are reviewed to obtain information about the status and prospects of important developments and to ascertain which companies and plants merit intensive field visits. Reports and publications of firms that produce particular types of equipment often are found useful in studies of industries that use such equipment.

Statistical data sources

Quantitative information about the status of specific technological developments is fragmentary and scarce. The Bureau makes use of available data from many public and private sources. Examples include: General Services Administration, annual inventory of computers in the Federal Government; International Trade Administration, *U.S. Industrial Outlook* (annual); American Bankers' Association, survey of banking automation; and American Machinist, inventory of metalworking machinery. The Bureau also analyzes data on diffusion of technology obtained in connection with selected industry wage surveys.

Statistical information on industrywide trends is useful in analyzing the economic implications of technological change. Among the important sources used are the Bureau's indexes of output per employee hour and related series on production, employment, and hours; BLS industry employment and occupational projections; the Bureau of the Census' data on plant and equipment expenditures and surveys of manufacturing technology; and the National Science Foundation's estimates of expenditures for research and development.

Plant records

In making detailed studies of the impact of technological change on individual workers within a plant, analysts sometimes can obtain data on the age, sex, and related personal characteristics of employees whose jobs are eliminated and the jobs in the plant held by each individual affected before and after the change. Similar data are sought for individuals who are selected for the positions created in connection with automated equipment.

Expert review

In preparing forecasts of technological trends, a critical step is the review of preliminary reports by outstanding experts in each industry. Drafts of industry reports are mailed to company executives, union research directors, trade association officials, technical journal editors, and university and government specialists for their assessment of the validity and adequacy of projected trends. Some experts also are visited personally to review draft statements in detail. Reports on technological prospects are designed to reflect, as much as possible, the authoritative views of a number of persons who have expert, firsthand knowledge of each industry.

Analysis and Interpretation

For a better understanding of research results in this field, it is important to keep in mind the meaning of certain key ideas and concepts. Some of the problems of interpretation and analysis, therefore, are set forth briefly.

Definition of technological change

Technological change is defined broadly in the BLS studies as encompassing significant changes in processes and equipment, products and services produced, and materials, fuels, and energy used. The technologies studied vary in complexity and include highly advanced, computerized and automatic systems often described as automation.

While BLS studies have often been concerned with developments in automation, particularly in anticipating long-term trends, they are not the only technological changes taking place that affect labor requirements and labor relations. For example, new ways of generating power, piggybacking in transportation, use of synthetic materials in manufacturing, mechanized methods of material handling, and faster steelmaking processes are important technological developments not usually covered by technical definitions of automation, but having significant employment implications.

Impact on productivity

Because one of the principal consequences of technological change, so far as use of the work force is concerned, is an increase in productivity (output per employee hour), special attention is given in BLS studies to analyzing changes in industry productivity. Such trend analysis is a useful method of measuring the pace of technological change. Changes in productivity, however, also reflect changes in capacity utilization and many other nontechnical factors. It is important to recognize that the productivity trend does not directly measure the rate of technological change in an industry.

In determining the impact of a specific technology, BLS studies try to indicate the reduction in unit labor requirements that the new process is designed to achieve. In some cases, estimates of labor savings are derived on the basis of comparisons with the estimated average technology of the industry under study; in others, with the best equipment that is available; or in actual plant studies, with the technology that is actually displaced.

It is also important to distinguish between the impact on productivity of the operation directly affected and on productivity of the plant as a whole. An advanced machine tool, for example, may result in a relatively large reduction in unit labor requirements in the machining operation, but would have little impact on finishing and assembling, and may, even require additional labor in engineering and maintenance work. The effect on plant productivity, therefore, may be considerably less than the effect on productivity of any department or operation directly affected.

Impact on employment

In assessing the effect of technological change on employment, it is necessary to consider the implications of plant policies and the effects of economic changes with which technological changes interact. Analysis of the impact of technological change purely in terms of machinery or equipment is incomplete.

At the plant level, for example, the substitution of machinery for labor may substantially reduce job opportunities in operations directly affected. If efforts are made, however, to eliminate these jobs by not filling vacancies or by transfer of affected workers to other positions in the plant or office, labor savings could be achieved without displacing the workers affected.

Moreover, the employment effect of technological change is also interrelated with the effects of the business cycle. Thus, workers whose jobs are eliminated by technological changes may not be displaced from a plant until a decline in demand results in layoffs--a long time after the change has been made in some cases. In the subsequent recovery, however, they may not be hired back because their jobs no longer exist.

The employment trend for the industry as a whole must also be examined. The plant which reduces its unit costs through technological improvement may be able to gain a larger share of the market and increase its employment, but at the expense of the less technically advanced competing plants, which may be forced to shut down, displacing workers far from the location of the change.

Because of the complex of economic factors that operate through the market, including changes in demand, location, foreign competition, corporate organization, and consumer taste, it is very difficult to isolate the effects of technological change.

Impact on occupations

Two aspects of occupational change resulting from technological changes are examined. Changes in job structure--the distribution of the plant or office work force by function or broad skill grouping--are studied to determine the extent of upgrading or downgrading. Because the content of jobs may be altered as a result of changes in equipment or processes, attention also is directed to intensive before-and-after analysis of job duties and the knowledge and abilities required to perform these duties as indicated by job descriptions and observation. The content of newly created jobs also is studied, and the qualifications required and personal characteristics of individuals selected for these new positions are described, so far as possible.

Adjustment to technological change

Technological change has important implications for personnel management and collective bargaining within plants. The introduction of new machinery, products, or processes often requires movement of workers among jobs. Often the adjustment proceeds according to rules established in advance through collective bargaining. Provisions to assist workers whose jobs are eliminated include severance pay, retraining, and early retirement. Besides analyzing the operation of formal provisions under collective bargaining, Bureau studies describe informal efforts to provide training, to utilize attrition, and to obtain jobs for displaced workers elsewhere. The limitations of these measures as well as their advantages are important matters studied.

Uses and Limitations

BLS studies and reports of technological change are useful to managers, union leaders, educators, economists, government officials, and others in planning policies to cushion the impact of change. The study of emerging technological trends and possible implications, moreover, provides a basis for more valid projections of producivity and economic growth. They also are useful in pinpointing employment problems and determining the most productive direction of future research to obtain possible solutions.

Some limitations of the Bureau's studies of technologal change must be kept in mind in assessing their appropriateness for particular uses. In general, it is important to recognize that judgments about the future direction and pace of technological change and its implications are necessarily complex and difficult. The rate of introduction of new technology depends not only on technical advantages but also on many economic factors, such as the volume of investment, market prospects, and the availability of trained workers, all of which are subject to significant variations. Moreover, since the period of introduction generally spans a number of years, the outlook must be reappraised from time to time in the light of new information.

Finally, studies of the impact of technological change deal primarily with changes within individual industries. But these changes often involve changes in the type and amount of goods and services purchased from other industries and could, therefore, have important implications for production and employment in industries supplying inputs. The accumulation of information on interindustry relationships, through the Bureau's economic growth studies, provides a quantitative basis for analyzing this aspect of technological change.

Technical References

Bureau of Labor Statistics

Mark, Jerome A. "Technology and Employment. Some Results of BLS Research," *Monthly Labor Review,* April 1987.
Highlights findings from the BLS research program on technological change including implications of new technology for employment and productivity.

Technology, Productivity, and Labor in the Bituminous Coal Industry, 1950-79, BLS Bulletin 2072, 1981.
Appraises some of the major structural and technological changes in the bituminous coal industry and their impact on labor in the industry.

The following bulletins appraise major technological changes emerging in key industries and discuss their impact on productivity over the next 5 to 10 years.

Outlook for Technology and Labor in Hospitals, BLS Bulletin 2404, 1992.

Technology and Its Impact on Employment in the Life and Health Insurance Industries, BLS Bulletin 2368, 1990.
This bulletin also includes findings of a BLS survey on the extent of use and impact of new technology, and the results of follow-up field visits.

Technology and Labor in Three Service Industries: Utilities, Retail Trade, and Lodging, BLS Bulletin 2367, 1990.

Outlook for Technology and Labor in Telephone Communications, BLS Bulletin 2357, 1990.

Technological Change and Its Labor Impact in Four Industries (contract construction, railroad transportation, air transportation, and petroleum pipeline transportation), BLS Bulletin 2316, 1988.

Technology and Labor Developments in Four Industries (lumber and wood products, footwear, hydraulic cement, wholesale trade), BLS Bulletin 2263, 1986.

Technology and Its Impact on Labor in Four Industries (tires, aluminum, aerospace, banking), BLS Bulletin 2242, 1986.

The Impact of Technology on Labor in Four Industries (textiles, paper and paperboard, steel, motor vehicles), BLS Bulletin 2228, 1985.

Technological Change and Its Labor Impact in Four Industries (hosiery, folding paperboard boxes, metal cans, laundry and cleaning), BLS Bulletin 2182, 1984.

The Impact of Technology on Labor in Five Industries (printing and publishing, water transportation, copper ore mining, fabricated structural metal, intercity trucking), BLS Bulletin 2137, 1982.

Technology and Labor Developments in Four Industries (meat products, foundries, metalworking machinery, electrical and electronic equipment), BLS Bulletin 2104, 1982.

Chapter 13. Foreign Labor Statistics

Background

From its inception, the Bureau has collected and published comparative statistical information on labor conditions and developments abroad. Foreign labor research and statistical analyses have been undertaken because (1) comparisons between U.S. and foreign labor conditions shed light on U.S. economic performance relative to other industrial nations; (2) comparisons provide information on the competitive position of the United States in foreign trade, which has an important influence on the U.S. economy and employment; (3) information on labor conditions published by a majority of foreign countries is not readily available to U.S. labor representatives, employers, Government officials, and others, and is often not available in English; and (4) often, only an expert can judge the quality and comparability of foreign statistical data.

Description of Measures

The emphasis of the current program is on the development of international comparisons of the labor force, employment, and unemployment; productivity and unit labor costs; hourly compensation costs of manufacturing production workers; indicators related to the family; gross domestic product per capita and per employed person; and consumer prices and other measures. The measures compiled relate primarily to the major industrial countries, but other countries or areas of importance to U.S. foreign trade are included in some of the measures. Most of the series are prepared on an annual average basis; comparative figures on unemployment and consumer prices are prepared monthly.

Labor force, employment, and unemployment. Comparative measures of the labor force, employment, unemployment, and related indicators are prepared regularly for the United States, Canada, Japan, Australia, France, Germany, Italy, the Netherlands, Sweden, and the United Kingdom. For most of the countries, the series begin with 1959. Unemployment rates, approximating U.S. concepts, are prepared monthly for most of the countries; the other measures are calculated annually. Some measures are calculated by sex or by age. Current research is directed toward the development of a series of comparative unemployment measures ranging from relatively narrow measures to measures encompassing employed persons working part time for economic reasons and discouraged workers.

Productivity and labor costs. Comparative trends in manufacturing labor productivity (output per hour), hourly compensation, unit labor costs (labor compensation per unit of output), and related measures are compiled on an annual average basis for the United States, Canada, Japan, Belgium, Denmark, France, Germany, Italy, the Netherlands, Norway, Sweden, and the United Kingdom. For the comparative measures of unit labor costs, Korea and Taiwan are added. The comparisons are limited to trend measures only; reliable comparisons of levels of manufacturing productivity and unit labor costs are not available.

BLS does not prepare comparisons of levels of manufacturing productivity and unit labor costs because of data problems in comparing the levels of manufacturing output among countries. To compare manufacturing output across countries, a common unit of measurement is needed, such as the U.S. dollar. Market exchange rates are not suitable as a basis for comparing output levels. What are needed are purchasing power parities (PPP's), that is, the number of foreign currency units required to buy goods and services equivalent to what can be bought with one unit of U.S. currency. Reasonably reliable PPP's are available for total gross domestic product (GDP). However, these were derived from the expenditure side of the national accounts and not from the output side. Therefore, the available data are not adequate for constructing industry-specific PPP's. PPP's for total GDP are also not suitable for component industries, such as manufacturing.

The trend measures are expressed in index form and as percent changes at annual rates. For most countries, the series begin with 1950. Indexes of unit labor costs for foreign countries are calculated on a U.S. dollar basis as well as in national currency terms to take account of relative changes in currency exchange rates. In addition to the individual country measures, the Bureau constructs relative trade-weighted measures of productivity and unit labor costs, that is, the U.S. measure relative to a trade-weighted average for the other economies or selected economies.

Comparative measures by broad industry within manufacturing have also been developed for Canada, Japan, France, and Germany. Current research is directed toward the expansion of the measures for several countries, including Japan and Germany, to include capital as well as labor inputs in the productivity measures.

Hourly compensation costs. Measures of total compensation per hour worked for production workers in all manufacturing and in 39 component manufacturing industries or industry groups are computed for over 30 countries or areas. The series are annual and begin with 1975 (1960 for total manufacturing in 10 industrial countries). For all manufacturing, measures of hourly direct pay and pay for time worked are also computed. The measures are computed in national currency and converted into U.S. dollars at prevailing market currency exchange rates. For total manufacturing, trade-weighted average measures of hourly compensation in U.S. dollars are computed for all foreign economies and for selected regional or economic groups.

Hourly compensation converted into U.S. dollars at market exchange rates is an appropriate measure for comparing levels of employer labor costs. It does not indicate relative living standards of workers or the purchasing power of their income. Prices of goods and services vary greatly among countries, and market exchange rates are not reliable indicators of relative differences in prices. PPP's must be used for meaningful international comparisons of the relative purchasing power of worker incomes.

The family. Indicators relating to the family are compiled for 10 countries. These indicators include marriage and divorce rates, births to unmarried women, the distribution of households by type, and the number of single-parent households. The series generally begin with 1960.

Real gross domestic product per capita and per employed person. Comparative levels (United States=100) and trends in gross domestic product (GDP), GDP per capita, and GDP per employed person are calculated on an annual average basis for the United States, Canada, Japan, Korea, and 10 European countries, generally beginning with 1950. The GDP level comparisons are based on purchasing power parities, that is, the number of foreign currency units required to buy goods and services equivalent to what can be bought with one unit of U.S. currency. A common practice has been to base such comparisons on market currency exchange rates. However, market exchange rates seldom reflect the relative purchasing powers of different currencies. Comparisons of GDP at market exchange rates are essentially comparisons of nominal values, that is, they reflect differences in price levels as well as differences in volumes.

Consumer prices and other measures. Indexes of consumer prices are compiled regularly for the United States and 14 foreign countries on a common base year. Annual indexes (since 1950) and monthly or quarterly indexes (since 1970) are available for most of the countries.

Other comparative measures, generally available on an annual basis, include the number of union members and union density ratios, as measured by union membership as a percent of civilian wage and salary workers, for 12 countries; indexes of real hourly and weekly compensation of manufacturing employees for 12 countries; and the number of work stoppages resulting from strikes and lockouts and their severity rates, as measured by days lost per thousand civilian wage and salary workers, for 15 countries.

Data Sources

Research on comparative labor statistics is based upon statistical data and other source materials from (a) statistical agencies of foreign countries; (b) international and supranational bodies such as the United Nations, International Labour Office (ILO), Organisation for Economic Cooperation and Development (OECD), and the Statistical Office of the European Communities (EUROSTAT); and (c) private agencies such as banks, industry associations, and research institutions. All data are drawn from secondary sources; the Bureau does not initiate surveys or data collection programs abroad.

Estimating Procedures

Because statistical concepts and methods vary from country to country, international comparisons of statistical data can be misleading. The Bureau attempts to derive meaningful comparisons by selecting a conceptual framework for comparative purposes; analyzing foreign statistical series and selecting those which most nearly match the desired concepts; and adjusting statistical series, where necessary and feasible, for greater intercountry comparability.

Labor force, employment, and unemployment. For these comparisons, the Bureau adjusts each country's published data, if necessary, to provide measures approximately consistent with U.S. definitions and standards. Although precise comparability may not be achieved, these adjusted figures provide a better basis for international comparisons than the figures regularly published by each country.

The foreign country data are adjusted as closely as possible to U.S. concepts, with the exception of age limits and the treatment of layoffs. The adjusted statistics have been adapted to the age at which compulsory schooling ends in each country, rather than to the U.S. standard of 16 years of age and over. Therefore, the adjusted statistics relate to the population age 16 and over in France, Sweden, and from 1973 onward, the United Kingdom; 15 and over in Canada, Australia, Japan, Germany, the Netherlands, and prior to 1973, the United Kingdom; and 14 and over in Italy.

In the U.S. labor force survey, persons on layoff who are awaiting recall to their job are classified as unemployed. European and Japanese layoff practices are quite different in nature from those in the United States; therefore, strict application of the U.S. definition has not been made on this point.

Under the U.S. definition, unpaid family workers who worked fewer than 15 hours a week are excluded from the labor force. This practice conformed to definitions recommended by the International Labour Office until 1982, when the ILO changed its recommendation to include all unpaid family workers regardless of the number of hours worked. Adjustments have been made to the U.S. definition on this point for Italy, Japan, Germany, and the Netherlands, but not for the other countries which follow the current ILO recommendation—Canada, Australia, France, Sweden (1987 onward), and the United Kingdom. The available information for these countries indicates that an adjustment for family workers would be very small.

The statistics for 6 of the 10 countries regularly studied—the United States, Canada, Australia, Japan, Italy, and Sweden—are obtained from monthly or quarterly household surveys. No adjustments are made to the published data for Canada and Australia, since their concepts and methods are virtually identical to those of the United States. Slight adjustments are made to the data for Japan and Sweden; a substantial adjustment is made to the Italian data.

Current unemployment measures for three of the other four countries studied—France, Germany, and the United Kingdom—are derived from monthly administrative data on the number of registrants at public employment offices. These countries also conduct periodic household surveys of the labor force (the United Kingdom conducts a monthly survey; however, because of the small sample size, figures are only published on an annual basis and for the larger spring survey; France and Germany conduct annual surveys) which contain benchmark data that are used to adjust the levels of the labor force, employment, and unemployment for greater comparability with U.S. concepts. Measures of current labor force, employment, and unemployment are obtained by applying adjustment factors from the most recent year's labor force surveys to published figures.

No monthly or quarterly estimates are currently made for the Netherlands because of the lack of reliable quarterly employment data. Beginning in 1988, the Dutch labor force survey, previously conducted biennially or annually, has been conducted on a monthly basis. BLS will investigate these results as a possible source of monthly data. However, several more years of observations are necessary to develop a reliable seasonal adjustment pattern.

Productivity and labor costs. Indexes of manufacturing labor productivity (output per hour), hourly compensation, and unit labor costs are constructed from three basic aggregative measures: Output, total labor hours, and total compensation. The hours and compensation measures refer to all employed persons, including the self-employed, in the United States and Canada and to all employees (wage and salary workers) in the other countries. Hours refer to hours worked in all countries. The figures for Canada are the official measures prepared by Statistics Canada.

In general, the measures relate to total manufacturing as defined by the International Standard Industrial Classification. However, the measures for France (beginning 1959), Italy (beginning 1970), and the United Kingdom (beginning 1971) refer to mining and manufacturing less energy-related products; the measures for Denmark include mining and exclude manufacturing handicrafts prior to 1966; and the measures for the Netherlands exclude petroleum refining and include coal mining from 1969 to 1976.

In general, the output measures are gross product originating in manufacturing (value added) in constant prices from the national accounts of each country. However, output for Japan prior to 1970 and the Netherlands prior to 1960 and from 1969 to 1977 are indexes of industrial production. The national accounts measures for the United Kingdom are essentially identical to their indexes of industrial production. While methods of deriving national accounts measures of manufacturing output differ substantially from country to country, and the British national accounts measures are essentially identical to their indexes of industrial production, the use of different procedures does not, in itself, connote lack of comparability. Rather, it reflects differences among countries in the availability and reliability of underlying data series.

The total hours measures are developed from statistics of manufacturing employment and average hours. The series used for France (from 1970 forward), Norway, and Sweden are official series published with their national accounts. Where official total hours series are not available, the measures are developed by the Bureau using employment figures published with the national accounts, or other comprehensive employment series, and estimates of annual hours worked.

For the Republic of Korea and Taiwan, the Bureau currently publishes only measures of unit labor costs and its components—output and total compensation. Total hours, and consequently productivity, are not computed for Korea and Taiwan because BLS has not yet developed adequate employment series for them.

The compensation (labor cost) measures are from the national accounts, except those for Belgium, which are developed by the Bureau using statistics on employment, average hours, and hourly compensation. Compensation includes all payments in cash or kind made directly to employees, plus employer expenditures for legally required insurance programs and contractual and private benefit plans. In addition, for some countries, compensation is increased to account for other significant taxes on payrolls or employment (or reduced to reflect subsidies), even if they are not for the direct benefit of workers, because such taxes are regarded as labor costs. Compensation does not include all items of labor cost, however. The costs of recruitment, employee training, and plant facilities and services-such as cafeterias and medical clinics—are not covered because data are not available for most countries. Self-employed workers are included in the U.S. and Canadian figures by assuming that their hourly compensation is equal to the average for wage and salary employees.

For all countries, the measures for recent years may be based on current indicators of manufacturing output, employment, average hours, and hourly compensation, until national accounts and other statistics used for the long-term measures become available.

Since the economies covered differ greatly in their relative importance to U.S. trade in manufactured products, the Bureau constructs trade-weighted measures of productivity and unit labor costs to take account of these differences. The trade weights were derived by rescaling a series for 21 economies that was developed by the International Monetary Fund. The International Monetary Fund weights used are based on disaggregated 1980 trade data for manufactured goods and take account of both bilateral trade and the relative importance of "third country" markets. Two summary measures are constructed: "Competitors" indexes, which are the trade-weighted geometric averages of the indexes for foriegn economies, and relative indexes, which are the ratios of the U.S. indexes to "competitors" indexes.

Hourly compensation costs. Measures of hourly compensation costs are prepared by the Bureau in order to provide a better basis for assessing international differences in employer labor costs. Comparisons based on the more readily available average earnings statistics published by many countries can be very misleading. National definitions of average earnings differ considerably, average earnings do not include all items of labor compensation, and the omitted items of compensation frequently represent a large proportion of total compensation.

Hourly compensation is defined as (1) all payments made directly to the worker—pay for time worked (basic time and piece rates plus overtime premiums, shift differentials, other premiums and bonuses paid regularly each pay period, and cost-of-living adjustments), pay for time not worked (vacations, holidays, and other leave), seasonal or irregular bonuses and other special payments, selected social allowances, and the cost of payments in kind—before payroll deductions of any kind, plus (2) employer expenditures for legally required insurance programs and contractual and private benefit plans. In addition, for some countries, compensation is adjusted for other taxes on payrolls or employment (or reduced to reflect subsidies), even if they are not for the direct benefit of workers, because such taxes are regarded as labor costs. For consistency, compensation is measured on an hours-worked basis for every country.

The BLS definition of hourly compensation costs is not the same as the International Labour Office definition of total labor costs. Hourly compensation costs do not include all items of labor costs. The costs of recruitment, employee training, and plant facilities and services—such as cafeterias and medical clinics—are not included because data are not available for most countries. The labor costs not included account for no more than 4 percent of total labor costs in any country for which the data are available.

The total compensation measures are computed by adjusting each country's average earnings series for items of direct pay not included in earnings and for employer expenditures for legally required insurance, contractual and private benefit plans, and other labor taxes or subsidies.

Earnings statistics are obtained from establishment surveys of employment, hours, and earnings for most countries. They are obtained from surveys or censuses of manufactures for six countries—Brazil, Mexico, Israel, Austria, Denmark, and Portugal. The surveys of employment, hours, and earnings are establishment stratified sample surveys for most countries (except they are full surveys of establishments covered for Singapore, Finland, Luxembourg, and Norway and a judgement sample for Switzerland). The surveys of manufactures are establishment stratified sample surveys of industrial production and other industrial statistics, including labor input and labor cost. Censuses are complete enumerations of establishments.

Adjustment factors are obtained from periodic labor cost surveys and interpolated or projected to nonsurvey years on the basis of other available information for most countries. The labor cost surveys are establishment stratified sample surveys (full surveys for Ireland and Luxembourg). The information used to interpolate or project the adjustment factors to non-labor-cost-survey years includes annual tabulations on employer social security contribution rates provided by the International Studies Staff of the U.S. Social Security Administration, information on contractual and legislated fringe benefit changes from ILO and national labor bulletins, and statistical series on indirect labor costs. The adjustment factors are obtained from the surveys of manufactures for Brazil, Mexico, and Portugal, and from reports on fringe benefit systems and social security for Hong Kong, Israel, New Zealand, Singapore, Sri Lanka, and Spain. For the United States, the adjustment factors are special calculations for international comparisons based on data from several surveys.

The statistics are also adjusted, where necessary, to account for major differences in worker coverage; differences in industrial classification systems; and changes over time in survey coverage, sample benchmarks, or frequency of surveys. Nevertheless, some differences in industrial coverage remain and, with the exception of the United

States, Canada, and several other countries, the data exclude very small establishments (fewer than 5 employees in Japan and fewer than 10 employees in most European and some other countries).

Special estimation procedures have been used for some countries because of incomplete data. Hourly earnings are computed from daily or monthly earnings using estimates of standard hours worked for Brazil and Israel. Earnings for production workers are estimated from all-employee earnings for Korea (1975-84), New Zealand, and Israel (1978 to present). The adjustment factors for additional compensation relate to all employees for Brazil, Mexico, Japan, Korea, Taiwan, France, Ireland, the Netherlands, Portugal, and the United Kingdom; they are constants or the midpoints of constant ranges for Hong Kong, Israel, and New Zealand.

Hourly compensation costs are converted to U.S. dollars using the average daily exchange rate for the reference period. Changes in hourly compensation in U.S. dollars from one period to another are therefore affected by changes in currency exchange rates as well as by changes in compensation. The exchange rates used are prevailing commercial market exchange rates as published by either the U.S. Federal Reserve Board or the International Monetary Fund.

The trade weights used to compute the average compensation cost measures for selected economic groups are based on the sum of U.S. imports of manufactured products for consumption (customs value) and U.S. domestic exports of manufactured products (f.a.s. value), as compiled by the U.S. Bureau of the Census. The import data have been adjusted by the Bureau to eliminate the U.S. value content of U.S. imports under items 806.30 and 807.00 of the *U.S. Tariff Schedules.* Those tariff items allow U.S. metals or manufactured components to be exported for foreign processing and duty to be paid only on the value added (value of imported product less the value of the U.S. metals or manufactured components) when the products are returned. A description of the trade weights and trade-weighted measures was published in *International Comparisons of Hourly Compensation Costs for Production Workers, 1975-87,* BLS Report 754 (August 1988).

The family. The regularly published statistics on marriage and divorce rates for each country have been adjusted to a common denominator. Thus, marriage rates are expressed as marriages per 1,000 population ages 15 to 64; divorce rates are expressed as divorces per 1,000 married women. Births to unmarried women are shown as a percent of all live births.

Concepts and definitions relating to household composition differ among countries, and adjustments have been made, where possible, for conformity with U.S. standards. In some instances, foreign statistical offices have retabulated their data on U.S. definitions. National definitions of households with children vary considerably because of differences in the age limits defining a child. In the United States, children are defined as all those under the age of 18; in the other countries, age limits for children vary from all those 16 and under to no upper age limit at all. Adjustment of the foreign country data to the U.S. age limit has been possible in most cases, at least for selected year.

Real gross domestic product per capita and per employed person. The Bureau's measures of comparative levels and trends of gross domestic product (GDP) per capita and per employed person are based on benchmark levels of GDP extrapolated to other years on the basis of relative changes in real GDP as measured by each country, and on annual population and employment estimates. The GDP level comparisons are based on purchasing power parities (PPP's). The benchmark level comparisons of GDP are from the United Nations International Comparison Project (UNICP). The benchmark figures are derived by comparing relative prices at detailed levels of expenditure (PPP's by item of expenditure) and aggregating these price relatives to derive overall PPP exchange rates for total GDP. These original volume measures of GDP are modified by BLS, where applicable, to account for subsequent revisions by countries of their national accounts. The Bureau also constructs PPP's for GDP for all years by applying relative changes in implicit price deflators for GDP, as measured by each country, to the benchmark PPP's.

Consumer prices and other measures. No adjustments are made to the overall consumer price indexes as published by each country except to convert them to a uniform base year.

Union membership statistics published by each country differ in sources, reporting techniques, definitions, and coverage. The U.S. data are derived from the Current Population Survey (CPS) from 1983 onward, with some CPS data also available for 1 month in a few earlier years. For 1980 and earlier, U.S. data were derived directly from the labor unions, via a biennial questionnaire. Other countries generally derive their union membership time series data from union reports rather than household surveys.

In order to enhance international comparisons, the reported union membership data for the European countries are adjusted to the CPS concept of coverage for selected years. This concept covers union members who are employed wage and salary workers. Thus, members who are retired, unemployed, or self-employed are excluded. For Australia and Canada, union membership data for selected recent years are taken directly from household surveys. No adjustments are made to the reported union membership data for Japan because they include very few non-wage and salary workers.

Indexes of real hourly or weekly compensation are constructed by deflating indexes of nominal compensation by each country's consumer price index. Work stoppages usually refer to strikes and lockouts, but the exact definition differs from country to country. The statistics are not adjusted for comparability.

Analysis and Presentation

Analyses of international labor statistics focus upon comparisons with U.S. data. Wherever possible, the foreign data are adjusted to U.S. definitions and concepts to facilitate comparisons; for example, the adjustment of foreign unemployment rates to approximate U.S. concepts and the adjustment of production worker earnings to total hourly compensation.

Labor force, employment, and unemployment data are analyzed to determine the sources or components of differences and changes in labor force measures. Shifts in labor force composition are analyzed by age, sex, and industrial sector. Productivity and unit labor cost data are analyzed to explain the relative contributions of changes in output, employment, average hours, compensation, and exchange rates to changes in the measures. Changes in production worker compensation are analyzed to determine the relative contributions of direct pay and the other elements of compensation.

The presentation of foreign labor statistics varies with the degree of analysis and major use of the data. Comprehensive bulletins have been published, covering manufacturing productivity and labor cost trends, steel productivity and costs, unemployment and labor force comparisons, and youth unemployment comparisons. For more current developments, articles are published periodically in the *Monthly Labor Review.* Some series are published regularly in the statistical section of the *Monthly Labor Review*; an annual news release is issued on comparative trends in manufacturing productivity and labor costs; and the hourly compensation cost measures for total manufacturing are issued in BLS reports. The BLS's *Handbook of Labor Statistics* and the Bureau of the Census' *Statistical Abstract of the United States* publish many of the principal foreign data series, and some series are published in the annual *Economic Report of the President.* Many unpublished tabulations of current comparative data are available on request. Many data series are also available on data tape or diskette.

Uses and Limitations

The principal uses of information on foreign labor statistics are (a) to assess U.S. economic performance relative to other industrial countries; (b) to inform Government and private officials of foreign economic developments that may affect U.S. international economic policy; (c) to evaluate the competitive position of the United States in international trade; (d) to review foreign experience for possible application domestically; and (e) to provide labor statistics and related information to individuals, corporations, labor unions, and others concerned with foreign investment and development.

Although considerable progress has been made in making international economic statistics more uniform among countries, e.g., through the work of international agencies such as the United Nations, the International Labour Office, the Organisation for Economic Cooperation and Development, and the Statistical Office of the European Community (EUROSTAT), international statistical comparisons should be used cautiously. Nevertheless, through careful analysis of each country's data, valid statistical comparisons can be made.

Whenever possible, BLS adjusts foreign data, if necessary, for greater consistency with U.S. measures; in some cases, data are sufficiently similar in definition and concept for valid comparisons without adjustment. Moreover, when conceptual differences are substantial, the Bureau attempts to describe the differences in sufficient detail, in publications and in notes to statistical tabulations, to provide guidance in the interpretation of the data.

The limitations of the data are less serious for the Bureau's published measures than for the unpublished tabulations, where either no adjustments are made to the foreign data or where the adjustments made do not deal with some fundamental deficiences. Despite their limitations, however, the unpublished tabulations are considered useful for analysis.

Technical References

General

International Labour Office. *Current International Recommendations on Labour Statistics*, 1988 Edition. Geneva, 1988.

Presents recommendations on standardizing labor statistics, includeing recommendations on employment and unemployment statistics, statistics, of labor costs, wage statistics, consumer price indices, and strikes and lockouts.

Labor force, employment, and unemployment

Chernyshev, Igor. "ILO-Comparable Employment and Unemployment Estimates: A Technical Guide." Geneva, International Labour Office, STAT Working Paper No. 91-3; and Chernyshev, Igor and Lawrence, S. "ILO-Comparable Annual Employment and Unemployment Estimates: Results and Short Methodological Presentation." *ILO Bulletin of Labour Statistics, 1990-4,* pp. *IX-XXXIX.*

The Technical Guide presents detailed descriptions of employment and unemployment data and adjustments made to ILO definitions for 26 countries in Eastern and Western Europe, the Far East, and Oceania. The Bulletin summarizes the ILO program and presents the annual average data for 1981-89, including breakdowns by sex and age.

Sorrentino, Constance. "Japan's Low Unemployment: An In-Depth Analysis," *Monthly Labor Review,* March 1984; "Japanese Unemployment: BLS Updates Its Analysis," *Monthly Labor Review,* June 1987; and "Adjusted Japanese Unemployment Rate Remains below 3 percent in 1987-88," *Monthly Labor Review,* June 1989.

Presents comparisons of U.S. and Japanese unemployment rates including persons on economic part time and discouraged workers.

Sorrentino, Constance. "The Uses of the European Community Labour Force Surveys for International Unemployment Comparisons," EUROSTAT, Conference on the European Community Labour Force Surveys in the Next Decade. Luxembourg, October 1987.

Investigates the uses of the European Community (EC) labor force surveys for purposes of international comparisons of unemployment and provides comparisons of alternative measures of unemployment for the EC countries, the United States, Canada, and Japan.

Moy, Joyanna and Sorrentino, Constance. "Unemployment, Labor Force Trends, and Layoff Practices in 10 Countries," *Monthly Labor Review,* December 1981.

Discusses the treatment of persons on layoff in the Bureau's international comparisons of unemployment.

U.S. Department of Labor, Bureau of Labor Statistics. *Youth Unemployment: An International Perspective,* Bulletin 2098, September 1981. Also, Sorrentino, Constance. "Youth Unemployment: An International Perspective," *Monthly Labor Review,* July 1981.

Examines the labor market experience of youth in the United States and eight other industrial countries from the early 1960's to the late 1970's.

U.S. Department of Labor, Bureau of Labor Statistics. *International Comparisons of Unemployment,* Bulletin 1979, August 1978, and subsequent unpublished country supplements and summaries.

Provides the conceptual framework and a comprehensive description of the Bureau's work on international unemployment comparisons, describes in detail the methods of adjusting foreign unemployment rates to U.S. concepts, and analyzes various factors contributing to differences in unemployment levels.

U.S. Department of Labor, Bureau of Labor Statistics. *Comparative Labor Force Statistics for Ten Countries.* Updates released in the spring and fall of each year.

Presents annual time series from 1959 or 1960 onward covering civilian working age population, labor force, employment, unemployment, and related variables.

Productivity and unit labor costs

Neef, Arthur and Kask, Christopher. "Manufacturing Productivity and Labor Costs in 14 Economies," *Monthly Labor Review,* December 1991.

The most current in a series of articles on comparative trends in labor productivity and unit labor costs.

Dean, Edwin; Darrough, Masako; and Neef, Arthur. "Alternative Measures of Capital Inputs for Computation of Multifactor Productivity Growth in Japanese Manufacturing." Charles R. Hulton, ed., *Productivity Growth in Japan and the United States.* National Bureau of Economic Research, 1990.

Examines and assesses the various data sources and methods available for measuring capital stock in Japanese-manufacturing.

Neef, Arthur. "Comparative Changes in Labor Productivity: United States and Western Europe," Atlantic Economic Conference, Session on Recent Developments in Major Nations. Williamsburg, Virginia, October 13, 1990.

Analyzes labor productivity growth in component manufacturing industries in three countries—the United States, France, and Germany—and the labor productivity slowdown each country has experienced since about 1973.

Neef, Arthur. "An International Comparison of Manufacturing Productivity and Unit Labor Cost Trends," Social Science Research Council Conference on International Productivity and Competitiveness. Palo Alto, California, October 28-30, 1988.

Analyzes comparative trends in manufacturing labor productivity and unit labor costs in 12 countries and comparative developments in labor productivity in component manufacturing industries in the United States, Japan, and Germany.

Maddison, Angus. "Growth and Slowdown in Advanced Capitalist Economies: Techniques of Quantitative Assessment," *Journal of Economic Literature,* Vol. 25, June 1987.

Examines economic growth and labor productivity developments since 1870 in the United States, Japan, and four European countries and factors which help to explain variations in growth rates.

Nelson, Richard R. "Research on Productivity Growth and productivity Differences: Dead Ends and New Departures," *The Journal of Economic Literature,* Vol. 19, September 1981.

Reviews the research on productivity growth over time and across countries.

Hill, T.P. *The Measurement of Real Product.* Paris, Organization for Economic Cooperation and Development, February 1971.

A theoretical and empirical analysis of the growth rates for different industries and countries.

Shelton, William C. and Chandler, John H. "Technical Note–International Comparisons of Unit Labor Cost: Concepts and Methods," *Monthly Labor Review,* May 1963.

Hourly compensation costs

U.S. Department of Labor, Bureau of Labor Statistics. *International Comparisons of Hourly Compensation Costs for Production Workers in Manufacturing,* BLS Report 82, June 5, 1991.

Latest in a series of reports issued twice yearly.

Capdevielle, Patricia. "International Comparisons of compensation Costs," *Monthly Labor Review,* August 1991.

Most recent research summary comparing hourly compensation costs for production workers in manufacturing. More detailed results are published in BLS reports issued twice yearly.

The Family

Sorrentino, Constance. "The Changing Family in International Perspective," *Monthly Labor Review,* March 1990.

Analyzes comparative developments in selected demographic, household, and labor force characteristics over 25-30 years in the United States, Canada, Japan, and seven Western European nations.

Real gross domestic product per capita and per employed person

Summers, Robert and Heston, Alan. "The Penn World Table (Mark 5): An Expanded Set of International Comparisons, 1950-1988," *The Quarterly Journal of Economics,* May 1991.

Extrapolations and estimates of purchasing power parities, comparative prices, and quantity comparisons of gross domestic product per capita for over 100 countries that have been benchmarked to the results of the United Nations International Comparison Program Project.

Blades, Derek and Roberts, David. "A Note on the New OECD Benchmark Purchasing Power Parities for 1985," Paris. Organisation for Economic Cooperation and Development, Economic Studies No. 9, Autumn 1987.

Provides a short description of how the 1985 purchasing power parities for OECD countries were calculated and how they differ from the 1980 benchmark estimates.

Organisation for Economic Cooperation and Development. *Purchasing Power Parities and Real Expenditures, 1985.* Paris, Organisation for Economic Cooperation and Development, 1987.

Methods and results of the 1985 benchmark comparisons for the member countries of the Organisation for Economic Cooperation and Development.

United Nations. *World Comparisons of Purchasing Power and Real Product for 1980.* Phase IV of the International Comparison Project. New York, 1986.

Kravis, Irving B. "Comparative Studies of National Incomes and Prices," *Journal of Economic Literature, Vol. XXII,* March 1984.

Summarizes developments in the study of comparative national incomes and price levels with special attention to the United Nations International Comparison Project.

Union membership

Chang, Clara and Sorrentino, Constance. "Union Membership Statistics in 12 Countries," *Monthly Labor Review,* December 1991, pp. 46-53.

Summarizes issues relating to international comparisons of union membership and presents statistics adjusted to an employed wage and salary worker basis for selected years.

Visser, Jelle. "Trends in Trade Union Membership." Chapter 4 in *OECD Employment Outlook.* Paris, Organisation for Economic Cooperation and Development, July 1991.

An analysis of union membership statistics covering both European and non-European OECD member countries.

Visser, Jelle. *European Trade Unions in Figures.* Boston, Kluwer Law and Taxation Publishers, 1989.

An analysis and compilation of trade union statistics for 10 European countries for the period 1913 to 1985.

Chapter 14. Occupational Safety and Health Statistics

Part I. Annual Survey of Occupational Injuries and Illnesses

Background

The Bureau of Labor Statistics has been developing data on safety and health conditions for workers on the job since 1912 when it introduced its series on industrial accidents in the iron and steel industries. Subsequent BLS studies reflected a growing concern for the worker disabled on the job and were helpful in the development of the present workers' compensation system.

It was not, however, until the passage of the Occupational Safety and Health Act of 1970 that the Bureau was delegated responsibility for developing a comprehensive statistical system covering all work-related deaths, injuries, and illnesses. In the words of the act, the Commissioner of the Bureau of Labor Statistics was responsible for "furthering the purposes of the Occupational Safety and Health Act by developing and maintaining an effective program of collection, compilation, analysis, and publication of occupational safety and health statistics." Shortly thereafter, the Bureau, in cooperation with many State governments, designed an annual survey to estimate the number and frequency of work-related injuries and illnesses nationwide and for participating States.

Twenty years after the act, this BLS Federal/State survey is undergoing major changes, following recent Congressional approval of a multi-year effort. Briefly stated, the annual survey will be expanded to report on the characteristics of workers and work hazards involved in injury and illness cases. A separate census of fatal occupational injuries also will be developed. (See "technical references" for reports of ongoing pilot work on this survey redesign.)

Survey Definitions

The following definitions of occupational injuries and illnesses and lost workdays used in the annual survey are the same as those used by employers to keep logs of such incidents throughout the survey (calendar) year. (See technical references for citations of instructional materials useful in understanding the types of cases to record under current recordkeeping guidelines.)

Recordable injuries and illnesses are:

1. Occupational deaths, regardless of the time between injury and death, or the length of the illness; or
2. Nonfatal occupational illnesses; or
3. Nonfatal occupational injuries which involve one or more of the following: Loss of consciousness, restriction of work or motion, transfer to another job, or medical treatment (other than first aid).

Occupational injury is any injury such as a cut, fracture, sprain, amputation, etc. which results from a work-related event or from a single instantaneous exposure in the work environment.

Occupational illness is any abnormal condition or disorder, other than one resulting from an occupational injury, caused by exposure to factors associated with employment. It includes acute and chronic illnesses or disease which may be caused by inhalation, absorption, ingestion, or direct contact.

The following listing gives the categories of occupational illnesses and disorders that are used to classify recordable illnesses. For purposes of information, examples of each category are given. These are typical examples, however, and are not to be considered the complete listing of the types of illnesses and disorders that are to be counted under each category.

a. *Occupational skin diseases or disorders.* Examples: Contact dermatitis, eczema, or rash caused by primary irritants and sensitizers or poisonous plants; oil acne; chrome ulcers; chemical burns or inflammations.
b. *Dust diseases of the lungs (pneumoconioses).* Examples: Silicosis, asbestosis and other asbestos-related diseases, coal worker's pneumoconiosis, byssinosis, siderosis, and other pneumoconioses.

c. *Respiratory conditions due to toxic agents.* Examples: Pneumonitis, pharyngitis, rhinitis or acute congestion due to chemicals, dust, gases, or fumes; farmer's lung.

d. *Poisoning (systemic effects of toxic materials).* Examples: Poisoning by lead, mercury, cadmium, arsenic, or other metals; poisoning by carbon monoxide, hydrogen sulfide, or other gases; poisoning by benzol, carbon tetrachloride, or other organic solvents; poisoning by insecticide sprays such as parathion and lead arsenate; poisoning by other chemicals such as formaldehyde, plastics, and resins.

e. *Disorders due to physical agents (other than toxic materials).* Examples: Heatstroke, sunstroke, heat exhaustion, and other effects of environmental heat; freezing, frostbite, and effects of ionizing radiation (isotopes, X-rays, radium); effects of nonionizing radiation (welding flash, ultraviolet rays, microwaves, sunburn).

f. *Disorders associated with repeated trauma.* Examples: Conditions due to repeated motion, vibration, or pressure, such as carpal tunnel syndrome; noise-induced hearing loss; synovitis, tenosynovitis, and bursitis; and Raynaud's phenomena.

g. *All other occupational illnesses.* Examples: Anthrax, brucellosis, infectious hepatitis, malignant and benign tumors, food poisoning, histoplasmosis, coccidioidomycosis.

Lost workday cases involving days away from work are those cases which result in days away from work, or a combinatoin of days away from work and days of restricted work activity.

Lost workday cases involving restricted work activity are those cases which result *only* in restricted work activity.

Lost workdays—away from work are the number of workdays (consecutive or not) on which the employee would have worked but could not because of occupational injury or illness.

Lost workdays—restricted work activity are the number of workdays (consecutive or not) on which, because of injury or illness:

1. The employee was assigned to another job on a temporary basis;
2. The employee worked at a permanent job less than full time; or
3. The employee worked at a permanently assigned job but could not perform all duties normally connected with it.

The number of days away from work or days of restricted work activity does not include the day of injury or onset of illness or any days on which the employee would not have worked even though able to work.

Survey Measures

Survey data are developed for three basic types of cases: (1) Fatalities, (2) lost workday cases, and (3) nonfatal cases without lost workdays. In addition, the number of workdays lost or restricted are tabulated as one measure of the severity of lost workday cases.

In addition to counting the number of injury and illness cases reported, the survey also records the frequency (incidence) of such cases. Incidence rates permit comparison among industries and establishments of varying sizes. They express various measures of injuries and illnesses in terms of a constant, i.e, exposure hours in the work environment (200,000 employee hours or the equivalent of 100 full-time employees working for 1 year), thus allowing for a common statistical base across industries regardless of employment size of establishments. In this way, a firm with 5 cases recorded for 70 employees can compare its injury and illness experience to that of an entire industry with 12,000 cases for 150,000 employees. (The method of calculating incidence rates is discussed in a later section.)

Comparisons may also be made to evaluate the performance of a particular industry over a period of time, similar establishments in the same industry, or establishments in the same industry but in different geographic areas. Further comparisons are possible using the different types of rates computed for each industry—total cases, cases that involve lost workdays, nonfatal cases that do not involve lost workdays, and the number of workdays lost or restricted. These measures are available for injuries, illnesses, and injuries and illnesses combined.

Scope of the Survey

The survey sample selected by BLS consists of approximately 250,000 units in private industry. Survey data are solicited from employers having 11 employees or more in agricultural production, and from all employers in agricultural services, forestry, and fishing; oil and gas extraction; construction; manufacturing; transportation and public utilities; wholesale trade; retail trade; finance, insurance, and real estate; and services (except private households). Data for employees covered by other Federal safety and health legislation are provided by the Mine Safety and Health Administration of the U.S. Department of Labor and the Federal Railroad Administration of the U.S. Department of Transportation. Although State and local government agencies are not surveyed for national estimates, several States have legislation which enables them to collect these data. (Self-employed persons are not considered to be employees under the 1970 act.)

State Participation

Federal grants covering about 50 percent of the operating cost permit States to develop estimates of occupational injuries and illnesses and to provide the data from which BLS produces national results. National data for selected States which do not have operational grants are collected directly by BLS and by the State agencies under contract. The participating State agencies collect and process the data and prepare estimates using standardized procedures established by BLS to insure uniformity and consistency among the States. To further insure comparability and reliability, BLS designs and identifies the survey sample for each State and, through its regional offices, validates the survey results, and provides technical assistance to the State agencies on a continuing basis.

Data Collection

State agencies mail report forms to selected employers in February to cover the previous calendar year's experience. For those States not participating in the program, reporting forms are mailed by BLS. Each employer completes a single report form which is used for both national and State estimates of occupational injuries and illnesses. This procedure eliminates duplicate reporting by respondents and, together with the use of identical survey techniques at the national and State levels, insures maximum comparability of estimates. (A copy of the reporting form, No. 200-S, is included at the end of the chapter.)

Information for the injury and illness portion of the report form is copied directly from employer logs. The form also contains questions about the number of employee hours worked (needed in the calculation of incidence rates), the reporting unit's principal products or activity, and average employment to insure that the establishment is classified in the correct industry and employment-size class. State agency personnel edit the completed report forms and verify apparent inconsistencies through phone calls, correspondence, or visits. The data are keypunched and mechanically edited. Reports which do not meet the computer screening criteria are verified with the employer.

By midsummer, the active collection phase of the survey is completed and the preparation of data for both national and State estimates of occupational injuries and illnesses begins.

Sample Design

Because the survey is a Federal-State cooperative program and the data must meet the needs of participating State agencies, an independent sample is selected for each State. The sample is selected to represent all private industries in the States and territories. The sample size for the survey is dependent upon (1) the characteristics for which estimates are needed, (2) the industries for which estimates are desired, (3) the characteristics of the population being sampled, (4) the target reliability of the estimates, and (5) the survey design employed.

While there are many characteristics upon which the sample design could be based, the Bureau elected to use the total recorded case incidence rate. This is considered to be one of the most significant characteristics and, importantly, the least variable; therefore, it requires the smallest sample size.

The salient features of the sample design employed are its use of stratified random sampling with a Neyman allocation and a ratio estimator. The characteristics used to stratify the establishments are the Standard Industrial Classification (SIC) code and employment. Since these characteristics are highly correlated with an establishment's number and rate of recorded injuries and illnesses, stratified sampling provides greater precision and, thus, results in a smaller sample size than simple random sampling. The Neyman allocation produces the minimum sample size which will provide an estimate with a given sampling variance. For the larger employment size classes, the allocation procedure places all of the establishments of the frame in the sample; as employment decreases, smaller and smaller proportions of establishments are included in the sample. The certainty strata are usually the size groups with more than 100 employees. The precision of the sample is further improved, hence permitting a reduction in sample size, by using the ratio estimator which in turn uses employment data that are correlated with the characteristics which are to be measured.

The sample is designed to produce data at the 2-digit SIC industry level in agriculture, forestry, and fishing; at the 3-digit level in oil and gas extraction; construction; transportation and public utilities; wholesale and retail trade; finance, insurance, and real estate; and services; and at the 4-digit level in manufacturing. Beginning with data for 1989, the *Standard Industrial Classification Manual*, 1987 edition, was used to classify industries.

Estimation Procedures

Weighting

By means of a weighting procedure, sample units are constructed to represent all units in their size class for a particular industry. The weight is determined by the inverse of the sampling ratio for the industry/employment-size class from which the unit was selected. Because a small proportion of survey forms are not returned, weights of responding employers in a sampling cell are adjusted to account for nonrespondents. The respondents are then shifted into the estimating cell determined by the employment and business activity reported. Data for each unit are multiplied by the appropriate weight and nonresponse adjustment factor. The products are then aggregated to obtain a total for the estimating cell.

Data for an individual estimating cell are weighted according to the following formula:

$$X_i = \sum_{j=1}^{n} W_{ij} X_{ij}$$

where:

X_i = weighted estimate of characteristics, e.g., number of cases reported, in size class i
W_{ij} = weight of sample unit (establishment) j, in size class i, adjusted for nonresponse
X_{ij} = characteristics reported by sample unit j, in size class i

Benchmarking

Because the universe file which provides the sample frame is not current to the reference year of the survey, it is necessary to adjust the data before publication to reflect current employment levels. This procedure is known as benchmarking. In the annual survey, all estimates of totals are adjusted by the benchmark factor at the estimating cell level. The benchmarking procedure requires a source of accurate employment data which can be converted into annual average employment figures for the cell level in which separate estimates are desired. Because industry/employment-size data are required for national estimates, benchmark factors are calculated using both industry level employment data and size class level employment data. The benchmark factors are applied to the size class "blow up" estimates.

Incidence rate calculation

Incidence rates are calculated using the total obtained through the weighting and benchmarking procedures. The adjusted estimates for a particular characteristic, for example injury cases involving lost workdays, are aggregated to the appropriate level of industry detail. The total is multiplied by 200,000 (the base of hours worked by 100 full-time employees for 1 year). The product is then divided by the weighted and benchmarked estimate of hours worked as reported in the survey for the industry segment.

The formula for calculating the incidence rate at the lowest level of industry detail is:

$$\text{Incidence rate} = \frac{\text{(Sum of characteristic reported) X 200,000}}{\text{Sum of number of hours worked}}$$

Incidence rates for higher levels of industry detail are produced using aggregated weighted and benchmarked totals. Rates may be computed by industry, employment size, geographic area, extent or outcome of case, number of lost workdays, etc.

Reliability of Estimates

All estimates derived from a sample survey are subject to sampling and nonsampling errors. Sampling errors occur because observations are made on a sample, not on the entire population. Estimates based on the different possible samples of the same size and sample design could differ. The relative standard errors, which are a measure of the sampling error in the estimates, are calculated as part of the survey's estimation process. For the all-industry estimate of the total occupational injuries and illnesses incidence rate, the sample size is set to insure that a year-to-year difference of 0.10 or more will be statistically significant at the 95-percent confidence level. Target relative sampling oerrors for year-to-year changes in the total injury and illness rate are also set for each industry. These targets vary from 7 percent to 38 percent, with the average being 11 percent, to give a 95-percent level of confidence. Both the estimates and the relative standard errors of the estimates are published in the BLS annual bulletin, *Occupational Injuries and Illnesses in the United States by Industry.*

Nonsampling errors in the estimates can be attributed to many sources, e.g., inability to obtain information about all cases in the sample, mistakes in recording or coding the data, definitional difficulties, and so forth. To minimize the nonsampling errors in the estimates, the completed forms are edited and apparent inconsistencies are checked with the employer. A small fraction of the sample does not submit usable data. To account for this missing information, nonresponse adjustment factors are applied at the appropriate industry and size class level.

Publication Guidelines

The estimating procedure generates occupational injury and illness estimates for approximately 900 SIC codes. Industry estimates are *not published* if one of the following situations occurred.

1. Estimates for the industry are based on reports from fewer than three companies. Or, if three or more companies report data for the industry, one firm employs more than 50 percent of the workers or two companies combined employ more than 75 percent.
2. Average employment for the industry was less than 10,000 in the survey year. However, data for an industry with an annual average employment of less than 10,000 are publishable if the majority of the employment was reported in the survey.
3. The relative standard error on total cases for the industry at 1 standard error was more than 20 percent.
4. Benchmark factor for the industry was less than 0.90 or greater than 1.49.

Data for an unpublished industry are included in the total for the broader industry level of which it is a part.

Also, selected items of data are suppressed for publishable industries if the sampling error for the estimate equals or exceeds 60 percent.

Presentation

Each year, BLS publishes a comprehensive bulletin covering national results. Selected national data also are published in a news release, a detailed industry summary, and periodically in *Monthly Labor Review* articles. The data are also available on BLS data diskettes. The data are published in safety and trade journals and in the President's *Annual Report on Occupational Safety and Health to the U.S. Congress.*

In addition, State data on microfiche are available from the National Technical Information Service, 5285 Port Royal Road, Springfield, VA 22161.

Uses and Limitations

National and State policymakers use the survey as an indicator of the magnitude of occupational safety and health problems. The Occupational Safety and Health Administration uses the statistics to help determine which industries have the greatest need to improve safety programs and to measure the effectiveness of the 1970 act in reducing work-related injuries and illnesses.

Both labor and management use the estimates in evaluating safety programs. Other users include insurance carriers involved in workers' compensation, industrial hygienists, manufacturers of safety equipment, researchers, and others concerned with job safety and health.

In terms of the recording and reporting of occupational illnesses, the statistics generated through the annual survey are a reliable measure of disease cases that are unequivocally visible. However, in terms of statistical validity, the data may be wanting because chronic diseases and diseases with long latency periods, although not totally excluded, are largely beyond the scope of the survey system. To this extent, an undercount exists in the illness estimates. There is, as yet, no reliable measure of that undercount. The only other comprehensive source of occupational disease statistics lies in State workers' compensation records. However, the same difficulties in establishing an occupational link apply to workers' compensation cases.

Part II. Supplementary Data System

The Supplementary Data System (SDS) of the Bureau of Labor Statistics is a comprehensive effort to standardize occupational injury and illness data from State workers' compensation information to achieve some degree of comparability. The SDS data are unique in the detail available, providing analysts with opportunities for more extensive research than heretofore possible.

Background

While the annual survey program provided the information required by the Occupational Safety and Health Act of 1970, there was an increasing demand for information about characteristics of the occupational injuries and illnesses and the workers to whom they were occurring. In 1973, in response to this demand, the Bureau began testing the feasibility of collecting such information through contracts with States.

Records routinely generated by State workers' compensation programs—employee and employer reports, medical reports, compensation award records, and so forth—were long recognized as potentially valuable sources of information about occupational injuries and illnesses. Most workers' compensation agencies were primarily concerned with administering claims systems, however, and were not particularly concerned with availability and accuracy of industry, occupation, or injury and illness data. Additionally, States processing such data had different coding systems, sometimes with identical terms being defined differently.

States were urged to supply the desired information in machine-readable form. The different classification systems and record formats resulted in noncomparabilities and processing difficulties, however. As a result, the Bureau revised the program to require participating States to use comparable record formats and classifications.

In 1976, the current structure of the Supplementary Data System was established. The name was chosen from the role SDS plays in providing supplementary information to the annual survey of injuries and illnesses. Although the SDS does not affect the variations in coverage and reporting requirements among States, it requires that participating States provide prescribed data elements, and use specific classification systems, standard record formats, and uniform procedures.

Description of SDS

The primary source of information for the SDS is a first report of injury or illness, which employers and insurance carriers submit to State workers' compensation agencies. All jurisdictions require such reports. There are four basic types of information on the report. The first identifies the employer and permits classification of the case by industry and geographic location. The second lists characteristics of the employee such as age, sex, salary, and occupation.

The third describes how the accident or exposure occurred, any objects or substances involved, the nature of the injury or illness, and the part of body affected. The fourth provides information on the workers' compensation carrier, possible disability, and other items needed to process the claim. Participating State agencies classify, code, and process the information from the various workers' compensation reports.

The prescribed data elements which must be uniformly defined and submitted by all participating States are:

State code
Reference year
Case number
Year and month of occurrence
Occupation of employee
Industry
Ownership (public or private industry)
Nature of injury or illness
Part of body affected
Source of injury or illness
Type of accident or exposure
Gender of employee

At their option, States may also submit other data elements, such as duration of employment, extent of disability, and weekly wages, some of which may be defined differently from State to State. For example, "duration of employment" may refer to time with an employer, in a particular occupation, or in a particular job. The following optional items as of 1988 may be submitted by participating States.

Day of occurrence
Hour of shift
Associated object or substance
Age of employee
Duration of employment
Weekly wages
Extent of disability (fatalities)
Kind of insurance

Classification systems used by all States in the SDS include: (1) the 1972 and 1987 *Standard Industrial Classification Manual* to code industry; (2) the 1980 *Bureau of the Census Alphabetical Index of Industries and Occupations* to code the occupation of the injured or ill employee; (3) the American National Standards Institute Z16.2—1962 *Method of Recording Basic Facts Relating to the Nature and Occurrence of Work Injuries* (with codes expanded and modified by the Bureau) to classify the nature of the injury or illness, the part of body affected, the source of the injury or illness, and the type of accident or exposure; and (4) a newly developed classification, the associated object or substance, which provides additional information about the factors associated with the injury or illness.

To achieve uniform data, the Bureau establishes conceptual and operational standards which are developed in consultation with the State agencies. Federal/State cooperation is achieved through specific actions and groups tailored toward improving the SDS. For example, State coding is periodically reviewed by regional and national office personnel for uniformity among all States. Uniformity is also achieved through State participation on the SDS Interpretations Committee, which resolves differences in coding difficult cases.

Presentation

SDS data are presented in two different formats, both available from the National Technical Information Service (NTIS). Injury and illness characteristics organized into groups of multistate tabulations are available in microfiche and paper copy. Individual case records, containing no information identifying employees or employers, are compiled into a multistate microdata file.

Uses and Limitations

The Supplementary Data System provides valuable information in three general areas: (1) Defining work-related safety and health problems for policymakers; (2) guiding professional investigations and research; and (3) making available information for the administration of workers' compensation programs.

Because SDS is a machine-readable categorization of workers' compensation information, it provides a State with the capability to analyze its cases in considerable detail, including the types of cases handled and the predominant types of affected workers and work situations. The data direct attention to problem areas which can be most effectively handled by safety and health standards, training, or compliance programs.

The Supplementary Data System standardizes the classification, processing, and tabulations of data. Nevertheless, it is not a complete census of occupational injuries and illnesses because, as of 1988, only 14 States were participating. In addition, coverage and reporting requirements variations reflect differences in State workers' compensation laws. Differences also exist because of statutory and administrative variations in workers covered and reports processed, and in the kinds of cases required to be reported to workers' compensation agencies.

Finally, occupational illness data from the SDS suffer from the same low degree of identification as that experienced in the annual survey of occupational injuries and illnesses. Recognition of occupational illness depends on the "state of the art." As medical knowledge increases, illness identification will improve in both data collection systems.

Part III. Work Injury Reports

Work Injury Reports (WIR), initiated in 1978, provide detailed information on the causes and effects of workplace injuries and illnesses obtained directly from individual injured workers. Such data are not available from the annual survey or the Supplementary Data System, which contain information primarily originating from individual business establishments.

Background

The annual survey produces measures of the incidence and severity of work-related injuries and illnesses, while the SDS complements the annual survey by providing information on selected general characteristics of the injured worker and the injury. Neither program, however, provides extensive information on the numerous, more detailed factors associated with certain types of injuries. When the Occupational Safety and Health Administration indicated a need for this type of data in 1978, BLS established the WIR program.

OSHA addresses a wide variety of issues, such as hazardous worksite conditions, the safe operation of tools or equipment, the use of protective equipment, and special industry standards. The WIR survey program, by allowing flexibility in both the survey subject matter and the data elements collected, is able to provide this information. A WIR survey is designed to identify patterns of accident causes, the activity of the worker at the time of the incident, the equipment used, the protective equipment worn, and any training received.

Because it would be difficult, if not impossible, for employers to provide some of the needed information, the decision was made to survey the injured worker directly. For example, questions regarding worker activity are so specific that, in the absence of witnesses, employers must question the injured worker. Similarly, only the worker could explain why protective equipment was or was not used. Finally, by surveying the worker directly, it is possible to expand the scope of questions on work being done when injured to include safety training and prior work experience, if any, provided by previous employers. Such information helps safety and health experts to zero in on the proportion of the injured workers who lacked any safety training on the work activity they performed when injured.

The Survey Process

Choosing a topic is the first phase of the survey process and is based on OSHA's assessment of data requirements. The WIR program permits substantial flexibility in subject matter because it uses the SDS source document, the State Workers' Compensation Report, from which the following injury or illness characteristics are available: Nature of injury, part of body affected, source of injury, and event or exposure. The report also identifies the industry and the worker's occupation. Any one of these characteristics can be selected for a specific study. WIR surveys have focused on industries such as oil and gas drilling and well servicing, logging, and longshore operations. Other surveys have been based on injuries to a particular part of the body (back, hand, eye, face, head, and foot injuries), or selected types of accidents (falls on stairs, falls from elevations, falls from scaffolds, falls from ladders, and contact with hazardous substances). Specific nature of injuries (upper extremity amputations, chemical burns, and heat burns), and occupations (construction laborers, warehouse workers) were the subjects of other Work Injury Reports. The scope of a WIR survey, however, can be expanded beyond the SDS classification categories. Three surveys have used worker activity, which is not coded in SDS, as a selection criterion (workers injured while welding, using power saws, and servicing equipment).

The questionnaire used in the WIR program is tailored to obtain information unique for each topic selected for study by OSHA. (See example attached.) Because development of the survey questionnaire requires close interaction with OSHA, a WIR task force was formed of representatives from the BLS Office of Occupational Safety and Health Statistics and the OSHA Offices of Compliance, Standards Development, Training, and Regulatory Analysis. Also included on the task force are representatives of the National Institute for Occupational Safety and Health (NIOSH), who provide expertise in the area of occupational injury and illness epidemiology. All proposed survey questions are discussed by the task force and, where possible, multiple choice responses are provided. Each questionnaire is designed to be brief to minimize the burden on respondents and encourage participation. In general, information is sought on how the injury occurred, the worker's activity and location, what hazardous conditions prevailed, the nature of the equipment involved, the safeguards used, and the extent of related safety training. Additionally, each questionnaire is tested on a small panel of workers before it used for the survey.

Respondents in current surveys are chosen by a systematic random sampling procedure, unless the expected population size is small enough to warrant a complete census. Survey parameters are estimated using a Horwitz-Thompson estimator with a nonresponse adjustment procedure. Based on a predicted population size, the sample size is targeted so that any estimate of a proportion of the entire universe will have a sampling error no greater than plus or minus 5 percent at the 2 sigma, or 95-percent, confidence level. Early WIR surveys were based on a purposive sample of about 750 respondents.

The universe of potential respondents generally includes all workers in the participating States who meet the criteria established for the survey. The survey period is usually limited to 1 month, but may be longer if the expected population is very small or if seasonality is a concern. Excluded from each survey are cases in the coal and metallic and nonmetallic mining industries, or government, because these sectors are not regulated by OSHA. Also excluded are cases involving fatalities or assaults.

Participating State agencies screen incoming first reports of injury for injury or illness cases that meet BLS criteria for defining the target population of injured workers to be surveyed. A table of sample selection numbers, generated by BLS for each survey, is used to determine cases to be sampled. A questionnaire prepared by BLS is mailed directly to the selected injured worker's home address.

Staff in the agencies of the participating States match returned questionnaires with the appropriate first report of injury forms, and code the primary SDS data elements, such as nature of injury, industry, occupation, age, and sex. All information which could identify a worker or an employer is deleted from the questionnaire and first report. At the completion of the data collection phase, all returned questionnaires are transmitted to BLS-Washington, together with refusals, nonmailables, and Post Office returns.

Questionnaires are manually edited by BLS-Washington for completion and consistency. Results of the survey are then keypunched and mechanically edited. Finally, tabulations are prepared and published with an accompanying text which highlights the findings.

Weighting and Estimation Procedures

Unless a census has been taken, the sample of injured workers is weighted to account for all injured workers within the scope of the survey in the participating States. The weight assigned is the inverse of the probability of selection, and is applied to each sample member's response.

Injured workers who do not return the questionnaires are referred to as unit nonrespondents and a weighting-class nonresponse adjustment procedure is used to reduce the potential bias due to nonresponse. This procedure partitions the sample into cells, and a unit nonresponse adjustment factor is calculated within each cell. This procedure is based on the assumption that, within each cell, the distribution of the variables of the unit nonrespondents would be the same as the distribution of the respondents.

To determine the set of cells for unit nonresponse adjustment, the following characteristics are compared for respondents and nonrespondents: Age, sex, nature of injury, part of body affected, source of injury, type of accident, industry, and occupation. If it is determined that there are differences in the distribution of a particular characteristic between respondents and nonrespondents, a partition based on this characteristic is used to adjust for unit nonresponse.

In addition to unit nonrespondents, each survey must adjust for a small number of workers who respond to the survey but do not answer all of the questions. These are referred to as item nonrespondents. To account for this type of nonresponse, it is assumed that the response distribution of the item nonrespondents would be the same as the response distribution of the item respondents.

For each question, a final weight for each respondent is calculated as the product of the original weight, the unit nonresponse factor, and the item nonresponse factor. The estimate of the total number of in-scope injured workers for each question is equal to the sum of the final weights of the respondents. The estimate of the percent of workers giving a particular answer to a question is the sum of the final weights of the respondents giving a particular answer divided by the estimate of the number of injured workers in the scope of the survey.

Reliability of Estimates

All estimates derived from a sample survey are subject to sampling and nonsampling errors. Sampling errors occur because observations are made on a sample, not on the universe. The standard errors, which are a measure of the sampling error in the estimates, are calculated as part of the survey's estimation process and are available upon request.

Nonsampling errors in the estimates can be attributed to many sources, e.g., inability to obtain information about all cases in the sample, mistakes in recording or coding the data, definitional difficulties, etc. To minimize the nonsampling errors in the estimates, the completed questionnaires are edited, and apparent inconsistencies are checked. Reweighting of respondents information, as described above, takes into account missing data from injured workers who did not respond.

Presentation

At the completion of each survey, the results are tabulated and published along with an analysis of the survey findings. As in other BLS programs, data are provided in summary form; no individual responses are identified. Since 1979, 20 survey reports have been published. The most recent reports are listed in the technical references.

Uses and Limitations

The flexibility in both the types of surveys done and the kind of information collected enables the surveys to produce a broad range of data on work-related incidents. The ways in which the data can be used, as well as the people who use it, are as varied as the information itself. OSHA, of course, is the primary user of WIR data.

WIR surveys can be used by OSHA in the development or revision of safety standards and in the planning of compliance strategy and training programs. In standards setting, WIR data can be used to test the need for a particular standard and to support the requirements of the standard. They can also be used to direct OSHA's attention to an area where a problem may exist and to assist in determining the corrective action that may need to be taken.

Once standards are approved, OSHA is responsible for their enforcement by compliance officers who inspect workplaces for adherence to them. Even on an aggregated basis, WIR survey data can provide useful information on how and why a particular type of accident occurs, and these data have proven a valuable tool in training compliance officers.

In training and education, OSHA needs information for targeting the categories of workers who might benefit the most by knowing the injury potential inherent in certain work situations. Once these areas are identified, OSHA can tailor educational programs to increase awareness of these problems. Because of the detailed information provided by WIR surveys, OSHA has been able to incorporate data from several surveys into their educational programs.

Other data users include employers and safety officials throughout private industry, government, and labor organizations. Special interest groups such as lawyers, consumer organizations, and manufacturers of safety equipment also find the information useful. For example, NIOSH uses data in conjunction with their testing procedures and special studies, while State government agencies use the data to evaluate standards specific to safety issues in their States.

In spite of the unprecedented amount of information provided through the program, there are limitations associated with the survey data. Data collection procedures limit coverage, for the most part, to those States which participate in the SDS program. For this reason, the WIR program does not produce national estimates. The program is also subject to differences in State workers' compensation reporting requirements. At the present time, the program does not permit detailed comparisons between injured workers and the rest of the working population. For example, there are no data on the use of protective equipment for workers who were not injured. Lack of data on workers who were exposed to the same hazards but not injured precludes the development of incidence rates as a measure of the relative risk by activity, occupation, etc. In addition, the data reflect the injury experience for a particular reference period ranging from 1 to 6 months.

Technical References

Toscano, Guy and Windau, Janice. "Further Test of a Census Approach to Compiling Data on Fatal Work Injuries," *Monthly Labor Review,* October 1991.

Windau, Janice and Goodrich, Donna. "Testing a Census Approach to Compiling Data on Fatal Work Injuries," *Monthly Labor Review,* December 1990.

Personick, Martin E. "Nursing Home Aides Experience Increase in Serious Injuries," *Monthly Labor Review,* February 1990.

Personick, Martin E. and Taylor-Shirley, Katherine. "Profiles in Safety and Health: Occupational Hazards of Meatpacking," *Monthly Labor Review,* January 1989.

Eisenberg, William M. and McDonald, Helen. "Evaluating Workplace Injury and Illness Records; Testing a Procedure," *Monthly Labor Review,* April 1988.

Root, Norman and Sebastian, Deborah. "BLS Develops Measure of Job Risk by Occupation," *Monthly Labor Review,* October 1981.

Hilaski, Harvey J. "Understanding Statistics on Occupational Illnesses," *Monthly Labor Review,* March 1981.

Root, Norman and Hoefer, Michael. "The First Work Injury Data Available From New BLS Study," *Monthly Labor Review,* January 1979.

Bureau of Labor Statistics.

Occupational Injuries and Illnesses in the United States by Industry. Bulletin issued yearly.

Technical References—Continued

Evaluating Your Firm's Injury and Illness Record: Construction Industries, April 1992.

This guide helps construction employers measure and evaluate their injury and illness experience compared with others in the industry. Similar guides for other industries, such as manufacturing, are also available.

Injury and Illness Data Available from 1988 Workers' Compensation Record, Announcement 90-2, September 1990.

Heat Burn Injuries, Bulletin 2358, May 1990; *Chemical Burn Injuries,* Bulletin 2353, October 1989; *and Injuries Involving Longshore Operations,* Bulletin 2326, May 1989.

The three most recent Work Injury Reports, all of which cite previous studies.

Recordkeeping Guidelines for Occupational Injuries and Illnesses, September 1986.

These Guidelines are the official Department of Labor interpretation of employer recordkeeping requirements under the Occupational Safety and Health Act of 1970 and 29 CFR Part 1904.

Dear Employer:

The Occupational Safety and Health Act of 1970 requires the Secretary of Labor to collect, compile, and analyze statistics on occupational injuries and illnesses. This is accomplished through a joint Federal/State survey program with States that have received Federal grants for collecting and compiling statistics. Establishments are selected for this survey on a sample basis with varying probabilities depending upon size. Certain establishments may be included in each year's sample because of their importance to the statistics for their industry.

You have been selected to participate in the nationwide Occupational Injuries and Illnesses Survey for 1990. Under the Occupational Safety and Health Act, your report is mandatory.

The following items are enclosed for your use: (1) Instructions for completing the form; (2) The OSHA No. 200-S form and a copy for your files; and (3) An addressed return envelope. Please complete the OSHA No. 200-S form and return it within thirty days in the envelope provided.

If you have any questions about this survey, contact the survey collection agency indicated on the OSHA No. 200-S form.

Thank you for your cooperation with this important survey.

Sincerely,

GERARD F. SCANNELL
Assistant Secretary for
Occupational Safety and Health

1990 OSHA No. 200–S

Annual Occupational Injuries and Illnesses Survey Covering Calendar Year 1990

U.S. Department of Labor

Bureau of Labor Statistics for the Occupational Safety and Health Administration

The information collected on this form will be used for statistical purposes only by the BLS, OSHA, and the cooperating State Agencies.

THIS REPORT IS MANDATORY UNDER PUBLIC LAW 91–596. FAILURE TO REPORT CAN RESULT IN THE ISSUANCE OF CITATIONS AND ASSESSMENT OF PENALTIES.

O.M.B. No. 1220–0045
Approval Exp. 9/30/92

St. Sch. No. Ck. Suf.

SIC

EDIT

Complete this report whether or not there were recordable occupational injuries or illnesses.

PLEASE READ THE ENCLOSED INSTRUCTIONS

Burden Statement Located in instructions

Complete and return ONLY THIS FORM within 30 days

OSHA NO. 200-S

I. ANNUAL AVERAGE EMPLOYMENT IN 1990

Enter the average number of employees who worked during calendar year 1990 in the establishment(s) covered by this report. Include all classes of employees: full–time, part–time, seasonal, temporary, etc. See the instructions for an example of an annual average employment calculation. ***(Round to the nearest whole number.)***

II. TOTAL HOURS WORKED IN 1990

Enter the total number of hours actually worked during 1990 by **all** employees covered by this report. DO NOT include any non–work time even though paid such as vacations, sick leave, etc. If employees worked low hours in 1990 due to lay–offs, strikes, fires, etc., explain under Comments (section VII). ***(Round to the nearest whole number.)***

III. NATURE OF BUSINESS IN 1990

A. Check the box which best describes the general type of activity performed by the establishment(s) included in this report.

- ☐ Agriculture
- ☐ Forestry
- ☐ Fishing
- ☐ Mining
- ☐ Construction
- ☐ Manufacturing
- ☐ Transportation
- ☐ Communication
- ☐ Public Utilities
- ☐ Wholesale Trade
- ☐ Retail Trade
- ☐ Finance
- ☐ Insurance
- ☐ Real Estate
- ☐ Services
- ☐ Public Administration

B. Enter in order of importance the principal products, lines of trade, services or other activities. For each entry also include the approximate percent of total 1990 annual value of production, sales or receipts.

________ %

________ %

________ %

C. If this report includes any establishment(s) which perform services for other units of your company, indicate the primary type of service or support provided. ***(Check as many as apply.)***

1. ☐ Central administration
2. ☐ Research, development and testing
3. ☐ Storage (warehouse)
4. ☐ Other (specify)

IV. TESTING FOR DRUG OR ALCOHOL USE

A. Did the establishment(s) covered by this report have a formal **written** policy to test job applicants and/or employees for drug or alcohol use during calendar year 1990?

1. ☐ No
2. ☐ Yes

B. Were any drug or alcohol tests administered at the company's request to any employees as the result of the occurrence of a recordable work–related injury or illness during calendar year 1990?

1. ☐ No
2. ☐ Yes

V. RECORDABLE INJURIES AND ILLNESSES

Did the establishment(s) have any recordable injuries or illnesses during calendar year 1990?

1. ☐ No (Please complete section VII.)
2. ☐ Yes (Please complete sections VI and VII.)

SEE REVERSE →

REPORT LOCATION AND IDENTIFICATION

Complete this report for the establishment(s) covered by the description below:

Please indicate any address changes below.

RETURN REPORT TO:

VA Department of Labor and Industry
VOSH Research and Analysis
P.O. Box 12064
Richmond, Virginia 23241

For Information Call:

(804) 786-5490
(804) 786-7616

OSHA No. 200–S (Revised December 1990)

VI. OCCUPATIONAL INJURY AND ILLNESS SUMMARY (Covering Calendar Year 1990)

- ***Complete this section by copying totals from the annual summary of your 1990 OSHA No. 200.***
- Remember to reverse the carbon insert before completing this side.
- Leave section VI blank if there were no OSHA recordable injuries or illnesses during 1990.
- ***Note: First aid for injuries even when administered by a doctor or nurse is not recordable.***
- Please check your figures to be certain that the sum of entries in columns (7a) + (7b) + (7c) + (7d) + (7e) + (7f) + (7g) = the sum of entries in columns (8) + (9) + (13).
- If you listed fatalities in columns (1) and/or (8), please give a brief description of the object or event which caused each fatality in the "Comments" section.

OCCUPATIONAL INJURY CASES

INJURY RELATED FATALITIES** (DEATHS)	INJURIES WITH LOST WORKDAYS				INJURIES WITHOUT LOST WORKDAYS*
	Injury cases with days away from work and/or restricted workdays	Injury cases with days away from work	Total days away from work	Total days of restricted activity	
Number of DEATHS in col. 1 of the log (OSHA No. 200)	Number of CHECKS in col. 2 of the log (OSHA No. 200)	Number of CHECKS in col. 3 of the log (OSHA No. 200)	Sum of the DAYS in col. 4 of the log (OSHA No. 200)	Sum of the DAYS in col. 5 of the log (OSHA No. 200)	Number of CHECKS in col. 6 of the log (OSHA No. 200)
(1)	(2)	(3)	(4)	(5)	(6)
DEATHS					

OCCUPATIONAL ILLNESS CASES

TYPE OF ILLNESS Enter the number of checks from the appropriate columns of the log (OSHA No. 200).							ILLNESS RELATED FATALITIES** (DEATHS)	ILLNESSES WITH LOST WORKDAYS				ILLNESSES WITHOUT LOST WORKDAYS*
Occupational skin diseases or disorders	Dust diseases of the lungs	Respiratory conditions due to toxic agents	Poisoning (systemic effects of toxic materials)	Disorders due to physical agents	Disorders associated with repeated trauma	All other occupational illnesses		Illness cases with days away from work and/or restricted workdays	Illness cases with days away from work	Total days away from work	Total days of restricted activity	
(7)							Number of DEATHS in col. 8 of the log (OSHA No. 200)	Number of CHECKS in col. 9 of the log (OSHA No. 200)	Number of CHECKS in col. 10 of the log (OSHA No. 200)	Sum of the DAYS in col. 11 of the log (OSHA No. 200)	Sum of the DAYS in col. 12 of the log (OSHA No. 200)	Number of CHECKS in col. 13 of the log (OSHA No. 200)
(a)	(b)	(c)	(d)	(e)	(f)	(g)	(8)	(9)	(10)	(11)	(12)	(13)
							DEATHS					

* WITHOUT LOST WORKDAYS—CASES (WITH NO DAYS LOST) RESULTING IN EITHER: DIAGNOSIS OF OCCUPATIONAL ILLNESS, LOSS OF CONSCIOUSNESS, RESTRICTION OF WORK OR MOTION (ON THE DAY OF OCCURRENCE), TRANSFER TO ANOTHER JOB, OR MEDICAL TREATMENT BEYOND FIRST AID.

VII. REPORT PREPARED BY (Please type or print)

NAME ______________________

TITLE ______________________

SIGNATURE ______________________

AREA CODE __________ PHONE ______________

DATE ______________________

** IF YOU LISTED FATALITIES IN COLUMNS (1) AND/OR (8), PLEASE GIVE A BRIEF DESCRIPTION OF THE OBJECT OR EVENT WHICH CAUSED EACH FATALITY IN THE "COMMENTS" SECTION BELOW.

COMMENTS ______________________

SURVEY REPORTING REGULATIONS

Title 29, Part 1904.20–22 of the Code of Federal Regulations requires that: each employer shall return the completed survey form, OSHA No. 200–S, within 30 days of receipt in accordance with the instructions shown below.

We estimate that it will take an average of 10 – 30 minutes to complete this form, including time for reviewing instructions, searching existing data sources, gathering and maintaining the data needed, and completing and reviewing this information. If you have any comments regarding these estimates or any other aspect of this survey, send them to the Bureau of Labor Statistics, Division of Management Systems (1220–0045), 441 G St. NW, Washington, DC 20212, and to the Office of Management and Budget, Paperwork Reduction Project (1220–0045), Washington, DC 20503.

INSTRUCTIONS FOR COMPLETING THE OSHA NO. 200–S FORM 1990 OCCUPATIONAL INJURIES AND ILLNESSES SURVEY (Covering Calendar Year 1990)

Change of Ownership – When there has been a change of ownership during the report period, only the records of the current owner are to be entered in the report. Explain fully under Comments (Section VII), and include the date of the ownership change and the time period this report covers.

Partial–Year Reporting – For any establishment(s) which was not in existence for the entire report year, the report should cover the portion of the period during which the establishment(s) was in existence. Explain fully under Comments (Section VII), including the time period this report covers.

ESTABLISHMENTS INCLUDED IN THE REPORT

This report should include only those establishments located in, or identified by, the Report Location and Identification designation which appears next to your mailing address. This designation may be a geographical area, usually a county or city, or it could be a brief description of your operation within a geographical area. If you have any questions concerning the coverage of this report, please contact the agency identified on the OSHA No. 200–S report form.

DEFINITION OF ESTABLISHMENT

An ESTABLISHMENT is defined as a single physical location where business is conducted or where services or industrial operations are performed. (For example: a factory, mill, store, hotel, restaurant, movie theatre, farm, ranch, bank, sales office, warehouse, or central administrative office.)

For firms engaged in activities such as construction, transportation, communication, or electric, gas and sanitary services, which may be physically dispersed, reports should cover the place to which employees normally report each day.

Reports for personnel who do not primarily report or work at a single establishment, such as traveling salespersons, technicians, engineers, etc., should cover the location from which they are paid or the base from which personnel operate to carry out their activities.

SECTION I. ANNUAL AVERAGE EMPLOYMENT IN 1990

Enter in Section I the **average** (not the total) number of full and part–time employees who worked during calendar year 1990 in the establishment(s) included in this report. If more than one establishment is included in this report, add together the annual average employment for each establishment and enter the sum. Include all classes of employees – seasonal, temporary, administrative, supervisory, clerical, professional, technical, sales, delivery, installation, construction and service personnel, as well as operators and related workers.

Annual Average employment should be computed by summing the employment from all pay periods during 1990 and then dividing that sum by the total number of such pay periods throughout the entire year, including periods with no employment. For example, if you had the following monthly employment – Jan.–10; Feb.–10; Mar.–10; Apr.–5; May–5; June–5; July–5; Aug.–0; Sept.–0; Oct.–0; Nov.–5; Dec.–5– you would sum the number of employees for each monthly pay period (in this case, 60) and then divide that total by 12 (the number of pay periods during the year) to derive an annual average employment of 5.

SECTION II. TOTAL HOURS WORKED IN 1990

Enter in Section II the **total** number of hours actually **worked** by all classes of employees during 1990. Be sure to include **only** time on duty. **DO NOT include any non–work time** even though paid, such as vacations, sick leave, holidays, etc. The hours worked figure should be obtained from payroll or other time records wherever possible; if **hours worked** are not maintained separately from **hours paid,** please enter your best estimate. If actual hours worked are not available for employees paid on commission, salary, by the mile, etc., hours worked may be estimated on the basis of scheduled hours or 8 hours per workday.

For example, if a group of 10 salaried employees worked an average of 8 hours per day, 5 days a week, for 50 weeks of the report period, the total hours worked for this group would be 10 x 8 x 5 x 50 = 20,000 hours for the report period.

SECTION III. NATURE OF BUSINESS IN 1990

In order to verify the nature of business code, we must have information about the specific economic activity carried on by the establishment(s) included in your report during calendar year 1990.

Complete Parts A, B and C as indicated in Section III on the OSHA No. 200–S form. Complete Part C **only** if supporting services are provided to other establishments of your company. Leave Part C blank if a) supporting services are not the primary function of any establishment(s) included in this report or b) supporting services are provided but only on a **contract or fee basis** for the general public or for other business firms. **(Instructions continued on page 2.)**

NOTE: If more than one establishment is included, information in Section III should reflect the combined activities of all such establishments. One code will be assigned which best indicates the nature of business of the group of establishments as a whole.

SECTION IV. TESTING FOR DRUG OR ALCOHOL USE

A. Check the appropriate box. Check "Yes" if your company had a formal written policy, during calendar year 1990, to test **JOB APPLICANTS and/or EMPLOYEES** for drug or alcohol use. Examples of testing policies include: "For cause", for selected jobs, random tests, as part of an annual physical, periodic tests, or testing all employees.

Drug Test--A test designed to detect the presence of metabolites or drugs in urine or blood specimens.

Drugs include opioids, cocaine, cannabinoids (such as marijuana or hashish), hallucinogens, and their derivatives. Drugs for which persons have prescriptions (whether or not the prescription was legally obtained) are excluded. Please answer part B.

B. Check the appropriate box. Check "Yes" only if an employee was **actually tested** for drug or alcohol use in connection with a work-related injury or illness, **EVEN IF THE EMPLOYEE WAS ONE OTHER THAN THE EMPLOYEE WHO WAS INJURED OR BECAME ILL**, during calendar year 1990. Only drug or alcohol tests administered at the request of the company, whether actually administered by the company or another organization, should be considered when answering this question.

SECTION V. RECORDABLE INJURIES AND ILLNESSES

Check the appropriate box. If you checked "Yes", complete Sections VI and VII on the back of the form. If you checked "No", complete only Section VII.

SECTION VI. OCCUPATIONAL INJURY AND ILLNESS SUMMARY

This section can be completed easily by copying the totals from the annual summary of your 1990 OSHA No. 200 form (Log and Summary of Occupational Injuries and Illnesses). Please note that if this report covers more than one establishment, the final totals on the "Log" for each must be added and the sums entered in Section VI.

Leave Section VI blank if the employees covered in this report experienced no recordable injuries or illnesses during 1990.

If there were recordable injuries or illnesses during the year, please review your OSHA No. 200 form for each establishment to be included in this report to make sure that all entries are correct and complete before completing Section VI. Each recordable case should be included on the "Log" in only one of the six main categories or injuries or illnesses:

1. INJURY - related deaths (Log column 1)
2. INJURIES with days away from work and/or restricted days (Log column 2)
3. INJURIES without lost workdays (Log column 6)
4. ILLNESS - related deaths (Log column 8)
5. ILLNESSES with days away from work and/or restricted days (Log column 9)
6. ILLNESSES without lost workdays (Log column 13)

Also review each case to ensure that the appropriate entries have been made for the other columns if applicable. For example, if the case is an injury with Lost Workdays, be sure that the check for an injury involving **days away from work** (Log column 3) is entered if necessary. Also verify that the correct number of days away from work (Log column 4) and/or days of restricted work activity (Log column 5) are recorded. A similar review should be made for a case which is an illness with Lost Workdays (including Log columns 10, 11 and 12). Please remember that if your employees' loss of workdays is still continuing at the time the annual summary for the year is completed, you should estimate the number of future workdays they will lose and add this estimate to the actual workdays already lost. Each partial day away from work, other than the day of the occurrence of the injury or onset of illness, should be entered as one full restricted workday.

Also, for each case which is an illness, make sure that the appropriate column indicating Type of Illness (Log columns 7a-7g) is checked.

After completing your review of the individual case entries on the "Log," please make sure that the "Totals" line has been completed by summarizing Columns 1 through 13 according to the instructions on the back of the "Log" form. Then, copy these "Totals" onto Section VI of the OSHA No. 200-S form. If you entered fatalities in columns (1) and/or (8), please include in the "Comments" section a brief description of the object or event which caused each fatality.

FIRST AID

Finally, please remember that all injuries which, in your judgement, required **only First Aid Treatment**, even when administered by a doctor or nurse, should not be included in this report. First Aid Treatment is defined as one-time treatment and subsequent observation of minor scratches, cuts, burns, splinters, etc., which do not ordinarily require medical care.

SECTION VII. COMMENTS AND IDENTIFICATION

Please complete all parts including your area code and telephone number. Then return the OSHA No. 200-S form in the pre-addressed envelope. **KEEP** your file copy.

Bureau of Labor Statistics
Work Injury Report—Chemical Burns

U.S. Department of Labor

The information collected on this form by the Bureau of Labor Statistics and the State Agencies cooperating in its statistical program will be held in confidence and will be used for statistical purposes only.

This report is authorized by law 29 U.S.C. 2. Your voluntary cooperation is needed to make the results of this survey comprehensive, accurate, and timely.

Form Approved
O.M.B. No. 1220-0047
Approval Expires 9/30/86

Survey Code | 2 | 8 | 5 | Case Number ________   Date of Accident ___ – ___ – ___

A. Describe what you were doing at the time of your injury, and how the injury occurred. (For example: Pouring chemical into mixer and it splashed into eye; cleaning restroom with spray cleaner and sprayed liquid onto hand; jumpstarting car battery when battery exploded and liquid burned chest and arms.)

____

B. Provide as much information as possible about the chemical or substance that burned you.

1. Name of chemical (e.g., Hydrofluoric acid, sulfuric acid, etc.) ______
2. Type of substance or product (e.g., Soap, cleanser, paint, battery acid, concrete mix, lime, etc.) ______
3. Brand name of product: ______

C. In your job, how often did you work with/near the chemical or substance that burned you? *(Check one.)*

1. ☐ First time you worked with this chemical or substance
2. ☐ Daily or almost every day
3. ☐ About once a week
4. ☐ About once a month
5. ☐ Seldom—less than once a month

D. Did you receive written or printed instructions from your employer on safe work practices for handling chemicals?

1. ☐ No 2. ☐ Yes

E. How long was the chemical or substance on your skin or eyes? *(Check one.)*

1. ☐ Less than 1 minute
2. ☐ 1 to 5 minutes
3. ☐ 5 to 10 minutes
4. ☐ 10 to 30 minutes
5. ☐ 30 minutes or more
6. ☐ Don't know

F. Were eyewashes, deluge showers, or other emergency treatment available at the jobsite?

1. ☐ No
2. ☐ Yes—emergency eyewashes
3. ☐ Yes—emergency deluge showers
4. ☐ Yes—other emergency treatment (For example: Sinks or other sources of water): *(Describe)* ______

IF YES:

a. How close were you to them when you were burned? *(Check one.)*

1. ☐ Less than 10 feet
2. ☐ 10 to 25 feet
3. ☐ 25 to 50 feet
4. ☐ 50 to 100 feet
5. ☐ 100 feet or more
6. ☐ Don't know

b. Did you use any of these at the time of your injury?

1. ☐ No
2. ☐ Yes: *(Describe)* ______

G. Were there any conditions at the worksite which you feel contributed to your accident? *(Check all that apply.)*

1. ☐ Equipment in bad condition
2. ☐ Using wrong equipment
3. ☐ Working in a limited space
4. ☐ Inadequate lighting
5. ☐ No warning of hazardous substance in work area
6. ☐ Cluttered work area
7. ☐ Inadequate cleaning of work materials or work area
8. ☐ Too noisy
9. ☐ Poor ventilation
10. ☐ Other: *(Describe)* ______
11. ☐ No worksite conditions contributed to accident

H. Were there any other factors which you feel contributed to your accident? *(Check all that apply.)*

1. ☐ Not aware chemical or substance could burn you
2. ☐ Upset, under stress, or tired
3. ☐ Inadequate labeling: *(Explain)* ______
4. ☐ Handling procedures for the chemical not followed
5. ☐ Co-worker's activity: *(Describe)* ______
6. ☐ Not paying attention to what you were doing
7. ☐ Careless in what you were doing
8. ☐ Working too fast
9. ☐ Wearing wrong type of protective equipment
10. ☐ Not given instructions on how to do job
11. ☐ Other: *(Describe)* ______
12. ☐ No other factors contributed to accident

I. Check EACH TYPE of personal protective equipment which you were *wearing* when injured and *describe the materials*, for example: Leather, cotton, PVC, neoprene, nitrile, natural rubber, latex, and tyvek.

1. ☐ Face shield
2. ☐ Safety glasses
3. ☐ Safety goggles
4. ☐ Respirator
5. ☐ Gloves: *(Describe material)* ______
6. ☐ Boots: *(Describe material)* ______
7. ☐ Protective apron: *(Describe material)* ______
8. ☐ Protective lab coat: *(Describe material)* ______
9. ☐ Protective jacket: *(Describe material)* ______
10. ☐ Protective pants or overalls: *(Describe material)* ______
11. ☐ Protective one-piece body suit (fully encapsulated): *(Describe material)* ______
12. ☐ Barrier cream: *(Describe type of cream)* ______
13. ☐ Other: *(Describe equipment and material)* ______
14. ☐ Not wearing any personal protective equipment

BLS 98K (April 1985)

J. Was any of the personal protective equipment you were wearing intended to prevent chemical burns? *(Check one.)*

1. ☐ No
2. ☐ Yes: Indicate which equipment was intended to prevent chemical burns ____________
3. ☐ Don't know
4. ☐ Not wearing personal protective equipment

K. Who pays for your personal protective equipment? *(Check one.)*

1. ☐ Employer
2. ☐ You
3. ☐ Both you and your employer: *(Explain)* ____________
4. ☐ Don't know

L. Was the part(s) of body where you were burned covered by personal protective equipment?

☐ NO: **Indicate reason(s):** *(Check all that apply.)*

1. ☐ Proper protective equipment was not provided by employer
2. ☐ Did not think it was needed
3. ☐ Using it slows down work
4. ☐ Too uncomfortable or hot to work with it on
5. ☐ Personal protective equipment does not cover burn area
6. ☐ Other *(Describe)* ____________

☐ YES: **Describe the equipment that covered the area where you were burned and complete a, b, and c:**

____

a. How did the chemical or substance burn this area? *(Check all that apply.)*

Chemical or substance:

1. ☐ Filtered or soaked through personal protective equipment
2. ☐ Filtered or soaked through seams in fabric
3. ☐ Passed under or around personal protective equipment
4. ☐ Dissolved or burned through personal protective equipment
5. ☐ Other: *(Describe)* ____________

b. Were there any other reasons why the personal protective equipment failed to prevent your burn? *(Check all that apply.)*

Personal protective equipment:

1. ☐ Was in bad condition (torn, etc.)
2. ☐ Did not fit properly (too loose, etc.)
3. ☐ Was not designed to protect against chemical burns
4. ☐ Was not cleaned or maintained properly
5. ☐ Was wrong style: *(Explain)* ____________
6. ☐ Had been reused too many times
7. ☐ Other reason(s): *(Describe)* ____________
8. ☐ No other reasons

c. What effect did the personal protective equipment have on your burn? *(Check all that apply.)*

1. ☐ No effect on burn
2. ☐ Reduced area burned
3. ☐ Reduced seriousness of burn
4. ☐ Made burn more serious: *(Explain)* ____________
5. ☐ Other: *(Describe)* ____________

M. What, if any, information were you given on wearing *chemical-resistant* protective equipment to prevent burns? *(Check all that apply.)*

1. ☐ Where and when to wear chemical resistant protective equipment
2. ☐ Written instructions on chemical-resistant protective equipment: *(Describe)* ____________
3. ☐ Which types of protective equipment are chemical-resistant
4. ☐ Limitations and advantages of chemical-resistant protective equipment
5. ☐ Other: *(Describe)* ____________
6. ☐ Did not receive information on wearing chemical-resistant protective equipment

N. From whom did you receive this information? *(Check all that apply.)*

1. ☐ Supervisor, employer, or safety supervisor
2. ☐ Co-worker
3. ☐ In school or other type of classroom instruction
4. ☐ From label or printed instructions on product that burned you
5. ☐ Printed instructions that came with protective equipment
6. ☐ Other: *(Describe)* ____________
7. ☐ Did not receive information on wearing chemical-resistant protective equipment

O. Did your injury cause you to lose time from work beyond the day of injury?

1. ☐ No 2. ☐ Yes

IF YES: **How long were you (or do you expect to be) out of work?** (NOTE: Do not count the day of injury, days on light duty work, normal days off, or holidays.)

____________ Workdays

P. Have you returned to work? *(Check one.)*

1. ☐ No—still off because of injury
2. ☐ Yes—returned to regular job duties
3. ☐ Yes—returned to restricted job duties (light duty). Indicate the number of days you were on light duty: ____________
4. ☐ Other: *(Describe)* ____________

Q. Did your injury require you to be hospitalized overnight or longer?

1. ☐ No 2. ☐ Yes

IF YES: **How long were you (or do you expect to be) in the hospital?**

____________ Nights

R. How do you think your accident could have been prevented? *(Check all that apply.)*

1. ☐ Wearing chemical-resistant protective equipment: *(Describe)* ____________
2. ☐ Wearing a better type of chemical-resistant protective equipment: *(Describe)* ____________
3. ☐ Using safer work procedures on your part
4. ☐ More time to do job
5. ☐ More or better safety training
6. ☐ Use of protective barriers (such as plexiglass screens, etc.): *(Describe)* ____________
7. ☐ Better labeling of product or chemical container
8. ☐ Having company enforce safe work practices
9. ☐ Using different or less hazardous chemical: *(Explain)* ____________
10. ☐ Using different or better work equipment
11. ☐ Other: *(Describe)* ____________
12. ☐ Do not think it could have been prevented

Chapter 15. Employment Projections

Part I. Overview

For more than 25 years, the Bureau of Labor Statistics has developed long-term (5-15 years) projections of likely employment patterns in the U.S. economy. Since the early 1970's, projections have been prepared on a 2-year cycle. These projections cover the future size and composition of the labor force, aggregate economic growth, detailed estimates of industrial production, and industrial and occupational employment. The resulting data serve the many users who need information on likely patterns of economic growth and their effects on employment. The information on future employment opportunities by occupation, for example, is used by counselors, educators, and others helping young persons choose a career, and by officials who plan education and training programs.

Over the years, the procedures used to develop these projections have undergone many changes as new data series became available and economic and statistical tools improved but, since the late 1970's, the basic methodology has been relatively unchanged. The procedures have centered around projections of an interindustry or input-output model which determines the chain of indirect job requirements associated with the production needs issuing from several possible scenarios.

Projecting employment in industry and occupational detail requires an integrated projection of the total economy and its various sectors. The BLS projections are developed in a series of six steps, each of which is based on separate projection procedures and models, and various related assumptions. These six steps, or analytical phases, are: (1) Labor force, (2) aggregate economy, (3) final demand (GNP) by sector and product, (4) interindustry relationships (input-output), (5) industry output and employment, and (6) occupational employment. They provide a sequenced, analytical framework needed to develop employment projections (see chart 1). Each phase is solved separately, with the results of each needed as input for the next phase and with some results feeding back to earlier steps. In each phase, many iterations are made to ensure internal consistency as assumptions and results are reviewed and revised.

(1) *Labor force projections* are determined by projections of the future age, sex, and racial composition of the population and by trends in the labor force participation rates—the percent of the specified group in the population who will be working or seeking work. The population projections, prepared by the U.S. Bureau of the Census, are based on trends in birth rates, death rates, and net migration. With the population projections in hand, BLS analyzes and projects changes in labor force participation rates for more than 100 age, sex, and race or Hispanic origin groups.

Projections of labor force participation rates for each group are developed by first estimating a trend rate of change based on participation rate behavior during the prior 15 year period. Second, the rate is modified when the time-series projections for the specific group appear inconsistent with the results of cross-sectional and cohort analyses. This second step ensures consistency in the projections across the various groups. Finally, the size of the anticipated labor force is calculated by multiplying the labor force participation rates by the population projections. The results are again reviewed for consistency.

(2) *Aggregate economic performance*—the second phase of the BLS projections process—develops projections of the gross national product (GNP—gross domestic product or GDP in future projections) and major categories of demand and income. These results provide control totals that are consistent with each other and with the various assumptions and conditions of the projections scenarios. The values generated for each demand sector and subsector are then used in the next phase in developing detailed purchases for personal consumption, business investment, foreign trade, and government.

These projections are accomplished using a macroeconomic model. The model basically consists of sets of equations that correlate various aspects of the economy with each other. It provides internally consistent, moderately detailed projections for each set of assumptions and goals. The *Outlook: 1990-2005* projections were based upon a long-term macro model developed by Data Resources, Inc. This model has approximately 400 equations which determine those factors affecting growth in the U.S. economy. The model is driven by a set of 213 exogenous variables, or values, which are specified by BLS. To provide a range of estimates, the macro model is solved for three economic scenarios representing low, moderate, and high growth possibilities.

(3) *Final demand.* The BLS projection procedure then moves from the aggregate to the industrial level. For the industry output projections, the economy is disaggregated into 228 producing sectors that cover the U.S. industrial structure, both public and private. The framework for this procedure is an input-output model. The initial input-output data used by BLS are prepared by the Bureau of Economic Analysis, U.S. Department of Commerce.

The development of projections of industry output begins with aggregate demand projections from the Data Resources model. In this model, projections are made for 7 major categories of consumption, 6 categories of investment, 13 end-use categories of foreign trade, and 3 categories of government spending. A further disaggregation of the values from the model is then undertaken. For example, personal consumption expenditures are estimated for 82 detailed categories.

Furthermore, to develop industry output projections, provision is made to allow for shifts in the commodity makeup of a given demand category. This is accomplished by projecting "bridge tables" relating individual types of demand to the actual industries supplying the goods. The bridge table is a percent distribution for each given demand category, such as the personal consumption or investment category, among each of the 228 sectors in the BLS input-output model. In projecting changes in these bridge tables, expected changes in technology, consumer tastes or buying patterns, the commodity pattern of exports and imports, the future composition of business investment, and other structural factors are considered.

(4) *Input-output.* The next stage in the projections process is the estimation of the intermediate flows of goods and services required to produce the projected GNP. Only final sales are counted in the GNP to avoid repeated counting of intermediate inputs. An industry's total employment depends on its total output whether that output is consumed as an intermediate input or used as a final good. This is accomplished using an interindustry or input-output model. This model mathematically solves for all levels of intermediate inputs given industry input relationships and final demand.

The BLS input-output model consists of two basic matrices for each year, a "use" and a "make" table. The principal table is the "use" table. This table shows the purchase of commodities by each industry as inputs into its production process. Projecting this table must take into account the changes in the input pattern or the way in which goods or services are produced by each industry. In general, two types of changes in these input patterns are made in developing a future input-output table: (a) Those made to the inputs of a specific industry (as, for example, the changes in inputs in the publishing industry); and, (b) those made to the inputs of a specific commodity in all or most industries (as for example increased use of business services across a wide spectrum of industries). The "make" table shows the commodity output of each industry. It allocates commodity output to the industry to which it is primary and to all other industries where the commodity is produced as a secondary product. The "use" table is the basis for the direct requirements table of coefficients showing the inputs required to produce one dollar of that industry's output. The "make" table is used to create a "market shares" table, which shows the values of the "make" table as coefficients. The coefficient tables are used to calculate the total requirements table which shows the direct and indirect requirements to produce a dollar's worth of final demand. Projection tables are based on historical tables and on studies of specific industries conducted internally or by other organizations both within and outside of government.

(5) *Industry employment.* The projected level of industry employment is based on the projected levels of industry output as well as other factors such as expected technological changes and their impact on labor productivity. After the initial industry output is calculated, employment is derived for each industry from the level of projected industry output based on trend analyses of industry employment, hours, and the ratio of output to hours. The employment projections by industry are constrained by the requirement that they sum to the aggregate employment level as determined by the aggregate projections.

(6) *Occupational employment.* The model used to develop the occupational employment projections is an industry-occupation matrix showing the distribution of employment for 258 industries and for more than 507 detailed occupations. Occupational staffing patterns for the industries are based on data collected by State employment security agencies and analyzed by BLS.

Staffing patterns of industries in the base-year industry-occupation matrix are projected to the target year to account for changes expected to occur in technology, shifts in product mix, and other factors. For example, one would expect greater employment of computer specialists as computer technology spreads across industries. In projecting the staffing patterns, the changes introduced into the input-output model for expected technological change are also analyzed to account for the impact of that technology on the future occupational staffing patterns of industries. The projected industry employment data are applied to the projected industry occupational staffing patterns, yielding employment by occupation for each industry. These data are aggregated across all industries to yield total occupational employment for the projected year.

Final review. An important element of the projection system is its comprehensive structure. To ensure the internal consistency of this large structure, the BLS projection procedure encompasses detailed review and analysis of the results at each stage for reasonableness and for consistency with the results from other stages of the BLS projections.

For example, changes in staffing patterns in the occupational model are closely related to changes in industry productivity, and technology projections are reviewed in detail by the BLS Office of Productivity and Technology. In short, the final results reflect innumerable interactions among staff members who focus on particular variables in the model. Because of this review, the projection process at BLS converges to an internally consistent set of employment projections across a substantial number of industries and occupations. The continued cross-checking of the assumptions and results makes it difficult to quantify the effects of each change in each variable.

The projection process at the Bureau of Labor Statistics does not end with the development and publication of a set of projections. Once the target year is reached, BLS evaluates the projections to determine what changes in assumptions or models would have made them more accurate. Knowing the sources of errors helps improve the projection process. It also highlights for users the imprecise nature of making statements about future economic conditions, industrial activity, or employment growth.

Assumptions

To carry out the projection process, the BLS makes many underlying assumptions. The projections themselves should be considered as likely outcomes in light of the assumptions. Three major types of assumptions were made by BLS economists in developing the projections for the year 2005.

First, assumptions are made concerning general economic or social conditions. The *Outlook: 1990-2005* projections, for instance, include the following assumptions: (1) Work patterns will not change significantly over the projection period; for example, the average workweek will not change markedly; (2) broad social and educational trends will continue; (3) there will be no major war; (4) there will be a significant change in the size of the Armed Forces; and (5) fluctuations in economic activity due to the business cycle will continue to occur.

The assumptions that fall into this first major category have both an overall and a particular impact. For example, the assumption that social trends will continue implies that our society will continue to provide for the education of the young in a way which is broadly similar to current practices. This would be considered the overall impact. The particular impact of this assumption would be to influence the projected level of local government expenditures for education and, consequently, the demand for teachers.

Second, BLS analysts determine the factors which previously have exerted a strong influence on the behavior of important projection results. Once the factors have been identified, the analysts decide whether those factors will continue to have a similar strong influence in the future.

During the 1970's and early 1980's, for example, employment of cashiers in retail stores grew at the expense of other sales occupations as these stores centralized their cashier services. This factor, in the judgment of BLS economists, will no longer cause changes in the types of workers retail stores hire because the shift to centralized cashier operations in the stores has been completed. These types of assumptions are fully documented in Part III of *Outlook 1990-2005*.

Finally, BLS economists set ranges of acceptability for variables normally considered as results of the various projection methods, such as the level and rate of growth of real gross national product (GNP), the unemployment rate, the rate of growth of labor productivity, and other key results of the various stages of the projection process. The purpose is to ensure consistent results rather than to impose absolute levels on the various items involved.

With these three classes of assumptions in mind, BLS economists then specify three alternative projection scenarios, a low, moderate, and high level of projected economic activity. By offering three scenarios, BLS allows the user of the projections to select that combination of assumptions which best represents the user's own notions of future economic potential.

Presentation

The projections are first published in the *Monthly Labor Review*, usually in the fall of odd-numbered years, and subsequently appear in BLS bulletins and the *Occupational Outlook Quarterly*, which also prints articles on such topics as new and emerging occupations and changing job market conditions for existing occupations.

Three bulletins are based on the 1990-2005 projections: *Outlook: 1990-2005*; the *1992-93 Occupational Outlook Handbook*; and *Occupational Projections and Training Data*, 1992 Edition. The first reprints the *Monthly Labor Review* articles and contains supplementary data, such as selected aggregate economic variables, the size of each labor force cohort, final demand by industry, gross output and employment by industry, and wage and salary employment by detailed industry. The *Occupational Outlook Handbook* discusses about 250 occupations; besides outlook data, it includes information on the nature of the work, training requirements, working conditions, and earnings. The *Handbook* is available in the vast majority of career information centers in the country's high schools, colleges, and libraries, where it is used as a primary source of information for people in the process of choosing a career. *Occupational Projections and Training Data* presents detailed statistics on employment, occupational separations, and education and training completions; most of the data are for the occupations included in the *Handbook*.

Limitations

For example, most analysts would agree that the use of robots and other computer-controlled machinery will affect employment in manufacturing industries, yet numerical estimates of the reduction in the proportion of assemblers and welders in an industry affected by this equipment could vary significantly among analysts. The Bureau attempts to address this dilemma by making clear all of the important assumptions underlying its projections, developing alternative versions that reflect some of the uncertainties and differing policy decisions about the future, and making projections on a regular 2-year cycle in order to incorporate new data and assumptions.

The Bureau also seeks to improve the projections process and to make users aware of their limitations by reviewing previous projections. Once the target year is reached, BLS evaluates the projections to determine the errors and to learn what changes in assumptions or models might have made them more accurate.

Part II. Labor Force

Labor force projections, the first step in the BLS projections sequence, depend upon an analysis of the current population and projections of its future size and composition, as well as the trends in labor force participation rates for different population groups. Projections are made for the labor force as a whole, for 96 separate age-sex-race groups, and for 18 age-sex groups of people of Hispanic origin.

The Bureau of the Census prepares the population projections by age, sex, race, and Hispanic origin. BLS develops data on participation rates based on the Current Population Survey (CPS), conducted for BLS by the Bureau of the Census.

Procedures

Various assumptions can be made for population growth and labor force participation. The size and composition of the population are affected by the interaction of three variables: Births, deaths, and net immigration. The Bureau of the Census makes three assumptions for each variable—preparing all possible combinations of these assumptions yields 27 scenarios. For analytic purposes, the Bureau of the Census also prepares three additional projections assuming zero net immigration.

For the 1990-2005 round of projections, BLS has selected the high net immigration and middle population scenarios as bases for the labor force and other projections. The size and composition of the population affect not only the labor force projections, but the projected composition of GNP and of the levels of employment in some occupations.

Three separate projections of the labor force are prepared, with the differences based on different assumptions about future participation rates. The moderate growth labor force scenario assumes labor force participation growth comparable to past years. The high growth labor force scenario assumes higher participation rates, and the low growth scenario assumes lower labor force participation rates.

BLS currently disaggregates whites, blacks, and Asians and others (Asians and Pacific Islanders, native Americans and Alaskan natives) into age groups by sex. Specifically, ages 16 and 17, 18 and 19, 20 and 21, 22 to 24, 25 to 29, . . ., 55 to 59, 60 and 61, 62 to 64, 65 to 69, 70 to 74, and 75 and older. For Hispanics more aggregated data are projected: Ages 16 and 17, 18 and 19, 20 to 24, 25 to 34, 35 to 44, 45 to 54, 55 to 59, 60 to 64, 65 and older. After the rates are assembled or computed, they are smoothed using a robust-resistant nonlinear filter.[1] Only the data for whites are not smoothed. To adjust labor force participation rates for the effects of the recession which began in the middle of 1990, the 1990 rates were adjusted using the end-value smoothing described *Exploratory Data Analysis*, Chapter 7, "Smoothing techniques."[2]

The next step is to transform the data into logits, or natural logs of the odds ratios or flogs (folded logs). The form of the flog is exp[(p-A)/(B-p)]. In the usual case for logits, A is zero and B is set to 1. As a result, when the projected logits are transformed back, they will not exceed 100 percent or drop below 0 percent. BLS generally constrains women's participation rates not to exceed the rates for men of the same age. By setting B to the rate for men in the target year, this is done automatically. Before doing this, the likely spread of women's rates is calculated to see if this is too limiting a constraint. The male rate is calculated to be 3 times the mean absolute deviation (MAD) greater than the median labor force rate over the period for which the estimates are made before B is set to the male rate. (The male participation rates are generally used.) If it is too close to the women's rate, then B is set to the median plus 3 times the MAD.

Once the data are transformed, they are extrapolated linearly by regressing the logit of the rate against time and then extending the fitted series to or beyond the target year. When the series are transformed back into participation rates, the projected path is nonlinear. Participation rates that have been changing slowly will continue to change slowly and the patterns will be linear. Participation rates that have been changing rapidly will continue to increase rapidly in the short run and then gradually decrease their rate of change. No rate will change slowly in the short run and then accelerate, though this is possible.

[1] Velleman, Paul F. "Definition and Comparison of Robust Nonlinear Data Smoothing Algorithms," *Journal of the American Statistical Association*, 1980, pp. 609-615.

[2] Tuckey, John W. *Exploratory Data Analysis*, (Reading, MA, Addison-Wesley Publishing, 1977), pp. 221-222.

After the labor force participation rates have been projected, they are reviewed. We consider the time-series, the cross-section in the target year, and cohort patterns of participation. The labor force level resulting from the projection is compared with the labor force derived from an econometric model that projects only the total civilian labor force. When a basic scenario is completed, high and low alternatives are projected using the confidence interval on the slope (or change) coefficient from the original regression.

Cross-sectional and cohort analyses are also conducted for each group. The cross-sectional analysis consists of reviewing the pattern of labor force participation rates for each sex-race group in the target year. The cohort analysis consists of reviewing the pattern of labor force participation by sex-race groups born in successive 5-year periods. The aggregated labor force resulting from the projection is compared with the labor force derived from an econometric model that projects only the total civilian labor force. In cases where these analyses show inconsistencies, the participation rate extrapolated from the time-series data is modified. The modification is greatest for black women and smallest for white men.

The projected participation rate for each age-sex-race group is then multiplied by the corresponding population projection to obtain the labor force projection for that group. The groups are then summed to obtain the total civilian labor force.

Part III. Aggregate Economy

Projections of the aggregate economy—the second stage in the BLS projections sequence—are made through use of a macroeconomic model, referred to as the macro model. The labor force projections made in the first stage of the BLS procedure are used along with many other variables to develop projections of GNP and major categories of demand and income. Because the variables are so numerous, sources of data are manifold. They include BLS itself, the U.S. Departments of Commerce and Energy, the Federal Reserve Board, and Data Resources, Inc.

Procedures

For the past few cycles of projections, BLS has used models of the economy—which are basically sets of equations that correlate different aspects of the economy with each other—created by other organizations. The specific equations used in a model may differ, but they work in similar ways to provide a framework for the preparation of a consistent set of economy-wide projections for a given set of assumptions and goals. The *Outlook:1990-2005* projections are based on a long-term macro model created by Data Resources, Inc. The macro model is a system of behavioral relationships and identities based on annual data and designed to allow an analyst to explore the determinants of growth in the U.S. economy. Made up of approximately 400 equations, the macro model is driven by a set of 213 exogenous variables—arithmetic values that can be manipulated by the equations in the macro model. BLS specifies the values of these variables.

The exogenous variables can be divided into three groups, according to the degree of certainty to which each can be determined. The first group consists of reliable, generally accepted values which are available for some variables, such as the future size of the population. Census population projections have proven to be highly accurate. The second group includes variables that involve policy decisions which, while subject to change, have remained fairly constant for many years; these include the amount of Federal transfer payments, the response of the monetary authority to economic growth, and the size of the Armed Forces. Finally, the last group contains exogenous variables that do not follow predictable relationships; these include the inflation rates in the economies of the major trading partners of the United States, the exchange value of the U.S. dollar, and energy prices.

Besides being governed by general assumptions, the projections are generally approached with certain goals or targets in mind. Because the goals relate to variables that are, strictly speaking, results of the aggregate model rather than inputs to it, they are attained by changes to the structure of the model itself. Such goals or target variables include the unemployment rate, the rate of growth of labor productivity, and general growth in prices.

Once the value of each exogenous variable has been determined, the macro model is run, that is, the equations are solved, producing projected values for numerous kinds of economic activity, such as GNP, purchases of consumer goods, and capital investment. BLS analysts review the aggregate results for soundness of logic and reasonableness. The review includes checks on internal consistency, evaluation of continuity with past trends, and comparisons with projections made by other organizations. Although the review tends to focus on such items as GNP, unemployment, and productivity, the macro model's framework ensures that other important measures of economic performance are not overlooked.

The major results of this second stage of the projections process, which are passed along to subsequent stages, are GNP, the major demand components of GNP, and aggregate employment, as well as certain other aggregate measures of economic performance used by the models in later stages of the projections. Demand detail generated by the macro model includes seven categories of personal consumption spending, six categories of investment spending, six categories of exports of goods and seven services, seven categories of imports of goods and services, and three categories of government purchases of goods and services.

Part IV. Final Demand by Product

Projections of final demand by product are the third stage of the BLS projections process. Final demand is one way to view GNP; it is GNP distributed among final users, broadly categorized into four groups: (1) Personal consumption expenditures (PCE), (2) business investment, (3) foreign trade, and (4) government purchases.

PCE represents demand on the part of persons and nonprofit institutions serving individuals. Rent and the imputed rental value of owner-occupied dwellings are included in this category, but the actual purchase of dwellings is classified as investment.

Investment includes both fixed capital goods—the purchase of durable equipment and structures by business and nonprofit institutions—and the value of changes in business inventories of raw materials, semifinished goods, and finished goods. Purchases by persons of owner-occupied and rental structures are included here.

Foreign trade includes both exports and imports of goods and services. These are analyzed separately; imports are subtracted at the final stage of the projections procedure to derive domestic production.

Government demand is defined as the goods and services purchased by all government units—local, State, and Federal. It includes employee compensation, but does not include transfer payments, interest payments, grants, or subsidies, all of which are accounted for under personal consumption expenditures or other categories of demand.

Final demand, along with intermediate flows of goods and services, determines total output at the commodity and industry level of detail. Industry output, in turn, is a key determining factor of employment demand. Because the purpose of production is the satisfaction of demand, variations in the demand for goods and services, and in the means of producing these goods and services, will generally result in changing patterns of employment demand in future time periods. Final demand is always expressed on a product, or commodity, basis. The translation from commodity demand to industry output takes place at a later stage of the projections.

Data sources

In general, projecting final demand entails the compilation of historical data in a form that helps determine the commodity distribution of detailed categories of GNP for some future year. Large amounts of data in various forms are available to analyze past trends in the composition of final demand. Much of it is provided by the Bureau of Economic Analysis (BEA) of the Department of Commerce as the basis for this data base. Although considerable data are collected annually, the creation of a list of specific purchases in its most complete detail is only done for years in which a benchmark input-output study of the economy is prepared. BEA produces these input-output tables once every 5 years, for years in which economic censuses are done. The historical series depends heavily, therefore, on the census years; more recent economic trends are incorporated into the projections through data series which rely heavily on data compiled as part of the National Income and Product Accounts (NIPA), which include detailed data on each broad category of final demand.

The latest 1982 input-output table developed by BEA and released in July 1991 was not available when BLS prepared the 2005 projections. Therefore, BLS used the 1977 BEA I/O definitions to develop the 1987 I/O table. The 1977 and 1987 data were used as a base to project 2005. Both the 1977 and 1987 I/O tables were based on the 1977 Standard Industrial Classification (SIC) basis while BLS converted the 1977 I/O table and developed the 1987 and 2005 I/O tables on the 1987 SIC basis. Conversion to the 1987 SIC scheme required a different industry classification from the original 1977 I/O table.

Personal consumption expenditures compiled by BEA are available annually from 1929, disaggregated into 82 expenditure categories. For example, data are available for several categories of expenditures on food. These include food purchased for off-premises consumption (including alcoholic beverages), purchased meals and beverages, food furnished employees (including military), and food produced and consumed on farms. BEA also produces a "bridge table" for each year that an input-output study is prepared which distributes each of the 82 PCE expenditure categories among over 500 commodities purchased. The bridge table thus allows BLS analysts to disaggregate the values for food purchased for off-premises consumption to the detailed products purchased at food stores.

The bridge table also allows the analysis to move one step further—to remove the trade and transportation costs associated with getting the food from the point of production to the point of sale to the final consumer. That is, BLS analysts use the bridge table to strip the trade and transportation margins from the published figures to arrive at the producer's valuation rather than the purchaser's valuation used in the NIPA. This is an important step in determining employment. If the revaluation were not done, it would be difficult, if not impossible, to determine the employment in the trade and transportation industries themselves.

The principal source of data for capital investment is also annual NIPA data, which yield information on both producers' durable equipment (PDE) and structures. PDE includes such expenditure categories as communication equipment; office, computing, and accounting machinery; furniture and fixtures; and tractors. BEA produces a bridge table for census years for the more than 20 categories of equipment purchases, allowing expenditure categories to be disaggregated to the specific goods purchased. NIPA data are also available for about 30 categories of structures, including industrial, commercial, religious, educational, hospital and institutional, and other buildings. Residential structures include single- and multi-family units, additions and alterations, and major replacements. In census years, BEA also produces a capital flows table, which shows the mix of investment goods purchased by each of 77 consuming industries. This allows BLS analysts to study the specific types of equipment and structures purchased by each of these industries.

For foreign trade, plentiful data on exports and imports are available annually in the detailed merchandise trade statistics of the Bureau of the Census. The Balance of Payments Division at BEA is the primary source of detail on services trade flows, as well as for the general accounting structure used to present U.S. international transactions.

Finally, BEA produces detailed information on government expenditures as part of the NIPA. For the Federal Government, detail is available for both defense and nondefense expenditures. Defense expenditure data are available for specific types of military hardware, as well as for compensation and many other types of expenditures. The detail for nondefense expenditures is not as great, but it is fairly extensive. State and local government expenditure data are available for 19 functional spending categories, such as sewerage, sanitation, police and fire protection, and highways. A detailed list of commodity purchases for each of the State and local government categories, which functions as a bridge table, is available as part of the BEA input-output studies.

Procedures

In order to project final demand, the same kinds of judgments and assumptions are made as those that enter into the macro model. For example, demand for residential construction in the macro model depends heavily on demographic and income forecasts. Breaking total residential construction down into the components of single-family, multi-family, and mobile homes depends on the same determining variables. Judgments are also made with regard to the effect of technological developments—such as computers and robots—on the mix of investment goods as well as on purchases by other components of final demand.

The initial projections of various categories of final demand generated by the early runs of the macro model provide a starting point for the analysts, who study all aspects of demand to ensure that the models remain balanced and consistent throughout the development of a new set of projections. Although the four categories of final demand are subject to different procedures, they have two basic steps in common. First, the detail available from the macro model is further disaggregated. For example, the 7 personal spending categories are expanded to the 82 NIPA product categories. Second, for each of the detailed categories of final demand, a projected distribution by commodity (the bridge table or bills of goods discussed earlier) is estimated and used to disaggregate by commodity the spending total developed in the first step.

The latest bridge tables, developed by BEA for 1977, are updated by BLS to 1987. These are then used to develop projected bridge tables for detailed categories to the 228 commodities projected (most are at a 3-digit SIC level). The projected bridge tables reflect such factors as expected changes in technology, consumer tastes or buying patterns, the industrial composition of exports and imports, and the composition of investment. Thus, the bridge tables allow the analyst to provide for shifts in the commodity makeup of a given demand category. Having the data at this level of detail allows finer adjustment for technological and economic change.

However, before the analyst can make use of the detailed bridge tables, the expenditure data from the macro model must be disaggregated to match the detail of the bridge tables. This is done differently for each of the major demand categories.

Personal consumption expenditures are initially projected by the macro model for seven major product groups. These are autos and parts; clothing and shoes, furniture and appliances, and other durable goods; gasoline and oil, fuel oil, and natural gas; food, beverages, and other nondurables; housing services; electricity consumption; and other consumer services. For this set of projections, a consumption submodel, developed by BLS analysts, is used to project consumption expenditures for the 82 NIPA expenditure categories. Each of the 82 equations is estimated as a function of real disposable income, the lagged value of that category, and the ratio of the price of the category to the price of total consumption. Then the 82 category estimates are aggregated and summed to their appropriate major product group from the macro model. The differences between these aggregated estimates and the original macro controls are then carefully examined and, generally, scaling adjustments are introduced at the 82-order level of detail in order to reproduce the macro model control values. Occasionally, estimates developed at the detailed level will use information not available to the macro model. In cases such as this, the macro model controls may themselves be modified in response to the more finely developed detail at this level of the projections.

Investment is initially projected by the macro model, which generates values for total investment in nonresidential durable equipment, residential investment, and nonresidential structures; nonresidential structures are further disaggregated by the macro model to public utilities, petroleum and other mining, and other building and nonbuilding facilities. These categories are then disaggregated even further, relying on historical data for each of the detailed categories available from NIPA. Each of the subcategories is plotted and regressions are estimated, resulting in initial estimates for 2005. The estimates are then aggregated to the macro level of detail and compared with the macro control values and adjusted, where necessary. The projected expenditures are also evaluated based on their relative growth rates and their shares of total investment spending. They are then distributed to producing sectors using projected bridge tables. The macro model also projects a total for change in business inventories, which is also distributed by commodity.

Foreign trade is initially projected by the macro model, which generates values for six major end-use categories of exports and seven major end-use categories of imports. These include foods, feeds, and beverages; industrial supplies and materials (with petroleum broken out of this category in the case of imports); capital goods; autos and parts; consumer and other goods; and services. The values are distributed among the 228 commodities in light of past trends, existing and expected shares of the domestic market, expected world economic conditions, and known trade agreements.

Total imports are divided into two categories: those competitive with domestic products and those that have no domestic counterparts, such as coffee and diamonds. Competitive imports are subtracted from final demand in order to derive domestic output on a commodity-by-commodity basis. For example, the projected value of imported automobiles is subtracted from total demand for autos so that the demand for autos, and therefore auto output, reflects only demand for domestic production. Noncompetitive imports are considered purchases by the industry that uses them; some noncompetitive imports which do not require further processing, such as bananas, are only included in the personal consumption category of final demand.

Historical data for exports and imports are among the most detailed maintained by BLS. Using the detailed trade data from Census and BEA, exports and imports are allocated by BLS to product definitions for each year from 1977 through 1988, in both current and constant dollars. The resulting time series allow for an extensive look at recent movements for specific goods, especially for changes in the relative importance of imports. An analysis of product distribution across the macro model end-use categories is performed, then projected to the year 2005 and used as the initial estimator for disaggregation of macro model controls to the full-order commodity detail. Further adjustments, based on the judgments of BLS analysts, are then made directly to the list of purchases in order to arrive at the final detailed projections of foreign trade.

Government demand is initially projected by the macro model for three categories: Federal defense, Federal nondefense, and State and local government. Historical data available from NIPA show more detail for each of the three major government categories.

There are 19 functional categories of State and local government spending identified by BEA: Elementary and secondary education; higher education; other education and libraries; health and hospitals; public assistance and relief; sewerage; sanitation; police protection; fire protection; corrections; highways; water and air facilities; transit utilities; other commerce and transportation; gas and electric utilities; water; urban renewal and community facilities; natural and agricultural resources and recreation; and other general government. The 19 categories are projected, along with a bridge table to break these expenditures down to the types of products purchased.

For the Federal Government, NIPA data are available on specific types of defense hardware purchases, as well as compensation and many other types of purchases. Bridge tables are created by BLS, using unpublished notes from BEA, at the greatest level of detail possible. The bridge tables and expenditure data are projected based upon past trends and expected changes. For defense, projections are made for seven categories of purchases of goods and services, plus compensation and structures. For nondefense, projections are made for compensation, structures, Commodity Credit Corporation inventory change, and all other purchases. Initial estimates are evaluated based on growth rates and shares of the total before they are distributed by the projected bridge tables to products purchased.

Part V. Input-Output

The fourth stage of the BLS projections process is the estimation of the intermediate flows of goods and services in the economy required to produce GNP. By definition, GNP reflects only sales to final purchasers. Intermediate material inputs, such as the steel incorporated into automobiles, are not explicitly reflected in the GNP estimates.

Therefore, in order to derive an estimate of the employment necessary to produce a given level of GNP, it is first necessary to translate that GNP to a total output concept.

Input-output accounting methods allow for just such a translation and, at the same time, allow BLS analysts to explicitly take into account other expected phenomena, such as technological changes, shortages or surpluses, or any other factors which affect the production process. Further, it is at this stage that the GNP estimates, broken down by commodity, are translated to total output estimates by industry.

Historical data prepared by the Department of Commerce, projected final demand data developed in the third stage of the projections process, and special studies of particular industries and commodities are all used to produce the projected input-output tables. BEA creates historical input-output tables based on data contained in the Census of Manufactures and other economic censuses. When the projections were prepared, the latest official table available from BEA was for 1977. BLS used data from more recent censuses and other sources in order to construct input-output tables for 1987. This table reflects changes which have occurred in the economy since 1977 but is developed based on 1977 BEA input-output definitions.

Procedures

The BLS input-output model consists of two basic matrices, or tables, and several other matrices calculated from these. The first, referred to as the "use" table, describes the sale of every commodity both as a finished product, for use in its unaltered state, and as an intermediate product, for use as an input to the production process of other industries. In the "use" table, the sum of the rows is equal to commodity output, while the sum of the columns (plus estimates of labor compensation and the return to capital) is equal to industry output. This table is so named because it reflects the use of commodities by industries.

The second table, called the "make" table, displays the production of commodities by each industry. In the "make" table, the sum of the rows is equal to industry output, while the sum of the columns is equal to commodity output. The "make" table allocates commodity output to the industry to which it is primary and to all other industries where the commodity is produced as a secondary product.

The "use" table is then used to create the direct requirements table. This table represents the values from the use table as coefficients, i.e., it shows, for each industry, the inputs required to produce $1 of that industry's output. Conversely, the market shares matrix presents the values of the "make" table as coefficients, i.e., it shows the percentage of each commodity produced in every industry. This table allows the translation of commodity output to industry output.

Finally, the total requirements table combines data from the direct requirements table and the market shares matrix; it shows total requirements—direct and indirect—to produce $1 of final demand and represents purchases throughout the entire production chain necessary to produce a final product.

BLS economists use the historical direct requirements tables and market shares matrices to project input-output relationships. The projected direct requirements and market shares tables are changed throughout the projections process for several reasons, including expected technological developments, changes in product mix or relative prices, and the availability of substitute inputs. Once these two tables have been projected to the target year, a projected total requirements matrix is calculated and the coefficients are analyzed and adjusted to ensure that they reflect the best information available and are consistent with other projections. As with the other steps, however, several reviews and interim projections are required before the final matrices are produced.

Part VI. Industry Employment

The fifth stage of the projections sequence is the analysis of trends in industry employment. The number of jobs, the average workweek, and the number of employee hours are projected for each of the 228 industries in the system. The projections of industry employment depend strongly on the projections of industry output, derived in the prior stage of the projections process.

Data sources

Historical data for the industry employment and output are developed from a wide variety of sources. Time series on output (in constant dollars) for manufacturing industries are estimated from the *Annual Survey of Manufactures* conducted by the Department of Commerce and from BLS industry and producer price indexes. For nonmanufacturing industries, the sources for the output and price data are diverse; they include NIPA, the *Services Annual Survey*, IRS data on business receipts, *Agricultural Statistics, Minerals Yearbook*, transportation statistics, and numerous others. The output data are benchmarked to the 1977 and 1987 estimates of industry output that are derived from the historical input-output tables, described in an earlier section.

Time series on employment and hours are derived from three BLS sources for different groups of workers: The Current Employment Statistics survey (or establishment survey) for nonagricultural wage and salary employment, production worker employment, and weekly hours; the Current Population Survey, (or household survey), for agricultural employment, self-employed and unpaid family worker jobs and hours, and private household workers; and unemployment insurance data for employment in industries not published in the establishment survey.

As was noted in the previous discussion of the BLS input-output tables, the historical data were converted to the 1987 SIC from the old 1977 SIC. Approximately one-third of the 228 sectors were affected by SIC redefinitions. Time series for these industries have been reconstructed where possibie. For output data, it was generally possible to identify the specific 4-, 5-, or 7-digit industry or product code redefined, and to calculate an adjustment based on 1972, 1977, and 1982 census data. Ratios from these census years were then used as a basis for interpolating the intervening years. For employment, series were adjusted based on the percentage of employment lost or gained in the first quarter of 1988 from Employment and Wages data, (which were reported for that quarter under both the old and new SIC codes); where possible, this 1988 percentage was extended back to 1972, 1977, and 1982 based on census data, and intervening year ratios were interpolated.

Procedures

With the most recent set of projections, the derivation of wage and salary employment by industry began with a trend analysis of employment. An initial estimate of employment was made by extrapolating the historical time series. Wage and salary hours were then calculated based on a trend projection of average weekly hours. The initial projection of wage and salary employment was then reviewed and revised with the analytical focus on the ratio of output to hours calculated from the projections of output and employment. The projection of self-employed and unpaid family worker component of employment was done based on analysis of individual industries and time series regressions.

The projections of industry employment are subject to specific industry assumptions as well as the general assumptions governing the macro model. For example, productivity in a particular industry may be assumed to equal, exceed, or fall short of the value projected by the time series regression. For a detailed review of the specific assumptions made for the last set of projections for the year 2005, see part III of *Outlook: 1990-2005*.

Adjustments to the initial projections of industry employment are based on detailed analyses of historical and recent trends, special industry studies conducted by the staff, a review of the occupational implications of the projections, and industry technology studies from the Bureau's Office of Productivity and Technology. In order to make all these adjustments and to balance total employment from the aggregate projections with the sum of the industry employment projections, a number of iterations of the process are necessary.

Part VII. Occupational Employment

The final stage in the BLS projection procedure is the development of occupational employment projections. To generate these data for wage and salary workers, an industry-occupation matrix, or table, showing the distribution of occupational employment by industry is constructed for the base year and projected to the target year. Base-year and projected data for self-employed workers and unpaid family workers are developed for the economy as a whole rather than by industry. The three classes of workers—wage and salary workers, self-employed, and unpaid family workers—are summed to derive the base-year and projected estimates of total employment for each occupation.

Data sources

Data needed to develop the base-year occupational employment estimates are derived from several sources. Information on the occupational distribution of wage and salary workers by industry (staffing patterns) is derived from the Occupational Employment Statistics (OES) surveys conducted by State employment security agencies under a BLS-State cooperative program for all but a few industries. The OES surveys are conducted on a 3-year cycle, with roughly a third of the economy covered in each year. Total industry employment to which the OES staffing patterns are applied to derive the base year employment estimates are obtained from the Bureau's Current Employment Statistics survey, (or establishment survey). Information on the staffing patterns of wage and salary workers in agriculture; forestry; and fishing, hunting, and trapping are derived from the latest Decennial Census of Population. Base-year total employment for these industries is obtained from the CPS. Staffing patterns and total employment of wage and salary workers for the private household industry are derived from the CPS. Economy-wide data on self-employed and unpaid family workers by occupation are also derived from the CPS. Information on staffing patterns for the Federal Government is developed by BLS from data compiled by the Office of Personnel Management (OPM). Total Federal Government employment for the base year matrix is obtained from the Current Employment Statistics survey.

Procedures

Base-year data. Occupations in the industry-occupation matrix are classified according to the system used in the OES surveys, which is compatible with the *Standard Occupational Classification Manual* (SOC). It is very similar to the system used to classify occupations in the Decennial Census of Population and the CPS.

The OES survey covers about 775 detailed occupations in 367 industries, nearly all at the 3-digit Standard Industrial Classification (SIC) level. In developing the base-year matrix, occupations having fewer than 5,000 workers were aggregated into similar larger occupations or appropriate residuals. Also, industries employing less than 50,000 workers were aggregated into residuals within the same 2-digit SIC, if their staffing patterns were comparable to the residual. As a result of this aggregation, the 1990-2005 projections cover 507 occupations in 258 industries.

In some industries adjustments are made to OES survey staffing patterns because some occupations are not listed separately in the survey questionnaire, but are included in a residual category. To develop economy-wide employment estimates for these occupations it is necessary to disaggregate data from OES survey residuals. Data from the decennial census are used for these adjustments.

Adjustments also have to be made to staffing patterns derived from sources other than the OES survey. For example, the occupational classifications used to classify Federal Government workers used by OPM are more detailed than the SOC, necessitating the aggregation of many occupations to make them comparable to the classification used in the matrix. Similarly, estimates of employment for self-employed and unpaid family workers derived from the CPS and decennial census must be adjusted to make them comparable to the occupational classification used in the matrix.

Once all these data have been reviewed, they are arrayed in a matrix that shows occupational employment distributed in percentages by industry. Because these percentages are derived from surveys conducted in different years, they are applied to total industry employment estimates for the base year in order to develop occupational employment estimates for the base year.

To develop estimates for 1990, data from the following OES survey rounds were used: 1987 surveys of wholesale and retail trade, regulated industries, and State and local governments; 1988 surveys of manufacturing industries and hospitals; and 1989 surveys of mining, construction, finance, and services. The ratios of occupational employment to total employment in each detailed industry covered by the surveys were applied to 1990 total employment estimates derived from the Bureau's Current Employment Statistics program. Annual average employment estimates for agriculture and private households were obtained from the 1990 CPS. Employment by occupation in the Federal Government for 1989 was obtained from the Office of Personnel Management and benchmarked to 1990 data from the Current Employment Statistics program. In order to derive the 1990 estimates of total employment by occupation, the detailed cells of the industry-occupation matrix were aggregated across all industries and added to estimates separately derived for self-employed and unpaid family workers by occupation.

Projections. When a matrix for the base year has been developed, a projected matrix for the target year can be made. Because staffing patterns of industries change over time, the projection method must account for these changes. This is done in a series of procedures. First, historical data are reviewed to identify trends. Then, factors underlying these trends are identified through analytical studies of specific industries and occupations, technological change, and a wide variety of other economic data. Finally, judgments are made as to how the pattern will change in the future. Factors underlying this change are numerous, including technological developments affecting production and products, innovations in the ways business is conducted, modifications of organizational patterns, responses to government policies, and decisions to add new products and services or stop offering old ones.

Some expected trends may not be evident in the historical data. For example, an analysis of the past would not point toward the future impact of robots on staffing because this technology has not been used much in most industries. However, robots are expected to have a significant impact on some occupations, especially in the automobile industry. Information of this nature is identified in studies conducted by the BLS Office of Productivity and Technology as well as other research-oriented organizations.

The industry-occupation matrix can display either the number employed or coefficients that show the proportion of workers in an industry that work in a particular occupation. The matrix of coefficients is used to project the staffing pattern of an industry. The change projected for a specific occupation may be small, moderate, or significant; the precise percentage reflects the judgment of the staff members based on the analyses described above that relate to that occupation. In general, changes in coefficients averaging about 10 percent are considered to be small changes, 20 percent to be moderate changes, and 30 percent or more to be significant changes. Part III of *Outlook: 1990-2005* provides detail on the assumptions developed for each of the occupations for which changes to the base-year coefficients were made in developing the 1990-2005 projections.

The projected coefficients are multiplied by projected estimates of total employment by detailed industry. The individual cells of the matrix are than summarized across all industries and added to estimates separately projected for self-employed and unpaid family workers by occupation to derive the projected estimates of total employment by occupation.

Several versions of the projected matrix are developed during the projection procedure. Each version is reviewed by members of the staff preparing the *Occupational Outlook Handbook* and economists working on other steps in the projection program; these reviews insure that all information available to the staff is brought to bear on the projections and that consistent assumptions are made for all the Bureau's projections. Knowledgeable people outside the Bureau are also asked to comment. The final matrix represents, therefore, a broad consensus on the part of all analysts working on the projections.

Technical References

U.S. Department of Labor, Bureau of Labor Statistics. *Occupational Outlook Quarterly*, quarterly.

U.S. Department of Labor, Bureau of Labor Statistics. *Occupational Outlook Handbook*, biennial.

U.S. Department of Labor, Bureau of Labor Statistics. *Occupational Projections and Training Data*, biennial.

Eck, Alan. "Research Summary—Improved Estimates of Future Occupational Replacement Needs," *Monthly Labor Review*, August 1992.

Fullerton, Howard N, Jr. "Evaluating BLS Projections for 1990—Labor Force, Population, and Participation Rates," *Monthly Labor Review*, August 1992.

Rosenthal, Neal H. "Evaluating BLS Projections for 1990—Occupational Employment," *Monthly Labor Review*, August 1992.

Saunders, Norman C. "Evaluating BLS Projections for 1990—Industry Employment," *Monthly Labor Review*, August 1992.

U.S. Department of Commerce, National Technical Information Service. *The National OES Survey-Based Industry-Occupational Employment Matrix, 1990 and Projected 2005.*

U.S. Department of Labor, Bureau of Labor Statistics. *Outlook: 1990-2005*, BLS Bulletin 2402, April 1992.

Carey, Max L. and Franklin, James C. "Industry Output, Job Growth Slowdown Continues," *Monthly Labor Review*, November 1991, reprinted in *Outlook: 1990-2005*, BLS Bulletin 2402, April 1992.

Fullerton, Howard N, Jr. "Labor Force Projections: The Baby Boom Moves On," *Monthly Labor Review*, November 1991, reprinted in *Outlook: 1990-2005*, BLS Bulletin 2402, April 1992.

Kutscher, Ronald E. "New BLS Projections: Findings and Implications," *Monthly Labor Review*, November 1991, reprinted in *Outlook: 1990-2005*, BLS Bulletin 2402, April 1992.

Saunders, Norman C. "The U.S. Economy into the 21st Century," *Monthly Labor Review*, November 1991, reprinted in *Outlook: 1990-2005*, (BLS Bulletin 2402), April 1992.

Silvestri, George, and Lukasiewicz, John. "Occupational Employment Projections," *Monthly Labor Review*, November 1991, reprinted in *Outlook: 1990-2005*, (BLS Bulletin 2402), April 1992.

U.S. Department of Labor, Bureau of Labor Statistics. *Total and Net Occupational Separations: A Report on Recent Research*, August 1991.

U.S. Department of Commerce, Bureau of the Census. *Projections of the Population of the United States, 1987 to 2080*, Current Population Reports, Series P-25, No. 1018, 1989.

U.S. Executive Office of the President, Office of Management and Budget. *Standard Industrial Classification Manual*, 1987.

U.S. Department of Commerce, Office of Federal Statistical Policy and Standards. *Standard Occupational Classification Manual*, 1980.

Chapter 16. Producer Prices

The Producer Price Index (PPI) measures average changes in selling prices received by domestic producers for their output. Most of the information used in calculating the Producer Price Index is obtained through the systematic sampling of virtually every industry in the mining and manufacturing sectors of the economy. The PPI program (also known as the industrial price program) includes some data from other sectors as well—agriculture, fishing, forestry, services, and gas and electricity. Thus the title "Producer Price Index" refers to an entire "family" or system of indexes.

As of January 1992, the PPI program contained:

- Price indexes for nearly 500 mining and manufacturing industries, including approximately 9,750 indexes for specific products and product categories;
- Over 3,200 commodity price indexes organized by type of product and end use;
- Approximately 500 indexes for specific outputs of industries in the services sector and other sectors that do not produce physical products; and
- Several major aggregate measures of price change organized by stage of processing, both commodity-based and industry-based.

Together, these elements constitute a system of price measures designed to meet the need for both aggregate information and detailed applications, such as following price trends in specific industries and products.

Measures of price change classified by industry form the basis of the program. These indexes reflect the price trends of a constant set of goods and services which represent the total output of an industry. Industry index codes are based upon the Standard Industrial Classification (SIC) system and provide comparability with a wide assortment of industry-based data for other economic phenomena, including productivity, production, employment, wages, and earnings.

Background

Known until 1978 as the Wholesale Price Index or WPI, the Producer Price Index is one of the oldest continuous systems of statistical data published by the Bureau of Labor Statistics, as well as one of the oldest economic time series compiled by the Federal Government. When first published in 1902, the index covered the years from 1890 through 1901. The origins of the index can be found in an 1891 U.S. Senate resolution authorizing the Senate Committee on Finance to investigate the effects of the tariff laws "upon the imports and exports, the growth, development, production, and prices of agricultural and manufactured articles at home and abroad."[1]

The first index, published on the base period 1890-99, was an unweighted average of price relatives for about 250 commodities. Since that time, many changes have been made in the sample of commodities, the base period, and the method of calculating the index. A system of weighting was first used in 1914, for example, and major sample expansions and reclassifications were implemented in 1952 and 1967.

When it was originally founded, the industrial price program was intended to measure changes in prices received for goods sold in primary markets of this country. The conceptual framework and economic theory guiding the program's evolution, while more implicit than explicit, concentrated on obtaining the price received by either a domestic producer or an importer for the first commercial transaction.

One of the major limitations of the traditional methodology was its reliance on judgment samples of commodities and producers. This practice resulted in a system that was too heavily composed of volume-selling products made by larger firms. The PPI therefore did not adequately reflect the behavior of the multitude of products whose individual transactions values might have been small but which collectively accounted for a sizable portion of the economy. Another result of judgment sampling was that the output of many industries was completely overlooked. Before the transition to the current methodology began, products covered by the PPI program only accounted for about half of the total value of output by the mining and manufacturing sectors. The practice of assigning equal weight to price reports from each producer of a given commodity, regardless of any disparity in size among these firms, may have caused some distortions.

Another limitation of the traditional PPI methodology was its commodity orientation, which, while important, did not provide compatability with the industry orien-

[1] Senate Committee on Finance, *Wholesale Prices, Wages, and Transportation,* Senate Report No. 1394, "The Aldrich Report," Part I, 52nd Congress, 2d sess., March 3, 1893; and U.S. Department of Labor, *Course of Wholesale Prices, 1890-1901,* Bulletin No. 39, March 1902, pp. 205-09.

tation of most other Federal economic time series. The PPI's unique commodity classification scheme made it difficult to compare producer price movements with data for most other economic variables that were expressed in terms of the Standard Industrial Classification.

These and other weaknesses in the industrial price program, combined with increased development of the theory of price indexes in preretail markets, spurred several changes in terminology and operations during the 1970's. The 1978 program name change from Wholesale Price Index to Producer Price Index, for example, was intended to reemphasize that the industrial price program continues to be based on prices received by producers from whoever makes the first purchase, rather than on prices paid to wholesalers by retailers or others further down the distribution chain. This new nomenclature was accompanied in 1978 by a shift in the Bureau's analytical focus from the all commodities price index (which was popularly called "the" Wholesale Price Index) to the Finished Goods Price Index and the other commodity-based stage-of-processing price indexes.

These changes were a prelude to the most comprehensive overhaul of industrial price methodology in the program's history. Also begun in 1978, this overhaul was phased in gradually until the transition to the current methodology was essentially completed in January 1986.

Description of Survey

Universe

The Producer Price Index universe consists of the output of all industries in the goods-producing sectors of the American economy—mining, manufacturing, agriculture, fishing, and forestry—as well as gas, electricity, and goods competitive with those made in the producing sectors, such as waste and scrap materials. Imports are no longer included within the PPI universe; however, the BLS International Price Program publishes price indexes for both imports and exports. (See chapter 18.) Domestic production of goods specifically made for the military is included, as are goods shipped between establishments owned by the same company (termed interplant or intracompany transfers).

The output of the services sector and other sectors that do not produce physical products is also conceptually within the PPI universe, although actual coverage is incomplete. As of January 1992, the PPI program publishes data for selected industries in the following industry groups: Railroad, water, and air transportation of freight; air passenger transportation; warehousing; U. S. Postal Service; petroleum pipe lines; services incidental to water transportation; tour operators and travel agencies; electrical power and natural gas utilities; automotive rental and leasing; and scrap and waste materials collection. While funding is currently insufficient to permit full coverage of services, key sectors have been targeted for inclusion. Over the next few years, coverage will be expanded to include significant representation of the health services, real estate, and business services industries. Areas wholly overlapping the Consumer Price Index, such as personal services, will not be targeted.

Prices

One crucial task in designing a price index is to define what constitutes the "price" whose changes are to be measured. A seemingly simple question such as "What is the price of steel?" is unanswerable until it is made more specific.

For the purposes of the industrial price program, a price is defined as the net revenue accruing to a specified producing establishment from a specified kind of buyer for a specified product shipped under specified transaction terms on a specified day of the month. This definition points up the several price-determining variables that must be clarified before a cooperating business establishment can report a meaningful price for any of its products to BLS. For example, if a company charges more for a red widget than a white one, color is one of the price-determining variables; if all widgets sell for the same price regardless of color, color is not a price-determining variable.

Because the PPI is meant to measure changes in net revenues received by producers, changes in excise taxes—revenues collected on behalf of the government—are not reflected. But changes in rebate programs, low-interest financing plans, and other sales promotion techniques are reflected to the extent that these policies affect the net proceeds ultimately realized by the producer for a unit sale. If an auto manufacturer offers retail customers a rebate of $500, the manufacturer's net proceeds are reduced by $500, and the PPI for new cars would reflect a lower price. (Conversely, termination of a rebate program would be treated as a price increase.) But if a retail car dealer offers retail customers an additional rebate whose cost is absorbed by the dealer rather than the manufacturer, such a rebate would not affect the PPI. (The Consumer Price Index, of course, would reflect a customer rebate regardless of whether it was sponsored by the manufacturer or the dealer.)

The statistical accuracy of Producer Price Indexes depends heavily on the quality of the information voluntarily provided by respondents. BLS emphasizes to cooperating businesses the need for reports of realistic transaction prices, including all discounts, premiums, rebates, allowances, etc., rather than list or book prices. The use of list prices in the industrial price program has been the exception rather than the rule. Even before the conversion to the current methodology, a BLS survey showed that only about 20 percent of traditional commodity indexes were based on list prices. Inasmuch as the current methodology is more systematic than the older methodology in concentrating on actual transaction prices, the use of list prices is even less frequent now.

Neither order prices nor "futures" prices are included, because the PPI tries to capture the selling price for output being shipped in that same month, not in some other time. Changes in transportation costs will be reflected in industry price indexes only when the producing company delivers the product itself without hiring a third party shipper.

Most prices refer to one particular day of the month, viz., the Tuesday of the week containing the 13th of the month; this pricing date can range between the 9th and the 15th. There are exceptions for some products, however. A number of farm products are priced on a day of the week other than Tuesday. Prices for some refined petroleum products are commonly an average of prices during the first 10 working days of the month or the prices received by oil refineries on the tenth working day. Price indexes for natural gas to pipelines, liquefied petroleum gas, and some industrial chemicals are still based on data for the calendar month as a whole and therefore lag 1 month behind other indexes. The November index for natural gas to pipelines, for example, would reflect price changes that actually occurred in October. Although most prices reported to the Bureau are the selling prices of selected producers, free on board (f.o.b.) point of production, some prices are those quoted on organized commodity exchanges or at central markets; this practice is most often found among farm products.

Product change and quality adjustment

Although the same product usually is priced month after month, it is necessary to provide a means for bridging over changes in detailed specifications so that only real price changes will be measured. An adjustment is especially important when one product is replaced by a new one. Even when companies report their selling prices based on altered transaction selling terms (e.g., price per 1,000 sold instead of price per 100), or when there is a change in the number or identity of companies reporting to BLS, routine steps are taken to ensure that only true price changes influence the index.

When a company respondent reports a price that reflects a physical change in a product, the Bureau uses one of several quality adjustment methods. The direct comparison method is used when the change in the physical specification is so minor that no product cost differences result; in this instance, the new price is directly compared to the last reported price under the former specifications, and the affected index reflects any price difference.

When changes in physical characteristics of a product cause product cost differences, however, the Bureau attempts to make an accurate assessment of real price change by taking systematic account of quality differences. The explicit quality adjustment method is especially important for automobiles, machinery, and other types of goods that undergo periodic model changes. For these goods the usual method for quality adjustment involves the collection of data from reporting companies on the costs they have incurred in connection with the quality change. If the selling price of a new model car is $500 more than the previous model year's version, but $200 of that increase is due to the extra product cost and normal margin associated with the addition of government-mandated safety equipment, then the real price has only risen by $300; the change in the passenger car index will reflect only that amount, not the nominal price rise of $500.

Unfortunately, it is not always possible to obtain a value for quality adjustment if, for example, the respondent is unable to estimate the production cost difference between an old item and a new one, or if an explicit comparison between an entirely new product and a previous product is not feasible. In such cases, the Bureau may have to assume that any difference in price between the old and the new items is entirely due to quality differences; the Bureau, therefore, employs the "overlap" method (if possible). Under this method, the Bureau collects prices for both the old and the new item over a period of time and chooses 1 month as the overlap month. The difference between the prices of the two items in the overlap month is assumed to represent the value of their quality differences. For purposes of calculating the official price index, the Bureau uses price changes for the old item through the overlap month but thereafter follows price changes only for the new item.

When resource cost information is absent from the reporter concerning product attributes that have changed, a different yardstick is employed to measure these missing values. It has been very difficult if not impossible to estimate the value of improvements or deteriorations in products manufactured by companies included in "high tech" industries such as computers, semiconductors, and so forth. These industries may frequently develop new products that are technologically superior and cost less. The conventional quality adjustment methodology is suitable for situations in which increased resource costs for producing a product are necessary for improved performance. This is the exact opposite of what typically happens in industries that manufacture sophisticated products comprised of electronic components. This inverse relationship between cost changes and quality changes requires many different techniques for index construction, especially in the area of quality adjustment.[2] An alternative quality adjustment technique using hedonic regressions has recently been incorporated into PPI adjustment processes. Hedonic regressions estimate the functional relationship between the characteristics embodied in the products in a market and the products' selling prices. They yield estimates of "implicit prices" for specified product characteristics that may be used to value the quality improvement resulting from changes in

[2] See "New Price Index for the Computer Industry," by James Sinclair and Brian Catron, *Monthly Labor Review*, October 1990.

the various characteristics embodied in a product. The value of the quality improvement can then be removed from the reported price change to obtain a measure of the pure price change appropriate for the PPI.

Since January 1991, the Bureau has published a computer price index incorporating these new quality adjustment procedures. In addition, series for other high-tech industries related to computers may also incorporate these new techniques of adjusting for embodied technological change.

Classification

The Producer Price Index family of indexes consists of several major classification systems, each with its own structure, history, and uses. However, indexes in all classification systems now draw from the same pool of price information provided to BLS by cooperating company reporters. The three most important classification structures are: (1) industry; (2) commodity; and (3) stage of processing.

Industry classification. A Producer Price Index for an industry is a measure of changes in prices received for the industry's output sold outside the industry (that is, its net output). As previously stated, the SIC 4-digit industry code is the basis for the industry price index system. Price indexes have also been available since 1985 for many more highly aggregated industry series at the 3- and 2-digit levels, as well as for total mining industries and total manufacturing industries.

Nearly every 4-digit industry price index is accompanied by detailed indexes representing price movements for the various products made in that industry. Code numbers for these indexes at the 5-digit (product class) and the 7-digit (individual product) levels often follow the product codes and titles established by the Census Bureau as extensions of the SIC structure. Sometimes, however, BLS assigns its own codes and titles.

In general, there may be as many as three kinds of product price indexes for a given industry. Every industry has primary product indexes to show changes in prices received by establishments classified in the industry for products made primarily, but not necessarily exclusively, by that industry. The industry under which an establishment is classified is determined by those products accounting for the largest share of its total value of shipments. In addition, most industries have secondary product indexes to show changes in prices received by establishments classified in the industry for products chiefly made in some other industry. Finally, some industries may have miscellaneous receipts indexes to show price changes in other sources of revenue received by establishments within the industry.

Commodity classification. The commodity classification structure of the Producer Price Index organizes products by similarity of end use or material composition, regardless of whether these products are classified as primary or secondary in their industry of origin. This system is unique to the PPI and does not match any other standard coding structure such as the SIC or the United Nations Standard International Trade Classification. Historical continuity of index series, the needs of index users, and a variety of ad hoc factors were important in developing the PPI commodity classifications.

Fifteen major commodity groupings (2-digit level) make up the all commodities index. Of these, 2 major commodity groupings form the index for farm products and processed foods and feeds, while the other 13 are grouped into the industrial commodities price index. Each major commodity grouping includes (in descending order of aggregation) subgroups (3-digit), product classes (4-digit), subproduct classes (6-digit), and individual items (8-digit). The structure of the traditional commodity classification system thus follows a strict, consistent hierarchy.

Corresponding indexes. Nearly all 8-digit commodities under the traditional commodity coding system are now derived from corresponding industry-classified product indexes. In such instances, movements in the traditional commodity price indexes are identical to movements of their counterparts. Although most traditional commodity price indexes continue to be published on their own original base period, the corresponding industry product price indexes are published on a base of the month of their introduction. Therefore, monthly percent changes for corresponding indexes will be virtually identical even though their respective index levels may differ.[3]

Specifications for 8-digit commodities priced under the current methodology generally follow Census Bureau definitions and are considerably broader than those formerly used for traditional commodity indexes. Because companies report prices for a broad range of commodity and transaction-term specifications within a given commodity index, it is not feasible to publish meaningful average prices for individual commodities. Price indexes are usually calculated by constructing an index for each reporting establishment's price and then averaging these indexes, with appropriate establishment weights, to derive the commodity index.

Commodity-based stage-of-processing classification. Commodity-based stage-of-processing (SOP) price indexes regroup commodities at the subproduct class (6-digit) level according to the class of buyer and the amount of physical processing or assembling the products have undergone.

[3] Lists of corresponding commodity codes and product codes appear in *Supplement to Producer Price Indexes, Data for 1990,* pp. 353-86.

Finished goods are defined as commodities that are ready for sale to the final-demand user, either an individual consumer or a business firm. In national income accounting terminology, the Finished Goods Price Index roughly measures changes in prices received by producers for two portions of the gross national product: (1) Personal consumption expenditures on goods, and (2) capital investment expenditures on equipment.[4] Within the Finished Goods Price Index, the consumer foods category includes unprocessed foods, such as eggs and fresh fruits, as well as processed foods, such as bakery products and meats. The finished energy goods component includes those types of energy to be sold to households—primarily gasoline, home heating oil, residential gas, and residential electricity. The category for consumer goods other than foods and energy includes durables such as passenger cars and household furniture, and nondurables such as apparel and prescription drugs. The capital equipment index measures changes in prices received by producers of durable investment goods such as heavy motor trucks, tractors, and machine tools.

The category for intermediate materials, supplies, and components consists partly of commodities that have been processed that still require further processing. Examples of such semifinished goods include flour, cotton yarn, steel mill products, and lumber. The intermediate goods category also encompasses nondurable, physically complete goods purchased by business firms as inputs for their operations. Examples include diesel fuel, belts and belting, paper boxes, and fertilizers.

Crude materials for further processing are defined as unprocessed commodities not sold directly to consumers. Crude foodstuffs and feedstuffs include items such as grains and livestock. The crude energy goods category consists of crude petroleum, natural gas to pipelines, and coal. Examples of crude nonfood materials other than energy include raw cotton, construction sand and gravel, and iron and steel scrap.

Many major commodity-based stage-of-processing price indexes exist continuously back to 1947. However, some special groupings within this system (such as finished goods less foods and energy) were first calculated in the 1970's and have no historical record before then.

Industry-based stage-of-process classification. The Bureau publishes industry-based stage-of-process indexes, with data beginning in June 1985. These industry-based SOP indexes combine industry price indexes with interindustry transaction data from the 1977 input/output tables of the U.S. Department of Commerce; the result is a rigorous price model of the industrial economy.

The industry-based SOP system is grounded on SIC industries, which are allocated to processing stages based on their transaction relationships to each other. The traditional SOP system is grounded on commodities, which are allocated to processing stages based on their degree of fabrication and on the class of their ultimate buyer.

Industry-based SOP data use net output and net input weights that exclude transactions internal to an SOP component and that limit measurement to include only those transactions which affect other SOP components. This practice systematically eliminates multiple counting of price change, a problem which affects some commodity-based SOP indexes, particularly within the Intermediate Goods category.

Industry-based SOP indexes are arranged to facilitate economic analysis of the inflation transmission process by maximizing the amount of frontflows within the system, i.e., transactions from industries classified in an earlier stage of process to industries classified in a later stage. Backflows (i.e., transactions from a later stage of process to an earlier stage) introduce circularity into what is ideally a sequential system.

There are four major output SOP indexes: (1) Crude processors; (2) primary processors; (3) semifinished processors; and (4) finished processors. There are also four major material input SOP indexes, with two major subindexes for final demand: (1) Material inputs to primary processors; (2) material inputs to semifinished processors; (3) material inputs to finished processors; and (4) material inputs to final demand, including separate indexes for material inputs to personal consumption and material inputs to capital investment.[5]

Other. There are several additional classification structures within the PPI family of indexes. For example, Producer Price Indexes are available by durability of product. Allocation of individual commodities to durability-of-product categories (such as durable manufactured goods and total nondurable goods) is based on the Census Bureau definition; products with an expected lifetime of less than 3 years are classified as nondurable, while products with a longer life expectancy are considered durable goods. Special commodity grouping indexes (such as fabricated metal products and selected textile mill products) rearrange PPI commodity data into different combinations of price series. In 1986, BLS began publication of indexes measuring changes in prices of material inputs to construction industries.

Most Producer Price Indexes, whether commodity-oriented or industry-oriented, are national rather than regional in scope. However, regional price indexes are published for a few selected items, such as electric power,

[4] The Producer Price Index universe excludes the consumer services portion of total consumption expenditures and the structures portion of investment expenditures.

[5] See "New Stage-of-Process Price System Developed for the Producer Price Index" by Robert Gaddie and Maureen Zoller, *Monthly Labor Review,* April 1988.

coal, sand and gravel, scrap metals, and cement, where regional markets are the rule rather than the exception.

Data Sources and Collection Methods

An industry as a whole is the basic starting point for sampling, and each industry has an individually designed and tailored sample. The first step in selecting a sample is to construct a universe frame of establishments classified within that industry. The primary source for compiling this universe of establishments is the Unemployment Insurance System, because most employers are legally required to participate. Supplementary information from multiple, publicly available lists is used to refine the industry's frame of establishments.

The next step in constructing an industry sample consists of clustering establishments into price-forming units. Each member of a price-forming unit must belong to the same industry; establishments in a profit center that belong to other industries are excluded in this step. An establishment is defined as a production entity in a single location. Two establishments may occupy the same or adjacent space if they are separable by physical identification, recordkeeping, or both. Establishments are the units for which production and employment data are usually collected; however, in many cases establishments are not the appropriate unit for the collection of producer price data. Several establishments owned by a single firm may be operated as a cluster and constitute a profit-maximizing center. In such cases, the business maximizes profits for the cluster as a whole rather than for any one establishment. A profit-maximizing center is therefore the price-forming unit.

Once a list of price-forming units in an industry has been compiled, the list may be stratified by variables appropriate for that industry. The criterion for identifying the sampling strata is whether price trends may be different for different values of a variable. For example, the size of the production unit may cause differences in production technologies and, thus, different responses to changes in demand or input costs. Some industries may be characterized by geographically independent markets, which may become strata. Within each stratum, units are usually ordered by size to ensure a proportionate distribution of the sample.

The next step is to assign the number of units to be selected in each stratum. This assignment may be in direct proportion to the value of shipments by units in each stratum. However, if there is evidence that some strata have more heterogeneity in price change, these strata will be assigned a greater proportion of the total sample than their simple shipment values would require. Each price-forming unit is selected systematically with a probability of selection proportionate to its size. Ideally, the proper measure of size would be the total revenue of the unit; however, in practice, employment is used as a proxy because employment information is usually more readily available.

Once an establishment or cluster of establishments is selected for pricing, a BLS field economist visits the unit to solicit its cooperation. The management of the unit is assured that their assistance is completely voluntary, and that any information they agree to provide to BLS will be safeguarded under the strictest guarantees of confidentiality. Current laws have consistently been interpreted to ensure that no one other than sworn BLS employees, including other government agencies, is allowed access either to individual company price information or to information that could identify reporting companies.

If the establishment agrees to participate in the Producer Price Index program, the BLS field economist proceeds to select those transactions to be priced through time from among all the unit's revenue-producing activities. A probability sampling technique called disaggregation is used to select those transactions. The disaggregation procedure assigns to each category of items shipped, and to each category of other types of receipts, a probability of selection proportionate to its value within the reporting unit. The categories selected are broken into additional detail in subsequent stages until unique items, or unique types of other receipts, are identified.

Even after a physically unique item has been selected, it is usually necessary to disaggregate further. If the same physical item is sold at more than one price, then the conditions that determine that price—such as the size of the order, the type of customer, etc.—must also be selected on the basis of probability. This method for identification of terms of sale (or transaction terms) both ensures that the same type of transaction is priced over time and eliminates any bias in the selection of the terms of sale.

To minimize the reporting burden on cooperating companies, the disaggregation process described above usually is completed within 2 hours in the initiation interview. (An example of the product checklists used in this process is shown at the end of this chapter.) Subsequently, reporting companies agree to supply prices for those items selected on an agreed-upon schedule, usually monthly but sometimes less often. BLS Form 473P, also shown at the end of this chapter, is used for reporting producer prices. The degree of cooperation generally remains high, although some companies decline to participate from the beginning and others may drop out of the program.

The publication of company-specific data in identifiable form is prohibited in the statistical and research work of BLS. Data from firms participating in the PPI survey are encrypted to ensure the respondent's confidentiality even within the Bureau, so that only those few staff members with an absolute need to know can identify a respondent. Furthermore, publication criteria have been established to prevent an inadvertent revelation of a respondent's identity to the public through the movement in a published index.

In most cases, publication of an index requires that: (1) There are at least three different respondents in the survey; (2) there is price information from at least two of these reporting units in any given month; and (3) no single respondent accounts for 50 percent or more of the total weight for that item. With few exceptions, indexes which do not meet these standards are not published. For series such as those for agriculture, whose price data are compiled from sources in the public domain, only one quote is required to pass the test for number of respondents. BLS industry analysts may allow an index to be published if they determine that confidentiality would not be compromised.

The BLS sample of each industry's producers and output must be updated every few years to account for changing market conditions. This procedure, called "resampling," takes place relatively often for industries marked by dynamic changes in production technology or industry structure. More stable industries need to undergo resampling less frequently. In practice, many of the reporting companies and products included in the sample may be the same both before and after resampling.

Data Processing

Producer Price Indexes are the output of a series of computer subsystems which automate most operations. Although previously limited to relying upon mainframe computers, PPI data processing has increasingly turned to microcomputer and local area network (LAN) technologies.

After BLS field representatives conduct an initial survey of each reporting establishment, the data collected are reviewed by the Bureau's regional offices to ensure consistency and completeness. These data are then subject to final review by the Bureau's national office staff. At that point, a survey can be prepared, tailored specifically for each establishment listing all price-determining variables and terms of sale for each selected product; these surveys are called repricing schedules. These repricing schedules are thereafter sent to those establishments on a regular basis.

In the Bureau's repricing system, the schedules returned by the respondents are scanned by an optical character reader, which logs in each form and captures the essential data elements. The Bureau's economists then verify the price information and check for changes that might have been missed by the optical character reader. The repricing system makes possible the collection and processing of current prices of over 80,000 items, as well as any changes in the price determining characteristics of those items.

The estimation system takes the item prices from the repricing system and calculates the published indexes, generating a variety of outputs used for production of printed statistical tables, floppy diskettes, and mainframe data tapes.

These automated data processing systems for the PPI facilitate the accuracy and timeliness of published PPI data and protect the confidentiality of data supplied by the respondents.

Estimating Procedures

Weights

If the Producer Price Index system were composed merely of indexes for individual products, with no grouping or summarization, there would be no need to devise a comprehensive weight structure. However, given the desire for numerous indexes for groupings of individual products, there is a need for a weight system that will let more important products have a greater impact on movements of groupings. Without a weighting structure, a 10-percent rise in gasoline prices would have no more significance than a 10-percent rise in greeting card prices.

Commodity and product aggregation weights. A price index for even the most finely detailed commodity or product (usually termed a "cell index") cannot be calculated without applying a policy for weighting the individual price reports received by BLS for each item. Reports of some establishments are given more weight than those from others in accordance with data on shipment values provided to BLS field representatives during the initiation interviews with reporting establishments, adjusted by BLS probability selection techniques.

To calculate both commodity and product indexes for levels of aggregation above the cell index, BLS compiles weights based on values of shipments derived from information provided by the Bureau of the Census and a few other sources.[6] Product index weights, however, are based only on values of shipments for those aggregations of products made within the same industry; thus, shipment values for the same products made in other industries are not counted.

Industry net output weights. In compiling price indexes for 4-digit SIC industries, as well as for more highly aggregated industry group indexes, BLS employs net output values of shipments as weights. Net output shipment values include only shipments from establishments in one industry to establishments classified in other industries or to final demand. By definition, then, net output shipment values differ from gross shipment values by excluding

[6] Information currently used for calculating weights throughout the PPI family of indexes is largely taken from the following censuses conducted by the Bureau of the Census of the U.S. Department of Commerce: (1) *Census of Manufactures;* (2) *Census of Mineral Industries* (which includes oil and gas production); (3) *Census of Agriculture;* and (4) *Census of Wholesale Trade.* Other current weight sources include the Energy Information Administration of the U.S. Department of Energy and the National Marine Fisheries Service of the U. S. Department of Commerce.

shipments among establishments within the same industry, even if those establishments are owned by separate and independent firms. The meaning of "net output" depends on the context of the index grouping. The net output for total manufacturing, for example, would be the value of manufactured output shipped outside the entire manufacturing sector, e.g., to the construction sector or to consumers. In addition to the value of shipments data supplied by the Census of Manufactures, BLS also constructs appropriate net output price indexes through the use of data on detailed industry flows from the input-output tables compiled by the Bureau of Economic Analysis of the U.S. Department of Commerce, and other detailed industry data. Currently, industry price indexes are calculated primarily with 1987 net output weights and 1977 input-output relationships.

Weights for traditional commodity groupings. Weights for individual commodity price indexes, and in turn for commodity grouping price indexes, are based on gross value of shipments data, as compiled by the Bureau of the Census and a few other sources. This is in contrast to the net output weights used for industry indexes. These commodity weights represent the total selling value of goods produced or processed in the United States, f.o.b. production point, exclusive of any excise taxes. Since January 1987, shipment values between establishments owned by the same company (termed interplant transfers) have been included in commodity and commodity grouping weights; interplant transfers had been excluded from the weight structure before then.

Commodity and commodity grouping weights are updated periodically to take into account changing production patterns. Since January 1992, these weights have been derived from the total net selling value of commodities reported in the 1987 economic censuses. From January 1987 through December 1991, 1982 shipment values formed the foundation for commodity and commodity grouping weights. 1972 weights were used between January 1976 and December 1986. Updated weights are incorporated into the PPI system in a manner that does not require recalculation of indexes for earlier periods.

BLS does not publish the actual values used as weights, but does publish what is called a relative importance for each commodity and commodity grouping. The relative importance of an item represents its basic value weight, including any imputations, multiplied by the relative of price change from the weight date to the date of the relative importance calculation, expressed as a percentage of the total value weight for the all commodities category. Data showing the relative importance of commodity groupings with respect to the three major stage-of-processing groupings are also available.

BLS calculates relative importance data for December of each year. Except when entirely new weights are introduced from the latest industrial censuses, or when there are sample changes affecting a given grouping, relative importance data usually change from one December to another solely because of relative price movements. The relative importance of a commodity will rise if its price rises faster than the all commodities index; conversely, a commodity whose price falls or rises less than the all commodities index will show a smaller relative importance. Published relative importance data are not used, however, as fixed inputs by the Bureau to calculate monthly price indexes. Rather, each commodity's actual weight value fluctuates each month in accordance with its previous price movements. Theoretically, the Bureau could calculate and publish a new set of relative importance data every month. Relative importance data for any given commodity grouping also change when its components are subjected to a sample change.

Commodity-based stage-of-processing indexes. For commodity-based stage-of-processing indexes, weights are allocated to detailed SOP indexes at the subproduct class (i.e., 6-digit) level of commodity code series. These detailed SOP indexes are in turn aggregated to broader SOP indexes, such as Finished Goods, and also to SOP special groupings, such as finished goods excluding foods and energy. Allocations of subproduct classes to detailed SOP indexes appear in a table of relative importance data published in the annual supplement to the monthly detailed report, *Producer Price Indexes.*

The value-weight of a single subproduct class may be allocated among several different commodity-based SOP categories to reflect different classes of buyers. For example, a portion of the value-weight of the citrus fruits index has been assigned to the index for crude foodstuffs and feedstuffs to represent the proportion of citrus fruit sold to food processors; most of the rest of the value-weight for this grouping has been assigned to the index for finished consumer foods. The allocations of these value-weights to various SOP categories are currently based on input-output studies for 1972 conducted by the Bureau of Economic Analysis. The relative value-weights within any subproduct class are the same as for those within the commodity classification scheme.

Industry-based stage-of-process indexes. For both sets of indexes within the industry-based stage-of-process system, industry data are weighted into SOP totals based on their 1987 Census value of shipments. Industry data may be allocated to more than one industry-based SOP, as in the commodity-based SOP system described above.

For net output industry-based SOPs, net ouput weights are allocated at the 4-digit industry level. The net output value includes only that portion of output value which goes to industries in other stages of process and excludes shipments among industries within a stage of process. A listing of the assignment of specific industries to the four net output SOP groupings appears in the methodology study by

Gaddie and Zoller referenced at the end of this chapter. BLS does not publish industry-level weights for either the net output or the material input industry-based SOP schemes.

For material input industry-based SOP groupings, weights are generally allocated at the 4-digit product class level (i.e., primary product class series for industry outputs); however, there are some exceptions where narrower product classes may be used. In either case, the weights for these product classes are assigned on a wherever-made basis, so that weights for secondary products are also included. Specifically, gross-weighted product classes that are contributed as inputs to each SOP category are weighted according to their proportionate use ratio, which indicates what portion of each product class is used collectively by industries assigned to that SOP category. Also, to eliminate transactions internal to an SOP industry, product figures representing SOP inputs originating from within the same SOP are given a net input weighting in addition to the proportionate use ratio which applies to all of the SOP input data. A net input ratio is applied which reflects the proportion of inputs received from industries outside the stage of process in question.

Seasonal adjustment

Direct and aggregative adjustment. PPI series are selected for seasonal adjustment if statistical tests indicate seasonality and if there is an economic rationale for the observed seasonality. Both indexes and rates of change can be published on a seasonally adjusted basis.

All commodity code series, and a few SOP series, that are seasonally adjusted are adjusted directly, by applying the X-11 procedure based on a multiplicative model to data for the latest 8 calendar years.[7] Seasonal factors for the latest full calendar year are used to generate adjusted data for the current year. Most commodity-based stage-of-processing series, however, are adjusted by the indirect or aggregative method, which is more appropriate than direct adjustment for broad categories whose component series show strongly different seasonal patterns. Under the aggregative method, direct adjustment is first applied to indexes at lower levels of detail, and thereafter the adjusted detail is aggregated up to yield the broad SOP index. (For those detailed series which have not been selected for seasonal adjustment, the original, unadjusted data are used in the aggregation process.)

Specifically, commodity groupings at the subproduct class level (i.e., 6-digit commodity codes) are usually first aggregated to detailed SOP series; after those detailed SOP series have been seasonally adjusted directly, they are aggregated to form the seasonally adjusted total SOP series. There are several exceptions to this general scheme, such as the energy and food groupings at all three major stages of processing, and all subproduct classes within the Finished Goods index; in these cases, the subproduct class data are adjusted directly rather than after first being aggregated to a detailed SOP series.

Intervention. Some index series show erratic behavior which can cause problems in making an accurate seasonal adjustment. An index series whose underlying trend has experienced a sharp and long-lasting shift will generate distorted results when put through the X-11 procedure. Trend shifts have been observed, for example, when petroleum prices have reacted to major policy changes instituted by the Organization of Petroleum Exporting Countries (OPEC) cartel—a recurring event which happens at infrequent and irregular intervals. Another kind of distorting change may occur when the seasonal pattern itself changes, such as when many firms within an industry decide to change the months of the year in which they will institute their regular price increases.

In order to compensate for those instances where such distortions are both substantial and identifiable, an established method of intervention analysis, developed at BLS, is sometimes applied.[8] In recent years, BLS has used intervention analysis in seasonal adjustment for various refined petroleum products, passenger cars, and tobacco products. Broad SOP indexes that are adjusted by the aggregative method and that have been affected by such distortions are corrected by applying intervention analysis to those component detailed series where the problem has been observed.

Other estimation procedures

Missing prices. If no price report from a participating company has been received in a particular month, then the change for that price will in general be estimated by averaging the price changes for the other items within the same cell (i.e., for the same kind of products) for which price reports have been received.

Rounding policy. Whenever rounding is performed to prepare PPI data for publication, the data are rounded to the nearest tenth of a decimal place. To derive monthly or annual average indexes, BLS bases its calculations onunrounded data; index figures are rounded at the final step only. Before 1991, annual averages for index series based on commodity code data were calculated by using the rounded published indexes for the individual months; this is no longer the case. Annual averages for industry and product indexes have always been based on unrounded indexes.

[7] A general description of how seasonal adjustment procedures are typically applied at BLS is given in appendix A at the end of this *Handbook.*

[8] See "On the Use of Intervention Analysis in Seasonal Adjustment" by J. A. Buszuwski and S. Scott, *Proceedings of the Business and Economics Section,* American Statistical Association, 1988.

To derive seasonally adjusted indexes, rounded published data which are unadjusted are divided by rounded seasonal factors; the seasonally adjusted index data which result are then rounded for publication. A methodology change scheduled for implementation soon will call for seasonally adjusted indexes to be calculated from unrounded data with respect to both the unadjusted index data and the seasonal factors.

When BLS displays percent changes in association with any index data (whether unadjusted or seasonally adjusted), these changes are calculated on the basis of the published, rounded indexes.

Index calculation

In concept, the Producer Price Index is calculated according to a modified Laspeyres formula:

$$I_i = (\Sigma Q_a P_i / \Sigma Q_a P_o) \times 100$$

where:

P_o is the price of a commodity in the comparison period;

P_i is its price currently; and

Q_a represents the quantity shipped during the weight-base period.

An alternative formula more closely approximates the actual computation procedure:

$$I_i = \left[(\Sigma Q_a P_o (P_i / P_o)) / \Sigma Q_a P_o \right] \times 100$$

In this form, the index is the weighted average of price relatives, i.e., price ratios for each item (P_i / P_o). The expression ($Q_a P_o$) represents the weights in value form, and the P and Q elements (both of which originally relate to period "a" but are adjusted for price change to period "o") are not derived separately. When specifications or samples change, the item relatives must be computed by linking (multiplying) the relatives for the separate periods for which the data are precisely comparable.

Analysis and Presentation

Analysis

In 1978, as the transition to the current methodology began, BLS also shifted its analytical focus. Prior to that time, the Bureau's economic analysis had focused on the all commodities index, the industrial commodities index, and other highly aggregated major commodity groupings. During the 1970's, however, when price changes were particularly volatile, it became clear that these indexes are subject to a bias from the multiple counting of price changes. In brief, a multiple-counting bias means that price changes for components that go through many stages of processing have an excessive impact on aggregate index series. This problem is common among highly aggregated traditional commodity groupings because they are calculated from price changes of commodities at several stages of processing, where each individual price change is weighted by its total gross value of shipments in the weight-base year.

To illustrate the multiple-counting problem, suppose that the price of cotton rises sharply. If this price increase is passed through by spinners of cotton yarn, then by weavers of gray cotton fabric, then by producers of finished cotton fabric, and finally by shirt manufacturers, the single price increase for the raw material cotton would have been included five times in the all commodities index and four times in both the industrial commodities category and in the major commodity group for textile products and apparel. Inasmuch as prices throughout the economy are always changing at different rates, multiple counting can result in rates of change for aggregated price indexes that are highly misleading, both because material prices tend to be more volatile than finished goods prices are and because gross output values are used as weights for major commodity groups. (Less aggregated commodity grouping indexes that cover only a single stage of processing are not affected by this multiple-counting defect.)

Commodity-based stage-of-processing indexes are currently the central classification structure used by the Bureau for analyzing price trends in the general economy because they minimize the multiple-counting problem. In particular, since 1978 the Finished Goods Price Index has been stressed by the Bureau as the single most important index. This index measures inflation in consumer and capital goods, upon which demand for materials and other inputs depends. Both this index and the index of Crude Materials for Further Processing are largely free of multiple-counting problems because they are rather strictly defined. The index for Intermediate Materials, Supplies, and Components, however, is a residual, encompassing everything that cannot fit into one of the other two major stage-of-processing categories. This index, therefore, includes several different stages of processing (three such stages in the shirt example above) and is affected by the multiple-counting problem. Industry-based stage-of-processing indexes provide another solution to the problems inherent in aggregated price indexes based upon a weighting structure using gross shipment values.

Presentation

Producer Price Indexes are usually issued in the second or third week of the month following the reference month. The specific monthly dates for each year are announced prior to the beginning of each calendar year and are determined by the pricing date of the previous month. The monthly summary PPI news release—available without charge from the Bureau—shows the most recent originally released and revised data for all commodity-based stage-of-processing indexes and for selected major commodity groupings that comprise the bulk of these indexes. While all indexes in the news release are shown on an unadjusted basis, seasonally adjusted monthly percent changes also are shown for many series; price changes over the last 12 months are also included. Even though the news release can display only a limited number of PPI series, all Producer Price Indexes are available at the time of the release and are considered officially published at that time.

The monthly detailed report, *Producer Price Indexes,* is printed several weeks after the news release date and is available to the public from the U.S. Government Printing Office on a paid subscription basis. The monthly detailed report currently includes most published indexes within the PPI family of indexes that are not seasonally adjusted; data for series which duplicate those whose codes appear in print are available only on request. The detailed report also shows yearly percent changes, both seasonally adjusted and unadjusted monthly percent changes, and a few seasonally adjusted indexes. In addition, it contains a narrative section explaining the most significant price movements within major stage-of-processing and industry groups for that month. When appropriate, additional narratives explain the latest sample changes (usually effective in January and July of each year), updates in seasonal adjustment factors or weights, or other changes in methodology or presentation. Occasionally, a longer narrative section provides a more in-depth explanation of the economic background underlying recently observed price movements.

A subscription to this periodical also includes an annual supplement. This supplement, commonly mailed to subscribers in the summer of the year following the reference year, provides final monthly indexes and annual averages for the calendar year, as well as tables of relative importance data effective for December of that year. Neither the monthly periodical nor the annual supplement includes information on actual dollar prices for any item.

Printouts of tables of historical price indexes for any PPI series are available from the Bureau on request, usually without charge. Two computer tapes are available at cost; one shows complete historical tables for all individual commodities and commodity groupings, commodity-based stage-of-processing groupings, durability-of-product groupings, and other indexes from older PPI structures, and the other shows complete historical records for industry-based SOP groupings and for industry and product indexes classified according to the SIC and the Census product codes. Complete historical records are also available on microfiche at cost. Monthly diskettes showing the latest monthly values and the previous 12 months of data for most series included within the PPI news release are also available. The monthly PPI news release may also be accessed on-line through the BLS Electronic News Service.

Seasonally adjusted data. Because price data are used for different purposes by different groups, BLS publishes seasonally adjusted as well as unadjusted data each month. For economic analysis of price trends, seasonally adjusted data are usually preferred because they are designed to eliminate the effect of changes that normally occur at about the same time and in about the same magnitude each year—such as price movements resulting from normal weather patterns, regular production and marketing cycles, model changeovers, seasonal discounts, and holidays. Data that are seasonally adjusted can therefore reveal more clearly long-term or cyclical trends.

The economic analysis that the Bureau conducts for PPI data are normally based on seasonally adjusted data. Unadjusted data are used for analysis when a series has not been selected for seasonal adjustment. Because seasonal adjustment is a tool for enhancing economic analysis, those index series which the Bureau deemphasizes for the purpose of economic analysis are deliberately not calculated on a seasonally adjusted basis. In particular, those PPIs which are subject to the multiple-counting problem described earlier, such as the all commodities index and the indexes for the major commodity groups, are not available on a seasonally adjusted basis.

The unadjusted version of PPI data are of primary interest to those who need information which can be more readily related to the dollar values of transactions. For example, unadjusted data are used in price escalation clauses of long-term sales or purchase contracts.

The latest 5 years of seasonally adjusted data are revised at the beginning of each year. This is in addition to the 4-month revision, discussed below, which applies to all PPI data both seasonally adjusted and unadjusted. The newly revised 5-year histories for seasonally adjusted data are made available with the release of January data in mid-February of each year.

Revised data. All unadjusted Producer Price Indexes are routinely subject to revision only once, 4 months after original publication, to reflect late reports and corrections by company respondents. Once revised, indexes are considered final. The Bureau does not use the term "preliminary" to describe the originally released PPI numbers, because "preliminary" usually describes data that are based on a small sample of information and that are typically subject to large revisions. When Producer Price Indexes are first released, they are typically based on a substantial portion of the total number of returns that will eventually be received from respondents; hence, subsequent revisions are normally minor, especially at the more highly aggregated grouping levels. "First published" or "originally released" are more appropriate term than "preliminary." Changes in previously published data caused by a processing error are so indicated in a subsequent news release and/or detailed report; such occurrences are rare.

Calculating index changes. Movements of price indexes from one month to another should usually be expressed as percent changes rather than as changes in index points because index point changes are affected by the level of the index in relation to its base period, while percent changes are not. Each index measures price changes from a reference period which is defined to equal 100.0. 1982 is currently the standard base period for most commodity-oriented PPI series, but many indexes that began after 1982 are based on the month of their introduction. The following tabulation shows an example of the computation of index point and percent changes.

Index point change

Finished Goods Price Index	121.3
Less previous index	118.5
Equals index point change	2.8

Index percent change

Index point change	2.8
Divided by previous index	118.5
Equals	0.024
Results multiplied by 100	0.024 x 100
Equals percent change	2.4

An increase of 20 percent from the reference base period in the Finished Goods Price Index, for example, is shown as 120.0. This change can be expressed in dollars as follows: Prices received by domestic producers of a systematic sample of finished goods have risen from $100 in 1982 to $120.00 today. Likewise, a current index of 133.3 would indicate that prices received by producers of finished goods today are one-third higher than what they were in 1982.

From time to time, the Bureau updates its standard reference base period. The change to the 1982=100 base occurred in January 1988; before that, the year 1967 was used as the standard reference base. For reasons explained above, any change of standard reference base periods leaves calculations of percent change for any index virtually unaffected. However, care must be taken to ensure that indexes on one base period are not being incorrectly compared against indexes for the same series expressed on a different base period.

Uses and Limitations

Producer Price Indexes are used for many purposes by government, business, labor, universities, and other kinds of organizations, as well as by members of the general public.

Economic indicator

The Finished Goods Price Index is one of the Nation's most closely watched indicators of economic health. Movements in this index are often considered to presage similar changes in inflation rates for retail markets, as measured by the Bureau's Consumer Price Index. While this may sometimes be the case, there are many reasons why short-term movements in the PPI and the CPI may diverge. For example, the Finished Goods Price Index by definition excludes services, which constitute a major portion of the CPI. The Producer Price Index does not measure changes in prices for imported goods, while the Consumer Price Index does include imports. Conversely, the CPI does not capture changes in capital equipment prices, a major component of the Finished Goods Price Index. Large swings in producer prices for foods and other items may be considerably dampened by the time retail prices are measured.

Other commodity-based stage-of-processing price indexes besides the Finished Goods Price Index are used for general economic analysis. Because prices for food and energy have tended to be so erratic in recent years, some economists prefer to focus attention on an index such as finished goods other than foods and energy as a better measure of the so-called "core" or "underlying" rate of inflation. The Index for Intermediate Materials, Supplies, and Components is closely followed as an indicator of material cost pressures that may later appear in the Finished Goods Price Index and/or the CPI. The index for crude materials other than foods and energy is quite sensitive to shifts in total demand and can be a leading indicator of the state of the economy; its limited scope, however, makes it less reliable as an indicator of the future status of inflation in general. The stage-of-processing structures are especially well suited for analysis of the inflation transmission process.

Deflator

Producer Price Index data for capital equipment are used by the U.S. Department of Commerce to help calculate the gross national product (GNP) deflator and many of its component deflators. PPI data at all levels of industry and commodity aggregation can be used to deflate dollar values expressed in current dollars to constant-dollar values for a variety of economic time series, such as inventories, sales, shipments, and capital equipment replacement costs. To illustrate the deflation concept, suppose that nominal shipment values for a given industry have doubled over a 10-year span. If the Producer Price Index for that same industry has tripled over the same time span, then the "real" (i.e., inflation-adjusted) value of shipments for that industry has actually declined; higher prices would more than account for the doubling of dollar shipment values, and physical volume would have implicitly fallen.

Private business uses

Private business firms use PPI data to assist their operations in a variety of ways, in addition to using these figures for general economic analysis or deflation as discussed above. Producer Price Indexes are frequently cited in price escalation clauses of long-term sales or purchase contracts as a means to protect both the buyer and the seller from unanticipated surges or drops in prices. For example, an escalation clause may specify that the price for x number of widgets being sold by company A to company B each year will go up or down by a specified fraction of the percentage of change in material costs, as measured by one or more specified Producer Price Indexes (often in conjunction with the change in a measure of labor costs, such as the Employment Cost Index). Hundreds of billions of dollars in contract values are tied to Producer Price Indexes through these price escalation clauses; such clauses are common in both government and private sector contracts.

Private companies can also use PPI data to compare changes in material costs they incur against changes in the PPI for that material. By the same token, they can compare changes in the selling prices they charge for their own output to changes in the PPI for the same kind of product. PPI information is also employed in econometric models, in forecasting, in market analysis, and in academic research. PPI's are frequently used in LIFO (Last-In, First-Out) inventory accounting systems by firms wishing to avoid the kind of "phantom profits" that might appear on their books with a FIFO (First-In, First-Out) system.

Discontinued data

Those wishing to follow PPI data for a particular series over a prolonged time span should be aware that highly detailed indexes are more vulnerable to discontinuation by BLS than are aggregated indexes. During the industry resampling process described earlier, for example, an industry index (4-digit level) is commonly kept continuous before and after the resampling process is completed, while indexes for detailed products within that industry may be discontinued and replaced by items that are new or that had not been selected for pricing before. Finely detailed indexes are also vulnerable to temporary suspension of publication. The Bureau's rules against disclosure of confidential information preclude publication of indexes when fewer than three companies are in the sample for a given product. Even if there are three firms in the sample for a given product, the Bureau will ordinarily publish that index only if at least two companies actually report prices and if no single reporter accounts for more than half of the market for that product. When a detailed index disappears either temporarily or permanently, the Bureau rountinely recommends that users who had been following than index either choose another detailed index within the same product grouping or else switch their attention to a more highly aggregated grouping index.

Technical References

Escalation and Producer Price Indexes: A Guide for Contracting Parties, Report 807. U.S. Department of Labor, Bureau of Labor Statistics, September 1991.

Supplement to Producer Price Indexes, Data for 1990. U.S. Department of Labor Bureau of Labor Statistics, August 1991.

Sinclair, James and Catron, Brian. "New Price Index for the Computer Industry," *Monthly Labor Review,* October 1990.

Buszuwski, J.A. and Scott, S. (1988), "On the Use of Intervention Analysis in Seasonal Adjustment," Proceedings of the Business and Economics Section, American Statistical Association.

Gaddie, Robert and Zoller, Maureen. "New Stage-of-Process Price System Developed for the Producer Price Index," *Monthly Labor Review,* April 1988.

Clem, Andrew and Thomas, William. "New Weight Structure Being Used in Producer Price Index," *Monthly Labor Review,* August 1987.

Gousen, Sarah; Monk, Kathy; and Gerduk, Irwin. *Producer Price Measurement: Concepts and Methods.* U.S. Department of Labor, Bureau of Labor Statistics, June 1986.

Tibbetts, Thomas R. "An Industrial Price Measurement Structure: The Universe Matrix of Producers and Products," *1978 Proceedings of the Section on Survey Research Methods.* American Statistical Association, Washington, DC, 1979.

Early, John F. "Improving the Measurement of Producer Price Change," *Monthly Labor Review,* April 1978.

Popkin, Joel. "Integration of a System of Price and Quantity Statistics with Data on Related Variables," *Review of Income and Wealth,* March 1978.

Archibald, Robert B. "On the Theory of Industrial Price Measurement: Output Price Indexes," *Annals of Economic and Social Measurement,* Winter 1977.

Council on Wage and Price Stability. *The Wholesale Price Index,* June 1977.

Bureau of Labor Statistics
Information for the Producer Price Indexes

U.S. Department of Labor

The information collected on this form by the Bureau of Labor Statistics will be held in the strictest confidence and will be used for statistical purposes only.

This report is authorized by law, 29 U.S.C. 2. Your voluntary cooperation is needed to make the results of this survey comprehensive, accurate, and timely.

Form Approved
O. M. B. No. 1220-0008

The Department estimates that the public reporting burden for this form varies from 1 to 30 minutes per response, with an average, of 18 minutes per response including time for searching, gathering, and maintaining the data needed and completing and reviewing the form. Send comments regarding the burden estimate or any other aspect of this form, including suggestions for reducing this burden to Department of Labor, Room N-1301, 200 Constitution Avenue, N.W., Washington, D.C. 20210 and to the Office of Management and Budget, Paperwork Reduction Project, Washington, D.C. 20503.

Dear Respondent,

Thank you for your continuing participation in the Producer Price Index (PPI) program. The data which you provide are used in computing the Producer Price Indexes and constitute the basis for analyzing industrial price changes.

Please use the enclosed postage free envelope to return the pricing forms. Your continued cooperation is greatly appreciated.

Commissioner of Labor Statistics

Instructions for completing a PPI pricing form:

Item and Transaction Description

If the Item Description or the Transaction Terms, or both, no longer apply, please select a substitute item or transaction terms. Item substitution should only occur when the item previously reported is no longer available because it is being or has been permanently discontinued. The substitute item should be as similar as possible to the current item and should be expected to remain available for some time. The substitute transaction terms should likewise be as similar as possible to the discontinued transaction terms.

Report these changes in the closest open area and provide current price information.

Adjustments to Price

Following is a list of the more common adjustments to price. The specific adjustments on the pricing form were selected originally and should be changed only when either the level of an existing adjustment changes or a new adjustment becomes applicable to the product and transaction described.

Deductions from price include:
1. Standard discounts (Cash, Seasonal, Cumulative Volume, and Trade)
2. Rebates
3. Other recurring discounts
4. Other nonrecurring discounts (Competitive and Negotiated)

Additions to price include
1. Surcharges
2. Other charges added to price

Taxes should always be excluded from the price. If this exclusion is not possible, note this in REMARKS.

Freight charges should be excluded from the price unless delivery was selected originally as part of the product. Make changes if the currently described freight terms no longer exist.

QUESTIONS

Answer whether changes have (YES) or have not (NO) been made to the item description, terms of transaction, or adjustments to price.

Answer YES or NO depending on whether the shipment price of the item described changed (YES) between the two dates listed or whether the shipment price did not change (NO) during the time period. If the answer is NO, the form has been completed and is ready for mailing.

DO NOT ENTER A PRICE IF THE PRICE HAS NOT CHANGED!

If the answer is YES, please enter the new price.

Write in any corrections to terms or address to whom this form should be sent in the future. Name and address changes need to be made on only one form.

Please complete and return within 5 business days all of the pricing forms mailed to you even if there are no changes.

If you anticipate a change in any of the information you provide, please indicate in REMARKS. List the anticipated changes and when they will occur.

Any questions you have regarding the pricing form or its completion may be resolved by calling the person listed on the reverse side of this form.

B2S 473P
rev. Jan, 1989

Have the Item Description, Terms of Transaction, or Adjustments to Price changed since your last report?
If "YES," please enter the necessary changes.

THIS FORM IS MACHINE PROCESSED. Limitations imposed by Bureau processing equipment restrict recognition of blue entries. Please use BLACK pen/pencil only.

This item has been selected for use in the Producer Price Index. You are asked to provide a price each month for the item described under the terms and adjustments shown.

Please review each section of this form. If your firm no longer sells this specific item under the terms and adjustments, revise the description, terms, and/or adjustments indicating when the changes were made.

If the change made to the description resulted in a change to your production costs, please provide an estimated value of the change for Bureau staff to use in making appropriate adjustments. This value is the production cost difference including your standard markup.

Further instructions are shown on the reverse side of this form. If you have any questions concerning completion of this form, please call collect:

Please use the enclosed postage-free envelope or send to:

U.S. Department of Labor
Bureau of Labor Statistics
600 E Street N.W. Code 47
Washington, D.C. 20212

PRICE INFORMATION

Please review the Previous Price Information. Enter missing prices if available or correct any Incorrect prices that are shown.

Please enter the current price in the boxes provided ONLY if there has been a change from the price you previously reported.

THE LATEST TYPE OF PRICE REPORTED WAS (Prices for actual shipments are desired):

PREVIOUSLY REPORTED PRICES *CORRECTIONS*

Did the price change between
If "YES," please report the price of the last shipment since
If there was no shipment in please estimate the
price you would have charged on

USE BLACK PEN/
PENCIL ONLY.
DO NOT USE BLUE.

CHECK THIS BOX *ONLY* IF THE ITEM DESCRIBED ABOVE IS BEING CLOSED OUT.
If the item is closed out, please provide a substitute item on this form.

The information collected on this form by the Bureau of Labor Statistics will be held in confidence and will be used for statistical purposes only.

This report is authorized by law 29 U.S.C. 2. Your voluntary cooperation is needed to make the results of this survey comprehensive, accurate, and timely

Form Approved
O. M. B. No. 1220-0008
Disclosure Statement
Located on Form 1810-A

Establishment Code

Quote Code

SIC 2064 - CANDY AND OTHER CONFECTIONERY PRODUCTS

PRODUCT CHECKLIST - Pages 2 - 3

Definitions - Pages 4 - 5

INDUSTRY DEFINITION - SIC 2064

This industry includes establishments primarily engaged in manufacturing candy, including chocolate candy, other confections, and related products. All chocolate products in this industry must be made from purchased chocolate.

NOTE:

Chocolate products made from cocoa beans, roasted and ground on the premises of the establishment are classified in SIC 2066, Chocolate and Cocoa Products.

Also excluded are the following similar products:

- Cookies and crackers (SIC 2052)
- Chewing gum (SIC 2067)
- Salted, roasted, dried, cooked, or canned nuts and seeds (SIC 2068)
- Retail sales of candy and other confections (SIC 5441)

SPECIAL INSTRUCTIONS

1) Chocolate or chocolate-type confectionery made of more than one ingredient must be coded as follows:

   - Under PRODUCT (codes 05-22) circle one code based on the primarily featured ingredient.
   - Under FILLING INGREDIENTS (codes 81-86) describe the secondary, other featured ingredients.

2) Centers panned (sprayed) with chocolate or sugar may be confused with those centers enrobed (coated) or molded with chocolate or sugar. Use the following general guidelines to distinguish between these types of products/processes:

   - Panned confectioneries have a thin, high gloss and often hard external shell and are made using comfit or revolving pans.
   - Enrobed confectioneries have a thick, dull, textured covering and are made using enrobing or coating machines.
   - Molded confectioneries often have a shiny surface and are made using shell forming and filling machines.

Establishment Code | Quote Code

(00) SIC Code B2064 | Industry Name CANDY AND OTHER CONFECTIONERY PRODUCTS

PRODUCT

CHOCOLATE AND CHOCOLATE-TYPE CONFECTIONERY

SOLID (without inclusions)
- 01 Bar
- 02 Character/animal (incl. hollow)
- 03 Stars
- 04 Other, ____

SOLID WITH INCLUSIONS
- 05 With dried fruit
- 06 With nuts
- 07 With rice
- 08 With other, ____

ENROBED/MOLDED WITH BAKERY PRODUCT CENTER
- 09 Cookie center
- 10 Wafer center
- 11 Other bakery product center, ____

ENROBED/MOLDED WITH NON-BAKERY PRODUCT CENTER
- 12 Caramel center
- 13 Nougat center
- 14 Other candy/candy-cream center, ____
- 15 Nut center
- 16 Fruit center

CHOCOLATE-PANNED
- 17 Bridge mix
- 18 Chocolate center
- 19 Nut center
- 20 Other center, ____

- 21 ASSORTMENT
- 22 OTHER, ____

NONCHOCOLATE/OTHER CONFECTIONERY

HARD CANDY
- 23 Brittle
- 24 Sucker/lollipop
- 25 Lemon drops
- 26 Sour balls
- 27 Candy canes
- 28 Mints
- 29 Other, ____

CHEWY CANDY
- 30 Toffee
- 31 Taffy
- 32 Caramel
- 33 Granola
- 34 Candied popcorn
- 35 Nougat
- 36 Other, ____

SOFT CANDY
- 37 Candy corn
- 38 Fruit slice
- 39 Fudge
- 40 Other, ____

ICED/COATED
- 41 Bonbons
- 42 White chocolate
- 43 Other, ____

LICORICE (Includes licorice-type)
- 44 Twists
- 45 Shoelaces
- 46 Nuggets
- 47 Other, ____

NONCHOCOLATE-PANNED
- 48 Boston baked beans
- 49 Jelly beans
- 50 Other, ____

OTHER
- 51 Candied fruit peels
- 52 Candied fruit
- 53 Cough drops (nonpharmaceutical)
- 54 Glazed nuts
- 55 Other, ____

56 ITEM IDENTIFICATION - NA
- 57 Brand name, ____
- 58 Product number, ____
- 59 Other, ____

TYPE OF PRODUCTION
- 501 Primary product
- 502 Resale

81 FILLING INGREDIENTS - NA
82 Nuts/seeds/cereal, ____________
83 Creams/pastes/butters, ____________
84 Fruit, ____________
85 Jellies/syrups/oils/liqueurs, ____________
86 Other, ____________

60 INDIVIDUAL ITEM WEIGHT - NA
61 ________ oz.
62 ________

64 ITEM COUNT - NA (Specify no. per pkg.)
65 ________ per package

66 PACKAGE WEIGHT - NA
67 ________ oz.
68 ________ lbs.
69 ________

70 PACKAGE TYPE - NA
71 Individually wrapped
72 Bags
73 Boxes
74 Bulk
75 Cans
76 Cartons
77 Rolls
78 Other, ____________

79 NUMBER OF PACKAGES PER CASE - NA
80 ________ packages per case

113 OTHER FEATURES - NA
114 ____________
115 ____________

** CHOCOLATE/CHOCOLATE-TYPE CONFECTIONERY **

100 TYPE OF CHOCOLATE - NA
101 Milk
102 Dark
103 Other, ____________

CHOCOLATE ORIGIN
104 Chocolate purchased from another establishment
105 Chocolate made from raw cocoa beans ground in the same establishment

** NONCHOCOLATE & OTHER CONFECTIONERY **

106 TYPE - NA
107 Solid
108 With filling

109 FLAVOR - NA
110 Assorted
111 Other, ____________

90 COMMENTS ____________
91 ____________

2064

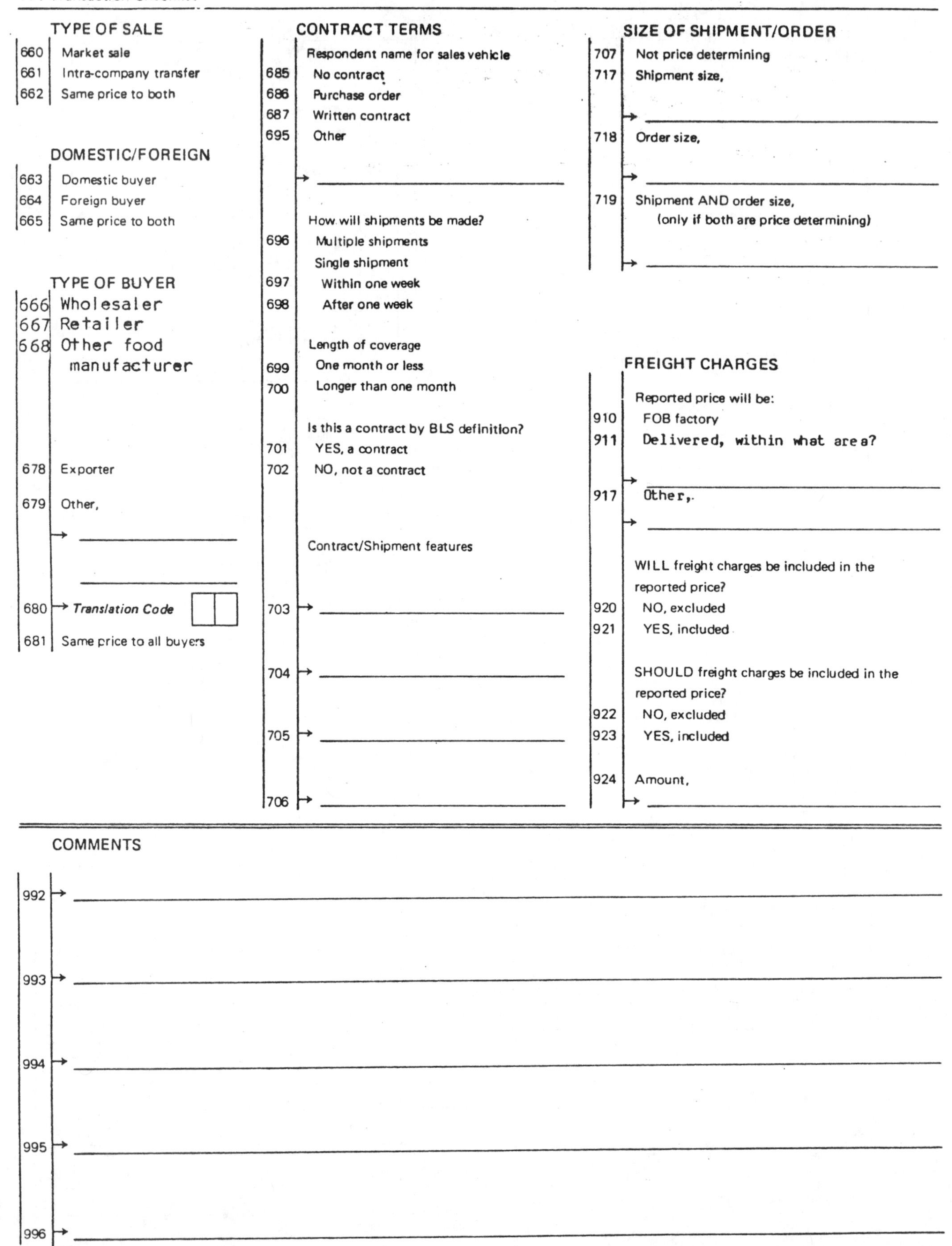

TYPE OF SALE

660 Market sale
661 Intra-company transfer
662 Same price to both

DOMESTIC/FOREIGN

663 Domestic buyer
664 Foreign buyer
665 Same price to both

TYPE OF BUYER

666 Wholesaler
667 Retailer
668 Other food manufacturer

678 Exporter
679 Other,
→ ______________
____
680 → *Translation Code* [|]
681 Same price to all buyers

CONTRACT TERMS

Respondent name for sales vehicle
685 No contract
686 Purchase order
687 Written contract
695 Other
→ ______________

How will shipments be made?
696 Multiple shipments
Single shipment
697 Within one week
698 After one week

Length of coverage
699 One month or less
700 Longer than one month

Is this a contract by BLS definition?
701 YES, a contract
702 NO, not a contract

Contract/Shipment features
703 → ______________
704 → ______________
705 → ______________
706 → ______________

SIZE OF SHIPMENT/ORDER

707 Not price determining
717 Shipment size,
→ ______________
718 Order size,
→ ______________
719 Shipment AND order size,
(only if both are price determining)
→ ______________

FREIGHT CHARGES

Reported price will be:
910 FOB factory
911 Delivered, within what area?
→ ______________
917 Other,
→ ______________

WILL freight charges be included in the reported price?
920 NO, excluded
921 YES, included

SHOULD freight charges be included in the reported price?
922 NO, excluded
923 YES, included

924 Amount,
→ ______________

COMMENTS

992 → ______________
993 → ______________
994 → ______________
995 → ______________
996 → ______________

ADJUSTMENTS TO PRICE

CASH DISCOUNT/CASH SURCHARGE

820 None regularly offered
821 Respondent name for discount,

→ ______________________

822 Complete cash discount structure,

→ ______________________

831 Respondent name for surcharge,

→ ______________________

832 Complete cash surcharge structure,

→ ______________________

COMPETITIVE DISCOUNT

840 None
841 Not currently in effect
990 Respondent refuses to provide information
842 Respondent name for discount,

→ ______________________

843 Standard discount,
844 Amount,

→ ______________________

845 Price reductions vary with market conditions
846 Reported price reflects market condition reductions
847 Typical amount,

→ ______________________

SEASONAL DISCOUNT

850 None regularly offered
851 Respondent name for discount,

→ ______________________

852 Discount on shipments
853 Discount on orders
Complete seasonal discount strueture,

854 → ______________________

855 → ______________________

For discounts on ORDERS only, % of revenue from shipments including seasonal discount, by month,

856 → ______________________

857 → ______________________

819 No discounts or surcharges apply

TRADE DISCOUNT

860 Respondent name for discount,

→ ______________________

861 Amount,

→ ______________________

862 Offered to,

→ ______________________

QUANTITY DISCOUNT

870 Respondent name for discount,

→ ______________________

871 Amount,

→ ______________________

872 Required size,

→ ______________________

OTHER DISCOUNT (#1)

880 Type of discount,

→ ______________________

881 Amount,

→ ______________________

882 Terms,

→ ______________________

OTHER DISCOUNT (#2)

890 Type of discount,

→ ______________________

891 Amount,

→ ______________________

892 Terms,

→ ______________________

OTHER SURCHARGE

900 Type of surcharge,

→ ______________________

901 Amount,

→ ______________________

902 Terms,

→ ______________________

HOW WILL RESPONDENT REPORT ADJUSTMENTS TO PRICE AT REPRICING?

	Applied by Respondent?	If NOT Applied by Respondent: Order	Varies?	Amount		
829 → Cash discount	Y N	1 2 3 4 5 6 7 8 9 10	Y N	$.	or	. %
839 → Cash surcharge	Y N	1 2 3 4 5 6 7 8 9 10	Y N	$.	or	. %
849 → Competitive	Y N	1 2 3 4 5 6 7 8 9 10	Y N	$.	or	. %
859 → Seasonal	Y N	1 2 3 4 5 6 7 8 9 10	Y	$.	or	. %
869 → Trade	Y N	1 2 3 4 5 6 7 8 9 10	Y N	$.	or	. %
879 → Quantity	Y N	1 2 3 4 5 6 7 8 9 10	Y N	$.	or	. %
889 → Other discount (#1)	Y N	1 2 3 4 5 6 7 8 9 10	Y N	$.	or	. %
899 → Other discount (#2)	Y N	1 2 3 4 5 6 7 8 9 10	Y N	$.	or	. %
909 → Other surcharge	Y N	1 2 3 4 5 6 7 8 9 10	Y N	$.	or	. %
919 → Freight charge	Y N	1 2 3 4 5 6 7 8 9 10	Y N	$.	or	. %
(14-16)	(21)	(23-24)	(26)	(28-37)		(39-44)

TYPE OF PRICE RESPONDENT WILL PROVIDE

NET PRICE

800 Actual shipment price

801 List price (all adjustments indicated)

802 Estimated price

803 CURRENT AVERAGE PRICE (enter basis of average in COMMENTS)

GROSS PRICE

804 List price (some adjustments indicated)

805 List price (no adjustments indicated)

806 LAGGED AVERAGE PRICE (enter basis of average in COMMENTS)

818 OTHER

→ ______________________

CURRENT PRICE (same type as at repricing)

770 → $ [ ][ ][ ],[ ][ ][ ],[ ][ ][ ].[ ][ ][ ][ ]

UNIT OF MEASURE

772 per bag

773 per box

774 per carton

775 per case

776 per pound

771 per, ______________________

COMMENTS

798 → ______________________

799 → ______________________

MAILING ADDRESS FOR REPRICING

760 → Same as QUOTE [A][ ][ ]

761 → Company name [ ]

762 → [ ]

763 → [ ]

764 → [ ]

765 → City (21-43) [ ] State (45-46) [ ][ ] Zip (48-56) [ ][ ][ ][ ][ ]–[ ][ ][ ][ ]

766 → TELEPHONE Area Code [ ][ ][ ]–[ ][ ][ ]–[ ][ ][ ][ ] Extension [ ][ ][ ][ ]

SEASONALITY

726 The product is NOT available for repricing in:

→ (21-32) [ ] JAN [ ] FEB [ ] MAR [ ] APR [ ] MAY [ ] JUNE [ ] JULY [ ] AUG [ ] SEPT [ ] OCT [ ] NOV [ ] DEC

OFF-CYCLE

743 Respondent refuses to report in:

→ (21-32) [ ] JAN [ ] FEB [ ] MAR [ ] APR [ ] MAY [ ] JUNE [ ] JULY [ ] AUG [ ] SEPT [ ] OCT [ ] NOV [ ] DEC

FREQUENCY OF SHIPMENT

Is the product actually shipped at least once every 3 months?

738 YES, when in season

If NO, when in season, will the respondent provide?

740 Estimated price

741 Quality adjustment data

742 Neither of these

COMMENTS

997 → ______________________

998 → ______________________

999 → ______________________

*U.S. GOVERNMENT PRINTING OFFICE: 1990--262-257/20060

Chapter 17. International Price Indexes

Background

The International Price Program (IPP) provides, as its primary output, price indexes for the foreign sector of U.S. merchandise trade. Additional outputs include international service sector indexes, foreign currency indexes, and international export price comparison measures. These data play a crucial role in the analysis of trends in U.S. trade and are also used in the analysis of domestic price levels.

Although the Bureau has collected international price data for a number of years, a complete set of international price indexes has been published only since the early 1980's. The first collection of import prices took place nearly 100 years ago as part of a one-time study of U.S. price competitiveness. The next effort occurred immediately following World War II, when to meet the need for accurate measures of price change within the expanding U.S. foreign trade sector, BLS initiated the limited development of export and import price indexes. However, budget restrictions in 1948 led to the termination of this effort. As a result, the development of foreign trade sector price indexes was postponed until 1967 when BLS began research on the feasibility of producing U.S. export and import price indexes. This research was among the early major products of the Division of Price and Index Number Research established in 1966 on the recommendation of the Price Statistics Review Committee of the National Bureau of Economic Research. This research resulted in congressional allocation of funds for IPP in fiscal year 1970.

A limited number of export price indexes were first published in June 1971 and selected import indexes followed in 1972. These introductory index series presented annual values until 1974 when collection and publication of quarterly price data began.

During the remainder of the 1970's and into the early 1980's, IPP steadily expanded its product coverage and the publication of export-import price indexes. The index covering all imports is available beginning with September 1982 data, and the all-export series begins in September 1983.

Beginning with data for January 1989 data, IPP began publishing monthly indexes for 16 aggregate end-use series. These indexes have been used since January 1990 by the Bureau of the Census to deflate the monthly merchandise trade balance figures, and have supplanted the unit value indexes of the Census as the only monthly measurement of U. S. international prices. Beginning with the release of data for January 1993, indexes by Standard Industrial Classification (SIC), end-use, Standard International Trade Classification (SITC), and Harmonized series will be available monthly.

In addition to its coverage of international trade in products, IPP tracks price movements in the services area of foreign trade. Late 1986 saw the initial publication of service sector indexes representing export air passenger fares and import electricity. The coverage of services has expanded to include published indexes for import tanker freight, air freight, and liner freight, and import air passenger markets. Currently IPP is developing an index for export air freight and is researching the measurement of prices for other transportation services.

The current indexes for both exports and imports reflect the market basket of internationally traded goods in the base year 1985. Beginning with the release of data for January 1993, the weights will be updated to reflect the market basket of goods traded in 1990.

Description of Survey

Concepts

The U.S. export and import price indexes are general-purpose indexes that measure changes in price levels within the foreign trade sector. The all-export index provides a measure of price change for domestically produced U.S. products shipped to other countries; the all-import index measures price change of goods purchased from other countries by U.S. residents. Since the indexes are intended to be used as deflators in the National Income and Product Accounts (NIPA), BLS has used balance-of-payments definitions, where appropriate, in its methodology.

In addition to the all-export and all-import indexes, indexes are published for a wide variety of product categories with several levels of detail. Currently, IPP publishes indexes for product categories which recorded at least $700 million of imports and $500 million of exports in 1985. Beginning in 1993, these limits will be raised to cover product categories with a 1990 value of $900 million for imports and $700 million for exports. Indexes that represent areas of trade with smaller dollar values are incorporated into the calculation of higher level indexes but are generally not published separately.

Data Sources and Calculation Methods

Product universe

The product universe of the export-import price indexes consists of all commodities exchanged between U.S. residents and foreign residents. ("Residents" refers to the NIPA definition; it includes corporations, businesses, and individuals but does not require either specific ownership or U.S. citizenship.) The export universe consists of products sold by U.S. residents to foreign buyers. The import universe covers products purchased from abroad by U.S. residents. The universe in each case includes raw materials, agricultural products, semi-finished manufactures, and finished manufactures, including both capital goods (electrical machinery, agricultural equipment, textile equipment, etc.) and consumer goods (appliances, electronic equipment, clothing, etc.).

Ideally, the total breadth of U.S. trade would be represented in the product universe. Items for which it is difficult to obtain consistent time series (works of art, commercial aircraft, ships, etc.) for comparable products are not included, however. Also, military goods are not priced in the indexes except to the extent that some nonmilitary products may be purchased on the open market for military use—e.g., automobiles, clothing, nonspecialized hardware, fuel, etc.

Sampling

The objective of the International Price Program sample design is to provide an unbiased measure of price change in each published index. A multistage survey design is employed to provide a sample of exporters and importers for specific product strata as well as specific items which can be repriced over time. The survey design is responsive to the constraints of both cost and the burden on firms. The cost constraints impose limits on the number of establishments selected in a sample, while the number of items priced in each establishment is controlled to limit respondent burden.

The two universes for the IPP are all exporters and all importers (and their respective products). A sampling frame for each universe is constructed from all documents filed during a specified reference period (generally 1 year). In the case of exports, these are the Shipper's Export Declarations (SED's) and, in the case of imports, the Consumption Entry Documents (CED's). These documents contain brief product descriptions, 10-digit Harmonized[1] product classification codes, value, quantity (where required), date, origin or destination, company name and address, and an establishment identification code.

[1] Harmonized product classification codes are defined in *Harmonized Tariff Schedule of the U.S. (1990)*, and are used for imports. *Statistical Classification of Domestic and Foreign Commodities Exported for the U.S. Schedule B* are used for export classifications.

The availability of an establishment identification code on both export and import records makes it possible to incorporate frequency of trade (consistency) into the sample design. Companies can be designated as either consistent or inconsistent exporters/importers of particular commodity classes. This information is used in each stage of sampling to increase the yield of usable time series prices.

The import frame, obtained from the Customs Bureau, contains a record of import transactions. Similarly, the export frame, provided by the Bureau of the Census, contains a record of export transactions.

The sample design for both exports and imports consists of three stages. The first is the selection of establishments; the second is the selection of Entry Level Items (ELI's—commodity classes within a sampling stratum); and the third is the selection of specific items (products) in the ELI. The system is identical for both exports and imports unless otherwise noted below.

The first step is to generate a measure of establishment size. To do this, dollar values on each document are aggregated to company-ELI, company-sample stratum, and company levels. They are also aggregated within an ELI, and for the stratum as a whole across all companies. A proportion is then calculated for each company-stratum by dividing the aggregated company-stratum dollar value by the aggregated dollar value within the stratum. This "company-stratum probability" is the proportion of dollar value that the company contributes to the particular stratum. The maximum-probability for each company is the maximum "company-stratum probability" for that company over all strata. In addition to a maximum-probability, a maximum-probability stratum (the stratum associated with the maximum-probability) is assigned to a company. The companies are then implicitly stratified by maximum-probability strata, and a systematic probability proportionate to size (PPS) selection of companies is made using the maximum-probability as the company's measure of size. The principal advantage of maximum-probability here is that a company's chance of selection is based on the product category for which it is most important; this is desirable since the indexes are calculated and published by product category.

When a company is selected in the first stage, it is selected for all its products, including those outside its maximum-probability stratum. In order to lessen the burden on respondents, it is then necessary to select a second-stage sample of ELI's within each company. The first step of this second stage is to ensure that publication requirements are met by selecting company ELI'S with certainty in some strata. The remaining ELI'S in each company are then sampled using a systematic PPS technique. The measure of size is the ELI-probability (the company-stratum probability distributed among the ELI's in the company in proportion to their dollar value contributions). This constitutes the sample of respondents and their selected ELI's.

After the sample of companies and ELI's has been selected, further sampling is needed to obtain a specific item for repricing. A probability selection method, referred to as disaggregation, was introduced in 1982. Under this method, the ELI is partitioned into subclasses, and a probability-proportionate-to-size selection is made among the subclasses using their proportion of trade in the establishment as the measure of size.[2] The process continues through the successive subdivisions of each selected subclass until an identifiable item is obtained that can be priced over time.

Probability sampling techniques have been used in IPP since 1976. Prior to that time, samples were based on nonstatistical, judgment samples of commodity groups. The judgmental criteria required that items selected in each company be repriceable and that their price movement be representative of the respondent's other products in that same ELI.

Starting in 1989, IPP divided the import and export sampling universes into halves, fielding one import and one export sample each year. Each half-universe, then, is resampled every 2 years. The sampled products are priced for about 4 years until they are replaced by a newer sample of the same half-universe.

The average sampling response rate is approximately 30 percent, that is, the IPP obtains initial price data for about 30 percent of the company-ELI's sampled. The major reason for nonresponse is that the company-ELI is traded infrequently or cannot be consistently repriced.

Collection

Prices are recorded on an IPP reporting form by firms at a visit initiated by a Bureau representative. (A copy of the price reporting forms appear at the end of this chapter.) During this visit, the reporting requirements are explained verbally and in writing, and the selection of products for which the firm will report price information is made. In the overwhelming majority of cases, prices are collected directly from the exporter or importer, although in a few cases prices are obtained from secondary sources.

Subsequent repricing is conducted by mail. If data clarification is required or if the form is not returned by the deadline, however, then the firm is contacted by telephone. IPP currently reprices all samples every quarter and a subsample each month to support the 16 monthly series. During 1993, IPP will be converting all samples to monthly repricing. The average repricing response rate for the survey is approximately 90 percent. That is, updates (either by mail or telephone) are obtained on about 90 percent of the forms that are sent out for repricing. Some of these updates may simply indicate that there was no trade for the product for that period, in which case the price of the product is imputed (based on price trends of other items in the same product category) for that pricing period.

[2] This "proportion of trade" estimate is provided by the respondent.

Pricing

The price reporting form asks firms to indicate all discounts, allowances, rebates, etc., applicable to the reported prices so that the price used in the calculation of the indexes is the actual transaction (or net) price for which the product was bought or sold. During the repricing process, respondents are reminded of this requirement in their repricing mail package and, if necessary, by a phone contact from an industry analyst on the IPP staff.

All prices collected are representative of actual transactions in the foreign-trade market. Average prices are not accepted in the IPP survey, with the exception of selected commodities where secondary source data are used.

The International Price Program's preferred pricing basis for exports is f.a.s. (free along side ship) U.S. port of exportation. When firms supply export prices that are on an f.o.b. (free on board) factory basis, an attempt is made to collect information on production point and freight to enable the IPP to calculate a shipment cost to the specified port of U.S. exportation. This information includes location of production point and port of exportation, size and weight of shipment, name of carrier, and routing. This shipment cost can then be added to the reported f.o.b. factory price in order to create a usable f.a.s. price. These adjustments are reviewed monthly for significant changes in transport costs.

In some product areas, for example finished manufactures, firms frequently provide prices only on an f.o.b. factory basis and are unable to supply freight information. As long as the firm can provide a consistent price series, IPP will include the product in the indexes.

For imports, IPP's preferred pricing basis has been c.i.f. at the U.S. port of importation. As with exports, however, any price basis is used if it can be maintained over time. IPP does attempt to collect import price data on both c.i.f. and f.o.b. foreign port bases. A c.i.f. price basis consists of the foreign selling price plus the other costs (insurance and freight) associated with bringing the product to the U.S. border. F.o.b. foreign port prices represent the cost of the item at the foreign port of exportation, and are consistent with the basis for valuation of imports in NIPA, where insurance and freight costs are tabulated separately in the services accounts. Import index calculation is performed on a duty-excluded basis. Import duty information, if necessary, is collected separately and, where appropriate, is deducted from the reported price.

Price index calculation requires that collected price data reflect the same item from period to period. To ensure this, the specifications for each product in the IPP survey include detailed physical and functional characteristics as well as the terms of transaction, e.g., number of units bought or sold, class of buyer or seller, etc. Any change in a product's specifications or terms of trade is reviewed to determine the significance of these changes. If the changes are cosmetic, product substitution is effected by direct price comparison, and any reported price change is reflected in the index. If the changes are substantive, product substitution is made by linking, which ensures that the index reflects only actual or "pure" price changes and is not affected by quality changes.

The following simplified example illustrates the principle of linking. The June reference period price for a specific imported automobile was $9,250.88. In the September reference period, a price of $10,108.77 was supplied for a new model of this automobile. It was determined that the new model was essentially comparable with the old, except that it had a bumper assembly that could only withstand a 2 1/2 m.p.h. impact without structural damage to the vehicle, whereas the former model was equipped with a 5 m.p.h. bumper. For linking purposes, the object is to determine the "appropriate" price that the new model would have commanded in the marketplace in the previous reference period. In this example, the new model was estimated to have a June price of $8,955.50 ($9,250.88, the June price of the former model, minus a $295.38 decrease in the value of the bumper assembly). The price comparison between June and September was based on the estimated June price of $8,955.50 and the reported September price of 10,108.77. Thus, a 12.9-percent increase was reflected in the September index, but the price change including the quality decrease (poorer quality bumper) was not reflected.

Linking is also used when products are added to or deleted from an index. When a completely new product series is added to a commodity grouping, the linking procedure discussed above is not feasible. Instead, the relative importance of each item in the commodity group is redistributed to include the new item, and the historical movement of the index is attributed to the new product. A change in the relative importance of a product also occurs when products are dropped from an index without being replaced.

Classification

Export-import price indexes are based on the nomenclature of Revision 2 of the Standard International Trade Classification of the United Nations.[3] Although primary indexes are calculated under the SITC, prices collected for the survey are classified by the basic product classification systems used for recording U.S. foreign trade. For exports, the 7-digit Schedule B classification system of the U.S. Department of Commerce[4] is used; for imports, the 7-digit Tariff Schedule of the United States Annotated (TSUSA)[5] is used. Concordance schemes are used for classifying Schedule B and TSUSA categories into the appropriate SITC's.[6] Beginning in 1993, the IPP will begin using the Harmonized TSUSA and Schedule B nomenclature which has been used by the Bureau of the Census and the Bureau of Customs since 1988 for the classification of import and export trade volumes.

By maintaining these detailed product classifications, BLS is able to prepare alternative indexes for groupings other than those afforded by the SITC. These additional indexes offer a wider variety of analytical uses for international price index data. Alternative groupings in published indexes include the industry-oriented Standard Industrial Classification based system and the Bureau of Economic Analysis' end-use system. Beginning with January 1993 data, the Harmonized nomenclature will be the primary system used to publish aggregate export and import price indexes.

Estimation Procedures

Formula

The export and import price indexes are weighted indexes of the Laspeyres type. Individual product price relatives are assigned equal importance within each weight-group category, and the weight-group relatives are then aggregated to the successive stratum index levels.

$$I_{x,t} = \frac{\Sigma_j \Sigma_i \left[\frac{P_i^t}{P_i^o}\right] \frac{w_j}{n_j}}{\Sigma_{jwj}}$$

where:

x = SITC group for which index is calculated
j = the weight categories within x (they are the Schedule B categories for exports, and the TSUSA categories for imports)
i = product within j
n = number of price relatives within j
t = time
w_j = share of the value of jth category in group x in the base year
P_{ti}/P_{oi} = price relative of product i in year t to base year o

The IPP weights represent the total dollar value of U.S. foreign trade in a designated base year and are distributed among several thousand 7-digit weight-group categories.

Values assigned to each of these weight group categories are based on trade value figures compiled by the Bureau of

[3] United Nations Statistical Office, *Standard International Trade Classification, Revised, Statistical Papers, Series M,* No. 34/Rev. 2 (New York, United Nations, 1975).

[4] Bureau of the Census, *Statistical Classification of Domestic and Foreign Commodities Exported From the United States, Schedule B,* January 1, 1978 edition and revisions.

[5] U.S. International Trade Commission, *Tariff Schedule of the United States Annotated,* 1980 edition and revisions.

[6] U.S. Bureau of the Census, *U.S. Foreign Trade Statistics Classifications and Cross Classifications,* 1980.

the Census for the base year.[7] In the case of the export price index the 7-digit weight group category is the Schedule B, and in the case of the import price index, it is the TSUSA. Beginning in January 1993, the weight-group categories will be the 6- 8- or 10-digit Harmonized Schedule B or TSUSA.

Each weight-group category is considered to be a relatively homogeneous commodity classification. Therefore, each product, or group of products, selected for the IPP survey within a weight-group category represents not only itself, but all products that fall within that weight-group. Due to budgetary limitations, not all weight-group categories are represented. Consequently, index trends of the represented categories are used to impute the movement of weight groups which are not covered.

Although earlier published indexes used weights from 1969, 1970, 1973, or 1975, all historical data were revised in February 1982 to reflect 1980 trade weights. Beginning with the release of the first quarter 1988 indexes, the base period was updated to 1985 and indexes were recalculated from 1985 to 1987. Data prior to 1985 continued to use 1980 weights. In 1993, the base period will be updated to 1990, but data prior to January 1993 will not be recomputed using these new weights.

Publication

All reporting is voluntary and confidential, and, therefore, no index is published in such a way as to reveal the name, price, or price behavior of any respondent. No index is published when fewer than three companies provide data; for the vast majority of indexes there are considerably more.

The quarterly export and import price indexes are published in BLS news releases 5 weeks after the third month of the quarter. The release includes a narrative summary as well as the SITC and end-use product indexes, service sector indexes, average rate and nominal foreign currency indexes, and import indexes by country or region of origin. A smaller monthly release covering data for the first 2 months of each quarter consists of 16 aggregate end-use groups. Comprehensive and specific historical tables are available and summary tables are published in the *Monthly Labor Review.* All of the index series are available on data diskette.

Where possible, the index base is 1985=100. In numerous cases where the price data are not supportive of a 1985 index base period, the indexes are presented with a more recent period. With the switch to 1990 weights in 1993, the index base will be shifted to 1990=100 for most series. At that time, Harmonized- and SIC-based indexes will be included in the press release which will, generally, provide data at the 2-digit level each month.

In addition to the export and import price indexes, reports are prepared at irregular intervals. These reports present index comparisons between the United States and the Federal Republic of Germany, and between the United States and Japan.[8] These comparisons measure price movements of U.S. exports relative to those of its major world competitors for similar commodities.

Uses and Limitations

The indexes published in this program are the only comprehensive indexes of prices related to the U.S. foreign trade sector. They provide monthly and quarterly measures of the price trend of U.S. products sold abroad and of products imported to the United States from other countries. The series enable analysts and policymakers to assess the effect of export and import price changes on the U.S. economy and its industrial sectors, as well as to analyze the effects of price changes on the balance of payments. The price measures provide a basis for calculating changes in the volume of exports and imports in the aggregate and for product groups.

Export price indexes provide a basis for measuring changes in the prices of U.S. products in relation to price trends of comparable products of other countries with which the United States competes for markets. They are also good tools for assessing changes in U.S. price competitiveness. Prices collected for exports, however, do not include overseas transportation, foreign duties, or other charges outside the United States.

Because import price indexes only measure the value of a product at a port (either domestic or foreign), special care must be taken in using these data to assess the effect of import prices on domestic inflation levels. First, an f.o.b. (free on board) foreign port series excludes international freight charges. Second, both an f.o.b. foreign port and a c.i.f. (cost-insurance-freight) U.S. port price series exclude duty as well as costs associated with domestic intermediaries (e.g., wholesalers and retailers). All of these factors may affect the final selling price.

Import and export price indexes are not seasonally adjusted. Consequently, price trends for commodities with seasonal patterns may require longer time spans for proper analysis.

[7] U.S. Bureau of the Census, *U.S. Foreign Trade Statistics Classifications and Cross Classifications,* 1980.

[8] The reports update *Comparisons of United States, German, and Japanese Export Price Indexes,* BLS Bulletin 2046 (1980).

Technical References

Pratt, Richard J. and Ferguson, Gwyn R. "Alternative Sample Designs in the International Price Program," *Proceedings of the Section on Survey Research Methods.* Washington, American Statistical Association, 1980.

U.S. Department of Labor, Bureau of Labor Statistics. *Comparisons of United States, German, and Japanese Export Price Indexes,* Bulletin 2046, February 1980.

Bureau of Labor Statistics
U.S. Export Price Information

U.S. Department of Labor

The information collected on this form by the Bureau of Labor Statistics will be held in confidence and will be used for statistical purposes only.

This report is authorized by law 29 U.S.C. 2. Your voluntary cooperation is needed to make the results of this survey comprehensive, accurate, and timely.

O.M.B. No. 1220-0025

We estimate that it will take an average of 30 minutes to complete this information form including time for reviewing instructions, searching existing data sources, gathering and maintaining the data needed, and completing and reviewing this information. If you have any statements regarding these estimates or any other aspect of this survey, send them to the Bureau of Labor Statistics, Division of Management Systems, Washington, D.C. 20212, and to the Office of Management and Budget Paperwork Reduction Project 1220-0026, Washington, D.C. 20503.

Schedule No.: ☐ ELI: ☐ Quote No.: ☐

Schedule B: ☐ If Multiple Hit, No. of Quotes Represented: ☐

Company/Reporter No.: ☐ Same Respondent as Quote No.: ☐ ☐ Currently Reporting Prices to IPP

Address Information

Company Name:

Division Name:

Respondent Name:

Respondent Title:

Mailing Address:

City: St: Zip:

Telephone: Extension:

I. Description

If off cycle,
mark month(s) priced

Jan	Feb	Mar	Apr	May	Jun	Jul	Aug	Sep	Oct	Nov	Dec

(Enter "X" in boxes which apply.)

☐ Price related to size of order. Specify: ______ ☐ Market sale

☐ Price related to class of buyer. Specify: ______ ☐ Intra-company transfer (Trends as market sale)

Comments: ______ ☐ Catalogue included

BLS 2894B (June 1990)

II. Export Price and Price Basis

Price Basis *(Enter code in the box below.)*

1. FAS/FOB Port/FOB Border
2. FOB Factory/ FOB Distribution Center/ FOB Mill/FOB Mine
3. Fly Away Factory (FAF)/ FOB Factory, Freight Allowed to Port or Border
4. Other (specify) ____________

Unit Priced *(Enter code in the box below.)*

Each (001)
Dozen (002)
Short Ton (003)
Metric Ton (004)
Long Ton (005)
Kilogram (006)
Pound (007)
Foot (008)
Meter (009)
Sq. Ft. (010)
Sq. Yd. (011)
Other (See appendix A.)

Date (YY) / (MM) [| | |]

Export Price [| | | | | | | | . | | |]

Country or Area of Destination

III. Discounts

[ ] No Discounts

(Enter percentage amount for each type and enter "Y" if already deducted, "N" if not already deducted.)

Distributor — [ ] Deducted — [| | . | |] %

Cash — [ ] Deducted — [| | . | |] %

Quantity — [ ] Deducted — [| | . | |] %

Other ________ — [ ] Deducted — [| | . | |] %

IV. Shipping Information

(Please complete the following if the reported price is not on the publication price basis.)

Typical Shipment from Factory or Distribution Center to U.S. Port or Border Point

Freight		Number Shipped*		Weight Shipped	
Charge	Unit Code	Number	Unit Code	Weight	Unit Code

Name of Original Carrier, if known ____________

Please check one of the following: [ ] Contract [ ] Common

Mode of Transportation to Port [ ]

1. Motor
2. Rail
3. Air
4. Barge
5. Freight Forwarder
6. UPS
7. U.S. Parcel Post
8. Pipeline
9. Other (specify) ____________

Typically Shipped By [ ]

1. Car Load Lot
2. Less Than Car Load Lot
3. Truck Load Lot
4. Less Than Truck Load Lot
5. Air Freight
6. Container
7. Other (specify) ____________

Location of Factory or Distribution Center ____________ City, State

Name of U.S. Port or Border Point Most Frequently Used for Export of this Product ____________ City, State

* If mixed shipment, leave blank and enter shipping weight of unit priced in description of Section I.

Comments: ____________

Bureau of Labor Statistics
U.S. Import Price Information

U.S. Department of Labor

The information collected on this form by the Bureau of Labor Statistics will be held in confidence and will be used for statistical purposes only.

This report is authorized by law 29 U.S.C. 2. Your voluntary cooperation is needed to make the results of this survey comprehensive, accurate, and timely.

O.M.B. No. 1220-0026

We estimate that it will take an average of 30 minutes to complete this information form including time for reviewing instructions, searching existing data sources, gathering and maintaining the data needed, and completing and reviewing this information. If you have any statements regarding these estimates or any other aspect of this survey, send them to the Bureau of Labor Statistics, Division of Management Systems, Washington, D.C. 20212, and to the Office of Management and Budget Paperwork Reduction Project 1220-0026, Washington, D.C. 20503.

Schedule No.: ELI: Quote No.:

TSUSA: If Multiple Hit, No. of Quotes Represented:

Company/Reporter No.: Same Respondent as Quote No.: ☐ Currently Reporting Prices to IPP

Address Information

Company Name:

Division Name:

Respondent Name:

Respondent Title:

Mailing Address:

City: St: Zip:

Telephone: Extension:

I. Description

If off cycle, mark month(s) priced

Jan	Feb	Mar	Apr	May	Jun	Jul	Aug	Sep	Oct	Nov	Dec

(Enter "X" in boxes which apply.)

☐ Price related to size of order. Specify: ______

☐ Price related to class of seller. Specify: ______

☐ Market sale

☐ Intra-company transfer (Trends as market sale)

Comments: ______

☐ Catalogue included

BLS 3007B (June 1990)

U.S. Import Price Information
Initiation

II. Import Price and Price Basis

Price Basis *(Enter code in the box below.)*

C. CIF U.S. Port
A. FOB Foreign Port
4. Other (specify) ______

Unit Priced *(Enter code in the box below.)*

Each (001)	Long Ton (005)	Meter (009)
Dozen (002)	Kilogram (006)	Sq. Ft. (010)
Short Ton (003)	Pound (007)	Sq. Yd. (011)
Metric Ton (004)	Foot (008)	Other (See appendix A.)

Date (YY)/(MM)

Import Price

Currency of Price

III. Price Factors

Name of U.S. Port or Border Point Most Frequently Used for Import of This Item

City, State

Country from which Item was Imported

IV. Duty

(Please complete the following if CIF price is reported.)

Duty Code

1. Duty included
2. Duty excluded
3. Duty free

Amount (Included in CIF price)

and/or

Percent of FOB Foreign Port price

. %

V. Discounts

No Discounts

(Enter percentage amount for each type and enter "Y" if already deducted, "N" if not already deducted.)

Distributor	Cash	Quantity	Other
Deducted	Deducted	Deducted	Deducted
. %	. %	. %	. %

Comments:

U.S. GOVERNMENT PRINTING OFFICE: 1990 0—262-098

Chapter 18. Consumer Expenditures and Income

Consumer expenditure surveys are specialized studies in which the primary emphasis is on collecting data relating to family expenditures for goods and services used in day-to-day living. Expenditure surveys of the Bureau of Labor Statistics (BLS) also collect information on the amount and sources of family income, changes in savings and debts, and demographic and economic characteristics of family members.

Background

The Bureau's studies of family living conditions rank among its oldest data-collecting functions. The first nationwide expenditure survey was conducted in 1888-91 to study workers' spending patterns as elements of production costs. With special reference to competition in foreign trade, it emphasized the worker's role as a producer rather than as a consumer. In response to rapid price changes prior to the turn of the century, a second survey was conducted in 1901. These data provided the weights for an index of prices of food purchased by workers, which was used as a deflator for workers' incomes and expenditures for all kinds of goods until World War I. A third survey, spanning 1917-19, provided weights for computing a cost-of-living index, now known as the Consumer Price Index (CPI). The next major survey, covering only urban wage earners and clerical workers, was conducted in 1934-36, primarily to revise these weights.

During the economic depression of the 1930's, the use of consumer surveys extended from the study of the welfare of selected groups to more general economic analysis. Concurrent with its 1934-36 investigation, the Bureau cooperated with four other Federal agencies in a fifth survey, the 1935-36 study of consumer purchases, which presented consumption estimates for both urban and rural segments of the population. The sixth survey, in 1950, was an abbreviated version of the 1935-36 study, covering only urban consumers. The seventh survey, the 1960-61 Survey of Consumer Expenditures, which once again included both urban and rural families, provided the basis for revising the CPI weights and also supplied material for broader economic, social, and market analysis.

The next major survey to collect information on expenditures of householders in the United States was conducted in 1972-73. That survey, while providing continuity with the content of the Bureau's previous survey, departed from the past in its collection techniques. Unlike earlier surveys, the Bureau of the Census, under contract with BLS, conducted all sample selection and field work. Another significant change was the use of two independent surveys, a Diary Survey and an Interview Panel Survey, to collect the information. A third major change was the switch from an annual recall to a quarterly recall (Interview Survey) and daily recordkeeping of expenditures (Diary Survey). These data were again used to revise the CPI weights.

It had been apparent for a long time that there was a need for more timely data than could be supplied by surveys conducted every 10-12 years. The rapidly changing economic conditions of the 1970's intensified this requirement. The continuing survey that was initiated in 1979 extended the BLS tradition of providing data describing the consumption behavior of American families.

The Current Survey

Unlike previous surveys, which occurred every 11 years or so, the latest survey has been continuous since late 1979. Data are now available quarterly and annually. The collection of data is carried out by the Bureau of the Census under contract with BLS. The objectives of the survey remain the same: to provide the basis for revising the weights and associated pricing samples for the CPI and to meet the need for timely and detailed information on consumption patterns of different types of families.

Like the 1972-73 survey, the current survey consists of two separate surveys, each with a different data collection technique and sample. In the Interview Survey, each consumer unit (CU) in the sample is interviewed every 3 months over five calendar quarters. The sample for each quarter is divided into three panels, with CU's being interviewed every 3 months in the same panel of every quarter. The Diary (or recordkeeping) Survey is completed at home by the respondent family for two consecutive 1-week periods.

The sample housing unit is notified in advance by a letter informing the occupants about the purpose of the survey and the upcoming visit by the interviewer. Both surveys are conducted by personal visits with telephone usage limited to appointment scheduling and follow-up calls for information missed at the time of the proposed interview. The interviewer uses a structured questionnaire to collect both the demographic and expenditure data in the Interview Survey. The demographic data in the Diary Survey are collected by the interviewer whereas the expenditure data are entered on the diary form by the respondent. Both surveys accept proxy responses from any eligible household member who is at least 16 years old if an adult is not available after a few attempts to contact that person.

The unit for which expenditure reports are collected is the set of eligible individuals constituting a consumer unit, which is defined as (1) all members of a particular housing unit who are related by blood, marriage, adoption, or some other legal arrangement, such as foster children; (2) a person living alone or sharing a household with others, or living as a roomer in a private home, lodging house, or in permanent living quarters in a hotel or motel, but who is financially independent; or (3) two or more unrelated persons living together who pool their income to make joint expenditure decisions. Students living in university-sponsored housing are also included in the sample as separate CU's.

The Interview Survey collects detailed data on an estimated 60 to 70 percent of total family expenditures. In addition, global estimates, i.e., estimated average expenditures for a 3-month period, are obtained for food and other selected items. These global estimates account for an additional 20 to 25 percent of total expenditures. On the average, it takes approximately 90 to 120 minutes to complete the interview.

In the Diary Survey, detailed data are collected on all expenditures made by consumer units during their participation in the survey. It is estimated that it takes approximately 20 minutes for the interviewer to collect the demographic data and to instruct the respondent on how to keep the diary. It is also estimated that it will take the respondent about 90 to 105 minutes each week to complete the diary.

There is a reinterview program established for the Consumer Expenditure Survey to provide quality control. It provides a means of evaluating individual interviewer performance to determine how well the procedures are being carried out in the field. The reinterview must be conducted by a member of the supervisory staff. A subsample of approximately 6 percent of households in the Interview Survey and 17 percent in the Diary Survey are reinterviewed on an ongoing basis.

All data collected in both surveys are subject to Census and BLS confidentiality requirements which prevent the disclosure of the respondents' identities. All employees have taken an oath to this effect.

Interview Survey

The Interview Survey is designed to collect data on the types of expenditures which respondents can be expected to recall for a period of 3 months or longer. In general, expenses reported in the Interview Survey are either relatively large, such as property, automobiles, or major appliances, or are expenses which occur on a fairly regular basis, such as rent, utility bills, or insurance premiums. Each occupied sample unit is interviewed once per quarter for five consecutive quarters. After the fifth interview, the sample unit is dropped from the survey and replaced by a new consumer unit. For the survey as a whole, 20 percent of the sample is dropped and a new group added each quarter. New families are introduced into the sample on a regular basis as other families complete their participation. Another feature of the current survey is that data collected in each quarter are considered independently, so that estimates are not dependent upon a family participating in the survey for a full five quarters.

For the initial interview, information is collected on demographic and family characteristics and on the inventory of major durable goods of each consumer unit. Expenditure information is also collected in this interview, using a 1-month recall, but is used, along with the inventory information, solely for bounding purposes, i.e, to classify the unit for analysis and to prevent duplicate reporting of expenditures in subsequent interviews.

The second through fifth interviews use uniform questionnaires to collect expenditure information in each quarter. Data collected in these questionnaires which are arranged by major expenditure component (e.g., housing, transportation, medical, education), form the basis of the expenditure estimates derived from the Interview Survey. In addition, information is obtained on the names of establishments (or outlets) from which selected commodities or services are purchased. Wage, salary, and other information on the employment of each CU member is also collected or updated in each of these interviews. The expenditure data are collected via two major types of questions asked. The first type of question asks for the purchase month directly for each reported expenditure. The second type of question asks for a quarterly amount of expenditures. The use of these two types of questions varies depending on the types of expenditures collected. Approximately 64 percent of the data were collected using the direct monthly method, whereas about 36 percent were collected using the quarterly recall approach.

In the fifth and final interview, an annual supplement is used to obtain a financial profile of the consumer unit. This profile consists of information on the income of the CU as a whole, including unemployment compensation; income from royalties, dividends, and estates; alimony and child support; etc. A 12-month recall period is used to collect income and asset type data.

Diary Survey

The primary objective of the Diary Survey is to obtain expenditure data on small, frequently purchased items which are normally difficult to recall. These items include detailed expenditures for food and beverages, both at home and in eating places; housekeeping supplies and services; nonprescription drugs; and personal care products and services. The Diary Survey is not limited to these types of expenditures, but rather, includes all expenses which the consumer unit incurs during the survey week. Expenses incurred by family members while away from home overnight and for credit and installment plan payments are excluded.

Two separate questionnaires are used to collect Diary data: a Household Characteristics Questionnaire and a Record of Daily Expenses. The Household Characteristics Questionnaire is used to record information pertaining to age, sex, race, marital status, and family composition, as well as information on the work experience and earnings of each CU member. This socioeconomic information is used by BLS to classify the consumer unit for publication of statistical tables and for economic analysis. Data on household characteristics also provide the link in the integration of Diary expenditure data with Interview expenditure data for publishing a full profile of consumer expenditures by demographic characteristics.

The daily expense record is designed as a self-reporting, product-oriented diary on which respondents record a detailed description of all expenses for two consecutive 1-week periods. Data collected each week are considered independently. The diary is divided by day of purchase and by broad classifications of goods and services—a breakdown designed to aid the respondent when recording daily purchases. The items reported are subsequently coded by the Bureau of the Census so that BLS can aggregate individual purchases for representation in the Consumer Price Index and for presentation in statistical tables.

Integrated survey data

The integrated data from the BLS Diary and Interview Surveys provide a complete accounting of consumer expenditures and income, which neither survey component alone is designed to do. Some expenditure items are collected only by either the Diary or Interview Survey. For example, the Diary collects data on detailed food expenditures, which are not collected in the Interview. The Interview collects data for expenditures on overnight travel and information on reimbursements for medical care costs, which are not collected in the Diary. For items unique to one or the other survey, the choice of which survey to use as the source of data was obvious. However, there is considerable overlap in coverage between the surveys. Because of the overlap in coverage, the integration of the data presented the problem of determining the appropriate survey component from which to select the expenditure items. When data were available from both survey sources, the more reliable of the two was selected as determined by statistical methods. The selection of items remains the same pending periodic review.

Processing

Due to differences in format and design, Diary and Interview Survey data are processed separately. Diary questionnaires are reviewed for completeness and consistency and are then transmitted to the Census Processing Center in Washington, DC, where computer processing is performed. In addition, missing or invalid data on demographic or work experience are imputed. No imputation is done for missing data on income. The families are assigned weights so that estimates can be derived that represent the total civilian noninstitutional population. Finally, monthly Diary data tapes are transmitted to the Bureau of Labor Statistics.

As the monthly Diary data tapes are received, BLS combines the tapes into separate data bases that form calendar quarters. The data on these quarterly tapes are screened selectively for invalid coding and inconsistent relationships as well as for extreme values that may affect the reasonableness of estimates after the data are aggregated. All errors of coding or extreme value are corrected before further processing.

Selected portions of the Diary data are also adjusted by automated imputation and allocation routines when respondents report insufficient detail to meet publication requirements. These procedures are performed annually on the data. The imputation routines assign qualifying information to data items when there is clear evidence of invalid nonresponse. For example, the qualifiers classify food expenditures by type of processing (i.e., fresh or frozen) and apparel expenditures by age and sex groupings of the members in the consumer units. Allocation routines are a means of transforming reports of nonspecific items into specific ones. For example, when respondents report expenditures for "meat" rather than beef or pork, allocations are performed using proportions derived from specific reports in other completed diaries to distribute the expenditure reported for "meat" to the specific items such as beef or pork.

Census processing of Interview Survey questionnaires proceeds along similar lines. The questionnaires are completed and returned to the regional offices, where codes are applied to identify demographic characteristics, expenditures, income and assets, and other items such as make and model of automobile, and trip destination. In addition, all outlets are coded uniquely by name. Upon completion of the clerical processing, the data are keyed and transmitted to Washington where they pass through a detailed computer pre-edit. Inconsistencies, errors, and identification of missing questionnaires are transmitted back to the regional offices for reconciliation by the field staff through office review or interviewer followup. Corrections are keyed and transmitted to Washington, and again cycled through the computer pre-edit. This continues until errors identified by the pre-edit no longer appear. Once the pre-edit process is completed for a given month, data necessary for bounding are transcribed to the next quarter's questionnaire. The current quarter's questionnaire is sent to a regional processing office for microfilming and storage.

The data then go through a series of complex computer edits and adjustments which include the identification and correction of data irregularities and inconsistencies throughout the questionnaire. Other adjustments convert mortgage and vehicle payments into principal and interest (given associated data on the interest rate and term of the loan), eliminate business and other reimbursed expenses, apply appropriate sales taxes, and derive weights for individual questionnaires. In addition, demographic and work-experience items (except income) are imputed when missing or invalid.

The Bureau of Labor Statistics, upon receipt of the data from the Bureau of Census, conducts an extensive review to ensure that severe data aberrations are corrected. The review takes place in several stages: A review of counts and means by region; a review of coding of family relationships for inconsistencies; a review of selected extreme values for expenditure and income categories; and a verification of the various data transformations performed by BLS. Cases of questionable data values or relationships are investigated by looking up questionnaires on microfilm. Any errors are corrected prior to release of the data for public use.

Data imputation routines are carried out in the Interview Survey to account for missing or inconsistent entries. The procedures are performed quarterly on the data . The routines, which affect all fields in the data base except income and assets, are intended to improve the estimates derived from the survey. Imputation in the Interview Survey is done at the cell level with cells defined by variables such as income class, family size, region, and so on. The methods used—hot deck, weighting class, and percent distribution—depend on the types of expenditures. In addition, allocation routines are applied to the Interview data in a fashion similar to that for the Diary data.

Sample Design

Selection of households

The Consumer Expenditure Survey is a national probability sample of households designed to represent the total civilian noninstitutional population. The selection of households begins with the selection of primary sampling units (PSU's), which consist of counties (or parts thereof), groups of counties, or independent cities. The set of sample PSU's used for the survey consists of 101 areas, of which 85 urban areas have also been selected by BLS for the Consumer Price Index program. The urban PSU's are classified according to the following four categories:

1. 29 "A" certainty PSU's that are Metropolitan Statistical Areas (MSA's) with nonfarm population greater than 1.2 million;
2. 20 "L" PSU's, which are medium-sized MSA's;
3. 24 "M" PSU's, which are small MSA's; or
4. 12 "R" PSU's, which are urban nonmetropolitan areas.

The population break between L and M PSU's is different by region. The breaks are: Northeast—500,000; Midwest—360,000; South—450,000; and West—330,000. Since these PSU's do not represent the entire rural part of the United States, 16 additional PSU's (denoted as "T") are selected to represent the rural nonmetropolitan areas.

The sampling frame (i.e., the list from which housing units are chosen) for this survey is now generated from the 1980 census 100-percent detail file, which is augmented by a sample drawn from new construction permits and coverage improvement techniques to eliminate recognized deficiencies in the census. In addition, the sample for the Diary Survey is doubled during the last 6 weeks of the year to collect expenditure data during the peak shopping period of the Christmas and New Year holidays.

The population of interest is the total U.S. civilian population. Within this framework, the eligible population includes all civilian noninstitutional persons (for example, those living in houses, condominiums, or apartments) and all people residing in group quarters such as housing facilities for students and workers. Military personnel living on base are not included.

The Bureau of the Census selected a sample of approximately 8,020 addresses to participate annually in the Diary Survey. This results in an effective annual sample size of 5,870 households, since many diaries are not completed due to refusals, vacancies, ineligibility, or the nonexistence of the household address. The actual workload of diaries is spaced over the 52 weeks of the year.

The Interview Survey is a rotating panel survey in which approximately 8,910 addresses are contacted in each of the calendar quarters. Allowing for bounding interviews, which are not included in the estimates, and for nonresponse (including vacancies), the number of completed interviews per quarter is targeted at 6,160. Each month, one-fifth of the units interviewed are new to the survey. Each panel is interviewed for five consecutive quarters and then dropped from the survey.

Cooperation levels

The response data for the Consumer Expenditure Survey are shown in text table 1 for the Interview and Diary Surveys. The results are based on 1990 data. For the Interview Survey, the total refers to housing units when a unique housing unit address is interviewed once each quarter for the year.

Type B or C nonresponses are housing units that are vacant, nonexistent, or ineligible for interview. Type A nonresponses are housing units which the interviewers were unable to contact or the respondents refused to participate in the survey. These response rates are based on the eligible housing units (i.e., the designated sample less type B and type C nonresponses).

Response data for 1990 CE Survey

Survey	Housing units designated for the survey	Type B or C nonresponse	Eligible			
			Total	Type A nonresponse	Responded	Response rate (percent)
Interview	29,064	5,135	23,929	3,412	20,517	86
Diary	8,467	1,615	6,852	985	5,867	86

Estimation

Each family included in the Consumer Expenditure Survey represents a given number of families in the U.S. civilian population, which is the universe. The translation of sample families into the universe of families is known as weighting. Several factors are involved in determining the weight for each consumer unit for which a usable report is received. One factor in assigning weights is the inverse of the probability of selection of the housing unit and the adjustment for subsampling in the field. For interviews which cannot be conducted in occupied sample households because of refusals or the fact that no one is home, a complex noninterview adjustment is made. Additional factors include a national-ratio estimate adjustment for age, sex, and race to known civilian noninstitutional population controls and an adjustment based upon CU family composition to determine a weight for the consumer unit. In the case of the Diary, an additional factor is also included to adjust the probability of selection to reflect the increase in sample size for the last 6 weeks of the year.

Beginning with 1984 data, an additional step in the weighting procedure was introduced to correct the inconsistent demographic estimates between the Diary and Interview Surveys. The new step is a ratio estimation procedure using the method of generalized least squares. It is used to narrow the difference between the consumer unit counts of the two surveys for selected published characteristics. While this new step equalizes the number of consumer unit counts of the two surveys, the impact on mean expenditures is small.

Presentation

Information from the Consumer Expenditure Survey is available in bulletins, reports, analytical papers, and on public-use tapes and diskettes. Publications may be obtained through the BLS Office of Publications, the Chicago regional office of BLS, or from the Government Printing Office. Information on public-use tapes can be obtained from the BLS Division of Consumer Expenditure Surveys.

Publications from the Consumer Expenditures Survey generally include tabulations of average expenditures and income arrayed by family characteristics. Integrated Diary and Interview Survey data are currently published on an annual basis while Interview data are published quarterly. Data tabulated for a given year or quarter are shown at a relatively aggregated level due to the small sample size of the survey. With several years of data from the current survey now available, however, estimates for several years may be combined to provide greater expenditure detail and additional classifications of families.

The public-use tapes contain the actual expenditure and income reports of each family but prevent identification of the family. In order to protect the identity of respondents, selected geographic detail is eliminated, thereby reducing the possibility that participating families may even be indirectly identified.

Diary and Interview Survey tapes are available from the current survey back to the 1980 survey. Integrated survey data are not available on tape. Beginning with the 1988 data, BLS has released expenditure tapes containing files created directly from all the sections of the quarterly Interview Survey. These are called the EXPN tapes and they include more detailed expenditure records than found on the Interview Survey tapes. Also, tabulations of integrated survey data for the years 1984 through the present are available on diskettes.

Standard error tables applicable to Consumer Expenditure Survey data are available from the BLS national office upon request. These are cell specific and therefore extensive. Call (202) 606-6900.

Evaluation Research

The surveys undergo continuous evaluation by comparing CES results with other data and by performing internal statistical analysis. In order to improve the expenditure estimates, research related to the data collection instruments and interview procedures began in the mid-1980's. During this time, BLS received funding from Congress to create a Survey Design Research Center. Shortly thereafter, in January 1987, a Questionnaire Design Advisory Conference was convened at the BLS. As a result of the recommendations received by the Bureau at this conference, combined with results from the underreporting studies, research on the cognitive aspects of the data collection process increased. Recent research has placed an emphasis on the use of cognitive techniques for investigating respondents' thought processes in response to survey questions, and developing alternative questionnaire formats and question phrasing. Attention has also been focused on the demands placed upon respondents' time.

The mortgage and trip sections of the Interview Survey questionnaire were redesigned using cognitive techniques. These changes were implemented in April 1991.

BLS is also studying how the public classifies food purchases. The Diary Survey currently provides two groupings for the respondent to use: Food for Home Consumption and Food Away from Home. With the proliferation of ready-to-eat food at grocery stores and restaurants, these categories need clarification or new definitions. Respondents will be questioned about their perceptions of what is included in each category.

Uses and Limitations

The survey data are of value to government and private agencies interested in studying the welfare of particular segments of the population, such as the elderly, low-income families, urban families, and those receiving food stamps. The survey data are used by economic policymakers interested in the effects of policy changes on levels of living among diverse socioeconomic groups. Econometricians find the data useful in constructing economic models. Market researchers find them valuable in analyzing the demand for groups of goods and services. The Department of Commerce uses the survey data as a source of information for revising its benchmark estimates of some of the personal consumption expenditure components of the gross national product.

As in the past, the revision of the Consumer Price Index remains a primary reason for undertaking such an extensive survey. The results of the Consumer Expenditure Survey have been used to select new market baskets of goods and services for the index, to determine the relative importance of components, and to derive new cost weights for the baskets.

Sample surveys are subject to two types of errors, nonsampling and sampling. Nonsampling errors can be attributed to many sources, such as definitional difficulties, differences in the interpretation of questions, inability or unwillingness of the respondent to provide correct information, mistakes in coding or recording the data obtained, and other errors of collection, response, processing, coverage, estimation for missing data, and interviewer variability.

For the Interview Survey, an analysis of time-in-sample and recall effects was done on the macro-level using the 1982-83 data. Minimal-to-moderate conditioning effects were found in less than half of the published means. However, recall length effects were widespread and substantial among the expenditure classes for which the expenditure month is collected. For the Diary Survey, research has examined the first-day bias and the use of recall. Comparisons between Diary and Interview Surveys have recently included an analysis of seasonal patterns. Research on nonsampling error will continue.

Sampling errors occur because observations are not taken from the entire population. The standard error, which is the accepted measure for sampling error, is an estimate of the difference between the sample data and the data that would have been obtained from a complete census. The methodology employed to calculate the sampling variance is balanced half-sample replication. Standard error tables applicable to published BLS data can be obtained from the BLS Division of Consumer Expenditure Surveys.

Chapter 19. The Consumer Price Index

Part I. The Index in Brief

The Consumer Price Index (CPI) is a measure of the average change in the prices paid by urban consumers for a fixed market basket of goods and services. The Bureau of Labor Statistics (BLS) calculates the CPI monthly and publishes it about two weeks after the end of the month to which it refers.

BLS calculates the CPI for two population groups, one consisting only of wage earners and clerical workers and the other consisting of all urban consumers.[1] The Consumer Price Index for Urban Wage Earners and Clerical Workers (CPI-W) is a continuation of the historical index that was introduced well over a half-century ago for use in wage negotiations. As new uses were developed for the CPI in recent years, the need for a broader and more representative index became apparent. The Consumer Price Index for All Urban Consumers (CPI-U) introduced in 1978 is representative of the buying habits of about 80 percent of the noninstitutional population of the United States, compared with 32 percent represented in the CPI-W. The methodology for producing the index is the same for both populations and is described in detail in part II of this chapter.

Background

The Consumer Price Index was initiated during World War I, when rapid increases in prices, particularly in shipbuilding centers, made such an index essential for calculating cost-of-living adjustments in wages. To provide appropriate weighting patterns for the index, so that it would reflect the relative importance of goods and services purchased by consumers, studies of family expenditures were conducted in 92 industrial centers in 1917-19. Periodic collection of prices was started, and, in 1919, the Bureau of Labor Statistics began publication of separate indexes for 32 cities. Regular publication of a national index, the U.S. city average, began in 1921, and indexes were estimated back to 1913.[2]

Because people's buying habits had changed substantially, a new study was made covering expenditures in the years 1934-36, which provided the basis for a comprehensively revised index introduced in 1940.

During World War II, when many commodities were scarce and goods were rationed, the index weights were adjusted temporarily to reflect these shortages. In 1951, the Bureau again made interim adjustments, based on surveys of consumer expenditures in seven cities between 1947 and 1949, to reflect the most important effects of immediate postwar changes in buying patterns.[3]

The first comprehensive postwar revision of the index was completed in January 1953, using weights from the 1950 expenditure survey.[4] At that time, not only were the weighting factors, list of items, and sources of price data updated (appendix 1), but many improvements in pricing and calculation methods were introduced. Medium-size and small cities were added to the city sample to make the index representative of prices paid by all urban wage-earner and clerical-worker families.

Another revision, completed in 1964, introduced new expenditure weights based on spending patterns in 1960-61 of single persons as well as families, and updated samples of cities, goods and services, and retail stores and service establishments.[5]

The 1978 revision reflected spending patterns based upon the surveys of consumer expenditures conducted in 1972-74. A new and expanded 85-area sample was selected based on the 1970 Census of Population. The Point-of-Purchase Survey (POPS) was also introduced. POPS eliminated reliance on outdated secondary sources for screening samples of establishments or outlets where prices are collected. A new store-specific approach to the item selection process was also introduced, as was a second index, the more broadly based CPI for All Urban Consumers. The CPI-U took into account the buying patterns of professional and salaried workers, part-time workers, the self-

[1] The all-urban-consumer population consists of all-urban households in Metropolitan Statistical Areas (MSA's) and in urban places of 2,500 inhabitants or more. Nonfarm consumers living in rural areas within MSA's are included, but the index excludes rural consumers and the military and institutional population. The urban wage earner and clerical worker population consists of consumer units with clerical workers, sales workers, craft workers, operatives, service workers, or laborers. More than one-half of the consumer unit's income has to be earned from the above occupations, and at least one of the members must be employed for 37 weeks or more in an eligible occupation.

[2] Collection of food prices back to 1890 had been initiated in 1903. During the course of the 1917-19 expenditure survey, retail prices for other articles were collected in 19 cities for December of each year back to 1914 and in 13 other cities back to December 1917 only. Retail prices of food and wholesale prices of other items were used to estimate price change from 1914 back to 1913.

[3] *Interim Adjustment of Consumers' Price Index*, Bulletin 1039, Bureau of Labor Statistics, 1951.

[4] *Consumer Prices in the United States*, 1953-58, Bulletin 1256, Bureau of Labor Statistics, 1959.

[5] *The Consumer Price Index: History and Techniques*, Bulletin 1517, Bureau of Labor Statistics, 1966.

employed, the unemployed, and retired people, in addition to wage earners and clerical workers.[6]

In January 1983, the Bureau changed the way in which homeownership costs were measured.[7] A rental equivalence method replaced the asset-price approach to homeownership costs for the CPI-U. In January 1985, the same change was made in the CPI-W. The central purpose of the change was to separate shelter costs from the investment component of homeownership so that the index would reflect only the cost of shelter services provided by owner-occupied homes.

The most recent revision of the CPI, completed in 1987, further improved sampling, data collection, processing, and statistical estimation. This revision stressed techniques that would make the production and calculation of the CPI more efficient, especially with respect to design and allocation of the samples. The updated samples of items, outlets, and areas were based upon data from the Survey of Consumer Expenditures for the years 1982, 1983, and 1984; the 1980 Census of Population; and the ongoing Point-of-Purchase Survey, which, beginning with 1985, reflected the new item and area design. The new technique of rolling in the new area, item, and outlet samples significantly reduced the cost of introducing new samples. In addition, the housing survey was redesigned to represent optimally both owners and renters, which improved the estimation method for shelter costs.

The improvements introduced over the years have reflected not only the Bureau's own experience and research, but also the criticisms and investigations of outsiders. A major study was conducted during World War II by the President's Committee on the Cost of Living.[8]

The House Committee on Education and Labor conducted a detailed examination of the index in 1951.[9]

A decade later, a study was made by the Price Statistics Review Committee, which was appointed by the National Bureau of Economic Research, at the request of the Office of Statistical Standards of the Bureau of the Budget, to review all Government price statistics.[10]

A continuing flow of articles in professional journals and books has also contributed to the assessment of the CPI's quality and of the ways in which it might be improved.[11]

[6] *The Consumer Price Index: Concepts and Content Over the Years,* Report 517, Bureau of Labor Statistics, 1978.

[7] "Changing the Homeownership Component of the Consumer Price Index to Rental Equivalence," *CPI Detailed Report,* January 1983, pp. 7-13.

[8] *Report of The President's Committee on the Cost of Living* (Washington, Office of Economic Stabilization, 1945).

[9] *Consumers' Price Index, Report of a Special Subcommittee of the Committee on Education and Labor,* U.S. Congress, House of Representatives, 82/1, Subcommittee Report No. 2 (Washington, U.S. Government Printing Office, 1951).

[10] *Government Price Statistics, Hearings before the Subcommittee on Economic Statistics,* U.S. Congress, Joint Economic Committee, 871. Part 1 (Washington, U.S. Government Printing Office, Jan. 24, 1961).

Concepts

Several key concept dictate how the Consumer Price Index should be calculated.

Prices and living costs

The CPI is based on a sample of prices of food, clothing, shelter and fuels, transportation, medical services, and other goods and services that people buy for day-to-day living. Price change is measured by repricing essentially the same market basket of goods and services at regular intervals and comparing aggregate costs with the costs of the same market basket in a selected base period.

A unifying framework for dealing with practical questions that arise in construction of the CPI is provided by the concept of the cost-of-living (COL) index.[12]

As it pertains to the CPI, the COL index for the current month is based on the answer to the following question: "What is the cost, at this month's market prices, of achieving the standard of living actually attained in the base period?" This cost is a hypothetical expenditure – the lowest expenditure level necessary at this month's prices to achieve the base-period's living standard. The ratio of this hypothetical cost to the actual cost of the base-period consumption basket in the base period is the COL index.[13]

The COL index is a measure of price change (it compares current-period and base-period prices). However, the concept is difficult to implement because it holds the standard of living constant, and the living standard must be estimated in some way.

The CPI uses a fixed market basket to hold the base-period living standard constant. The CPI equals the ratio of the cost of the base-period basket at this month's prices to the actual cost of the base-period basket in the base period. The formula used for calculating the CPI is the one known in price index literature as the Laspeyres index. (See part II.) The CPI provides an approximation to a COL index as a measure of consumption costs. It is sometimes said that the CPI's Laspeyres formula provides an "upper bound" on the COL index.

Note that both the CPI and the COL index that were defined above measure changes in expenditures. Neither one measures the change in income required to maintain the base-period living standard. For this reason, neither the COL index nor the CPI are affected by changes in

[11] For a list of published papers on the CPI, see the technical references at the end of this chapter.

[12] On the use of a cost-of-living index as a conceptual framework for practical decision making in putting together a price index, see Robert Gillingham, "A Conceptual Framework for the Revised Consumer Price Index," *Proceedings of the Business and Economic Statistics Section,* American Statistical Association, 1974, pp. 46-52.

[13] For more information on the cost-of-living index concept, see the technical references at the end of this chapter.

income taxes, but both will include the effects of changes in sales taxes and other indirect taxes.

For certain purposes, one might want to define price indexes to include, rather than exclude, income taxes. One could develop either a COL index or a Laspeyres index along these lines. Such indexes would provide an answer to a different question from the one for which the present CPI is relevant, and would be appropriate for different uses. For a research measure of a consumption index inclusive of income taxes and Social Security contributions, see Gillingham and Greenlees.[14]

Sampling

Since it is not practical to obtain prices for all consumer transactions in the United States, the CPI is estimated from a set of samples. These samples, which use statistical procedures to make the CPI representative of the prices paid for all goods and services purchased by consumers in all urban areas of the United States, are:

- Urban areas selected from all U.S. urban areas,
- Consumer units within each selected urban area,
- Outlets from which these consumer units purchased goods and services,
- Specific, unique items—goods and services—purchased by these consumer units, and
- Housing units in each urban area for the shelter component of the CPI.

Weights and relative importance

The weight of an item in the CPI is derived from the expenditure on that item as estimated by the Consumer Expenditure Survey. This survey provides data on the average expenditure on selected items, such as white bread, gasoline, and so on, that were purchased by the index population during the survey period. In a fixed-weight index such as the CPI, the implicit quantity of any item used in calculating the index remains the same from month to month.

A related concept is the relative importance of an item. The relative importance shows the share of total expenditure that would occur if quantities consumed were unaffected by changes in relative prices and actually remained constant. Although the implicit quantity weights remain fixed, the relative importance changes over time, reflecting the effect of price changes. Items registering a greater than average price increase (or smaller decrease) become relatively more important. Conversely, items registering a smaller than average price increase (or larger decrease) become relatively less important. Thus, the relative importance of medical care in the index for all urban consumers, which was 6.0 percent in December 1982, was 6.9 percent in December 1986. During the same period, the relative importance of energy fell from 12.4 percent to 8.9 percent. The published data on relative importance are often used to answer such questions as: What was the direct effect on the overall CPI of a particular price change (e.g., gasoline prices) for a particular period? (See appendix 2.)

[14] Gillingham, Robert F. and Greenlees, John. "The Impact of Direct Taxes on the Cost of Living," *Journal of Political Economy*, 95(4), August 1987.

Owners' equivalent rent

The concept of owners' equivalent rent used to measure homeowner shelter costs was introduced in the CPI-U in January 1983 and in the CPI-W in January 1985. The owners' equivalent rent index measures the change in the cost of renting housing services equivalent to those services provided by owner-occupied housing.

Prior to the introduction of owners' equivalent rent, homeowners' shelter costs in the CPI were represented by five elements: (1) House prices, (2) mortgage interest costs, (3) property taxes, (4) homeowner insurance charges, and (5) maintenance and repair costs. These constitute the major costs associated with purchasing and maintaining the physical asset of a house.

This "asset price" approach to homeowner costs failed to distinguish the investment aspect of owning a home from the consumption aspect. The basic concept of the CPI is as a measure of the average change in the prices paid by consumers for consumption goods and services. Investment purchases, such as stocks and bonds, are conceptually out of the scope of the index and are excluded. A house is not consumed at the time of purchase. It is a long-lived asset (investment), but it also provides the owner with a flow of shelter services over time. Thus, it is the cost of this shelter service provided by the asset that is the conceptually appropriate element of the CPI.

To implement the new concept, the old homeownership component was replaced with two items: (1) Owners' equivalent rent; and (2) household insurance, which contains those parts of homeowners' insurance that do not insure the structure.

In addition, the previous maintenance and repairs component was made a new component covering both renters' expenses and owners' expenses—exclusive of those estimated to be part of owners' equivalent rent. Also, the weight for household appliances was reduced to remove those expenses in homeowners' costs for appliances included with the house.

Scope and Calculation

Prices for the goods and services used to calculate the index are collected in 85 urban areas throughout the country and from about 21,000 retail and service establishments—supermarkets, department stores, gasoline stations, hospitals, etc. In addition, data on rents are collected from about 40,000 landlords or tenants and 20,000 owner occupants are asked about their housing units.

Food, fuels, and a few other items are priced monthly in all 85 locations. Prices of most other goods and services are collected monthly in the five largest urban areas and bimonthly in the remaining areas. Trained BLS field representatives collect all price information through visits or telephone calls.

The index is the average of the price changes for all the various items within each area. The averaging process uses weights which represent the importance of the items in the spending pattern of the appropriate population group in that area. Separate indexes are compiled for: the urban United States, 4 regions, 4 size classes, 13 groups cross-classified by region and population size, and 29 local metropolitan statistical areas.

Movements of the indexes from one month to another are usually expressed as percent changes rather than changes in index points. Index point changes are affected by the level of the index in relation to its base period while percent changes are not. The example in the tabulation illustrates the computation of index points and percent changes:

Index point change

CPI	136.0
Less CPI for previous period	129.9
Equals index point change	6.1

Percent change

Index point difference	6.1
Divided by the previous index	129.9
Equals	0.047
Results multiplied by 100.0	0.047 x 100
Equals percent change	4.7

Percent changes for periods that are less than 1 year can be expressed as annual rates and are computed according to the standard formula for compound growth rates. These data indicate what the percent change would be if the average rate for the period was maintained for a 12-month period.

Uses

Almost all Americans are affected by the Consumer Price Index because of the many ways that it is used. Three major uses are:

As an economic indicator. As the most widely used measure of inflation, the CPI is an indicator of the effectiveness of government economic policy. The President, Congress, and the Federal Reserve Board use trends in the CPI to aid in formulating fiscal and monetary policies. In addition, business executives, labor leaders, and other private citizens use the index as a guide in making economic decisions.

As a deflator of other economic series. The CPI and its components are used to adjust other economic series for price changes and to translate these series into inflation-free dollars. Examples of series adjusted by the CPI include retail sales, hourly and weekly earnings, and components of the gross domestic product.

As a means of adjusting income payments. Almost 3 million workers are covered by collective bargaining agreements which tie wages to the CPI. The index affects the income of more than 70 million persons as a result of statutory action: 43.1 million Social Security beneficiaries, about 3.9 million military and Federal Civil Service retirees and survivors, and about 22.6 million food stamp recipients. Changes in the CPI also affect the cost of lunches for the 24.2 million children who eat lunch at school. Some private firms and individuals use the index to keep rents, royalties, alimony, and child support payments in line with changing prices. Finally, since 1985, the CPI has been used to adjust the Federal income tax structure to prevent inflation-induced increases in tax rates.

Analysis and Presentation

CPI data are issued initially in a news release about 2 weeks following the reference month. Summary tables are sent to persons on the mailing list at that time. The *CPI Detailed Report*, available about 3 weeks after the initial release, provides detailed indexes and a monthly analysis of U.S. price movements. *The Monthly Labor Review* also contains much of the CPI data each month and provides regular analyses of recent price movements as well as of long-term trends.

Seasonally adjusted data—primarily of use for current economic analysis—are presented in addition to the unadjusted data.

Limitations of the Index

CPI users should understand that the CPI may not be applicable to all questions about price movements for all population groups. For example, the indexes represent the average movement of prices for the U.S. urban population and, thus, may not be appropriate for use by nonurban residents. Also, the CPI does not provide data separately for the rate of inflation experienced by any demographic subgroups of the population, such as the elderly, which may purchase different consumer items and face different rates of inflation.

In addition, the indexes cannot be used to determine relative living costs. The change in an index for individual geographic area index measures how much prices have changed in that particular area. It does not show whether prices or living costs are higher or lower in that area relative to another.

A further limitation is that the CPI is not a complete measure of price change. Because the index is estimated from a sample of consumer purchases, the results may deviate slightly from those which would be obtained if all consumer transactions were covered. These estimating or sampling errors are statistical limitations of the index.

A different kind of error in the CPI can occur when a respondent provides BLS field representatives with inaccurate or incomplete information. The Bureau attempts to minimize these errors by obtaining prices by personal observation wherever possible, and by correcting errors immediately upon discovery. The field representatives, technicians, and commodity specialists who collect, process, and analyze the data are trained to watch for deviations in reported prices which might be due to errors. Also, an independent audit staff conducts a systematic evaluation of all CPI collection and processing activities. The goal is to develop long-term quality improvement in all aspects of the index calculation.

A fuller discussion of the varieties and sources of possible error in the index is presented in part III of this chapter, "Precision of Estimates."

Part II. Construction of the Index

The construction of the Consumer Price Index is based on a series of samples and on estimation procedures described below.

Definition of the Index

The CPI is defined as a fixed-quantity price index, that is, a measure of the price change in a fixed market basket of consumption goods and services of constant quantity and quality bought on average by urban consumers, either for all urban consumers (CPI-U) or for urban wage earners and clerical workers (CPI-W). It is a ratio of the costs of purchasing a set of items (i) of constant quality and constant quantity in two different time periods. We denote the index by $I_{t,0}$, where t is the comparison period for which a new index number is to be calculated and 0, the reference period:

$$I_{t,0} = \frac{\sum_i P_{it} Q_{ib}}{\sum_i P_{i0} Q_{ib}} \times 100.0$$

where:

- P_{it} is the price for the ith item in comparison period t
- P_{i0} is the price for the ith item in reference period 0
- Q_{ib} is the quantity of the ith item consumed in the expenditure base period b.

When the expenditure base (b) and reference period (0) coincide, this becomes the Laspeyres price index formula. For the 1987 revision of the CPI, however, they did not coincide and the formula was modified. The expenditure data, $\sum P_{ib} Q_{ib}$, from the 1982-84 Consumer Expenditure Survey (described later in this chapter) were updated for relative price changes (P_{ip}/P_{ib}) to November or December 1986, the respective pivot periods, p, when they were introduced into the CPI. Expenditure data for index areas priced bimonthly in the odd-numbered months were updated to November 1986. Expenditure data for the index areas priced monthly or bimonthly in the even-numbered months were updated to December 1986. Price relatives from the midpoint (June 1983) of the Consumer Expenditure Survey collection period to November or December 1986 were calculated from the appropriate detailed indexes for the period. The price relatives were applied to the corresponding expenditure data, thereby updating the expenditures to the end of 1986. Continuity with the pre-1987 version of the CPI was maintained in the published version by modifying the above formula to:

$$I_{t,0} = \frac{\sum_i P_{it} Q_{ib}}{\sum_i P_{ip} Q_{ib}} \times I_{p,1967}$$

where $I_{p,1967}$ is the 1967-based value of the CPI for the pivot month, November or December 1986.

NOTE: The base period for the expenditure weights, 1982-84, should not be confused with the numeric reference base period, although both are currently 1982-84=100. A new numeric reference base period for the index was established effective with the release of the index for January 1988, when the index was rebased to 1982-84=100. The previous numeric reference base was 1967=100. Such changes in numeric bases are achieved by dividing all indexes in a series by the appropriate average index on the old base for the time period of the new base.

Index Calculation

For sampling and index computation purposes, the set of all retail consumer expenditures by the target population for a given index area has been subdivided into 207 classes of similar items (see appendix 4) called item strata. The item strata are mutually exclusive and exhaustive of all consumer expenditures. They are defined identically for both index populations.

There are currently 88 areas (see appendix 3) which combine to yield the 41 basic areas—29 self-representing areas plus 12 region- and population-size class cross-classifications for non-self-representing areas. Thus there are 8487 (207 times 41) basic CPI strata. Each month BLS calculates indexes for these basic strata and aggregates these indexes to higher area and item groups.

The CPI is computed by a chaining process in which the index for the previous month, $I_{hzt-1,0}$, for each basic area (h) and item stratum (z) is multiplied by an estimate of the relative change in price from the previous month to the current month to provide the current-month index for that area and item stratum:

$$I_{hzt,0} = I_{hzt-1,0} \times R_{hzt,t-1}$$

where $R_{hzt,t-1}$ is an estimate of the one-period price change in the hth basic area for the zth item stratum. Basic area and item stratum indexes are then aggregated using aggregation weights to form desired aggregate area and item indexes, $I_{HZt,0}$:

$$I_{HZt,0} = \frac{\sum_{h \in H} \sum_{z \in Z} A_{hz} I_{hzt,0}}{A_{HZ}}$$

where A_{hz} is the aggregation weight for the hth basic area and z^{th} item stratum A_{HZ} is the aggregate weight for the aggregate area and item index, and where H and Z represent the set of h areas and z items, respectively.

The U.S. city average all items CPI is computed by aggregating all basic component area and item aggregate indexes:

$$I_{ust,0} = \frac{\sum_{h \in US} \sum_{z \in US} A_{hz} I_{hzt,0}}{A_{US}} \quad \text{for all h,z}$$

Aggregation weights for a given area Z and item stratum H combination are calculated as the expenditures for the pivot period divided by the corresponding index in the pivot period, that is,

$$A_{hz} = \sum_{h \in H} \sum_{z \in Z} P_{hzp} Q_{hzb} / I_{hzp,r}$$

where p is November or December 1986 and r is the numerical base, currently the same as b (the weight-base), equal to the average of 1982-84. The pivot period is the time when revised CPI is attached to the previous CPI to create a continuous series.

The formula for the aggregation weights of high level item and area indexes is:

$$A_{HZ} = \sum_{h} \sum_{z} P_{hzp} Q_{hzP} / I_{HZp}$$

The aggregation weight for higher level indexes is not, in general, equal to the same of the aggregation weights of its elements.

The computation of the index using one-period price relatives based on identical item specifications in adjacent periods allows the requisite flexibility to update the samples of outlets and specifications to reflect an updated distribution of purchases within an item stratum within a local area. The form of the estimator for a one-period price change, $R_{hzt,t-1}$, depends on the procedures used for selecting the samples of outlets and items and are designed to provide approximate unbiased estimators of price changes. When the samples are selected with each unit having a probability proportional to quantity, the estimator of $R_{hzt,t-1}$ is:

$$R_{hzt,t-1} = \frac{\sum_{z \in Z} W_{hz} P_{hit}}{\sum_{z \in Z} W_{hz} P_{hi,t-1}}$$

This is the ratio of the summation of weighted prices, where the weights (W_{hz}) reflect the probability of selection of the item being priced and a noninterview adjustment. Noninterview adjustment is a statistical procedure designed to adjust for nonresponse. This form of the estimator is used in the rent and owners' equivalent rent item strata.

When the samples of outlets and items are selected with probability proportional to expenditure, the estimator of $R_{hzt,t-1}$ is:

$$R_{hzt,t-1} = \frac{\sum_{z \in Z} W_{hz} P_{hz,t} / P_{hia}}{\sum_{z \in Z} W_{hz} P_{hz,t-1} / P_{hia}}$$

where P_{hza} is an estimate of the price of the selected item in period a, corresponding to the expenditures used in outlet sampling.

This is the ratio of the summation of weighted price ratios, where the weights reflect the probability of selection of the item being priced and noninterview adjustments. It is used for all commodity and service item strata.

Thus, construction of the CPI is a twofold estimation process. First, the aggregation weights, A_{hz}, must be estimated. These estimates are derived from the Consumer Expenditure Survey (CE) as explained in the next section. Second, the one-period price changes, $R_{hzt,t-1}$, must be estimated for each pricing period. The methodology for estimating price changes is explained in later sections.

Estimation of expenditure-population weights

The aggregation weights for each of the index areas, for each item stratum, and for both the CPI-U and CPI-W populations, require an estimate of expenditure that serves as its weight in the market basket of goods and services. When divided by their respective index for the pivot period, the expenditures weight becomes the aggregate weight. Each expenditure weight is the product of the mean annual expenditure per consumer unit (estimated from the 1982-84 CE Survey) and the number of consumer units (obtained from a special tabulation of the 1980 census).

Calculation of mean expenditures consists of three steps: (1) Preliminary estimation of expenditures and their relative importance, (2) final estimation of relative importance data, using a composite estimation procedure, (3) final estimation of mean expenditures using a raking process on the mean expenditures derived from the relative importance data determined in (2). The design criterion for this estimation procedure is to minimize the average mean square error of the relative importance of the expenditure weights for the index areas. The relative importance is a stratum's share (usually expressed as a percent) of the total expenditure for consumption.

Preliminary mean expenditures and relative importance. Preliminary mean expenditures and their relative importance were calculated for each area-item stratum and expenditure class, for each population, index area, replicate,[15] and major geographic area from each survey source—the CE Interview or Diary Surveys. Composite estimation reduced the variance of these preliminary relative importance data by averaging them with the relative importance of their major geographic areas. There were eight major geographic areas (index area aggregates), each consisting of either the self-representing or non-self-representing index areas[16] in each Census region. The mean expenditures are estimated using information from the 1982, 1983, and 1984 CE Surveys. They are the simple weighted averages (overall consumer units in the population desired) of the expenditures for the particular stratum or expenditure class. The consumer unit weights are those described in the section on the CE Survey.

The relative importance of stratum or expenditure class is the proportion of total consumption expenditures that the consumer units in a population index area (or major area), and replicate spend for that structure or class.

Composite estimation. Composite estimation is a method used to decrease the mean square error (MSE) of the relative importance of area-item strata by using data from the corresponding major areas. It is implemented separately for data from the Diary and Interview Surveys. The composite estimated relative importance of a particular area-item stratum, or expenditure class is a weighted average of the two preliminary relative importance estimators, RI, one for the index area and major area.

To calculate the composite estimator, let the relative importance for the particular item stratum (or EC) at the index area and one for the major area be RI_h and RI_m, respectively. The initial composite estimator, ICRI, is a weighted average of the PSU level and major area. It is calculated as:

$$ICRI = B_h \cdot RI_m + (1-B_h) \cdot RI_h$$

where:

$$B_h = \frac{Var\ RI_h - Cov\ RI_h}{ESD\ RI_h}$$

where:

$Var\ RI_h$, is the estimated variance of the relative importance for index area h,

$Cov\ RI_h$, is the estimated covariance of the relative importance RI_h and RI_m, and

$ESD\ RI_h$, is the estimated expected squared differences of the relative importance RI_h and RI_m.

If $B_h < 0$, then B_h is set equal to 0. If $B_h > 1.0$, then B_h is set equal to 1.0.

The above composite estimation procedure defines a "shrinkage" estimator. A further refinement to defining the final composite estimator, CRI, limits the shrinkage. Let $SDRI_h$ be the square root of the $Var\ RI_h$. The final composite estimator is calculated as:

$$CRI_h = ICRI_h \quad \text{if } ICRI_h - RI_h < K_{m,mg} \cdot SDRI_h$$

$$CRI_h = RI_h - K_{m,mg} \cdot SDRI_h \quad \text{if } RI_h - ICRI_h \geq K_{m,mg} \cdot SDRI_h$$

$$CRI_h = RI_h + K_{m,mg} \cdot SDRI_h \quad \text{if } ICRI_h - RI_h \geq K_{m,mg} \cdot SDRI_h$$

where $K_{m,\ mg}$ is a limiting factor defined for each major area, m, and major item group, mg. The parameter, $K_{m,mg}$, was determined by testing alternative values on the 1972-73 CE data. The value which maximized the reduction of the MSE and minimized the change for expenditure estimates at the major group level was selected.

Raking. To reestablish data consistency between item strata and EC levels and to reflect the special consumer unit weights, an iterative ratio estimation procedure (raking) was performed. That is, the sum of the expenditures for all item strata within an EC for an index area was forced to equal the total expenditures for the EC in the index area. The sum of the expenditures for a specific item stratum across all index areas in a major area was forced to equal the major area estimate of average expenditures for the item stratum times the special consumer unit weights. After composite estimation of the relative importance, initial total expenditure estimates, TE, for each item stratum and expenditure class, population, index area, and replicate for the Diary and Interview Surveys were calculated as:

$$TE_{hz} = CRI_{hz} \cdot ES_z$$

where ES_Z is the sum of preliminary mean expenditures across all item strata for index area z. Similarly, total expenditure estimates were calculated for each item stratum and EC at the major area level.

Expenditures from the Diary and Interview Surveys were then integrated. Each item has as its expenditure source either the Diary or Interview Survey. All of the processing activities described above were performed separately by survey. After composite estimation and raking

[15] A single selection of entry level items and outlets for all item strata assigned to a primary sampling unit is called a replicate. For further information, see the section on sampling.

[16] Self-representing and non-self-representing index areas are defined in the section on sample and publication areas.

were completed, expenditures from the two surveys were combined to form the set of total expenditures.

The raked, composite estimated expenditures were converted to aggregation weights in a two-step process. First, item strata expenditures were updated from June 1983, (the midpoint of the 1982-84 CE period) to December 1986 (the pivot month) for the index area. (November 1986 for bimonthly index areas published in odd months.) Each expenditure weight was multiplied by a long-term price change from the CPI for the time interval:

$$E_{hz8612} = E_{hz8306} \cdot \frac{I_{hz8612}}{I_{hz8306}}$$

where:

E_{hz8612} is the updated expenditure for the item strata in the hth area for December 1986,

E_{hz8306} is the raked composite estimated expenditure for the zth item strata in the hth area for June 1983,

I_{hz8612} is the CPI index for the z^{zh} item strata for the hth area for December 1986, and

I_{hz8306} is the CPI index for the zth item strata for the hth area for June 1983.

Updated item strata expenditures were summed to arrive at the required updated expenditures for aggregate items and areas. In the second step, the updated expenditure weights were divided by a corresponding index for the pivot period, yielding the aggregation weight:

$$A_{hz} = \frac{E_{hz8612}}{I_{hz8612}}$$

Special expenditure-weight procedures. As a result of the 1987 revision, the cost-weight definitions for new and used vehicles and for medical care item strata were changed significantly. In the former CPI, all expenditures for vehicles were valued at the net transaction price—the negotiated price less any trade-in value. In the revised CPI, the treatment of trade-ins and outright sales of used vehicles was changed. Trade-ins at their market value continue to be netted out of the price of used vehicles. However, the total market value of trade-ins on new vehicles is now netted from used vehicle purchases, rather than new vehicles. Sales of vehicles from one consumer to another are netted against the corresponding purchase because the transaction is really an intrapopulation exchange of wealth; there is no net change in the consumption of used vehicles. As a result of these changes, the expenditure weight for used vehicles represents: (1) Purchases of used vehicles that are entering the consumer sector for the first time (that is, purchases from private industry, including auto rental companies, and from public agencies; as well as purchases of used vehicles that enter the U.S. market from abroad as used vehicles); and (2) the difference between, (a) the price a consumer receives when he sells (or trades-in) a vehicle to an auto dealer, and (b) the price another consumer pays when he buys the vehicle from that (or a different) auto dealer.

In medical care, the way health insurance premiums were represented changed in the expenditures weights. While this change has no effect on the final index result and is mathematically equivalent to the former procedure, the new structure provides a clearer picture of the role of health insurance in the CPI. In both the former and current CPI, the health insurance weight is only expenditures by consumers for premiums; it does not include employers' contributions, just as other medical care expenditures are out-of-pocket payments by consumers. Insurance premiums can be viewed as purchasing two things: (1) the medical care for which benefits are paid, and (2) the services of the insurance carrier in administering the policy and bearing risk. This second element has been labeled retained earnings and refers to operating costs and any profit of the insurance carrier.

In the former CPI, within health insurance, the insurance expenditure weight was broken into item strata for each type of benefit and for the retained earnings associated with each type of benefit. The price movement for a health insurance benefit stratum (for example, insurance-paid hospital rooms) was the same as the price movement for the corresponding medical items in the CPI (hospital rooms). The price movement for a retained earnings stratum was the combination of price change for the relevant medical care items and an estimate of changes in retained earnings as a proportion of premiums.

In the current CPI, using the same example, instead of using the price change for both the hospital room index and the hospital-room-paid-by-insurance index, the expenditures for the two types of hospital payment are combined into a single index. The cost-weight for each medical care item is the combination of direct out-of-pocket expense for the item and indirect out-of-pocket expense for the item paid from consumer-purchased health insurance. The health insurance cost weight is the sum of all retained earnings.

Annual and semiannual average index estimation

Annual average CPI values use 12 successive months of CPI values as:

$$I_{12av} = \sum_{t=1}^{12} I_{t,0} / 12$$

Semiannual average indexes are computed for the first half of the year (January-June) and for the second half of the year (July-December) using 6 successive months of CPI values as:

$$I_{6av} = \sum_{t=1}^{6} I_{t,0} / 6$$

where the value of each monthly index is real or interpolated, depending on availability.[17]

For bimonthly indexes, the intermediate indexes are calculated using a geometric mean of the values in the months adjacent to the one being estimated.

Sampling: Areas, Items, and Outlets

The 1987 CPI area sample defined 91 geographic areas from which 94 PSUs were selected. In 1988 due to budget constraints, 6 PSUs were dropped from the design leaving 88 PSUs in 85 areas. The following sections describe the sample as it was designed for the 1987 revision. Where changes have occurred due to the 1988 budget constraints, the resulting numbers will be noted in parenthesis next to the original numbers. See appendix 3 for more details.

Area sample

Pricing for the CPI is conducted in 94 (88) primary sampling units (PSU's) in 91 (85) geographic areas. (The New York area has three PSU's and the Los Angeles area has two PSU's.) The area design[18] and sampling are summarized as follows: The urban was divided into 1,088 PSU's. Except in New England where they are groups of cities and towns, a PSU is a county or a group of contiguous counties. The basis of the PSU definition was the geographic areas defined by the Bureau of the Census for the Current Population Survey in 1980 with population estimates from the 1980 census. Each Consolidated Metropolitan Statistical Area (CMSA) or Metropolitan Statistical Area (MSA) as defined by the Office of Management and Budget in 1983 is a PSU. BLS grouped the remaining non-MSA counties containing any urban population to form PSU's. Rural areas of the non-MSA counties were excluded. (See appendix 3.)

The urban U.S. was partitioned into 91 geographic strata. The strata were sets of similar PSU's combined according to the following characteristics, which were found to be highly correlated with price change:

a. Region, population size, MSA vs. non-MSA,
b. Mean interest and dividend income per housing unit,
c. Mean wage and salary income per housing unit,
d. Percent of housing units heated by electricity,
e. Percent of housing units heated by fuel oil,
f. Percent black, and
g. Percent retired.

[17] To be published, a semiannual average must have at least two noninterpolated index values with sufficient samples. An annual average must have at least four noninterpolated index values with sufficient samples.

[18] Dippo, Cathryn S. and Jacobs, Curtis A. "Area Sample Redesign for the Consumer Price Index," Proceedings of the Survey Research Methods Section, American Statistical Association, 1983, pp 118-123.

The Census Bureau defined the four regions: the Northeast, the Midwest, the South, and the West. These characteristics along with preference factors for each characteristic, the number of strata, and the limits on strata size were the input to a program which used a modified Friedman-Rubin clustering algorithm to determine the stratification. This algorithm attempts to identify the best partition of sampling units into strata by minimizing the between PSU variance.

This area design resulted in 31 strata with one pricing area per stratum (self-representing PSU's) and 60 non-self-representing strata. (The three New York PSU's and two Los Angeles PSU's are also self-representing.) One sample PSU was selected from the PSU's in each non-self-representing stratum. A controlled selection program was used to insure that the sample areas were distributed geographically across the United States and to increase the overlap between the old area sample and the new area sample.

Since 39 of the 94 PSU's selected were new to the CPI, the new area sample for the CPI was introduced over a 2-year period. Twenty new PSU's were initiated during 1986 and have been used in CPI index calculations since January 1987. Sixteen of the remaining new PSU's were initiated during 1987, and the final three were initiated in 1988. Each of the 19 old PSU's continued to be priced until the new PSU which corresponded to it was initiated and linked into the index.

The CPI area design defines 37 (36) publication areas, that is, areas for which a CPI is published. Twenty-seven of the self-representing areas were defined as publication areas. Eight (seven – the B size class in the West is no longer published due to budgetary constraints) additional publication areas were defined by crossing the two city-size classes (non-self-representing MSA areas) by the four Census regions. The non-MSA areas in the Midwest and South were also defined as publication areas. Each of these region-by-size publication areas has 4, 6, or 10 strata. Only two strata were defined in the non-MSA areas in the West and Northeast, which made them ineligible for publication. Indexes are also published for the U.S. total as well as for region and city-size class totals.

Indexes for the U.S. total, the 10 (9) region-by-size class areas, and the 5 largest local areas are published monthly. Indexes for the 10 next largest areas are published bimonthly, and indexes for the smaller self-representing areas are published only as semiannual and annual averages.

Every 2 months the CPI prices 134 (126) replicates. One replicate is approximately 1,100 price quotes for commodities and services and 390 housing units for shelter. The allocation of the replicates is proportional to the population represented by the PSU, with at least one replicate assigned to each PSU. The actual allocation of replicates to PSUs is provided in the next section.

Item and outlet samples: Commodities and services other than shelter

Item structure and sampling. The CPI item structure has four levels of classification. The 7 major groups are made up of 69 expenditure classes (EC's), which in turn are divided into 207 item strata. Within each item stratum, one or more substrata, called entry level items (ELI's), are defined. There are 364 entry level items. (See appendix 4 for a complete list of EC's, item strata, and ELI's.) The major groups are primarily for emphasis in publication. The Expenditure categories are needed to smooth the weights of the item strata during composite estimation. (See above.) The CPI uses the item strata at the CPI area level to calculate the index each month. The ELI's are the ultimate sampling units for items as selected by the BLS national office. They are the level of item definition at which the data collectors begin item sampling within each sample outlet.

To enable the CPI to reflect changes in the marketplace, new item and outlet samples are selected each year for 20 percent of the PSU's on a rotating basis. Each year, four regional item-universes are tabulated from the two most recent years of Consumer Expenditure Survey data. An independent sample of ELI's is selected for each item stratum for each PSU-replicate scheduled for rotation that year from the corresponding regional item universe. For the complete 5-year cycle, 134 samples of ELI's are selected nationally. Within each region, each ELI sample uses a systematic sampling procedure, in which each ELI has a probability of selection proportional to the CPI-U population expenditures for the ELI within its stratum. Selection of outlet samples is described in the following section.

Item and outlet sample design. The CPI uses two separate sample designs, one for rent and owners' equivalent rent and one for all other commodities and services. The methodology employed to determine the commodities and services item and outlet sample design is presented here. Those for the rent and owners' equivalent rent components are described later.

For the development of the sample design, all commodities and services item strata were grouped into eight major groups:

Food and beverages	Transportation
Fuels and utilities	Medical care
Household services and furnishings	Entertainment
Apparel and upkeep	Other commodities and services

The objective of the sample design methodology was to determine, by major group, the number of ELI's to be sampled and the number of outlets to be selected per PSU replicate. There were four major activities in the design project. First, a variance function projected the variance of price change as a function of the above variables for the commodity and service components. Second, a cost function modeled the total annual cost of the commodities and services components of the CPI. Third, values for all coefficients of the two functions were estimated (including estimates of outlet overlap). Fourth, nonlinear programming techniques were used to determine approximately optimal sizes for the item and outlet samples to minimize the CPI variance under varying assumptions of annual price change subject to cost constraints.

The variance and cost functions for the CPI were modeled for 10 PSU groups:

1. New York City
2. New York, New Jersey suburbs
3. Los Angeles City
4. Los Angeles suburbs
5. Chicago
6. Philadelphia
7. San Francisco, Detroit
8. Large self-representing PSU's
9. Small self-representing PSU's
10. Non-self-representing PSU's

A detailed discussion of the sample allocation methodology is provided in appendix 5.

The solution of the design problem yielded the following number of item strata selections per PSU replicate by major item group:

CPI expenditure categories	*Item strata selections (ELI's)*
Food and beverages	73
Fuel and utilities	12
Household services and furnishings	66
Apparel and upkeep	47
Transportation	34
Medical care	18
Entertainment	27
Other commodities and services	21

The number of outlets selected for each Point-of-Purchase-Survey category (see below) for each major item group by PSU group is as follows:

POPS expenditure categories	*PSU group*									
	1	*2*	*3*	*4*	*5*	*6*	*7*	*8*	*9*	*10*
Food and beverages	6	7	6	6	8	9	9	4	2	6
Fuel and utilities	7	8	4	4	7	8	6	4	2	6
Household services and furnishings	1	1	1	1	1	1	1	1	1	1
Apparel and upkeep	2	2	2	2	2	3	3	2	1	2
Transportation	2	4	3	3	3	4	4	3	1	3
Medical care	3	3	3	3	3	5	3	3	1	4
Entertainment	1	1	1	1	1	1	1	1	1	1
Other commodities and services	1	1	1	1	1	2	1	1	1	1

The PSU groups are as defined earlier. With this allocation, outlets and quotes will be initiated each year under sample rotation. For ongoing pricing, there will be about 25,000 outlets visited each month, with prices collected for 95,000 items.

Outlet and price surveys. BLS field representatives collect prices monthly for food, energy items, and a small number of other commodity and service item strata in all PSU's. Prices are collected monthly for all commodity and service item strata in the five largest index areas (New York, Los Angeles, Chicago, Philadelphia, and San Francisco). Prices are collected bimonthly for the item strata not cited above in the remaining index areas. Each bi-monthly PSU was assigned to either the even- or odd-numbered months for pricing.

Point-of-Purchase Survey. The Bureau of the Census conducts the Continuing Point-of-Purchase Survey (CPOPS) for BLS. It furnishes current data on retail outlets from which urban households made purchases of defined groups of commodities and services. Data from the survey provide the sampling frame of outlets for food and most commodities and services to be priced in the CPI. CPOPS is the source of the outlet sampling frame for about 90 percent of the commodities and services items by expenditure weight. (See appendix 6 for a list of CPOPS categories. See appendix 7 for a complete list of items not covered by the CPOPS.)

The Point-of-Purchase Survey conducted in 1974 was the source of the outlet sampling frame in the 87 PSU's defined for the 1978 CPI revision. It was based on the 1970 census. From 1977 to 1984, the Continuing Point-of-Purchase Survey was conducted in approximately one-fifth of these PSU's on a rotating basis, so that the outlet sample for any PSU was never more than 5 years old. Since 1985, the survey has been based on the 1980 census and covers the 94 PSU's defined for the 1987 CPI.

Various methods have been tested to determine the sample of households to be interviewed in the survey. In 1974, a highly clustered sample of households was selected on the assumption that, if families tended to buy in the areas where they live, the outlets given as responses to the survey would also be clustered. In order to increase the expected chance of clustering the outlets, the household clusters were formed (where possible) around central business districts, shopping centers, and other retail centers. These large clusters were called secondary sampling units (SSU's). Within a cluster of tracts, a sample of Census enumeration districts (ED's) was selected, and, within the selected ED's, the sampled households were dispersed evenly. Five housing units were selected in each ED, and, since the desired sample size per cluster was 40 housing units, about 8 ED's were sampled from each cluster. In areas that issue permits for new construction, construction units were selected from the list of permits issued; in other areas, selection was made from area segments. This sampling approach was used, with minor modifications, in 1977 and 1978.

From 1979 through 1984, unclustered samples of households were selected for the survey. Since 1985, households have been selected on the basis of a noncompact clustering procedure which is modeled after the sample design for the Consumer Expenditure Survey. There are five sample frames: Unit, special place, area, block, and permit. The 1980 Census 100-Percent Edited Detail File is used as the source for all frames, except new construction in permit areas. For this frame, an unclustered sample of units is chosen from the permits issued since January 1980. For the unit, special place, area, and block frames, ED's are selected first. Then, a systematic sample of four or five units from each chosen ED is selected.

The Continuing Point-of-Purchase Survey is conducted annually over a period of 4 to 6 weeks, usually beginning in April, in approximately one-fifth of the PSU's in the CPI. The eligible population for the survey is the same as for the CE Survey: All civilian, noninstitutional persons, including persons residing in boarding houses, housing facilities for students and workers, mobile home parks, permanent-type living quarters in hotels and motels, and staff residing in institutions. The interviews, conducted in selected housing units, consist of two parts. First, the interviewer elicits information on the demographic and socioeconomic characteristics of the household. This information is used to analyze the shopping patterns of various segments of the population. It is also used to determine how many consumer units reside in the housing unit and should be interviewed. A consumer unit (CU) consists of all members of a particular housing unit or other type of living quarters who are related by blood, marriage, adoption, or some other legal arrangement, such as foster children, or who are unrelated but financially dependent upon each other for major living expenses, such as housing or food.

In the second part of the interview, the respondent is asked whether or not the CU purchased categories of goods and services within a specified recall period. Commodities and services are grouped into sampling categories called POPS categories based on entry level items as defined in the CPI classification structure. Some POPS categories consist of only one ELI, while others consist of combinations of ELI's. ELI's are combined into a single POPS category when the commodities or services are generally sold in the same outlets. For example, POPS category 106, Meat and Poultry, consists of eight beef ELI's, six pork ELI's, four ELI's for other meats, and three poultry ELI's. These ELI's are combined because an outlet that sells beef also tends to sell other meats.

Recall periods for POPS categories vary from 1 week to 5 years. The recall period for a specific POPS category is defined to produce a sufficient, but not excessive, number of outlets for sampling purposes. Since consumer units tend to purchase food items, tobacco products, and gasoline frequently throughout the year, a 1- or 2-week recall period is used. In contrast, CU's tend to purchase cars, hard-surface flooring, and funeral services infrequently; therefore, a 5-year recall period is assigned to these categories.

In the 1987 survey design, there are 170 POPS categories. Two different checklists of POPS categories are used by interviewers-each checklist is used in one-half of all sample households in the total nationwide sample. Each checklist consists of a subsample of 147 POPS categories. Most categories are included on both checklists. However, some of the short-recall-period categories are included on only one checklist. Subsampling on two checklists is used to control the expected number of responses received from a household and to minimize respondent burden. The combination of sample size and reference period for a given POPS category is designed to generate 6 to 12, not necessarily unique, outlets reported for a given PSU/POPS category. For each POPS category on the designated checklist, the respondent for a CU is asked whether purchases were made within the stated recall period and, if so, the names and locations of all places of purchase and the expenditure amounts.

From the results of the annual household survey, a new sample of outlets is selected for approximately one-fifth of the PSU's in the CPI. In the year following the survey, BLS initiates these new outlets, selects items for pricing from each, and replaces the former set of items in the CPI from each surveyed city with the new outlets and items.

Outlet sampling procedures. As indicated earlier, item samples and outlet samples are selected each year for 20 percent of the PSU's on a rotating basis. In self-representing PSU's, sample households for the POPS are divided into two or more independent groups by the first-stage order of selection, which defines two or more frames of outlets for outlet selection. The independent groups or replicates are needed for variance estimation. A single selection of ELI's and outlets for all item strata assigned to a PSU is called a replicate. For a given PSU, POPS category and replicate, the total expenditures reported for a given outlet are edited. If a purchase is reported for an outlet but the amount of expenditures is not reported, then, to ensure a chance of selection for the outlet, the mean expenditure for the PSU, replicate, and category is assigned. If large expenditures are reported for an outlet, then the amount is restricted to 20 percent of the total expenditure for the PSU, replicate, and category.

Outlet samples are selected independently for each PSU, replicate, and POPS category using a systematic sampling procedure. Each outlet on the frame has a probability of selection proportional to the amount of expenditures reported in the POPS. In each PSU replicate, all ELI's selected in the item sampling process are assigned for pricing to each sample outlet for the corresponding POPS category. When multiple selections of the sample outlet occur, a commensurate increase is made in the number of quotes priced for the outlet. The designated sample size for a given POPS category within each major item group for each replicate within a PSU group was presented in the section on item and outlet sample designs. The designated sample size is the number of outlet selections and not the number of unique outlets. The number of replicates by PSU group is presented below. There are 134 (126) replicates included in the CPI.

	PSU group	*Number of replicates*
1.	New York City	4
2.	New York suburbs, New Jersey suburbs	4
3.	Los Angeles City	4
4.	Los Angeles suburbs	2
5.	Chicago	4
6.	Philadelphia	2
7.	San Francisco, Detroit	4
8.	Large self-representing PSU's	18
9.	Small self-representing PSU's	32 (28)
10.	Non-self-representing PSU's	60 (56)

Outlet sampling procedures for commodities and services not included in the POPS. Some commodity and service items were excluded from the POPS either because existing sampling frames were adequate or it was apparent that the POPS would not yield an adequate sampling frame. (See appendix 7.) For each non-POPS item, BLS either construct the sampling frame or acquired it from another source. Each non-POPS item has its own sample design. The frames consist of all outlets providing the commodity or service in each sample area. A measure of size was associated with each outlet on the sampling frame. Ideally, this measure of size was the amount of revenue generated by the outlet for the item for the CPI-U population in the sample area. Whenever revenue was not available, an alternative measure of size, such as employment, number of customers, or sales volume, was substituted. All samples were selected using systematic sampling techniques with probability proportional to the measure of size.

The source of the sampling frame, the definition of the sampling unit, the measure of size employed, the final pricing unit, and the number of designated outlets and quotes for each non-POPS item are presented in appendix 7.

Augmentation. BLS monitors the sample of outlets for sufficiency on a regular basis. A sample of outlets for a given PSU replicate and POPS category is sufficient if at least one-half of the designated outlets are still active; that is, prices are being collected in at least one-half of the originally specified sample. When a sample no longer meets the sufficiency criteria, BLS augments it, linking new outlets into the index. These augmentation samples are selected from the same universe as the original sample and have the same number of outlets designated. The newly initiated outlets and quotes are used in addition to any remaining outlets and quotes from the original sample. This process allows BLS to maintain a sufficiently large sample for each

PSU, replicate and POPS category between the normal 5-year rotation cycle. Current BLS plans call for augmentation to occur on an annual basis.

Merging item and outlet samples. Since the item and outlet samples are selected separately, they must be merged before data collection. A concordance that maps ELIs to Point-of-Purchase categories allows each sampled ELI to be assigned for price collection to the outlet sample selected for the POPS category that contains it. The number of price quotes for an ELI in each outlet equals the number of times the ELI was selected for pricing in the PSU replicate during the item sampling process.

The item/outlet sample merge determines the number of price quotes assigned for collection in each sample outlet. In the outlet sampling process, if the expenditures reported for the outlet are large, an outlet may be selected more than once for a given POPS category. An outlet may also be selected for more than one POPS category. If an outlet is selected multiple times for a given POPS category, the same multiple of price quotes is assigned for collection for each sample ELI matching the category. If an outlet is selected for more than one POPS category, price quotes are assigned for collection for all ELI's selected in each category.

Selection procedures within outlets. A BLS field representative visits each selected outlet. For each ELI assigned to the outlet for price collection, the field representative uses a multistage probability selection technique to select a specific item from among all the items the outlet sells that fall within the ELI definition. The field representative first identifies all of the items included in the ELI definition and offered for sale by the outlet. When there is a large number of items in the ELI, they group them by common characteristics, such as brand, style, size, or type of packaging. With the assistance of the respondent for the outlet, the field representative assigns probabilities of selection to each group.

The probabilities of selection are proportional to the sales of the items included in each group. The field representatives may use any of four alternative procedures for determining the proportion of sales. In order of preference, they are:

a. Obtaining the proportions directly from a respondent;
b. Ranking the groups by importance of sales as indicated by the respondent and then obtaining the proportions directly or using preassigned proportions;
c. Using shelf space to estimate the proportions where applicable; and
d. Using equal probability.

After assigning probabilities of selection, the field representative uses a random number table to select one group. The field representative then identifies all items included in the selected group, forms groups of those items based on the in-common characteristics, assigns probabilities to each group, and uses a random number table to select one. The field representative repeats this process through successive stages until reaching a unique item. The field representative describes the selected unique item on a checklist for the ELI. Checklists contain the descriptive characteristics necessary to identify the item among all items defined within the ELI.

These selection procedures insure that there is an objective and efficient probability sampling of CPI items other than shelter. They also allow broad definitions of ELI's so that the same tight specification need not be priced everywhere. The wide variety of specific items greatly reduces the within-item component of variance, reduces the correlation of price movement between areas, and allows a substantial reduction in the number of quotes required to achieve a given variance. Another important benefit from the broader ELI's is a significantly higher likelihood of finding a priceable item within the definition of the ELI within the sample outlet.

This selection process is completed at the initial visit to the outlet to obtain the price for the selected item. Overtime, subsequent personal visits or telephone calls are made either monthly or bimonthly, to ascertain that the item is still sold and to obtain its current price.

Item and outlet samples: shelter

The CPI housing unit sample is the source of information on price change for the two principal shelter indexes—the residential rent index and the owners' equivalent rent index. The shelter indexes account for approximately 25 percent of the total CPI weight. The housing unit sample is a stratified, systematic, multistage, cluster sample that was designed to consist of approximately 40,000 rental units and 20,000 owner units. BLS selected housing units constructed before 1980 with data developed from the 1980 Census of Population and Housing. For housing constructed since 1980, the Bureau of the Census supplies an annual sample of new units from building permits data.

Stratification. BLS used two variables, average rent level and tenure (percent renter occupied), to select the stratifying area clusters called segments; these variables correlate with rent change. Using them for sampling stratification served to make the sample sizes within clusters more consistent, uniform, and homogeneous.

Stratification accomplished two goals. First, stratifying by variables associated with rent change insured sample coverage for important characteristics that correlate with rent. Second, stratification by percent renter occupied produced the clustering and the consistent sample sizes of renter and owner housing units within clusters. It is this geographic clustering that permitted the assignment or "matching" of renter-occupied units in the sample to the owner units in the sample. Matching is the mechanism that provides the basis for measuring price change of owner housing that is used in the owners' equivalent rent index.

To meet the stratification goals, BLS stratified at the lowest published Census areas within the 94 (88) CPI PSU's. In many cases, this was the block group or block level. In CPI areas where the Census Bureau provided data only by enumeration district (ED), BLS stratified at the ED level. Before stratifying areas where both block group and block data was available, BLS defined partial block groups (PBG's). Individual blocks within a block group were established as independent PBG's when they had a high percentage of renters and a large enough number of housing units to stand as an individual cluster. The balance of each original block group was also designated in total as a PBG. Less than 5 percent of the block groups were affected by this process. The use of this process, however, significantly reduced the cases where large numbers of renters were selected in a single building. The resulting PBG's were generally far more homogeneous in terms of percent renter occupied and structure type than the original block groups.

Strata boundaries were defined, and the PBG's and ED's were sorted into the strata defined on the basis of the two variables, average rent level and tenure (percent renter occupied). Eighteen strata were defined for each PSU, using three rent ranges and six tenure ranges. An important enhancement from previous CPI housing samples was that strata boundaries were defined differently for each PSU to insure that each stratum contained roughly the same number of housing units and allowed for between-PSU differences in rent levels and housing characteristics. BLS sampled PBG/ED's within each stratum, thereby insuring that the survey included housing clusters of all rent and tenure levels. Stratifying by tenure also permitted BLS to vary the sample rate for owners and renters in each cluster to obtain consistent sample sizes by tenure within the clusters.

Sample allocation to PSU's and strata. BLS allocated the sample to minimize a value Z, which is proportional to the sum of the variance of the rent and owners' equivalent rent indexes. This value is expressed as:

$$Z = \sum_{i=1}^{s} \left[O_i^2 \left(\left(\frac{\sigma_w^2}{o_i} \right) + \left(\frac{L}{r_i} \right) \right) + R_i^2 \left(\frac{L}{r_i} \right) \right]$$

where:

- S = number of strata,
- O_i = number of owner units in the ith strata,
- R_i = number of renter units in the ith strata,
- L = the total unit variance,
- σ_w^2 = within cluster variance,
- o_i = number of owners allocated to i^{th} strata,
- r_i = the number of renters allocated to i^{th} strata.

BLS determined the strata sample sizes, o_i and r_i, subject to the sample size constraints, by finding the values for o_i and r_i that minimize Z.[19] This produced an optimal sample for the given resource constraints for the two indexes.

BLS determined an initial allocation simultaneously across all strata and PSU's based on a criterion requiring a minimum sample size for each published index. If a publication PSU was not allocated the minimum sample, it was assigned a designated number of units large enough to meet publication standards. This minimum sample was allocated applying the above formula for Z among the strata within the PSU. A single process reallocated the remaining sample to the remaining PSU's.

The budget for the CPI Housing survey dictated a sample of 10,000 clusters (called segments) and 100,000 pricings per year for the pre-1980 sample portion of the survey. BLS added 900 more segments to compensate for an expected 9-percent sample loss that results from differences in the Census Bureau and CPI definitions of housing units. In contrast to the Census definition, the CPI excludes public housing, institutional housing, and military housing.

Sample selection within strata. BLS selected sample clusters in each stratum using a systematic probability-proportional-to-size (PPS) sample selection method. Each partial block group within a stratum was assigned a measure of size according to the total number of housing units, with controls on the maximum and minimum percent renter occupied. BLS sorted the PBG's geographically and, using the measures of size, allocated the sample of PBG's systematically.

Next, BLS partitioned each selected PBG into a number of clusters, depending on the PBG's size, and selected one at random. When a single Census block contained more than one cluster and one of these was a selected cluster, BLS field representatives defined the individual cluster following strict procedures derived from the sampling plan. For example, suppose that the sample design determined that a segment began 10.1 percent of the way into a block and ended at 23.8 percent into the block. If the block was not too big, the BLS representative would enumerate the entire block and then define the segment using these percentages. In large blocks, the field representative prescreened the blocks and sent the information to the BLS national office which determined the segment.

A field screening determined the final selection of housing units in the sample. In the first step of this process, called listing, BLS field representatives enumerated in order on listing forms every housing unit or potential housing unit they saw in each segment. The national office prepared unique selection sheets that indicated the sequence number of each unit to be screened and its

[19] For a full derivation of Z, see W. F. Lane and J. P. Sommers, "Improved Measures of Shelter Costs," *Proceedings of the Business and Economic Statistics Section,* American Statistical Association, 1984.

"desired tenure" (whether the unit needed to be owner or renter occupied to pass screening and remain in the survey). Using these selection sheets, the field representatives identified on the listing forms the units to be screened and their desired tenure.

The selection sheets for each segment took into account each segment's proportion that was renter occupied according to the 1980 census to determine how many units to screen, and how many to require of each tenure to yield an approximately optimal sample of renter and owner units for the CPI Housing survey. The two within-segment sampling rates determined how many renters and owners should be in the final sample. These rates were based on the final desired probability of selection for each tenure, the number of renters and owners in each stratum, and the number of selected segments and total segments in each stratum.

Thus, before the field agents contacted survey respondents for the first time, the units in each segment had already been assigned to one of four cases:

(1) Screen but initiate only if the unit is renter occupied;
(2) Screen but initiate only if the unit is owner occupied;
(3) Screen and initiate if either owner or renter occupied; or
(4) Do not contact for screening or initiation.

During screening, the field representatives contacted an eligible respondent for each housing unit to be screened and determined that the unit met the tenure criteria for the survey as well as other criteria such as being a year-round housing unit, built before 1980, and that it was someone's primary residence. Units that passed screening were immediately initiated into the sample.

Initiation is the process of collecting a first-time interview. Units that did not pass screening were not initiated; however, they may be recontacted at a later date to augment or to rotate the sample.

As planned, only about one-fourth of the units interviewed for screening met the tenure and other eligibility criteria required to pass screening and be initiated into the CPI Housing survey. Because renters were allocated according to total units and each cluster was allocated an equal number of renters, most of the units contacted in areas known from the Census Bureau to be mostly owner occupied failed screening. However, this process located the sparse renters in these areas for the survey and added "extra" renter units to the rent sample in owner areas. Although they represent few renters in the renter universe and, consequently, have very low weight in the rent index, they serve as the main source of rental units to match with owner units. It is their movement that primarily drives the owners' equivalent rent index.

Sample augmentation and rotation. In 1989, BLS augmented the renter sample in those strata containing a balanced mix of owner and renter units. Additional renter units in segments within these strata were selected, screened, and initiated, and the sampling weights for these segments were appropriately adjusted. The augmentation resulted in a 5-percent increase in the overall number of renters in the CPI housing survey and specifically added units that support both the rent and owner's equivalent rent indexes.

In 1992, BLS began rotating/rescreening segments in heavily owner-occupied strata, primarily to support the owner's equivalent rent index. Sampled rental units in heavily owner-occupied areas have demonstrated a substantial propenstity to change tenure from renter to owner during the past 5 years. Through rotation, BLS will regain renters in these areas by rescreening these segments to locate units that were owner-occupied during the original screening process but have since become rentals. This rotation will also result in a new sample of owner units in these segments.

Estimation of Price Change

Commodities and services other than shelter

At the end of each pricing period, the estimate of the one-period (t-1 to t) price change (price relative) is computed for each item-area stratum. Only price quotes obtained in both the current and previous pricing periods for the same or comparable items are used in the estimate. Where appropriate, price items are converted to a price per unit of measure before they are used in the estimation of price change. The same quote weights are used both for the current- and previous-period price quotes. The estimate of the one-period price change for the hth index area for the zth item stratum for a given market basket is computed as:

$$R_{hzt,1} = \frac{R_{hzt,a}}{R_{hzt-1,\,a}} = \frac{\sum_{i \in z} W_{hi}\, P_{hit} / P_{hia}}{\sum_{i \in z} W_{hi}\, P_{hit-1} / P_{hia}}$$

where:

P_{hit} is the price of the ith quote in the current pricing period, t, for item stratum z in index area h;

P_{hit-1} is the price of the ith quote in the previous pricing period, t-1, for item stratum z in index area h;

P_{hia} is the estimated price for the ith quote for item stratum 2 in the time period, a, of the POPS in index area h;

$W_{hi,}$ is the quote weight for the ith quote for item stratum z in index area h. It is computed as:

$$W_{hi} = \alpha\, Efg/MB$$

where:

α is the percent of sales of the ELI to the total sales of the POPS category in the outlet;

E is an estimate of the total daily expenditure for the POPS category, for the index area replicate and the CPI-U population;

f is a duplication factor to reflect any special subsampling of outlets or quotes;

g is a geographic factor to reflect the difference in coverage for the index area for the pre-1987 area definitions to the 1987 area definitions;

M is the number of usable quotes for the ELI/PSU replicate within the item stratum; and

B is the proportion of the expenditures for the selected ELI is of the total expenditures for the item stratum in the region (the probability of selection for the ELI).

NOTE: The geographic factor is 1.000 for all samples selected using the 1987 area definitions. See the section on outlet sampling procedures for an explanation of sample rotation.

Item substitution, quality adjustments, and imputation

One of the more difficult conceptual problems faced in compiling a price index is the accurate measurement and treatment of quality change due to changing product specifications and consumption patterns. The concept of the CPI requires that BLS measures through time, the cost of purchasing a fixed, constant-quality market basket of goods and services. In reality, products frequently disappear, products are replaced with new versions, and new products emerge. BLS uses several methods to adjust for quality change and to account for the change in item specifications. These methods may be categorized as 1) directly comparable, 2) direct quality adjustment, and 3) imputation. In all cases, it is necessary to estimate a new base-period price in order to use the new item specification in future periods. The base-period price (called P_{hia} in the above formula) is an estimate of the item's price at the time it was reported on the POPS.

Directly comparable. If the new and old item specifications are considered directly comparable, i.e., the characteristics of the new item are essentially the same as the old item's characteristics, the base-period price for the new specification is set equal to the base-period price for the old specification, and the price comparison between the items is used in the index. It is assumed that no quality difference has occurred.

Direct quality adjustment. This is the most explicit measure for dealing with specification changes. Direct quality adjustments are frequently made for the automobile and apparel components of the CPI.

The most frequently cited example of direct quality adjustment is the annual model changeover for new cars and trucks. Each year, price adjustments are made to account for the quality differences between the old and the new models. In some cases, the adjustments are based on the previous model's retail price for optional equipment. In other cases, the quality adjustments must be derived from production cost data supplied by the manufacturers. These data are adjusted by estimated manufacturer and retailer markup rates to derive retail values for the quality changes.

Adjustments for quality change in the CPI new car index include structural and engineering changes that affect safety, environment, reliability, performance, durability, economy, carrying capacity, maneuverability, comfort, and convenience. Although antipollution equipment on automobiles does not directly increase the quality of the automobile for the buyer, these devices do improve the quality for consumers in general. Consequently, quality adjustments are made for pollution controls to automobiles on the assumption that, by legislative definition, the cost of installing antipollution devices was no more than the value derived from them.

Quality adjustments of new cars exclude changes in style or appearance, such as chrome trim, unless these features have been offered as options and purchased by customers. Also, new technology sometimes results in better quality at the same or reduced cost. Usually no satisfactory value can be developed for such a change. In such cases, it is ignored, and prices are compared directly.

In addition to quality adjustments for physical changes to cars and trucks, adjustments are made for changes in the warranty coverage provided by auto manufacturers when sufficient data are available to derive estimates of their values.

The marketing of apparel items have historically caused a number of problems in the maintenance of a constant quality market basket of apparel commodities in the CPI. Many apparel items are seasonal and subject to frequent style changes. In addition, heated competition in the marketing of apparel commodities has led to increasingly rapid turnover of styles available in retail outlets. Until recently, these factors have meant that, when new styles replace old ones, many substitutions were deemed not comparable. Marketing practices for apparel generally entail introducing such goods at high regular prices and marking them down to lower "sale" prices throughout their shelf life. Therefore, the inability to compare prices at the time the new goods are introduced (when price increases are normally passed along to the consumer) precludes capturing any pure price change which accompanies the style changes. As a result, during the early to mid-1980's, apparel indexes understated price change. Research undertaken to to correct this problem delineate the critical determined apparel quality characteristics to hold constant in the substitution process. When an outlet discontinues an apparel item, the field representative follows the CPI substitution procedures to find the closest substitute it offers for sale. The procedure insures that as many as possible of the critical quality characteristics of the substitute are the same as those of the discontinued item. For those that are not the same, CPI apparel experts estimate the value of the difference and directly adjust the price to account for them.

Hedonic regression modeling is the technique which was used to determine the importance of the various quality characteristics which add value to a particular good. In this approach, an item can be viewed as a collection of characteristics which, taken together, provide satisfaction or value to the consumer. In other words, a women's suit can be considered an aggregation of its components, such as a jacket and skirt or pants, each of which contributes to the value of the suit in the eyes of the consumer. In addition, certain aspects of the suit, such as its fiber content, its construction, etc., will add or detract value from the consumer's standpoint. Hedonic regression modeling is a tool which allows the researcher to estimate which factors are the most important price-determining characteristics of these goods. In the CPI, this research resulted in better data collection documents and procedures for pricing apparel commodities. By noting the most important quality characteristics on the data collection document, the field agents who collect data for the CPI can try to hold constant these important characteristics even when other details change. This improvement in the collection documents resulted in a remarkable increase in the number of comparable substitutions chosen for apparel commodities.

As additional research led to further improvements in the modeling process, steps were taken to further reduce the number of substitute items deemed not comparable to the old items. Tests on the data which are collected for apparel goods determined that direct quality adjustments could be made using the estimates of the values of the different components of the apparel items. If, for example, a two-piece men's suit had been priced but was no longer available, all the two-piece suits having been replaced by the new three-piece style, the value of the vest can be added to the price of the old two-piece suit and the quality-adjusted price of the old suit compared directly with the price of the new three-piece suit. Alternatively, if fiber percentages vary between two items, quality adjustment can account for the quality difference to permit comparison of the prices of the two goods. Other differences which have been shown to be statistically significant can also be factored out to permit constant quality price comparisons of apparel items. This critical change allows another incremental step forward in decreasing the number of substitutions which can not be compared due to differences in quality characteristics. While this change has its greatest impact in apparel, since apparel has been plagued with low comparability rates, this same research is underway in all other areas of the CPI so that marginal improvements in comparability in other areas can be expected in the next few years.

The hedonic approach to quality adjustment used for apparel is in contrast to the approach used for new cars, which is based on manufacturers costs. While those estimates of the value of the quality change are based on the manufacturers' cost differentials adjusted for retail markups, the quality adjustments in apparel are based on the average consumers' valuation of the change as well as on the manufacturers' costs to produce the goods. This valuation is what the hedonic modeling technique-based on the prices paid by consumers for the goods for which the CPI collects prices, implicitly estimates. As this research continues, BLS expects to make further improvements in the quality adjustment process.

In general, if the new item specification is similar to the previous one but has changed one or more of its component parts, a quality adjustment can establish comparability between their prices. A synthetic previous-period price for the new item ($P^*_{i,t-1}$) is calculated as follows:

$$P^*_{i,t-1} = P_{i,t-1} + QA$$

where:

$P_{i,t-1}$ is the actual previous-period price of the previous item and QA is the dollar value of the quality change, which may be either positive or negative.

After the above calculation is made, the base-period price for the new item ($P^*_{i,a}$) is computed as:

$$P^*_{i,a} = \frac{P_{i,a} P^*_{i,t-1}}{P_{i,t-1}}$$

where:

$P_{i,a}$ is the base-period price for the previous item.

$$P^*_{i,t-1} = P_{i,t-1} \left[P_{i,t} / (P_{i,t} - QA) \right]$$

Imputation. For some item specification changes, however, BLS has not yet determined how to make quality adjustments. Substitute items that can neither be directly compared nor quality-adjusted are called noncomparable. For noncomparable substitutions, an estimate of constant-quality price change is made by imputation.

There are two types of imputation used for commodities and services. The first type of imputation is prevalent for noncomparable substitutions that occur for food and service items. In this type of imputation, the rate of price change between the old item and the noncomparable new item is assumed to be the same as the average price change of all similar items used in CPI calculations that month for the same geographic area.

To execute this imputation or "link," two estimates of price change for the item-stratum are required: ($R_{zt-1,a}$) the long-term change from the CPOPS period a, to the previous pricing period t-1 and ($R_{zt,t-1}$) the 1-month change from the previous period to the current month. A new base-period price ($P^*_{zi,a}$) for item i, in item stratum z is computed as follows:

The value of $R_{zt-1,a}$ is estimated at either the item level by using the ratio of the previous-period price to the base

$$P^*_{zi,a} = \frac{P_{zi,t}}{R_{zt-1,a} * R_{zt,t-1}}$$

price, or at the item stratum level by using the ratio of indexes for the item-area stratum where:

$$R_{zt-1,a} = \frac{I_{z,t-1}}{I_{z,a}}$$

$I_{hz,t-1}$ is the index of the previous pricing period for the item-area stratum h_z,

$I_{hz,a}$ is the base-period index for the CPOPS period (or other frame reference), and

$R_{hzt,t-1}$ is the one-period price change relative for the item-strata stratum.

The quality difference between the items in this case is assumed to be the difference between the price of the new variety and the imputed price for the old variety.

For many other items, however, price change is closely associated with the annual or periodic introduction of new lines or models. For example, price changes for new cars often accompany the introduction of new models. Price changes for cars within the same model year, then, are not the best estimate of price change for noncomparable substitutions that occur between model years. Rather, the average price change that occurs between model year changeovers used in CPI calculations provides a superior approximation of price change for noncomparable new car models. Therefore, since October 1989, price changes for noncomparable new model vehicles have been imputed using only constant-quality price change of comparable model changeovers. Price changes recorded within the same model year are excluded from the estimate. This type of imputation—using price changes for substitutions of comparable quality to estimate price change for noncomparable substitutions—will become increasingly prevalent for nonfood commodities.

In order to impute noncomparable substitutions by the price change for comparable substitutions, a current-period "overlap" price ($P^*_{i,t}$) is estimated for the old specification of the item as follows:

$$P^*_{i,t} = P_{i,t-1}\, R_{ct,t-1}$$

where $R_{ct,t-1}$ is the current one-period relative for all comparable and quality-adjusted substitutions in the same item-area stratum.

When a price is obtained for the old ($P_{i,t}$) item specification, and imputed for the new ($P^*_{i,t}$) specification in the same period (overlap pricing), the estimation of the base-period price is based on the same-period price relationship of the two specifications. The new base-period price ($P^*_{i,a}$) is estimated as follows:

$$P^*_{i,a} = P^*_{i,t}\, (P_{i,a} / P_{i,t})$$

For the current month, the price comparison used in the index is $P_{i,t-1}$ to $P^*_{i,t}$ At the next pricing, the comparison will be made on the new item. The quality difference is assumed to be the difference in the prices of the old and new varieties in the current month.

Medical care. Another area in which quality adjustment presents particular difficulties is medical care. Not all factors affecting the quality of medical care services can be accounted for in the description of the item being priced. Quite often the respondent does not have knowledge of many price-determining quality factors. For example, hospital room modifications, changes in the nurse-to-patient ratio, or the availability of new equipment are all likely to contribute to determining the price level of the room service priced. Such changes are normally reflected as price movement because BLS either is not aware of the changes or has no method available to deal with the change. Improved technologies and procedures can lead to quality changes that cannot necessarily be measured by BLS. For instance, new advances in the development of porous materials in the manufacturing of prosthetic implants, such as in hip replacement surgery, allow the bone to grow around the prosthesis. This is not the case with the nonporous materials that have been commonly used in hip replacement prosthetic implants. Many doctors view this porous implant as an improvement in the results of hip replacement surgery. In pricing total hip replacement surgery, the quality impact of shifting from a nonporous to a porous implant would not be factored out of the index, as BLS has no methodology to account for the value of the quality difference.

There are, however, certain areas in medical care where the quality difference can be measured and adjustments made for changes in the quality of priced services. For example, the CPI might be pricing a limited visit to a physician's office for treatment of a sore throat, and the physician changed the fee schedule so that a throat culture was always performed and the price included in the cost of the visit. The addition of the throat culture would not be reflected as a price increase, because it was not in the described service and would be considered a substitution. If the physician identifies the cost of the office visit for the current month, a price change in the cost of the office visit can be reflected from the previous month. For subsequent pricing comparisons, the new service would include the office visit and throat culture. If a hospital introduces a separate admitting charge that previously was included in the room rate, BLS prorates the admission charge to a per-day basis using an appropriate hospital-provided length-of-stay measure. The prorated admission charge is then added to the room rate priced to reflect the price movement in the index.

Other price adjustments

Bonus merchandise adjustments. Sometimes products are offered with free merchandise included with the purchase of the original item. Such "bonus" items may provide additional satisfaction to consumers, and BLS will, therefore, make adjustments to the purchase price to take into consideration the value of the bonus merchandise. The adjustment made depends on the type of merchandise offered and the perceived value of the bonus to the consumer.

If the bonus merchandise consists of more of the same item, the adjustment is reflected in the price of the item. For example, if a manufacturer offers two ounces of toothpaste "free with the purchase of the regular six-ounce tube," then the item's price will be adjusted to reflect a decrease in the per-ounce price. When the bonus is removed, the price per ounce will return to its prior level, and a price increase will be recorded. In this instance, the value to the consumer is assumed to be one-third greater.

If the bonus merchandise consists of an item that has some significant value to the consumer, and the item is of a different genre, an adjustment will be made to account for the value of the free item when feasible to do so.

When bonus merchandise adjustments occur, base prices are not adjusted since there is no difference in the quantity or quality of the original item being priced.

Utility refunds. Sometimes public utility commissions require that utilities such as telephone, natural gas, or electricity companies make rebates to their customers. These rebates may arise from a number of different causes. For example, a utility may be permitted to use a new rate schedule temporarily until a final determination is made. If the final rates set by the commission are lower than the temporary ones, the difference must be refunded for consumption during the period. The utility bills priced for the CPI will reflect the full amount of these refunds in the month(s) they are credited to the customers.

Manufacturers' rebates. When product manufacturers offer cash rebates to consumers for purchases of items priced in the CPI, these rebates will be reflected in the index as price reductions. The amount of the rebate adjustment usually depends on the percentage of purchasers who take advantage of the rebate offer. For example, when auto manufacturers offer a $500 rebate on the purchase of a new car or reduced-rate financing, the price of each car eligible for the rebate is reduced by the proportion of customers who opt for the rebate. If 70 percent of customers choose rebates for a particular model, then the price of each quote for that model in the CPI will be reduced by $350, and the index will reflect the price decline. The reduced interest rates chosen by the remaining customers will be reflected in the auto financing component of the CPI. For mail-in rebate offers, an attempt is made to determine the proportion of customers who take advantage of the rebate, and the reported prices are adjusted accordingly.

Cents-off coupons. Generally, no adjustments are made for coupons presented by customers as price reductions at the time of payment. One exception is when the coupons are attached to the product for immediate redemption at the point of purchase. BLS field representatives are instructed in this latter situation to deduct the amount of the coupon from the price of the item.

Seasonal items

Seasonal items are those commodities and services that are not available year round but are available only at certain times of the year. Heavyweight coats, tents, and fresh peaches are examples of seasonal items. Special procedures are employed when selecting and pricing these types of items to ensure they are appropriately represented in the sample and price changes are correctly included in the calculation of the CPI. In particular, the procedures prevent substituting away from a seasonal item when it is out of season.

Although seasonal items can exist in any ELI, some ELI's include an especially large percentage of items that are seasonal and, consequently, receive special treatment. These seasonal ELI's include most apparel items, fresh fruit, and sports and recreational equipment. The designation of an ELI as seasonal or nonseasonal was made at the regional level, using the four geographic Census regions in the CPI design. It is not uncommon for some items that are seasonal in the Northeast region, for example, to be sold year round in the South.

After the samples for these seasonal ELI's are selected following the normal sample selection procedure, the number of quotes is doubled to ensure that, despite the seasonal disappearance of a large number of quotes, a large enough number of in-season quotes will remain to calculate the index.

The quotes in these ELI's are paired; that is, for each original quote that is selected, a second quote in the same ELI and outlet is initiated and priced 6 months later. In the fresh fruit ELI's, one quote of each pair is designated January-June, and the other quote is designated July-December. In all other seasonal ELI's, one quote of each pair is designated fall/winter, and one quote is designated spring/summer. The fall/winter and spring/summer designations are used for the nonfood quotes because these are the distinctions that are most commonly used by the retailing industry to categorize seasonal merchandise. These seasonal designations are used to help establish the specific items eligible for each quote so that year-round items and items from each season are initiated in their proper proportions.

For every specific commodity and service priced in the CPI, including year-round items, BLS field representatives collect—at the time they initiate the item and every time they must find a substitute for it—its in-season months. These data become a part of the item description and are updated if there is a change. Field representatives attempt to price every item in each period it is designated for collection, even during those months when the item may be out of its indicated season. If the item is available, the price is collected and used in the calculation of the CPI. If the item is unavailable because it is out of season, no substitute item is selected nor is any further action taken, and that item is not used in the calculation of the CPI that month. Its price is imputed using standard imputation procedures.

When an item becomes permanently unavailable, the standard procedure is to substitute the most similar item. In the case of a year-round item not in a seasonal ELI, this process takes place as soon as the item is permanently unavailable. For items in seasonal ELI's and seasonal items in ELI's that are not designated seasonal, however, the period during which a substitution can take place is restricted to those months when a full selection of appropriate seasonal merchandise is available.

These special initiation, pricing, and substitution procedures are intended to ensure that an adequate sample of items is available every month, and the correct balance of seasonal and year-round items is maintained. As a result, the estimates of price movement for the ELI's that include seasonal items are hoped to reflect price changes for the universe of items included in those ELI's correctly.

Special estimation procedures

A number of special estimation procedures are used in compiling price information for selected categories of items in the CPI.

New vehicles. Prices for new cars and trucks selected for inclusion in the CPI pose a special problem since the manufacturer's suggested retail (sticker) price does not represent the transaction price for most new vehicles. Most automotive dealers offer customers concessions on the sticker price, or, at those times when models are in high demand, the dealers will charge an additional markup beyond the sticker price. When pricing new vehicles, BLS field representatives obtain separately the base price and the prices for options, dealer preparation, transportation, etc. In addition, they obtain from the dealer the average concession and/or markup during the preceding 30 days. This enables BLS to estimate the true transaction price for each vehicle after concessions/markups.

Used cars. The only expenditures on used cars included in the CPI market basket are those for previously owned cars consumers purchased from the business or government sectors and the profit of dealers on the sale of used cars. (See special expenditure weight issues above.) The used car sample was selected from types of cars purchased for use by businesses and governments. The sample consists of 2- through 6-year-old models. Average wholesale prices of clean cars sold at used car auctions are published by the National Automotive Dealers Association. The average of these prices is adjusted for depreciation using the difference in prices between model years for the same model car. The prices used in the index are a 3-month moving average of the average wholesale prices adjusted for depreciation.

Natural gas. The energy value of natural gas varies according to the quality of the gas supplied. BLS attempts to price a constant amount of energy consumption for natural gas. When natural gas is sold by volume—e.g., cubic feet—the amount of gas needed to produce a constant amount of energy will vary depending on the heating value of the gas. To ensure that a constant amount of energy is being priced, the amount of gas consumed is adjusted each month based on the current heating value. Thus, through time, a constant amount of energy is priced. The current adjusted consumption is calculated as follows:

Current adjusted consumption = original consumption x (original heat value/current heat value).

Health insurance. Health insurance is not directly priced in the CPI. The price change is imputed from the price movement of the various services that are covered by health insurance and from the change in the ratio of retained earnings to benefits paid by type of health insurance carrier—Blue Cross/Blue Shield or other. (For additional detail, see special expenditure weight procedures.) Thus, the price change for health insurance, by type of carrier, is estimated each month by the product of two relatives—one for the change in the various assigned medical care items (e.g., physician services, hospital rooms, etc.) and the other for the change in the retained earnings ratio of the carrier.

Automobile finance charges. The price used in the CPI for automobile finance charges represents the amount paid for financing a loan with fixed characteristics such as down-payment percentage, term of the loan, type and model of car, etc. The price change is affected by two items—the interest rate on the loan and the changes in the amount financed due to price movement for new cars. The automobile financing charges index is estimated each month by the product of two relatives, one for changes in interest rates charged on new-car loans and the other for changes in new-car prices.

Quantity discounts. Many items in the CPI are sold both individually and in quantity. When consumers are able to purchase an amount greater than a single unit at a discounted price, the first multiple unit price is reported for use in the CPI. For example, if the 12-ounce can of corn being priced can be purchased at 25 cents for a single can, three cans for 69 cents, or five cans for $1, the price used in the CPI will be the per-ounce price of the three cans.

Unit-priced fruits and vegetables. When pricing fresh fruits and vegetables that are sold on a unit basis, two of the items are weighed to determine an average weight for the item. This helps to reduce the variability in the size that occurs among individual, loose-produce items and is not overly burdensome for the data collection process. For example, if the item being priced is Red Delicious apples and the price is 50 cents each, the BLS field staff will report the price of one apple and the combined weight of two Red Delicious apples taken from the produce rack. In computing the price per ounce, the weight of the two apples is divided by two and the price of an apple is divided by this average weight.

Bottle deposits. BLS collects information on bottle deposits for a variety of nonalcoholic and alcoholic beverages in order to calculate the influence of changes in bottle legislation on price change. Consumers who purchase throwaway containers are considered to be purchasing both the product itself and the convenience of throwing the container away. When a local jurisdiction enacts bottle legislation and no longer allows stores to sell throwaway containers, those consumers who were previously purchasing throwaway containers may experience a change in the price of the convenience. The price of the same size bottle of product plus its deposit establishes an upper bound for the price change since the consumer could retain the former convenience by now purchasing returnables and simply throwing them away. In similar fashion, information about deposits and the status of bottle legislation can be used to estimate price change when a bottle bill is repealed. Changes due to bottle bills are shown in the month the legislation is effective.

Sales taxes. The CPI includes all applicable taxes paid by consumers for services and products purchased. A number of prices for services and products used to calculate the CPI are collected with taxes included because this is the manner in which they are sold. Other prices are collected excluding applicable taxes with those taxes subsequently added in the Washington office. The tax rates for these items are determined from secondary sources based on the State and local tax structure governing the sale of the service or product at the point of purchase. BLS currently is studying the effects of taxes on the monthly movement of the CPI.

Shelter: residential rent and owners' equivalent rent

The residential rent and owners' equivalent rent indexes measure the change in the cost of shelter for renters and owners, respectively. Price change data for these two indexes come from the CPI Housing survey. Each month, BLS field representatives gather information from renter units on the rent for the current month the previous month and on what services are provided. From owners' units, they obtain an estimated or implicit rent and from all units they collect information on characteristics of the sample housing units and respondents.

Residential rent. The rent estimates used in the CPI are "contract rents:" they are the payment for all services the landlord provides in exchange for the rent. For example, if the landlord provides electricity, it is part of the contract rent. The CPI item expenditure weights also include the full contract rent payment. The CPI rents are calculated as the amounts the tenants pay their landlords plus any rent reductions tenants receive for performing services for the landlord (sometimes called "rent as pay") plus any subsidy payment paid to the landlord. If the rent is lower than prevailing market rents because the renter is related to the landlord, the unit is not used in the calculation. Reductions for any other reasons are not considered part of the rent.

BLS makes two preliminary estimates of the rent index for each CPI area: Its current month's index is estimated, first, by applying estimates of 1-month change to its next index for the previous month and, second, by applying estimates of 6-months rent change to its index for 6 months earlier. The estimate of the 1-month rent change is the sum of the current month's rents—weighted and adjusted for 1 month of aging—divided by the previous month's sum of weighted rents. The estimate of the 6-month rent change is the sum of the current month's rents—weighted and adjusted for 6 months of aging—divided by the sum of weighted rents for the previous 6 months. The final rent index for the current month is a weighted average of the previous month's rent index moved forward by the estimate of 1-month rent change and the rent index from 6 months earlier advanced by the estimate of 6-month change.

To put this in the form of an equation, let S_1 be the set of rental units in the CPI Housing survey in a CPI area with valid comparable rents in both time t and in time t-1; and let S_6 be the set of units interviewed in time t with valid comparable rent values in both time t and time t-6. Vacant units that were previously renter occupied are also included in S_1 and S_6 and have current (t) and previous (t-1) month's rents assigned using a vacancy imputation process. Let the rent for rental unit i in time t be r_{it}, and let a_i be the factor, which is discussed below, that adjusts for the estimated small loss in quality due to the aging that the unit experienced between t-1 and t. The 1-month and 6-month estimates of rent change, $R_{t,t-1}$ and $R_{t,t-6}$, are calculated by:

$$R_{t,t-1} = \frac{\sum_{i \in S_1} (r_{i,t} + a_i r_{i,t-1}) W_{i1}}{\sum_{i \in S_1} r_{i,t-1} W_{i1}} \qquad R_{t,t-6} = \frac{\sum_{i \in S_6} (r_{i,t} + 6 a_i r_{i,t-6}) W_i}{\sum_{i \in S_6} r_{i,t-6} W_{i6}}$$

where:

W_{i1} and W_{i6} are the sampling weights, which are the inverse of the renter units' probability of selection adjusted for nonresponse.

Using $R_{t,t-1}$ and $R_{t,t-6}$ and the indexes for the previous month I_{t-1}, and for the 6 months previous, I_{t-6}, BLS computes two preliminary estimates ($I_{t-1}R_{t,t-1}$ and $I_{t-6}R_{t,t-6}$) of the current month's rent index, I_t, for each market basket. The final rent index for month t for each market basket is the weighted average of the two preliminary estimates:

$$I_t = A(I_{t-1} R_{t,t-1}) + (1-A)(I_{t-6} R_{t,t-6})$$

where:

A = 0.65, the value that simulation studies determined to minimize the mean squared error of the estimate.[20]

Vacancy imputation. Vacant units which were previously renter occupied are used in the calculation of $R_{t,t-1}$ and $R_{t,t-6}$. The vacancy imputation process incorporates several assumptions about the unobserved rents of vacant units. It is assumed that rents tend to change at a different rate for units that become vacant (and are, therefore, in the process of changing tenants) than for other units. The vacancy imputation model assumes that, after an initial lease period, expected rents change at a steady rate until the old tenant moves out of the unit. When there is a change in occupant or a unit becomes vacant, its rent is assumed to "jump" at some rate, referred to as the "jump rate." In markets with generally rising rents, this jump rate is usually greater than the average rate of change for occupied units. BLS estimates the jump rate based on nonvacant sample units in the PSU which have had a change in tenant between t and t-6. Nonvacant units without a tenant change are used to calculate the average continuous rate of change. These values are used to impute rents for vacant units for periods t and t-1 from their rent in t-6.[21]

In general, the imputed rents, $r_{i,t}$ and $r_{i,t-1}$, of the ith vacant rental unit in t and t-1 are:

$$r_{i,t-1} = r_{i,t-6} C^5 \text{ and } r_{i,t} = r_{i,t-1} J$$

where J is the jump rate for the PSU calculated, and C is the steady rate of change.

The imputation of vacant rents ensures that the unobserved rent change that occurs when a unit becomes vacant will be reflected in the final rent index. The 6-month rent-change estimates will capture these changes once the units become occupied, however, they will be missed in 1-month rent-change estimates without vacancy imputation. Because the final rent index is calculated using both 1- and 6-month change estimates, omission or misstatement of rent estimates for vacant units would lead to BLS missing part of rent changes in the CPI.

Aging adjustment. The aging adjustment accounts for the small loss in quality as housing units age (or depreciate) between interviews. The aging adjustment factors, a_i, can be thought of as 1/(1-d) where d is the monthly rate of physical depreciation. BLS computes factors for each housing unit with regression-based formulas. The formulas account for the age of the unit and a number of structural characteristics.[22] The aging adjustment procedure was introduced into the CPI in 1988.

Quality adjustment. Quality adjustments made to the cost of rental housing are used in the rent and owners' equivalent rent indexes. In addition to collecting the rent charged, BLS also collects a description of major services and facilities provided by the landlord. If the services and facilities differ between two collection periods when rents are compared, the rent for the current period is adjusted to reflect the differences in services between the time periods. For instance, if the owner no longer provides a certain utility, BLS calculates an estimate of the value of that utility and adds it to the current rent in order to have an adjusted rent value. This adjusted rent is the current cost of the same set of services provided for the previous rent.

To make quality adjustments in costs of utilities, BLS uses data from the Department of Energy's Residential Energy Consumption Survey to develop formulas to estimate utility usage for various types and sizes of housing, in various climates, with different types of heating and air conditioning, hot water, and so on. Prices for utilities come from the CPI average price program. A similar, simpler formula is used to estimate water costs.

Using data calculated yearly from the aging adjustment regressions, quality adjustments for major structural changes (i.e., the number of bedrooms, bathrooms, or other rooms and central air conditioning) have been made since February 1989.[23] Previously, when such major changes occurred, BLS omitted these observations from the calculation for estimation of price change for that time period.

Owners' equivalent rent. In Part I of this chapter, the concept of using owners' equivalent rent to measure homeowner shelter costs was discussed. BLS estimates the own-

[20] For a derivation of the optimal value of A, see C. L. Kosary, J., P. Sommers, and J. M. Branscome, "Evaluation Alternatives to the Rent Estimator," *Proceedings of the Business and Economic Statistics Section,* American Statistical Association, 1984.

[21] For more information on vacancy imputation, see J. P. Sommers and J. D. Rivers, "Vacancy Imputation Methology for Rents in the CPI," *Proceedings of the Business and Economic Statistics Section,* American Statistical Association, 1983.

[22] For further information, see Lane, Walter F.; Randolph, William C.; and Berenson, Stephen A.; "Adjusting the CPI Shelter Index to Compensate for Effect of Depreciation," *Monthly Labor Review,* October 1988, pp. 34-37.

[23] For additional information on quality adjustments in housing, see Henderson, Steven W. and Berenson, Stephen A. "Quality Adjustments for Structural Changes in the CPI Housing Sample," *Monthly Labor Review,* November 1990, pp. 40-42.

ers' equivalent rent index[24] by estimating the owners' implicit rent, m_j for each owner unit, j, in the sample. In contrast to the contract rent concept used in the rent index, the implicit rent is a "pure rent"; that is, it excludes payments for extra services such as utilities and furniture. Once the implicit rents are estimated, the calculation of the owners' equivalent rent index essentially follows that of the rent index.

The initial value derived for time t for $m_{j,t}$, is an estimate of the rent the owner-occupied housing units in the Housing survey would bring if they were rented. The estimate is based on the answer to the question, "How much do you think you could rent this house out for monthly, not including utilities?" For owner-occupied units whose owners are unable to estimate their unit's implicit rent, BLS uses estimates provided by its field representatives based on their knowledge of the rental market in that area. If this information cannot be obtained, BLS uses an imputation procedure that assigns the implicit rent from a similar unit to any that have missing values.

To get subsequent values of implicit rent each month, BLS assigns a set of renters, Q_j, to each owner unit, j. This assignment is done on the basis of location within the PSU, structure type, and structural characteristics. BLS first tries to match owners with renters that fit for all variables. For those owners for whom a matching set of renters is not obtained at the first stage, BLS relaxes the constraints one at a time until a satisfactory set of renters is found for all the owners. In general, a single renter may be assigned to sets for estimating no more than three owner equivalents. When several renters, say n_j are assigned to owner j, this counts as only $1/n_j$ toward each renter's maximum of three owners. Renters are only checked against their maximum after a round of matching, however, so it is possible for a renter to move more than three owner equivalents if the renter is matched to more than three during one round. The sample selection process, which sampled renters in owner areas at a very high rate, facilitated the matching of renters to owners. (See the section on item and outlet samples for shelter.) BLS estimates the pure rent, $P_{i,t}$, for all the rental units in Q_j. This pure rent estimate, $P_{i,t}$, is $r_{i,t}$ minus an estimate of the value of any utilities or furniture the landlord provides.

Q_{j1} is the subset of the renters in Q_j that have valid comparable rents in both t and t-1. Q_{j6} is the subset with valid rents in both t and t-6. Vacant, previously renter-occupied housing units are eligible for Q_{j1} and Q_{j6}. The implicit rent, m_{jt} for owner j in time t is estimated from the implicit rent for t-6 and the average change in the pure rent of the units in Q_{j6}:

$$m_{j,t} = m_{j,t-6} \sum_{i \in Q_{j6}} \left(\frac{P_{i,t}}{P_{i,t-6}} + 6a_i \right) \Big/ n_{j6}$$

where $p_{i,t}$ is the ith rental unit's pure rent, a_i is the aging adjustment factor, and n_{j6} is the number of rental units in Q_{j6}.

The 1-month previous implicit rent is the current month's implicit rent moved back 1 month with the pure rents in Q_{j6}:

$$m_{j,t-1} = m_{jt} \sum_{i \in Q_{j1}} \left(\frac{P_{i,t-1}}{P_{i,t} + a_i P_{i,t-1}} \right) \Big/ n_{j1}$$

Once BLS obtains estimates of current, 1-month-ago, and 6-months-ago implicit rents for all owners, it proceeds to estimate the owners' equivalent rent index for the current month. The process is similar to that used for the rent index. There is no problem here with missing price change for vacant units or aging since the calculation of implicit rent already adjusts for these considerations.

BLS makes 1-month and 6-month estimates of change in the owners' shelter cost for each market basket as follows: Let S_1 be the set of owner units with implicit rents in both time t and time t-1 and S_6 the set of owner units with implicit rents in t and t-6. Note that owner units may not be in S_1 or S_6 if their sets Q_{j1} or Q_{j6} are empty. The 1-month and 6-month estimates of price change for owner units in each market basket are:

$$R_{t,t-1} = \frac{\sum_{j \in S_1} m_{jt} w_{j1}}{\sum_{j \in S_1} m_{j,t-1} w_{j1}} \qquad R_{i,t-6} = \frac{\sum_{i \in S_6} m_{jt} w_{j6}}{\sum_{i \in S_6} m_{j,t-6} w_{j6}}$$

where w_{j1} and w_{j6} are the owner units' inverse probability of selection adjusted for nonresponse.

As in the rent index, two preliminary estimates of the current month's price index for each market basket ($I_{t-1}R_{t,t-1}$ and $I_{t-6}R_{t,t-6}$) are averaged together to get the final estimate I_t:

$$I_t = A\,(I_{t-1}\,R_{t,t-1}) + (1-A)\,(I_{t-6}R_{t,t-6})$$

Again, $A = 0.65$ is a value that reduces the mean squared error.

Estimation of seasonal effects

Seasonal adjustment. Seasonal adjustment removes the estimated effect of changes that normally occur at the same time every year (such as price movements resulting from changing climatic conditions, production cycles, model changeovers, holidays, sales, etc.). CPI series are selected for seasonal adjustment if they pass certain statistical criteria and if there is an economic rationale for the observed seasonality. Seasonal factors used in computing the season-

[24] Substantial changes in the method of measuring price change of owner-occupied housing were introduced with the index for January 1983 (January 1985 for the CPI-W). For information on the change and the old method, see "Changing the Homeownership Component of the Consumer Price Index to Rental Equivalence," *CPI Detailed Report,* January 1983.

ally adjusted indexes are derived using the ARIMA option of the X-11 variant of the Census Method II Seasonal Adjustment Program. In some cases, intervention analysis seasonal adjustment is used in combination with X-11-ARIMA to derive more accurate seasonal factors. Consumer price indexes may be adjusted directly or aggregatively depending on the level of aggregation of the index, and the behavior of the component series. [25]

Intervention analysis seasonal adjustment. Some index series that show occasional erratic behavior known as a "trend shift," which can cause problems in making an accurate seasonal adjustment. An index series whose underlying trend has experienced a sharp and permanent shift will generate distorted results when put through the X-11-ARIMA procedure. Trend shifts have been observed, for example, when gasoline prices have reacted to major changes instituted by the Organization of Petroleum Exporting Countries cartel—a recurring event which happens at infrequent and irregular intervals. Another kind of distorting change may occur when the seasonal pattern itself changes.

In order to compensate for those instances in which such distortions are both substantial and identifiable, an established method of intervention analysis, developed at BLS, is applied when appropriate.[26] In recent years, BLS has used intervention analysis seasonal adjustment for various indexes—gasoline, fuel oil, new vehicle, women's apparel, and tobacco and smoking products.

Direct and aggregative adjustment. Each year BLS seasonally adjusts eligible lower level CPI index series independently with the X-11-ARIMA multiplicative model on to data for the latest 5 to 8 calendar years. This product's seasonal factors that will be used to generate seasonal adjusted indexes for the current year. BLS recalculates and publishes seasonally adjusted indexes for the previous 5 years.

Most higher level index series are adjusted by the indirect, or aggregative, method, which is more appropriate for broad categories whose component indexes show strongly different seasonal patterns. Under the aggregative method, direct adjustment is first applied to indexes at lower levels of detail, and thereafter the adjusted detail is aggregated up to yield the higher level seasonally adjusted indexes. If intervention analysis is indicated, it will be used in adjusting selected lower level indexes prior to aggregation. For those series which have not been selected for seasonal adjustment, the original, unadjusted data are used in the aggregation process.

[25] See appendix A for an explanation of BLS seasonal adjustment methods.

[26] Buszuwski, J.A. and Scott, S. (1988), "On the Use of Intervention Analysis in Seasonal Adjustment," *Proceedings of the Business and Economics Section,* American Statistical Association.

Revision. The seasonal factors are updated annually. BLS recalculates and publishes seasonally adjusted indexes for the previous 5 years.

Average Prices

Average prices are estimated from CPI data for selected food items, gasoline, utility (piped) gas, electricity, and fuel oil in order to support the research and analytic needs of CPI data users. For each food item, the average price for a specified unit of size (i.e., pound, gallon, etc.) are published monthly for the U.S. city average and for the four regions—Northeast, Midwest (formerly the North Central), South, and West. The regional definitions are those of the Bureau of the Census. Metric equivalent sizes are noted as well.

Average prices for gasoline, utility (piped) gas, electricity, and fuel oil are published monthly for the U.S. city average, the 4 regions, the 4 population size classes, 13 of 16 region/size-class cross classifications, 4 population size classes, and the 15 largest index areas. For utility (piped) gas, average prices per therm, per 40 therms, and per 100 therms are published. For electricity, average prices per kilowatt-hour (kwh) and per 500 kwh are published. For fuel oil and gasoline, the average price per gallon is published. Average prices for popular grades of gasoline are published.

Price quotes for 40 therms and 100 therms of utility gas and for 500 kWh of electricity are collected in sample outlets for use in the average price programs only. Since they are for prespecified consumption amounts, they are not used in the CPI. All other price quotes used for average price estimation are regular CPI data.

With the exception of the 40 therms, 100 therms, and 500 kWh price quotes, all prices are converted to a price-per-normalized quantity. For example, prices for gallons, quarts, or pints of milk are converted to prices per ounce. All prices are then used to estimate a price for a defined fixed quantity. That is, a price per ounce of milk is estimated and multiplied by 64 to yield a price per half gallon, the published quantity.

The average price for collection period t is estimated as:

$$\overline{P}_t = \frac{\sum_i W_{it} P_{it} / P_{ia}}{\sum_i W_{it} / P_{ia}}$$

where W_{it} is the quote weight as defined in the estimation of price change modified to reflect the number of quotes usable for average price estimation for the ELI/PSU/replicate. (Imputed prices are used in estimating average prices.)

In the equation, W_{it} is an expenditure weight. Dividing the expenditure weight by the price, P_{ia}, for a given quote yields an implicit estimate of quantity. Thus, the average price is, conceptually, a weighted average of prices where the weights are quantity amounts.

Part III. Precision of Estimates

An important advantage of probability sampling methods is that a measure of the sampling error of survey estimates can be computed directly from the sample data. The CPI sample design accommodates error estimation by making two or more selections (replicates) of items and outlets within an index area. Therefore, two or more samples of quotes in each self-representing PSU and one in each non-self-representing PSU are available. With this structure, which reflects all stages of the sample design, variance estimation techniques using replicated samples can be used.

Different methods of variance estimation were used for the CPI during the period 1978-86 than are used in the current CPI. The sampling of areas, outlets, and items for the CPI for both periods followed replicated sample designs. The 1982-84 CE Survey also employed a replicated sample design. However, the 1972-73 CE Survey, which provided the expenditure weights for the 1978-86 CPI, did not use a replicated sample design. Thus it was necessary to perform two additional steps in total variance estimation for 1978-86 to include the contribution to the variance from the 1972-73 CE that were not necessary in estimating total sampling variance for 1987 forward. Both methods are described below.

1978-86 CPI Variance Estimation

The method used to estimate CPI variances for geographic aggregates for 1978-86 depends upon the statistical independence of the estimated indexes for individual index areas. The independence assumption does not hold entirely for the 1978-86 time period because during that time period, the same item sample of ELI's was used in more than one index area within a region. However, since the selection of specific items to be priced involved considerable subsampling of the ELI's within outlets, the local index area indexes were regarded as statistically independent for variance estimation. For each index area, two independent estimates of the index were constructed using the replicates specified in the design. This required calculation of price relatives by replicate for each item stratum for each time period, application of the replicate relatives to the previous-period replicate index for each item stratum, and aggregation across item strata to produce replicate indexes for item aggregates in each index area.

Squared differences of these indexes (properly scaled) provided preliminary estimates of the variance of the area index. These variance estimates were conditional on the values of the December 1977 expenditures which were updated from estimates from the 1972-73 CE Survey. Unconditional estimates of index variances, which include a component attributable to variation in expenditure weight estimates, were then computed using the conditional index variances and December 1977 expenditure weight variances which were estimated separately. Variance estimates were computed for all items and for major groups and selected item subcategories.

As noted earlier, in CPI estimation price relatives are computed for each item stratum for each index area of the CPI. Variance estimation required that price relatives also be computed for each item stratum for each index area and replicate. The methodology for computing the price relatives was the same for the full index area as for the replicates. All replicate computations were for the CPI-U population with sales and excise taxes included.

For commodities and services, each replicate sample was selected independently within each index area. In the shelter survey, for each self-representing PSU, each rental unit was assigned to one of two replicates. For non-self-representing index areas, the index PSU determined the replicate for a given rental unit.

For relative computation for rent and owners' equivalent rent, preliminary replicate cost weights for each index area replicate were constructed to provide a basis for weighting the 1-month and 6-month relatives together. For replicate j, item stratum i (rent or owners' equivalent rent), in index area m, let:

$r_j(i,m,t,t\text{-}1)$ denote the corresponding 1-month relative between months t and t-1,
$CW_j(i,m,t)$ denote the cost weight at month t, and
$r_j(i,m,t,t\text{-}6)$ denote the corresponding 6-month relative between months t and t-6.

Then $CW_j\,(i,m,t)$ is computed by:

$$CW_j(i,m,t) = 0.65\ CW_j\,(i,m,t\text{-}1)\ r_j(i,m,t,t\text{-}1) + 0.35\ CW_j\,(i,m,t\text{-}6)\ r_j(i,m,t,t\text{-}6)$$

The final shelter relative, $R_j(i,m,t,t\text{-}1)$, is computed by:

$$R_j(i,m,t,t\text{-}1) = CW_j(i,m,t)\ /\ CW_j(i,m,t\text{-}1)$$

The CPI for any item stratum in any index area is computed by a chaining process in which the estimate of expenditure for the previous month for the item stratum is multiplied by its 1-month price relative to provide an estimate of the current month's expenditure for the stratum. Item stratum expenditure values, called cost weights and denoted by CW(i,m,t) are then aggregated and compared to the total expenditure in the reference period denoted by 0. Thus, for a single item stratum index the sequence of computations would be:

$$CW(i,m,t) = CW(i,m,t\text{-}1) \cdot R(i,m,t,t\text{-}1)$$

and

$$IX(i,m,t) = 100 \cdot [CW(i,m,t)\ /\ CW(i,m,0)].$$

Estimating Variances of the Index and Price Change

Estimates of the variance of the index, conditional on the December 1977 expenditure weights, for all items or a subset of items at the national, regional, or area level, were calculated using a random group estimation method. As noted above, the sample for the CPI in any index area is partitioned into two or more disjoint replicate panels, also termed random groups. In self-representing index areas comprising only one PSU, these replicate panels are disjoint subsets of the sample for the PSU. The sample for most self-representing index areas consists of two replicates. In non-self-representing index areas, each replicate consists of the sample for one or more of the sample PSUs in the index area. The number of replicates for non-self-representing index areas in this time period ranged from two to four.

Beginning in January 1978, price relatives for each item stratum were computed separately for the full sample and for each replicate in every CPI index area to produce separate cost weight series for all item strata for each replicate as well as the full sample for each area.

Cost weights for higher level item aggregates were constructed for each index area at full sample and replicate levels using the index aggregation methodology described earlier. Item stratum and item aggregate index variance estimates were then computed for each index area using the following formula:

$$Var_c[IX(I,m,t)] = \frac{\sum_{j=1}^{r}[CW_j(I,m,t)-CW_f(I,m,t)]^2}{r(r-1)\,CW(I,m,0)^2}$$

where I denotes the item or item aggregate, r denotes the total number of replicates in the index area, and $CW_f(I,m,t)$ and $CW_j(I,m,t)$ denote the cost weights for the full sample and replicate j, respectively, in the index area m.

Conditional mixed index covariances between item strata i and l and periods t and t-k were estimated analogously:

$$Cov_c\,[IX\,(i,m,t),\,IX\,(l,m,t\text{-}k)] = \frac{\sum_{j=1}^{r}[CW_j(i,m,t)-CW_f(i,m,t)][CW_j(l,m,t\text{-}k)-CW_f(l,m,t\text{-}k)]}{r\,(r-1)CW(i,m,0)[CW(l,m,0)]}$$

The December 1977 cost weights for the full sample and all replicates for any series in any index area were equal in value. Variances computed using these cost weight series alone are termed conditional because they do not reflect the variance of the index or price change due to sampling variation of the December 1977 expenditure estimates. That is, they are conditional on the values of December 1977 expenditure estimates. Also for 1978-86, base period expenditure estimates were not separately estimated for full and replicate samples, and thus were not distinguished.

In addition, for the database from which these variances were estimated, cost weights for the Homeowner's Equivalent Rent (REQ) item stratum were computed for every month in the 9-year period, even though the REQ stratum was not officially incorporated in the index before January 1983. These REQ cost weights were used in computation of the index and price change and their variances for All Items and Housing for each month. Thus the estimates of the index and price change for All Items, Housing, and Shelter used in variance estimation for 1978-82 do not correspond exactly with their published values.

Expenditure weight variances and covariances were estimated using balanced repeated replication (see Wolter, 1985). Consumer unit expenditures were collected for each index area and item stratum in either or both the Diary and Quarterly Consumer Expenditure Surveys for 1972-73. Expenditure data for REQ were obtained from the 1974 CE surveys. Each consumer unit was assigned a full sample weight and a set of 36 replicate weights. For each replicate, region, index area, and stratum the estimation of final mean expenditures was accomplished using three steps:

(1) preliminary estimation of expenditures,

(2) estimation of mean expenditures using a composite estimation procedure which combined index area and regional expenditure estimates,

(3) estimation of final mean expenditures using a raking process on the mean expenditures determined in (2).

For each item-area, the final raked mean expenditures were combined from the Diary and Quarterly Surveys. Final raked mean expenditures were then adjusted to reflect the new item strata structure which was revised in 1977. This was done by applying ratio adjustment factors to obtain mean expenditure estimates for newly introduced item strata. Inflation factors were then applied to estimate expenditures for December 1977, denoted 7712 below.

Cost weight variances for 7712 were estimated for each index area-stratum combination by:

$$Var\,[CW(i,m,7712)] = [\sum_{j=1}^{36}(RME_j\,(i) - RME_f\,(i))^2]/36$$

where $RME_j(i)$ is the estimated raked mean expenditure for a given index area m, item stratum i, and replicate j, and $RME_f(i)$ is an estimate of final raked full sample mean expenditure. Similarly, between item strata covariances were estimated by:

$$Cov\,[CW(i,m,7712),CW(l,m,7712)] = \Big\{\sum_{j=1}^{36}[RME_j\,(i,m,7712)-RME_f\,(i,m,7712)]\cdot[RME_j\,(l,m,7712)-RME_f\,(l,m,7712)]\Big\}/36$$

Cost weight variance estimates were then combined with conditional variances to produce unconditional estimates of index and price change variances. The unconditional variance of the index for time t was estimated by:

$$Var[IX(I,m,t)] = [100 / CW(I,m,0)]^2 \cdot \{Var[CW(I,m,t)] + [CW(I,m,t)/CW(I,m,7712)]^2 \cdot Var[CW(I,m,7712)] - 2 \cdot [(CW(I,m,t))/CW(I,m,7712)] \cdot Cov[CW(I,m,t),CW(I,m,7712)]\}$$

Similarly, the unconditional variance of price change from period t-k to period t,

$$PC(I,m,t,t\text{-}k) = 100 \cdot [(CW(I,m,t)/CW(I,m,t\text{-}k))-1],$$

was approximated as the variance of a first order Taylor expansion of the ratio of cost weights at times t and t-k:

$$Var[PC(I,m,t,t\text{-}k)] = [100/CW(I,m,t\text{-}k)]^2 \cdot \{Var[CW(I,m,t)] + [CW(I,m,t)/CW(I,m,t\text{-}k)]^2 \cdot Var[CW(I,m,t\text{-}k)] -2 \cdot [CW(I,m,t)/CW(I,m,t\text{-}k)]\ Cov[CW(I,m,t),CW(I,m,t\text{-}k)]\}$$

Here Var[CW(I,m,7712)] is as defined above and Var[CW(I,m,t)] and Cov[CW(I,m,t),CW(I,m,t-k)] are the unconditional cost weight variances and covariances for item or item aggregate I, index area m, and times t and t-k, estimated via the equality:

$$Var[CW(I,m,t)] = Var\{E[CW(I,m,t) \mid CW(I,m,7712)]\} + E\{Var[CW(I,m,t) \mid CW(I,m,7712)]\}$$

which gives:

$$Var[CW(I,m,t)] = (CW(I,m,0)/100)^2 \cdot Var_C[IX(I,m,t)] + \sum_{i \in I} \sum_{j \in I} \{[IX(i,m,7712) \cdot IX(j,m,7712)]^{-1} \cdot [IX(i,m,t)] \cdot IX(j,m,t) - Cov_C[IX(i,m,t),IX(j,m,t)] \cdot Cov[CW(i,m,7712),CW(j,m,7712)]\}$$

and

$$Cov[CW(I,m,t),CW(I,m,t\text{-}k)] = (CW(I,m,0)/100)^2 \cdot Cov_C[IX(I,m,t),IX(I,m,t\text{-}k)] + \sum_{i \in I} \sum_{j \in I} \{[(IX(i,m,7712) \cdot IX(j,m,7712)]^{-1} \cdot [IX(i,m,t)] \cdot IX(j,m,t\text{-}k) - Cov_C[IX(i,m,t),IX(j,m,t\text{-}k)] \cdot Cov[CW(i,m,7712),CW(j,m,7712)]\}.$$

Index and price change total variance estimates for higher level geographic aggregates were computed, assuming independence of indexes between areas, by summing cost weight variances and covariances over index areas within the geographic aggregate M:

$$Var[IX(I,M,t)] = [100/CW(I,M,0)]^2 \cdot \{Var[CW(I,M,t)] + [CW(I,M,t)/CW(I,M,7712)]^2 \cdot Var[CW(I,M,7712)] - 2 \cdot [(CW(I,M,t)/CW(I,M,7712)] \cdot Cov[CW(I,M,t),CW(I,M,7712)]\},$$

and

$$Var[PC(I,M,t,t\text{-}k)] = [100/CW(I,M,t\text{-}k)]^2 \{Var[CW(I,M,t)] + [CW(I,M,t)/CW(I,M,t\text{-}k)]^2 \cdot Var[CW(I,M,t\text{-}k)] - 2 \cdot [CW(I,M,t)/CW(I,M,t\text{-}k)] \cdot Cov[CW(I,M,t), CW(I,M,t\text{-}k)]\}$$

where:

$$Var[CW(I,M,t)] = \sum_{m \in M} Var[CW(I,m,t)], \text{ and}$$

$$Cov[CW(I,M,t),CW(I,M,t\text{-}k)] = \sum_{m \in M} Cov[CW(I,m,t),CW(I,m,t\text{-}k)].$$

Estimating Variances of the Index and of Price Change, Starting in 1987

There are two important differences between the variance estimates for the CPI series starting with the 1987 revision and those computed for 1978-86. The first difference between the estimates derives from the fact that the December 1986 revision expenditure estimates based on the 1982-84 Consumer Expenditure Survey were independently estimated for each replicate. Thus the variances computed for the 1987 revision index series directly incorporate the contribution to sampling variance attributable to the estimation of expenditure weights from the 1982-84 CE Survey, and so are unconditional estimators of the variance of the index or price change.

The second difference between the estimates is that the 1987 revised CPI variances incorporate between-index-area covariances in estimates for higher level geographic area aggregates such as regions, city-size classes, and All Cities.

As with the 1978-86 index series, BLS will be estimating variances for the index series for the CPI-U population with sales and excise taxes included. Expenditure weights used in revising item-area weights for the index for this period were derived from the 1982-84 Consumer Expenditure Survey.

As before, the variance estimators given here depend on the aggregation structure of the index which supports the construction of indexes for higher levels of aggregation such as item groups, regions, and All Cities from those for basic item strata and index areas. The estimators also depend on the replicate structure of the index sample. Use of replicates provides a means of measuring the overall variation of the index from those computed over subsets of the sample. The full sample for each index area comprises two or more replicate panels, half of which were designated "odd" and the other half "even."

Each index area is in one of four Census regions. Each region can further be divided into two major areas, one composed of the self-representing (A) index areas and one composed of the non-self-representing (non-A) index areas. Hence, there are eight major areas in the Nation. For each area aggregate larger than one index area, estimates of between-index-area covariances for each pair of different index areas in the same major area in the same area aggregate were included in index and price change computation.

Variance estimates for the index-

To estimate the unconditional variance of an index, consider the 2n x 1 vector $\mathbf{CW}_f(IMA,t,t')$ of full sample cost weights for an item or item aggregate I, whose elements are the cost weights for each of n index areas in major area MA in months t and t':

$$\mathbf{CW}_f(I,MA,t,t') =$$

$$[CW_f(I,m_1,t),...,CW_f(I,m_n,t),CW_f(I,m_1,t'),...,CW_f(I,m_n,t')]^T$$

Similarly denote $\mathbf{CW}_1(I,MA,t,t')$ and $\mathbf{CW}_2(I,MA,t,t')$ to be the corresponding vectors of average replicate cost weights for the item and major area, with 1 denoting the average of r/2 odd replicates and 2 denoting the average of r/2 even replicates:

$$\mathbf{CW}_1(I,MA,t,t') = 2/r \sum_{j\ odd} \mathbf{CW}_j(I,MA,t,t')$$

$$\mathbf{CW}_2(I,MA,t,t') = 2/r \sum_{j\ even} \mathbf{CW}_j(I,MA,t,t')$$

Let $\mathbf{A}_{M,MA}$ be the 2 x 2n area aggregation matrix for any area aggregate M with component index areas belonging to major area MA where:

$A_{M,MA}(1,j) = 1$ if index area $j \in M$, 0 otherwise; $j=1,...,n$
$A_{M,MA}(1,j) = 0$; $j=n+1,...,2n$
$A_{M,MA}(2,j) = 0$; $j=1,...,n$, and
$A_{M,MA}(2,j) = 1$ if index area $j \in M$, 0 otherwise; $j=n+1,...,2n$.

The covariance matrix of cost weights for any area aggregate M within a major area MA, $\mathbf{W}(I,M,MA,t,t')$, is estimated by:

$$\mathbf{W}(I,M,MA,t,t') =$$

$$A_{M,MA}\ 1/2[\sum_{j=1}^{2} \mathbf{DCW}_j(I,MA,t,t')\ \mathbf{DCW}_j(I,MA,t,t')^T]\ A_{M,MA}^T$$

where $\mathbf{DCW}_j(I,MA,t,t')$ is the diffcerence vector:

$$\mathbf{DCW}_j(I,MA,t,t') = [\mathbf{CW}_j(I,MA,t,t') - \mathbf{CW}_f(I,MA,t,t')],\ j=1,2.$$

Under the assumption that the cost weights for index areas are independent between major areas, the cost weight covariance matrix $\mathbf{W}(I,M,t,t')$ for any area aggregate M comprising index areas in more than one major area, such as All Cities, regions, and size classes, is computed by summing $\mathbf{W}(I,M,MA,t,t')$ over all major areas:

$$\mathbf{W}(I,M,t,t') = \sum_{MA=1}^{8} \mathbf{W}(I,M,MA,t,t')$$

Given the cost weight covariance matrix $\mathbf{W}$, the variance of the index or price change can be estimated by a first order Taylor series approximation of the ratio of two cost weights at times t and t'. The exact expansions are given below.

For the variance of the index at time t, t' is December 1986, denoted 8612. Let $\mathbf{L}(I,M,t,8612)$ represent 1 x 2 the linear transformation vector:

$$L(I,M,t,8612) = IX(I,M,8612) \cdot \{1/CW(I,M,8612), -CW(I,M,t)/[CW(I,M,8612)]^2\}.$$

Then the variance of IX(i,m,t) is estimated by:

$$Var[IX(I,M,t)] = \mathbf{L}(I,M,t,8612)\ \mathbf{W}(I,M,t,8612)\ \mathbf{L}(I,M,t,8612)^T$$

Variance estimates for price change

An estimate of k-month price change, PC(I,M,t,t-k), from month t-k to month t for item aggregate I and area aggregate M is computed by:

$$PC(I,M,t,t\text{-}k) = 100 \cdot \{[CW(I,M,t)/CW(I,M,t\text{-}k)]-1\}.$$

Thus, price change is also a simple function of the ratio of cost weights for two time periods. Its variance can be estimated by:

$$Var[PC(I,M,t,t\text{-}k)] = \mathbf{L}(I,M,t,t\text{-}k)\ \mathbf{W}(I,M,t,t\text{-}k)\ \mathbf{L}(I,M,t,t\text{-}k)^T$$

where $\mathbf{W}(I,M,t,t\text{-}k)$ is as defined above and the linear transformation vector $\mathbf{L}(I,M,t,t\text{-}k)$ is given by:

$$L(I,M,t,t\text{-}k) = 100 \cdot \{1/CW(I,M,t\text{-}k), -CW(I,M,t)/[CW(I,M,t\text{-}k)]^2\}.$$

Nonsampling Error

CPI estimates are subject to nonsampling error as well as sampling error. Surveys involve many operations that must be performed in order to produce the final results. All of these are potential sources of nonsampling error. The errors arise from the survey process regardless of whether the data are collected from the entire universe or from a sample of the population. The most general categories of nonsampling error are coverage error, nonresponse error, response error, processing error, and estimation error.

Coverage error in an estimate results from the omission of part of the target population (undercoverage) or the inclusion of units from outside of the target population (overcoverage). Coverage errors result from the omission of cities, households, outlets, and items that are part of the target populations from the relevant sampling frames or from the double counting or inclusion of them in the frames when they should not be. A potential source of coverage error is the timelag between the Point-of-Purchase Survey and the initiation of price collection for commodities and services at resampled outlets. Because of the timelag, the products offered by the outlet at the time pricing is initiated may not coincide with the set from which the POPS respondents were purchasing.

Nonresponse error results when data are not collected for some sampled units because of the failure to interview households or outlets. This can occur when selected households and outlets cannot be contacted or refuse to participate in the survey. Nonresponse rates at initiation for the CPI commodities and services and housing surveys are shown in table 3. This nonresponse could bias the CPI if the rate of price change at the nonresponding survey units differed from the rate of price change at the survey units successfully initiated. Nonresponse rates during monthly pricing for the CPI commodities and services and housing surveys are shown in tables 1 and 2.

Response error results from the collection and use in estimation of incorrect, inconsistent, or incomplete data. Response error may arise because of the collection of data from inappropriate respondents, respondent memory or recall errors, deliberate distortion of responses, interviewer effects, misrecording of responses, pricing of wrong items, misunderstanding or misapplication of data collection procedures, or misunderstanding of the survey needs and/or lack of cooperation from respondents. The pricing methodology in the commodities and services component of the CPI allows the previous period's price to be available at the time of collection. This dependent pricing methodology is believed to reduce response variance for measuring change, but may cause response bias and lag. The housing component of the CPI, however, employs an independent pricing methodology specifically to avoid potential response bias.

In 1986 BLS established a program called Process Audit to investigate various kinds of response variance in the CPI. Process auditors independently recollect pricing information for a subsample of outlets and ELI's drawn from the regular commodities and services sample. The primary objective has been to determine where and to what extent discrepancies occur between the Process Audit collections and the routine submissions from the field. Discrepancies are not just errors but also contain actual price changes that occur in the brief time period between field and process audit collections and cannot be easily identified. Studies have revealed that these pricing discrepancies tend to be related to certain pricing characteristics of the item, such as the amount of interaction required between the data collector and the respondent in order to collect the data, those items that have multiple components to be priced, the length of the checklist that is used to fully describe the item, and the degree of price volatility of the item. A recent redesign of the Process Audit sample will allow for a tracking of these discrepancy rates from year to year making it possible to measure the impact of process improvements and to identify new or existing problems in the pricing process.

Processing error arises from incorrect editing, coding, and data transfer. Survey data are converted into machine-readable form by two independent key entry operators, and discrepancies are resolved by a third person. Processing errors can be introduced by an incorrect resolution or by an identical miskeying of an element by two operators. Errors can also result from software problems in the computer processing which cause correctly keyed data to be lost. Computer screening and professional review of the data provide checks on processing accuracy. Occasional studies of these processing errors in the CPI have shown them to be extremely small.

Estimation error results when the survey process does not accurately measure what is intended. Such errors may be conceptual or procedural in nature, arising from a misunderstanding of the underlying survey measurement concepts or a misapplication of rules and procedures. A source of estimation error due to conceptual problems was the treatment of housing before 1983, which failed to distinguish between the consumption and investment aspects of homeownership. Prior to implementation of the change to the owners' equivalent rent, an experimental measure using rental equivalence diverged considerably from the official CPI.[27]

Substitutions and adjustments for quality change in the items priced for the CPI are possible sources of estimation error due to procedural difficulties. Ideally, CPI data collection forms and procedures would yield all information

[27] See Gillingham, Robert and Lane, Walter. "Changing the Treatment of Shelter Costs for Homeowners in the Consumer Price Index," *Statistical Reporter*, December 1981.

necessary to determine or explain price and quality differences for all items defined within an ELI. Since such perfect information is not available, BLS economists supplement directly collected data with secondary data. Estimation error will result if the BLS adjustment process, which may require significant judgment or lack key data, is misapplied, or if it consistently overestimates or underestimates quality change for particular kinds of items. While individual problems arising from estimating quality change have been identified, the evidence to date is that on average there is no systematic bias from this process. Cases where price change is overestimated are about as frequent as those where it is underestimated.

The effect of the aging of housing units is an example of potential estimation error, which is similar to the issue of quality change in commodities and services. Until 1988, BLS did not adjust for the slow depreciation of houses and apartments over time. Current BLS research indicates that annual changes for the residential rent and owners' equivalent rent indexes would have been 0.1 to 0.2 percent larger if some type of aging adjustment had been included.

The total nonsampling error of the CPI results from errors in the type of data collected, the methods of collection, the data processing routines, and the estimation processes. The cumulative nonsampling error can be much greater than the sampling error.

Response rates

Response rates are calculated for the CPI-U at the data collection phase and at the index estimation phase for ongoing pricing. The response rate at the data collection phase is the number of responding sample units divided by the sum of (1) the number of eligible sample units and, (2) the number of sample units with eligibility not determined. A sample unit is eligible if it belongs to the defined target population and responses should be collected from the unit for one or more items. The response rate at estimation is defined as the number of sample units used in estimation divided by the sum of (1) the number of eligible sample units and, (2) the number of sample units with eligibility not determined.

Commodities and services items (any except rent and owner's equivalent rent) are further broken down into outlets and quotes. An "outlet" is a generic term used by the CPI to describe places where prices are collected. A "quote" is a specific item to be priced in a specific outlet. There may be from 1 to more than 50 quotes priced in an outlet. In table 1, it is important to note the relatively low percentages of quotes reported collected and used in estimation for apparel and upkeep. Low rates for these items can be largely attributed to the design of the apparel sample. Because apparel items are commonly in stores only during certain times of the year, most of the apparel sample is doubled, with each half of the sample designated for pricing during part of the year. Thus, at any particular time of the year a large number of apparel quotes, althougheligibile, are designated out of season and prices are not collected. For further information see the section above on seasonal items.

Table 1. Response rates for commodities and services for the CPI-U, U.S. City Average, by major group, 1990

Commodities and services	Eligible	Collected	Percent collected	Used in estimation	Percent in estimation
Outlets	240,212	231,613	96.4	222,284	92.5
Total quotes	962,322	845,657	87.9	828,988	86.1
Food	526,600	484,871	92.1	477,945	90.8
Housing (excluding shelter)	119,725	111,799	93.4	109,212	91.2
Apparel and upkeep	131,547	79,465	60.4	75,181	57.2
Transportation	73,062	67,805	92.8	66,799	91.4
Medical care	44,623	41,418	92.8	40,833	91.5
Entertainment	37,363	31,644	84.7	30,630	82.0
Other goods and services	30,507	28,685	94.0	28,388	93.1

The response rates for housing (shelter) shown in table 2 include categories for owners, renters, and those for whom the tenure status is unknown. A unit qualifies as an owner or renter if its tenure status is known either by previous knowledge or is collected in the current interview period. The number of responses is higher than the total sample size because some of the sample is priced twice a year. The response rates at the data collection phase for housing (shelter) are separated into three categories. If usable information is obtained, the unit is designated *collected, data reported.* If the assigned unit is located but is unoccupied, the unit is designated *collected, found vacant.* In instances where the unit is eligible but no data are available (e.g. refusals), the unit is designated *no data at collection or other.*

Table 2. Response rates for housing for the CPI-U, U.S. City Average, 1990

Housing (shelter)	Eligible	Collected, data reported	Collected, found vacant	No Data at collection or other	Used in estimation
Number of total units	107,059	82,643	6,699	17,717	82,465
Percent of eligible units	100.0	77.2	6.3	16.5	77.0
Number of owners	31,664	26,945	838	3,881	27,069
Percent of eligible owners	100.0	85.1	2.6	12.3	85.5
Number of renters	69,900	55,569	5,636	8,695	55,396
Percent of eligible renters	100.0	79.5	8.1	12.4	79.3
Number of unknown	5,495	129	225	5,141	0
Percent of eligible unknown	100.0	2.3	4.1	93.6	0.0

Data for initiation of commodities and services (table 3) are for those areas which underwent sample rotation in 1990. Approximately one-fifth of the areas (primary sampling units) are rotated each year. The response rate data for initiation reflect the rate of success in attempting to price the new designated sample for the first time. These data are unique in that the outlets and quotes are only counted once, as opposed to the repeated (monthly or bimonthly) pricing that is reflected in table 1.

Table 3. Response rates at initiation of commodities and services for the CPI-U, U.S. City Average,1990

Commodities and services	Eligible	Collected	Percent collected
Outlets	3,820	3,403	89.1
Quotes	16,360	12,080	73.8

Technical References

Leaver, Sylvia G., and Swanson, David L., "Estimating Variances for the U.S. Consumer Price Index for 1987-1991," *Proceedings of the Survey Research Methods Section,* American Statistical Association, forthcoming.

Liegey Jr., Paul R. "Adjusting Apparel Indexes in the CPI for Quality Differences," *Price Measurements and their Uses,* Murray F. Foss, Marilyn Manser, and Allan Young, eds. NBER-University of Chicago Press, 1992.

Armknecht, Paul A., and Ginsburg, Daniel H. "Improvements in Measuring Price Changes in Consumer Services: Past, Present, and Future," *Output Measurement in the Services Sector,* Zvi Griliches, ed. Unviersity of Chicago Press, 1992, pp. 109-156.

Leaver, Sylvia G., Johnstone, James E., and Archer, Kenneth P., "Estimating Unconditional Variances of the U.S. Consumer Price Index for 1978-86," *Proceedings of the Survey Research Methods Section,* American Statistical Association, 1991.

Primont, Diane F., and Kokoski, Mary F., "*Comparing Prices Across Cities: A Hedonic Approach,*" BLS Working Paper 204, May, 1990.

Leaver, Sylvia G. "Estimating Conditional Variances of the U.S. Consumer Price Index for 1978-86," *Proceedings of the Survey Research Methods Section,* American Statistical Association, 1990, pp. 290-295.

Armknecht, Paul A. and Weyback, Donald. "Adjustments for Quality Change in the U.S. Consumer Price Index," *Journal of Official Statistics.* Vol. 5, No. 2, 1989, pp. 107-123.

Leaver, Sylvia G.; Weber, William L.; Cohen, Michael F.; and Archer, Kenneth F. "Determining an Optimal Item-Outlet Sample Design for the 1987 U.S. Consumer Price Index Revision," *Proceeding, International Statistical Institute.* Tokyo, 1989, Vol. 3, pp. 173-185.

Pollak, Robert A. *The Theory of the Cost-of-Living Index.* Oxford University Press, 1989.

Kokoski, Mary F. *Experimental Cost-of-Living Index Measures,* BLS Report 751, June 1988.

Ford, Ina K., and Sturm, Phillip, "CPI Revision Provides more Accuracy in the Medical Care Services Component," *Monthly Labor Review,* April 1988, pp. 17-26.

Randolph, William C. "Estimation of Housing Depreciation: Long-Term Vintage Effects," *Journal of Urban Economics,* Vol. 23, March 1988, pp. 162-178.

Early, John F. and Galvin, John M. "Comprehensive Quality Measurement in the Consumer Price Index," Proceedings of the 1987 Juran Instittute Inc., Annual Quality Management Conference.

Kosary, Carol L. and Sommers, John F. "The Effect of Computer Assisted Telephone Interviewing on Response Inconsistency," *Proceedings of the Survey Research Methods Section,* American Statistical Association, 1987, pp. 627-632.

Randolph, William C. and Zieschang, Kimberly D. "Aggregation Consistent Restriction-Based Improvement of Local Area Estimation," *Proceedings of the Business and Economic Statistics Section,* American Statistical Association, 1987.

Gillingham, Robert F. and Greenlees, John S. "The Impact of Direct Taxes on the Cost of Living," *Journal of Political Economy,* 95(4), August 1987.

Kokoski, Mary F. "Consumer Price Indexes by Demographic Group," BLS Working Paper 167, April 1987.

Randolph, William C. "Housing Depreciation and Aging Bias in the Consumer Price Index," BLS Working Paper 166, April 1987.

Helliwell, John. "New Network Behind Improved CPI," *PC Week,* February 3, 1987, pp. C/4-C/lo.

Early, John F. and Dmytrow, Eric D. "Managing Information Qualty in the CPI," *Fortieth Anniversary Quality Congress Transactions,* American Society for Quality Control, 1986, pp. 2-9.

Marcoot, John L. "Revision of the Consumer Price Index Now Underway," *Monthly Labor Review,* April 1985, pp. 27-38.

Armknecht, Paul A. "Quality Adjustment in the CPI and Methods to Improve It," *Proceedings of the Business and Economic Statistics Section,* American Statistical Association, 1984, pp. 57-63.

Technical References—Continued

Blanciforti, Laura A. and Galvin, John M. "New Approaches for Automobiles in the CPI, " *Proceedings of the Business and Economic Statistics Section*, American Statistical Association, 1984, pp. 64-73.

Cohn, Michael P. and Sommers, John P. "Evaluation of the Methods of Composite Estimation of Cost Weights for the CPI," *Proceedings of the Business and Economic Statistics Section*, American Statistical Association, 1984, pp. 466-71.

Kosary, Carol L.; Sommers, John F.; and Branscome, James M. "Evaluating Alternatives to the Rent Estimator," *Proceedings of the Business and Economic Statistics Section*, American Statistical Association, 1984, pp. 410-12.

Lane, Walter F. and Sommers, John F. "Improved Measures of Shelter Costs," *Proceedings of the Business and Economic Statistics Section*, American Statistical Association, 1984, pp. 49-56.

Dippo, Cathryn S. and Jacobs, Curtis A. "Area Sample Redesign for the Consumer Price Index," *Proceedings of the Survey Research Methods Section*, American Statistical Association, 1983, pp. 118-23

Early, John F. and Sinclair, James H. "Quality Adjustment in the Producer Price Indexes," *The U.S. National Income and Product Accounts Selected Topics*, Murray F. Foss, ed. University of Chicago Press, 1983.

Gillingham, Robert F. "Measuring the Cost of Shelter for Homeowners: Theoretical and Empirical Considerations," *The Review of Economics and Statistics, 1983, pp. 254-65.*

Sommers, John P. and Rivers, Joseph D. "Vacancy Imputation Methodology for Rent, in the CPI," *Proceeding of the Business, and Economic Statistics Section*, American Statistical Association, 1983, pp. 201-05.

Gillingham, Robert F. and Lane, Walter. "Changing the Treatment of Shelter Costs for Homeowners in the CPI," *Monthly Labor Review*, June 1982, pp. 9-14.

Hageman, Robert F. "The Variability of Inflation Rates Across Household Types," *Journal of Money, Credit and Banking*, Vol. 14:4, 1982, pp, 494-510.

Triplett, Jack E. "Reconciling the CPI and PCE Deflator," *Monthly Labor Review*, September 1981, pp. 3-15.

Diewert, W.E. "The Economic Theory of Index Numbers, a Survey," *Essays in the Theory and Measurement of Consumer Behavior in Honor of Richard Stone.* Cambridge University Press, 1981, pp. 163-208.

Braithwait, S.D. "The Substitution Bias of the Laspeyeres Price Index: An Analysis Using Estimated Cost-of-Living Indexes," *American Economic Review*, March 1980.

Gillingham, Robert F. "Estimating the User Cost of Owner-Occupied Housing," *Monthly Labor Review*, February 1980, pp. 31-35.

Blackorby, C.; Primont, D.; and Russell, R.R. *Duality, Separability, and Functional Structure: Theory and Economic Applications.* American Elsevier, 1978.

Afriat, S. *The Price Index.* Cambridge University Press, 1977.

Triplett, Jack E. and McDonald, Richard J. "Assessing the Quality Error in Output Measures: The Case of Refrigerators," *Review of Income and Wealth*, 23, June 1977.

Diewert, W.E. "Exact and Superlative Index Numbers," *Journal of Econometrics*, Vol. 4, 1976, pp. 115-45.

Manser, M.E. "A Note on Cost-of-living Indexes and Price Indexes for U.S. Food Consumption, 1948-1973," BLS Working Paper 57, January 1976.

Allen, R.G.D. *Index Numbers in Theory and Practice.* Macmillan, 1975.

Christensen, L.R. and Manser, M.E. "Cost-of-Living Indexes and Price Indexes for U.S. Meat and Produce, 1947-71," *Household Production and Consumption*, Nestor Terleckyj, ed., Studies in Income and Wealth, 40. National Bureau of Economic Research, 1975.

Banerjee, K.S. *Cost of Living Index Numbers: Practice, Precision, and Theory.* Marcel Dekker, Inc., 1975.

Frisch, R. "Annual Survey of Economic Theory: The Problem of Index Numbers," *Econometrica*, Vol. 4, January 1936.

CPI Appendix 1. Chronology of changes in the Consumer Price Index, 1890 to date

Date	Survey providing expenditure weight		Base period	Census providing population weights	Number of areas included	Family composition	Earnings of chief earner	Source and amount of family income	Length of employment	Economic level, length of residence, nativity, and race	Title(s)
	Group weights	Item weights									
1890[1] ...	None	1901	Varied	None	Varied	Two or more persons.	Salaried worker earning $1,200 or less during year. No limitation on wage earners.	No limitation.	No limitation.	No limitation.	
1919	1917-19	1917-19	1913								
Feb. 1921					[2]32	Minimum of husband, wife, and 1 child who was not a boarder or lodger. No boarders nor more than 3 lodgers present.	Salaried worker earning $2,000 or less. No limitation on wage earners.	At least 75 percent from principal earner or others who contributed all earnings to family fund.		No slum or charity families; white only; in area entire year and in the United States 5 years or more; no non-English speaking families.	Cost of living.
Sept. ... 1935				[3]Average 1920-30							
Dec. .... 1935[4]			1923-25								
Aug. .... 1940[5]	1934-36	[6]1934-36	1935-39	1930	[7]33	Two or more persons. Not more than 2 boarders or lodgers, or guests for more than 26 guest-weeks.	At least $300. Salaried worker earning less than $2,000 during year or less than $200 during any month. No upper limitation on wage earners.	At least $500. Less than one-fourth from interest, dividends, royalties, speculative gains, rents, gifts, or income in kind. No rent in payment of services. Less than 3 months' free rent. No subsidiary clerical worker earning $2,000 or over.	At least 1,008 hours spread over 36 weeks.	No relief families, either on direct or work relief; white only, except where black population was significant part of total; in area 9 months or more.	Indexes of the cost of living of wage earners and lower-salaried workers in large cities.
May .... 1941[8]					34						
July 1943				[9]1940							
Sept. ... 1945											Consumer's Price Index for Moderate Income Families in Large Cities.
Jan. .... 1951[10]	1947-49	[11]1934-36		1950		Two or more persons.	No limitation. (Family income not in excess of $10,000.)	Family income under $10,000 after taxes in the survey year. No minimum income limit, except that families with no income from wages or salaries were excluded.	Family head must have been employed at least 26 weeks.	No exclusion for receipt of relief as such, but only families with wage or salary earnings included. No length of residence, nativity, or racial limitations.	

See footnotes at end of table.

CPI Appendix 1. Chronology of changes in the Consumer Price Index, 1890 to date—Continued

Date	Survey providing expenditure weight		Base period	Census providing population weights	Number of areas included	Family composition	Earnings of chief earner	Source and amount of family income	Length of employment	Economic level, length of residence, nativity, and race	Title(s)
	Group weights	Item weights									
Jan. .... 1953[12]	[13]1950	[13]1950	[14]1947-49		46				No specific requirement, but major portion of income of family head must be from employment as wage earner or salaried clerical worker.	Short title. Consumer Price Index Complete name: Index of Change in Prices of Goods and Services Purchased by City Wage-Earner and Clerical-Worker Families to Maintain Their Level of Living.	
Jan. 1962			[15]1957-59								
Jan. .... 1964[16]	[17]1960-61	[17]1960-61		1960	50	Families of 2 or more persons and single workers; at least 1 full-time wage earner.	No limitation.	More than half of combined family income from wage-earner or clerical-worker occupation.	A minimum of 37 weeks for at least 1 family member.	No restriction on other than the wage-earner and clerical-worker definition.	Consumer Price Index for Urban Wage Earners and Clerical Workers.
Jan. .... 1966[18]					56						
Jan. .... 1971[19]			1967								
Jan. .... 1978[20]	[21]1972-73	[21]1972-73		1970	85	Same as above for earner and clerical-worker index. No limitation for urban consumer index.		Same as above for wage-earner and clerical-worker index. No limitation for urban-consumer index.	Same as above for wage-earner and clerical-worker index. No employment required for urban-consumer index.	Same as above for wage-earner and clerical-worker index. No limitation for urban-consumer index.[22]	1) Consumer Price Index for Urban Wage Earners and Clerical Workers (CPI-W). 2) Consumer Price Index for All Urban Consumers (CPI-U).
Jan. .... 1987[23]	[24]1982-84	[24]1982-84		1980	91	Similar to above except that students residing in college-regulated housing are treated as separate family units.					
Jan. 1988			[25]1982-84								

[1] Food price index only

[2] For 19 cities, data were available back to December 1914 and for 13 cities, back to 1917. For the United States, data were available back to the 1913 annual average.

[3] Indexes between 1918-29 were recomputed retroactively with population weights based on the average of the 1920 and 1930 censuses.

[4] Index published in December 1935 for July 15, 1935; indexes were also calculated on the 1913=100 base.

[5] Indexes between 1925-29 were recomputed retroactively with group weights based on the average of 1917-19 and 1934-36, indexes between March 15, 1930, and March 15, 1940, were recomputed retroactively using 1934-36 group weights.

[6] During World War II, weights were adjusted to account for rationing and shortages.

[7] 51-56 cities included in the food index.

[8] Index published in May 1941 for March 14, 1941. Food indexes were based on 51 cities.

[9] 1940 census data were supplemented by ration book registration data.

[10] Index published in March 1951 for January 1951.

[11] Indexes between January 1950 and January 1951 were revised retroactively for all items and group indexes. Indexes for rent and all items were corrected for the new unit bias from 1940. Old series also published through 1952.

[12] Item weights were revised for only the 7 cities for which 1947-49 expenditure data were available. Index published in February for January 1953. Linked to old series as of December 1952. Old series also published for a 6-month overlap period.

[13] Data were adjusted to 1952 for weight derivation.

[14] Indexes were also calculated on the base of 1935-39=100 through December 1957.

[15] Index published in February for January 1962. Indexes were also calculated on bases of 1947-49=100 and 1939=100.

[16] Index published March 3 for January 1964. Linked to old series as of December 1963. Old series also published for a 6-month overlap period.

[17] Data were adjusted to December 1963 for weight derivation.

[18] Index published in February for January 1966. Linked to old series as of December 1965.

[19] Index published in February for January 1971. Indexes were also calculated on the 1957-59=100 base.

[20] Index published in February for January 1978. Linked to old series as of December 1977. Old series also published for a 6-month overlap period.

[21] Data were adjusted to December 1977 for weight deriviation.

[22] Coverage was expanded to include wage earners and clerical workers in the entire non-farm parts of the metropolitan areas in addition to those living within the urbanized areas of the metropolitan areas and urban places of 2,500 or more inhabitants.

[23] Index published in February for January 1987, linked to old series as of December 1986. Old series also published for a 6-month overlap period.

[24] Data were adjusted to December 1986 for weight derivation.

[25] Index published in February for January 1988. Indexes also calculated on the 1967=100 base.

CPI Appendix 2. Relative importance of components in the Consumer Price Indexes: U.S. city average, December 1991

(Percent of all items)

Item and group	U.S. City Average	
	All Urban Consumers (CPI-U)	Urban Wage Earners and Clerical Workers (CPI-W)
All items	100.000	100.000
Food and beverages	17.627	19.547
Food	16.007	17.811
Food at home	9.921	11.244
Cereals and bakery products	1.426	1.625
Cereals and cereal products	.461	.533
Flour and prepared flour mixes	.072	.085
Cereal	.288	.331
Rice, pasta, and cornmeal	.100	.117
Bakery products	.965	1.092
White bread	.229	.283
Fresh other bread, biscuits, rolls, and muffins	.217	.227
Cookies, fresh cakes, and cupcakes	.250	.295
Other bakery products	.269	.287
Meats, poultry, fish, and eggs	3.030	3.559
Meats, poultry, and fish	2.851	3.350
Meats	2.050	2.470
Beef and veal	1.050	1.261
Ground beef other than canned	.370	.461
Chuck roast	.093	.109
Round roast	.055	.063
Round steak	.089	.116
Sirloin steak	.078	.097
Other beef and veal	.365	.415
Pork	.585	.716
Bacon	.089	.106
Chops	.145	.181
Ham	.143	.175
Other pork, including sausage	.207	.254
Other meats	.415	.494
Poultry	.431	.481
Fresh whole chicken	.141	.168
Fresh and frozen chicken parts	.210	.229
Other poultry	.080	.085
Fish and seafood	.371	.399
Canned fish and seafood	.077	.085
Fresh and frozen fish and seafood	.294	.314
Eggs	.179	.210
Dairy products	1.229	1.363
Fresh milk and cream	.608	.713
Fresh whole milk	.355	.442
Other fresh milk and cream	.253	.271
Processed dairy products	.621	.650
Cheese	.361	.372
Ice cream and related products	.158	.171
Other dairy products, including butter	.102	.106

See footnotes at end of table.

CPI Appendix 2. Relative importance of components in the Consumer Price Indexes: U.S. city average, December 1991—Continued

(Percent of all items)

Item and group	U.S. City Average	
	All Urban Consumers (CPI-U)	Urban Wage Earners and Clerical Workers (CPI-W)
Fruits and vegetables	1.854	1.958
Fresh fruits and vegetables	1.225	1.286
Fresh fruits	.682	.713
Apples	.119	.130
Bananas	.066	.070
Oranges, including tangerines	.097	.118
Other fresh fruits	.400	.394
Fresh vegetables	.542	.573
Potatoes	.087	.097
Lettuce	.070	.074
Tomatoes	.066	.077
Other fresh vegetables	.319	.325
Processed fruits and vegetables	.629	.672
Processed fruits	.362	.365
Fruit juices and frozen fruit	.284	.291
Canned and dried fruits	.078	.074
Processed vegetables	.267	.307
Frozen vegetables	.089	.098
Other processed vegetables	.178	.209
Other food at home	2.382	2.738
Sugar and sweets	.344	.387
Sugar and artificial sweeteners	.088	.110
Sweets, including candy	.256	.277
Fats and oils	.260	.298
Nonalcoholic beverages	.739	.861
Carbonated drinks	.393	.484
Coffee	.201	.212
Other noncarbonated drinks	.145	.165
Other prepared food	1.039	1.192
Canned and packaged soup	.088	.097
Frozen prepared food	.183	.203
Snacks	.205	.233
Seasonings, condiments, sauces, and spices	.270	.306
Miscellaneous prepared food, including baby food	.293	.352
Food away from home	6.085	6.567
Lunch	2.154	2.445
Dinner	2.587	2.675
Other meals and snacks	1.028	1.220
Unpriced items	.317	.227
Alcoholic beverages	1.621	1.737
Alcoholic beverages at home	.882	.968
Beer and ale	.457	.574
Distilled spirits	.225	.214
Wine at home	.199	.180
Alcoholic beverages away from home	.739	.768

See footnotes at end of table.

CPI Appendix 2. Relative importance of components in the Consumer Price Indexes: U.S. city average, December 1991—Continued

(Percent of all items)

Item and group	U.S. City Average	
	All Urban Consumers (CPI-U)	Urban Wage Earners and Clerical Workers (CPI-W)
Housing	41.544	39.078
Shelter	27.894	25.593
Renters' costs	8.003	8.115
Rent, residential	5.835	6.678
Other renters' costs	2.168	1.437
Lodging while out of town	1.923	1.276
Lodging while at school	.211	.134
Tenants' insurance	.033	.027
Homeowners' costs	19.683	17.275
Owners' equivalent rent	19.303	16.953
Household insurance	.380	.322
Maintenance and repairs	.208	.202
Maintenance and repair services	.125	.109
Maintenance and repair commodities	.083	.093
Materials, supplies, and equipment for home repairs	.037	.041
Other maintenance and repair commodities	.046	.052
Fuel and other utilities	7.327	7.553
Fuels	4.057	4.149
Fuel oil and other household fuel commodities	.419	.383
Fuel oil	.292	.251
Other household fuel commodities	.127	.132
Gas (piped) and electricity (energy services)	3.638	3.766
Electricity	2.520	2.589
Utility (piped) gas	1.118	1.177
Other utilities and public services	3.270	3.403
Telephone services	1.821	1.849
Local charges	1.235	1.259
Interstate toll calls	.324	.323
Intrastate toll calls	.261	.266
Water and sewerage maintenance	.722	.746
Cable television	.526	.608
Refuse collection	.202	.200
Household furnishings and operation	6.323	5.932
Housefurnishings	3.699	3.615
Textile housefurnishings	.376	.354
Furniture and bedding	1.109	1.079
Bedroom furniture	.361	.402
Sofas	.219	.210
Living room chairs and tables	.183	.174
Other furniture	.346	.294
Appliances, including electronic equipment	.969	1.016
Video and audio products	.522	.571
Televisions	.181	.205
Video products other than televisions	.100	.103
Audio products	.241	.263
Unpriced items	.000	.000
Major household appliances	.311	.343
Refrigerators and home freezers	.092	.101
Laundry equipment	.100	.116
Stoves, ovens, dishwashers, and air conditioners	.119	.125
Information processing equipment	.136	.103
Other housefurnishings	1.245	1.165
Floor and window coverings, infants', laundry, cleaning, and outdoor equipment	.178	.150
Clocks, lamps, and decor items	.249	.199
Tableware, serving pieces, and nonelectric kitchenware	.221	.198
Lawn equipment, power tools, and other hardware	.190	.231
Sewing, floor cleaning, small kitchen, and portable heating appliances	.143	.150
Indoor plants and fresh cut flowers	.175	.155
Unpriced items	.089	.080

See footnotes at end of table.

CPI Appendix 2. Relative importance of components in the Consumer Price Indexes: U.S. city average, December 1991—Continued

(Percent of all items)

Item and group	U.S. City Average	
	All Urban Consumers (CPI-U)	Urban Wage Earners and Clerical Workers (CPI-W)
Housekeeping supplies	1.154	1.189
Laundry and cleaning products, including soap	.417	.481
Household paper products and stationery supplies	.370	.367
Other household, lawn, and garden supplies	.366	.341
Housekeeping services	1.469	1.128
Postage	.269	.262
Appliance and furniture repair	.175	.137
Gardening and other household services	.380	.215
Babysitting	.245	.316
Domestic services	.233	.067
Care of invalids, elderly, and convalescents	.052	.040
Unpriced items	.115	.090
Apparel and upkeep	6.097	6.092
Apparel commodities	5.535	5.566
Apparel commodities less footwear	4.735	4.682
Men's and boys'	1.451	1.445
Men's	1.191	1.124
Suits, sport coats, coats, and jackets	.353	.273
Furnishings and special clothing	.274	.263
Shirts	.305	.305
Dungarees, jeans, and trousers	.243	.264
Unpriced items	.016	.020
Boys'	.260	.321
Women's and girls'	2.517	2.452
Women's	2.137	2.016
Coats and jackets	.202	.162
Dresses	.359	.359
Separates and sportswear	1.014	.996
Underwear, nightwear, hosiery, and accessories	.346	.349
Suits	.184	.121
Unpriced items	.031	.028
Girls'	.380	.436
Infants' and toddlers'	.218	.283
Other apparel commodities	.550	.502
Sewing materials, notions, and luggage	.096	.084
Watches and jewelry	.454	.417
Watches	.085	.080
Jewelry	.369	.337
Footwear	.800	.884
Men's	.258	.302
Boys' and girls'	.166	.214
Women's	.376	.368
Apparel services	.562	.526
Laundry and dry cleaning other than coin operated	.294	.226
Other apparel services	.268	.300

CPI Appendix 2. Relative importance of components in the Consumer Price Indexes: U.S. city average, December 1991—Continued

(Percent of all items)

Item and group	U.S. City Average	
	All Urban Consumers (CPI-U)	Urban Wage Earners and Clerical Workers (CPI-W)
Transportation	17.013	18.939
Private	15.523	17.800
New vehicles	5.032	4.924
New cars	4.055	3.614
New trucks	.895	1.162
New motorcycles	.082	.149
Used cars	1.135	2.040
Motor fuel	3.304	4.068
Automobile maintenance and repair	1.520	1.594
Body work	.158	.164
Automobile drive train, brake, and miscellaneous mechanical repair	.439	.480
Maintenance and servicing	.504	.484
Power plant repair	.396	.446
Unpriced items	.023	.021
Other private transportation	4.533	5.173
Other private transportation commodities	.678	.856
Motor oil, coolant, and other products	.061	.078
Automobile parts and equipment	.616	.778
Tires	.307	.364
Other parts and equipment	.310	.414
Other private transportation services	3.855	4.317
Automobile insurance	2.415	2.737
Automobile finance charges	.691	.871
Automobile fees	.749	.710
Automobile registration, licensing, and inspection fees	.379	.411
Other automobile-related fees	.345	.282
Unpriced items	.026	.017
Public transportation	1.490	1.139
Airline fares	.967	.608
Other intercity transportation	.159	.111
Intracity public transportation	.353	.411
Unpriced items	.011	.010
Medical care	6.689	5.674
Medical care commodities	1.256	1.034
Prescription drugs [1]	.862	.692
Nonprescription drugs and medical supplies	.393	.342
Internal and respiratory over-the-counter drugs	.254	.256
Nonprescription medical equipment and supplies	.139	.086
Medical care services	5.433	4.640
Professional medical services	3.213	2.735
Physicians' services [2]	1.729	1.476
Dental services [3]	.974	.873
Eye care [4]	.340	.284
Services by other medical professionals [5]	.170	.103
Hospital and related services	1.947	1.708
Hospital rooms [6]	.763	.720
Other inpatient services [7]	.747	.642
Outpatient services [8]	.431	.342
Unpriced items	.005	.003
Health insurance [9]	.274	.197

CPI Appendix 2. Relative importance of components in the Consumer Price Indexes: U.S. city average, December 1991—Continued

(Percent of all items)

Item and group	U.S. City Average	
	All Urban Consumers (CPI-U)	Urban Wage Earners and Clerical Workers (CPI-W)
Entertainment	4.357	4.027
Entertainment commodities	2.026	2.110
Reading materials	.698	.613
Newspapers	.347	.321
Magazines, periodicals, and books	.352	.292
Unpriced items	.000	.000
Sporting goods and equipment	.447	.546
Sport vehicles, including bicycles	.201	.314
Other sporting goods	.246	.232
Toys, hobbies, and other entertainment	.881	.951
Toys, hobbies, and music equipment	.400	.437
Photographic supplies and equipment	.126	.113
Pet supplies and expense	.345	.386
Unpriced items	.011	.014
Entertainment services	2.330	1.917
Club memberships	.381	.211
Fees for participant sports, excluding club memberships	.366	.326
Admissions	.683	.584
Fees for lessons or instructions	.227	.163
Other entertainment services	.652	.619
Unpriced items	.022	.013
Other goods and services	6.674	6.643
Tobacco and smoking products	1.665	2.196
Personal care	1.187	1.146
Toilet goods and personal care appliances	.632	.652
Other toilet goods and small personal care appliances, including hair and dental products	.362	.397
Cosmetics, bath and nail preparations, manicure and eye makeup implements	.270	.255
Personal care services	.555	.494
Beauty parlor services for females	.443	.390
Haircuts and other barber shop services for males	.112	.103
Unpriced items	.000	.000
Personal and educational expenses	3.822	3.302
School books and supplies	.243	.211
School books and supplies for college	.171	.138
Elementary and high school books and supplies	.059	.060
Unpriced items	.013	.013
Personal and educational services	3.579	3.091
Tuition and other school fees	2.339	1.974
College tuition	1.340	.995
Elementary and high school tuition	.418	.336
Day care and nursery school	.350	.425
Tuition for technical, business, and other schools	.136	.137
Unpriced items	.094	.081
Personal expenses	1.241	1.118
Legal service fees	.457	.390
Personal financial services	.336	.276
Funeral expenses	.350	.359
Unpriced items	.098	.092

CPI Appendix 2. Relative importance of components in the Consumer Price Indexes: U.S. city average, December 1991—Continued

(Percent of all items)

Item and group	U.S. City Average	
	All Urban Consumers (CPI-U)	Urban Wage Earners and Clerical Workers (CPI-W)
Commodity and service group		
All items	100.000	100.000
Commodities	44.487	48.484
Food and beverages	17.627	19.547
Commodities less food and beverages	26.860	28.937
Nondurables less food and beverages	16.224	17.295
Apparel commodities	5.535	5.566
Nondurables less food, beverages, and apparel	10.689	11.729
Durables	10.636	11.642
Services	55.513	51.516
Rent of shelter	27.273	25.041
Rent of residential	5.835	6.678
Household services less rent of shelter	8.915	8.756
Transportation services	6.864	7.051
Medical care services	5.433	4.640
Other services	7.027	6.028
Special indexes		
All items less food	83.993	82.189
All items less shelter	72.106	74.407
All items less homeowners' costs	80.317	82.725
All items less medical care	93.311	94.326
Commodities less food	28.480	30.674
Nondurables less food	17.844	19.031
Nondurables less food and apparel	12.310	13.465
Nondurables	33.851	36.842
Services less rent of shelter	28.241	26.475
Services less medical care services	50.080	46.876
Domestically produced farm food	8.746	9.914
Selected beef cuts	.705	.869
Motor fuel, motor oil, coolant, and other products	3.365	4.146
Utilities and public transportation	8.397	8.309
Housekeeping and home maintenance services	1.595	1.237
Energy	7.361	8.217
All items less energy	92.639	91.783
All items less food and energy	76.633	73.972
Commodities less food and energy commodities	24.757	26.222
Energy commodities	3.723	4.451
Services less energy services	51.876	47.750

[1] Benefits provided by consumer-paid health insurance constitute 5.9 percent of the relative importance for the U-population and 6.3 percent for the W population.

[2] Benefits provided by consumer-paid health insurance constitute 35.1 percent of the relative importance for the U-population and 30.8 percent for the W population.

[3] Benefits provided by consumer-paid health insurance constitute 8.7 percent of the relative importance for the U-population and 8.7 percent for the W population.

[4] Benefits provided by consumer-paid health insurance constitute 0.7 percent of the relative importance for the U-population and 0.7 percent for the W population.

[5] Benefits provided by consumer-paid health insurance constitute 24.7 percent of the relative importance for the U-population and 29.3 percent for the W population.

[6] Benefits provided by consumer-paid health insurance constitute 61.0 percent of the relative importance for the U-population and 54.4 percent for the W population.

[7] Benefits provided by consumer-paid health insurance constitute 62.6 percent of the relative importance for the U-population and 62.8 percent for the W population.

[8] Benefits provided by consumer-paid health insurance constitute 57.0 percent of the relative importance for the U-population and 53.4 percent for the W population.

[9] Only health insurance premiums paid by the consumer are included in the CPI. The health insurance relative importance includes only that portion of the premium that is retained by the insurance carrier for administrative cost and profit, 9.7 percent of the total premiums for the U population and 10.6 percent for the W population. The portions that are paid as benefits have been assigned to the relevant medical care relative importances.

CPI Appendix 3. Sample areas, population weights, and pricing cycles

PSU	Sample areas and counties	Percent of index population	Pricing cycle Odd	Pricing cycle Even
	Northeast Region			
	New York-Northern New Jersey-Long Island, NY-NJ-CT, CMSA:			
109	New York City Bronx, Kings, New York, Queens, Richmond	4.115	X	X
110	New York-Connecticut Suburbs New York Portion: Nassau, Orange, Putnam, Rockland, Suffolk, Westchester Connecticut Portion: Fairfield, Litchfield (part), New Haven (part)	2.375	X	X
111	New Jersey Suburbs Bergen, Essex, Hudson, Hunterdon, Middlesex, Monmouth, Morris, Ocean, Passaic, Somerset, Sussex, Union	2.762	X	X
102	Philadelphia-Wilmington-Trenton, PA-DE-NJ-MD, CMSA Pennsylvania Portion: Bucks, Chester, Delaware, Montgomery, Philadelphia New Jersey Portion: Burlington, Camden, Cumberland, Gloucester, Mercer, Salem Delaware Portion: New Castle Maryland Portion: Cecil	2.920	X	X
103	Boston-Lawrence-Salem, MA-NH, CMSA Massachusetts Portion: Bristol (part), Essex, Middlesex (part), Norfolk (part), Plymouth (part), Suffolk, Worcester (part) New Hampshire Portion: Hillsborough (part), Rockingham (part)	2.141	X	
.04	Pittsburgh-Beaver Valley, PA, CMSA Allegheny, Beaver, Fayette, Washington, Westmoreland	1.276		X
.05	Buffalo-Niagara Falls, NY, CMSA Erie, Niagara	0.653		X
.02	Hartford-New Britain-Middletown, CT, CMSA Hartford (part), Litchfield (part) Middlesex (part), New London (part) Tolland (part)	0.991	X	
04	Syracuse, NY, Madison, Onondaga	0.767	X	
L106	Springfield, MA, MSA Hampden (part), Hampshire (part)	0.847		X
L108	Scranton--Wilkes-Barre, PA Columbia, Lackawanna, Luzerne, Wyoming	0.974		X
M102	Williamsport, PA, MSA Lycoming	0.824	X	
M104	Lancaster, PA, MSA Lancaster	0.746	X	
M106	Johnstown, PA, MSA Cambria, Somerset	0.756		X
M108	Poughkeepsie, NY, MSA Dutchess	0.771		X
R102	St. Lawrence Co, NY Urban parts of: St. Lawrence	0.545	X	
R104	Augusta, ME Urban parts of: Kennebec, Lincoln	0.535		X
	Midwest Region			
A207	Chicago-Gary-Lake County, IL-IN-WI, CMSA Illinois Portion: Cook, Du Page, Grundy, Kane, Kendall, Lake, McHenry, Will Indiana Portion: Lake, Porter Wisconsin Portion: Kenosha	4.039	X	X
A208	Detroit-Ann Arbor, MI Lapeer, Livingston, Macomb, Oakland, St. Clair, Washtenaw, Wayne	2.363		X
A209	St. Louis-East St. Louis, MO-IL, CMSA Missouri Portion: Franklin, Jefferson, St. Charles, St. Louis, St. Louis City Illinois Portion: Clinton, Jersey, Madison, Monroe, St. Clair	1.201	X	
A210	Cleveland-Akron-Lorain, OH, CMSA Cuyahoga, Geauga, Lake, Lorain, Medina, Portage, Summit	1.478	X	
A211	Minneapolis-St. Paul, MN-WI, MSA Minnesota Portion: Anoka, Carver, Chisago, Dakota, Hennepin, Isanti, Ramsey, Scott, Washington, Wright Wisconsin Portion: St. Croix	1.155	X	

CPI Appendix 3. Sample areas, population weights, and pricing cycles—Continued

PSU	Sample areas and counties	Percent of index population	Pricing cycle Odd	Pricing cycle Even
A212	Milwaukee, WI,* PMSA Milwaukee, Ozaukee, Washington, Waukesha	0.740		X
A213	Cincinnati-Hamilton, OH-KY-IN, CMSA Ohio Portion: Butler, Clermont, Hamilton, Warren Kentucky Portion: Boone, Campbell, Kenton Indiana Portion: Dearborn	0.855	X	
A214	Kansas City, MO-Kansas City, KS, CMSA Missouri Portion: Cass, Clay, Jackson, Lafayette, Platte, Ray Kansas Portion: Johnson, Leavenworth, Miami, Wyandotte	0.754		X
A215	Columbus, OH,* MSA Delaware, Fairfield, Franklin, Licking, Madison, Pickaway, Union	0.677		X
L210	Flint, MI, MSA Genesee	0.709		X
L212	Dayton-Springfield, OH, MSA Clark, Greene, Miami, Montgomery	0.871		X
L214	Youngstown-Warren, OH MSA Mahoning, Trumbull	0.769	X	
L216	Indianapolis, IN, MSA Boone, Hamilton, Hancock, Hendricks, Johnson, Marion, Morgan, Shelby	0.840	X	
M210	Steubenville-Weirton, OH-WV, MSA Ohio Portion: Jefferson West Virginia Portion: Brooke, Hancock	0.794		X
M212	Racine, WI, PMSA Racine	0.792	X	
M214	Waterloo-Cedar Falls, IA, MSA Black Hawk, Bremer	0.839		X
M216	Lawrence, KS, MSA Douglas	1.004	X	
M218	Terre Haute, IN, MSA Clay, Vigo	0.838		X
M220	Elkhart-Goshen, IN, MSA Elkhart	0.809	X	
R206	Grand Island, NE Urban parts of: Hall, Hamilton, Howard, Merrick	0.779	X	
R208	Kennett, MO Urban parts of: Dunklin, Pemiscot	0.739		X
R210	Mexico, MO Urban parts of: Audrain, Lincoln, Pike, Ralls	0.801	X	
R212	Ft. Dodge, IA Urban parts of: Calhoun, Hamilton, Webster	0.761		X
	South Region			
A315	Washington, DC-MD-VA, MSA District of Columbia Portion: Washington Maryland Portion: Calvert, Charles, Frederick, Montgomery, Prince Georges Virginia Portion: Arlington, Fairfax, Loudoun, Prince William, Stafford, Alexandria City, Fairfax City, Falls Church City, Manassas City, Manassas Park City	1.766	X	
A316	Dallas-Fort Worth, TX, CMSA Collin, Dallas, Denton, Ellis, Johnson, Kaufman, Parker, Rockwall, Tarrant,	1.556		X
A317	Baltimore, MD, MSA Anne Arundel, Baltimore, Carroll, Harford, Howard, Queen Annes, Baltimore City	1.124	X	
A318	Houston-Galveston-Brazoria, TX, CMSA Brazoria, Fort Bend, Galveston, Harris, Liberty, Montgomery, Waller	1.621		X
A319	Atlanta, GA, MSA Barrow, Butts, Cherokee, Clayton, Cobb, Coweta, De Kalb, Douglas, Fayette, Forsyth, Fulton, Gwinnett, Henry, Newton, Paulding, Rockdale, Spalding, Walton	1.118		X
A320	Miami-Fort Lauderdale, FL, CMSA Broward, Dade	1.526	X	
A321	Tampa-St. Petersburg-Clearwater, FL, MSA Hernando, Hillsborough, Pasco, Pinellas	0.953		X

*See footnote at end of table.

SU	Sample areas and counties	Percent of index population	Pricing cycle Odd	Even
322	New Orleans, LA, MSA Jefferson, Orleans, St. Bernard, St. Charles, St. John the Baptist, St. Tammany	0.639	X	
318	Richmond, VA Charles City, Chesterfield, Goochland, Hanover, Henrico, New Kent, Powhatan, Richmond City	0.792		X
320	Jacksonville, FL, MSA Clay, Duval, Nassau, St. Johns	0.812		X
322	Charlotte-Gastonia-Rock Hill, NC-SC, MSA North Carolina Portion: Cabarrus, Gaston, Lincoln, Mecklenburg, Rowan, Union South Carolina Portion: York	0.800	X	
324	Tulsa, OK, MSA Creek, Osage, Rogers, Tulsa, Wagoner	0.836	X	
326	Raleigh-Durham, NC, MSA Durham, Franklin, Orange, Wake	0.897		X
328	Norfolk-VA Beach-Newport News, VA, MSA Gloucester, James City, York, Chesapeake City, Hampton City, Newport News City, Norfolk City, Poquoson City, Portsmouth City, Suffolk City, Virginia Beach City, Williamsburg	0.761		X
330	Nashville, TN, MSA Cheatham, Davidson, Dickson, Robertson, Rutherford, Sumner, Williamson, Wilson	0.909	X	
332	El Paso, TX, MSA El Paso	0.664	X	
334	Birmingham, AL, MSA Blount, Jefferson, St. Clair, Shelby, Walker	0.747	X	
336	Orlando, FL, MSA Orange, Osceola, Seminole	0.720		X
322	Corpus Christi, TX, MSA Nueces, San Patricio	0.817	X	
324	Pine Bluff, AR, MSA Jefferson	0.774		X
326	Fort Smith, AR Crawford, Sebastian	0.811	X	
328	Brownsville-Harlingen, TX, MSA Cameron	0.612	X	

PSU	Sample areas and counties	Percent of index population	Pricing cycle Odd	Even
M330	Albany, GA, MSA Dougherty, Lee	0.793		X
M332	Florence, SC, MSA Florence	0.826		X
M334	Gainesville, FL, MSA Alachua, Bradford	0.785	X	
M336	Huntsville, AL, MSA Madison	0.788		X
M338	Beaumont-Port Arthur, TX, MSA Hardin, Jefferson, Orange	0.778		X
M340	Ocala, FL, MSA Marion	0.897	X	
R314	Cleveland, TN* Urban parts of: Bradley, Polk		0.654	
R316	Hammond, LA* Urban parts of: East Feliciana, St. Helena, Tangipahoa	0.693	X	
R318	Raeford, NC* Urban parts of: Hoke, Scotland	0.680	X	
R320	Pontotoc, MS Urban parts of: Benton, Pontotoc, Tippah, Union	0.688	X	
R322	Halifax, NC Urban parts of: Halifax	0.627		X
R324	Central KY* Urban parts of: Breathitt, Estill, Garrard, Jackson, Lee, Madison, Montgomery, Owsley, Powell, Rockcastle	0.631		X
	West Region			
	Los Angeles-Anaheim-Riverside, CA, CMSA:			
A419	Los Angeles City Los Angeles	4.189	X	X
A420	Greater Los Angeles Orange, Riverside, San Bernardino, Ventura	2.102	X	X
A422	San Francisco-Oakland-San Jose, CA, CMSA Alameda, Contra Costa, Marin, Napa, San Francisco, San Mateo, Santa Clara, Santa Cruz, Solano, Sonoma	3.156	X	X
A423	Seattle-Tacoma, WA, CMSA King, Pierce, Snohomish	1.193		X
A424	San Diego, CA, MSA San Diego	0.987	X	

CPI Appendix 3. Sample areas, population weights, and pricing cycles—Continued

PSU	Sample areas and counties	Percent of index population	Pricing cycle Odd	Pricing cycle Even
A425	Portland-Vancouver, OR-WA,* CMSA Oregon Portion: Clackamas, Multnomah, Washington, Yamhill Washington Portion: Clark	0.744	X	
A426	Honolulu, HI, MSA Honolulu	0.320		X
A427	Anchorage, AK, MSA Anchorage Borough	0.086		X
A429	Phoenix, AZ,* MSA Maricopa	0.816	X	
A433	Denver-Boulder, CO, CMSA Adams, Arapahoe, Boulder, Denver, Douglas, Jefferson	0.929		X
L438	Sacramento, CA,* MSA El Dorado, Placer, Sacramento, Yolo	0.814	X	
L440	Salt Lake City-Ogden, UT,* MSA Davis, Salt Lake, Weber	0.619		X
L442	Tucson, AZ,* MSA Pima	0.521	X	
L444	Fresno, CA,* MSA Fresno	0.513		X
M442	Redding, CA, MSA Shasta	0.642	X	
M444	Colorado Springs, CO, MSA El Paso	0.581	X	
M446	Yakima, WA, MSA Yakima	0.654		X
M448	Provo-Orem, UT, MSA Utah	0.647		X
R426	Alamogordo, NM Urban parts of: Otero	0.892		X
R428	Yuma, AZ Urban parts of: Yuma, La Paz	0.893	X	

*See footnote below.

* Due to budgetary constraints, 6 PSUs in the original 1987 CPI design were deleted from pricing in 1988. The 6 PSUs listed below were dropped, and the population represented was shifted to the paired PSU indicated.

Dropped PSU	Paired PSU	New population Percent
A215	A212	1.417
R318	R316	1.393
R324	R314	1.285
A429	A425	1.560
L438	L442	1.335
L440	L444	1.132

CPI Appendix 4. Expenditure classes, item strata, and entry level items

EC 01 Cereals and cereal products
0101 Flour and prepared flour mixes
01011 Flour

01012 Prepared flour mixes

0102 Cereal
01021 Cereal

0103 Rice, pasta, and cornmeal
01031 Rice

01032 Macaroni, similar products, and cornmeal

EC 02 Bakery products
0201 White bread
02011 White bread

0202 Other breads, rolls, biscuits, and muffins
02021 Bread other than white

02022 Rolls, biscuits, muffins (excluding frozen)

0204 Cakes, cupcakes, and cookies
02041 Cakes and cupcakes (excluding frozen)

02042 Cookies

0206 Other bakery products
02061 Crackers

02062 Bread and cracker products

02063 Sweetrolls, coffee cake, and doughnuts (excluding frozen)

02064 Frozen bakery products and frozen/refrigerated doughs and batters

02065 Pies, tarts, turnovers (excluding frozen)

EC 03 Beef and veal
0301 Ground beef
03011 Ground beef

0302 Chuck roast
03021 Chuck roast

0303 Round roast
03031 Round roast

0304 Other steak, roast, and other beef
03041 Other roasts (excluding chuck and round)

03042 Other steak (excluding round and sirloin)

03043 Other beef

0305 Round steak
03051 Round steak

0306 Sirloin steak
03061 Sirloin steak

EC 04 Pork
0401 Bacon
04011 Bacon

0402 Pork chops
04021 Pork chops

0403 Ham
04031 Ham (excluding canned)

04032 Canned ham

0404 Other pork, including sausage
04041 Pork roasts, picnics, other pork

04042 Pork sausage

EC 05 Other meats
0501 Lunchmeat, lamb, organ meats, and game

05011 Frankfurters

05012 Bologna, liverwurst, salami

05013 Other lunchmeats (excluding bologna, liverwurst, salami)

05014 Lamb, organ meats, and game

EC 06 Poultry
0601 Fresh whole chicken
06011 Fresh whole chicken

0602 Fresh or frozen chicken parts
06021 Fresh or frozen chicken parts

0603 Other poultry
06031 Other poultry

EC 07 Fish and seafood
0701 Canned fish and seafood
07011 Canned fish or seafood

0702 Fresh or frozen fish and seafood
07021 Shellfish (excluding canned)

07022 Fish (excluding canned)

EC 08 Eggs
0801 Eggs
08011 Eggs

EC 09 Fresh milk and cream
0901 Fresh whole milk
09011 Fresh whole milk

0902 Other fresh milk and cream
09021 Other fresh milk and cream

EC 10 Processed dairy products
1001 Butter and other dairy products (excluding cheese, ice cream)
10011 Butter

10012 Other dairy products

1002 Cheese
10021 Cheese

1004 Ice cream and related products
10041 Ice cream and related products

EC 11 Fresh fruits
1101 Apples
11011 Apples

1102 Bananas
11021 Bananas

1103 Oranges
11031 Oranges

1104 Other fresh fruits
11041 Other fresh fruits

EC 12 Fresh vegetables
1201 Potatoes
12011 Potatoes

1202 Lettuce
12021 Lettuce

1203 Tomatoes
12031 Tomatoes

1204 Other fresh vegetables
12041 Other fresh vegetables

EC 13 Processed fruits
1301 Fruit juices and frozen fruits
13011 Frozen orange juice

13012 Other frozen fruits and fruit juices

13013 Fresh, canned/or bottled fruit juices

1303 Canned and dried fruits
13031 Canned and dried fruits

EC 14 Processed vegetables
1401 Frozen vegetables
14011 Frozen vegetables

1402 Canned and other processed vegetables
14021 Canned beans other than lima beans

14022 Canned cut corn

14023 Other processed vegetables

EC 15 Sugar and sweets
1501 Candy and other sweets
15011 Candy and chewing gum

15012 Other sweets (excluding candy and gum)

1502 Sugar and artificial sweeteners
15021 Sugar and artificial sweeteners

EC 16 Fats and oils
1601 Fats and oils
16011 Margarine

16012 Other fats and oils

16013 Nondairy cream substitutes

16014 Peanut butter

EC 17 Nonalcoholic beverages
1701 Carbonated drinks
17011 Cola drinks

17012 Carbonated drinks other than cola

1703 Coffee
17031 Roasted coffee

17032 Instant and freeze dried coffee

1705 Other noncarbonated drinks
17051 Noncarbonated fruit-flavored drinks

17052 Tea

17053 Other noncarbonated drinks

EC 18 Other prepared foods
1801 Canned and packaged soup
18011 Canned and packaged soup

1802 Frozen prepared foods
18021 Frozen prepared meals

18022 Frozen prepared foods other than meals

1803 Snacks
18031 Potato chips and other snacks

18032 Nuts

1804 Spices, seasonings, condiments, sauces
18041 Salt and other seasonings and spices

18042 Olives, pickles, relishes

18043 Sauces and gravies

18044 Other condiments (excluding olives, pickles, relishes)

1806 Other prepared food
18061 Canned or packaged salads and desserts

18062 Baby food

18063 Other canned or packaged prepared foods

EC 19 Food away from home
1901 Lunch
19011 Lunch

1902 Dinner
19021 Dinner

1903 Other meals and snacks
19031 Snacks and nonalcoholic beverages
19032 Breakfast or brunch

1909 Unpriced board and catered affairs
19090 Unpriced items

EC 20 Alcoholic beverages
2001 Beer, ale, and other alcoholic malt beverages at home
20011 Beer, ale, and other alcoholic malt beverages at home

2002 Distilled spirits at home
20021 Whiskey at home

20022 Distilled spirits at home (excluding whiskey)

2003 Wine at home
20031 Wine at home

2005 Alcoholic beverages away from home
20051 Beer, ale, and other alcoholic malt beverages away from home

20052 Wine away from home

20053 Distilled spirits away from home

EC 21 Pure rent-renter occupied
2101 Rent of dwelling
21011 Rent of dwelling

2102 Lodging while out of town
21021 Lodging while out of town

2103 Lodging while at school
21031 Housing at school, excluding board

EC 22 Rental equivalence and household insurance
2201 Owners' equivalent rent
22011 Owners' equivalent rent

2202 Household insurance
22021 Household insurance

EC 23 Maintenance and repair services
2301 Property maintenance and repair services
23011 Inside home maintenance and repair services

23012 Repair/replacement of hard surface flooring

23013 Replacement of installed wall-to-wall carpet

23014 Repair of disposal, built-in dishwasher, range hood

EC 24 Maintenance and repair commodities
2401 Materials, supplies, equipment for home repairs
24011 Paint, wallpaper and supplies

24012 Tools and equipment for painting

24013 Lumber, paneling, wall and ceiling tile; awnings, glass

24014 Blacktop and masonry materials

24015 Plumbing supplies and equipment

24016 Electrical supplies, heating and cooling equipment

2404 Other property maintenance commodities
24041 Miscellaneous supplies and equipment

24042 Hard surface floor covering

24043 Landscaping items

EC 25 Fuel oil and other fuels
2501 Fuel oil
25011 Fuel oil

2502 Other fuels
25021 Bottled or tank gas

25022 Coal

25023 Other fuels

EC 26 Gas (piped) and electricity
2601 Electricity
26011 Electricity

2602 Utility natural gas service
26021 Utility natural gas service

EC 27 Other utilities and public services
2701 Telephone services, local charges
27011 Telephone services, local charges

2702 Water and sewerage maintenance
27021 Residential water and sewer service

2703 Community antenna and cable television
27031 Community antenna or cable TV

2704 Garbage and trash collection
27041 Garbage and trash collection

2705 Interstate telephone services
27051 Interstate telephone services

2706 Intrastate telephone services
27061 Intrastate telephone services

EC 28 Textile housefurnishings
2801 Linens, curtains, drapes, sewing materials
28011 Bathroom linens

28012 Bedroom linens

28013 Kitchen and dining room linens

28014 Curtains and drapes

28015 Slipcovers and decorative pillows

28016 Sewing materials for household items

EC 29 Furniture and bedding
2901 Bedroom furniture
29011 Mattress and springs

29012 Bedroom furniture other than mattress/and springs

2902 Sofas
29021 Sofas

2903 Living room chairs and tables
29031 Living room chairs

29032 Living room tables

2904 Other furniture
29041 Kitchen and dining room furniture

29042 Infants' furniture

29043 Outdoor furniture

29044 Occasional furniture

EC 30 Household appliances
3001 Refrigerators and home freezers
30011 Refrigerators and home freezers

3002 Laundry equipment
30021 Washers

30022 Dryers

3003 Stoves, ovens, portable dishwashers, window air-conditioners

30031 Stoves and ovens (excluding microwave ovens)

30032 Microwave ovens

30033 Portable dishwashers

30034 Window air-conditioners

EC 31 Television and sound equipment
3101 Television sets
31011 Television sets

3102 Video cassette recorders, disc players, and tapes
31021 Video cassette recorders, disc players, cameras, and accessories

31022 Video cassettes and discs, blank and prerecorded

31023 Video game hardware, software and accessories

3103 Audio components, radios, recordings, and other audio equipment
31031 Radios, phonographs, and tape recorders/players

31032 Components and other sound equipment

31033 Records and tapes, prerecorded and blank

3109 Unpriced accessories for electronic equipment
31090 Unpriced items

EC 32 Other household equipment and furnishings
3201 Floor/window coverings, outdoor/infant/laundry/cleaning equipment
32011 Floor coverings

32012 Window coverings

32013 Infants' equipment

32014 Laundry and cleaning equipment

32015 Outdoor equipment

3202 Clocks, lamps, and decorator items
32021 Clocks

32022 Lamps and lighting fixtures

32023 Household decorative items

3203 Tableware, serving pieces, nonelectric kitchenware
32031 Plastic dinnerware

32032 China and other dinnerware

32033 Flatware

32034 Glassware

32035 Silver serving pieces

32036 Serving pieces other than silver or glass

32037 Nonelectric cookingware

32038 Tableware and nonelectric kitchenware

3204 Lawn and garden equipment, tools, hardware
32041 Lawn and garden equipment

32042 Power tools

32043 Other hardware

32044 Nonpowered handtools

3205 Small kitchen appliances, sewing machines, portable heating/cooling equipment
32051 Floor cleaning equipment and sewing machines

32052 Portable heating/cooling equipment, small electric kitchen appliances

3206 Indoor plants and fresh cut flowers
32061 Indoor plants and fresh cut flowers

3209 Unpriced household equipment parts, small furnishings
32090 Unpriced items

EC 33 Housekeeping supplies
3301 Laundry and cleaning products
33011 Soaps and detergents

33012 Other laundry and cleaning products

3303 Household paper products, including stationery
33031 Cleansing and toilet tissue, paper towels, napkins

33032 Stationery, stationery supplies, gift wrap

3305 Other household products, lawn and garden supplies
33051 Miscellaneous household products

33052 Lawn and garden supplies

EC 34 Housekeeping services
3401 Postage
34011 Postage

3402 Babysitting
34021 Babysitting services

3403 Domestic service
34031 Domestic services

3404 Other household services
34041 Gardening and lawncare services

34042 Water softening service

34043 Moving, storage, freight expense

34044 Household laundry and drycleaning, excluding coin operated

34045 Coin-operated household laundry and drycleaning

3406 Appliance and furniture repair
34061 Repair of television, radio, and sound equipment

34062 Repair of household appliances

34063 Reupholstery of furniture

3407 Care of invalids, elderly, and convalescents in the home
34071 Care of invalids, elderly, and convalescents in the home

3409 Unpriced rent/repair of household equipment, sound equipment
34090 Unpriced items

34091 Unpriced items

EC 35 Tenants' insurance
3501 Tenants' insurance
35011 Tenants' insurance

EC 36 Men's apparel

3601 Men's suits, coats, sportcoats, jackets
36011 Men's suits

36012 Men's sport coats and tailored jackets

36013 Men's coats and jackets

3603 Men's furnishings
36031 Men's underwear and hosiery

36032 Men's nightwear

36033 Men's accessories

36034 Men's sweaters

36035 Men's active sportswear

3604 Men's shirts
36041 Men's shirts

3605 Men's pants and shorts
36051 Men's pants and shorts

3609 Unpriced men's uniforms and other clothing
36090 Unpriced items

EC 37 Boys' apparel
3701 Boys' apparel
37011 Boys' coats and jackets

37012 Boys' sweaters

37013 Boys' shirts

37014 Boys' underwear, nightwear, and hosiery

37015 Boys' accessories

37016 Boys' suits, sport coats, and pants

37017 Boys' active sportswear

3709 Unpriced boys' uniforms and other clothing
37090 Unpriced items

EC 38 Women's apparel
3801 Women's coats and jackets
38011 Women's coats and jackets

3802 Women's dresses
38021 Women's dresses

3803 Women's separates, sportswear
38031 Women's tops

38032 Women's skirts

38033 Women's pants and shorts

38034 Women's active sportswear

3804 Women's underwear, nightwear, accessories
38041 Women's nightwear

38042 Women's underwear

38043 Women's hosiery

38044 Women's accessories

3805 Women's suits
38051 Women's suits

3809 Unpriced women's uniforms and other clothing
38090 Unpriced items

EC 39 Girls' apparel
3901 Girls' apparel
39011 Girls' coats and jackets

39012 Girls' dresses and suits

39013 Girls' tops

39014 Girls' skirts and pants

39015 Girls' active sportswear

39016 Girls' underwear and nightwear

39017 Girls' hosiery and accessories

3909 Unpriced girls' uniforms and other clothing
39090 Unpriced items

EC 40 Footwear
4001 Men's footwear
40011 Men's footwear

4002 Boys' and girls' footwear
40021 Boys' footwear

40022 Girls' footwear

4003 Women's footwear
40031 Women's footwear

EC 41 Infants' and toddlers' apparel
4101 Infants' and toddlers' apparel
41011 Infants' and toddlers' outerwear

41012 Infants' and toddlers' play and dresswear

41013 Infants' and toddlers' underwear

41014 Infants' and toddlers' sleepwear

4109 Unpriced infants' accessories and other clothing
41090 Unpriced items

EC 42 Sewing materials and luggage
4201 Sewing materials, notions, luggage
42011 Fabric for making clothes

42012 Sewing notions and patterns

42013 Luggage

EC 43 Jewelry
4301 Watches
43011 Watches

4302 Jewelry
43021 Jewelry

EC 44 Apparel services
4401 Other apparel services
44011 Shoe repair and other shoe services

44012 Coin-operated apparel laundry and drycleaning

44013 Alterations and repairs

44014 Clothing rental

44015 Watch and jewelry repair

4402 Apparel laundry and drycleaning, excluding coin operated
44021 Apparel laundry and drycleaning, excluding coin operated

EC 45 New vehicles
4501 New cars
45011 New cars

4502 New trucks
45021 New trucks

4503 New motorcycles
45031 New motorcycles

EC 46 Used vehicles
4601 Used cars
46011 Used cars

4609 Unpriced other used motor vehicles
46090 Unpriced items

EC 47 Motor fuel, motor oil, coolant, and fluids
4701 Motor fuel
47011 Motor fuels

4702 Motor oil, coolant, and other fluids

47021 Motor oil

47022 Coolant, brake fluid, transmission fluid, additives

EC 48 Automobile parts and equipment
4801 Tires
48011 Tires

4802 Vehicle parts and equipment other than tires
48021 Vehicle parts and equipment other than tires

EC 49 Automobile maintenance and repair
4901 Automotive body work
49011 Automotive body work

4902 Automotive drive-train, front end repair
49021 Automotive drive-train repair

49022 Automotive brake work

49023 Repair to steering, front end, cooling system, and air-conditioning

4903 Automotive maintenance and servicing
49031 Automotive maintenance and servicing

4904 Automotive power plant repair
49041 Automotive power plant repair

4909 Unpriced automotive repair service policy
49090 Unpriced items

EC 50 Automobile insurance
5001 Automobile insurance
50011 Automobile insurance

EC 51 Vehicle finance charges
5101 Automobile finance charges
51011 Automobile finance charges

5109 Unpriced other vehicle finance charges
51090 Unpriced items

EC 52 Vehicle rental, registration, and inspection
5201 State and local automobile registration, license, inspection
52011 State automobile registration

52012 Local automobile registration

52013 Driver's license

52014 Vehicle inspection

5205 Other automobile-related fees
52051 Automobile rental

52052 Truck rental

52053 Parking fees

52054 Vehicle tolls

52055 Automobile towing charges

52056 Other vehicle rentals

5209 Unpriced docking and landing fees
52090 Unpriced items

EC 53 Public transportation
5301 Airline fare
53011 Airline fare

5302 Other intercity transportation
53021 Intercity bus fare

53022 Intercity train fare

53023 Ship fares

5303 Intracity transportation
53031 Intracity mass transit

53032 Taxi fare

53033 Car and van pools

5309 Unpriced school bus
53090 Unpriced items

EC 54 Prescription drugs and medical supplies
5401 Prescription drugs and medical supplies
54011 Prescription drugs and medical supplies

EC 55 Nonprescription drugs and medical supplies
5502 Internal and respiratory over-the-counter drugs
55021 Internal and respiratory over-the-counter drugs

5503 Nonprescription medical equipment and supplies
55031 Topicals and dressings

55032 Medical equipment for general use

55033 Supportive and convalescent medical equipment

55034 Hearing aids

5509 Unpriced drugs
55090 Unpriced items

EC 56 Professional services
5601 Physicians' services
56011 Physicians' services

5602 Dental services
56021 Dental services

5603 Eyeglasses and eye care
56031 Eyeglasses and eye care

5604 Services by other medical professionals
56041 Services by other medical professionals

EC 57 Hospital and other medical care services
5701 Hospital room, in-patient
57011 Hospital room, in-patient

5702 Other in-patient services
57021 Hospital in-patient services other than room

57022 Nursing and convalescent home care

5703 Hospital out-patient services
57031 Hospital out-patient services

5709 Unpriced rent or repair of medical equipment
57090 Unpriced items

EC 58 Health insurance
5811 Commercial health insurance retained earnings-prescription drugs
58111 Commercial health insurance retained earnings-prescription drugs

5812 Commercial health insurance retained earnings-physicians' services
58121 Commercial health insurance retained earnings-physicians' services

5813 Commercial health insurance retained earnings-dental services
58131 Commercial health insurance retained earnings-dental services

5814 Commercial health insurance retained earnings-eye care services
58141 Commercial health insurance retained earnings-eye care services

5815 Commercial health insurance retained earnings-other professional services
58151 Commercial health insurance retained earnings-other professional services

5816 Commercial health insurance retained earnings-hospital room
58161 Commercial health insurance retained earnings-hospital room

5817 Commercial health insurance retained earnings-other in-patient hospital services
58171 Commercial health insurance retained earnings-other in-patient hospital services

5818 Commercial health insurance retained earnings-out-patient hosp services
58181 Commercial health insurance retained earnings-out-patient hosp services

58211 Blue Cross/Blue Shield retained earnings-prescription drugs

5822Blue Cross/Blue Shield retained earnings-physicians' services
58221 Blue Cross/Blue Shield retained earnings-physicians' services

5823 Blue Cross/Blue Shield retained earnings-dental services
58231 Blue Cross/Blue Shield retained earnings-dental services

5824 Blue Cross/Blue Shield retained earnings-eye care services
58241 Blue Cross/Blue Shield retained earnings-eye care services

5825 Blue Cross/Blue Shield retained earnings-other professionals' services
58251 Blue Cross/Blue Shield retained earnings-other professionals' services

5826 Blue Cross/Blue Shield retained earnings-hospital room
58261 Blue Cross/Blue Shield retained earnings-hospital room

5827 Blue Cross/Blue Shield retained earnings-other in-patient hospital services
58271 Blue Cross/Blue Shield retained earnings-other in-patient hospital services

5828 Blue Cross/Blue Shield retained earnings-out-patient hospital services
58281 Blue Cross/Blue Shield retained earnings-out-patient hospital services

5831HMO retained earnings-prescription drugs
583117 HMO retained earnings-prescription drugs

5832 HMO retained earnings-physicians' services
58321 HMO retained earnings-physicians' services

5833 HMO retained earnings-dental services
58331 HMO retained earnings-dental services

5834 HMO retained earnings-eyecare services
58341 HMO retained earnings-eyecare services

5835 HMO retained earnings-other professionals' services
58351 HMO retained earnings-other professionals' services

5836 HMO retained earnings-hospital room
58361 HMO retained earnings-hospital room

5837 HMO retained earnings-other in-patient hospital services
58371 HMO retained earnings-other in-patient hospital services

5838 HMO retained earnings-out-patient hospital services
58381 HMO retained earnings-out-patient hospital services

5841 Other health insurance retained earnings-prescription drugs
58411 Other health insurance retained earnings-prescription drugs

5842 Other health insurance retained earnings-physicians' services
58421 Other health insurance retained earnings-physicians' services

5843 Other health insurance retained earnings-dental services
58431 Other health insurance retained earnings-dental services

5844 Other health insurance retained earnings-eyecare services
58441 Other health insurance retained earnings-eyecare services

5845 Other health insurance retained earnings-other professionals' services
58451 Other health insurance retained earnings-other professionals' services

5846 Other health insurance retained earnings-hospital room
58461 Other health insurance retained earnings-hospital room

5847 Other health insurance retained earnings-other in-patient hospital services
58471 Other health insurance retained earnings-other in-patient hospital services

5848 Other health insurance retained earnings-out-patient hospital services
58481 Other health insurance retained earnings-out-patient hospital services

EC 59 Reading materials
5901 Newspapers
59011 Newspapers

5902 Magazines, periodicals, and books
59021 Magazines

59022 Books purchased through book clubs

59023 Books not purchased through book clubs

5909 Unpriced newsletters
59090 Unpriced items

EC 60 Sporting goods and equipment
6001 Sports vehicles, including bicycles
60011 Outboard motors and powered sports vehicles

60012 Unpowered boats and trailers

60013 Bicycles

6002 Sports equipment
60021 Indoor, warm weather, and winter sports equipment

60022 Hunting, fishing, and camping equipment

EC 61 Toys, hobbies, and other entertainment commodities
6101 Toys, hobbles, and music equipment
61011 Toys, games, and hobbies

61012 Playground equipment

61013 Music instruments and accessories

6102 Photographic supplies and equipment
61021 Film

61022 Photographic and darkroom supplies

61023 Photographic equipment

6103 Pets and pet products
61031 Pet food

61032 Purchase of pets, pet supplies, accessories

6109 Unpriced souvenirs, fireworks, optic goods
61090 Unpriced items

EC 62 Entertainment services
6201 Club membership dues and fees
62011 Club membership dues and fees

6202 Fees for participant sports
62021 Fees for participant sports

6203 Admissions
62031 Admission to movies, theaters, and concerts

62032 Admission to sporting events

6204 Fees for lessons or instructions
62041 Fees for lessons or instructions

6205 Photographers, film processing, pet services
62051 Photographer fees

62052 Film processing

62053 Pet services

62054 Veterinarian services

62055 Other entertainment services

6209 Unpriced rental of recreational vehicles
62090 Unpriced items

EC 63 Tobacco products
6301 Tobacco and smoking supplies
63011 Cigarettes

63012 Tobacco products other than cigarettes

63013 Smoking accessories

6309 Unpriced smoking products
63090 Unpriced items

EC 64 Toilet goods and personal care appliances
6401 Hair, dental, shaving, miscellaneous personal care products
64011 Products for the hair

64012 Nonelectric articles for the hair

64013 Woman's hair pieces and wigs

64014 Dental products, nonelectric dental articles

64015 Shaving products, nonelectric shaving articles

64016 Deodorant/suntan preparations, sanitary/footcare products

64017 Electric personal care appliances

6403 Cosmetics/bath/nail preparations and implements
64031 Cosmetics, bath/nail/make-up preparations and implements

EC 65 Personal care services
6501 Beauty parlor services for females
65011 Beauty parlor services for females

6502 Haircuts and other barber shop services for males

65021 Haircuts and other barber shop services for males

6509 Unpriced repair of personal care appliances
65090 Unpriced items

EC 66 School books and supplies
6601 School books and supplies for college
66011 College textbooks

6602 Reference books and elementary and high school books
66021 Elementary and high school books and supplies

66022 Encyclopedias and other sets of reference books

6609 Unpriced miscellaneous school purchases
66090 Unpriced items

EC 67 Daycare, tuition, and other school fees
6701 College tuition and fees
67011 College tuition and fixed fees

6702 Elementary and high school tuition and fees
67021 Elementary and high school tuition and fixed fees

6703 Child daycare, nursery school
67031 Daycare and nursery school

6704 Other tuition and fees
67041 Technical and business school tuition and fixed fees

6709 Unpriced miscellaneous school items, rentals and other services
67090 Unpriced items

EC 68 Legal, financial, and funeral services
6801 Legal fees
68011 Legal fees

6802 Banking and accounting expenses
68021 Safe deposit box rental

68022 Checking accounts and special check services

68023 Tax return preparation and other accounting fees

6803 Cemetery lots and funeral expenses
68031 Funeral expenses

68032 Cemetery lots and crypts

6809 Unpriced miscellaneous personal services
68090 Unpriced items

EC 69 Information processing equipment
6901 Information processing equipment
69011 Personal computers and peripheral equipment

69012 Computer software and accessories

69013 Telephone, peripheral equipment, and accessories

69014 Calculators, adding machines, and typewriters

69015 Other information processing equipment

EC 72 Utility average prices
7260 Utility natural gas, 40 therms
72601 Utility natural gas, 40 therms

7261 Utility natural gas, 100 therms
72611 Utility natural gas, 100 therms

7262 Electricity, 500 kilowatt hours
72621 Electricity, 500 kilowatt hours

CPI Appendix 5. Sample Allocation Methodology for Commodities and Services

Introduction

The objective of the item-outlet sample design for the commodities and services component of the CPI revision was to determine the sample resource allocation by PSU, replicate, item stratum, and POPS category which would minimize the sampling variance of price change from the CPI at the U.S. level, while at the same time meeting certain budgetary constraints on total expenditures and total travel expenditures. To meet this objective, models were developed to express the CPI survey sampling variance and operational costs in terms of sample design variables. Nonlinear programming methods were then used to solve for design variables which minimized total price change sampling variance while meeting bugetary constraints.

Certain simplifying assumptions were made to render this problem manageable. First, all item strata were divided into eight major groups.

Food and beverages	Fuel and utilities
Household furnishings	Apparel and upkeep
Transportation	Medical care
Entertainment	Other commodities and services

Second, all sample PSU's were divided into 10 groups. Further, it was decided that the number of item selections in each major group would remain the same across all sample PSU's, and that the number of outlet selections per POPS category would remain the same within a PSU-major group. This reduced the design problem to one in 88 variables, $\{M_{ij}\}$ and $\{K_j\}$, i=1,...,10, j=1...,8, where M_{ij} represents the designated outlet sample size per POPS category for PSU group i and major group j, and K_j represents the designated item sample size for major group j.

Sampling variance and cost functions were developed in terms of these design variables.

The sampling variance function

The variance function for the CPI revision was modeled for index areas, i.e., geographic areas defined by PSU's or groups of PSU's. Each self-representing PSU constitutes a single index area. Non-self-representing PSU's were grouped into 12 index areas, each composed of 2 to 10 PSU's. The variance model chosen for the item-outlet redesign assumed that the total variance of price change for major commodity group j within index area k can be expressed as the sum of four components.

$$\sigma^2_{j,k} = \sigma^2_{p,j,k} + \sigma^2_{e,j,k} + \sigma^2_{o,j,k} + \sigma^2_{r,j,k}$$

where:

$\sigma^2_{p,j,k}$ is the component of variance due to the sampling of PSU's,

$\sigma^2_{e,j,k}$ is the component of variance due to the sampling of ELI's within item strata,

$\sigma^2_{o,j,k}$ is the component of variance due to the sampling of outlets, and

$\sigma^2_{r,j,k}$ is the residual component of variance.

Similarly, it was assumed that the variance of price change of a sample unit (i.e., a single price change observation or quote) within a major group j can be given by:

$$\sigma^2_{unit,j} = \sigma^2_{p,unit,j} + \sigma^2_{e,unit,j} + \sigma^2_{o,unit,j} + \sigma^2_{r,unit,j}$$

where:

$\sigma^2_{p,unit,j}$ is the component of unit variance due to the sampling of PSU's,

$\sigma^2_{e,unit,j}$ is the component of unit variance due to the sampling of ELI's within item strata,

$\sigma^2_{o,unit,j}$ is the component of unit variance due to the sampling of outlets, and

$\sigma^2_{r,unit,j}$ is the residual component of unit variance.

Under these assumptions, it follows that each component of $\sigma^2_{j,k}$ can be expressed in terms of its corresponding unit variance components:

$$\sigma^2_{p,j,k} = \sigma^2_{p,unit,j}/N'_k$$

where:

N'_k is the number of non-self-representing PSU's in the index area (Note: $\sigma^2_{p,j,k}$ is 0 for self-representing PSU's);

$$\sigma^2_{e,j,k} = (\sigma^2_{e,unit,j}/N_k \cdot H_k \cdot K_j) \cdot fpc_j \cdot NC_j$$

where:

N_k is the number of PSU's,

H_k is the number of replicates per PSU in the index area,

fpc_j $= (1-K_j/TI_j)$ is a finite population correction factor,

TI_j is the number of ELI's in the major group,

NC_j is the percent of the strata in the major group which are noncertainty strata, i.e., containing more than one ELI;

$$\sigma^2_{o,j,k} = \sigma^2_{o,unit,j}/(N_k \cdot H_k \cdot M'_{j,k} \cdot P_j)$$

where:

$M'_{j,k}$ is the number of unique inscope outlets selected per PSU-replicate per POPS category,

P_j is the number of POPS categories in the major group, and

$$\sigma^2_{r,j,k} = \sigma^2_{r,unit,j}/(N_k \cdot H_k \cdot M_{j,k} \cdot K_j \cdot P_j)$$

This gives the sampling variance of the national commodities and services index as:

$$\sigma^2_{TOTAL} = \sum_j (relimp_j)^2 \sum_k (w_k)^2 \sigma^2_{j,k}$$

where:

w_k is the population weight of index area k, and
$relimp_j$ is the relative importance of major group j.

The relative importance of an item stratum or major group was obtained from the Consumer Expenditure Survey and represents the percentage of total expenditures on all items which are expenditures on items in the stratum or major group. In this application, the relative importance data used were index area averages.

The cost function

The total annual cost of the commodities and services components of the CPI revision includes costs of initiation data collection, processing and review, personal visit and telephone pricing, and pricing processing and review. The costs of initiation of data collection, processing, and review were developed as either outlet- or quote-related costs. For PSU group i and major group j, outlet-related costs for initiation are:

$$CI_O(M_{ij}, K_j) = .2N_i \cdot H_i \cdot (C_{O,j} + C_{T,j}) \cdot (a_{ij} M_{ij}^2 + b_{ij} M_{ij} + c_{ij}) \cdot P_j$$

and quote-related costs for initiation are:

$$CI_Q(M_{ij}, K_j) = .2\, N_i \cdot H_i \cdot (C_{Q,j} + C'_{Q,j}) \cdot M_{ij} \cdot K_j \cdot NR_j$$

where:

N_i is the number of PSU's in PSU group i,
H_i is the number of replicates per PSU in PSU group i,
$C_{O,j}$ is the initiation cost per outlet for major group j,
$C_{T,j}$ is the travel cost at initiation per outlet for major group j,
$(a_{ij} M_{ij}^2 + b_{ij} M_{ij} + c_{ij})$ is a quadratic overlap function used to predict the number of unique sample outlets, accounting for the overlap of elements in the outlet sample within and between major groups for a PSU-replicate,
P_j is the number of POPS categories in major group j,
$C'_{Q,j}$ is the initiation cost per quote for major group j,
$C_{Q,j}$ is the initiation processing cost per quote for major group j,
NR_j is the outlet in-scope rate for major group j.

The 0.2 factor in the above cost formulas accounts for the rotation or reinitiation of the outlet sample in one-fifth of the sample PSU's each year. Note that the expected number of quotes per PSU-replicate-major group is estimated by the product of the number of designated outlets and the number of item strata hits, $M_{ij} \cdot K_j$.

The costs of ongoing price data collection, processing, and review were also developed as either outlet- or quote-related costs. For PSU group i and major group j, outlet-related costs for ongoing pricing are:

$$CP_O(M_{i,j}, K_j) = MB_{i,j} \cdot N_i \cdot H_i \cdot NR_j \cdot (a_{ij} M_{ij}^2 + b_{ij} M_{ij} + c_{ij}) \cdot P_j \cdot [(C_{PV,O,j} + C_{PV,T,j}) \cdot (1 - R_{T,O,j}) + C_{T,O,j} \cdot R_{T,O,j}]$$

and quote-related costs for ongoing pricing are:

$$CP_Q(M_{ij}, K_j) = MB_{ij} \cdot N_i \cdot H_i \cdot M_{ij}\, K_j \cdot [C_{PV,Q,j} \cdot (1 - R_{T,Q,j}) + C_{T,Q,j} \cdot R_{T,Q,j} + C_{P,Q}]$$

where:

$C_{PV,O,j}$ is the cost for a personal visit for pricing per outlet for major group j,
$C_{PV,T,j}$ is the travel cost for a personal visit for pricing per outlet for major group j,
$R_{T,O,j}$ is the proportion of outlets priced by telephone for major group j,
$C_{T,O,j}$ is the cost for telephone collection per outlet for major group j;
MB_{ij} is a factor to adjust for the monthly/bimonthly mix of outlets and quotes by PSU and major product group,
$C_{PV,Q,j}$ is the per quote cost for a personal visit for pricing,
$R_{T,Q,j}$ is the proportion of telephone collected quotes for major group j,
$C_{T,Q,j}$ is the per quote cost for telephone collection for major group j, and
$C_{P,Q}$ is the per quote cost for processing repricing data.

The total cost function associated with data collection and processing for the commodities and services index, summed over all major groups and PSU groups, is then given by:

$$TCOST = \sum_{ij} CI_O(M_{ij}, K_j) + CI_Q(M_{ij}, K_j) + CP_O(M_{ij}, K_j) + CP_Q(M_{ij}, K_j)$$

The total travel cost function depends only on the expected number of unique outlets in the sample and is a subtotal of the above, namely:

$$TRCOST = \sum_{ij} N_i \cdot H_i \cdot P_j \{.2C_{T,j} \cdot (a_{ij} M_{ij}^2 + b_{ij} M_{ij} + c_{ij}) + MB_{ij} \cdot NR_j \cdot (a_{ij} M_{ij}^2 + b_{ij} M_{ij} + c_{ij}) \cdot C_{PV,T,j}(1 - R_{T,O,j})\}$$

Note that the variance and total cost functions are nonlinear in the sample design variables $\{M_{ij}\}$ and $\{K_j\}$. The total travel cost function, however, is linear in the variables $\{M_{ij}\}$ and does not depend on the $\{K_j\}$.

Thus the sample design problem can be expressed as:

$$\begin{array}{lll} \text{minimize} & & \sigma^2_{TOTAL} \\ \{M_{ij}\},\{K_j\} \text{ integer} & & \\ \text{subject to} & TCOST \leq & TCLIM, \\ & TRCOST \leq & TRAVLIM, \\ & M_{ij} \geq 1, & i=1,\ldots, 10, \\ & & j=1,\ldots, 8, \\ & K_j \geq STRATA_j, & j=1,\ldots, 8, \\ & K_i \leq TI_j, & j=1,\ldots, 8. \end{array}$$

Here, TCLIM and TRAVLIM are the design parameters representing total expenditure and total travel expenditure ceilings, respectively, and $STRATA_j$ and TI_j are the design parameters denoting the number of item strata and total number of ELI's, respectively, in the jth major group.

Model coefficients

Estimates of components of the cost function were developed from agency administrative records and directly collected studies of travel time and within-outlet time. Response rates for each major group were developed from past initiation and pricing experience. Overlap functions, used to project the number of unique outlets, were developed by modeling the number of unique outlets obtained in simulations of the sampling procedures for each PSU group. Since outlet samples are selected independently for each point-of-purchase category, an individual outlet may be selected for more than one category. For example, a grocery store could be selected for both bakery products and dairy products. The number of unique outlets yielded by the sampling process is needed to project outlet-related costs.

Estimates of the components of the variance function were developed as follows. The total variance of price change for 2- and 6-month changes was computed by major group and for all items less housing using CPI data for January 1980 through December 1982. Components of the variance of price change for each major group were estimated using three-way analysis of variance methods. The total unit variance and unit components of variance were computed by multiplying the total variance and components of variance by the sample sizes employed for the respective indexes for each time period. The component unit variances and the total unit variance computed as the sum of the components were ratio-adjusted to the total unit variance computed directly from the CPI data to assure data consistency. Finally, generalized unit variance functions were developed by modeling observations of the unit variance of price change as a function of price change by major group. Estimates of the total unit variance of price change used in the solution of the sample design problem were generated from the generalized unit variance functions.

Components of unit relative variances as percentages of total unit relative variance were obtained from models of the component unit relative variances for each major group. Relative variances were computed for the PSU, outlet, and ELI components by dividing their corresponding unit variances by the squared price change. Components of relative variance were then modeled as functions of price change with the functional form:

$$Y = b1\, X^{b2}$$

where:

Y = the PSU, item, or outlet component of relative variance and

X = price change.

Percentages were then calculated by dividing the components of relative variance by their sum for each price change of interest. Final estimates of components of relative variance for a given time change and inflation rate were then obtained by multiplying modeled unit relative variances by their corresponding modeled estimates of percentage components of variance.

The solution

A sequential unconstrained minimization technique,[1] implemented in the nonlinear programming code Symbolic Factorable SUMT[2] was used to solve the design problem. Solution values of the sets $\{M_{ij}\}$ and $\{K_j\}$ were computed for various values of TCLIM and TRAVLIM and for modeled estimates of components of variance computed for various annual inflation rates and time periods. For each major group j, K_j was bounded below by the number of item strata in the major group and above by the number of ELI's in the major group. For the food and beverages group, a lower constraint of 73 item strata selections was imposed in order to support estimation of average food prices.

Unit variance and components of variance estimates used in the initial model development and design solution were for a 6-month price change at a 10-percent annual rate of inflation. Design solutions were also found using model estimates for 2-month price changes for both 8-percent and 10-percent annual rates. Only minor differences were observed between the problem solutions found with variance estimates for the 6-month price change at 8-percent and 10-percent annual rates. The problem solution found for a 6-month price change at a 10-percent annual rate of inflation was selected as the final sample design because the estimates of unit variances and components of variance for some major groups were slightly less stable at the 8-percent annual rate. Solutions using estimates for 2-month price change were not used since some major groups have little or no price change in a short period.

[1] Fiacco, A. V. and McCormick, G. P. *Nonlinear Programming: Sequential Unconstrained Minimization Techniques* (New York, Wiley, 1968).

[2] Ghaemi, A. and McCormick, G. P. "Factorable SUMT: What Is It? How is It Used?" Technical Paper Serial T-402 (Washington, DC. The George Washington University, Institute for Management Science and Engineering, 1979).

CPI Appendix 6. POPS Categories

001 Prescription drugs

54011 Prescription drugs and medical supplies

002 Over-the-counter drugs, medicines, and medical supplies

55021 Internal and respiratory over-the-counter drugs
55031 Topicals and dressings
55032 Medical equipment for general use
55033 Supportive and convalescent medical equipment
55034 Hearing aids

003 Personal care services for female

65011 Beauty parlor services for females

004 Women's hosiery

38043 Women's hosiery

005 Personal care services for males

65021 Haircuts and other barber shop services for males

006 Laundry and drycleaning, not coin operated

34044 Household laundry and drycleaning, excluding coin operated
44021 Apparel laundry and drycleaning, excluding coin operated

007 Laundry and drycleaning, self-service

34045 Coin-operated household laundry and drycleaning
44012 Coin-operated apparel laundry and drycleaning

008 Stationery, greeting cards, gift wrap, wrap accessories

33032 Stationery, stationery supplies, gift wrap

009 Admissions to movies, theaters, concerts: combined season and single (367)

62031 Admission to movies, theaters, and concerts

010 Fees for participant sports

62021 Fees for participant sports

011 Wine for home use

20031 Wine at home

012 Whiskey and other liquors for home use

20021 Whiskey at home
20022 Distilled spirits at home (excluding whiskey)

013 Beer and ale for home use

20011 Beer, ale, and other alcoholic malt beverages at home

014 Alcoholic beverages purchased in restaurants and bars

20051 Beer, ale, and other alcoholic malt beverages away from home
20052 Wine away from home
20053 Distilled spirits away from home

015 Toys, games, hobbies, tricycles, and battery-powered riders

61011 Toys, games, and hobbies

016 Eye examination, eye care, glasses, contact lenses

56031 Eyeglasses and eye care

017 Medical/surgical care by general practitioners and specialists

56011 Physicians' services

018 Women's accessories

38044 Women's accessories

019 Women's sleepwear

38041 Women's nightwear

020 Men's accessories

36033 Men's accessories

021 Men's trousers

36051 Men's pants and shorts

022 Records, tapes, needles

31033 Records and tapes, prerecorded and blank

023 Repair of TV, radio, other sound equipment

34061 Repair of television, radio, and sound equipment

024 Household linens

28011 Bathroom linens
28012 Bedroom linens
28013 Kitchen and dining room linens

025 Dinnerware, glassware, flatware, and serving pieces

32031 Plastic dinnerware
32032 China and other dinnerware
32033 Flatware
32034 Glassware
32035 Silver serving pieces
32036 Serving pieces other than silver or glass

026 Indoor/outdoor plants and garden supplies

24043 Landscaping items
32061 Indoor plants and fresh cut flowers
33052 Lawn and garden supplies

027 Men's suits

36011 Men's suits

028 Men's sportcoats and tailored jackets

36012 Men's sport coats and tailored jackets

029 Men's overcoats, topcoats, raincoats, jackets

36013 Men's coats and jackets

030 Women's suits, including pantsuits

38051 Women's suits

031 Women's dresses

38021 Women's dresses

032 Women's coats, jackets, raincoats

38011 Women's coats and jackets

034 Women's active sportswear and playwear

38034 Women's active sportswear

035 Boys' clothing and accessories

37011 Boys' coats and jackets
37012 Boys' sweaters
37013 Boys' shirts
37014 Boys' underwear, nightwear, and hosiery
37015 Boys' accessories
37016 Boys' suits, sport coats, and pants
37017 Boys' active sportswear

036 Boys' footwear

40021 Boys' footwear

037 Girls' clothing and accessories

39011 Girls' coats and jackets
39012 Girls' dresses and suits
39013 Girls' tops
39014 Girls' skirts and pants
39015 Girls' active sportswear
39016 Girls' underwear and nightwear
39017 Girls' hosiery and accessories

038 Girls' footwear

40022 Girls' footwear

039 Infants' and toddlers' clothing and accessories

41011 Infants' and toddlers' outerwear
41012 Infants' and toddlers' play and dresswear
41013 Infants' and toddlers' underwear
41014 Infants' and toddlers' sleepwear

041 Shoe repair and other shoe services

44011 Shoe repair and other shoe services

042 Repair of household appliances, except radio, TV, sound equipment

23014 Repair of disposal, built-in dishwasher, range hood
34062 Repair of household appliances

043 Major household appliances

30011 Refrigerators and home freezers
30021 Washers
30022 Dryers
30031 Stoves and ovens excluding microwave ovens
30032 Microwave ovens
30033 Portable dishwashers
30034 Window air-conditioners
32051 Floor cleaning equipment and sewing machines
69015 Other information processing equipment

044 Small electric appliances for kitchen, personal care, etc.

32052 Portable cool/heat equipment, small electric kitchen appliances
64017 Electric personal care appliances

045 Soft surface floor covering

23013 Replacement of installed wall-to-wall carpet
32011 Floor coverings

046 Window and furniture coverings, upholstery, decorative pillows

28014 Curtains and drapes
28015 Slipcovers and decorative pillows
32012 Window coverings
34063 Reupholstery of furniture

047 Automotive body repair

49011 Automotive body work

048 Inside repair, replacement, installation, and maintenance of property

23011 Inside home maintenance and repair services

049 Radios, tape recorders/players, and phonographs

31021 Video cassette recorders, disc players, cameras, and accessories
31031 Radios phonographs, and tape recorders/players
31032 Components and other sound equipment

051 Photographic equipment

61023 Photographic equipment

052 Lamps and lighting fixtures

32022 Lamps and lighting fixtures

053 Pictures, mirrors, clocks, and other home decorations

32021 Clocks
32023 Household decorative items

054 Household furniture

29011 Mattress and springs
29012 Bedroom furniture other than mattress and springs
29021 Sofas
29031 Living room chairs
29032 Living room tables
29041 Kitchen and dining room furniture
29044 Occasional furniture

055 TV and TV combinations

31011 Television sets

056 Lawn mowing and other yard equipment

32041 Lawn and garden equipment

057 Men's sweaters and vests

36034 Men's sweaters

058 Moving expenses, including freight and storage

34043 Moving, storage, freight expense

059 Hospital care

57011 Hospital room, in-patient
57021 Hospital, in-patient services other than room
57031 Hospital out-patient services

060 New cars

45011 New cars

062 Office equipment for home use such as typewriters, etc.

69014 Calculators, adding machines, and typewriters

063 Men's active sportswear and playwear

36035 Men's active sportswear

064 Power tools

32042 Power tools

065 Bicycles, bicycle parts and accessories, and bicycle repair

60013 Bicycles

066 Playground equipment

61012 Playground equipment

067 Sports equipment, including unpowered sports vehicles

60012 Unpowered boats and trailers
60021 Indoor, warm weather, and winter sports equipment
60022 Hunting, fishing, and camping equipment

068 Musical instruments and accessories, including sheet music

61013 Music instruments and accessories

069 Infants' furniture and equipment

29042 Infants' furniture
32013 Infants' equipment

070 Patio, porch, other outdoor furniture and equipment

29043 Outdoor furniture
32015 Outdoor equipment

072 Hard surface flooring and floor covering

23012 Repair/replacement of hard surface flooring
24042 Hard surface floor covering

073 Used cars

46011 Used cars

076 Nonelectric cookware, kitchen utensils, laundry and cleaning equipment, closet-storage items

32014 Laundry and cleaning equipment
32037 Nonelectric cookingware
32038 Tableware and nonelectric kitchenware

077 Automotive repair to engine and related equipment

49021 Automotive drive train repair
49041 Automotive power plant repair

078 Miscellaneous automotive repair, maintenance, servicing

49022 Automotive brake work
49023 Repair to steering, front end, cooling system, and air-conditioning
49031 Automotive maintenance and servicing
52055 Automobile towing charges

079 Automotive parts, accessories, and products, excluding tires

47021 Motor oil
47022 Coolant, brake fluid, transmission fluid, additives
48021 Vehicle parts and equipment other than tires

080 Luggage

42013 Luggage

081 Wigs and hairpieces for females

64013 Women's hair pieces and wigs

082 Fish and seafood

07011 Canned fish or seafood
07021 Shellfish (excluding canned)
07022 Fish (excluding canned)

083 Processed fruits and vegetables

13011 Frozen orange juice
13012 Other frozen fruits and fruit juices
13013 Fresh, canned, or bottled fruit juices
13031 Canned and dried fruits
14011 Frozen vegetables
14021 Canned beans other than lima beans
14022 Canned cut corn
14023 Other processed vegetables

084 Fats, oils, peanut butter, salad dressings, dairy product substitutes

16011 Margarine
16012 Other fats and oils
16013 Nondairy cream substitutes
16014 Peanut butter

085 Sugar and other sweets, for home use

15011 Candy and chewing gun
15012 Other sweets (excluding candy and gum)
15021 Sugar and artificial sweeteners

086 Coffee, tea, fruit flavored drinks, other noncarbonated beverages

17031 Roasted coffee
17032 Instant and freeze dried coffee
17051 Noncarbonated fruit flavored drinks
17052 Tea
17053 Other noncarbonated drinks

087 Apparel and accessory alteration, repair, and rental

44013 Alterations and repairs
44014 Clothing rental

088 Watches, jewelry, and repair
43011 Watches
43021 Jewelry
44015 Watch and jewelry repair

090 Tickets to sporting events: combined season and single tickets (366)

62032 Admissions to sporting events

101 Gasoline and other vehicle fuels

47011 Motor fuels

102 Tobacco products

63011 Cigarettes
63012 Tobacco products other than cigarettes

103 Personal care items

64011 Products for the hair
64012 Nonelectric articles for the hair
64014 Dental products, nonelectric dental articles
64015 Shaving products, nonelectric shaving articles
64016 Deodorant/suntan preparations, sanitary/footcare products
64031 Cosmetics, bath/nail/makeup preparations and implements

104 Cleaning and laundry products, paper supplies, other household supplies

33011 Soaps and detergents
33012 Other laundry and cleaning products
33031 Cleansing and toilet tissue, paper towels, napkins
33051 Miscellaneous household products

105 Bakery products

02011 White bread
02021 Bread other than white
02022 Rolls, biscuits, muffins (excluding frozen)
02041 Cakes and cupcakes (excluding frozen)
02042 Cookies
02061 Crackers
02062 Bread and cracker products
02063 Sweetrolls, coffee cake and doughnuts (excluding frozen)

02064 Frozen bakery products and frozen/refrigerated doughs and batters
02065 Pies, tarts, turnovers (excluding frozen)

106 Meats and poultry

03011 Ground beef
03021 Chuck roast
03031 Round roast
03041 Other roasts (excluding chuck and round)
03042 Other steak (excluding round and sirloin)
03043 Other beef
03051 Round steak
03061 Sirloin steak
04011 Bacon
04021 Pork chops
04031 Ham (excluding canned)
04032 Canned ham
04041 Pork roasts, picnics, other pork
04042 Pork sausage
05011 Frankfurters
05012 Bologna, liverwurst, salami
05013 Other lunchmeats (excluding bologna, liverwurst, salami)
05014 Lamb, organ meats, and game
06011 Fresh whole chicken
06021 Fresh or frozen chicken parts
06031 Other poultry

107 Dairy products, including eggs

08011 Eggs
09011 Fresh whole milk
09021 Other fresh milk and cream
10011 Butter
10012 Other dairy products
10021 Cheese
10041 Ice cream and related products

108 Fresh fruits and vegetables

11011 Apples
11021 Bananas
11031 Oranges
11041 Other fresh fruits
12011 Potatoes
12021 Lettuce
12031 Tomatoes
12041 Other fresh vegetables

109 Carbonated beverages for home use

17011 Cola drinks
17012 Carbonated drinks other than cola

110 Miscellaneous prepared foods, cereals, condiments, and seasonings

01011 Flour
01012 Prepared flour mixes
01021 Cereal
01031 Rice
01032 Macaroni, similar products, and cornmeal
18011 Canned and packaged soup
18021 Frozen prepared meals
18022 Frozen prepared foods other than meals
18031 Potato chips and other snacks
18032 Nuts
18041 Salt and other seasonings and spices
18042 Olives, pickles, relishes
18043 Other condiments (excluding olives, pickles, relishes)
18044 Sauces and gravies
18061 Canned or packaged salads and desserts
18062 Baby food
18063 Other canned or packaged prepared foods

111 Meals in restaurants, cafeterias, carryouts, drive-ins

19011 Lunch
19021 Dinner
19032 Breakfast or brunch

112 Snacks and beverages away from home

19031 Snacks and nonalcoholic beverages

113 Pet food.

61031 Pet food

114 Footwear for men

40011 Men's footwear

115 Shirts for men

36041 Men's shirts

117 Socks, underwear, sleepwear, and bathrobes for men

36031 Men's underwear and hosiery
36032 Men's nightwear

118 Footwear for women

40031 Women's footwear

120 Separates and coordinates for women

38031 Women's tops
38032 Women's skirts
38033 Women's pants and shorts

122 Underwear for women

38042 Women's underwear

123 Sewing materials and notions

28016 Sewing materials for household items
42011 Fabric for making clothes
42012 Sewing notions and patterns

124 Dental care

56021 Dental services

126 Film and film processing

61021 Film
62052 Film processing

127 Materials and supplies for major home repairs

24013 Lumber, paneling, wall and ceiling tile, awnings, glass
24014 Blacktop and masonry materials

128 Automobile tires

48011 Tires

129 Hardware items, handtools, and other materials for minor home repairs

24011 Paint, wallpaper and supplies
24012 Tools and equipment for painting
24015 Plumbing supplies and equipment
24016 Electrical supplies, heating and cooling equipment
24041 Miscellaneous supplies and equipment
32043 Other hardware
32044 Nonpowered handtools

131 Pet services

62053 Pet services

132 Veterinarian services

62054 Veterinarian services

133 Personal income tax preparation fees and other accounting fees

68023 Tax return preparation and other accounting fees

134 Business and technical schools

67041 Technical and business school tuition and fixed fees

137 Local telephone service

27011 Telephone services, local charges

140 Other vehicle rentals

52056 Other vehicle rentals

141 Passenger ship carriers

53023 Ship fares

142 Van and carpools used for commuting

53033 Car and van pools

144 Water softening service

34042 Water softening service

146 Elementary and high school books and supplies

66021 Elementary and high school books and supplies

301 Automobile insurance

50011 Automobile insurance

302 Pipes, lighters, lighter fuel, and other smoking accessories

63013 Smoking accessories

303 College tuition and fixed fees

67011 College tuition and fixed fees

304 Housing at school (excluding board)

21031 Housing at school (excluding board)

305 Electricity

26011 Electricity

307 Homeowners' and tenants' insurance

35011 Tenants' insurance

308 Utility natural gas service

26021 Utility natural gas service

309 Rental of miscellaneous equipment

62055 Other entertainment services

310 Fuel oil, kerosene, bottled or tank gas, coal, and wood

25011 Fuel oil
25021 Bottled or tank gas
25022 Coal
25023 Other fuels

311 Electronic equipment for nonbusiness use in the home

31023 Video game hardware, software, and accessories
69011 Personal computers and peripheral equipment
69012 Computer software and accessories

312 Telephones and accessories

69013 Telephone peripheral equipment, and accessories

313 Long-distance telephone service

27051 Interstate telephone services
27061 Intrastate telephone services

314 Finance charges for automobiles and other vehicles

51011 Automobile finance charges

315 State vehicle registration

52011 State automobile registration

316 Local automobile registration (not State)

52012 Local automobile registration

318 Driver's license

52013 Driver's license

319 Vehicle inspection

52014 Vehicle inspection

321 Automobile rental

52051 Automobile rental

322 Truck and van rental

52052 Truck rental

323 Automobile parking

52053 Parking fees

324 Vehicle tolls

52054 Vehicle tolls

326 Airline fares

53011 Airline fares

327 Intercity bus fares

53021 Intercity bus fares

328 Intracity mass transit

53031 Intracity mass transit

330 College textbooks

66011 College textbooks

331 Elementary and high school tuition and fixed fees

67021 Elementary and high school tuition and fixed fees

333 Legal services, excluding closing costs for purchase of real estate

68011 Legal fees

334 Bank services

68021 Safe deposit box rental
68022 Checking accounts and special check services

336 Funeral services

68031 Funeral expenses

337 Water and sewer maintenance

27021 Residential water and sewer service

338 Taxicabs

53032 Taxi fares

339 Community antenna and cable TV

27031 Community antenna or cable TV

341 Garbage and trash collection

27041 Garbage and trash collection

342 Lodging away from home

21021 Lodging while out of town

344 Cemetery lots and crypts

68032 Cemetery lots and crypts

346 Services by practitioners other than physicians

56041 Services by other medical professionals

347 Postage

34011 Postage

348 Babysitting services

34021 Babysitting services

349 Child daycare services and nursery school

67031 Daycare and nursery school

350 Video cassettes, tapes, and discs

31022 Video cassettes and discs, blank and prerecorded

351 Flashbulbs/cubes, darkroom supplies, and other photographic supplies

61022 Photographic and darkroom supplies

352 New motorcycles

45031 New motorcycles

354 Nursing and convalescent home care

57022 Nursing and convalescent home care

355 Books purchased through book clubs and sets of reference books

59022 Books purchased through book clubs
66022 Encyclopedias and other sets of reference books

356 Powered sports vehicles, such as boats, dunebuggies, golf carts, snowmobiles

60011 Outboard motors and powered sports vehicles

357 Purchase of pets, pet accessories, and pet supplies (excluding food)

61032 Purchase of pets, pet supplies, accessories

360 New trucks and vans

45021 New trucks

361 Newspapers: combined single copies and subscriptions (377)

59011 Newspapers

362 Magazines: combined single copies and subscriptions (378)

59021 Magazines

363 Domestic household services

34031 Domestic services
34071 Care of invalids, elderly, and convalescents in the home

364 Garden or lawn services

34041 Gardening and lawncare services

365 Membership dues and fees

62011 Club membership dues and fees

368 Lessons or instructions in golf, swimming, piano, dancing, crafts, hobbies

62041 Fees for lessons or instructions

371 Intercity train fares

53022 Intercity train fares

375 Individual books not purchased through clubs

59023 Books not purchased through book clubs

376 Photographers

62051 Photographer fees

For each non-POPS entry level item (electricity, for example), the following information is given below:

1. Source of the universe data
2. Sampling unit for outlets
3. Measure of size
4. Desired final pricing unit
5. Number of designated outlets and designated quotes.

21031 Housing while at school

1. Schools reported for college tuition in the Point-of-Purchase Survey.
2. Schools reported for college tuition by consumers in each CPI sample area.
3. Expenditures reported for college tuition.
4. Specific housing fee for the college.
5. Outlets 132; quotes 132.

26011 Electricity

1. a. Consumer Expenditure Survey (CE).
   b. Department of Energy publication: *Typical Electric Bills-January 1, 1984*.
   c. Department of Energy publication: *Financial Statistics of Selected Electric Utilities, 1982*.
   d. *American Public Power Association 1986 Directory*.
2. Electric utility companies reported in the CE survey or electric utility companies serving each of the CPI sample areas.
3. Expenditures reported for electricity in the CE survey or annual revenue from sales to residents of the respective sample areas.
4. Specific type of service for a specific number of kilowatt hours.
5. CPI: Outlets 205; quotes 1350. Average Prices: 452 additional quotes.

26021 Utility natural gas

1. a. Consumer Expenditure Survey (CE).
   b. *Brown's Directory of North American and International Gas Companies*.
2. Gas utility companies reported in the CE survey or gas companies serving each of the CPI sample areas.
3. Expenditures reported for natural gas in the CE survey or annual revenue from sales to residents of the respective sample areas.
4. Specific type of service and specific number of cubic feet or therms of gas.
5. CPI: Outlets 165; quotes 1065. Average Prices: 588 additional quotes.

27011 Local telephone charges

1. a. Consumer Expenditure Survey (CE).
   b. *Telephony's Directory and Buyers Guide*.
2. Telephone companies reported in the CE survey or companies providing service in each CPI sample area.
3. Expenditures reported for local telephone service in the CE survey or number of residential customers.
4. Specific service such as main station costs, additional message units, extension costs, etc.
5. Outlets 135; quotes 612.

34011 Postage

1. The distribution of household mail by type of postal service and postal zone as determined by the postal service in the *Household Mailstream Study, Final Report*, prepared for the US Postal Service.

2. U.S. Postal Service.

3. Postal revenue for each type of service and postal zone.

4. Specific postal service and zones traveled.

5. Outlets 1; quotes 132.

35011/50011 insurance--auto and tenants

1. Data file of insurance companies obtained from A.M. Best Data Center.

2. Insurance companies serving the states in which the CPI sample areas are located.

3. Total revenue for noncommercial policies by type of insurance.

4. Specific policy within the sample area.

5. Auto: Outlets 325; quotes 665.
   Tenants: Outlets 390; quotes 400.

46011 Used cars

1. *1985/86 Survey and analysis of Business Car Policies and Costs*, published by Rungheimer International.

2. Selection of used car prices in *The Official Used Car Trade-In Guide*, published by National Automobile Dealers Association.

3. Total sales of used cars from the business and government sectors to the consumer sector.

4. Specific used cars with specific options.

5. Outlets 340; quotes 340.

52011/52013/52014 State vehicle registration, Driver's license, and State vehicle inspection

1. *Digest of Motor Laws.*

2. State motor vehicle departments in each CPI sample area.

3. Revenue generated by each type of fee.

4. Specific class/vehicle registration, type of license, or inspection service.

5. State vehicle registration: Outlets 110; quotes 110.
   Driver's license: Outlets 20; quotes 20.
   State vehicle inspection: Outlets 12; quotes 12.

53011 Airline fares

1. Civil Aeronautics Board data file consisting of a 10-percent sample of all passenger itineraries originating in the U.S.

2. All airlines providing service from any CPI sample area.

3. Number of non-business passengers per airline, per trip itinerary, per fare class.

4. Specific trip itinerary and fare class for the selected airline.

5. Outlets 870; quotes 870.

53021 Intercity bus service

1. *Russell's Official National Motor Coach Guide.*

2. Bus companies serving each of the CPI sample areas.

3. Number of trips per week.

4. Specific trip (origin and destination) and class of service.

5. Outlets 100; quotes 160.

53022 Intercity train service

1. Data file of intercity train trips provided by Amtrak and the Alaskan Railroad.
2. Amtrak and the Alaskan Railroad.
3. Number of tickets sold.
4. Specific trip and class.
5. Outlets 2; quotes 115.

57022 Nursing and convalescent home care

1. National Center for Health Statistics data file consisting of an inventory of long term car facilities in the U.S.
2. Facilities providing nursing home care in each CPI sample area.
3. Number of beds.
4. Specific accommodations and services provided.
5. Outlets 45; quotes 115.

Chapter 20. National Longitudinal Surveys

Background

The National Longitudinal Surveys (NLS) are a set of data on the labor force experience (current labor force and employment status, work history, and characteristics of currentlast job) of five groups of the United States population. BLS contracts with the Center for Human Resource Research of The Ohio State University to manage the surveys and provide user services. The NLS was begun in the mid 1960's with the drawing of four samples: Young Men who were 14-24 years old as of January 1, 1966, Young Women who were 14-24 years old as of January 1, 1968, Older Men who were 45-59 years old as of January 1, 1966, and Mature Women who were 30-44 years old as of January 1, 1967. Each sample originally had about 5,000 individuals with overrepresentation of blacks. In the early 1980's, the Young Men and Older Men surveys were discontinued.[1] The two women's surveys continue and are currently collected on a biannual cycle.

In 1979, a new cohort was begun with a sample of over 12,000 young men and women who were 14-21 years of age as of January 1, 1979. It included oversamples of blacks, Hispanics, economically disadvantaged nonblacks/non-Hispanics, and youth in the military. The military oversample was discontinued after the 1984 survey and the economically disadvantaged nonblack/non-Hispanic oversample was discontinued in 1990. This survey is called the Youth cohort and it has been interviewed every year since it began.

Along with information of labor force experience, additional information has been gathered on a regular basis on a range of factors potentially affecting labor market behavior: Investments in education and training; geographic region of residence and local labor market conditions; the formative influence of parents; current marital status and family responsibilities; financial characteristics; work-related attitudes and aspirations; and such potentially delimiting factors as health problems and job discrimination.

[1] In 1990, the National Institute on Aging, through a contract with The Ohio State University Research Foundation, reinterviewed living members of the Older Men's cohort and widows or next-of-kin of deceased cohort members.

With the advent of the Youth cohort in the late 1970's, the content of the surveys expanded and diversified reflecting the interests of other governmental agencies in addition to the Department of Labor. Support from the Department of Defense and Armed Services made possible interviews with 1,280 youth enlisted in the military in 1979-84. In a 1980 study jointly sponsored by the Departments of Defense and Labor, the Armed Services Vocational Aptitude Battery was administered to the civilian and military youth samples. Beginning in 1979, a 5-year cooperative effort with the National Center for Research in Vocational Education was begun. This effort resulted in surveys of the high schools of the civilian youth respondent, and detailed transcript information was collected on young persons completing high school. In 1981, the National Institute of Education sponsored a set of time-use questions. Alcohol and substance abuse questions were added to the 1982-85, 1988, and 1989 Youth surveys with funding from the National Institute on Alcohol Abuse and Alcoholism and the National Institute on Drug Abuse. Also, the National Institute of Child Health and Human Development sponsored the administration of a battery of cognitive and socioemotional assessment instruments to children of female Youth respondents in 1986, 1988, and 1990, as well as the 1982-86, 1988, 1990 fertility components, and the 1982-86, and 1988 child-care components of the Youth surveys.

The primary responsibility for tasks such as sample selection, field work, and editing of data files, has resided since the project's inception within two separate organizations: The Bureau of the Census for the original cohorts and National Opinion Research Center (NORC) at the University of Chicago for the Youth cohort. The methods used by each are coordinated by BLS and the Center for Human Resource Research.

Sampling

Each of the four original NLS samples were designed to represent the civilian noninstitutionalized population of the United States at the time of the initial survey. Each age-sex cohort is represented by a multi-stage probability sample located in 235 sample areas containing 485 counties and independent cities representing every State and the District of Columbia. The samples were drawn by the Bureau of the Census from the primary sampling units (PSU's) that had been selected for the experimental Monthly Labor Survey conducted between early 1964 and 1966. A primary sample unit is composed of either a single county or group of counties (SMSA). In certain special situations, State-defined units are termed "independent cities" or "parishes." In these instances, such units are used in the definition of primary sample units. The 235 sample areas were selected by grouping all of the Nation's counties and independent cities into about 1,900 PSU's and further forming 235 strata of one or more PSU's that are relatively homogeneous according to socioeconomic characteristics. Within each of the strata, a single PSU was selected to represent the stratum. Within each PSU, a probability sample of housing units was selected to represent the civilian noninstitiutionalized population.

Since one of the survey requirements was to provide separate reliable statistics for blacks, households in predominantly black enumeration districts (ED's) were selected at a rate between 3 and 4 times that for the households in predominantly white ED's. The sample was designed to provide approximately 5,000 interviews for each of the four cohorts—about 1,500 blacks and 3,500 whites.

For the Youth cohort, the following three independent probability samples, which were designed to represent the entire population of youth born in the United States between 1957 and 1964, were drawn: (1) A cross-sectional sample designed to be representative of the noninstitutionalized civilian segment of American young people aged 14-21 as of January 1, 1979; (2) a supplemental sample designed to overrepresent civilian Hispanic, black, and economically disadvantaged non-Hispanic, nonblack youth; and (3) a military sample designed to represent the population aged 17-21 as of January 1, 1979 and serving in the military as of September 30, 1978.

All sample selection was done through a multi-stage stratified area probability sample of dwelling units and group quarter units, except for individuals on active military duty. A screening interview was administered in approximately 75,000 dwellings and group quarters distributed among 1,818 sample segments in 202 PSU's (inclusive of most of the 50 States and the District of Columbia). Included in this screening interview was information which would allow the identification of persons for sample membership.

Members on active military duty as of September 30, 1978, were sampled from rosters provided by the Department of Defense. Sample selection was accomplished in two stages. In the first stage, a sample of approximately 200 "military units" was selected. These units were selected with probabilities proportional to the number of persons age 14-21 within the unit. Within selected units, persons age 14-21 were subsampled with probabilities inversely proportional to the first-stage selection probability. Females were oversampled at a rate approximately 6 times that of the males in order to produce approximately equal numbers of males and females. Within each sex, the sample was stratified on the basis of military service (Army, Navy, Air Force, and Marine Corps) and geographic location.

Initial interviews with each of the four original cohorts occurred between 1966 and 1968, and initial interviews for the Youth cohort occurred in 1979. About 90 percent of the individuals designated for interviewing responded to each of the first-year interviews: 5,020 (91 percent) of the Older Men and 5,225 (92 percent) of the Young Men were interviewed in 1966; 5,083 (94 percent) or the Mature Women were interviewed in 1967; 5,159 (93 percent) of the designated Young Women were interviewed in 1968; 12,686 (90 percent) of the Youth were interviewed in 1979. Completion rates for the initial and latest survey years of each of the cohorts are summarized in table 1.

Questionnaire Design

Development of each survey instrument involves a review of earlier questionnaires, analysis of field notes from the previous round, examination of problems encountered during the fielding of other cohort's surveys, and identification of new topics and/or questions for inclusion in the current survey. Development of the first draft of the questionnaire typically begins 6 to 12 months prior to fielding. Close examination at the early developmental stage occurs on issues such as placement of questions, overall format of the questionnaire, survey timing, and sensitive questions. Advice on question inclusion as well as review of the draft survey instrument is sought from technical review committees and other agencies which regularly use these data. In an effort to promote comparability across surveys, new questions, whenever possible, follow the language and format of already developed questions from other surveys.

Table 1. Completion rates by NLS cohort for the initial and latest survey years

NLS cohort	Designated for interviewing	Number and percent interviewed initial survey year			Number and percent interviewed last/latest survey year		
		Number	Percent	Year	Number	Percent	Year
Older Men	5,518	5,020	91	1966	2,091	42	1990[2]
Mature Women	5,393	5,083	94	1967	3,094	61	1989
Young Men	5,713	5,225	92	1966	3,398	65	1981
Young Women	5,533	5,159	93	1968	3,405	66	1991
Youth total	14,574	12,686	87	1979	9,018	91	1991[3]
Cross-section sample	6,812	6,111	90	1979	5,556	91	1991
Supplemental sample	5,969	5,295	89	1979	3,281	90	1991[4]
Military sample	1,793	1,280	72	1979	181	90	1991[5]

[1] Calculated as the percent of respondents interviewed during the initial survey year. Includes certain out-of-scope respondents notably deceased, institutionalized, and respondents enlisted in the military.

[2] In 1990, interviews were completed with 2,091 surviving members of the original sample and with 1,341 widows and 865 other next-of-kin of decendents from whom information was obtained about the decendent (including work experience prior to death and cause of death). A total of 4,297 interviews were completed, representing information about 86 percent of the original sample. These interviews were sponsored by the National Institute on Aging through a contract with The Ohio State University Research Foundation.

[3] After the 1984 survey, 1,079 respondents in the military subsample were not eligible for interview. After the 1990 survey, 1,643 economically disdavantaged nonblack/non-Hispanic respondents in the supplemental sample were not eligible for interview. Youth retention calculations are based on the total number of respondents eligible for interview (9,964).

[4] Calculated as a percent of the 3,652 supplemental sample respondents who were retained for interviewing after 1990.

[5] Calculated as a percent of the 201 military respondents who were retained for intervierviewing after 1984.

The central focus of each cohort's survey has, to some extent, been determined by the particular stage of labor market attachment that each of these five unique age-sex groups was experiencing. Each survey instrument is organized around a core sets of questions: Employment, education, training, work experience, income, marital status, health, attitudes toward work, as well as occupational and geographic mobility. In addition, for each cohort, there are special set of questions that are specific to that cohort. Over the years, for example, the surveys of Older Men have focused on plans for their future, specifically retirement, pension plans, and health. Special topics for the Mature Women's cohort have included questions on volunteer work, household activities, plans for retirement, child care, care of parents, health insurance, commuting time and costs, attitudes toward women working, and perceived job discrimination. The surveys of both the Young Men and Young Womens' cohorts have focused on educational goals, high school and college experiences, characteristics of their high school, and future job plans.[2] Surveys of the Young Men have, in addition, collected information on military service and union membership, while special topics for the Young Women's cohort have included fertility, child care, responsibility for household tasks, attitudes toward women working, and perceived job discrimination.

The Youth survey instruments contain core sets of questions on the following topics: (1) Marital history; (2) schooling; (3) current labor force status; (4) jobs and employer information; (5) training; (6) work experience and attitudes; (7) military service; (8) health limitations; (9) fertility; (10) income and assets; and (11) geographic residence. While information on these topical areas has been collected during each survey year, users should be aware that the number of questions on any given topic as well as the wording and universes for each question may differ from year to year.

Additional sets of questions on a variety of factors which may affect a young person's labor force attachment have been included during selected years. During the initial year of the Youth survey, information was collected on family background, knowledge of the world of work, a retrospective evaluation of labor market experience, the influence of family and friends, and an abbreviated Rotter locus of control scale.[3] Subsequent surveys have included questions on job search methods, migration, attitudes towards work,

[2] In 1968, a supplemental survey of the last secondary school attended by respondents of the Young Men and Young Women cohorts was conducted. This special survey was designed to collect information on the academic performances and intelligence scores of respondents as well as the programs and facilities of their high schools.

[3] The Rotter scale used in the Youth survey is a four-item abbreviated version of the longer scale developed by Julian Rotter in 1966. The scale was designed to measure the extent to which an individual believes that he/she has control over his/her own life through self-motivation or self-determination as opposed to the extent that the individual believes that the environment controls his/her life.

educational and occupational aspirations and expectations, school discipline, self-esteem, child care, pre- and post-natal health behavior, drug and alcohol use, delinquency, time use, AIDS knowledge, and childhood residences.

Collection Methods

The respondents selected for interviewing each year, with the exceptions noted below, are those who had participated in the initial year interviews and who were alive at the interview date. For the original cohorts, subsequent to the first-year interview, those respondents who had refused to be interviewed were dropped from the sample. Beginning with the third interview year, respondents who had not been interviewed for any reason for 2 consecutive years also were eliminated from the sample. However, this noninterview exclusion was not applied to those members of the Young Men's cohort who were subsequently inducted into the Armed Forces. No interviews were attempted with this group while they were on active military duty. They were, however, retained in the sample and interviewed as soon as they left active military service. Beginning in the mid 1980's, Census modified the procedures to select respondents for interviewing and no longer dropped refusals and those not interviewed for 2 survey years.

In the Youth survey, attempts are made to reach all individuals within the active samples. No respondents have been routinely excluded from locator efforts with the exception of respondents who have died. The permanent Youth sample designated for interviewing during the 1979-84 interview years consisted of all civilian and military youth who were interviewed in the base year and who were alive at the survey date. In 1985, when interviewing of the full military sample ceased, the total Youth sample size dropped from 12,686 to 11,607. Retained for interviewing were the original 11,406 civilian respondents as well as 201 military respondents.

While personal interviews have been the method used for most of the survey years, at times telephone interviews also were conducted. In addition, interviews by mail were conducted for the 1968 Older Men and Mature Women surveys. Telephone contact may occur in cases where the respondent resides in a remote area or the field staff determines that it is the preferred method of interviewing a respondent. Interview schedules and retention rates for the original four cohorts and the Youth cohort are listed in tables 2 and 3, respectively.

Estimation

The NLS surveys are based upon stratified, multistage random samples with oversamples of blacks, and in the case of the Youth cohort, Hispanics, poor whites, and youth in the military. Data from each interview year include a weight specific to that year. When this weight is applied, the number of sample cases is translated into the number of persons in the population which those observations represent.

The assignment of individual respondent weights involves at least three stages. The first stage involves the reciprocal of the probability of selection at the baseline interview. Specifically, this probability of selection is a function of the probability of selection associated with the household in which the respondent was located as well as the subsampling (if any) applied to individuals identified in screening. The second stage of weighting adjusts for differential response (cooperation) rates in both the screening phase and baseline interview. Differential cooperation rates are computed (and adjusted) on the basis of geographic location, group membership, and within group, subclassification. The third stage of weighting attempts to adjust for certain types of random variation associated with sampling as well as sample "undercoverage." This ratio estimation is used to conform the sample to independently derived population totals.

Subsequent to the initial interview of each cohort, reductions in sample size have occurred due to noninterviews. In order to compensate for these losses, the sampling weights of the individuals who were interviewed had to be revised. A revised weight for each respondent was calculated for each interview year using the same method described above. Sampling weights for each respondent can be found on the corresponding public data tape or CD-ROM.

In the event one wishes to tabulate characteristics of the sample for a single interview year in order to describe the population being represented, it is necessary to weight the observations using the weights provided. For example, to compute the average hours worked in 1987 by individuals in the Youth cohort (persons 14-21 as of January 1, 1979), simply weight average hours worked by the 1987 sample weight. These weights are correct when used in this way.

Often users confine their analysis to subsamples for which respondents provided valid answers to certain questions. Weighted means here will not represent the entire population, but rather those persons in the population who would have given a valid response to the specified questions. Item nonresponse because of

Table 2. Interview schedules and retention rates[1]: original four cohorts

Year	Older Men 45-59 in 1966			Mature Women 30-44 in 1967		
	Type of interview	Total	Retention rate	Type of interview	Total	Retention rate
1966	Personal	[2] 5,020	100.0			
1967	Personal	4,744	94.5	Personal	5,083	100.0
1968	Mail	4,648	92.6	Mail	4,910	96.6
1969	Personal	4,381	87.4	Personal	4,712	92.7
1970						
1971	Personal	4,175	83.2	Personal	4,575	90.0
1972				Personal	4,471	88.0
1973	Telephone	3,951	78.7			
1974				Telephone	4,322	85.0
1975	Telephone	3,732	74.3			
1976	Personal	3,487	69.5	Telephone	4,172	82.1
1977				Personal	3,964	78.0
1978	Telephone	3,219	64.1			
1979				Telephone	3,812	75.0
1980	Telephone	3,001	59.8			
1981	Personal	2,832	56.4	Telephone	3,677	72.3
1982				Personal	3,542	69.7
1983	Telephone	2,633	52.5			
1984				Telephone	3,422	67.3
1985						
1986				Telephone	3,335	65.6
1987				Personal	3,241	63.7
1988						
1989				Personal	3,094	60.9
1990	Personal	[3] 2,092	41.5			
1991						
1992				Personal		

Year	Young Men 14-24 in 1966			Young Women 14-24 in 1968		
	Type of Interview	Total	Retention rate	Type interview	Total	Retention rate
1966	Personal	5,225				
1967	Personal	4,790				
1968	Personal	4,318	82.6	Personal	5,159	100.0
1969	Personal	4,033	77.2	Personal	4,930	95.6
1970	Personal	3,993	76.4	Personal	4,766	92.4
1971	Personal	3,987	76.3	Personal	4,714	91.4
1972				Personal	4,625	89.6
1973	Telephone	4,014	76.8	Personal	4,424	85.8
1974						
1975	Telephone	3,977	76.1	Telephone	4,243	82.2
1976	Personal	3,695	70.7			
1977				Telephone	4,108	79.6
1978	Telephone	3,538	67.7	Personal	3,902	75.6
1979						
1980	Telephone	3,438	65.8	Telephone	3,801	73.7
1981	Personal	3,398	64.9			
1982				Telephone	3,650	70.8
1983				Personal	3,547	68.7
1984						
1985				Telephone	3,720	72.1
1986						
1987				Telephone	3,639	70.5
1988				Personal	3,508	68.0
1989						
1990						
1991				Personal	3,405	66.0
1992						

[1] Retention rate is defined as the percent of the base-year respondents who were interviewed in any given survey year. Included in the calculations are deceased and institutionalized respondents as well as those serving in the military.

[2] Data were originally collected on 5,027 respondents. However, seven of the records were determined unusable and dropped from the survey.

[3] In addition to the 2,092 surviving members of the original sample interviewed during 1990, interviews were also completed with 1,341 widows or next-of-kin of deceased respondents.

Table 3. Interview schedules and retention rates: Youth cohort

Year	Type of Interview	Youth age 14-21 on January 1, 1979					
		Civilian sample		Military sample		Total sample	
		Total	Retention rate[1]	Total	Retention rate[1]	Total	Retention rate[1]
1979	Personal	11,406	100.0	1,280	100.0	12,686	100.0
1980	Personal	10,948	96.0	1,193	93.2	12,141	95.7
1981	Personal	11,000	96.4	1,195	93.4	12,195	96.1
1982	Personal	10,912	95.7	1,211	94.6	12,123	95.6
1983	Personal	10,995	96.4	1,226	95.8	12,221	96.3
1984	Personal	10,854	95.2	1,215	94.9	12,069	95.1
1985	Personal	10,708	93.9	[2] 186	92.5	[3]10,894	93.9
1986	Personal	10,472	91.8	183	91.1	10,655	91.8
1987	Telephone	10,306	90.4	179	89.1	10,485	90.3
1988	Personal	10,291	90.2	175	87.1	10,465	90.2
1989	Personal	10,424	91.4	181	90.0	10,605	91.4
1990	Personal	10,253	89.9	183	91.0	10,436	89.9
1991	Personal	8,837	90.5	181	90.0	[4]9,018	90.5

[1] Retention rate is defined as the percent of the base-year respondents within each sample type who were interviewed in any given survey year.

[2] A total of 201 military respondents were retained from the original military sample of 1,280.

[3] The total number of civilian and military respondents in the Youth cohort at the initiation of the 1985 survey was 11,607.

[4] The total number of civilian and military respondents in the Youth cohort at the initiation of the 1991 survey was 9,964.

refusals or invalid skips is usually quite small, so the degree to which the weights are incorrect is probably also quite small. In these instances, while the population estimates may be moderately in error, the population distributions (including means, medians and proportions) are reasonably accurate. Exceptions to this might be for data items that have relatively high nonresponse rates such as family income.

Uses and Limitations

NLS data have served for 20 years as an important tool for economists, sociologists, and other researchers in the study of the determinants of labor supply, earnings and income distribution, job search and separation, labor market inequities, and human capital investments. In addition, these data have been used to study the effect of governmental policies/programs and various social-psychological factors on labor force participation.

The broad range of core NLS data coupled with the recent topical expansion of the Youth surveys, the ongoing longitudinal nature of the data, and the replication of cohorts across time make the NLS a rich and yet-to-be fully exploited source of data for the continued study of such issues as: Life cycle changes, the family, the aging process, retirement decisions, geographic and occupational mobility, as well as a host of other topical and methodological analyses.

Several comprehensive reviews of NLS research (Bielby, Hawley, and Bils, 1979; Daymont and Andrisani, 1983) and annotated bibliographies of NLS research summarize much of the work that has been conducted by the NLS since the mid-1960's. The continued relevance of the NLS for policy makers at the Federal, State, and local levels, as well as the research community is summarized in *The Future of the NLS: A Report from the NSF Conference on the Future of the NLS and the NLS Technical Review Committee* (Center for Human Resource Research, 1989). A summary of some uses of the NLS made by the Federal Government can be found in *How the Federal Government Uses Data from the National Longitudinal Surveys* (Pergamit, 1991).

It is important to note that each survey is designed to be nationally representative of the specified age group (when properly weighted), not the entire population. The estimates from the survey are subject to sampling errors, or errors which arise from the fact that the estimates are drawn from a sample rather than the entire population. Also, the surveys are subject to errors due to nonresponse. Although the weights are adjusted to account for noninterviews, nonresponse is still a possible source of bias. In addition, the surveys are subject to processing errors, although these are minimized through controlled patterns of coding, editing, and cleaning procedures.

Presentation and Availability

BLS publishes a regular report entitled *Work and Family* which is based on data that focuses on various issues of public interest. Also, articles using NLS data appear periodically in the *Monthly Labor Review.* NLS data files are available to the public in the form of compact disc-read only memory (CD-ROM) and magnetic tape. To order NLS data files, contact the NLS Public User's Office, Center for Human Resource Research, The Ohio State University, 921 Chatham Lane, Suite 200, Columbus, Ohio 43221-2418, or call (614) 442-7300.

Technical References

Pergamit, Michael, *How the Federal Governement Uses Data from the National Longitudinal Surveys,* Report NLS 92-1, Bureau of Labor Statistics, 1991.

Center for Human Resource Research, *NLS Handbook 1991,* Columbus, OH: The Ohio State University, 1991.

Manser, Marilyn; Pergamit, Michael, and Peterson, Wanda Bland, "National Longitudinal Surveys: development and uses," *Monthly Labor Review,* July 1990.

Center for Human Resource Research, "Technical Sampling Report Addendum: Standard Errors and Deft Factors for Rounds IV through XI," 1990.

Center for Human Resource Research, *The Future of the NLS: A Report from the NSF Conference on the Future of the NLS and the NLS Technical Review Committee,* Columbus, OH, The Ohio State University, 1989.

Rhoton, Patricia. "Attrition and the National Longitudinal Surveys of Labor Market Experience: Avoidance, Control, and Correction," Columbus, OH, Center for Human Resource Research, The Ohio State University, 1984.

Daymont, Thomas N. and Andrisani, Paul J. "The Research Uses of the National Longitudinal Surveys: An Update," *Review of Public Data Use,* October 1983.

Frankel, Martin R.; McWilliams, Harold A; and Spencer, Bruce D. "Technical Sampling Report," *National Longitudinal Survey of Labor Force Behavior,* Chicago, IL, NORC-University of Chicago, 1983.

Bielby, William T., Hawley, Clifford B., and Bils, David. "Research Uses of the National Longitudinal Surveys," R&D Monograph 62, U.S. Department of Labor, 1979.

Grasso, John T. and Kohen, Andrew I. "The National Longitudinal Surveys Data Processing System," *The Survey of Income and Program Participation: Proceedings of the Workshop on Data Processing,* D. Kasprzyk, et. al., eds., U.S. Department of Health, Education, and Welfare, 1978.

National Opinion Research Center (NORC), *Household Screening Interviewer's Reference Manual. National Longitudinal Survey of Labor Force Behavior,* Chicago, IL, University of Chicago, 1978.

Appendix A. Seasonal Adjustment Methodology at BLS

An economic time series may be affected by regular intrayearly (seasonal) movements which result from climatic conditions, model changeovers, vacation practices, holidays, and similar factors. Often such effects are large enough to mask the short-term, underlying movements of the series. If the effect of such intrayearly repetitive movements can be isolated and removed, the evaluation of a series may be made more perceptive.

Seasonal movements are found in almost all economic time series. They may be regular, yet they do show variation from year to year and are subject to changes in pattern over time. Because these intrayearly patterns are combined with the underlying growth or decline and cyclical movements of the series (trend-cycle) and also random irregularities, it is difficult to estimate the pattern with exactness.

More than a half-century ago, attempts were made to isolate seasonal factors from time series. Some early methods depended upon smoothing curves by using personal judgment. Other formal approaches were periodogram analysis, regression analysis, and correlation analysis. Because these methods involved a large amount of work, relatively little application of seasonal factor adjustment procedures was carried out.

In the mid-1950's, new electronic equipment made more elaborate approaches feasible in seasonal factor methods as well as in other areas. The Bureau of the Census developed computer-based seasonal factors based on a ratio-to-moving-average approach. This was a major step forward, as it made possible the uniform application of a method to a large number of series at a relatively low cost.[1] Subsequent improvements in methods and in computer technology have led to more refined procedures which are both faster and cheaper than the original technique.

The Bureau of Labor Statistics began work on seasonal factor methods in 1959. Prior to that time, when additional data became available and seasonal factors were generated from the lengthened series, the new factors sometimes differed markedly from the corresponding factors based on the shorter series. This difference could affect any portion of the series. It was difficult to accept a process by which the addition of recent information could affect significantly the seasonal factors for periods as much as 15 years earlier, especially since this meant that factors could never become final. The first BLS method, pas introduced in 1960, had two goals: First, to stabilize the seasonal factors for the earlier part of the series; second, to minimize the revisions in the factors for the recent period. Since 1960, the Bureau has made numerous changes and improvements in its techniques and in methods of applying them. Thus far, all the changes relating to the seasonal adjustment of monthly series have been made within the scope of the ratio-to-moving-average or difference-from-moving-average types of approaches. The BLS 1960 method, entitled "The BLS Seasonal Factor Method," was further refined, with the final version being introduced in 1966. It was in continuous use for many Bureau series (especially employment series based on the establishment data) until 1980. In 1967, the Bureau of the Census introduced "The X-11 Variant of the Census Method II Seasonal Adjustment Program," better known as simply X-11. The X-11 provided some useful analytical measures along with many more options than the BLS method. Taking advantage of the X-11's additional flexibility, BLS began making increasing use of the X-11 method in the early 1970's, especially for seasonal adjustment of the labor force data based on the household survey. Later in the 1970's, Statistics Canada, the Canadian national statistical agency, developed an extension of the X-11 called "The X-11 ARIMA Seasonal Adjustment Method." The X-11 ARIMA (Auto-Regressive Integrated Moving Average) provided the option of using modeling and forecasting techniques to extrapolate some extra data at the end of a time series to be seasonally adjusted. The extrapolated data help to alleviate the effects of the inherent limitations of the moving average techniques at the ends of series. After extensive testing and research showed that use of X-11 ARIMA would help to further minimize revisions in factors for recent periods, BLS began using the X-11 ARIMA procedure in 1980 for most of its official seasonal adjustment.

The standard practice at BLS for current seasonal adjustment of data, as it is initially released, is to use projected seasonal factors which are published ahead of time. The time series are generally run through the seasonal adjustment program once a year to provide the projected factors for the ensuing months and the revised seasonally adjusted data for the recent history of the series, usually the last 5 years. It has generally been unnecessary to revise any

[1] Shiskin, Julius. *Electronic Computers and Business Indicators,* Occasional Paper No. 57, New York, National Bureau of Economic Research, 1957.

further back in time because the programs which have been used have all accomplished the objective of stabilizing the factors for the earlier part of the series, and any further revisions would produce only trivial changes. For the projected factors, the factors for the last complete year of actual data were selected when the X-11 or the BLS method programs were used.

With the X-11 ARIMA procedure, the projected year-ahead factors produced by the program are normally used. For the labor force data since 1980, only the factors for the January-June period are projected from the annual run—a special midyear run of the program is done, with up-to-date data included, to project the factors for the July-December period.

Since 1989, projected factors are also calculated twice a year for use in seasonally adjusted establishment-based employment, hours, and earnings data. Factors are projected for the May through October period and introduced concurrent with the annual benchmark adjustments, and again for the November-April period. In 1989, BLS also developed an extension of X-11 ARIMA to allow it to adjust more adequately for the effects of the presence or absence of religious holidays in the April survey reference period and of Labor Day in the September reference period. This extension was initially applied in 1989 to three persons-at-work labor force series. Since early 1990, the extension has been used for the adjustment of many of the establishment-based series on average weekly hours and manufacturing overtime.

An alternative to the use of projected factors is concurrent adjustment, where all data are run through the seasonal adjustment program each month, and the current observation participates in the calculation of the current factor. Of course, the concurrent approach precludes the prior publication of factors and requires substantially more staff and computer resources to run, monitor, and evaluate the seasonal adjustment process. However, recent research has shown potentially significant technical advantages in the area of minimization of factor revisions that are possible with concurrent adjustment. If future findings suggest the desirability of a change to a concurrent procedure or to some other type of methodology, such a change will be seriously considered in consultation with the Government's working group on statistics.

In applying any method of seasonal adjustment, the user should be aware that the result of combining series which have been adjusted separately will usually be a little different from the direct adjustment of the combined series. For example, the quotient of seasonally adjusted unemployment divided by seasonally adjusted labor force will not be quite the same as when the unemployment rate is adjusted directly. Similarly, the sum of seasonally adjusted unemployment and seasonally adjusted employment will not quite match the directly adjusted labor force. Separate adjustment of components and summing of them to the total usually provides series that are easier to analyze; it is also generally preferable in cases where the relative weights among components with greatly different seasonal factors may shift radically. For other series, however, it may be better to adjust the total directly if high irregularity among some of the components makes a good adjustment of all components difficult.

Finally, it is worth noting that the availability of a fast, efficient procedure for making seasonal adjustment computations can easily lead to the processing of large numbers of series without allotting enough time to review the results. No standard procedure can take the place of careful review and evaluation by skilled analysts. A review of all results is strongly recommended. And it should also be remembered that, whenever one applies seasonal factors and analyzes seasonally adjusted data, seasonal adjustment is a process which estimates a set of not directly observable components (seasonal, trend-cycle, irregular) from the observed series and is, therefore, subject to error. Because of the complex nature of methods such as X-11 ARIMA, the precise statistical properties of these errors are not known.

Technical References

U.S. Department of Labor, Bureau of Labor Statistics. *Employment and Earnings*, January and June 1992.

Dagum, Estela Bee. *The X-11 ARIMA Seasonal Adjustment Method.* Ottawa, Statistics Canada, January 1983 (Statistics Canada Catalogue No. 12-564E).

U.S. Department of Commerce, Bureau of the Census. *Seasonal Analysis of Economic Time Series,* Economic Research Report, ER-l, issued December 1978.

Proceedings of a 1976 conference jointly sponsored by the National Bureau of Economic Research and the Bureau of the Census.

U.S. Department of Commerce, Bureau of the Census. *The X-11 Variant of the Census Method II Seasonal Adjustment Program.* Technical Paper No. 15 (1967 revision).

U.S. Department of Labor, Bureau of Labor Statistics. *The BLS Seasonal Factor Method, 1966.*

Organization for Economic Cooperation and Development. *Seasonal Adjustment on Electronic Computers.* Paris, 1961.

The report and proceedings of an international conference held in November 1960. Describes experience in the United States, Canada, and several European countries. Includes theoretical sections relating to calendar (trading day) variation and general properties of moving averages.

Shiskin, Julius. *Electronic Computers and Business Indicators,* Occasional Paper No. 57. New York, National Bureau of Economic Research, 1957. Also published in *Journal of Business,* Vol. 30, October 1957.

Describes applications of the first widely used computer program for making seasonal adjustments.

Macaulay, Frederick R. *The Smoothing of Time Series,* NBER No. 19. New York, National Bureau of Economic Research, 1931.

An early discussion of moving averages and of the criteria for choosing one average rather than another.

Barton, H. C., Jr. "Adjustment for Seasonal Variation," *Federal Reserve Bulletin,* June 1941.

The classic account of the FRB ratio-to-moving-average method, in which the analyst uses skilled judgment to draw freehand curves at key stages of the procedure.

Appendix B. Industrial Classification

BLS and other Federal and State agencies follow as closely as possible a single system to define and classify industries in the U.S. economy. The Office of Management and Budget, in the Executive Office of the President, publishes the *Standard Industrial Classification* (SIC) *Manual* based on principles set forth by a technical group made up of government and industry experts. The Bureau of Labor Statistics participated in the initial development of the classification and continues to work with the Office of Management and Budget and other agencies in seeking to improve it. The manual is revised periodically to reflect the economy's changing industrial composition and organization.

Three basic principles are followed in developing the SIC: (1) The classification should conform to the existing structure of American industry; (2) each establishment is to be classified according to its primary activity; and (3) to be recognized as an industry, the group of establishments constituting the proposed classification must be statistically significant in the number of persons employed, the volume of business done, and other measures of economic activity.

As there are thousands of products and activities, the SIC provides for grouping these into categories, both narrow and broad, to enhance the value of industrial statistics for users interested in different levels of detail. The most recent revision of the SIC system occurred in 1987. The revision took into account such factors as the development and growth in products and services due to technological changes; institutional changes such as deregulation in the banking, communications, and transportation industries; and tremendous expansion in the services section.

In the 1987 edition of the *SIC Manual,* the broadest grouping divides the economy into 11 major industry divisions: Agriculture, forestry, and fishing; mining; construction; manufacturing; transportation, communications, electric, gas, and sanitary services; wholesale trade; retail trade; finance, insurance, and real estate; services; public administration; and nonclassifiable establishments.

Overall, the 1987 revision did not change the total number of industries (1,005), but many industry classifications were added, deleted, or modified. New industries were created by subdividing or restructuring existing ones, and some industries were merged to reflect declines in their importance or size. In addition, various industries were revised by transfers of individual activities, primarily to increase the accuracy, consistency, and usefulness of the classifications.

At the 2-digit level, all products and services are combined into 84 "major groups." For example, in the manufacturing division, establishments engaged in manufacturing machinery, apparatus, and supplies for the generation, storage, transmission, transformation, and utilization of electrical energy are combined into Major Group 36—Electronic and other electrical equipment.

The 3-digit level provides 416 categories. In the electronic and other electrical equipment major group, the SIC provides eight groups of industries: Electric distribution equipment (SIC 361); electrical industrial apparatus (SIC 362); household appliances (SIC 363); electric lighting and wiring equipment (SIC 364); household audio and video equipment (SIC 365); communications equipment (SIC 366); electronic components and accessories (SIC 367); and miscellaneous electrical equipment and supplies (SIC 369).

Thousands of products and activities are distinguished at the 4-digit level. For example, in Group 367, eight industries are defined: Electron tubes; printed circuit boards; semiconductors and related devices; electronic capacitors; electronic resistors; electronic coils and transformers; electronic connectors; and electronic components, not elsewhere classified.

The Bureau classifies reports from survey respondents, usually based on an establishment concept, according to their primary product or activity. The same SIC coding concept is used in the same way by the State employment security agencies (SESA's) that supply the Bureau, through the ES-202 program (chapter 5), with universe and benchmark data. The correctness of SIC codes assigned by the supplying SESA's is ensured through an annual Federal-State cooperative survey. Each year on a rotational basis, one-third of all establishments covered by the unemployment insurance (UI) program, are surveyed to collect information concerning their economic activity. This information is used to verify or correct, if necessary, the SIC code assigned to their establishments. Hence, a high degree of orderliness and consistency is attained, which benefits not only the users of all BLS establishment statistics, but also the users of Government figures.

An establishment is an economic unit, generally at a single physical location, where business is conducted or where services or industrial operations are performed (for example: A factory, mill, store, hotel, movie theater, mine, etc.)

Where separate economic activities are performed at a single physical location (such as construction activities operated out of the same location as a lumber yard), each activity should be treated as a separate establishment wherever (1) no one industry description in the classification includes such combined activities; (2) the employment in each such economic activity is significant; and (3) reports can be prepared on the number of employees, their wages and salaries, sales or receipts, and other establishment type data.

For activities such as construction and similar physically dispersed operations, establishments are represented by those relatively permanent main or branch offices, terminals, stations, etc., which are either (1) directly responsible for supervising such activities, or (2) the base from which personnel operate to carry out these activities. Hence, the individual sites, projects, fields, networks, lines, or systems of such dispersed activities are not ordinarily considered to be establishments.

An establishment is not necessarily identical with an enterprise or company, which may consist of one or more establishments. Also, it is to be distinguished from subunits, departments, or divisions. Supplemental interpretations of the definition of an establishment are included in the industry descriptions of the *Standard Industrial Classification Manual* where appropriate.

All private sector and most government sector establishments primarily engaged in the same kind of economic activity are classified in the same 4-digit industry, regardless of the type of ownership. Hence, their owners may include such diverse organizations as corporations, partnerships, individual proprietors, government agencies, joint ventures, etc.

Technical References

U.S. Department of Labor, Bureau of Labor Statistics. *1987 SIC Coding Interpretations Manual*, September 1991.

U.S. Department of Labor, Bureau of Labor Statistics. "Establishment Estimates Revised to March 1989 Benchmarks and 1987 SIC Codes," *Employment and Earnings,* September 1990.

U.S. Department of Labor, Bureau of Labor Statistics. *Employment Data Under the New Standard Industrial Classification, First Quarter 1988*, Report 772, October 1989.

Office of Management and Budget, Statistical Policy Division. *Standard Industrial Classification Manual,* 1987.

Statistical Policy Office, Office of Information and Regulatory Affairs, and Office of Management and Budget. *A Review of Industry Coding Systems.* Statistical Policy Working Paper II, 1984.

Hostetter, S. "The Verification Method as a Solution to the Industry Coding Problem," *Proceedings of the Section on Survey Research Methods.* American Statistical Association, Washington, DC, 1983.

Appendix C. Geographic Classification

The geographic detail for which BLS publishes data varies with the scope and size of the surveys it undertakes. In addition to national summaries, the Bureau publishes data for four regions; individual States, the District of Columbia, and outlying areas (Guam, Puerto Rico, and the Virgin Islands); Metropolitan Statistical Areas (MSA's); Labor Market Areas (LMA's); individual cities; and other area designations developed to meet specific survey objectives. (See table C-1.)

BLS regions

For survey estimates and indexes (including estimates of the civilian labor force and unemployment, Area Wage Surveys,[1] Employment Cost Index, productivity surveys, and the Consumer Price Index), BLS generally uses a four-region classification system[2] as follows:

Northeast: Connecticut, Maine, Massachusetts, New Hampshire, New Jersey, New York, Pennsylvania, Rhode Island, and Vermont;

Midwest: Illinois, Indiana, Iowa, Kansas, Michigan, Minnesota, Missouri, Nebraska, North Dakota, Ohio, South Dakota, and Wisconsin;

South: Alabama, Arkansas, Delaware, District of Columbia, Florida, Georgia, Kentucky, Louisiana, Maryland, Mississippi, North Carolina, Oklahoma, South Carolina, Tennessee, Texas, Virginia, and West Virginia;

West: Alaska, Arizona, California, Colorado, Hawaii, Idaho, Montana, Nevada, New Mexico, Oregon, Utah, Washington, and Wyoming.

Data for the Industry Wage Surveys are published for nine regions.[3]

Metropolitan Statistical Areas

Metropolitan areas are designated by the Office of Management and Budget through the Federal Executive Committee on Metropolitan Areas. BLS is represented on this committee along with other organizations.[4]

[1] Alaska and Hawaii are not covered in the Area Wage Surveys.

[2] This classification is the same as the four regions used by the Bureau of the Census.

[3] *New England*: Connecticut, Maine, Massachusetts, New Hampshire, Rhode Island, and Vermont; *Middle Atlantic*: New Jersey, New York, and Pennsylvania; *Border States*: Delaware, District of Columbia, Kentucky, Maryland, Virginia, and West Virginia; *Southeast*: Alabama, Florida, Georgia, Mississippi, North Carolina, South Carolina, and Tennessee; *Southwest*: Arkansas, Louisiana, Oklahoma, and Texas; *Great Lakes*: Illinois, Indiana, Michigan, Minnesota, Ohio, and Wisconsin; *Middle West*: Iowa, Kansas, Missouri, Nebraska, North Dakota, and South Dakota; *Mountain*: Arizona, Colorado, Idaho, Montana, New Mexico, Utah, and Wyoming; *Pacific*: Alaska, California, Hawaii, Nevada, Oregon, and Washington.

The general concept of a metropolitan area is one of a large population nucleus together with adjacent communities which have a high degree of economic and social integration with that nucleus.

Areas qualifying for recognition as metropolitan statistical areas have either a city with a population of at least 50,000 or a Bureau of the Census urbanized area of at least 50,000 and a total metropolitan statistical area population of at least 100,000.

Each metropolitan statistical area has one or more central counties, containing the area's main population concentration. A metropolitan statistical area may also include outlying counties which have close economic and social relationships with the central counties. Such counties must have a specified level of commuting to the central counties and must meet certain standards regarding metropolitan character, such as population density. In New England, metropolitan statistical areas are composed of cities and towns, rather than whole counties. Under specified conditions, two adjacent areas may be combined into a single metropolitan statistical area.

Each metropolitan statistical area has at least one central city. The titles of metropolitan statistical areas include up to three central city names, as well as the name of each State into which the metropolitan statistical area extends.

Each metropolitan statistical area is categorized in one of the following levels based on total population:

- Level A - Metropolitan Statistical Areas of 1 million or more.
- Level B - Metropolitan Statistical Areas of 250,000 to 1 million.
- Level C - Metropolitan Statistical Areas of 100,000 to 250,000.
- Level D - Metropolitan Statistical Areas of fewer than 100,000.

Areas assigned to Levels B, C, or D are designated as metropolitan statistical areas. In areas with over 1 million population (Level A), primary metropolitan statistical areas may be identified. These areas consist of a large urbanized county, or cluster of counties, that demonstrate very strong internal economic and social links, in addition to close ties to neighboring areas. When primary metropolitan statistical areas are defined, the large area of which

[4] Included among the other organizations are the Department of Housing and Urban Development, the Bureau of the Census, the Bureau of Economic Analysis, the Federal Reserve Board, the Department of Agriculture, and the Department of Transportation. The committee is chaired by a representative of the Office of Management and Budget.

they are components is designated a consolidated metropolitan statistical area.[5]

Labor market areas

A labor market area (LMA) is defined by the Bureau of Labor Statistics as a geographic area consisting of a central community and contiguous areas which are economically integrated into that community. Within a labor market area, workers generally can change jobs without relocating. BLS defines LMA's in terms of entire counties, except in New England where cities and towns are used. LMA's are categorized as either "major," which is usually coterminous with a metropolitan statistical area, or as "small." A "small" labor market area is defined as a county or group of counties with a central community of at least 5,000 population and which meets commuting requirements. Generally, LMA's do not cross State boundaries. Counties which are not included in labor market areas are designated as "estimating areas." (In New England, estimating areas are made up of cities or towns, or groups of cities or towns.)

More detailed information on the definitions and the geographic boundaries of labor market and estimating areas will be available in the Bureau of Labor Statistics forthcoming publication, *Directory of Labor Market Areas.*

[5] *Federal Register*, Vol. 55, No. 62, March 30, 1990, pp. 12154-12160.

Table C-1. Geographic areas currently used in selected BLS programs

Program and major publication	Nation	Region	State	MSA	Labor Market Area	Other areas[1]	Cities
Employment and Unemployment Statistics							
Labor Force, Employment, and Unemployment:							
Employment and Earnings	x						
Nonfarm Employment, Hours, and Earnings:							
Employment and Earnings	x		x	x	x		
Occupational Employment:							
Occupational Employment in Manufacturing	x		x				
Occupational Employment in Selected Nonmanufacturing Industries	x		x				
Local Area Unemployment Statistics:							
Employment and Earnings			x	x	x	x	x
Geographic Profile of Employment and Unemployment	x	([2])	x	x		x	x
Employment and Wages:							
Employment and Wages	x		x				
Mass Layoff Statistics:							
Mass Layoffs			x	x		x	
Price and Living Conditions							
Consumer Expenditures and Income:							
Consumer Expenditure Survey	x	([2])		x			
International Prices:							
U.S. Import Price Indexes; U.S. Export Price Indexes	x						
Consumer Prices:							
CPI Detailed Report	x	([2])		x		x	
Producer Prices:							
Producer Price Indexes	x						
Compensation and Working Conditions							
Survey of Professional, Administrative, Technical, and Clerical Pay:							
The National Survey of Professional, Administrative, Technical, and Clerical Pay	x						
Area Wage Surveys:							
Area Wage Surveys	x	([2])		x			
Industry Wage Surveys:							
Industry Wage Surveys	x	([3])	x	x			
Employment Benefits Survey:							
Employment Benefits Survey	x						
Employment Cost Index:							
Current Wage Developments	x	([2])					
Productivity and Technology							
Productivity Research:							
Productivity and Costs	x						
Multifactor Productivity Measures	x						
Industry Productivity and Technology Studies:							
Productivity Measures for Selected Industries	x						
Foreign Labor Statistics:							
International Comparisons of Manufacturing and Labor Force Trends						x	
Occupational Safety and Health Occupational Safety and Health Statistics:							
Occupational Injuries and Illnesses	x		x				

[1] Defined according to survey objectives.

[2] Four-region classification designated in "BLS regions."

[3] Nine-region classification designated in footnote 3 of text.

Chapter Index

Page

Chapter 1. Labor Force, Employment, and Unemployment from the Current Population Survey

Background 3
Description of survey 3
Concepts 4
Employment 4
Unemployment 4
Civilian labor force 4
Not in the labor force 4
Sampling 4
Selection of sample areas 5
Selection of sample households 5
Rotation of sample 6
Collection methods 6
Estimation methods 7
Noninterview adjustment 7
Ratio adjustment 7
First-stage ratio adjustment 7
Second-stage ratio adjustment 7
Composite estimate 8
Seasonal adjustment 8
Presentation and uses 8
Limitations 9
Geographic 9
Sources of errors in the survey estimates 9
Nonresponse 9
Processing errors 10
Measuring the accuracy of results 10
Planned changes for the CPS 10
The new CPS questionnaire 10
Computer-assisted interviewing 11
Redesign of the CPS sample 11
Technical references 11

Chapter 2. Employment, Hours, and Earnings from the Establishment Survey

Background 14
Concepts 14
Establishment 14
Employment 14
Production workers 15
Employment benchmark 15
Hours and earnings 15
Aggregate payrolls 15
Total hours 15
Overtime hours 15
Average hourly earnings 16
Real earnings 16
Straight-time average hourly earnings 16
Industrial classification 16
Data sources and collection methods 16
Sample data 16
Benchmark data 17

Page

Sample design 17
Estimation procedures 18
Employment 18
Hours and earnings 19
Average weekly hours and average hourly earnings 19
Overtime hours 20
Average weekly earnings in 1977 dollars 20
Average weekly earnings, excluding overtime for manufacturing industries 20
Hourly earnings indexes 20
Indexes of aggregate weekly worker hours and payrolls 20
Indexes of diffusion of changes in the number of employees on nonagricultural payrolls 20
Seasonally adjusted series 20
Presentation 20
Comparison with the Current Population Survey 21
Uses 23
Reliability of estimates 23
Technical references 24

Chapter 3. Occupational Employment Statistics

Background 29
Concepts 29
Industrial classification 29
Occupational classification 29
Data sources and collection methods 30
Sampling 30
Estimating procedures 30
Presentation 31
Uses and limitations 31
Technical references 31

Chapter 4. Measurement of Unemployment In States and Local Areas

Background 32
Estimation methodology 33
Estimates for States 33
Employment level 33
Unemployment rate models 33
Benchmarking 33
Estimates for sub-State areas—the Handbook method 34
Unemployment 34
Employments 34
Sub-State adjustment for consistency and additivity 34
Producing estimates for parts of LMA's 35
Uses and limitations 35
Technical references 36

Chapter 5. Employment and Wages Covered by Unemployment Insurance

Background 37

Page

Concepts and methodology 37
Scope of coverage 37
Reporting units and establishments 37
Employment 38
Total wages 38
Taxable wages and contributions 38
Industrial classification 39
Collection methods 39
Comparison of the ES-202 program with other series 40
County business patterns reports 40
Current employment statistics 40
Office of personnel management 40
Current population survey 40
Presentation 41
Uses 41
Technical references 41

Chapter 6. Occupational Pay and Employee Benefits

Background 42
Description of surveys 42
White-collar pay survey 44
Industry wage surveys 44
Concepts 44
Survey methods 45
Planning 45
Questionnaires 46
Data collection 46
Sampling 46
Estimating procedures 47
Analysis and presentation 47
Uses and limitations 48
Technical references 50

Chapter 7. Negotiated Wage and Benefit Changes

Background 51
Description of statistical series 51
Coverage 51
Private industry agreements 51
State and local government agreements 51
Data presented 51
Wage-rate changes 51
Compensation changes 52
Data sources 52
Estimating rates and costs 52
Expressing rates and costs 53
Wage and compensation rate changes under settlements 53
Compensation cost changes 53
Wage-rate changes under all contracts 54
Presentation 54
Uses and limitations 54
Technical reference 55

Chapter 8. Employment Cost Indexed

Background 56
Description of the ECI 56
Major features 56
Occupational classification 58
Industrial classification 58
Geographic classification 58
Union classification 58
Data Sources and Collection Methods 58

Page

Survey Design 59
Private sector—respondent universe and sample design 59
Public sector—respondent universe and sample design 60
Sample replacement 60
Adjustments for sample nonresponse 60
Index computation 60
Seasonal adjustment 62
Reliability of the estimates 62
Presentation 63
Uses and limitations 63
Technical references 64

Chapter 9. The Employee Benefits Survey

Background 67
Description of the survey 68
Professional, technical, and related 68
Clerical and sales 68
Regular employees 68
Teachers 68
Police and firefighters 68
Survey design 69
Data collection 69
Survey response 70
Data processing 70
Estimation 70
Reliability of the estimates 71
Presentation 71
Uses and limitations 71
Quality control and future research 74

Chapter 10. Productivity Measures: Business Sector and Major Subsectors

Background 78
Description of measures 78
Data sources and estimation procedures 79
Output per hour measures 79
Output 79
Labor input 79
Compensation and labor costs 80
Multifactor productivity measures for major sectors 80
Multifactor productivity measures for manufacturing industries 81
Analysis and presentation 81
Compensation and labor costs 82
Unit labor and nonlabor costs 82
Availability of results 82
Calculation procedures 82
Labor productivity 82
Multifactor productivity 83
Uses and limitations 84
Technical references 84

Chapter 11. Productivity Measures: Industries and Government

Background 89
Labor productivity measures 89
Concepts 89
Methods and sources 90
Industries 90
Output 90
Weights 90

Benchmark indexes ... 91
Annual indexes ... 91
Sources ... 92
Employee hours ... 92
Comparability of output and employee hours data ... 93
Government ... 94
Federal ... 94
State and local ... 94
Multifactor productivity measures ... 94
Concepts ... 94
Methods and sources ... 95
Output ... 95
Employee hours ... 95
Capital ... 95
Intermediate purchases ... 96
Weights for major input components ... 96
Presentation ... 96
Uses and limitations ... 97
Technical references ... 98

Chapter 12. Technological change

Background ... 99
Description of Studies ... 99
Data Sources and collection methods ... 99
Personal interviews ... 99
Trade and technical publications ... 100
Statistical data sources ... 100
Plant records ... 100
Expert review ... 100
Analysis and interpretation ... 100
Definition of technological change ... 100
Impact on productivity ... 100
Impact on employment ... 101
Impact on occupations ... 101
Adjustment to technological change ... 101
Uses and limitations ... 101
Technical references ... 102

Chapter 13. Foreign Labor Statistics

Background ... 103
Description of measures ... 103
Labor force, employment, and unemployment ... 103
Productivity and labor costs ... 103
Hourly compensation cost ... 104
The family ... 104
Real gross domestic product per capita and per employed person ... 104
Consumer prices and other measures ... 104
Data sources ... 104
Estimating procedures ... 104
Labor force, employment, and unemployment ... 104
Productivity and labor costs ... 105
Hourly compensation costs ... 106
The family ... 107
Real gross domestic product per capita and per employed person ... 107
Consumer prices and other measures ... 107
Analysis and Presentation ... 108
Uses and limitations ... 108
Technical references ... 109

Chapter 14. Occupational Safety and Health Statistics

Annual survey of occupational injuries and illnesses ... 111
Background ... 111
Survey definitions ... 111
Survey measures ... 112
Scope of the survey ... 112
State participation ... 113
Data collection ... 113
Sample design ... 113
Estimation procedures ... 113
Weighting ... 113
Benchmarking ... 114
Incidence rate calculation ... 114
Reliability of estimates ... 114
Publication guidelines ... 114
Presentation ... 115
Uses and limitations ... 115
Supplementary data system ... 115
Background ... 115
Description of SDS ... 115
Presentation ... 116
Uses and limitations ... 116
Work injury reports ... 117
Background ... 117
The survey process ... 117
Weighting and estimation procedures ... 118
Reliability of the estimates ... 118
Presentation ... 118
Uses and limitations ... 119
Technical references ... 119

Chapter 15. Employment projections

Overview ... 128
Labor force projections ... 128
Aggregate economic performance ... 128
Final demand ... 129
Input-output ... 129
Industry employment ... 129
Occupational employment ... 129
Final review ... 129
Assumptions ... 130
Presentation ... 130
Limitations ... 130
Labor force ... 131
Aggregate Economy ... 132
Final demand by product ... 133
Data sources ... 133
Procedures ... 134
Personal consumption expenditures ... 134
Investment ... 135
Government ... 135
Input-output ... 135
Industry employment ... 136
Data sources ... 136
Procedures ... 137
Occupational Employment ... 137
Data sources ... 137
Procedures ... 138
Base-year data ... 138
Projections ... 138
Technical references ... 139

Page

Chapter 16. Producer Prices
Background ... 140
Description of survey ... 141
Universe ... 141
Prices ... 141
Product change and quality adjustment ... 141
Classification ... 143
Industry classification ... 143
Commodity classification ... 143
Corresponding indexes ... 143
Commodity-based stage-of-processing classification ... 144
Industry-based stage-of-process classification ... 144
Other ... 144
Data sources and collection methods ... 145
Data processing ... 146
Estimation procedures ... 146
Weights ... 146
Commodity and product aggregation weight ... 146
Industry net output weights ... 146
Weights for traditional commodity groupings ... 147
Commodity-based stage-of-processing indexes ... 147
Industry-based stage-of-process indexes ... 147
Seasonal adjustment ... 148
Direct and aggregating adjustment ... 148
Intervention ... 148
Other estimation procedures ... 148
Missing prices ... 148
Rounding policy ... 148
Index calculation ... 149
Analysis and presentation ... 149
Analysis ... 149
Presentation ... 149
Seasonally adjusted data ... 150
Revised data ... 150
Calculating index changes ... 151
Uses and limitations ... 151
Economic indicator ... 151
Deflator ... 151
Private business uses ... 152
Discontinued data ... 152
Technical references ... 152

Chapter 17. International Prices Indexes
Background ... 161
Description of Survey ... 161
Concepts ... 161
Data sources and calculation methods ... 162
Product universe ... 162
Sampling ... 162
Collection ... 163
Pricing ... 163
Classification ... 164
Estimation Procedures ... 164
Formula ... 164
Publication ... 165
Uses and limitations ... 165
Technical references ... 165
The current survey ... 165

Page

Chapter 18. Consumer Expenditures and Income
Background ... 170
Interview survey ... 171
Diary survey ... 171
Integrated survey data ... 172
Processing ... 172
Sample design ... 173
Selection of households ... 173
Cooperation levels ... 173
Estimation ... 174
Presentation ... 174
Evaluation research ... 174
Uses and limitations ... 175

Chapter 19. Consumer Price Indexes
The index in brief ... 176
Background ... 176
Concepts ... 177
Prices and living costs ... 177
Sampling ... 178
Weights and relative importance ... 178
Owners' equivalent rent ... 178
Scope and calculation ... 178
Uses ... 179
As an economic indicator ... 179
As a deflator of other economic series ... 179
As a means of adjusting income payments ... 179
Analysis and presentation ... 179
Limitations of the index ... 179
Construction of the index ... 180
Definition of the index ... 180
Index calculation ... 180
Estimation of expenditure-population weights . 181
Preliminary mean expenditures and relative importance ... 182
Composite estimation ... 182
Raking ... 182
Special expenditure-weight procedures ... 183
Annual and semiannual average index estimation ... 183
Sampling: areas, items, and outlets ... 184
Area sample ... 184
Item and outlet samples: commodities and services other than shelter ... 185
Item structure and sampling ... 185
Item and outlet sample design ... 185
Outlet and price surveys ... 186
Point-of-purchase survey ... 186
Outlet sampling procedures ... 187
Outlet sampling procedures for commodities and services not included in the POPS ... 187
Augmentation ... 187
Merging item and outlet samples ... 188
Selection procedures within outlets ... 188
Item and outlet samples: shelter ... 188
Stratification ... 188
Sample selection within strata ... 189
Sample allocation to PSU's and strata ... 189
Sample augmentation and rotation ... 190
Estimation of price change ... 190
Commodities and services other than shelter .. 190
Item substitution, quality adjustments, and imputation ... 191
Directly comparable ... 191
Direct quality adjustment ... 191

Page

Imputation ... 192
Medical care ... 193
Other price adjustments ... 194
Bonus merchandise adjustments ... 194
Utility refunds ... 194
Manufacturers' rebates ... 194
Cents-off coupons ... 194
Seasonal items ... 194
Special estimation procedures ... 195
New vehicles ... 195
Used cars ... 195
Natural gas ... 195
Health insurance ... 195
Automobile finance charges ... 195
Quantity discounts ... 195
Unit-priced fruits and vegetables ... 196
Bottle deposits ... 196
Sales taxes ... 196
Shelter: rent and owners' equivalent rent ... 196
Residential rent ... 196
Vacancy imputation ... 197
Aging adjustment ... 197
Quality adjustment ... 197
Owners' equivalent rent ... 197
Estimation of seasonal effects ... 198
Seasonal adjustment ... 198

Page

Intervention analysis seasonal adjustment .. 199
Direct and aggregate adjustment ... 199
Revision ... 199
Average prices ... 199
Precision estimates ... 200
1989-90 CPI variance estimation ... 200
Estimating variances of the index and price change ... 201
Nonsampling error ... 203
Coverage error ... 204
Nonresponse error ... 204
Response error ... 204
Processing error ... 204
Estimation error ... 204
Response rates: commodities and services ... 205
Technical references ... 206

Chapter 20. National Longitudinal Surveys

Background ... 236
Sampling ... 236
Questionnaire design ... 237
Collection methods ... 239
Estimation ... 239
Uses and limitations ... 240
Presentation and availability ... 240
Technical references ... 241z

☆ U.S. GOVERNMENT PRINTING OFFICE: 1992—3 1 2 -4 0 8 / 7 4 5 8 5

ISBN 0-16-038205-X
90000
9 780160 382055

U.S. Department of Labor
Bureau of Labor Statistics
Washington, DC 20212

Official Business
Penalty for Private Use, $300
RETURN POSTAGE GUARANTEED